Equipment Leasing

Peter K. Nevitt
President
Mitsui Nevitt Capital Corporation

Frank J. Fabozzi
Visiting Professor
Sloan School of Management
Massachusetts Institute of Technology

Third Edition

Dow Jones-Irwin
Homewood, Illinois 60430

©DOW JONES-IRWIN, 1981, 1985, and 1988

This book was set in 10/12 Century Schoolbook by Carlisle Communications Limited.
The editors were Richard A. Luecke, Paula M. Buschman, Joan A. Hopkins.
The production manager was Carma W. Fazio.
The drawings were done by Jill Smith.
Arcata Graphics/Kingsport was the printer and binder.

ISBN 1-55623-058-3

Library of Congress Catalog Card No. 87–71671

Printed in the United States of America

1 2 3 4 5 6 7 8 9 0 K 5 4 3 2 1 0 9 8

PKN's corner
To my wife

FJF's corner
To my parents

Preface

This book provides the reader with a practical overview of equipment leasing as it is conducted today in the United States. We have attempted to cover the subject matter in sufficient depth to provide useful and practical information, concepts, and insights for the reader. At the same time, we have tried to keep the text readable, understandable, and useful for persons unfamiliar with many aspects of leasing. Our aim has been to produce a simple treatise on equipment leasing which will be valuable to lessors as well as lessees; to lawyers as well as nonlawyers; to accountants and financial analysts as well as nonfinancial people; and to persons experienced and well-versed in leasing as well as people new to leasing.

Equipment leasing has experienced an amazing growth. Twenty years ago only a small fraction of new equipment was financed by leasing. Today more equipment is financed by equipment leasing than by bank loans or any other method of financing. The volume of equipment leasing is expected to continue to increase in the future.

From time to time over the past 20 years, the future of equipment leasing has sometimes seemed threatened by changes in tax laws or accounting rules. However, leasing has emerged from each threat stronger and more widely used than before.

In 1986 Congress drastically revised the tax laws and changed many provisions affecting equipment leasing; once again lessees and lessors have quickly adjusted to the changes, and the volume and growth of equipment leasing continues unabated. If the past is prologue lessees and lessors will adjust to new changes in tax laws and accounting rules as they occur, the volume of equipment leasing will further increase in the future, and the general principles of equipment leasing as outlined in this book will continue to be applicable as in the past.

Despite the rapid growth and wide use of leases to finance equipment, there is a surprising lack of text material on many aspects of leasing. Excellent articles appear from time to time on specific subjects of current interest. A few books have been published addressing particular aspects of leasing. Symposiums have been published on legal technicalities of leasing. However, there are few books that provide a broad overview of equipment leasing. The objective of this book is to provide the reader with such an overview.

The authors acknowledge the thoughtful suggestions, counsel, and help provided by Cheryl Knowles in connection with the chapters on lease documentation. Peter Nevitt acknowledges the advice and counsel he has received over the years from his friends and associates in the leasing business and particularly Richard Harris, Richard Michalik, Hiroshi Aoki, Steve Alexander, William Reed, James Kempenich, Bruce Koppe, Jack Hawkes, Peter Leiter, John Geist, Alfred Youngwood, Stewart Odell, Richard Bronstein, and John Stewart. He also acknowledges the forbearance of his wife in putting up with the hours of weekend work that preparing this book entailed. Frank Fabozzi thanks his secretary, Jean Marie DeJordy, for her administrative assistance.

Peter K. Nevitt
Frank J. Fabozzi

Contents

SECTION II
Operating a Leasing Company

SECTION III
Lease Documentation for a Nonleveraged Lease Transaction

SECTION IV
Leveraged Leases

Treatment of an Owner Trust Acting as a Lessor. Debt for Leveraged Leases. Facility Leases. Construction Financing. Credit Exposure of Equity Participants. Points of Contention between Lenders and Equity Participants. Tax Indemnification for Future Changes in Tax Law. Leveraged Leases with Individual Investors.

SECTION I

Background and Fundamentals of Equipment Leasing

1

The Fundamentals of
Equipment Leasing

More equipment is financed today by equipment leases than by bank loans, private placements, or any other method of equipment financing. Nearly any asset that can be purchased can also be leased: from aircraft, ships, satellites, computers, refineries, and steam-generating plants, on the one hand, to typewriters, duplicating equipment, automobiles, and dairy cattle, on the other hand. According to the American Association of Equipment Lessors, 80 percent of American companies currently use leasing each year to acquire the use of over $100 billion of capital equipment.

In order to compare leasing with other methods of financing, it is necessary to understand the basics of how leasing works and the differences among the general categories of equipment leases. This will be explained in the present chapter, followed by a critical evaluation of the reasons often cited for leasing. In this chapter we also discuss the types of lessors, the factors that should be considered in selecting a lessor, and the various types of lease programs available.

BACKGROUND

A lease is a contract wherein, over the term of the lease, the lessor (owner) permits the lessee (user) the use of an asset in exchange for a promise by the latter to pay a series of lease payments. Most corporate financial executives recognize that earnings are derived from the use of an asset, not its ownership, and that leasing is simply an alternative financing method. While this recognition seems axiomatic today, it was not always a belief shared by financial executives. Except for the transportation industry, where leasing had long been employed for railroad rolling stock, until the 1970s the ownership ethic dominated equipment financing decisions. Leasing was regarded as a last resort form of financial transaction that prestigious and financially strong companies simply did not undertake.

HOW LEASING WORKS

A typical leasing transaction works as follows. The user-lessee first decides on the equipment needed. The lessee then decides on the manufacturer, the make, and the model. The lessee specifies any special features desired, the terms of warranties, guaranties, delivery, installation, and services. The lessee also negotiates the price. After the equipment and terms have been specified and the sales contract negotiated, the lessee enters into a lease agreement with the lessor. The lessee negotiates with the lessor on the length of the lease; the rental; whether sales tax, delivery, and installation charges should be included in the lease; and other optional considerations.

After the lease has been signed, the lessee assigns its purchase rights to the lessor, which then buys the equipment exactly as specified by the lessee. When the property is delivered, the lessee formally accepts the equipment to make sure it gets exactly what was ordered. The lessor then pays for the equipment, and the lease goes into effect. Rentals are usually net to the leasing company. Except in short-term operating leases, discussed later, taxes, service, insurance, and maintenance are the responsibility of the lessee and may not be deducted from rentals.

At the end of the lease term, the lessee usually has the option to renew the lease, to buy the equipment, or to terminate the agreement and return the equipment. As we shall see in later chapters, the options available to the lessee at the end of the lease are very significant in that the dimensions of such options determine the nature of the lease for tax purposes and the classification of the lease for financial accounting purposes.

When all costs associated with the use of the equipment are to be paid by the lessee and not included in the lease payments, the lease is called a *net lease*. Examples of such costs are property taxes, insurance, and maintenance. Most long-term lease financing transactions are net leases.

TYPES OF EQUIPMENT LEASES

Equipment leases fall into three general categories, each with a different type of purchase option.

1. *Non-tax-oriented leases* (also called *conditional sale leases, leases intended as security, hire-purchase leases, money-over-money leases,* and *pseudoleases*), which either have nominal purchase options or automatically pass title to the lessee at the end of the lease.
2. *Tax-oriented true leases* (also sometimes called *guideline leases*), which either contain no purchase option or have a purchase option based on fair market value. There are two types of tax-oriented true leases: single-investor leases (also called *direct leases*) and leveraged leases.
3. *Tax-oriented TRAC leases for licensed over-the-road vehicles* (also called *open-end leases*), which have terminal rental adjustment clauses that shift the entire residual risk to the lessee but may permit the lessee to acquire the equipment at a fixed price at the end of the lease.

The Non-Tax-Oriented Lease or Conditional Sale Lease

A conditional sale lease transfers all incidents of ownership of the leased property to the lessee and usually gives the lessee a bargain purchase option or renewal option not based on fair market value at the time of exercise. Although generally the lessee has both legal title and tax title in a conditional sale lease, the tax rules and legal rules for determining when a lease constitutes a true lease or conditional sale are not always the same. Conditional sale leases for tax purposes may include leases for a lease term of more than 80 percent of the original useful life of the leased property or for a term whereby the estimated fair market value of the leased property at the end of the lease term is less than 20 percent of the original cost. The lessee under a conditional sale lease treats the property as owned, depreciates the property for tax purposes, claims any tax credit which may be available, and deducts the interest portion of rent payments for tax purposes. The lessor under a conditional sale lease treats the transaction as a loan and cannot offer the low lease rates associated with a true lease since the lessor does not retain the ownership tax benefits.

Equipment financing offered by vendors is often in the form of conditional sale leases. Most leasing done outside the United States is structured similarly to a conditional sale lease, although the tax implications may not be the same as in the United States.

The Tax-Oriented True Leases

The true lease offers all of the primary benefits commonly attributed to leasing. Substantial cost savings can often be achieved through the use of tax-oriented true leases in which the lessor claims and retains the tax benefits of ownership and passes through to the lessee most of such tax benefits in the form of reduced lease payments. The lessor claims depreciation deductions, and the lessee deducts the full lease payment as an expense. If investment tax credit (ITC) is available it may be claimed by the lessor or, by agreement, the lessee.[1] The lessor in a true lease owns the leased equipment at the end of the lease term.

The principal advantage to a lessee of using a true lease to finance an equipment acquisition is the economic benefit that comes from the indirect realization of tax benefits that would otherwise be lost.

If the lessee is unable to generate a sufficient tax liability to currently use fully tax benefits, such as depreciation, associated with equipment ownership, the cost of owning new equipment will effectively be higher than leasing the equipment under a true lease. Under these conditions leasing is usually a less costly alternative because the lessor uses the tax benefits from the acquisition and passes on most of these benefits to the lessee through a lower lease payment.

There are two categories of true leases: single-investor leases (or direct leases) and leveraged leases. Single-investor leases are essentially two-party transactions, with the lessor purchasing the leased equipment with its own funds and being at risk for 100 percent of the funds used to purchase the equipment. In a leveraged lease, on the other hand, there are three parties to the transaction: a lessee, a lessor (equity participant), and a long-term lender. In a leveraged lease the lessor provides only a portion of the purchase price of the leased equipment from its own funds (typically 20 to 25 percent), borrows the remainder of the purchase price (typically 75 to 80 percent) from third-party lenders on a nonrecourse basis, claims tax benefits on 100 percent of the purchase price, and receives 100 percent of the residual value. The leveraged use of tax benefits and profit from the residual value constitutes the "leverage" in a leveraged lease. The greater benefits to the lessor enable the lessor to pass through greater benefits indirectly to the lessee in the form of reduced rents. Leveraged leases are discussed in greater depth in Chapters 16, 17, and 18.

---

[1] ITC was repealed effective December 31, 1985, except for certain property on firm order as of that date and except for certain "transitional property" designated by Congress.

The lower cost of leasing realized by a lessee throughout the lease term in a true lease must be weighted against the loss of the leased asset's residual value at the end of the lease term. A framework for evaluating the tax and timing effects is presented in Appendix C of the book. In an absolute sense, the give-up of residual value is of small significance as long as the lessor assumes a realistic residual value for pricing purposes, the lease term constitutes a substantial portion of the economic life of the asset, and renewal options permit continuity of control for its economic life.

The Internal Revenue Service is well aware that parties to a lending transaction may find it more advantageous from a tax point of view to characterize an agreement as a "lease" rather than as a conditional sales agreement. Therefore, guidelines have been established by the IRS to distinguish between a true lease and a conditional sales agreement. These guidelines are discussed in Chapter 5.

TRAC Leases

The Deficit Reduction Act of 1984 authorized a new type of lease for over-the-road motor vehicles called a "TRAC lease" that combined the benefits of a true lease and a conditional sale. The name *TRAC lease* is derived from the fact that a TRAC lease contains a "terminal rental adjustment clause." Properly structured, a TRAC lease can be used to provide a lessee with true tax-oriented lease rates even though the lease contains a terminal rental adjustment clause which is comparable to a fixed-price purchase option.

TRAC leases can be used to finance motor vehicles used in a trade or business. While the statute is not entirely clear on the subject, the term *motor vehicles* most likely includes only motor vehicles such as trucks, truck tractors and trailer rigs, automobiles, and buses. On the other hand, vehicles such as farm tractors, construction equipment, and forklifts are probably not eligible for TRAC leases. TRAC leases are discussed further in Chapter 5.

OPERATING LEASES

Thus far, the leases we have discussed are comparable to equipment financing transactions in that the lease term is for a substantial portion of the economic life of the leased equipment. Other types of leases called *operating leases,* on the other hand, are not financing transactions. Operating leases may be for only a fraction of the life of the asset. The name is derived from the fact that it originally described a lease in which equipment was furnished along with an operator on a lease service arrangement, as, for example, with a piece of construction equipment, a ship, or an airplane.

An operating lease is a true lease for tax purposes. That is, the lessor is entitled to all the tax benefits associated with ownership, and the lessee is entitled to deduct the rental payments.

Historically in the equipment leasing business the term *operating lease* was used fairly exclusively to describe short-term leases for a small fraction of the economic life of an asset. When *FASB Statement No. 13* was enacted, it adopted that term as an accounting definition for leases with lease terms equal to as much as 75 percent of the economic life of the leased asset.

We shall explain later in this chapter, and in more depth in Chapter 3, the special meaning the term *operating lease* has for financial accounting purposes. Transactions classified as operating leases are not disclosed in the body of the balance sheet as financial obligations. Instead, they are shown in the footnotes to the financial statement as fixed obligations. This classification may arise despite the fact that the transaction is to all intents and purposes a financing transaction.

REASONS FOR LEASING

Leasing is an alternative to purchasing. Since the lessee is obligated to make a series of payments, a lease arrangement resembles a debt contract. Thus, the advantages cited for leasing are often based on a comparison between leasing and purchasing using borrowed funds on an intermediate-term (maturity between 3 and 10 years) or long-term (maturity greater than 10 years) basis.

Cost

Many lessees find true leasing attractive because of its apparent low cost. This is particularly evident where a lessee cannot currently use tax benefits associated with equipment ownership due to such factors as lack of currently taxable income, net operating loss carryforwards, or being subject to the alternative minimum tax.

Financial economists have demonstrated that if it were not for the different tax treatment for owning and leasing an asset, the costs would be identical in an efficient capital market.[2] However, due to the different tax treatment as well as the diverse abilities of tax entities to

---

[2] See Merton H. Miller and Charles W. Upton, "Leasing, Buying, and the Cost of Capital Services," *Journal of Finance,* June 1976, pp. 761–87; and Wilbur G. Lewellen, Michael S. Long, and John J. McConnell, "Asset Leasing in Competitive Capital Markets," *Journal of Finance,* June 1976, pp. 787–98.

currently utilize the tax benefits associated with ownership, no set rule can be offered as to whether borrowing to buy or a true lease is the cheaper form of financing. Various factors must be analyzed to assess the least costly financing method. A framework for such an analysis is given in Appendix C.

The cost of a true lease depends on the size of the transaction and whether the lease is tax-oriented or non-tax-oriented. The equipment leasing market can be classified into the following three categories:[3] (1) small-ticket retail market with transactions in the $5,000 to $100,000 range, (2) middle market with large-ticket items covering transactions between $100,000 and $5 million, and (3) special products market involving equipment cost in excess of $5 million.

Tax-oriented leases generally fall into the second and third markets. Most of the leveraged lease transactions are found in the third market and the upper range of the second market. The effective interest cost implied by these lease arrangements is considerably below that of prevailing interest rates charged on borrowed funds. Even so, the potential lessee must weigh the lost economic benefits from owning the asset against the economic benefits to be obtained from leasing.

Non-tax-oriented leases fall primarily into the small-ticket retail market and the lower range of the second market. *There is no real cost savings associated with these leases compared to traditional borrowing arrangements.* In most cases, however, cost is not the dominant motive of the firm that employs this method of financing.

From a tax perspective, leasing has advantages under the following circumstances that lead to a reduction in cost.

1. A company may be in a tax loss carryforward position and consequently be unable to claim tax benefits associated with equipment ownership currently or for several years in the future.

2. A company may be subject to alternative minimum tax and, therefore, be unable to make efficient use of ACRS depreciation deductions.

3. Leasing is ideal for joint venture partnerships in which tax benefits are not available to one or more of the joint venturers because of the way in which the joint venture is structured or because of the particular tax situation of one or more of the joint venture partners. In such cases, the lessor may utilize the tax benefits that would otherwise be wasted and pass those benefits through to the joint venturers in the form of lower lease payments.

---

[3] Karl M. Parrish, "The Operation and Management of a Bank-Affiliated Leasing Company," in *Equipment Leasing-Leverage Leasing,* ed. Bruce E. Fritch and Albert F. Reisman (New York: Practicing Law Institute, 1980).

4. Leasing also works well for project financings structured through subsidiaries not consolidated for tax purposes and, consequently, not usually in a position to claim and use tax benefits from equipment acquisitions.

5. A company with foreign tax credits may find it difficult to claim tax deductions and any available tax credits under the tax formula for claiming the foreign tax credit.

6. Where costs of plant and equipment expected to be financed by tax-free industrial revenue bonds exceed statutory limits, equipment can often be acquired through a lease to keep the remainder of the project within the bond limits. This is very important in preserving the tax-free characteristics of the bonds.

Sale-and-Leasebacks to Lock in Deferred Tax

Companies concerned that tax rates may rise in the future may wish to do a sale-and-leaseback of property that is subject to a large deferred income tax liability resulting from prior accelerated depreciation deductions, in order to "lock in" the future deferred taxes at the current tax rate. The lease rate may, of course, reflect the lessor's view as to possible tax rate changes in the future. If the lessee were to indemnify the lessor for future tax rate changes, the economics would be less attractive for the lessee.

Conservation of Working Capital

The most frequent advantage cited by leasing company representatives and lessees is that leasing conserves working capital. The reasoning is as follows: When a firm borrows money to purchase equipment, the lending institution very rarely provides an amount equal to the entire price of the asset to be financed. Instead, the lender requires the borrowing firm to take an equity position in the asset by making a down payment. The amount of the down payment will depend on such factors as the type of asset, the creditworthiness of the borrower, and prevailing economic conditions. Leasing, on the other hand, typically provides 100 percent financing since it does not require the firm to make a down payment.[4] Moreover, costs incurred to acquire the equipment, such as delivery and installation charges, are not usually covered by a loan agreement. They may, however, be structured into a lease agreement.

The validity of this argument for financially sound firms during normal economic conditions is questionable. Such firms can simply

---

[4] The Internal Revenue Service does not permit an investment by the lessee in any event. See Chapter 5.

obtain a loan for 100 percent of the equipment or borrow the down payment from another source that provides unsecured credit. On the other hand, it is questionable that the funds needed by a small firm for a down payment can be borrowed, particularly during tight money periods. Also, some leases do, in fact, require a down payment in the form of advance lease payments or security deposits at the beginning of the lease term.

Preservation of Credit Capacity by Avoiding Capitalization

Prior to 1973 financial reporting standards did not mandate the disclosure of lease obligations. Thus, leasing was commonly referred to as "off-balance sheet financing." As we shall explain in Chapter 3, current financial reporting standards for leases require that lease obligations classified as capital leases be capitalized as a liability on the balance sheet. According to *FASB Statement No. 13*, the principle for classifying a lease as a capital lease for financial reporting purposes is as follows:

> A lease that transfers substantially all of the benefits and risks incident to ownership of property should be accounted for as the acquisition of an asset and the incurrence of an obligation by the lessee.

FASB Statement No. 13 specifies four criteria for classifying a lease as a capital lease. Leases not classified as capital leases are considered operating leases. Unlike a capital lease, an operating lease is not capitalized. Instead, certain information regarding such leases must be disclosed in a footnote to the financial statement.

Many chief financial officers are of the opinion that avoiding capitalization of a lease will enhance the financial image of their corporations. Since there is generally ample room for designing lease arrangements so as to avoid having a lease classified as a capital lease, CFOs generally prefer that lease agreements be structured as operating leases. However, is there any empirical evidence to support or refute the concern of CFOs that capitalization of leases influences the evaluation of financial analysts, stockholders, lenders, and bond-rating agencies? Moody's and Standard and Poor's capitalize most operating leases in making their credit evaluations. Two interesting behavioral studies may shed some further light on this question.

In a 1979 study sponsored by the National Association of Accountants and the Society of Management Accountants of Canada, the investigators interviewed two bond raters.[5] They asked the raters whether

---

[5] William L. Ferrara, James B. Thies, and Mark W. Dirsmith, *The Lease-Purchase Decision* (New York: National Association of Accountants and the Society of Management Accountants of Canada, 1980), pp. 23–24.

the FASB requirement produced lower bond ratings if a firm now had to capitalize its lease whereas it did not have to prior to *Statement No. 13*. The raters' response was that because they had already given effect to the capitalization of leases prior to *Statement No. 13* in determining the bond rating of an issuer, the requirement did not produce lower bond ratings. In fact, one of the rating agencies indicated that not only had it capitalized leases now covered by *Statement No. 13* but that it had also been capitalizing lease obligations not covered by *Statement No. 13* and take-or-pay contracts.[6] According to this bond rater, the real question is "whether the facility or asset involved is essential to the ongoing business operation, e.g., warehousing (we need it) or a retail store (we need it). Regardless of legal term, it must be renewed to keep the business going."[7]

In an FASB-sponsored study dealing with the impact on lessees of *Statement No. 13, "Accounting for Leases,"* the researchers found the following:

> The majority of analysts and bankers responding to the straightforward survey questions claimed that there are not substantive grounds for the assertion that they changed their evaluation of the companies affected by capitalization of leases. However, that response was not validated when analysts and bankers were asked to respond to a similar question indirectly. The indirect approach consisted of a request (as part of the survey) to evaluate two (economically) identical companies that differed only in the method of accounting for leases. The condensed financial statements of the two companies were produced side by side and respondents *were told that they "are almost identical (the difference lies in their method of accounting for leases)."* The results were quite a surprise: Over 40 percent of the responding financial analysts and commercial bank loan officers considered the company that did not capitalize the 20-year noncancelable lease more profitable, whereas only about 8 percent considered the other company more profitable, and about 50 percent considered them equally profitable. Since, by design, the two companies were identical in real terms, respondents who favored one over the other did so based on the numbers shown on the face of the financial statements.[8]

Moreover, more than 25 percent of the analysts and bankers responding to the survey indicated that the company that kept leases off the balance sheet had a better debt-paying ability. The researchers concluded:

---

[6] Of course, this assumes that the raters were aware of the operating leases, which may not have always been the case prior to *Statement No. 13*.

[7] Ibid.

[8] A. Rashad Abdel-khalik et al., *The Economic Effects on Lessees of FASB Statement No. 13, Accounting for Leases* (Stamford, Conn.: Financial Accounting Standards Board, 1981), pp. 23–24.

It is evident from these results that what responding users *say* they do and what they *actually* do may be substantially different. Note that the indirect question resembled a financial analyst's task more closely than the direct one. Taken by itself, that evidence is not unequivocal. However, it tends to support the concern that some preparers of financial statements have indicated, namely that the evaluation of their success indicators by users is quite often influenced by cosmetic accounting changes.[9]

As a practical matter, in the experience of the authors, 80 to 90 percent of all long-term true leases (payout type leases for the lessors) are structured as operating leases for financial accounting purposes at the request of the lessees.

Risk of Obsolescence and Disposal of Equipment

When a firm owns equipment, it faces the possibility that at some future time the asset may not be as efficient as more recently manufactured equipment. The owner may then elect to sell the original equipment and purchase the newer, more technologically efficient version. The sale of the equipment, however, may produce only a small fraction of its book value. By leasing, it is argued, the firm may avoid the risk of obsolescence and the problems of asset disposal. The validity of this argument depends on the type of lease and the provisions therein.

With a cancelable operating lease, the lessee can avoid the risk of obsolescence by terminating the contract. However, the avoidance of risk is not without a cost since the rental under such lease arrangements reflects the risk of obsolescence perceived by the lessor.[10] At the end of the lease term, the disposal of the obsolete equipment becomes the problem of the lessor. The risk of loss in residual value that the lessee passes on to the lessor is embodied in the cost of the lease.

The risk of disposal faced by some lessors, however, may not be as great as the risk that would be encountered by the lessee. A manufacturer-lessor has less investment exposure since its manufacturing costs will be significantly less than the retail price. Also, it is often equipped to handle reconditioning and redesigning due to technological improvements. Moreover, the manufacturer-lessor will be more active in the resale market for the equipment and thus be in a

---

[9] Ibid.

[10] Some full payout leases also provide for early termination should the leased property become obsolete to the lessee's needs. However, the lessee in a full payout lease is then liable for a termination payment which reflects the difference between the then value of the equipment and the lessor's unrecovered investment, costs, and contemplated profit on the transaction.

better position to find users for equipment that may be obsolete to one firm but still satisfactory to another. IBM is the best example of a manufacturer-lessor that has combined its financing, manufacturing, and marketing talents to reduce the risk of disposal. This reduced risk of disposal, compared with that faced by the lessee, is presumably passed along to the lessee in the form of a reduced lease cost.

Restrictions on Management

When a lender provides funds to a firm for an extended period of time, provisions to protect the lender are included in the debt contract. The purpose of protective provisions, or protective covenants, is to ensure that the borrower remains creditworthy during the period over which the funds are borrowed. Protective provisions impose restrictions on the borrower. Failure to satisfy such a protective covenant usually creates an event of default that, if not cured upon notice, gives the lenders certain additional rights and remedies under the loan agreement, including the right to perfect a security agreement or to demand the immediate repayment of the principal. In practice, the remedy and ability to cure vary with the seriousness of the event of default.

Three general types of protective provisions are imposed by lenders regardless of whether the funds borrowed are provided by a financial institution, such as a bank or life insurance company, or via a bond issue.[11] One type of protective provision seeks to safeguard the liquidity of the borrower. Four examples of general provisions to safeguard liquidity are (1) minimum working capital requirements. (2) cash dividend and repurchase-of-stock restrictions, (3) capital expenditure limitations, and (4) limitations on other indebtedness. The specific dollar amounts imposed by these restrictions depend on the financial characteristics of the individual borrower and the borrower's industry.

Routine provisions are a second type of protective covenant. These provisions include such requirements as providing periodic financial statements, restrictions on the sale or pledging of assets, and payment of other obligations. Most important for our discussion is the inclusion of a provision that prohibits the borrower from circumventing the restriction on indebtedness and capital expenditures by leasing. A limit may be imposed on the dollar amount, the term, or the type of leasing obligations.[12]

---

[11] James Van Horne, *Financial Management and Policy* (Englewood Cliffs, N.J.: Prentice-Hall, 1977), pp. 472–75. Covenants in public bond issues tend to be more general and less restrictive because of the difficulty in obtaining waivers or consents if some event of default should arise.

[12] Ibid., p. 474.

Finally, specific protective provisions may address particular situations. Examples of such provisions are: specification of how the funds borrowed will be used by the borrower, a management clause that mandates the continued employment of key officers during the borrowing period, and an after-acquired property clause. The last provision specifies that collateral for the borrowed funds is not only that which is indicated in the loan agreement or bond indenture but also includes any similar property acquired by the borrower in the future. Such a provision makes it difficult for the borrower to obtain additional financing, since it prohibits management from using property to be acquired in the future as collateral for a new loan.

An advantage of leasing is that leases typically do not impose financial covenants and restrictions on management as does a loan agreement used to finance the purchase of equipment. The historic reason for this in true leases is that the Internal Revenue Service discouraged true leases from having attributes of loan agreements. Leases may contain restrictions as to location of the property and additional investments by the lessee in the leased equipment in order to ensure compliance with tax laws.

Flexibility and Convenience

In addition to the flexibility and convenience that may result from leasing due to fewer restrictions being imposed on management, five other reasons are often cited for leasing. These reasons are characterized by flexibility and convenience.

1. Tailor-Made Lease Payments. Lease payment schedules can sometimes be designed to meet the specific needs of the lessee. For example, lease payments can be reduced or not scheduled during the period when the firm has its greatest needs for working capital. Payments can be set higher during the later years of the lease and lower in the earlier years, subject to Internal Revenue requirements, where the lessee's objective is a low present value cost. Although it may be possible to structure a term loan in the same way, it is generally difficult to do so. Moreover, the term for a true lease can usually be structured for a longer period than is customary for conventional loan agreements. Lessors can offer longer terms than bank term loans because of longer-term borrowing to fund activities and faster return of capital as a result of cash flow generated by tax benefits.

2. Speed in Obtaining Financing. A lease for a small-ticket item can generally be arranged more quickly than financing with other sources of intermediate-term debt. Documentation is usually simpler for closing leasing deals than for other arrangements. However, where large-ticket items are financed using a leveraged lease, it may take just as much time, or possibly longer, to put together an acceptable package for all parties as it would take to structure a term loan or arrange a private placement of bonds.

Some lessors write *master leases* to facilitate quick handling of a series of deliveries of various equipment. A master lease agreement works like a line of credit. Such an arrangement permits the lessee to acquire equipment when needed without having to negotiate a new lease agreement each time equipment is acquired. A restriction is placed on both the dollar amount of equipment to be leased and the time period over which the master lease is to apply. Generally, the time period is less than one year. The interest rate is either agreed to at the outset or is indexed to a reference interest rate at the time of acceptance. As equipment is delivered and accepted by the lessee, the lessee and lessor sign a schedule describing the equipment and lease term which is then incorporated into the master lease agreement by reference. One major advantage to the lessee is that financing costs and conditions of the lease are known in advance. Another advantage is the simple documentation requirements after the master lease agreement is in place.

3. Regulatory Ease

a. Public disclosure of financial information and confidential trade information is not required in connection with a lease transaction, as is the case with a prospectus for a public offering of debt or equity and as is sometimes the case with a private offering prospectus or memorandum.

b. Compliance by the lessee with SEC regulations governing the issuance of securities is not required under a lease. A special financial audit is not usually necessary.

c. Since lease obligations are not "securities" as defined by the Interstate Commerce Act, leasing enables railroads and other companies subject to ICC regulation to avoid obtaining ICC approval and competitive bidding requirements.

4. Getting around Budget Limitations.

Acquisition of equipment not contemplated by a capital expenditure budget can sometimes be accomplished through use of a lease, with lease payments structured to be classified as an operating expense. This is a common reason for leasing where a company (or a division of a company) has its capital budget in place and desires to acquire equipment to take advantage of a profit opportunity. Rather than go back to the board, the chairman, and so forth, to reopen the budget, the company leases the equipment and reflects it as an expense.

A particularly noteworthy example of this occurred in 1984 when the U.S. Navy leased a fleet of tankers and support vessels with the apparent intent of expensing such equipment rather than including the equipment in its capital (appropriations) budget.

In many firms division managers may be authorized to make current expenditures but not capital expenditures, which are usually reserved to corporate management. Leasing provides a way to circumvent this budgeting restriction for small-ticket items.

5. Eliminates Maintenance Problems. Of course, for a lease structured as a net lease, maintenance problems are not eliminated but are the responsibility of the lessee. Although an operating lease in which the lessor agrees to maintain the equipment eliminates maintenance problems for the lessee, the cost of maintenance is reflected in the lessor's pricing of the lease. If the lessor under an operating lease is the manufacturer and provides a service contract if the equipment is purchased, the relative unbundled maintenance cost implied in the lease must be compared with the same cost if the equipment is purchased in conjunction with a service contract in order to determine the least expensive operating lease arrangement.

Impact on Cash Flow and Book Earnings

In a properly structured true lease arrangement, the lower lease payment from leasing rather than borrowing can provide a lessee with a superior cash flow. Whether the cash flow stream on an after-tax basis after taking the residual value of the equipment into account is superior on a present value basis must be ascertained. The concept of present value and an analysis of cash flows from leasing versus borrowing to purchase are explained in Appendixes B and C.

Lease payments under a true lease will usually have less impact on book earnings during the early years of the lease than will depreciation and interest payments associated with the purchase of the same equipment.

TYPES OF LESSORS

Corporate lessors may be generally categorized as bank holding companies and commercial banks or their subsidiaries, independent leasing companies, captive leasing subsidiary companies of nonfinance companies, finance companies or their subsidiaries, investment banking firms, and subsidiaries of life or casualty companies.

Commercial banks that were national banks were first permitted to engage in equipment leasing in 1963 when the Comptroller of the

Currency ruled that national banks could become owners and lessors of personal property.[13] Subsidiaries of bank holding companies were first permitted to engage in equipment leasing in 1971 with the enactment of the Bank Holding Company Act. Many banks and bank holding companies or their subsidiaries participate indirectly in leasing through working relationships with independent and captive leasing companies.[14]

Independent leasing companies engage in equipment leasing the same as banks. After purchasing and taking title to the equipment requested by the lessee, such companies lease the equipment to the lessee on a "net" lease basis. Larger leasing companies can acquire funds to finance their operations from bank loans, commercial paper, and the issuance of securities. Smaller leasing companies obtain short-term funds from banks or finance companies to purchase leased equipment and then sell or discount their leases or "paper" to a third party, usually the bank or finance company providing the original funding for the transaction. A commission fee is received by the leasing company when the paper is sold or discounted to a third party.[15] When the leasing company sells or discounts the paper, it is acting in a brokerage capacity. Specialized leasing companies provide leasing and servicing of specific equipment in a particular industry. For example, many independent leasing companies concentrate on data processing equipment.

Captive leasing or finance companies are generally subsidiaries of equipment manufacturers, and their primary purpose is to secure financing for the customers of the parent company. Captives may also be involved in the lease financing of equipment other than that manufactured by their parent company. In addition to providing a marketing vehicle for the parent's products, the leasing activity of captives allows a parent with substantial taxable income to shelter a portion of that income.

In recent years, many nonfinance industrial and service companies without a need to finance their own products have established captive leasing companies to engage in tax-oriented leasing of equipment. These companies have become important participants in the market. They

---

[13] Except for certain specified purposes, commercial banks are barred from acting as lessors of real property. Bank holding companies may lease real property.

[14] For a detailed discussion of bank and bank holding company regulations see Chapter 10 of Peter K. Nevitt, Frank J. Fabozzi, and Edmond J. Seifried, *Equipment Leasing for Commercial Bankers* (Philadelphia, Penn.: Robert Morris Associates, 1987).

[15] The commission fee depends on the credit rating of the lessee, the length of the lease term, prevailing interest rates, the rate implicit in the lease (after considering residual value in the case of a true lease), and the yield sought by the lender for holding the paper in its portfolio.

have hired talented people, and in some cases their cost of funds is lower than most banks.

Captive leasing companies are usually funded initially by their parents. As their portfolio grows, matures, and establishes a track record, the funding is shifted to conventional borrowing sources such as discounting, bank loans, commercial paper, and private placements which are not supported by their parent.

LEASE BROKERS AND FINANCIAL ADVISERS

The growth of the leasing industry has produced a demand for intermediaries to assist lessors in servicing lessees. Lease brokers and financial advisers serve as architects or packagers of lease transactions by bringing together lessors, lessees, and, in the case of a leveraged lease, third-party lenders. Investment bankers, commercial banks, and small independent leasing companies have all played an important role as lease brokers and financial advisers.[16]

Lease brokers and financial advisers can perform a useful service for both lessees and lessors in arranging equipment leases. They can be especially helpful to a lessee by obtaining attractive pricing from a legitimate investor and advising the lessee in structuring and negotiating the transaction. While lease brokers and financial advisers typically represent lessees, they can be helpful to a lessor in finding solutions to negotiating issues.

The services performed by skilled brokers and financial advisers represent real value-added services which result in lower costs for lessees.

For its services as an intermediary, the lease broker or financial adviser receives a brokerage commission. The amount of the remuneration can vary widely, depending on the complexity of the deal and the attractiveness of the deal to the lessor in the prevailing economic environment. The standard fee usually ranges from ½ percent to 4 percent of the cost of the equipment, depending on the services performed or provided by the broker and the size and difficulty of the transaction.[17] In some brokered transactions, the lease broker or financial adviser may also receive at least a portion of its compensation in the form of an interest in the residual value of the leased equipment. And in still other situations the broker or financial adviser will work for a flat fee.

---

[16] See Chapter 17.

[17] In leases brokered to individuals in limited partnerships or wrap leases (discussed in Chapter 5), brokerage fees of 8 to 20 percent are not unusual.

In some instances a broker may assume some equipment risk by purchasing equipment on speculation for lease. Where a broker assumes such equipment risks, the rewards can be substantial. For example, suppose a lease broker purchases an asset such as an executive jet aircraft that requires a two-year lead time for delivery. When the airplane is delivered its market value may be greater than the purchase price paid by the lease broker two years earlier. The lease broker will then line up a lessee who needs the services of the airplane but cannot wait two years for delivery and a lessor interested in a tax-sheltered lease. The lease broker then assigns its purchase contract for the aircraft to the lessor and structures the lease payments so that the latter receives the necessary after-tax rate of return necessary to make the deal attractive. The lease broker's compensation in this transaction will consist of two parts: (1) a brokerage fee and (2) profit realized from the sale of its purchase contract. Of course, the lease broker in its position as an equipment speculator may realize a loss rather than a profit. Needless to say, speculation on future values of equipment such as aircraft is risky.

SELECTING A LESSOR OR FINANCIAL ADVISER TO ARRANGE A LEASE

Because of the low entry cost and easy access by lessors into the leasing industry, the potential lessee should exert caution in selecting a lessor, lease broker, or financial adviser. Negotiating a lease with a lessor or lease broker who is incapable of satisfying the lessee's objectives wastes management's time and delays the acquisition of the asset the firm seeks to lease. Moreover, even if a deal is consummated, the lease terms may fail to satisfy a tax and/or financial accounting result sought by the lessee.

Some lessors and lease brokers or packagers tend to quote unrealistically low lease rates only to request a renegotiation at a later time. The low lease rate may not always be a ploy to deceive the potential lessee. Sometimes it may simply be due to a lessor's or packager's belief that a deal can be put together on favorable terms, but subsequent changes in economic or market conditions may make the initial goal impossible.

The lessee should have a feel for prevailing lease rates. In the highly competitive leasing industry, the lease rates quoted should not vary significantly among lessors and packagers.[18]

---

[18] In the 1984, 1985, and 1986 navy ship leases, for example, the lease rates fell into a range of a few basis points so closely clustered that lessors with fiscal years shortly after the ship deliveries often won the transactions. (A basis point is equal to .01 percent. One percent is therefore equal to 100 basis points.) The U.S. Navy was skillfully represented by Argent Group in those lease transactions.

The dollar size of the transaction and the type of equipment will influence the selection of a lessor or lease broker. Lessors or lease brokers generally establish minimum dollar amounts for transactions they are willing to consider. Lessors will usually go below their minimum target in order to foster a relationship with a new client who may generate more financing activity in the future.

Companies may wish to employ lease financing for equipment to be used in operations by overseas subsidiaries. Because legal and tax aspects of lease transactions differ in every country, most lessors do not have the skills to engage in international leasing.[19] The larger commercial banks with international branches have some expertise in writing international leases. A lessee, however, need not rely solely on a U.S. lessor when seeking to lease equipment that will be used in a foreign country. Foreign banks and leasing companies throughout the world provide equipment lease financing. To facilitate the introduction of lessees in one country to lessors in another country, several international equipment lease clubs have been formed.[20]

Exhibit 1 lists questions that a potential lessee should consider before selecting a leasing company.

LEASE PROGRAMS

Lessors can structure lease transactions to suit the needs of most companies. Examples of various lease programs available are described below.

A *standard lease* provides 100 percent long-term financing with level payments over the term of the lease. Standard documentation facilitates quick handling and closing of the lease transaction. Installation costs, delivery charges, transportation expense, and taxes applicable to the purchase of the equipment may be included as part of the lease financing package.

A *custom lease* contains special provisions designed to meet particular needs of a lessee. It may, for example, schedule lease payments to fit cash flow. Such a lease can be particularly helpful to a seasonal business.

A *master lease,* as discussed earlier, works like a line of credit. It is an agreement that allows the lessee to acquire during a fixed period of time assets as needed without having to renegotiate a new lease contract for each item. With this arrangement, the lessee and lessor agree to the fixed terms and conditions that will apply for various

---

[19] A lease agreement that established the rights of a lessor in one country, for example, may imperil them in another.

[20] When the lessee and lessor are domiciled in different countries, the leasing arrangement is referred to as "transnational" or "cross-border" leasing.

EXHIBIT 1   Evaluating a Lessor, Broker, or Financial Adviser

---

In evaluating the choice of a lessor, broker, or financial adviser, a lessee should ask the following questions regarding the firms being considered. Every "no" answer regarding a prospective lessor, broker, or financial adviser should make the lessee apprehensive regarding the capacity of that lessor, broker, or financial adviser to perform as represented and in a manner satisfactory to the lessee. Furthermore, the degree of risk rises with the number of "no" answers.

		Yes	No
1.	If the firm is a lessor, rather than a broker, will sign a firm commitment subject only to documentation.		
2.	Will not broker the transaction to a third party who will be unreasonable to deal with. If problems develop with the proposed investor the broker will locate another investor at no additional cost.		
3.	Is adequately capitalized to back up any firm commitment.		
4.	Will furnish an audited statement; will state net worth.		
5.	Is substantial from a financial and management point of view.		
6.	Is experienced and has a clear history in the equipment leasing business. Has a good track record.		
7.	Has a good anticipated future in equipment leasing and will be available for consultation throughout the term of the lease.		
8.	Is not a promoter type who will disappear after payment of his fee.		
9.	Is familiar with the special legal problems related to a lease.		
10.	Understands and can correctly analyze the income tax considerations.		
11.	Will disclose the full amount of any fees he will receive in the transaction.		
12.	The "leasing company" has not purposely submitted a "low-ball" bid.		

classifications of equipment for a specified period, usually six months to one year. At any time within that period, the lessee can add equipment to the lease up to an agreed maximum, knowing in advance the rate to be paid and the leasing conditions.

Designed as a sales tool for equipment manufacturers or distributors, a *vendor lease* program permits suppliers to offer financing in the form of true or conditional sale leases. Vendor leases may be structured as tax-oriented or non-tax-oriented leases. They may be either short-term operating leases or full payout leases. Vendor lease programs can be offered directly by manufacturers and distributors or in conjunction with a third-party leasing company. Vendor leases are discussed in Chapter 10.

EXHIBIT 1   *(concluded)*

13. All material facts will be presented in obtaining any needed tax ruling since the ruling may be valueless if this is not the case and the lessee may then be liable under the tax indemnity clause.		
14. The transaction may be booked for financial accounting purposes as presented.		
15. If a lessor, has sufficient financial resources to do follow-on lease financing of retrofits, improvements, or additions.		
16. Will not broker the lease to a syndicate of parties, not one of whom can bind the others and who will be difficult to deal with as a group if changes are later needed.		
17. Will not disrupt the lessee's credit standing by indiscriminately contacting financial debt and credit sources all over the country in attempting to broker the transaction.		
18. If the commitment is not firm, the broker or financial adviser will disclose in advance how he will go about finding equity participants and whom he will contact.		
19. If the broker or financial adviser intends to bring in other brokers to help find equity participants, he will disclose who they are, whom they will contact, the amount of their fees, and who will pay the fees.		
20. The broker or financial adviser will make correct representations to the equity participants so that they will thoroughly understand their rights and obligations under the lease and not become disgruntled investors with whom it will be difficult to deal should the need arise.		
21. The equity participants will be financially able to meet their obligations to the owner trustee.		
22. The services to be performed by the broker or financial adviser represent real value-added services that result in a lower overall cost for the lessee than the lessee could achieve by dealing directly with a lessor. This is the most important test.		

An *offshore lease* is an agreement to lease equipment to be used outside the United States. Offshore lease programs offer leases calling for payments in U.S. dollars or local currencies for equipment used abroad. Both true leases and conditional sale leases can be arranged for firms requiring capital equipment in overseas operations. However, the tax benefits to U.S. lessors are insignificant since little depreciation is available on equipment located outside of the United States.

Sale-and-leaseback transactions can be used by a company to convert owned property and equipment into cash. The asset is purchased by the lessor and then leased back to the seller. (Care must be taken to comply with bulk sales laws and similar provisions of the commercial code. Usury laws should also be reviewed and sales tax consequences should be understood.)

Under a *facility lease,* an entire facility—a plant and its equipment—can be leased. Under this arrangement a lessor may provide or arrange construction financing for a facility. Interest costs during construction can often be capitalized into the lease. The lease commences when the completed facility has been accepted by the lessee.

An industrial revenue bond *overrun lease* can be used where the costs of a plant exceed the dollar limits of industrial revenue bonds. In such a situation a true lease can be used to finance the equipment portion of the project to keep those costs within statutory limits. Leases can also be structured using industrial revenue bonds as leveraged debt.

Lease agreements designed for specific assets are also available. For example, *computer leases* permitting additions of memory core, upgrades, and special features during the course of the initial lease can be arranged. *Ship leases* utilizing a leveraged lease and Title XI guaranteed debt can be arranged. There are *fleet leases* for cars and trucks, including *TRAC leases* containing terminal rental adjustment clauses.

SUMMARY

This introductory chapter has been intended to give the reader a brief overview of equipment leasing. Each of the subjects touched on in this chapter will be discussed in detail in the ensuing chapters. The logical place to begin a study of this widely used and important method of financing is with a review of the history of leasing.

2

History of Leasing

Leasing of personal property has experienced rapid growth in the United States, Europe, and Asia over the past 20 years and is generally thought of as a relatively new device for financing capital equipment. However, leasing is actually a very ancient form of commercial transaction. Modern leasing has roots that date back thousands of years. In this chapter we shall present a history of leasing that will provide a background and perspective on equipment leasing as it is conducted today.[1]

LEASING IN ANCIENT TIMES

The earliest record of equipment leasing occurred in the ancient Samarian city of Ur in about 2010 B.C. These leases involved rentals of agricultural tools to farmers by the priests who were, in effect, the government officials. Ur was a thriving commercial center, and both land and tools were leased. These transactions were recorded on clay tablets that were discovered in 1984.

---

[1] "Those who ignore the past may be condemned to repeat it." Santayana. Appendix A of this book lists the milestone events in the history of equipment leasing.

Later an ancient and powerful Babylonian king named Hammurabi, who ruled about 1750 B.C., acknowledged the existence of leases of personal property in his famous code of laws. The ancient Egyptians engaged in leases of both personal property and real property. The Greeks and Romans also leased personal property and in about 550 A.D. the Justinian Codex went so far as to distinguish between finance leases and short-term rentals of equipment.

Ships have been chartered from the time of the ancient Phoenicians. Ship charters were actually a very pure form of equipment leases. Short-term time charters and trip charters were the same as operating leases in which a crew is provided with a ship. Long-term bareboat charters were equivalent to net finance leases since the charters were for most of the useful life of the asset and the lessee had many of the benefits and obligations of ownership. Net lease provisions in modern leases are known as "pay come hell or high water" clauses because such provisions originated in ship charter agreements. Shipowners, acting as lessors, and ship users (charter parties), acting as lessees, have been negotiating their various duties, rights, and obligations under ship charters for thousands of years. The issues that have arisen in such transactions over the years are not dissimilar from the issues that arise today in commercial leases of personal property.

For hundreds of years personal property leasing was not recognized under English common law, although real property was leased extensively and sometimes involved very complex structures. Under English common law, the possession of personal property implied ownership. Eventually, the English courts recognized the need for commercial use of personal property by nonowners and developed a law of bailments based on European law. Personal property leases were called "bailments for hire" and "hire purchase agreements."

EARLY LEASING IN THE UNITED STATES

The first recorded leases of personal property in the United States seem to have been leases of horses, teams of horses, buggies, and wagons by liverymen or livery stables in the 1700s. Modern equipment leasing in the United States had its significant beginnings in the 1870s in connection with the financing of barges, railroad cars, and railroad locomotives under equipment trust certificates.

Consumer leasing in the United States began on a large scale with leases of sewing machines by the Singer Sewing Machine Company. Singer sewing machines were sold for $5 down and $5 a month under an instrument resembling a conditional sale lease.

EARLY RAILROAD EQUIPMENT LEASES

Railroad equipment was commonly financed during the 1800s under an arrangement whereby a railroad contracted with a manufacturer for the purchase of railroad cars, with the purchase price to be paid under a contract closely resembling a conditional sale contract. Typically, the equipment was financed over several years, with the purchase price paid in installments, plus interest, at set intervals over the term. Title passed to the railroad when the purchase price was entirely paid. From the standpoint of the railroad, needed equipment was acquired and paid for as it generated earnings. This type of financing was used by railroads because they could not qualify for conventional financing and were unable to provide a first mortgage as debt security.

Manufacturers of railroad cars, however, were not well capitalized or inclined to carry large amounts of receivables from railroads. Therefore, a railroad wishing to purchase railroad cars arranged through investment bankers to borrow funds from investors willing to finance the equipment. Upon delivery of the equipment, these investors transferred the funds needed to purchase the equipment to a bank or trust company acting on their behalf as agent. The bank or trust company then paid the purchase price to the manufacturer, took an assignment of the conditional sale agreement, and issued participation certificates to investors that were identical to the payment schedule called for under the conditional sale agreement. The bank or trust company held title to the equipment until the entire purchase price was paid, at which time title passed to the railroad. This method of financing was sometimes referred to as the "New York Plan."

There were serious drawbacks to this method of financing. Some state laws, particularly the laws of Pennsylvania, did not at that time recognize conditional sales on the ground that the holder of title to property under a conditional sale contract was not protected against claims of creditors of the purchaser who lacked knowledge of the conditional sale arrangement. Presumably, a creditor of a railroad subject to a conditional sale arrangement, or even a purchaser of property from such a railroad, would have a claim against railroad cars placed in the custody of the railroad under a conditional sale contract if that creditor or purchaser was not aware of the contract. This gave rise to the "Pennsylvania bailment lease" and eventually to a new method of financing railroad equipment known as the "Philadelphia Plan."

Under the Philadelphia Plan, the railroad desiring to purchase equipment arranged through investment bankers for investors to purchase "equipment trust certificates" that provided for repayment of the principal amount of the certificates plus "dividends" equivalent to interest payments over a specified period of time. Instead of an assignment of a conditional sale contract, as under the New York Plan, investors contributed funds to a bank or trust company acting as trustee for the purchase of equipment trust certificates. Upon receipt of such funds, the bank or trust company purchased the equipment from the manufacturer and "leased" it to the railroad for a term of years that equaled the principal and "dividends" due on the equipment trust certificates. The lease and the right to receive rentals were held by the trustee for the benefit of the holders of the equipment trust certificates. The creditor rights of the holder of an equipment trust certificate were usually bolstered by the direct guarantee of the railroad, which was enforceable in the event of a default on the lease and which enabled the equipment trust certificate holder to proceed directly against the railroad without having to exhaust his remedies under the "lease" agreement. As in the New York Plan, the railroad eventually acquired title to the equipment upon payment of all amounts due under the trust certificates. Investors generally preferred the Philadelphia Plan trust certificates to the New York Plan participation certificates.

Thus, the Philadelphia Plan, utilizing a direct lease, a trust, and equipment trust certificates, is the forerunner of modern-day conditional sale leasing.

In the early 1900s another form of railroad car leasing evolved in which the lessor retained title to the equipment at the end of the lease term. Railroad car leasing companies, such as GATX, Union Tank Car, and North American Car, rose from modest beginnings to be major owners and lessors of railroad cars by leasing them on a basis whereby they retained ownership of the railroad cars at the conclusion of the lease term. Although railroads were to some extent lessees under these arrangements, the major lessees were shippers who needed railroad cars dedicated to transporting their products. Also, such shippers often needed someone to manage the operation and maintenance of their cars. In many instances shippers did not desire long-term leases, although in practice they regularly renewed their leases. In any event a new industry arose in which railroad lessors purchased or manufactured railroad cars for lease to shipper lessees under arrangements whereby the lessor would maintain the cars and own them at the end of the lease term. These leases were among the first "true leases" and "operating leases" of equipment other than ships. It is also interesting to note that such railroad car lessors sometimes used Philadelphia Plan equipment trust certificates to finance their own fleets.

EARLY EQUIPMENT LEASES OTHER THAN LEASES OF RAILROAD ROLLING STOCK

Vendor leasing began to evolve in the 1920s as manufacturers sought to encourage sales of their equipment. Manufacturers promoted sales of their products with installment sales contracts that were then discounted to banks and finance companies.

Leasing was also used by manufacturers seeking to maintain monopoly control over the use of machinery with unique characteristics that made it superior to other machinery performing the same function. In such situations, leasing was sometimes used as a substitution for a licensing arrangement. U.S. Shoe Machinery was an early user of leases to control its products.

During World War II, a new stimulus to leasing arose from the terms of government "cost-plus contracts" for the manufacture and production of war materials. The theory of cost-plus contracts was to limit the profit a company could realize from manufacturing goods for the war effort. However, a manufacturer was permitted to make a small profit in excess of its costs. The government recognized that costs were beyond the control of a manufacturer due to shortages and difficulties in obtaining materials. Consequently, the establishment of costs for the purpose of computing the profits to which a manufacturer was entitled was very important. Manufacturers under cost-plus contracts did not want to invest in production equipment that could not be used at the end of the war. Such manufacturers were concerned that attempts to depreciate equipment of this kind over a fairly short period might not be recognized for purposes of figuring costs. Therefore, leases of production equipment for the life of a cost-plus contract became popular where doubt existed as to the manufacturer's ability to otherwise write off the equipment over the life of a contract. In some instances, the government acted as the lessor where large specialized machinery and tools were leased to manufacturers. The same concept continues today where specialized equipment is required for a particular contract with a duration shorter than the life of the equipment. Cost-plus contracts are also used today by contractors working on projects located in remote locations where transportation of equipment from the construction site will not be feasible from a cost standpoint at the conclusion of a contract.

Another form of short-term lease that developed involved the lease of equipment with an operator, such as a truck with a driver or construction equipment with an operator. These leases were called operating leases because an operator was furnished. Over time, the term *operating lease* has come to refer to a wide variety of short-term leases. The Financial Accounting Standards Board eventually adopted a precise definition for operating leases and a special set of rules for both lessees and lessors to account for operating leases.

The car rental business had its origins in 1918 when Walter Jacobs acquired 12 Model T Fords and formed Rent-a-Car, Inc., which he sold five years later to John D. Hertz. In 1941, an automobile dealer in Chicago named Zollie Frank commenced long-term fleet leasing of automobiles. He is generally credited with being the originator of automobile leasing as it is conducted today with a total volume of over $20 billion a year.

During the late 1940s, significant automobile leasing began on both an individual basis and a fleet basis. Short-term rentals by Avis, Hertz, and National Car Rental all grew rapidly during the 1950s. Airport locations by rent-a-car companies changed the entire character of that business. Automobile leases were the first introduction to equipment leasing for many businesspeople.

EARLY TRUE LEASE STRUCTURES

The first significant long-term true leases of equipment occurred in the late 1940s. These were leases of railroad equipment. Certain insurance companies were willing to assume a residual risk in railroad equipment at the end of a lease term and to reflect the expected residual value by lowering lease rentals during the lease term. The railroad lessee under such an arrangement had to rationalize the loss of the residual value at the end of the lease term and accept the modern-day underlying rationale for true leasing, that the use of the equipment rather than ownership makes economic sense to a lessee where a lower rental rate reflects a reasonable value for the residual. Sometimes the residual risk to the lessee in such leases was protected by a purchase option at a price higher than a nominal price. Tax benefits did not produce a positive cash flow for the lessor in these early transactions and were not a factor in the lease pricing.

However, the railroads taking advantage of such true lease arrangements benefited in that rental obligations under these leases were not classified as "fixed charges," as was interest on equipment trust certificates or conditional sales. Also, the financing was off balance sheet, outside the restrictions of loan covenants, and not considered to be "after-acquired property" under open-end basket security provisions of indentures whereby assets acquired after an indenture was in effect would be deemed to be subject to the security interest granted under the earlier lending agreement. In addition, certain restrictions on the issuance of new securities under the Interstate Commerce Act could be avoided by using the lease device.

In 1949, the Equitable Life Assurance Society developed an imaginative arrangement for financing railroad cars that was an early forerunner of modern leveraged leasing. Equitable purchased railroad cars from a manufacturer on terms under which Equitable paid 80 percent of the cost on delivery and 20 percent in installments over a five-year period. Equitable simultaneously leased the railroad cars to a railroad for 15 years at rents that were sufficient to retire the 20 percent debt balance owed by Equitable to the manufacturer over the five-year term of the debt and also to return Equitable's 80 percent investment with profit over the 15-year lease term. Equitable's payments on the 20 percent debt balance to the manufacturer were contingent upon receipt of payments under the lease. The manufacturer did not have a lien on the equipment except for an option to repurchase it for an amount equal to Equitable's investment in the event of a default by the lessee. The lease was drafted as a net lease in a manner that shielded Equitable from ownership risks.

Banks also began utilizing trust structures to invest in lease equity positions in railroad equipment financial leases. Legal title to the equipment was held by a trustee because federal and state laws were then interpreted to prohibit banks from leasing.

MODERN EQUIPMENT LEASING COMPANIES

If modern equipment leasing has a founder, that person would have to be Henry Schoenfeld. In 1954, U.S. Leasing Corporation, established by Henry Schoenfeld, became the first company formed to engage in general equipment leasing along the general lines on which such businesses are conducted today. The leases were net leases in which the lessee paid all the expenses of maintenance, insurance, taxes, and so forth associated with equipment ownership. The lessee generally retained a nominal purchase option. Lease rental payments were sufficient to cover the cost of the lessor purchasing and financing the purchase of the leased equipment.

In 1956, Boothe Leasing Corporation, a spin-off of U.S. Leasing personnel, was formed by D. P. Boothe to engage in general equipment leasing. (Boothe Leasing Corporation was acquired by the Greyhound Corporation in 1962 and became known as Greyhound Leasing and Financial Corporation.) In 1957, Chandler Leasing was formed. (It was acquired by Pepsi-Cola in 1967.) General Electric Credit Corporation, Commercial Credit Corporation, and National Equipment Leasing Corporation began to engage in the leasing of personal property in the 1950s. These companies along with U.S. Leasing Corporation and a few others were the forerunners of the hundreds of equipment leasing companies that exist today. Their alumni span the industry.

The groundwork for use of nonrecourse leveraged debt in true leases dates from 1947 when the U.S. Supreme Court held in the landmark case of *Crane* v. *Commissioner,* 331 U.S. 1, that the owner of qualifying property could include in his property cost amounts that had been borrowed on the security of the property and that the owner was not personally obligated to repay. This was not terribly significant until the potential tax benefits for lessors under equipment leases were increased by accelerated depreciation provisions in the Internal Revenue Code of 1954.

National Equipment Leasing Corporation was among the first to recognize the possibilities of leveraging these tax benefits, and in the middle 1950s it arranged some limited partnerships of individual investors to assume equity positions in equipment leases. Debt was provided by institutional lenders. National acted as a trustee.

General Motors adapted the National Equipment structure to lease diesel railroad engines that it manufactured. The equipment was leased directly to the railroads, utilizing a General Motors subsidiary formed for that purpose, with recourse on the subsidiary's debt limited to the assets of the subsidiary consisting of the rents and rights under the lease agreement.

LEASING FROM 1960 TO 1970

The American Association of Equipment Lessors was formed in 1962 as a trade association to promote leasing and to monitor federal and state laws and regulations affecting leasing. The pioneer leasing companies represented at the initial meeting to form the AAEL and their representatives at this meeting were as follows:

D. P. Boothe of Boothe Leasing Corporation, based in San Francisco. Boothe Leasing Corporation later became Greyhound Leasing and Financial Corporation.

Spencer Clawson of Security Leasing Company, based in Salt Lake City. This company is now part of Equitable Life.

Robert Sheridan of Nationwide Leasing, based in Chicago.

Edward F. Monahan of Indiana-Michigan Corporation of Chicago, now based in Oak Brook, Illinois.

Ed Herman and Ben Kelts of Chandler Leasing Corporation of Waltham, Massachusetts, later Pepsico Leasing Corporation.

Daniel Cavanaugh of American Industrial Leasing Company, New York.

Henry Shoenfeld of U.S. Leasing Corporation of San Francisco.

Carl Hutman of Public Service Leasing, based in Baltimore, Maryland.

Patrick H. Pringel of First National Leasing Corporation, based in Milwaukee.

Henry Shoenfeld of U.S. Leasing Corporation attended as an observer. Ellis Lyons was present as legal counsel.

In the early 1960s, both Greyhound Leasing and Financial Corporation and General Electric Credit Corporation began to engage in large-scale leasing in which they assumed a residual risk that they passed through to the lessee in the form of lower rents than would have been payable under a conditional sale agreement. The leases were made to airlines and railroads as well as to other equipment lessees. They were net leases that sometimes contained purchase options of 15 to 25 percent. Nevertheless, tax counsel at the time was of the opinion that the downside residual risk made them true leases. Tax benefits from accelerated depreciation were claimed by Greyhound and General Electric Credit Corporation. These leases were upheld as true leases after sometimes lengthy audit by the Internal Revenue Service.

A stimulus to tax-oriented leasing was provided in 1962 when Congress inadvertently changed the whole character of the equipment leasing business by passing income tax legislation designed to foster investment in capital equipment. The stimulus took the form of a 7 percent investment tax credit and an increased deduction for tax depreciation. Greyhound and General Electric Credit discovered (to their surprise) that as lessors and owners of equipment they were entitled to substantial tax benefits under committed true leases in which the lessee did not have a right to acquire the equipment at the end of the lease term for a nominal purchase option. They also became aware that they could substantially reduce rentals to lessees in future leases by passing through a portion of the tax benefits to lessees. These lower rentals made leasing more attractive for lessees that had little taxable income to shelter and consequently could not claim the tax benefits on their own tax returns. Most airlines and railroads were in this situation. Other major finance companies, such as Commercial Credit Corporation, CIT, and Ford Motor Credit, quickly recognized the implications of the new tax laws and became active in tax-oriented leasing.

Another important stimulus to equipment leasing was provided in 1963, when the U.S. Comptroller of the Currency issued a ruling that permitted national banks to own and lease personal property.[2] Prior

---

[2] Interpretive Ruling No. 400, 12 CFR Sec. 7.300, since revised.

to that time, banks had invested in equipment trust certificates and discounted receivables under financial leases written by independent leasing companies. The profitability of tax-oriented true leases written by Greyhound and General Electric Credit had not gone unnoticed by the major commercial banks lending to those companies. Since such banks, like the parent companies of Greyhound Leasing and Financial Corporation and General Electric Credit Corporation, had substantial tax liability to shelter, they recognized tax-oriented true leases of equipment as an attractive product to offer for financing equipment. The initial leasing efforts of banks were aimed at the railroads, which were in perpetual need of equipment, and at the airlines, which were rapidly adding routes and acquiring jet aircraft to meet their expansion needs. Most railroads and airlines were not in a taxpaying position to claim the ITC or accelerated depreciation associated with equipment ownership.

The entry of banks into the leasing business was responsible for the standard method used today for computing lease yields on a pretax basis after taking cash flows from tax benefits into account. This method was introduced because banks wanted to compare lease yields with loan yields. Brokers seeking to sell lease transactions to banks saw the advantage of providing a method for easy comparison of leases to loans and therefore promoted the pretax-posttax yield analysis method. Before banks got into leasing, more conventional methods of calculating return on investment or equity were used by nonbank leasing companies.

A very major event of the late 1960s was the development of modern leveraged lease structures in which the lessor provided only a portion of the purchase price of the asset, borrowed the remainder of the purchase price from institutional lenders on a nonrecourse basis, but claimed tax benefits on 100 percent of the purchase price of the leased equipment. Lessors computed their yields, including expected residual values, on their equity investments rather than the entire equipment cost, thus enabling lessors to offer more attractive lease rates to lessees than were offered under unleveraged true leases. This major breakthrough in pricing made leasing attractive to a much broader market and significantly stimulated the growth of leasing.

Tax-oriented leasing suffered some setbacks in the 1960s when Congress first suspended the investment tax credit (ITC) in 1966, then reinstated it in 1967, and again repealed it in 1969, before enacting it again in 1971.[3]

In the late 1960s, individual investors began to become involved as equity participants in limited partnerships structured with nonre-

---

[3] ITC remained in effect until it was repealed by the Tax Reform Act of 1986.

course debt. With individuals in 70 percent tax brackets, banks and finance companies found themselves in danger of being unable to compete from a price standpoint with syndicates of individual lessors offering leveraged lease financing. However, with the reenactment of the ITC in 1971, Congress imposed restrictions that effectively limited the availability of investment tax credit to individuals and eliminated syndicates of individuals as significant investors in leveraged leases until the early 1980s, when changes in the tax laws improved conditions for individuals acting as lessors.[4]

In another leasing development of the 1960s, IBM and Xerox began to significantly utilize equipment leases as a marketing strategy for realizing maximum revenue from their products. IBM and Xerox recognized that substantial sums could be made from the financing of their equipment. Also, by adjusting the prices of rentals and purchase prices, the mix of machines rented or purchased could be varied to produce a more orderly growth of reported profits. In addition, the strategy offered a means to remove obsolete machines from the marketplace and control the resale market. IBM and Xerox assumed the risk of property taxes and the cost of insurance and provided maintenance, all as a "bundled" charge for rental. From the customer's standpoint, the short-term lease rate was reasonable, was off balance sheet, and offered protection against obsolescence due to fast-developing technology. Other manufacturers of computers, copying equipment, and office equipment offered similar terms in order to meet the competition of IBM and Xerox.

Vendor leasing by manufacturers of all kinds of equipment came into wide use during the 1970s as equipment users began to demand financing as part of the purchase package.

Computer leasing by independent third-party leasing companies became popular during the 1960s. Computer leasing companies operated on the premise that they could purchase new IBM equipment, rent the equipment to users for short terms at less than IBM rentals, and still keep the equipment long enough after the initial lease terms to recover their investment and return a profit after the payment of all expenses. During the late 1960s, over 50 computer leasing companies engaged in the purchase and lease of IBM 360 computers. Unfortunately, the introduction of the IBM 370 computer resulted in the obsolescence of the 360 computers, a drastic reduction in rentals, and financial failure for many of these companies. It is interesting to note that a few companies tried the same pricing and leasing strategy with IBM 370 computers with much the same result. Residual insurance under Lloyd's "J" policies was used to support the residuals of some companies, with

---

[4] The Deficit Reduction Act of 1984 and Tax Reform Act of 1986 made equipment leasing unattractive for individual lessors.

the result that Lloyd's suffered huge losses and has since been reluctant to offer residual insurance for any type of equipment.

The substantial leasing of computers and office equipment that occurred during the 1960s was a significant factor in the growth of leasing, since many companies were exposed to equipment leasing for the first time when they leased such equipment.

Until the early 1970s, however, leasing remained something of a novelty for most companies. Although most airlines and railroads utilized leases in financing major portions of their equipment needs, most nontransportation companies still did not utilize leasing except for short-term operating leases of computers, office copiers, and transportation equipment. In most cases these leases were not even handled by their finance departments but, instead, were handled by the operating departments involved. Since leasing competed with conventional sources of financing, such as loans offered by banks and insurance companies, those financial institutions often discouraged their nontransportation customers from using leases. Equipment leasing was still regarded as "last-resort financing" that a company did not use so long as conventional financing was available.

BANK HOLDING COMPANY LEGISLATION

The general attitude of banks toward leasing changed in 1970 when Congress amended the Bank Holding Company Act to permit banks to form holding companies and to engage in a number of activities in addition to lending. These permitted activities included equipment leasing. This legislation was enacted in response to a lobbying effort by banks to be permitted to engage in types of activities other than lending in order to compete with major finance companies that banks felt were making inroads into their traditional markets. Banks asked permission to compete on equal terms with major finance companies and offer the same broad range of services, including leasing, that were offered by the finance companies. The amendment of the Bank Holding Company Act in 1970, the amendment of Regulation Y in 1971, and the more specific amendment of Regulation Y in 1974 resulted from these efforts.

In response to this legislation, most large banks formed holding companies to engage in nonbanking activities. This was expensive. The formation of holding companies involved board of directors and stockholder approval, the expense of substituting new stock certificates, and large legal fees. As a result, bank managements became understandably concerned about quickly launching some new and profitable operations within their holding company structures to justify the expense. Since leasing was one of the permissible activities outlined in the Bank Holding Company Act and in Regulation Y, as amended in 1970 and 1971, since bank managements felt somewhat comfortable with leasing because of its similarity to lending, and since some banks had had some leasing experience under the earlier Comptroller of the Currency ruling, the establishment of subsidiaries of bank holding companies to engage in leasing suddenly became the vogue.

Bank holding company leasing subsidiaries offered true leases, purchase option leases, and conditional sale leases for all kinds of equipment. In some instances, small leasing companies engaged in money-over-money kinds of leasing were acquired by banks to gain portfolios and expertise. In other instances, banks hired persons with leasing experience to head up and manage their leasing operations. And in still other instances, banks staffed their new leasing corporations with bright young loan officers who relied heavily on brokers and finders for the generation of lease business.

Suddenly leasing became a very respectable method of financing equipment. Prior to the formation of bank holding company subsidiaries engaged in leasing, banks had generally encouraged their customers to view leasing as a source of funds to be used only by a company unable to borrow funds, as equivalent to a borrowing of last resort, and as something "nice companies didn't do." As bank holding companies entered the business, leasing became not only respectable but also a type of "creative financing" that smart companies took advantage of. Banks instructed their loan officers to encourage their customers to lease and to refer such business to their new leasing subsidiaries. Bank loan officers and other conventional lenders ceased downgrading leasing as a method of financing. Within the next few years, most companies in the United States were exposed to leasing, and many companies began using leases on a regular basis to finance major equipment needs.

In 1979, the Comptroller of the Currency revised the regulations describing the leasing activities permitted by banks and bank subsidiaries. These detailed regulations were pretty much identical to Regulation Y, which applied to bank holding companies, and certainly endorsed the proposition that equipment leasing was a good and legitimate business for banks.

Whereas in the early 1970s few financial officers had been exposed to leasing, by the late 1970s most financial officers were very familiar with leasing and had seriously considered leasing even if they had not, in fact, used leasing to finance equipment.

DEVELOPMENT OF ACCOUNTING STANDARDS FOR LESSEES AND LESSORS

The rapid growth of tax-oriented true leases in the 1960s and early 1970s raised serious questions as to the correct accounting for such transactions. Although *APB 5,* issued in 1964, required a lessee to capitalize a lease if it contained a nominal purchase option and was comparable to a purchase, accounting for leases by lessees was not uniform or consistent. In 1972, the Securities and Exchange Commission brought the matter to a head by threatening regulatory action if the accounting profession failed to clarify the situation. Consequently, *APB 31,* issued in 1973, required footnote disclosure of minimum and contingent rent obligation for the current year and succeeding years. The SEC was still not satisfied and continued to pressure the newly formed Financial Accounting Standards Board for comprehensive lessee and lessor accounting rules. In 1976, the Financial Accounting Standards Board issued *Statement of Financial Accounting Standards No. 13 (FAS 13),* which set forth comprehensive guidelines for lease accounting by both lessees and lessors. *FAS 13* is discussed in Chapter 3.

At the time *FAS 13* was issued, lessees and lessors were very fearful that its requirement that lessees capitalize leases under certain circumstances would discourage leasing and reduce volume. However, the net effect was just the opposite. The guidelines were fairly drawn and liberally interpreted by the accounting profession. The net result was that *FAS 13* provided much greater uniformity in reporting and defining lease accounting. Consequently, *FAS 13* gave greater respectability and acceptability to leasing. Over the next few years, the FASB issued several statements, interpretations, and technical bulletins explaining and interpreting *FAS 13.* Nevertheless, its provisions have remained unchanged, providing continuity and additional respectability for leasing and lease accounting.

INCREASED TAX BENEFITS DURING THE 1970s

During the 1970s, Congress became concerned regarding the adequacy of tax deductions for depreciation in view of the inflationary cost of new equipment. In response to this problem Congress in 1971 shortened the depreciable lives of equipment (ADR guidelines), permitted accelerated depreciation, and restored the 7 percent ITC (investment tax credit), which had been repealed in 1969. Congress recognized that companies unable to directly utilize the tax benefits of depreciation deductions and the ITC because they were not in a taxpaying position could indirectly obtain most of the tax benefits associated with equipment ownership through true leases in which the lessor claimed such benefits. Later, in 1975, Congress increased the ITC from 7 percent to 10 percent. The increased tax benefits enacted by Congress in 1971 and 1975 made tax-oriented true leasing more attractive for lessees unable to claim such benefits directly.

TAX LAW CLARIFICATIONS DURING THE 1970s

As leasing volume began to experience rapid growth in the early 1970s, the Internal Revenue Service was besieged with requests for private revenue rulings pertaining to proposed transactions. There was no statutory law or case law defining true leases. The Internal Revenue Service had issued Revenue Ruling 55–540 in 1955, which provided guidance on simple true leases, but this ruling was very general and of little help to lessees, lessors, or their tax counsel in addressing the complex structures of leveraged leases that were beginning to arise with great frequency.

The Internal Revenue Service found itself in a very uncomfortable position. It was besieged with ruling requests. Large, complex commercial transactions were entered into conditioned upon obtaining favorable rulings, which created tremendous pressure for approval as closing and delivery deadlines approached. The ability of the Internal Revenue Service to respond was further hampered by the small IRS staff available to review and act upon ruling requests.

Furthermore, an unhealthy "old boy" network was developing. Since private rulings were not publicized at that time, a tax counsel with knowledge of recent private tax rulings through his experience or his contacts with other tax counsel was at a tremendous advantage in anticipating what structures the IRS would approve. Tax counsel with such inside knowledge was at a distinct advantage in arguing with the IRS for approval based on private ruling precedents.

In response to this situation, the IRS issued Revenue Procedure 75–21, setting forth "guidelines" for obtaining favorable tax rulings on leveraged lease transactions. If the guidelines of Revenue Procedure 75–21 were met, a favorable ruling was assured. Further clarifications of Revenue Procedure 75–21 were contained in Revenue Procedures 75–28, 76–30, and 79–48.

Lessees and lessors were very apprehensive regarding Revenue Procedure 75–21. They feared it would be difficult to comply with the lengthy and complex requirements. The procedure made requesting a ruling difficult and expensive by requiring vast amounts of detailed information. Also, since Revenue Procedure 75–21 set forth requirements that tax counsel regarded as stricter than the requirements of statutory or case law, lessees and lessors were concerned that Revenue Procedure 75–21 might assume the importance and substance of tax regulation criteria for true lease status for both leveraged and non-leveraged leases. Furthermore, there was the risk that the guidelines of Revenue Procedure 75–21 would be used as requirements for true leases by Internal Revenue agents in conducting tax audits.

However, most of the concerns initially expressed regarding Revenue Procedure 75–21 have failed to materialize. In most cases, it has been possible to comply with the guidelines without undue problems for either the lessee or the lessor. In most cases lease transactions are completed without obtaining a favorable tax ruling because the parties feel comfortable that their transactions comply with Revenue Procedure 75–21.

Consequently, Revenue Procedure 75–21 actually helped and encouraged leasing by standardizing requirements for a true lease and by eliminating the expense and uncertainty of obtaining a tax ruling or negotiating complex tax indemnity or unwind agreements.

THE FRANK LYON CASE

In a landmark decision in 1978, the U.S. Supreme Court, in the case of *Frank Lyon & Co.* v. *United States,* 435 U.S. 561, considered the criteria for a true lease and particularly the significance of a purchase option in determining whether a lease constituted a true lease. The court affirmed the general rule that a lease would be characterized as a true lease for federal tax purposes if the parties intended to enter into a lease rather than a loan. The court indicated that this could be determined by ascertaining whether at the time of the execution of the lease it was reasonable to suppose that the lessor would retain a substantial economic or proprietary interest in the leased property. The court declared that key factors indicating the intent of the parties are the parties' estimates at the time of the execution of the lease that the value and remaining economic life of the leased property will be substantial rather than nominal.

The *Frank Lyon* case went on to hold that since the trial court had made a factual finding that the option price was a reasonable estimate of fair market value at the time the option was exercised, the appellate court could not conclude that the option would be exercised.

The net effect of the ruling in the *Frank Lyon* case has been to give considerable comfort to the position that a true lease can contain a fixed-price purchase option despite the fact that Revenue Procedure 75–21 indicates that a favorable ruling will not be given to a lease containing a fixed-price purchase option. However, any fixed-price purchase option would appear to have to take into consideration the 20 percent at-risk rules and inflationary factors as a minimum safe level for a fixed-price purchase option. Tax counsel relying on the *Frank Lyon* case have given favorable opinions on true lease status for leveraged leases containing options in the range of 40 to 50 percent of the original cost.

ECONOMIC RECOVERY TAX ACT OF 1981

The Economic Recovery Tax Act of 1981 (ERTA) contained provisions that dramatically changed equipment leasing and financing until those provisions were repealed in 1982 and 1983.

For many years, Congress had been concerned with providing business with more effective incentives for capital spending. The 10 percent ITC coupled with accelerated tax depreciation achieved this result for companies with annual federal tax liability large enough to take advantage of such tax benefits. However, a great many creditworthy companies did not have sufficient tax liability to claim the ITC and tax depreciation deductions. These included most companies engaged in heavy capital spending programs, such as steel companies, automotive companies, railroads, airlines, mining companies, forest products companies, and utilities. These were the very industries that many congressmen were most interested in helping. Furthermore, these industries formed an effective lobby to obtain government subsidies.

Tax-oriented leasing companies had provided true leases as an indirect means for nontaxpaying, capital-intensive companies to obtain and enjoy the benefits of the ITC and tax depreciation on their equipment acquisitions. However, as previously discussed, the tax laws and regulations required lessors under true leases to retain certain attributes of ownership that were objectionable to many lessees. In true leases, lessees were not permitted by Revenue Procedure 75–21 to have bargain purchase options, to lease limited-use property, to finance any part of the purchase price, or to lease equipment for more than 80 percent of its useful life. Although leasing had grown dramatically during the 1970s, these requirements, and particularly the inability to have a bargain purchase option, discouraged many companies from using true leases to obtain indirectly the advantages of tax benefits associated with equipment ownership. Many of the companies that did utilize true leases nevertheless resented the lack of a bargain purchase option.

Alternatives to true leases for the pass-through of ITC benefits to companies not in a taxpaying position had been informally considered from time to time by Congress. One method was "ITC refundability," whereby a company unable to utilize the ITC would instead be paid an equivalent amount by the Internal Revenue Service when it filed its income tax return claiming such credit. A similar proposal involved "ITC certificates" that would be issued by the Internal Revenue Service to a company entitled to ITC but unable to obtain the benefit of tax credits when filing its own return. These certificates could then be sold at a price near their face value to corporations able to claim such benefits. Serious flaws in both of these approaches, however, were the difficulties in administering such programs so as to provide timely ITC refunds while at the same time preventing fraud. Also, these proposals did not result in a transfer of tax depreciation deductions.

Safe-Harbor Leasing

In 1981, Congress devised and included in ERTA the "safe-harbor leasing" of equipment as a new and clever method for paying amounts equivalent to ITC and tax depreciation to companies unable to claim such benefits. Safe-harbor leasing permitted relatively free transferability of tax benefits from lessees to "nominal lessors." In safe-harbor leases of equipment acquired by lessees, nominal lessors were held responsible for proof of the legitimacy of their claims for the ITC and depreciation. The definition of a lease for which a lessor could claim tax benefits was broadened to include leases with fixed-price bargain purchase options, leases in which the lessee lent the lessor up to 90 percent of the purchase price, leases for longer terms than those authorized in true leases, and leases of limited-use property. Furthermore, permission was given for a streamlined form of safe-harbor lease called a "tax benefit transfer lease" (TBT lease) in which rental payments exactly equaled and offset debt payments. Under a TBT lease, compensation for tax benefits could be paid by the nominal lessor to the lessee in a single lump-sum payment at the beginning of the lease. TBT leases were, in effect, simply sales of tax shelters by lessees to lessors.

Safe-harbor leasing made it easy for any corporation with tax liability to act as a nominal lessor. It was also possible for almost any equipment purchase to be structured as a safe-harbor tax-oriented lease in which a nominal lessor could claim the ITC and tax depreciation and pay the lessee for such benefits either in a single lump-sum payment or in reduced rental payments.

Safe-harbor leasing was enthusiastically received and utilized by companies unable to use tax benefits currently. A large volume of equipment was leased under the new law. Most safe-harbor leases were structured as TBT leases that, in substance, were sales of tax shelters.

Increased Tax Benefits under ERTA

ERTA also contained provisions that dramatically increased tax benefits to owners of equipment, including lessors. ACRS depreciation permitted most equipment to be depreciated in five years on an accelerated basis. ITC vested in just five years (for five-year ACRS property) at the rate of 2 percent per year.

Increased Lease Volume by Individual Lessors

Prior to ERTA, equipment leasing was not a particularly attractive tax shelter for individual lessors as compared to alternative investments. ITC was not available to individuals except on short-term leases, and depreciation deductions alone were not large enough to make such leases competitive with leases offered by corporate lessors. ACRS deductions changed the economics of leasing for individual lessors and made leases offered by individuals attractive where ITC was not a factor. This gave rise to limited partnerships and some fairly exotic structures for equipment leases that were competitively priced.

TAX EQUITY AND FISCAL RESPONSIBILITY ACT OF 1982— REPEAL OF SAFE-HARBOR LEASES AND INTRODUCTION OF FINANCE LEASES

The overall results of safe-harbor leasing under ERTA proved to be very controversial. The volume of safe-harbor leasing was larger than expected. The revenue loss to the Treasury Department was higher than projected. Most of the benefits were channeled to large creditworthy lessees, while many small- and medium-sized eligible companies were unable to take advantage of the legislation. Some large taxpaying corporations were able to substantially reduce their taxes by acting as nominal lessors in safe-harbor leases.

This led many commentators to characterize safe-harbor leasing as wasteful, unfair, and a raid on the federal Treasury. Such criticism caused Congress to have serious second thoughts regarding the merits of this legislation. Furthermore, the rising federal deficits made the safe-harbor leasing provisions an attractive target for revision to provide a source of increased tax revenue.

As a result, Congress enacted the Tax Equity and Fiscal Responsibility Act of 1982 (TEFRA), which contained provisions that discontinued safe-harbor leasing by:

1. Repealing and phasing out safe-harbor and TBT leasing in 1982 and 1983.
2. Substituting and establishing a new type of tax-oriented lease called a "finance lease," effective January 1, 1984.

In establishing finance leases as a part of TEFRA, Congress provided a compromise lease structure. It eliminated the excessive liberalization of safe-harbor leasing but provided a solution to the major objection that many lessees had to be true leases by eliminating the requirement for a fair-market-value purchase option or a fixed-price purchase option based on estimated fair market value.

Finance leases differed from true leases in two major respects:

1. A finance lease could include a fixed-price purchase option equal to 10 percent, or more of the purchase price, whereas a true lease could contain only a fair-market-value purchase option.
2. Special-purpose or limited-use property could be leased under a finance lease, whereas such property could not be leased under a true lease.

Congress imposed certain restrictions on using finance leases or claiming tax benefits attributable to finance leases in 1984 and 1985. These restrictions were aimed at phasing in finance leases slowly and raising tax revenue in those years:

1. During 1984 and until September 30, 1985, the lessor in a finance lease could claim only 20 percent of eligible ITC in the year that the property was placed in service and 20 percent in each of the next four years.
2. A lessor could reduce its federal income tax by only 50 percent in each of the years 1984 and 1985 as a result of tax benefits generated from finance leases or safe-harbor leases, including depreciation attributable to such leases entered into in earlier taxable years. This limitation expired for property placed in service after September 30, 1985, in taxable years beginning after that date.
3. The amount of equipment that a lessee could lease using finance leases in 1984 and 1985 was limited to 40 percent of otherwise eligible property in each year. There was no limit on the amount of eligible property that a lessee could lease after 1985.
4. Only corporate lessors could offer finance leases.

True lease structures were not changed by ERTA and TEFRA. Moreover, the legislative history of TEFRA reviewed in detail the Internal Revenue Service guidelines for a true lease set forth in Revenue Procedure 75–21, and by implication endorsed those criteria.

TREASURY ATTEMPT TO LIBERALIZE TAX RULES REBUFFED

The Treasury Department made no secret of the fact that it favored safe-harbor leasing and was disappointed with the congressional repeal of it.

In 1983, the Treasury Department sought to indirectly resurrect safe-harbor leasing by liberalizing the requirements for true leases through regulations permitting fixed-price purchase options at fairly nominal amounts and reducing at-risk investment requirements. Although these regulations were never formally proposed, drafts were leaked and openly discussed. This effort to liberalize the requirements for true leases was stopped as a result of communications to the Treasury by the House Ways and Means Committee. Chairman Rostenkowski and other congressmen expressed strong displeasure with the proposed regulations, which they felt were contrary to the expressed intent of Congress in repealing safe-harbor leasing.

DEFICIT REDUCTION ACT OF 1984

In 1983 and 1984, Congress became increasingly concerned about the mounting federal budget deficit. As a result, it passed the Deficit Reduction Act of 1984, which was aimed primarily at raising revenue by raising taxes. Finance leases, which were to become effective on January 1, 1984, were identified by Congress as revenue losers and were consequently postponed for four years, until January 1, 1988. All of the special phase-in rules applicable to finance leases that had been due to take effect in 1985 and subsequent years were likewise postponed for four years.

True tax-oriented leases to foreign airlines, foreign companies, or government entities, 50 percent of the income of which was not subject to U.S. income tax, were also made ineligible for tax-oriented leases. True tax-oriented leases to not-for-profit corporations such as hospitals were restricted to certain short-life equipment.

On the other hand, TRAC leases containing terminal rental adjustment clauses for registered vehicles were made eligible for true lease treatment by the Deficit Reduction Act of 1984. This change created significant new tax-oriented lease opportunities for lessees and lessors.

Congress again approved true leases by favorable reference and implication in its committee reports. Furthermore, the committee reports contain language intended to prevent the Treasury Department from issuing regulations liberalizing the requirements for true leases.

The Deficit Reduction Act of 1984 contained very little to discourage leases of equipment by individuals. In the meantime, however, the Internal Revenue Service became concerned about claimed abuses in the structures of equipment leases by individuals and instituted an audit drive aimed at overturning and discouraging such equipment leases if they lacked economic substance.

TAX SIMPLIFICATION PROPOSAL

In December of 1984, the U.S. Treasury Department proposed a tax simplification plan for consideration by Congress. Among other things, this proposal eliminated ITC, eliminated ACRS, and indexed interest rate deductions to the excess over the inflation rate. Interestingly enough, the proposals did not eliminate or index deductions for lease rental payments.

During 1985, the administration presented two revised plans for tax revision modifying and expanding upon the 1984 proposal. The common objective agreed to by Congress and the administration was that any new comprehensive tax bill should achieve the objectives of being fair, simple, and revenue neutral.

THE TAX REFORM ACT OF 1986 (TRA)

In the fall of 1985, the House of Representatives began serious consideration of the tax bill proposed by the administration. After numerous changes and in the closing hours of the 1985 session of the House of Representatives, the House approved a tax bill (by voice vote) which eliminated ITC and most accelerated depreciation while reducing individual and corporate tax rates.

During 1986, the Senate considered and passed a tax law which repealed ITC, generally rearranged, but essentially retained, ACRS accelerated depreciation deductions, expanded the corporate minimum tax, and further reduced corporate and individual tax rates. Differences between the House and Senate bills were resolved, with the result that Congress passed and President Reagan signed into law on October 22, 1986, the most far-reaching revision of the tax laws in the history of the country. This new tax law was named the Tax Reform Act of 1986 (TRA) and was embodied in the newly designated Internal Revenue Code 1986. Unfortunately, the original idealistic objectives of fairness, simplicity, and revenue neutrality were not reflected in the final bill, which met none of those criteria.

Briefly stated, changes made by the TRA which particularly affected equipment leasing were as follows:

1. The corporate tax rate was reduced from 46 percent in 1986 to approximately 40 percent in 1987 and to 34 percent in 1988 and subsequent years.
2. Investment tax credit was repealed after December 31, 1985, except for certain property subject to binding contract which was excepted under transition rules.
3. Deductions for depreciation were changed for property placed in service after December 31, 1986, with certain exceptions

under transition rules. The deductions were increased for some types of equipment and decreased for other types of equipment.

4. An alternative minimum tax (AMT) was enacted which greatly reduced the accelerated depreciation deductions of companies subject to AMT and created immense administrative burdens for all corporations to maintain a new set of AMT books.

1987

The cost of acquiring equipment by lease or by purchase increased significantly as a result of the changes in the TRA. However, the cost differential between leasing and purchasing is much less under the new law. Furthermore, where a prospective lessee is in a loss-carry-forward position or is subject to AMT, leasing equipment quickly becomes significantly less expensive under the TRA than purchasing equipment. Experience in the marketplace quickly demonstrated a continuing market for tax-oriented equipment leasing. Most companies that found leasing attractive prior to TRA continued to lease.

Other effects of the new tax became apparent in 1987. Companies subject to AMT became good lease prospects and poor candidates to engage in leasing as lessors. Some lessors that formerly found equipment leasing attractive because of the large tax benefits thrown off by ITC no longer engaged in equipment leasing. A market for purchasing and brokering lease portfolios developed. Leveraged leases were more highly leveraged in the 75 to 80 percent range. Single investor leases began being used for larger transactions.

Another development during 1987 was the amendment of the National Bank Act to permit national banks to engage in short term operating leases.

The SEC requirement (SAB No. 70, June 10, 1987) that nonrecourse borrowings involving assignment of a security interest in a lease and/ or property subject to a lease do not result in recognition "as if" a sale had occurred; further, SAB 70 does not allow an offsetting of the lease receivables and nonrecourse debt.

AFTER 1987

If the past is prologue, the future of leasing seems assured.

Numerous threats to the leasing business have arisen in the past. On each occasion, the industry has faced up to the challenge, adjusted to the new rules, and emerged stronger than ever. Changes have created new opportunities as well as problems. The people engaged in leasing have been quick to take advantage of the opportunities.

3

Financial Reporting Requirements for Lease Transactions

Financial reporting considerations are important for most lessees and potential lessees. At one time, lessees needed only to disclose information regarding lease commitments in footnotes to their financial statements. Hence, leasing was often referred to as "off balance sheet financing." With the issuance by the Financial Accounting Standards Board (FASB) of *Statement of Financial Accounting Standards No. 13 (FAS 13)*, the accounting treatment of lease commitments changed.[1] *FAS 13* required that certain leases be recorded on the lessee's balance sheet as a liability and the leased property reported as an asset. This procedure is called "capitalizing a lease" or "lease capitalization." For leases that fail to meet the test specified by *FAS 13*, the lessee need only disclose certain information regarding lease commitments in a footnote.

The purpose of this chapter is to explain the rule set forth in *FAS 13* for determining whether a lease must be capitalized and then to

---

[1] FASB, *Statement of Financial Accounting Standards No. 13*, "Accounting for Leases" (Stamford, Conn., November 1976), as amended and interpreted.

compare the financial reporting requirements of capitalized and non-capitalized leases. Although *FAS 13* does not change economic reality, it will change certain key financial measures normally utilized by investors, creditors, and rating services to assess the financial position of the lessee. The impact of *FAS 13* on certain key financial measures will be discussed in this chapter. In addition, the chapter will explain how the lessee's judgment in gathering information so that its auditors can implement *FAS 13* may allow the lessee to influence the classification of a lease. We conclude this chapter with a discussion of lease defeasance.

THE RULE MAKERS

The auditors' opinion paragraph in a financial statement will more than likely state:

> In our opinion, the financial statements referred to above present fairly the financial position of X Company as of December 31, 19XX, and the results of its financial position for the year then ended, in conformity with *generally accepted accounting principles* applied on a basis consistent with that of the preceding year.[2]

But what exactly are generally accepted accounting principles (GAAP)?

Prior to 1964 the pronouncements of the Committee on Accounting Procedure and the Accounting Principles Board were viewed by practitioners as *recommendations* of GAAP. But, lacking enforcement power, accountants did not necessarily comply with the recommendations of GAAP. This "I can do what I want approach" to accounting led external users of financial reports to look suspiciously upon the accountant's product.

In 1964, therefore, the Council of the American Institute of Certified Public Accountants incorporated Rule 203 into its rules of ethics. Rule 203 states:

> A member shall not express an opinion that financial statements are presented in conformity with generally accepted accounting principles if such statements contain any departure from an accounting principle promulgated by the body designated by Council to establish such principles which has a material effect on the statements taken as a whole,

---

[2] AICPA, *Codification of Statements on Auditing Standards* (New York, 1977), AU Sec. 509.07. (Emphasis added.)

The AICPA has proposed changing this innocent-sounding statement of opinion. The proposed change has sparked considerable debate in the accounting profession. A corporate auditor paraphrased the proposed auditor's opinion this way: "It's not ours. We only looked at it a little, so don't blame us." See Arlene Hershman, "Auditor's Letter: Them's Fighting Words," *Dun's Review,* January 1981, pp. 71–73.

unless the member can demonstrate that due to unusual circumstances the financial statements would otherwise have been misleading. In such cases his report must describe the departure, the approximate effects thereof, if practicable, and the reasons why compliance with the principle would result in a misleading statement.

The eagerness of financial statement users to litigate, the economics of litigation defense, and the desire of accountants to keep their licenses compelled accountants to comply with GAAP.[3]

GAAP is now "manufactured" by the Financial Accounting Standards Board (FASB). The FASB was established in early 1973 as a result of the recommendation of a study group commonly known as the Wheat Committee. Its "plant" is located in Stamford, Connecticut. The FASB replaced the Accounting Principles Board, the 13-year-old group that previously "manufactured" GAAP but whose productivity was questioned by members of the accounting and financial community and, more importantly, by government regulatory agencies ready in the wings to regulate accounting activity.

One of the products "manufactured" by the FASB was *FAS 13*. This standard, published in November 1976 (and discussed in the next section) is now GAAP for the treatment of leases. The Securities and Exchange Commission has also established disclosure rules for the financial reporting of leases.[4]

CLASSIFICATION OF LEASES

According to *FAS 13,* a lease is classified as either an operating lease or a capital lease. The principle for classifying a lease as either operating or capital for reporting purposes is as follows:

> [A] lease that transfers substantially all of the benefits and risks incident to ownership of property should be accounted for as the acquisition of an asset and the incurrence of an obligation by the lessee. ... All other leases should be accounted for as operating leases.[5]

But how should the accountant interpret when substantially all of the benefits and risks of ownership are transferred? *FAS 13* specifies that

---

[3] A more precise definition of GAAP is given in paragraph 138 of *Accounting Principles Board Opinion No. 4* (October 1970):

> Generally accepted accounting principles encompass the conventions, rules, and procedures necessary to define accepted accounting practice at a particular time. The standard of "generally accepted accounting principles" includes not only broad guidelines of general application but also detailed practices and procedures.

[4] Securities and Exchange Commission, *Accounting Series Release No. 147,* "Notices of Adoption of Amendments to Regulation S-X Requiring Improved Disclosure of Leases" (October 5, 1973).

[5] Paragraph 60 of *FAS 13.*

if one or more of the following four criteria are met for a noncancelable lease at the date of the lease agreement, the lease is to be accounted for as a capital lease:

1. The lease transfers ownership of the property to the lessee by the end of the lease term.
2. The lease contains a bargain purchase option.
3. The lease term is equal to 75 percent or more of the estimated economic life of the leased property.[6]
4. The present value of the minimum lease payments (excluding executory costs) equals or exceeds 90 percent of the fair value of the leased property.[7]

A lease that does not satisfy at least one of the above four criteria is classified as an operating lease.

For reasons to be discussed below, lessees prefer a lease to be classified as an operating lease. While it may appear that *FAS 13* prevents management from manipulating how a lease will be treated for financial reporting purposes, this is not true in practice. There are several ways in which a lessee can get around the spirit of *FAS 13*, as will be discussed later.

ACCOUNTING TREATMENT OF LEASES

Operating Lease

Since an operating lease does not represent the transfer of substantially all of the benefits and risks of ownership, the leased property is not capitalized, nor is the lease obligation shown as a liability on the balance sheet. Instead, operating lease payments are charged to expense over the lease term as they become payable.[8]

Although neither the leased asset nor the obligation appears in the balance sheet, the lessee must disclose the following information in footnotes to its financial statements: (1) a general description of the leasing arrangement, which would include restrictions imposed by the lease arrangement, the existence of renewal or purchase options, and

---

[6] This criterion and the next do not apply for a lease that commences within the last 25 percent of the total estimated economic life of the leased property.

[7] Present value is discussed in Appendix B. Minimum lease payments and executory costs are defined later in this chapter.

[8] Even if the lease payments are not uniform, for example, when there are advances or prepayments, they are normally expensed on a straight-line basis (i.e., constant dollar amount). A method other than the straight-line basis can be employed if that method is more representative of the time pattern in which use benefit is derived from the leased property.

EXHIBIT 1 Lease Commitments Footnote Disclosure in 1983 Annual
Report of Nabisco Brands, Inc.

Leases–Amounts included in Property, plant and
equipment under capital leases as of December 31
were as follows:

(In millions)	1983	1982
Buildings	$ 68.0	$ 68.0
Machinery and equipment	50.0	44.1
	118.0	112.1
Less, accumulated depreciation	33.7	28.1
Total	$ 84.3	$ 84.0

Capital leases relate to administrative facilities, warehousing facilities and manufacturing equipment. Operating leases cover facilities and equipment used by the
Company for warehousing, transportation, administration and manufacturing. Future minimum payments
under noncancelable leases with terms in excess of
one year are:

(In millions)	Capital Leases	Operating Leases
1984	$ 10.3	$ 29.0
1985	9.7	21.7
1986	9.5	18.0
1987	9.4	16.7
1988	8.9	15.6
1989 and thereafter	123.9	70.3
Total minimum lease payments	171.7	$171.3
Less, amounts representing interest and executory costs	87.0	
Present value of minimum lease payments	$ 84.7	

escalation clauses; (2) the lease expense for each year in which an
income statement is presented; and (3) future minimum lease payments
required in the aggregate and separately for each of the next five years.[9]

Exhibit 1 is an illustration of a footnote disclosure of lease commitments taken from the 1983 annual report of Nabisco Brands, Inc.
The disclosure of commitments for both operating and capital leases
is shown. The latter disclosure requirements are explained in the next
section.

---

[9] When the lessee has entered into a noncancelable sublease (i.e., leases the leased
asset to another party), then the total minimum lease payments to be received in such
arrangements must be disclosed.

Capital Lease

A capital lease is treated for accounting purposes as if the asset were purchased and financed over time. The question then arises as to how the value of the leased asset and the corresponding liability should be recorded on the lessee's books at the inception of the lease.

FAS 13 requires that these amounts be recorded at the inception of the lease as the lower of (1) the present value of the minimum lease payments during the lease term or (2) the fair market value of the leased asset. The minimum lease payments are defined as the sum of (*i*) the minimum lease payments required during the lease term and (*ii*) the amount of any bargain purchase option. In the absence of a bargain purchase option the amount of any guarantee of the residual value[10] and the amount specified for failure to extend or renew the lease are used in lieu of (*ii*). Excluded from the minimum lease payments are insurance, maintenance, and property taxes (known as executory costs) where these are required to be paid by the lessee to the lessor. Precisely what present value means and how it is computed are the subject of Appendix B.

Once the asset and liability at the inception of the lease have been determined, the depreciation charge[11] and the interest expense associated with the liability must be determined. Although the amounts of the asset and liability are the same at the inception of the lease, the subsequent depreciation and interest expense are computed independently.[12]

The following example illustrates the financial reporting requirement for a capital lease.

Best Dress Company and American Leasing Company sign a lease agreement on January 1, 19X1. The lease agreement specifies the following:

- The lease is noncancelable.
- Six annual payments of $54,291 are to be made by Best Dress, with the first payment due on January 1, 19X1.

---

[10] If the lease agreement calls for the guarantee of the residual value attributable to damage, excessive use, or extraordinary wear and tear, it is not to be included in the minimum lease payments. (*FASB Interpretation No. 19*, "Lessee Guarantee of the Residual Value of Leased Property" [Stamford, Conn., 1977], para. 3.)

[11] *FAS 13* refers to the allocation expense associated with the leased property as amortization instead of depreciation because the leased property is an intangible. Yet when considering substance over form, as is done when the lease is capitalized, depreciation seems more appropriate. This is the terminology employed in this chapter.

[12] For purposes of depreciating the leased asset, the useful life is determined by the following rule: When the lease is capitalized because it satisfies either the third or fourth criterion, the useful life is the lease term. However, should either of the first two criteria be satisfied, the useful life is the economic life of the leased asset.

- The lease is a net lease and, therefore, there are no executory costs included in the lease payments of $54,291.
- At the end of the lease term, the leased asset reverts to American Leasing. There are no bargain purchase options, renewal options, or guarantees of a minimum residual value.

Additional information needed to report the lease follows:

- The lessee has determined that the leased asset has a fair market value as of January 1, 19X1, of $250,000. This is the price the lessee would have paid had it purchased the asset.
- The lessor believes that the residual value of the asset will be negligible.
- The lessee has determined that the implicit rate that will be realized by American Leasing from the lease arrangement is 12 percent.[13]
- Best Dress Company's incremental borrowing rate is 15 percent.
- For financial reporting purposes, the asset would be depreciated using the straight-line method of depreciation.
- The expected economic life of the leased asset is six years.
- Best Dress Company's fiscal year is from January 1 to December 31.

The lease qualifies as a capital lease because it satisfies two of the four criteria specified in *FAS 13*. First, the lease term is more than 75 percent of the economic life of the leased asset. Second, the present value of the minimum lease payments is $250,000, which also happens to be the fair market value.[14] Since the present value of the minimum lease payments equals the fair market value, it satisfies the "90 percent recovery criterion" (criterion 4).

On January 1, 19X1, Best Dress Company would record on its books an asset of $250,000 and a liability obligation of the same amount. The value of the leased asset on the balance sheet would decline over the lease life by the amount of the annual depreciation. Table 1 shows the amount of the leased asset that would be reported in the balance sheet in each year. Table 2 presents the annual interest expense and reduction in lease obligation for each of the six years.

---

[13] The interest rate implicit in the lease is defined later in this chapter. How it is computed is illustrated in Appendix B.

[14] See Appendix B for the computation of the present value of the minimum lease payments.

TABLE 1 Best Dress Company: Determination of Amount to Be Reported as an Asset in the Balance Sheet

Fiscal year	Depreciation expense*	Shown on year-end balance sheet as a leased asset†
19X1	$41,667	$208,333
19X2	41,667	166,666
19X3	41,667	124,999
19X4	41,667	83,332
19X5	41,667	41,665
19X6	41,665	–0–

* Straight-line depreciation = $250,000 ÷ 6
= $ 41,667

For illustration purposes, $41,667 is used in the first five years and $41,665 in the last year.
† $250,000 minus accumulated depreciation.

TABLE 2 Best Dress Company: Determination of Interest Expense and Annual Lease Obligation

Date	Annual lease payment	Interest on unpaid balance (12%)	Reduction of lease obligation*	Balance of lease obligation
1/1/X1				$250,000
1/1/X1	$54,291	$ —0—	$54,291	195,709
1/1/X2	54,291	23,485	30,806	164,903
1/1/X3	54,291	19,788	34,503	130,400
1/1/X4	54,291	15,648	38,643	91,757
1/1/X5	54,291	11,011	43,280	48,477
1/1/X6	54,291	5,814	48,477	–0–

* Annual lease payment minus interest on unpaid balance.

Table 3 summarizes how this capital lease would be reported in the balance sheet and income statement.[15] Notice that the liability obligation is divided into two parts: (1) current liability and (2) noncurrent liability. The current liability is the amount by which the total liability obligation will be reduced in the next fiscal year. For example, for the 19X2 fiscal year the total lease obligation is $164,903. On January 1, 19X3, the lease payment of $54,291 will reduce the total lease obli-

---

[15] The impact on equity is not considered here. The effect will depend on the lessee's marginal tax bracket and dividend policy. The result will also be complicated by the treatment of deferred taxes.

TABLE 3   Best Dress Company: Balance Sheet and Income Statement
Effects of a Capital Lease

| | | Balance sheet* | | | | Income statement | |
| | | Lease obligation | | | | Expenses | |
Fiscal year	Leased asset	Total	Current	Noncurrent	Dep.	Interest	Total
19X1	$208,333	$195,709	$30,806	$164,903	$41,667	$23,485	$65,152
19X2	166,666	164,903	34,503	130,400	41,667	19,788	61,455
19X3	124,999	130,400	38,643	91,757	41,667	15,648	57,315
19X4	83,332	91,757	43,280	48,477	41,667	11,011	52,678
19X5	41,665	48,477	48,477	-0-	41,667	5,814	47,481
19X6	-0-	-0-	-0-	-0-	41,665	-0-	41,665

* Impact on equity not shown.

gation by $34,503, as shown in Table 2. This amount is treated by the accountant as a current liability and recorded as such in the balance sheet for the 19X2 fiscal year. The impact of this treatment on net working capital and liquidity ratios is discussed below.

In addition, the following footnote disclosures for capital leases are required in the lessee's financial statement:

1. The gross amount of assets recorded under capital leases presented by major classes according to nature or function. The lessee can combine this information for owned assets, which the company must also disclose.
2. Future minimum lease payments in the aggregate and for each of the five succeeding years (excluding executory costs) and the amount of imputed interest in reducing the minimum lease payments to present value.
3. Total contingent lease payments[16] actually incurred for each period for which an income statement is presented.[17]
4. A general description of the leasing arrangement, which would include restrictions imposed by the lease arrangement, the existence of renewal or purchase options, and escalation clauses.

Exhibit 1 illustrates the footnote disclosure for capital lease commitments.

---

[16] Contingent lease payments are those that are dependent on some factor other than the mere passage of time.

[17] The lessee must also disclose the total of minimum sublease payments from noncancelable subleases to be received in the future.

Comparison of Reporting Capital and Operating Leases[18]

The accounting treatment of a lease will have an impact on key financial measures used by investors, creditors, and rating agencies. The lessee must also be cognizant of the impact of the accounting treatment of a lease on any financial measures governed by a covenant in a previous lending transaction. For example, an outstanding loan agreement may establish a minimum current ratio that the firm agrees to maintain during the life of the loan.

Table 4 shows the difference in total annual expenses that would be reported in the income statement if the lease agreement between Best Dress Company and American Leasing were an operating lease rather than a capital lease. In the first three years the total annual expenses with a capital lease would exceed the total expenses with an operating lease; therefore, net income would be greater with an operating lease in the first three years. The reverse is true in the last three years. Note that over the lease period the aggregate total annual expenses are the same, $325,746, regardless of the accounting treatment of the lease.

Because of the adverse impact on reported income in the earlier years, lessees may prefer not to have a lease classified as a capital lease. In fact, as long as a company continues to add to the number of leases that are classified as capital leases, a reversal will not occur within any reasonable number of years. For example, if Best Dress Company added an identical $250,000 lease each year, the difference in total annual expenses between capital and operating leases for years 19X1 to 19X5 would be as follows:

19X1	$10,861
19X2	18,164
19X3	21,049
19X4	19,439
19X5	12,626

From 19X6 on, the total annual expenses for both the capital and operating leases would be equal. For financial reporting purposes, however, management is generally much more concerned with shorter run performance.

Operating income is another income statement measure employed by investors and creditors in analyzing the performance of management and in computing certain financial ratios. Operating income considers depreciation and lease payments as part of operating expenses. Since interest is not an operating expense, the difference between op-

---

[18] This section benefited from the following article: Monroe Ingberman, Joshua Ronen, and George H. Sorter, "How Lease Capitalization under FASB Statement No. 13 Will Affect Financial Ratios," *Financial Analysts Journal,* January–February 1979, pp. 28–31.

TABLE 4 Best Dress Company: Comparison of Total Expenses of a Capital and Operating Lease

Fiscal year	Total expenses: Capital lease	Total expenses: Operating lease	Difference
19X1	$ 65,152	$ 54,291	$10,861
19X2	61,455	54,291	7,164
19X3	57,315	54,291	3,024
19X4	52,678	54,291	(1,613)
19X5	47,481	54,291	(6,810)
19X6	41,665	54,291	(12,626)
Total	$325,746	$325,746	$ –0–

erating income for a capital lease and an operating lease will be the difference between depreciation expense and the lease payment. In the Best Dress lease agreement, annual depreciation expense is $41,667 for the capital lease, while the lease payment expense for the operating lease is $54,291; hence, operating income in each year will be $10,624 greater for a capital lease compared to an operating lease, even though net income is greater for an operating lease in the first three years.

An important measure employed by investors and creditors in assessing the ability of a company to pay interest, repay debt obligations, pay dividends, expand operations, and so forth, is the firm's cash flow. *Regardless of whether a lease is treated as a capital lease or an operating lease, the actual cash flow will not change; however, because cash flow is measured from income statement numbers, the accounting treatment will have an impact on the cash flow measured by financial statement users even though the economic reality does not change.* Table 5 shows the difference before tax considerations between the cash flow measured from income statement numbers if the lease is treated as a capital lease rather than an operating lease. The cash flow is greater for the capital lease, and the difference in the cash flow increases over the lease period.

The impact of the accounting treatment of leases on reported income is usually minimal.[19] The primary concern of management is, therefore, not with the impact on reported income but with the effect on the firm's debt-to-equity ratio. This ratio is commonly employed by creditors and investors to determine whether a company is overburdened with debt. With a capital lease, the debt-to-equity ratio will be greater than if the lease is treated as an operating lease because of the lease obligation reported in the balance sheet.

---

[19] Further evidence of the minimal impact of the accounting treatment of leases on income is cited later in this chapter.

TABLE 5   Best Dress Company: Difference in Cash Flow before Taxes
between a Capital and Operating Lease

Fiscal year	Difference in net income between capital and operating lease*	Depreciation— capital lease	Difference in cash flow between capital and operating lease†
19X1	($10,861)	$41,667	$30,806
19X2	(7,164)	41,667	34,503
19X3	(3,024)	41,667	38,643
19X4	1,613	41,667	43,280
19X5	6,810	41,667	48,477
19X6	12,626	41,665	54,291

* Parentheses indicate that net income is higher for the operating lease. See Table 4.
† Sum of the two previous columns.

It may be naive to assume that market participants are untutored about the impact of noncapitalized leases on the debt-equity ratio.[20] A recent study based on interviews with bond-rating agencies found that these agencies have not only capitalized leases prior to *FAS 13* but have been capitalizing lease-type commitments not currently covered by *FAS 13*.[21] This finding is contrary to the belief shared by some in the leasing industry that rating agencies such as Moody's and Standard & Poor's do not consider noncapitalized leases until the value of such leases reaches a certain percentage of the company's capitalization.[22]

Some bankers may require a loan applicant to furnish the present value of noncapitalized leases.[23] Yet greater flexibility is afforded a loan officer if the debt-equity ratio acceptable to the bank would be

---

[20] The following study found that the SEC lease disclosure requirements did have an impact on the price of the lessee's common stock: Ryung T. Ro, "The Disclosure of Capitalized Lease Information and Stock Prices," *Journal of Accounting Research,* Autumn 1978, pp. 315–40. The following study, however, found that the firm's risk characteristics were not altered by the new lease disclosure requirements promulgated by the SEC and the FASB: Joseph E. Finnerty, Rick N. Fitzsimmons, and Thomas W. Oliver, "Lease Capitalization and Systematic Risk," *Accounting Review,* October 1980, pp. 631–39.

[21] William L. Ferrara, James B. Thies, and Mark W. Dirsmith, *The Lease-Purchase Decision* (New York: National Association of Accountants and the Society of Management of Canada, 1980), pp. 23–24.

[22] Another surprising finding of the Ferrara, Thies, and Dirsmith study was that except for retailing firms, the rating agencies did not encounter much in the way of "rewriting" leases to avoid capitalization of leases. This was not a conclusion reached by the authors of this book based on their experiences.

[23] Dan Palmon and Michael Kwatinetz, "The Significant Role Interpretation Plays in the Implementation of SFAS No. 13," *Journal of Accounting, Auditing & Finance,* Spring 1980, p. 219.

exceeded if all noncapitalized loans were capitalized.[24] This flexibility is important since the loan officer may still want to extend the loan if he or she is confident that the applicant would be capable of repayment despite the potentially high debt-equity ratio.

Because a portion of the lease obligation is treated as a current liability, the company's net working capital (that is, current assets minus current liabilities) will be reduced. Likewise, the current ratio (that is, current assets divided by current liabilities) will be reduced because of the increase in current liabilities.

Exhibit 2 illustrates the impact of lease capitalization on certain key financial ratios. The exhibit is taken from an article by Monroe Ingberman, Joshua Ronen, and George H. Sorter.[25] The authors assumed in preparing the exhibit that all earnings were paid out before year-end.

Sale-and-Leaseback Transaction

A sale-and-leaseback transaction involves the sale of an asset by the owner to another party and the simultaneous execution of a lease agreement whereby the original owner agrees to lease the asset from the new owner. The most common types of property in a sale-and-leaseback transaction are buildings, plants, and other facilities.

The four criteria of *FAS 13* are used to determine the accounting treatment of the lease regardless of whether the transaction is a sale-and-leaseback arrangement; however, because the sales price of the asset usually differs from the book value that it was carried at in the original owner's balance sheet, it is necessary to know how any profit or loss is treated for accounting purposes.

When the sales price is greater than the book value, any profit after considering the costs associated with the transaction (for example, legal expenses and finder's fees) must be deferred by the lessee and amortized in proportion to the lease payments should the lease be classified as an operating lease or in proportion to depreciation expenses should the lease be capitalized.[26] If the sales price exceeds the book value but a loss results because of the costs associated with the transaction, the lessee must defer the loss in the same manner as that described for the treatment of any profit. However, if a loss arises

---

[24] Recall that the lessee need only disclose in a footnote the future minimum lease payments of operating leases for the following five years and the aggregate amount for the remaining years. The payments disclosed are not cast in terms of present value.

[25] Ingberman, Ronen and Sorter, "Lease Capitalization," p. 29.

[26] If the asset in the sale-and-leaseback transaction is land, amortization should be on a straight-line basis.

EXHIBIT 2   Financial Measures and Ratios: Effects of Capitalization on
              Financial Ratios

	First year	Trend over time	Difference between capital and operating lease over time
Current assets / Current liabilities	Decreases	Decreases	Increases
Quick ratio	Decreases	Decreases	Decreases
Cash flow / Assets	Indeterminate	Increases	Indeterminate
Cash flow / Net worth	Increases	Constant	Constant
Cash flow / Liabilities	Indeterminate	Increases	Indeterminate
Net worth / Fixed assets	Decreases	Decreases	Decreases
Operating income / Interest	Decreases	Increases	Indeterminate
Sales / Working capital	Increases	Increases	Increases
Operating income / Sales	Increases	Constant	Constant
Net income / Sales	Decreases	Increases	Increases
Sales / Fixed assets	Decreases	Increases	Decreases
Net income / Net worth	Decreases	Increases	Reverses
Operating income / Assets	Decreases	Increases	Indeterminate
Operating income / Total debt	Decreases	Increases	Indeterminate
Debt / Equity	Increases	Decreases	Decreases
Income / Assets	Decreases	Increases	Reverses
Income before interest / Interest	Decreases	Increases	Indeterminate

Source: Monroe Ingberman, Joshua Ronen, and George H. Sorter, "How Lease Capitalization under FASB No. 13 Will Affect Financial Ratios," *Financial Analysts Journal*, January–February 1979, p. 31.

because the sales price is less than the book value, the lessee must recognize the loss in the period in which the transaction is consummated.

For example, suppose that the lease transaction between Best Dress Company and American Leasing Company is a sale-and-leaseback arrangement. Suppose, further, that the sales price of the asset is $250,000 and that the book value of the asset on Best Dress Company's balance sheet is $130,000. Assuming no transaction costs, the profit of $120,000 would be recognized at the rate of $20,000 per year ($120,000 divided by six years) if the lease payments are uniform. If the lease payments are uneven, the proportion of each payment to the total lease payments would determine the amount recognized in each year. That is, suppose the last two lease payments were to be $65,149 and $43,433 rather than $54,291 each. The total lease payments would still be $325,746; however, the proportion of the lease payments in the fifth and sixth years would be 20 percent and 13⅓ percent, respectively. The profit of $120,000 would then be recognized as follows: (1) $20,000 per year for the first four years, (2) $24,000 in the fifth year (20 percent times $120,000), and (3) $16,000 in the sixth year (13⅓ percent times $120,000).

Had the lease been capitalized, the recognition of the $120,000 would be $20,000 per year if straight-line depreciation were used. If sum-of-the-years' digits were selected for depreciating the leased asset by the lessee (Best Dress Company), the recognition of the profit in each fiscal year would be as shown in Table 6.

DATA COLLECTION FOR LEASE CLASSIFICATION AND MATERIALITY[27]

To classify a lease as friend (operating) or foe (capital), the company's auditors need information to apply the classification test. When the firm has a substantial number of leases, the data collection can be time-consuming and expensive. A sample questionnaire employed for gathering information about a lease is shown as Exhibit 3.

Because of the resources that must be committed to collect the required data, a lessee must resolve whether the terms of a lease are such that it is immaterial whether the lease is classified as an operating or capital lease. Two criteria commonly employed to determine materiality are the length of the lease term and the dollar value of the lease payments.

Lessees generally classify all leases shorter than a predetermined lease life as operating leases since capitalizing would have a negligible

---

[27] This section and the one to follow draw heavily from the article by Palmon and Kwatinetz. The illustrations, however, are not those of Palmon and Kwatinetz.

TABLE 6   Recognition of Profit in Sale-and-Leaseback Transaction for Capitalized Lease with Depreciation Based on Sum-of-the-Years' Digits

Fiscal year	Proportion of depreciation allocated using sum-of-the-years' digits	Total profit to be recognized	Profit to be recognized in fiscal year
19X1	6/21	$120,000	$ 34,286
19X2	5/21	120,000	28,571
19X3	4/21	120,000	22,857
19X4	3/21	120,000	17,143
19X5	2/21	120,000	11,429
19X6	1/21	120,000	5,714
Total	21/21		$120,000

impact on the lessee's financial statements. A typical cutoff point is 12 months. It is also immaterial how a lease is classified if the total lease payments are small relative to the size of the lessee's total assets and income. Consequently, lessees will specify a minimum total lease payment, usually based on a percentage of some financial measure of size, such as assets, equity, sales, or profits, for the classification test to be applied. A lease whose total lease payment is below management's cutoff point is classified as an operating lease. When applying the size criterion for materiality, however, management must resolve whether leases for similar assets should be treated on a lease-by-lease basis or aggregated.

THE ROLE OF INTERPRETATION IN THE IMPLEMENTATION OF *FAS 13*

The test set forth in *FAS 13* may suggest that the lessee cannot manipulate the classification of a lease. Every CPA knows how to classify a lease given the required information about the lease. But there's the rub! All but the first criterion, transfer of ownership by the end of the lease term, require sufficient judgment by the individual gathering the data so that some behind-the-scenes messaging of information can influence the classification. Let's look at the last three criteria to see how this is possible.

Bargain Purchase Option—Criterion 2

To say that an option to purchase some asset at a future date is a bargain purchase requires judgment as to the expected projected fair

---

EXHIBIT 3   Sample Questionnaire to Implement *FAS 13*

LEASE BRIEF DATA SHEET	Lease Identification Number .... (Corporate Office Will Assign)
Subsidiary/Division	Lessor Name
City & State of Leased Property	Lessor Street Address
	Lessor City & Street

SECTION I

1. Type of Property—Check One
   - Machinery and Equipment ....
   - Land ....
   - Building ....
   - Office Space ....
   - Other (specify) ....

2. Lease Term
   See lease term definition. Enter the "inception date" (or if this is a "renewal lease", enter the "renewal date") of the lease.

Month	Year
....	....

   a. Bargain Purchase Option (see definition)
   If the lease contains a bargain option, enter the "number of months" between inception of the lease and the date bargain purchase becomes exercisable.

   $$\text{OR} \ldots$$
   ....

   b. No Bargain Purchase Option
   If the lease does not contain a bargain purchase option, add together the following periods (in months) to arrive at the lease term:

---

market value at the exercise date. What you may perceive as a bargain purchase given your projected fair market value may not be a bargain to another individual who has determined a different projected fair market value for the same product. We constantly observe differences of opinion of projected future values in the marketplace for real and financial assets.

The person responsible for gathering the data shown in Exhibit 3 must resolve whether a bargain purchase option exists (question 2a).

EXHIBIT 3   (*continued*)

(1) Fixed non-cancelable term of the lease ....

(2) Additional period covered by bargain renewal options ....

(3) Additional period for which termination penalty assures renewal ....

(4) Additional period covered by renewals or extensions at lessor's option ....

(5) Additional period during which lessee guarantees lessor's debt related to leased property ....

TOTAL ==========

c. Enter the "lease term" as derived in either "2a" or "2b" above. . . . .

d. Explaining the provision of the lease, if applicable as they relate to the answers provided for items "2b(2)" through "2b(5)":

3. Payment Schedule

For the lease term as specified in item "2c," enter on the first line of the following schedule the information requested. If the amount of the lease payment changes (other than the executory cost increases), fill out an additional line for each change. Exclude contingent rentals (such as those based on usage or sales).

a.

Amount of Payment Per Period	First Payment Date			No. of Periods	No. of Months Per Period
	Month	Day	Year		
....	....	....	....	....	....
....	....	....	....	....	....
....	....	....	....	....	....

b. Total of all lease payments shown ....

4. Sublease Terms

If the lease property is completely or partially sublet by your division/subsidiary to another company, fill in the schedule below:

Sublease Payment Schedule

a.

Amount of Payment Per Period	First Payment Date			No. of Periods	No. of Months Per Period
	Month	Day	Year		
....	....	....	....	....	....
....	....	....	....	....	....
....	....	....	....	....	....

b. Total of all sublease payments shown ....

5. Contingent Rentals

If contingent rentals (such as those based on usage or sales) are provided for in this lease, give amounts below:

....
Fiscal 1976   Fiscal 1977*

* Estimate if necessary.

6. Lease Length, Dollar Levels

Answer "yes" or "no"—a through c

EXHIBIT 3   *(continued)*

a. Is the original or remaining term of this lease 12 months or less? ....

b. Are the total lease payments (see 3b) less than $4,000? ....

c. Is this lease for office space *only* where you rent less than 50% of the total office space of the premises? ....

Note: If the answer to any part of Item 6 is yes, do not complete SECTION II of this questionnaire.

SECTION II

1. Transfer of Ownership

Is the ownership of the property transferred to the division/subsidiary by the end of the lease term?

....

2. Purchase Option

a. If the lease contains a purchase option fill in the following data.

Date of Option	Amount of Option	Expected "Fair Market Value" (See Definition) on Option Date
Month Day Year		
....	................................,	....

b. Explain how Expected "Fair Market Value" on Option Date was determined.

3. Economic and Depreciable Life

At the inception of the lease, the "age" (if it is used property), the "remaining economic life" (see definition) and "remaining depreciable life" (see definition) of the property were:

Age	Remaining Economic Life	Remaining Depreciable Life
....	....	....
Number of Months	Number of Months	Number of Months

4. Fair Market Value

Enter the "fair market value" of the property and any investment tax credits retained by the lessor at the inception of the lease.

Fair Market Value	Investment Tax Credit
....	....

5. Executory Costs

Indicate (or estimate, if necessary) the amount which, at the inception of the lease, was included in each payment in item 3, Section I, if any, for "executory costs (see definition) paid by the lessee:

a. Executory Costs* Per Period	First Cost Date Month	Year	Number of Periods
.................................,	...............,	...............,	....
.................................,	...............,	...............,	....
.................................,	...............,	...............,	....

b. Total of all Executory Costs ....,

* Do not contact any government authority or taxing agency for estimates of taxes.

EXHIBIT 3   (*concluded*)

6. Salvage Value

   At the end of the lease term what is the "expected salvage value" (see definition) of the property?

   ....

7. Guarantee of Residual Value or Penalty

   a. At the end of the lease term:

      —If the company guarantees the "residual value" (see definition) of the property enter GUA

      ....

      —If there is no guarantee but there is a penalty for failure to renew the lease enter PEN

      ....

   b. Amount of guaranteed residual or penalty

      ....

Source: Dan Palmon and Michael Kwatinetz, "The Significant Role Interpretation Plays in the Implementation of SFAS No. 13," *Journal of Accounting, Auditing & Finance,* Spring 1980, pp. 221–24.

Even if the projected fair market value could be estimated with some degree of certainty, internally or externally from expert appraisers, judgment is still required to determine whether it is a bargain. Is the option to buy a leased asset for $400,000 five years from now when the projected fair market value has been estimated to be $405,000 a bargain? To resolve this question, management must specify criteria for the presence of a bargain purchase. An extreme case would categorize a bargain purchase when the option price is less than the projected fair market value. More than likely, management will arbitrarily set a minimum percentage for the purchase option price to the projected fair market value.

What seems to be a very simple criterion can now be seen to require considerable judgment by management and the individual designated to gather the information.

Lease Term to Estimated Economic Life Ratio—Criterion 3

FAS 13 classifies a lease as a capital lease if the lease term is 75 percent or more of the estimated economic life of the leased asset. At first, it may appear that the lease term is readily available from the lease agreement but that judgment is required to estimate the economic life. In fact, both permit managerial discretion in implementation in the absence of a bargain purchase option.

When a bargain purchase option exists, the lease term is defined as the period between the inception of the lease and the date on which the bargain purchase option becomes exercisable. In any case, the lease will be a capital lease since a bargain purchase option exists. The lease term in the absence of a bargain purchase option is the sum of (1) the fixed noncancelable term of the lease, (2) the additional period during which the lessee guarantees the lessor's debt related to the leased property, (3) the additional period covered by renewals at the lessor's option, (4) the additional period covered by bargain renewal options, and (5) the additional period for which a termination penalty assures renewal. Although the first three periods can be obtained from the lease agreement, the last two require the lessee to hold the scales.

The problems associated with estimating the economic life of the leased asset are the same as those experienced by management when estimating the economic life of owned assets it must depreciate. For certain types of assets, this task may not be difficult because of company or industry experience. For other assets, different estimates may exist for the same asset. "Playing" with the estimated economic life will influence the outcome of the third criterion for classification. Does this really happen in practice? The SEC thinks it may. It questioned the practice of four big retailers, J. C. Penney Company, K mart Corporation, Associated Dry Goods Corporation, and Montgomery Ward & Co., about the possibility that they overestimated the useful life of leased facilities.[28]

Ninety Percent Recovery Criterion—Criterion 4

The computation of the present value of the minimum lease payments requires that the minimum lease payments be discounted at a certain interest rate. The process of discounting or, equivalently, determining the present value, is explained in Appendix B. The selection of the appropriate interest rate, called the discount rate, is specified in *FAS 13*. The discount rate is the lower of the interest rate implicit in the lease and the lessee's incremental borrowing rate.

Before discussing the interest rate implicit in the lease and the lessee's incremental borrowing rate, let's see why the selection of the discount rate is important. The lease between Best Dress Company and American Leasing will be used to illustrate the sensitivity of the accounting treatment to the selection of the discount rate.

Recall that the Best Dress Company lease was a capital lease where the minimum lease payments were discounted at the implicit rate in

---

[28] "SEC Asking Four Big Retailers to Justify Interpretation of an Audit Rule," *The Wall Street Journal,* January 17, 1979.

TABLE 7 Best Dress Company: Comparison of Balance Sheet and Income Statement Effects of Capitalizing Lease at 12 Percent and 15 Percent

| | Balance sheet | | | | | |
| | Leased asset | | | Liability obligation | | |
Fiscal year	12 percent	15 percent	Difference	12 percent	15 percent	Difference
19X1	$208,333	$196,904	$11,429	$195,709	$181,994	$13,715
19X2	166,666	157,523	9,143	164,903	155,002	9,901
19X3	124,999	118,142	6,857	130,400	123,961	6,439
19X4	83,332	78,761	4,571	91,757	88,264	3,493
19X5	41,665	39,380	2,285	48,477	47,213	1,264
19X6	–0–	–0–	–0–	–0–	–0–	–0–

| | Income statement | | | | | | |
| | Expenses at 12 percent | | | Expenses at 15 percent | | | |
Fiscal year	Dep.	Interest	Total	Dep.	Interest	Total	Difference
19X1	$ 41,667	$23,485	$ 65,152	$ 39,381	$27,299	$ 66,680	($1,528)
19X2	41,667	19,788	61,455	39,381	23,250	62,631	(1,176)
19X3	41,667	15,648	57,315	39,381	18,594	57,975	(660)
19X4	41,667	11,011	52,678	39,381	13,240	52,621	57
19X5	41,667	5,814	47,481	39,381	7,078	46,459	1,022
19X6	41,665	–0–	41,665	39,380	–0–	39,380	2,285
Total	$250,000	$75,746	$325,746	$236,285	$89,461	$325,746	$ –0–

the lease of 12 percent. The implicit rate was assumed to be lower than the lessee's incremental borrowing rate. Suppose, instead, that the minimum lease payments had been discounted at 15 percent rather than 12 percent. Table 7 compares the balance sheet and income statement for the six years of the lease when the 12 percent and 15 percent rates are employed. The present value of the minimum lease payments is $236,285 using a 15 percent discount rate rather than $250,000 using a 12 percent rate.[29] Although the 90 percent recovery criterion is still met in this illustration, the use of a higher discount rate increases the likelihood that this criterion would be flunked. Even though the fourth criterion is passed, the liability reported in the balance sheet is less using the higher discount rate. The reason the present value of the minimum lease payments declines with the use of a higher discount rate will be explained in Appendix B.

[29] The computation is shown in Appendix B. Note that the present value of the minimum lease payments is now 94.5 percent of the fair value.

As for the impact on reported income, because the leased asset is carried on the balance sheet at a lower amount using the higher discount rate, depreciation expense is lower. However, the higher discount rate results in greater interest expense each year. Total expenses in the first three years will be greater when the lease is capitalized at 15 percent rather than 12 percent. In the last three years, the reverse is true. The aggregate total annual expenses over the six years will be the same regardless of the discount rate used to capitalize the lease.

Although the lessee cannot plead total ignorance of the interest rate implicit in the lease, the lessee's judgment of the residual value of the leased asset will influence the estimate of the rate. To understand why, let's see how the interest rate implicit in the lease is defined.

FAS 13 defines the interest rate implicit in the lease as the discount rate that equates the present value of both the minimum lease payments and the *unguaranteed residual value* accruing to the benefit of the lessor to the lessor's net investment.[30] The point is that to compute the interest rate implicit in the lease, the lessee must estimate the residual value if this value is not disclosed by the lessor. The greater the estimated residual value, the higher is the interest rate implicit in the lease. Since forecasting residual value is not an exact science, the lessee's judgment permits it to influence the interest rate implicit in the lease.

To illustrate the importance of the estimated residual value, suppose that Best Dress was not told, as initially assumed, that the residual value of the leased property would be negligible. Rather, Best Dress Company's management believes the residual value will be $43,723. Since the lessee does not guarantee any portion of the residual value, the interest rate implicit in the lease would be 16 percent.[31] Should Best Dress Company's incremental borrowing rate be 15 percent, then 15 percent would be employed to discount the minimum lease payments since it is less than the computed interest rate of 16 percent implicit in the lease.

An alternative approach to computing the interest rate implicit in the lease when the lessor does not disclose the rate or residual value it assumes is to ask the lessor for the rate. Those firms that have asked the lessor for the rate and have also computed the interest rate implicit in the lease have found material differences in the two rates![32]

---

[30] *FAS 13*, paragraph 5k. The net investment is the fair value less the investment tax credit if retained by the lessor. The definition of the interest rate implicit in the lease is generally called the yield on the investment (from the lessor's perspective). The FASB does note, however, that other factors will affect the lessor's yield (see paragraph 44).

[31] For the computations, see Appendix B.

[32] Palmon and Kwatinetz, "Significant Role," p. 214.

The incremental borrowing rate of the lessee is much easier to ascertain, right? Wrong! In the absence of specific guidelines as to how to determine the incremental borrowing rate, some firms have used the borrowing rate based on recent loans, others have used the prime rate plus an appropriate number of points at the inception of the lease, while others have used the average of the prime rate over the first year of the lease plus an appropriate number of points. The lessee can take its pick in trying to flunk the 90 percent recovery criterion or, at least, to minimize the liability that must be reported in the balance sheet.

The minimum lease payments also require judgment since the lessee must subtract executory costs. There is no problem with a net lease; however, when a gross lease is involved, executory costs must be estimated if these are not disclosed by the lessor.[33]

Once the discount rate has been selected and the minimum lease payments have been determined, there is still the problem of estimating the fair market value of the leased asset. It is this value that the auditor compares with the present value of the minimum lease payments to determine whether the 90 percent recovery criterion has been met. The fair market value at the inception of the lease is not always observable in the marketplace. In instances where the fair market value is unavailable from external sources, the individual collecting the information for the auditor will be able to influence the outcome of the 90 percent recovery criterion.[34]

Lessors are generally willing to work with lessees so that if the lessee desires a lease to be noncapitalized as an operating lease under FASB 13, the terms of the lease can be constructed accordingly. In addition to refusing to disclose information about residual values, executory costs, and the interest rate implicit in the lease (on the legitimate grounds such information is proprietary), the lessor can be of assistance to the lessee by designing lease payments in such a manner

---

[33] Contingent lease payments can also be played with to reduce the present value of the minimum lease payments. According to *FAS 13*, such payments are excluded from the minimum lease payments and are to be charged to expense as incurred. Many retail space lease agreements contain both a base lease payment and an override based on sales. The latter payment is a contingent lease payment. By drafting the lease agreement so that the base lease payment is reduced slightly and the override increased slightly, the present value of the minimum lease payments can be reduced to less than 90 percent of fair value. This action will increase the lessor's risk by a minuscule amount. (See Richard Dieter, "Is Lessee Accounting Working?" *CPA Journal*, August 1979, p. 15.)

[34] For leases involving part of a building such as floors of a multistory office building and retail space in a shopping mall, there are difficulties in measuring the fair value. Lessees have interpreted the special rules devised in *FAS 13* in the case of such leases to mean that the 90 percent recovery criterion should not be used. As a result, no capitalization seems to be occurring for the vast majority of leases involving only part of a building. (See Dieter, "Lessee Accounting," p. 14.)

that the lessor earns its targeted rate of return while justifiable assumptions by the lessee concerning the unknown factors will result in the lease failing to satisfy the 90 percent recovery criterion.

Of course, the lessor will be watching out for its own financial statements, which are also governed by *FAS 13*. Sometimes a conflict between the lessor and the lessee may occur because of the desire of each to look good for reporting purposes. Yet because there is no requirement of symmetry with respect to lease classification by the lessor and the lessee (that is, an operating lease for the lessee need not be an operating lease for the lessor), the use of judgment with respect to the factors discussed in this chapter can result in both classifying a lease to their own benefit.

One approach sometimes employed in the leasing industry so that the lessee and lessor can meet their respective financial reporting objectives is to have some or all of the residual value normally guaranteed by the lessee guaranteed by a third party.[35] Recall that the minimum lease payments in the absence of a bargain purchase option consist of the lease payments plus any guarantee of the residual value by the lessee. Any portion guaranteed by a third party is not considered part of the minimum lease payments.

To illustrate how this approach works, suppose that a machine with a fair market value of $56,535 is leased for $10,000 per year for five years, with the first payment due one year from now. Suppose, further, that the lessor estimates a residual value of $30,000 and wants the lessee to guarantee $26,000 of the residual value. The interest rate implicit in the lease if the lessee knows the lessor's estimated residual value of $30,000 would be 10 percent. Assuming, further, that 10 percent is also the appropriate rate for the lessee to discount the minimum lease payments, the present value of the minimum lease payments would be $54,051. The 90 percent recovery test would be passed and this lease capitalized. However, if the lessee guaranteed only $15,000 and a third party guaranteed the remaining $11,000, the present value of the minimum lease payments would be $47,222. Under this arrangement the lease would not satisfy the 90 percent recovery criterion for the lessor because the present value of the minimum lease payments would be only 83.5 percent of the fair market value of the leased asset. In fact, as long as the amount guaranteed by the lessee is less than $20,895, the lease will not pass the 90 percent recovery criterion.

But where can a lessee find a third party that will guarantee the residual value? An industry has emerged that performs exactly this

---

[35] Care must be used in residual guarantees lest Revenue Procedure 75–21, discussed in Chapter 5, be violated. Residual values insured by insurance companies have been widely used and are apparently satisfactory under Revenue Procedure 75–21.

function. The experience of Lloyd's of London in guaranteeing residual values in the U.S. computer leasing industry, however, has made firms in the "third-party guarantor" industry cautious with respect to their position with respect to equipment subject to rapid technological change.[36]

Even without third-party guarantees, the willingness of a lessor to accept a specific dollar limitation on the residual value deficiency that a lessee must guarantee will change the accounting treatment of the lease. For example, suppose that in our previous illustration the lessee agrees to make up the difference between $26,000 and $11,000. The lessor in agreeing to such an arrangement is thereby betting that the residual value will not be below $11,000. From the lessee's perspective the residual value guarantee that must be included in the minimum lease payments is limited to the specific maximum deficiency of $15,000 that it may have to make up at the end of the lease period.[37] The present value of the minimum lease payments would then be $47,222, as noted above, and the lease then would not satisfy the 90 percent recovery criterion for a capital lease.[38]

Some Empirical Evidence of How Interpretation Affects Financial Statements

In their discussion of the role that interpretation plays in the implementation of *FAS 13*, Dan Palmon and Michael Kwatinetz analyzed a sample of 28 lessee companies. All were audited by one of the Big Eight accounting firms. Most of the companies in their sample were listed companies, and several were in the Fortune 500.

Palmon and Kwatinetz reclassified the leases of each company using the most conservative interpretation, that is, an interpretation of the factors discussed in this chapter that would lead to more leases being capitalized. The impact on earnings of reclassification was minimal. No company would have realized a decline in earnings of more than 5 percent. The reduction in earnings for most of the companies would have been between 0 percent and 3 percent. Those firms that would have had the largest decline in recomputed earnings were the firms that had new leases whose value far exceeded the value of old leases.

Unlike the impact on earnings, however, the amount of the liabilities that would have been reported under the most conservative interpretation of *FAS 13* was substantial. Increases between 15 percent and

---

[36] See: "Lloyd's Biggest Disaster," *Forbes,* May 28, 1979, p. 38.

[37] *FASB Interpretation No. 19.*

[38] Lessors in the automobile leasing industry usually use this approach in getting around the spirit of *FAS 13*. (See Dieter, "Lessee Accounting," pp. 14–15.)

30 percent of equity were estimated. In some cases the increases would have exceeded equity.

DOWN THE ROAD

The following from *FAS 13* is prophetic of the direction in which the Financial Accounting Standards Board may move with respect to the financial accounting treatment of leases:

> *Some members* of the Board who support this Statement hold the view that, *regardless of whether all the benefits and risks of ownership are transferred,* a lease, in transferring for its term the right to use property, gives rise to the acquisition of an asset and the incurrence of an obligation by the lessee which should be reflected in his financial statements.[39]

At its March 6, 1979, board meeting, the FASB sent out the following message:

> *A majority* of the Board members expressed their tentative view that, if SFAS 13 were to be reconsidered, they would support a property-right approach in which all leases would be included as rights to the use of property and as lease obligations in the lessee's balance sheet.[40]

In 1986, the FASB considered reopening *FAS 13* to a complete review. It tabled the idea indefinitely, however.

Would the adoption by the FASB of the property-right approach for leases mean that the game is over? Not according to Michael Bohan, partner of the accounting firm of Touche, Ross & Co. Those seeking to avoid lease capitalization may find solace in the following observation of Mr. Bohan:

> Do you really think that accounting under the property-right approach will be substantially better than it would be if all adhered to the spirit of SFAS No. 13? While the author believes the property-right approach is conceptually preferable, he wonders if inventive users will not eventually concoct new transactions to circumvent the spirit of any new approach.[41]

The questions listed in Mr. Bohan's article that must be answered in order to implement a property-right approach are similar to those discussed in this chapter for implementing *FAS 13*.

---

[39] *FAS 13,* paragraph 63.

[40] *FASB Action Alert,* March 8, 1979.

[41] Michael P. Bohan, "New Directions in Lease Accounting," *Journal of Accounting, Auditing & Finance,* Spring 1980, p. 269.

DEFEASANCE OF CAPITALIZED LEASES

An in-substance defeasance of a capitalized lease obligation offers lessee companies an opportunity to reduce their liabilities, clean up their balance sheets, improve ratios, and protect their debt ratings. It may also result in income for financial reporting purposes. While many companies have considered defeasance of debt, many have overlooked the fact that capitalized leases as well as debt can be the subject of an in-substance defeasance. *Statement of Financial Accounting Standards No. 76 (FAS 76)*, "Extinguishment of Debt," indicates in paragraph 37 that "the provisions for in-substance defeasance generally apply to capitalized lease obligations if the lease has a specified maturity and a fixed payment schedule."

In-substance defeasance of capitalized lease obligations works pretty much the same as defeasance of debt obligations. *FAS 76* states in paragraph 3 that a debtor shall consider debt to be extinguished for financial reporting purposes where the debtor irrevocably places cash or other assets in a trust to be used solely for satisfying scheduled payments of both interest and principal of a specific debt obligation. The assets placed in trust must be sufficient to provide funds for the required payments, and the possibility that the debtor will be required to make any additional future payments with respect to such debt must be remote. Under such circumstances, debt is extinguished even though the debtor is not legally released from being the primary obligor under the debt obligation.

Likewise, a lessee can extinguish a capitalized lease obligation by placing assets irrevocably in a trust to be used solely to make scheduled rent payments under the lease.

FAS 76 describes in paragraph 4 the requirements as to the nature of the assets to be held by a trust that qualify for effecting an extinguishment of debt or of a capitalized lease:

a. The trust shall be restricted to owning only monetary assets[42] that are essentially risk-free as to the amount, timing, and collection of interest and principal. The monetary assets shall be denominated in the currency in which the debt is payable.

For debt denominated in U.S. dollars, essentially risk-free monetary assets shall be limited to:

1. Direct obligations of the U.S. government.
2. Obligations guaranteed by the U.S. government.

---

[42] The term *monetary assets* is defined as "money or a claim to receive a sum of money that is fixed and determinable without reference to future prices of specific goods or services."

3. Securities that are backed by the U.S. government obligations as collateral under an arrangement by which the interest and principal payments on the collateral generally flow immediately through to the holder of the security. However, some securities described in the previous sentence can be paid prior to scheduled maturity and so are not essentially risk-free as to the timing of the collection of interest and principal; thus, they do not qualify for ownership by the trust.

b. The monetary assets held by the trust shall provide cash flows (from interest and maturity of those assets) that approximately coincide, as to timing and amount, with the scheduled interest and principal payments on the debt that is being extinguished.

Defeasance of capitalized leases (or debt) is required to be disclosed in a footnote to the balance sheet, which must contain a general description of the transaction, including the amount of the liability that is considered to be extinguished.

The SEC concurred with *FAS 76* in *SEC Financial Reporting Release No. 15,* with the provision that the assets placed in trust to satisfy the debt requirements be risk-free. The SEC expressed a preference for direct obligations of the U.S. government.

Companies That Should Consider a Lease Defeasance

Any company that entered into a lease agreement required to be capitalized on its balance sheet in which the effective interest rate used to report the capitalized lease liability is significantly less than that of U.S. Treasury bonds with similar maturities ought to consider a defeasance of the lease obligation, provided it has adequate cash resources to purchase Treasury bonds with maturities and values equivalent to the lease rental obligations.

In the past, the balance sheet book liabilities for capitalized lease obligations were usually computed using either the rate implicit in the lease or (in more recent times) the lessee's incremental debt rate for similar maturities. In some instances in such situations the resulting liability is much greater than the cost of the Treasury bonds that will provide a stream of revenue equal to the rental obligations under the lease. Such capitalized leases are candidates for defeasance. This will be especially true when current interest rates are high.

While capitalized true leases are logical subjects for an in-substance defeasance, older non-tax-oriented leases and foreign leases required to be capitalized may also be candidates for defeasance.

How an In-Substance Defeasance of a Lease Works

Defeasance of a capitalized lease obligation works as follows: The lessee sets up an irrevocable trust or escrow account with a trustee to pay fixed rental payments to the lessor under a lease as the rental payments come due. The company funds the escrow fund by purchasing and delivering to the trustee U.S. Treasury bonds that will produce a cash flow matching the rental payments due under the lease. Interest on the Treasury bonds may be stripped to aid in matching the cash flow of the bonds against the rents. The trustee pays the rentals as they become due from the assets deposited with it for that purpose by the lessee. The possibility that the lessee will be required to make future payments under the lease in addition to those provided by the trust assets must be remote.

Exhibit 4 illustrates the parties, agreements, and cash flows in a typical defeasance of a lease. An explanation of Exhibit 4 follows:

1. The lessee corporation entered into a true lease several years ago with the lessor. The lessee capitalized the lease on its balance sheet.
2. The lessee establishes an irrevocable trust or escrow agreement with a bank.
3. The lessee purchases and deposits into escrow Treasury notes with maturities that match the cash needed to pay rents as they become due. Interest may be stripped from the Treasury notes. The debt is removed from the lessee's books.
4. The escrow agent pays rents on the lease as they become due.
5. The lease is completely paid at maturity, canceled, and returned to the lessee with any excess funds in the escrow.
6. Since a true lease is involved, the lessee must negotiate a purchase or renewal of the lease if it wishes to retain possession.

Financial Reporting Consequences

An in-substance defeasance of a capitalized lease enables a lessee to remove the capitalized lease as a liability on its balance sheet. (As noted earlier, a description of the defeasance of a capitalized lease is required to be disclosed in a footnote.)

The lessee realizes booked income for financial accounting purposes at the time the escrow trust is established. The amount of income recognized is measured by the difference between the amount paid to extinguish the debt and the net carrying amount of the debt. The amount paid to extinguish the debt is, in this example, the cost of the Treasury securities.

EXHIBIT 4   Defeasance of a Capitalized Lease

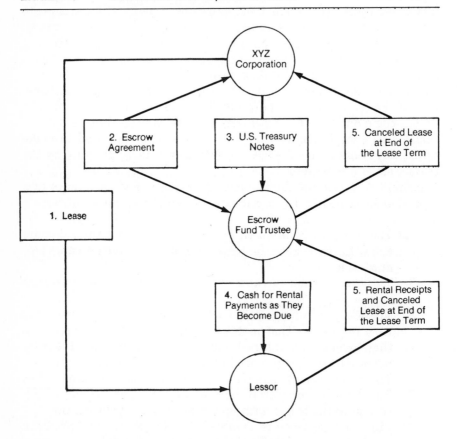

The net results are reduced liabilities, improved debt-to-equity ratios, and an addition to current net income.

Effect on Debt Rating

Standard & Poor's has indicated in the case of an in-substance defeasance of debt that it will disregard the original debt issue and related interest expense, along with escrowed assets, from financial measures such as pretax interest coverage and return on capital. Presumably, the same rules would be followed for an in-substance defeasance of a capitalized lease. Moody's will upgrade a defeased obligation if the security position of the bondholder is improved. However, the rating services must be consulted on a case-by-case basis where this is a concern.

Tax Consequences

The lessee in an in-substance defeasance realizes interest income on the bonds and claims a deduction for lease rentals.

The use of the bonds to pay rental obligations under the lease by the trustee will be treated as a sale of the bonds by the lessee and taxed accordingly. (The tax on a cash purchase of a debt or lease obligation at a discount is ordinary income.)

Immediate Defeasance

When *FAS 76* was issued the language seemed to permit an immediate defeasance of a capitalized lease. (Such simultaneous defeasances are also called same-day defeasances or 24-hour defeasances.) However, the FASB issued a *Technical Bulletin* dated February 16, 1984, which indicated that simultaneous defeasances were not permitted by *FAS 76*. It is not clear, though, how much time must elapse between capitalization of a lease and its defeasance in order to gain the benefits of *FAS 76*. Presumably, a reasonable period of time, such as at least a year, will suffice.

Lease Defeasances That Do Not Qualify under FAS 76

A lessee with a large cash position but unable to claim tax benefits currently might find a simultaneous defeasance of a true lease attractive even though book income cannot be claimed immediately under *FAS 76*. The lessee in such a situation realizes in cash an amount equal to the tax benefits reflected in the lease rate.

For example, assume that Treasury bonds costing 85 percent of the capitalized cost (or the purchase price of the leased asset) are sufficient to pay the rentals under the lease. The lessee can realize the equivalent of a 15 percent discount by setting up an escrow fund with Treasury bonds to pay the rents. Furthermore, since the benefits of *FAS 76* are not sought, the lessee can use securities paying higher rates than Treasury bonds to fund the escrow amount, thus decreasing the cost of the securities needed for the escrow.

4

Tax Benefits and Tax Laws Affecting Ownership and Leasing of Equipment: The Effect of the Tax Reform Act of 1986 upon Leasing

---

When an equipment lease agreement qualifies as a true lease for federal income tax purposes, the lessor is treated as the owner of the leased property and, as such, is entitled to all the income tax benefits associated with ownership of the leased equipment. The lessee under a true lease is entitled to deduct the lease payments paid to the lessor for the use of the leased equipment. Since the lessor in a true lease passes through to the lessee an amount equal to the value of most of the tax benefits it has claimed in the form of reduced lease payments, both the lessee and the lessor must have an understanding of the tax benefits associated with leasing in order to determine the most effective method of financing equipment.

In this chapter we describe the tax benefits associated with the ownership of equipment (consisting of tax depreciation deductions, interest deductions, and possibly, investment tax credit) and the effect of the Tax Reform Act of 1986 upon ownership and leasing equipment. In the next chapter we discuss the requirements a lease transaction must satisfy in order to qualify as a true lease.

TAX REFORM ACT OF 1986 (TRA); REVIEW OF MAJOR CHANGES THAT AFFECT LEASING

Briefly and generally stated, the major provisions of the Tax Reform Act of 1986 (TRA) that affect equipment leasing are as follows:

1. The corporate tax rate is reduced for a calendar year taxpayer from 46 percent in 1986, to 40 percent in 1987, and to 34 percent in 1988 and subsequent years. The tax rate in 1987 is a blended rate and is actually 39.95068 percent for a calendar year taxpayer. However, for convenience in this chapter the tax rate for 1987 is referred to as 40 percent.

2. Investment tax credit (ITC) is repealed for equipment placed in service after December 31, 1985, unless such equipment is subject to a binding written contract in effect on December 31, 1985, and at all times thereafter, provided the placed-in-service date occurs within certain time limits. ITC on qualified transition property for a calendar year taxpayer is equal to 100 percent of cost in 1986, 82.5 percent in 1987, and 65 percent of cost thereafter.

3. Deductions for depreciation are changed for equipment placed in service after December 31, 1986. The benefits are increased for some types of equipment and decreased for other types of equipment.

4. A newly enacted 20 percent alternative minimum tax for corporations will reduce the ability of corporations to claim tax benefits from depreciation and certain other tax deductions which create a difference between taxable income and book income.

5. A mid-quarter convention rather than half-year convention must be used for ACRS deductions if in any year more than 40 percent of all property of a taxpayer acquired during that year is placed in service during the fourth quarter of that taxable year.

These changes are discussed in detail in this chapter.

ITC REPEALED

The Tax Reform Act of 1986 repealed investment tax credit (ITC). Generally, any property placed in service after December 31, 1985, is not eligible for ITC.

The investment tax credit was a very powerful tax incentive enacted by Congress to encourage investment in equipment used in a trade or business. For companies able to claim and take advantage of ITC on equipment acquisitions, it was equivalent to a discount on the cost of the acquired equipment.[1]

Although revenue raising is the primary objective of the Internal Revenue Code, it has not always been the sole purpose. The tax law has also been used to accomplish economic, equity, social, and political objectives. The investment tax credit is an example of how tax legislation has been used to stimulate economic activity, foster capital formation, and create employment. The repeal of ITC reflects a basic policy decision by Congress to remove incentives for investment in capital equipment. The trade-off in the Tax Reform Act of 1986 was a tax system with lower tax rates for corporations and individuals.

Transition Rules for ITC

Although investment tax credit was repealed effective January 1, 1986, reduced ITC continues to be available under "transition rules" for property that was subject to a binding written contract in effect on December 31, 1985, and at all times thereafter, provided the transition property is (or was) placed in service on or before certain dates:

ADR midpoint	*Date by which transition property must be placed in service*
Less than 5 years	06-30-86
At least 5 but less than 7 years	12-31-86
7 years but less than 20 years	12-31-88
20 years or more	12-31-90

The law contains an exception for commercial aircraft which provides a placed-in-service date of December 31, 1989. In addition, Congress made eligible for ITC a large number of specific equipment acquisitions that would not otherwise qualify under the transition rules.

---

[1] A tax credit, such as the ITC, is a dollar reduction of the taxpayer's tax liability. By contrast, a tax deduction reduces the taxpayer's tax liability by shielding income from taxation. An illustration will clarify the difference between a tax credit and a tax deduction.

Suppose a taxpayer has taxable income of $100,000. Let's compare a tax credit of $20,000 with an additional tax deduction of a like amount. To simplify the illustration, assume that all taxable income up to $100,000 is taxed at a rate of 34 percent. Hence, the taxpayer's marginal tax rate is 34 percent. The taxpayer's tax liability would be $34,000. If the taxpayer is entitled to an additional tax deduction of $20,000, taxable income would be reduced to $80,000. The tax liability would be $27,200, a reduction of $6,800. Note that the reduction in taxes is the additional tax deduction of $20,000 multiplied by 34 percent (the marginal tax rate). On the other hand, a tax credit of $20,000 reduces the taxpayer's tax liability by $20,000.

Consequently, while ITC is not generally available in the future for new equipment acquisitions, ITC will continue to be available to lessees and lessors in certain specific transactions that qualify under the transition rules.

ITC Available under Prior Law and Transition Rules

The amount of ITC available on eligible property[2] under the law prior to the Tax Reform Act of 1986 was 10 percent on properties with a class life of five years or more and 6 percent on property with a class life of three years.[3]

In general, property used predominantly outside the United States does not qualify for the ITC. Also, property used by any state or political division of the United States does not qualify as Section 38 property.

For a taxpayer with a taxable year the same as a calendar year, ITC is discounted by 17.5 percent for property placed in service during 1987 and by 35 percent for property placed in service after December 31, 1987. ITC carryforwards are also discounted by 17.5 percent for taxable years beginning in 1987 and by 35 percent for taxable years beginning in 1988 and thereafter. The purpose of this "hair cut" is to make the

---

[2] Section 38 of the IRC describes the property on which ITC can be claimed. In general, Section 38 property means:

    (A) tangible personal property (other than an air conditioning or heating unit) or
    (B) other tangible property (not including a building and its structural components) but only if such property—
        (i) is used as an integral part of manufacturing, production, or extraction, or furnishing transportation, communication, electrical energy, gas, water, or sewage disposal services, or
        (ii) constitutes a research facility used in connection with any of the activities referred to in clause (i), or
    (C) elevators and escalators, but only if certain restrictions are satisfied. (Section 48(a)(1) of the IRC.)

[3] The Tax Equity and Fiscal Responsibility Act of 1982 (TEFRA) required that a basis adjustment be made for ITC claimed in computing depreciation. Specifically, TEFRA required that the amount by which an asset can be depreciated be reduced by one half of the amount of the ITC taken. For example, suppose a machine with a cost of $1 million was purchased and the machine qualified for the five-year class. The purchaser was required to adjust the amount by which the machine was depreciated by one half of the ITC. Since the ITC would be $100,000, the machine could be depreciated by an amount equal to $950,000 ($1 million minus $50,000).

TEFRA permitted an alternative to the above rule. It allowed a 2 percentage point reduction in the ITC that a firm could claim rather than reducing the tax basis. Specifically, for an asset that qualified for the 3-year class, a taxpayer could take a 4 percent ITC instead of a 6 percent ITC. For 5-year, 10-year, and 15-year class property, the taxpayer could take an 8 percent ITC (instead of a 10 percent ITC).

As noted in the text, under the TRA a basis adjustment for the entire amount of ITC claimed under transitional rules is required.

amount claimed for ITC consistent with the benefits from the tax rate reductions effective in those years.

A basis adjustment is required for the full amount of ITC claimed on transition property.

Binding Contract Definition

For purposes of eligibility for ITC under the "binding contract" transition rules, the Joint Tax Committee Report explains that the new rules do not apply to "property that is constructed, reconstructed, or acquired by a taxpayer pursuant to a written contract that was binding as of December 31, 1985, and at all times thereafter." A contract enforceable under state law is considered to be binding. Design changes for reasons of technical or economic efficiencies that cause an insignificant increase in the original price will not adversely affect the status of a binding contract. New supply contracts that fail to designate the amount or design specifications of property to be purchased will not qualify as a binding contract until a purchase order referring to the supply contract that designates a specific number of properties is placed.

Equipped Building Rule and Plant Facility Rule

Where construction of an "equipped building" or plant facility was begun on or before December 31, 1985, pursuant to a written specific plan, and more than one half of the equipped building cost (including cost of machinery and equipment for use in the building) or plant facility cost was incurred or committed by December 31, 1985, the entire equipped building project or plant facility and incidental appurtenances are considered to be transitional property eligible for ITC.

Limitation on Amount of ITC That May Be Claimed in Any Year

There is a limitation on the amount of the ITC that can be claimed against a company's regular corporate tax for a given taxable year. The limitation is based on the taxpayer's regular corporate tax liability and alternative minimum tax liability.

The regular corporate tax liability against which the ITC can be applied is the income tax after applying another tax credit known as the foreign tax credit. The ITC can offset the first $25,000 of tax liability plus 75 percent of the tax liability in excess of $25,000. Any unused

ITC can be carried back 3 years and forward 15 years.[4] Domestic steel companies were granted a 15-year carryback of 50 percent of their unused ITC carryforwards in existence as of the beginning of the first tax year after 1985.

The alternative minimum tax imposes a more restrictive limit upon companies with unused ITC carryforwards and transitional-rule ITC. The TRA limits ITC to a 25 percent reduction in precredit AMT liability.

ITC Recapture from Early Disposal

The Internal Revenue Code provides for recapture of ITC in the event of early disposition of property on which ITC was claimed. For each full year after the property is placed in service, the taxpayer is entitled to 20 percent of the ITC in the case of five-year or longer class property and $33\frac{1}{3}$ percent of the ITC in the case of three-year class property. Therefore, for example, five-year class property for which ITC was claimed, but which is disposed of prior to five years after it was placed in service, will result in recapture.

Leased Property—Lessee or Lessor May Claim ITC

As a general rule, the owner of the property is entitled to ITC. In the case of a true lease, the lessor is the owner of the leased property and consequently is entitled to the ITC if certain conditions are satisfied. However, the Internal Revenue Code permits the lessor and lessee in a true lease to agree that the lessee is to be treated as the owner of the leased property for the sole purpose of claiming the ITC.[5]

---

[4] To illustrate this limitation, suppose a firm has a tax liability of $300,000 for a taxable year. The maximum ITC allowable for that taxable year is $231,250 ($25,000 plus 75 percent of $275,000). If this firm acquires $5 million of equipment that qualifies for the full 10 percent, its ITC is $325,000 after the 35 percent reduction required by the Tax Reform Act of 1986. However, only $231,250 may be used for the taxable year in which the equipment is acquired. The unused ITC of $93,750 ($325,000 less $231,250) can be carried back to offset the tax liability for the 3 previous years or carried forward to offset future tax liabilities for the next 15 years. Specific rules are given for the order in which the unused ITC can be applied to reduce past or future tax liabilities.

[5] Section 48(d)(1) of the IRC. Proper election of the pass-through of the ITC is important for the lessee. The election is irrevocable. The election must be filed by the lessor with the lessee on or before the due date of the lessee's tax return. The election must be made in the lessee's tax year in which possession of the property is transferred to the lessee. Regulation 1.48(9) provides information regarding the election. The lessee's investment that is used to determine the amount of the ITC the lessee is entitled to claim is generally the cost of the equipment but in some instances may be the fair market value of property if that is higher.

ENERGY TAX CREDITS

The Tax Reform Act of 1986 extended certain energy tax credits that expired at the end of 1986, as follows:

	Solar	Geothermal	Ocean thermal	Biomass
1985	15%	15%	15%	10%
1986	15	15	15	15
1987	12	10	15	10
1988	10	10	15	None

A 15 percent energy credit for wind energy property and an 11 percent energy credit for small hydroelectric generating property were not extended. The basis of property is reduced by 100 percent of energy tax credits claimed.

DEPRECIATION

A company acquiring property with a useful life in excess of one year is entitled to annual tax deductions for capital cost recovery, more commonly referred to as tax depreciation deductions. Such deductions have the effect of deferring income tax the company would otherwise have to pay, and tax depreciation deductions consequently have value as a cost-free source of cash until the tax is payable. Where a company is in a loss-carryforward position or is subject to AMT, it cannot realize the benefits of tax depreciation deductions. Leasing in which the lessor claims depreciation deductions on the leased equipment permits a lessee to indirectly receive comparable benefits through reduced rental payments.[6]

---

[6] Because depreciation is a tax-deductible expense, it provides a shield against taxes. The dollar amount of the tax shield provided by depreciation is an important factor in determining whether to purchase or lease an asset.

The dollar amount of the depreciation tax shield can be computed by multiplying the firm's marginal tax rate by the depreciation allowance. That is,

Depreciation tax shield = Depreciation allowance × Marginal tax rate

To understand why, consider a firm with sales of $100,000, operating expenses (excluding depreciation) of $75,000, and depreciation of $2,000. Taxable income is then $23,000, and assuming a marginal tax rate of 34 percent, income taxes would be $7,820. Without depreciation, taxable income would increase by $2,000, to $25,000, and income taxes would be $8,500. The reduction of income taxes by $680 ($8,500 minus $7,820) is the amount of tax shield associated with the $2,000 depreciation allowance. The depreciation tax shield of $680 could also be computed by multiplying the marginal tax rate of 34 percent by the depreciation allowance of $2,000.

Does depreciation always provide a tax shield? Suppose in the example that sales were $70,000 instead of $100,000. Then there would be a loss of $7,000. The firm would not have a tax liability. Depreciation in this instance will not provide a tax shield unless

Deductions for tax depreciation are determined under the Accelerated Cost Recovery System (ACRS) contained in the Internal Revenue Code of 1986. (Sometimes called MACRS for Modified Accelerated Cost Recovery System.)

The TRA made significant changes in the class lives and depreciation deductions available on various kinds of equipment. Some of these changes increased the tax benefits available to taxpayers acquiring equipment, and some of the changes decreased the benefits.

Inasmuch as the new ACRS deductions permitted under the Tax Reform Act of 1986 rely upon the pre-1981 ADR guidelines as the primary basis for classifying assets into various class lives, a review of the historic development of tax depreciation is helpful in understanding current ACRS deductions permitted under the Internal Revenue Code.

Tax Treatment prior to the Economic Recovery Tax Act of 1981

Prior to the passage of the Economic Recovery Tax Act of 1981 (ERTA), annual depreciation deductions were based on:

1. The cost of the asset.
2. The useful life of the asset.
3. The depreciation method selected.
4. The estimated salvage value.

General guidelines were set forth by the IRS for estimating the useful life of an asset. Since the useful life of an asset was only an estimate, disagreements arose between the estimated life used by a taxpayer and that which the IRS was willing to accept as reasonable. To reduce the number of disputes the IRS adopted a schedule of useful lives for a wide variety of property based on industry averages. This schedule is known as the class life Asset Depreciation Range (ADR) System.

Guidelines were also set forth for determining the depreciation method the owner of the property could use to compute a reasonable

---

the loss can be carried back to offset taxable income in the previous three years. However, if that is not possible, the loss can be carried forward 15 years to shield future taxable income. If the loss can be carried back, it will generate an immediate tax shield. However, if the loss must be carried forward, the value of the tax shield will depend on (1) the prospects of sufficient future taxable income to absorb the unused tax shield, (2) when the benefits of the tax shield are expected, and (3) the marginal tax rate at the time.

Suppose, further, that the company were subject to AMT. Depreciation deductions are greatly reduced under AMT so that depreciation will provide little tax shield.

Leasing allows a company that cannot realize the maximum benefits associated with the depreciation tax shield to transfer those benefits to a lessor that can realize them.

annual depreciation. The intent of these guidelines was to prevent the owner of property from writing off an asset too quickly for tax purposes. One restriction, for example, was that the method adopted could not during the first two thirds of the property's useful life produce total depreciation in excess of that which would have been permissible under a specific depreciation method known as the declining-balance method.

Three depreciation methods were specifically stated in the Internal Revenue Code as permissible: (1) the straight-line method, (2) the declining-balance method, and (3) the sum-of-the-years'-digits method. The latter two are known as accelerated depreciation methods because they allow for a faster write-off of an asset as compared to the straight-line method. When the declining-balance method was employed, the maximum percentage permissible depended on whether the property was new or used. Other depreciation methods were also permissible as long as they satisfied the criteria set forth by the IRS.

There was also a restriction on the total depreciation that might be taken for an asset. The total depreciation could not exceed the asset's original cost less the estimated salvage value.[7] For example, if the original cost of an asset was $100,000 and the estimated salvage value associated with that asset was $25,000, then the total depreciation allowed for that asset was $75,000 ($100,000 minus $25,000). No consideration of salvage value was necessary if the estimated salvage value did not exceed 10 percent of the original cost.

Tax Treatment under the Economic Recovery Tax Act of 1981 as Amended by the Tax Equity and Fiscal Responsibility Act of 1982

ERTA provided for an unprecedented liberalization of depreciation allowances for assets placed in service after December 31, 1980, by permitting a faster write-off of depreciable assets. ERTA substituted the Accelerated Cost Recovery System (ACRS) for the class life ADR System.

Under ACRS as originally established under ERTA were four recovery period classes for personal property[8] used in a trade or busi-

---

[7] The IRS defined salvage value as "the amount (determined at the time of acquisition) which it is estimated will be realizable on a sale or other disposition of an asset when it is no longer useful in the taxpayer's trade or business or in the production of his income and is to be retired from service" (Reg. § 1.167(a)–1, CCH§1712).

[8] Personal property refers to property other than real estate. Antichurning rules prevented ACRS deductions being available on the sale-and-leaseback of property acquired before 1981. Recovery property excluded property leased to a person (or related person) who owned or used the property during 1980.

EXHIBIT 1   ACRS Recovery Period Classes for Personal Property under ERTA

3-year	5-year
Automobiles Light trucks Equipment and machinery used in connection with research and development Machinery and equipment with an ADR midpoint class life of four years or less	All other property not included in the other classes Public utility property with an ADR midpoint class life of more than 4 years but less than 18 years
10-year	**15-year**
Public utility property with an ADR midpoint class life of more than 18 years but not more than 25 years Railroad tank cars Certain "qualified" coal utilization property	Public utility property with an ADR midpoint class life greater than 25 years Elevators and escalators

ness—3-year, 5-year, 10-year, and 15-year classes.[9] Most equipment qualified as 5-year property as shown in Exhibit 1.

Allowable ACRS deductions under ERTA were set forth in the Internal Revenue Code and were equal to the 150 percent declining-balance method of depreciation, with half-year convention in the first year, as shown in Exhibit 2. The same percentages applied to both new and used property. Salvage value was not taken into consideration. Investment tax credit did not reduce the owner's tax basis under ERTA, but the Tax Equity and Fiscal Responsibility Act of 1982 (TEFRA) required that the amount of an owner's tax basis for depreciation be reduced by one half of the credit taken. Alternatively, the taxpayer could elect to reduce the amount of the ITC by 2 percent and depreciate the total cost of the asset.

MODIFIED ACRS DEPRECIATION UNDER THE TRA

The Tax Reform Act of 1986 adopted a modified ACRS which makes a number of significant changes to the existing ACRS, effective January 1, 1987. Briefly stated, the major changes are as follows:

---

[9] A taxpayer could elect a cost recovery period based on straight-line depreciation over the statutory recovery period or an optional longer recovery period. A taxpayer could also elect to use a depreciation method not expressed in terms of years (for example, the units-of-production method).

1. The TRA established new cost recovery system classes which are set forth in Exhibit 3.
2. Assets eligible for tax depreciation are generally assigned into 3-, 5-, 7-, 10-, 15-, or 20-year class lives according to their present ADR midpoint life. These are illustrated in Exhibit 4.
3. A new 7-year class is created for equipment with an ADR midpoint life of 10 through 15 years, and a new 20-year class is created for equipment with an ADR midpoint life of 25 years or more.
4. Any equipment without an ADR midpoint life and not otherwise classified is included in the new 7-year class.
5. Three-year, 5-year, 7-year, and 10-year class property use the 200 percent declining-balance method. Fifteen-year and 20-year class property use the 150 percent declining-balance method.
6. Property included in the 3-, 5-, 7-, 10-, 15-, and 20-year cost recovery classes which is eligible for the 200 percent or 150 percent declining balance-method, switches to straight line at a time appropriate to achieve a maximum depreciation deduction. Depreciation is determined using zero salvage value.
7. Taxpayers can elect to use the straight-line method of depreciation on a class-by-class basis.
8. Certain long-lived equipment constructed or acquired by a contract binding as of March 1, 1986, may use the old rules provided the equipment is placed in service by January 1, 1989,

---

EXHIBIT 2   ACRS Annual Percentage Deduction Allowances for Personal Property under ERTA

Recovery year	3 years	5 years	10 years	15 years (public utility)
1	25%	15%	8%	5%
2	38	22	14	10
3	37	21	12	9
4		21	10	8
5		21	10	7
6			10	7
7			9	6
8			9	6
9			9	6
10			9	6
11				6
12				6
13				6
14				6
15				6

EXHIBIT 3 ACRS Classes and Method

Cost recovery class	DDB method	ADR midpoint criteria
3 years	200%	4 years or less excluding automobiles and light trucks.
5 years	200	More than 4 years and less than 10 years including automobiles, light trucks, certain qualified technological equipment, computer-based central office switching equipment, renewable energy and biomass properties that are small power production facilities, semiconductor manufacturing equipment, and research and experimentation property.
7 years	200	10 years and less than 16 years or not otherwise classified for ADR.
10 years	200	16 years and less than 20 years.
15 years	150	20 years and less than 25 years including sewage treatment plants, telephone distribution plants, and comparable equipment for two-way exchange of data and voice communications.
20 years	150	25 years and more.
27.5 years	Straight line	Residential rental property.
31.5 years	Straight line	Commercial real estate.

for property with an ADR midpoint of more than 7 years and less than 20 years (January 1, 1990, for commercial aircraft); and before January 1, 1991, for property with a midpoint life longer than 20 years.

9. Since in some instances the new ACRS rules are more favorable than the old ACRS rules, antichurning rules prevent taxpayers from transferring ownership to bring property within the scope of the new rules where there is no change in the economic relationship of the lessee to the property.

Alternative Depreciation System for Leases to Tax-Exempt Entities, for Foreign Use, or by Electing Taxpayers

An alternative depreciation system (ADS) is established to be used for foreign-use property, property leased to a tax-exempt entity, and tax-exempt bond-financed property. Certain property, including predominantly foreign-use property (with exceptions), tax-exempt use property, and tax-exempt bond-financed property is subject to straight-line depreciation generally over the ADR midpoint (125 percent of the lease term, if longer, in the case of tax-exempt use property). Property

---

EXHIBIT 4   Cost Recovery Class of Equipment under the Tax Reform Act of 1986*

	ADR midpoint (years)
3-year class—ADR midpoint less than 4 years except automobiles and light trucks:	
Manufacture of glass,products—special tools	2.5
Special tools, manufacture of fabricated metal products or motor vehicles	3
Manufacture of food and beverages—special handling devices	4
Manufacture of rubber products—special tools and devices	4
Tractor units for over-the-road use	4
5-year class—ADR midpoint more than 4 years and less than 10 years but including automobiles and light trucks:	
Automobiles and taxis	3
Light general-purpose trucks	4
Semiconductor manufacturing equipment	5
Electric utility nuclear fuel assemblies	5
Computers	6
Data handling equipment, except computers	6
Airplanes (airframes and engines) noncommercial	6
Heavy general-purpose trucks	6
Trailers and trucks mounted containers	6
Drilling of oil and gas wells	6
Construction	6
Helicopters (airframes and engines)	6
Timber-cutting equipment	6
Sawing of dimensional stock from logs, portable units	6
Manufacture of electronic components, products, and systems (except semiconductors)	6
Air transport (restricted)	6
Radio and television broadcastings	6
Manufacture of primary nonferrous metals—special tools	6.5
Ship and boat building—special tools	6.5
Offshore drilling	7.5
Manufacture of knitted goods	7.5
Manufacture of textured yarns	8
Motor transport—freight	8
Satellite space segment property	8
CATV—service and test equipment	8.5
Buses	9
Manufacture of carpets and dyeing, finishing and packaging of textile products	9
Manufacture of apparel and other finished products	9
CATV—program origination	9
Manufacture of chemicals	9.5
CATV—microwave systems	9.5
Computer-based central office switching equipment	9.5
7-year class—ADR midpoint of 10 years or more and less than 16 years, or not otherwise classified for ADR:	
Railroad track	10
Office furniture, fixtures, and equipment	10

*The Internal Revenue Service has continuing authority to reassign class lives, unless Congress has specifically assigned a class life to an asset (that is, automobiles) in which case the recovery class can not be changed until 1992.

EXHIBIT 4 *(continued)*

	ADR midpoint (years)
Agriculture	10
Mining	10
Sawing of dimensional stock from logs (permanent mills)	10
Manufacture of wood products and furniture	10
Manufacture of converted paper, paperboard and pulp products	10
Manufacture of electrical and nonelectrical machinery and other mechanical products	10
Manufacture of aerospace products	10
Telephone station equipment	10
Satellite ground segment property	10
CATV—subscriber connection and distribution systems	10
Waste reduction and resource recovery plant	10
Computerized switching, channeling, and associated control equipment	10.5
Manufacture of yarn, thread, and woven fabric	11
Printing, publishing equipment	11
Manufacture of leather and leather products	11
Manufacture of locomotives	11.5
Cotton, ginning assets	12
Manufacture of other food and kindred products	12
Manufacture of fabricated metal products	12
Manufacture of motor vehicles	12
Ship and boat-building machinery and equipment	12
Manufacture of railroad cars	12
Manufacture of athletic, jewelry, and other goods	12
Aircraft (commercial)	12
Assets with no ADR midpoint that are deemed to have a 12-year midpoint, e.g., ship containers and railroad track	12
Theme and amusement parks	12.5
Manufacture of pulp and paper	13
TOCS high frequency radio and microwave systems	13
TOCS support and service equipment	13.5
Exploration for and production of petroleum and natural gas deposits	14
Manufacture of rubber products	14
Manufacture of glass products	14
Manufacture of primary nonferrous metals	14
Manufacture of foundry products	14
Railroad machinery and equipment (other than tank cars)	14
Gas utility substitute natural gas (SNG) production plants	14
Natural gas production plants	14
Manufacture of tobacco and tobacco products	15
Manufacture of stone and clay products	15
Single-purpose agricultural and horticultural structure	15
Manufactured homes	14 or 15
Qualified coal utilization property	14 or 15
Section 1250 property with an ADR midpoint of 12.5 years or less	14 or 15
10-year class—ADR midpoint 16 years or more and less than 20 years:	
Petroleum refining	16
TOCSC—central office control equipment	16.5
Manufacture of grain and grain mill products	17
Vessels, barges, tugs, and similar water transportation equipment (except those used in marine contract construction)	18

EXHIBIT 4 *(concluded)*

	ADR midpoint (years)
Manufacture of sugar and sugar products	18
Manufacture of vegetable oil and vegetable oil products	18
Substitute natural gas—coal gasification	18
Telephone central office equipment (except computer-based equipment)	18
Electric power generating and distribution systems	19

15-year class—ADR midpoint 20 years or more and less than 25 years, including sewage treatment plants, telephone distribution plants, and comparable plants for two-way communication of data and voice:

Manufacture of cement	20
Railroad wharves and docks (Section 1245 property only)	20
Distributive trade and services—billboard, service station buildings, and petroleum marketing land improvements (Section 1245 property only)	20
Land improvements (Section 1245 property only)	20
Water transportation	20
Electric utility nuclear production plant	20
Electric utility combustion turbine production plant	20
Industrial steam and electric generation and/or distribution systems	22
Pipeline transportation	22
Gas utility trunk pipelines and related storage facilities	22
Liquified natural gas plant	22
Telephone distribution plant and comparable equipment	24

---

specifically assigned to a class will be treated as having the same recovery period as used for regular depreciation purposes. Property with no assigned midpoint will use a 12-year recovery period. A taxpayer may also elect to use the alternative depreciation system.

Half-Year Convention. Half-year convention is to be used at both the beginning and end of a class life in computing deductions under the new cost recovery system. In other words, cost recovery deductions available for five-year class property, for example, will actually extend into the sixth year.

Mid-Quarter Convention—Forty Percent Rule. A mid-quarter convention is applicable to all property of a taxpayer if more than 40 percent of all property (other than class 10 property and low income housing) is placed in service by a taxpayer during the last three months of its taxable year. Under the mid-quarter convention, all property placed in service during any quarter of a taxable year is treated as being placed in service on the midpoint of such quarter. The 40 percent test is determined on an affiliated group basis.

If the property placed in service is subject to both ACRS under the old law and to modified ACRS under the new law, the 40 percent determination is made with respect to all such property. Under such circumstances, the mid-quarter convention only applies to property subject to the modified ACRS.

Comparison of Modified ACRS Deductions with Old Law

Exhibit 5 compares ACRS deductions under the old law with modified ACRS deductions under the new law for a $10,000 piece of equipment which would qualify as 3-, 5-, or 7-year class property under the new law.

TRANSITION RULE FOR PRE-TRA ACRS

As noted earlier, in some instances ACRS deductions under the tax law prior to the Tax Reform Act of 1986 may be more favorable for a taxpayer. Under a general transition rule of the TRA, the new ACRS rules need not apply to property constructed, reconstructed, or acquired by a taxpayer pursuant to a written contract that was binding as of March 1, 1986, and at all times thereafter, provided the property is placed in service by January 1, 1989, for property with an ADR midpoint of more than 7 years and less than 20 years; and before

EXHIBIT 5 ACRS Deductions under TRA Compared to Prior Law ·

	3-year ACRS		5-year ACRS		7-year ACRS	
Year	Old law	New law	Old law	New law	Old law	New law
1	$ 2,500	$ 3,334	$ 1,500	$ 2,000	$ 1,500	$ 1,428
2	3,800	4,444	2,200	3,200	2,200	2,449
3	3,700	1,481	2,100	1,920	2,100	1,749
4		741	2,100	1,152	2,100	1,250
5			2,100	1,152	2,100	892
6				576		892
7						892
8						448
Total	$10,000	$10,000	$10,000	$10,000	$10,000	$10,000
Present value @ 8%	$ 9,191	$ 9,306	$ 8,550	$ 8,762	$ 8,550	$ 8,273

· The analysis assumes that 3-year class property under the new law would have been 3-year class property under the old law and that 5- and 7-year class property under the new law would have been 5-year class property under the old law. Generally this will be the case.

January 1, 1991, for property with a midpoint life longer than 20 years. A special in-service date of January 1, 1990, applies to commercial aircraft. A contract enforceable under state law is considered to be binding. Design changes for reasons of technical or economic efficiencies that cause an insignificant increase in the original price will not adversely affect the status of a binding contract. New supply contracts that fail to designate amount or design specifications of property to be purchased will not qualify as a binding contract until a purchase order referring to the supply contract which designates a specific number of properties has been placed.

Equipped Building Rule and Plant Facility Rule

Where construction of an "equipped building" is begun on or before March 1, 1986, pursuant to a written specific plan and more than one half of the equipped building cost (including cost of machinery and equipment for use in the building) was incurred or committed by that date, the entire equipped building project and incidental appurtenances are transitional property eligible for ACRS under the law prior to the TRA. A similar rule applies with regard to plant facilities.

Effect of Transitional Rule on Sale-and-Leasebacks and Three-Month Window

Property is treated as meeting the requirements of a transitional rule or a general effective date rule if: (1) the property is placed in service by a taxpayer who acquired the property from a person in whose hands the property would qualify under a transitional or general effective date rule; (2) the property is leased back by the taxpayer to such person; and (3) the leaseback occurs within three months after such property was originally placed in service but no later than the applicable date. The legislative intent was that the special rule for sale-leasebacks apply to any property that qualifies for transitional relief under the act or that was originally placed in service by the lessee under the sale-leaseback before the general effective date.

Other Transitional Rules

Congress also enacted numerous special transitional rules preserving old ACRS deductions and ITC for particular projects or property that did not otherwise qualify as transitional property.

Antichurning Rules

Antichurning rules prevent property placed in service prior to 1987 from being depreciated under the new system. These rules generally prevent a taxpayer from transferring property to a related party or a lessor in a sale-leaseback transaction to obtain the benefits of more accelerated cost recovery.

Antichurning rules contained in ERTA that relate to property placed in service prior to 1981 continue in effect so that pre-1981 property cannot qualify for the new ACRS if it is transferred to a related party or a lessor.

THE ALTERNATIVE MINIMUM TAX

The new alternative minimum tax (AMT) contained in the TRA is the most significant business tax change enacted by Congress in many years. The AMT is applicable to taxable years beginning after December 31, 1986, and will have far-reaching consequences for the equipment leasing business, including two immediate effects:

> First, the AMT will motivate companies subject to AMT to lease equipment because rental payments will be deductible, and tax depreciation deductions will be curtailed by a longer depreciation life, a lower depreciation rate, a lower marginal tax rate, and a lower book depreciation rate.

> Second, the AMT will result in some lessors eliminating or curtailing their leasing activities.

The alternative minimum tax requires companies to compute their income tax twice—once under the standard corporate income tax and again under the AMT provisions. Companies pay the amount of the excess of "minimum tax" over the regular tax (in addition to remaining liable for regular tax). The AMT liability is computed at a 20 percent rate applied to alternative minimum taxable income (AMTI). An exemption amount of $40,000 is provided, subject to a phaseout which makes its value meaningless for most companies.

Briefly stated, the AMT has fewer deductions and a broader base of categories of income than the regular corporate income tax. The most far-reaching aspect of the AMT is that it brings financial accounting principles into the tax system. For many corporations, the AMT will be the predominant tax with which they will be concerned.

AMT income is equal to the sum of the taxpayer's regular taxable income or loss plus items of tax preference. Among the preferences are accelerated depreciation; 50 percent of the difference between taxable

---

EXHIBIT 6   Method for Computing the Alternative Minimum Tax

1. Begin with regular taxable income.
2. Add AMT preferences (including the book income adjustment).
3. Adjust the regular taxable income for any item that requires a substitute AMT method.
4. Make net operating loss adjustments (NOL) and reduce the base by the AMT NOL.
5. The sum of Items 1 through 4 results in the alternative minimum taxable income (AMTI).
6. Reduce the AMTI by any allowable exemption amount to determine the net AMTI.
7. Compute the 20 percent tax on the net AMTI to establish AMT before credits.
8. Subtract any allowable foreign tax credit and/or investment tax credit.
9. Pay AMT to the extent it exceeds the regular corporate income tax.
10. Compute the allowable AMT credit to carry over for use against regular corporate income tax in succeeding year(s).

---

income and book unreported profits (BURP); the completed contract method of accounting; and certain tax-exempt interest.[10] Exhibit 6 provides a summary of the method to be used for computing AMT.

Depreciation for equipment is recomputed under the AMT using the 150 percent declining-balance method over the ADR midpoint lives,

---

[10] Under AMT investment related preference adjustments, the cost recovery period will more closely approximate the investment's useful life by adjustments to:

- Depreciation of real and personal property.
- Amortization of pollution-control facilities.
- Mining exploration costs.

and by adding to AMT base:

- Expensed intangible drilling costs.
- Percentage depletion.

Timing adjustments are made by recognizing income earlier for:

- Income deferred under completed contract method.
- Income deferred under the installment method.
- Book income adjustment.
- Capital construction funds.
- Certain insurance company deductions.

and by adding to AMT base:

- Bad debt reserves for financial institutions.

Certain income excluded from regular taxable income is included in AMTI:

- Tax-exempt interest.
- Charitable contributions of appreciated property.

with special rules for selected assets. The effect of this is to reduce significantly the depreciation deduction available to the taxpayer by:

1. Lengthening the depreciation life.
2. Reducing the depreciation rate from 200 percent declining-balance method to 150 percent declining-balance method.

The BURP preference is determined by consolidating the book income of those corporations that are consolidated for tax purposes. Among other things this means that book depreciation can have a tax impact. Fifty percent of the excess of a taxpayer's pre-tax book profits over alternate minimum taxable income is a preference. Since most companies depreciate assets using the straight-line method for book purposes (thus increasing book income), the effect of the BURP preference is to further reduce the value of ACRS depreciation deductions to a taxpayer.

The BURP preference computed in this manner is only effective for three years. After such time a similar preference applies but is based on a more complex concept of "adjusted current earnings" which, among other things, further reduces depreciation deductions.

Depreciation on transition property that is eligible for ITC under the ITC transition rules is not subject to the AMT.

A corporation that pays AMT is entitled to a credit against future regular corporate tax liability. The credit is attributable to preference items that deferred the regular corporate tax liability, such as ACRS. The credit can be used to reduce regular tax liability in subsequent years to the extent the regular tax liability would otherwise exceed the tentative minimum tax. The credit can be carried forward indefinitely.

Three other features of AMT are of general interest. Companies can use 65 percent of unused carryover ITC to offset up to 25 percent of its AMT liability in a single year or, alternately, apply such carryover ITC to reduce regular tax liability. Adjusted operating loss carryforwards can be used to offset up to 90 percent of the alternate minimum taxable income. In general, no more than 90 percent of tentative minimum tax (before net operating losses and foreign tax credit) can be offset by AMT foreign tax credit.

The AMT results in increased tax liability for capital-intensive companies that are now only marginally taxable, greatly complicates their financial planning, and increases their administrative costs of conducting business.

The AMT is very complex, and a comprehensive discussion of the AMT would of necessity be quite lengthy and is beyond the scope of this book. However, the effect of AMT on corporate taxpayers is very important since it reduces the efficiency of ACRS depreciation deductions and will create leasing needs for companies seeking to avoid AMTI.

RESEARCH AND EXPERIMENTATION CREDIT

Prior to the TRA, rental expense was a qualified expense eligible for the 20 percent research and experimentation credit. Effective January 1, 1986, the TRA eliminated rental expense as a qualified R&E expense, except for certain very short-term rentals of equipment.

FINANCE LEASES

Finance leases, which were first authorized by TEFRA to become effective in 1984 and then were largely postponed in early 1984 by the DRA until 1988, were repealed effective January 1, 1987, except for certain very limited property eligible under certain prior transition rules.

TREASURY REGULATIONS

Most likely, little help for clarification of the TRA can be expected in the immediate future from Treasury Department regulations. The small Treasury Department staff responsible for issuing regulations is already years behind in promulgating regulations for prior laws, although Treasury has promised to accelerate the regulatory process with respect to the new act.

TRA COMPARED WITH FORMER LAW

Exhibit 7 compares provisions of the Tax Reform Act of 1986 that relate to equipment leasing with similar provisions of the former law and notes instances in which the law is unchanged.

EXHIBIT 7 Comparison of Provisions of Tax Reform Act of 1986 Affecting Equipment Leasing with Prior Tax Law

Old Law	Tax Reform Act of 1986
INTERNAL REVENUE CODE OF 1954	
The name of the general tax law is the Internal Revenue Code of 1954.	The name of the general tax law is now the Internal Revenue Code of 1986. The Section numbers remain the same as under the Internal Revenue Code of 1954.

EXHIBIT 7   (*continued*)

Old Law	Tax Reform Act of 1986

REVENUE PROCEDURE 75-21

General requirements outlined in Revenue Procedure 75-21 to qualify an equipment lease as a true lease.

No change from present guideline lease rules.

CORPORATE TAX RATE

Corporate income tax rate 46%.

Corporate income tax rate 46% in 1986; 40% in 1987 and 34% in 1988 and subsequent years. Graduated rates for small business.

CAPITAL GAINS TAX

Capital gains tax rate of 28%.

Capital gains taxed at the corporate income tax rate. The preferential alternate tax rate for net capital gains of corporations is eliminated.

INVESTMENT TAX CREDIT

Investment tax credit equal to 6% of equipment cost on 3 year class property and 10% of equipment cost on 5 year and longer class life property, subject to basis adjustment of one half ITC claimed.

ITC repealed effective December 31, 1985, unless subject to firm contract as of December 31, 1985, in which case a calendar year taxpayer can claim 100% of otherwise eligible ITC in 1986, 82.5 percent in 1987, and 65% in 1988 and subsequent years. A basis adjustment is required for the full amount of ITC. To be eligible under this transition rule, transition property must be placed in service by the following dates according to its ADR life: Less than 5 years, 6-30-86; at least 5 but less than 10 years, by 12-31-86; at least 7 years but less than 20 years, by 12-31-88; and 20 years or more, by 12-31-90. By exception, commercial aircraft by 12-31-89.

EXHIBIT 7 *(continued)*

Old Law	Tax Reform Act of 1986

MAXIMUM INVESTMENT TAX CREDIT

ITC applies against the first $25,000 of tax liability and up to 85% of tax liability in excess of $25,000.

ITC applies against the first $25,000 of tax liability and up to 75% of tax liability in excess of $25,000, for taxable years after 1985, or can be used to offset up to 25% of alternative minimum tax liability.

DEPRECIATION

ACRS depreciation with five asset classes: 3, 5, 10, 15 and 19 years. Most equipment other than public utility equipment was 5 year class. (Cars and light trucks were 3 year) Allowable depreciation was 150% declining balance switching to straight line with six month convention in the first year.

ACRS modified by providing for 8 asset classes from 3 to 31.5 years; 3, 5, 7 and 10 year classes use 200% declining balance method switching to straight line; some class lives for equipment remained the same as for ACRS and some class lives were lengthened. Half-year convention used in first and last year (for a 5 year class asset, for example, some depreciation is claimed in the 6th year). New rules apply to plant and equipment placed into service after December 31, 1986, provided that certain long lived equipment constructed or acquired by a contract that was binding as of March 1, 1986, may use the old rules provided the property is placed in service before January 1, 1989, for property with an ADR midpoint of more than 7 years and less than 20 years, and before January 1, 1991, for property with an ADR midpoint of 20 years or longer.

THREE MONTH WINDOW

Property retained its status as new equipment eligible for ITC if sold and leased back within three months of being placed in service.

Property retains its transitional property status for ITC and ACRS if sold and leased back within three months of being placed in service.

EXHIBIT 7   (*continued*)

Old Law	Tax Reform Act of 1986

40 PERCENT RULE ON DEPRECIATION

Property delivering in the last quarter of the year is eligible for regular ACRS, with six month convention in the first year.

If 40% or more of all property acquired in any taxable year is placed in service during the final quarter, the taxpayer must use a midquarter convention (one-half of one quarter's depreciation) in computing its allowable deduction in the first year. Under this midquarter convention, all property placed in service during any quarter of the taxable year is treated as being placed in service on the midpoint of such quarter. The 40% computation is determined on an affiliated group basis.

ALTERNATE MINIMUM TAX

Minimum taxes were assessed through application of an add-on minimum tax. None of the preference items added on significantly adversely affected lessors. The excess of acelerated depreciation on equipment over straight line is a preference item only for personal holding companies.

A new Alternate Minimum Tax ("AMT") requires corporations to compute their income tax twice: once under the standard corporate tax and again under the AMT. The AMT allows fewer deductions and more categories of income. The Corporate tax rate is 40 percent in 1987 and 34 percent in 1988 and thereafter, whereas the AMT rate is 20%. Corporations pay whichever method results in the larger tax. Depreciation is recomputed using 150% declining balance method over the ADR midpoint lives. AMT income equals the regular taxable income plus certain preference items which include 50 percent of the excess of pre tax book profit over AMT income. Thus, book depreciation has a tax impact under AMT.

TRAC LEASES

TRAC leases, which have true lease characteristics even though providing lessees with the equivalent of a fixed price purchase option under a Terminal Rental adjustment clause, were authorized for over the road vehicles by the Deficit Reduction Act of 1984.

TRAC leases survived the TRA without significant change.

EXHIBIT 7   (*continued*)

<table>
<tr><td align="center">Old Law</td><td align="center">Tax Reform Act of 1986</td></tr>
</table>

INSTALLMENT SALES

Profits on an installment sale by a parent to its subsidiary or to its customers are deferred until payments are received.

The installment sale method of reporting income is repealed for revolving credit plans and is limited for other installment sales based upon a debt to equity formula.

The DRA generally denies use of the installment method for a portion of a dealer's sales and for a portion of sales of business or rental property with a selling price exceeding $150,000, by treating a portion of the taxpayer's outstanding indebtedness for a year as payments on those sales.

The DRA designates a portion of a taxpayer's indebtedness as allocable installment indebtedness (AII). AII is generally defined as a portion of the taxpayer's average quarterly debt, in the same ratio to that debt as the taxpayer's applicable installment obligations bear to the taxpayer's installment obligations and adjusted bases in other assets. Certain related parties will be treated as one for purposes of these rules. This AII amount will be treated as a payment on the installment obligation, immediately before year-end, resulting in gain being recognized currently on the obligation. In each later year, gain will be recognized on an applicable installment obligation only to the extent payments exceed the AII allocated to the obligation in the earlier years; if gain is recognized, it will be accounted for under the ordinary installment method rule. The new law is effective as of January 1, 1987, for sales made after February 28, 1986.

FINANCE LEASES

Finance leases authorized by TEFRA for a few months in 1984 and then delayed until 1988 by the Deficit Reduction Act of 1984.

Finance leases are repealed effective January 1, 1987, except for property eligible under certain transition rules.

EXHIBIT 7   (*continued*)

Old Law	Tax Reform Act of 1986

DIVIDEND RECEIVED CREDIT

Dividends received by corporations are entitled to an 85 percent credit against corporate income tax.

The dividend received credit is reduced from 85 percent to 80 percent over 10 years beginning in 1987. The maximum rate will, therefore, be 6.8 percent under a 34 percent tax rate as compared to 6.9 percent under a 46 percent tax rate.

ENERGY TAX CREDITS

Expired after 1985.

Renewable solar extended through 1988; 15% in 1986, 12% in 1987 and 10% in 1988. Geothermal extended through 1988; 15% in 1986, 10% in 1987 and 1988. Biomass extended through 1987; 15% in 1986 and 10% in 1987. Wind energy and small hydro electric generating property expired after 1985.

ACCOUNTING METHOD

A corporate taxpayer could elect either the cash or accrual method.

Corporations with cash receipts of more than $5 million must use the accrual method of accounting for tax purposes effective for taxable years beginning after December 31, 1986. Income from leases entered into on or before September 25, 1985, will not be subject to change, provided the lessor makes an election to use the cash basis.

RESEARCH AND EXPERIMENTATION CREDIT

A 25 percent credit was allowed for certain qualified incremental expenditures for research and experimentation. Rental expense for use of personal property was treated as a qualified expenditure. The credit expired December 31, 1985.

The credit was reduced to 20 percent and extended to December 31, 1988. However, rental expense for use of personal property is no longer a qualified expense.

EXHIBIT 7   (*continued*)

<table>
<tr><td align="center">Old Law</td><td align="center">Tax Reform Act of 1986</td></tr>
</table>

**INDIVIDUALS DEDUCTIONS
FOR TAX SHELTERS**

Individuals who invested in leases of equipment as Lessors could deduct depreciation and interest for which they were at risk against passive income such as salaries, dividends and interest income.	Individuals can deduct passive tax losses for which they are at risk, such as, depreciation and interest expense incurred in investing in an equipment lease where the investor is not regularly involved in the management of the property, only as an offset against passive income from similar investments. Passive losses from investments where the activity has commenced at the date the law signed, October 22, 1986, may be deducted:

100% in 1986
65% in 1987
40% in 1988
20% in 1989
10% in 1990

FOREIGN SOURCE INCOME

Income or loss from rental of aircraft or ships was treated as U.S. source income if the property was leased to a U.S. person and the aircraft or ship was manufactured in the United States.	Ships and aircraft are now subject to the same rules as for sourcing transportation income. Income between two points in the U.S. is U.S. income. Income between two foreign points is foreign income. Income between a U.S. and a foreign point is half and half determined on a daily basis. Property held by a taxpayer as of January 1, 1986, is covered by the old rules.

**LOCAL GOVERNMENT TAX
EXEMPT BONDS OR LEASES**

Tax exempt bonds or leases issued by or on behalf of state and local governments to finance their traditional governmental activities are exempt from federal income tax.	Tax exempt bonds and leases issued by state and local governments for traditional governmental activities continue to be exempt from federal income tax.

EXHIBIT 7   (*continued*)

Old Law	Tax Reform Act of 1986

SMALL ISSUE INDUSTRIAL REVENUE BONDS

Interest on certain small issue $1 million and $10 million industrial revenue bonds for manufacturing and non-manufacturing facilities were exempt from federal income tax, with the exemption for new issues to expire December 31, 1986.

The law continues the exemption for $1 million and $10 million small-issue IDBs, while retaining the present-law sunset date for nonmanufacturing facilities (i.e., December 31, 1986), and extending the sunset date for manufacturing facilities to December 31, 1989. Also, for purposes of qualifying as small-issue IDBs, bonds for first-time farmers will be treated as bonds for manufacturing facilities and thus may be issued through 1989.

EXEMPT FACILITY INDUSTRIAL REVENUE BONDS

Tax exempt industrial revenue bond issues for amounts in excess of $10 million could be used to finance any of a number of designated types of facilities or structures.

Activities for which tax-exempt IDBs will continue to be allowed (subject to some modifications limiting the financing to the precise named purpose or function) include airport, dock, and wharf facilities; sewage and solid waste disposal facilities (except for certain alcohol and steam generation facilities); facilities for the furnishing of water, including irrigation systems; electric and gas local furnishing facilities; local district heating and cooling systems; hazardous waste disposal facilities; and mass commuting facilities. Tax-exempt IDB financing is no longer allowed for the following facilities; sports facilities; convention or trade show facilities; hydroelectric generating facilities, parking facilities (unless subordinate to other exempt facilities); and air and water pollution control facilities. The new law applies to bonds issued after September 1, 1986.

EXHIBIT 7   (*concluded*)

Old Law	Tax Reform Act of 1986
INTEREST EXPENSE DEDUCTIONS FOR INTEREST USED TO FINANCE INVESTMENT IN TAX EXEMPT OBLIGATIONS	
Financial institutions in the past were able to deduct without limit interest expense used to finance investments in tax exempt bonds and leases issued by state and local governments. 20% of such deductions were disallowed after January 1, 1983.	The law disallows 100 percent of any otherwise allowable interest expense that is deemed allocable to tax-exempt obligations acquired after August 7, 1986, effective for taxable years ending after December 31, 1986 (subject to certain binding commitment exceptions). The allocable interest amount is determined by multiplying the institution's otherwise allowable interest expense (prior to the 20 percent disallowance) by the ratio of the institution's average adjusted basis of tax-exempt obligations acquired after August 7, 1986, to the average adjusted basis of all its assets.
	The 20 percent disallowance is retained for interest expense allocable to tax-exempt obligations acquired between January 1, 1983, and August 7, 1986. Calendar year financial institutions are subject to the 20 percent disallowance for the balance of 1986 on all obligations acquired after December 31, 1982.
	The law provides an exemption from the 100 percent interest expense disallowance for certain tax-exempt issues by small municipal issuers. Financial institutions that acquire these small-issuer obligations will remain subject to the 20 percent interest expense disallowance of present law with respect to these obligations.
	Interest income from certain non-governmental purpose bonds is also a preference item for purposes of computing the new corporate alternative minimum tax.

EFFECT OF THE TRA UPON EQUIPMENT LEASING

The Tax Reform Act of 1986 (TRA) has changed equipment leasing and the effect on lessees and lessors in a number of ways, as follows.

The cost of acquiring equipment either by lease or by purchase increased significantly as a result of the changes in tax laws contained in the Tax Reform Act of 1986. However, the cost differential between leasing and purchasing where the lessee is able to claim tax benefits currently is much less under the new law. Moreover, leasing equipment quickly becomes less expensive than purchasing equipment when a taxpayer cannot use ACRS depreciation tax benefits in the year in which equipment is placed in service so that tax loss must be carried forward. Further, this effect is accelerated for a company subject to paying the alternative minimum tax. As a result of the TRA, many companies will find leasing attractive even though they may not have leased in the past.

Chapter 6 contains detailed analyses of the economics of lease versus purchase decisions under the old law and the new law for automobiles, computers, manufacturing equipment, and commercial aircraft.

Among other things, these analyses illustrate that leasing equipment is less expensive than purchasing equipment for a company unable to currently claim ACRS deductions under the TRA due to loss carryforwards and/or the AMT, and that leasing is more attractive from a cost standpoint at an earlier date under the new law as compared to the old law.

Exhibit 8 shows comparisons of typical lease rates (based on the assumptions presented) for leases of various types of equipment that

---

EXHIBIT 8   Lease Rates and Present Values of Lease Rentals under the Tax Reform Act of 1986 as Compared to Prior Law*

Assumptions:

	1985	1986	1987	1988
Equipment cost:	$1,000,000	$1,000,000	$1,000,000	$1,000,000
Transaction fee:	1.0%	1.0%	1.0%	1.0%
Tax Rate:	46%	46%/ 39.95%/34%	39.95%/34%	34%
ITC:	10%	0%	0%	0%
Debt Rate:	9%	9%	9%	9%
Rent Payments:		Quarterly in arrears		
Delivery & Commence- ment of Lease:	9/1/85	9/1/86	9/1/87	9/1/88
Depreciation:	ACRS	ACRS	200DB-SL/ 150DB-SL	200DB-SL/ 150DB-SL
Lessor's Yield:	7.0%AT	7.0%AT	7.0%AT	7.0%AT

*The authors acknowledge the help of Gail Niemi and Candice Field in preparing this exhibit.

EXHIBIT 8   *(continued)*

Equipment	ADR Class	ADR Mid-life	Lease Term	Residual Assumed for Pricing	Old ACRS Recovery Period	New ACRS Recovery Period
AIRLINES						
Commercial aircraft	45.0	12	20	20	5	7
Business aircraft	45.0	6	8	20	5	5
COMMUNICATION						
Telephone switching equipment	48.12	9.5	5	10	5	5
Fiber optic lines	48.14	24	5	10	5	15
Satellite communications	48.2	6	8	2.5	5	5
COMPUTERS						
Main frame	00.12	6	5	0	5	5
Disk drive	00.12	6	5	10	5	5
CONSTRUCTION						
D-9 caterpiller tractor	15.0	6	5	20	5	5
Cranes	15.0	6	5	20	5	5
DEPARTMENT STORE						
Cash registers	57.0	9	7	5	5	5
Store fixtures	57.0	9	7	5	5	5
ENERGY RELATED (other than public utility)						
Co-generation (electricity)	00.4	22	15	5	5	15
Waste to energy	49.5	10	20	0	5	7
HOSPITALS						
CAT Scanner	57.0	9	5	10	5	5
Kidney dialysis machine	57.0	9	5	10	5	5
Hospital bed	57.0	9	5	0	5	5
MANUFACTURING						
Press brake	33.4	15	5	20	5	7
Lathe	33.4	15	5	20	5	7
Automatic welder	33.4	15	5	20	5	7
Overhead crane	33.4	15	5	20	5	7
Steel rolling mill	33.4	15	5	20	5	7
Automated warehouse	33.4	15	5	20	5	7

(1) It should be noted that these results are presented for comparison purposes. Actual lease rates for a lessee will vary with the lessee's credit standing, prevailing interest rates, competitive factors, date of delivery, the lessor's estimate of residual value and other factors.

EXHIBIT 8   (*continued*)

Implicit or Interest Equivalent Lease Rate				Present Value				Approximate Leverage			
1985	1986	1987	1988	1985	1986	1987	1988	1985	1986	1987	1988
3.82	5.74	6.26	6.40	66.25	77.98	81.28	82.24	55/45	70	74	75
0.74	3.83	4.77	5.07	72.94	82.47	85.53	86.49	60/40	75	80	80
(.099)	5.11	5.08	5.64	79.61	90.95	90.89	92.15	73/27	79	79	79
(.099)	5.11	8.27	8.24	79.61	90.95	98.27	98.18	73/27	79	72	71
3.42	6.68	6.85	7.26	81.17	91.88	92.49	93.87	70/30	80	80	80
1.08	8.15	8.02	8.53	86.13	97.99	97.67	98.88	80/20	80	80	80
(.099)	5.11	5.08	5.64	79.61	90.95	90.89	92.15	73/27	79	79	79
(2.33)	1.97	2.04	2.64	75.02	84.00	84.16	85.46	59/41	80	80	80
(2.33)	1.97	2.04	2.64	75.02	84.00	84.16	85.46	59/41	80	80	80
2.60	6.39	6.56	6.98	80.74	91.86	92.37	93.67	72/28	80	80	80
2.60	6.39	6.56	6.98	80.74	91.86	92.37	93.67	72/28	80	80	80
4.29	6.25	8.37	8.42	74.32	84.51	96.33	96.60	62/38	75	80	80
4.56	6.40	6.89	7.03	70.65	82.18	85.42	86.37	59/41	73	77	78
(.099)	5.11	5.08	5.64	79.61	90.95	90.89	92.15	73/27	79	79	79
(.099)	5.11	5.08	5.64	79.61	90.95	90.89	92.15	73/27	79	79	79
2.94	8.15	8.02	8.53	86.13	97.99	97.67	98.88	80/20	80	80	80
(2.33)	1.97	3.06	3.43	75.02	84.00	86.39	87.20	59/41	80	80	80
(2.33)	1.97	3.06	3.43	75.02	84.00	86.39	87.20	59/41	80	80	80
(2.33)	1.97	3.06	3.43	75.02	84.00	86.39	87.20	59/41	80	80	80
(2.33)	1.97	3.06	3.43	75.02	84.00	86.39	87.20	59/41	80	80	80
(2.33)	1.97	3.06	3.43	75.02	84.00	86.39	87.20	59/41	80	80	80
(2.33)	1.97	3.06	3.43	75.02	84.00	86.39	87.20	59/41	80	80	80

EXHIBIT 8   (*continued*)

Equipment	ADR Class	ADR Mid-Life	Lease Term	Residual Assumed for Pricing	Old ACRS Recovery Period	New ACRS Recovery Period
MINING EQUIPMENT						
Dragline	10.0	10	20	20	5	7
Coal side wall miner	10.0	10	5	0	5	7
Conveyor system	10.0	10	5	0	5	7
PETRO CHEMICAL						
Oil refinery	13.3	16	20	5	5	10
On shore drilling rig	13.1	6	15	0	5	5
Pipeline	46.0	22	10	0	5	15
PUBLIC UTILITY						
Electric utility steam production plant	49.13	28	30	5	15	20
Nuclear electric generator	49.12	20	30	0	10	15
RAILROADS						
Track	NEW	10	20	5	5	7
Container flatcar	40.1	14	12	20	5	7
Locomotive	40.1	14	15	20	5	7
SHIPPING						
Container ship	00.28	18	25	0	5	10
Containers (trailer-mounted)	00.27	6	10	20	5	5
TRUCKING COMPANIES						
Tractor trailers	00.27	6	5	20	5	5
Light panel trucks	00.241	4	5	15	3	5
Heavy duty trucks	00.242	6	7	10	5	5
VEHICLES (other than trucks)						
Automobile	00.22	3	5	20	3	5
Buses	00.23	9	5	20	5	5

(1) It should be noted that these results are presented for comparison purposes. Actual lease rates for a lessee will vary with the lessee's credit standing, prevailing interest rates, competitive factors, date of delivery, the lessor's estimate of residual value and other factors.

EXHIBIT 8   (*concluded*)

Implicit or Interest Equivalent Lease Rate				Present Value				Approximate Leverage			
1985	1986	1987	1988	1985	1986	1987	1988	1985	1986	1987	1988
3.82	5.74	6.26	6.40	66.25	77.98	81.28	82.24	56/44	70	74	75
2.94	8.15	8.95	9.24	86.13	97.99	99.87	100.58	80/20	80	78	78
2.94	8.15	8.95	9.24	86.13	97.99	99.87	100.58	80/20	80	78	78
4.51	6.22	7.10	7.20	70.34	81.06	86.86	87.54	59/41	72	80	80
4.44	6.53	6.72	6.97	75.03	86.00	87.03	88.42	61/39	75	77	78
4.14	6.81	9.54	9.58	80.29	90.85	102.33	102.51	66/34	79	80	80
5.86	7.37	7.90	7.92	73.39	85.78	90.32	90.55	69/31	80	80	80
5.37	6.94	7.60	7.64	69.59	82.23	87.76	88.09	63/37	77	80	80
4.44	6.53	6.72	6.97	75.03	86.00	87.03	88.42	61/39	75	77	78
4.51	6.22	6.71	6.86	70.34	81.06	84.28	85.22	59/41	72	77	78
2.47	4.96	5.66	5.87	70.42	80.99	84.13	85.10	54/46	72	78	79
3.13	5.37	5.99	6.17	68.62	79.85	83.08	84.06	57/43	70	76	77
4.63	6.32	7.09	7.17	67.10	79.16	84.89	85.54	57/43	71	79	80
1.79	4.51	4.74	5.10	71.65	81.73	82.60	84.01	56/44	73	75	76
(2.33)	1.97	2.04	2.64	75.02	84.00	84.16	85.46	59/41	80	80	80
(.468)	0.95	3.57	4.15	78.84	81.84	87.51	88.80	67/33	74	80	79
1.72	5.32	5.48	5.94	78.29	88.63	89.13	90.50	70/30	80	80	80
(1.96)	(.582)	2.04	2.64	75.77	78.60	84.16	85.46	51/49	64	80	80
(2.33)	1.97	2.04	2.64	75.02	84.00	84.16	85.46	59/41	80	80	80

commence during 1986, 1987, and 1988, as compared to 1985 when ITC and old ACRS were available.

Fewer Lessors That Are Subsidiaries of Large Industrial Companies Due to AMT

Companies subject to AMT are no longer able to utilize tax depreciation deductions efficiently. The depreciation rate is lower for AMT. The difference between tax depreciation and book depreciation also affects AMT. Some companies subject to AMT which have been leading or significant lessors are no longer able to price competitively as lessors in tax-oriented leases for obvious economic reasons.

Fewer Small Independent Leasing Companies Are Engaged in Tax Leasing Due to AMT

Small independent leasing companies that have had taxable income and engaged in tax-oriented leasing in the past are finding it more difficult or impossible to offer competitively priced true leases due to AMT.

Fewer Lessors Due to Loss of ITC

Some casual lessor investors found leasing attractive because of the rapid recovery of their cash investment as a result of ITC. Without ITC, the time and funding exposure for a lessor to recover its investment is significantly longer. Some casual lessors find this exposure unacceptable and consequently have ceased to act as lessors.

New Lessors among Multinational Companies

Multinationals are encouraged to move taxable income to the United States from countries with higher tax rates. They may find engaging in leasing as a lessor to be an attractive method of shielding their higher U.S. taxable income.

Fewer Individual Lessors

In the past, individuals have been significant equipment lessors through limited partnerships. The TRA severely limits the attractiveness of tax-oriented equipment leasing for individuals. Tax deductions associated with passive ownership of equipment can only be offset against "passive income" from similar investments.

More Bank Lessors

Changes in tax laws relating to limits on deductions for interest used to purchase tax-exempt municipal bonds and deductions for loan loss reserves are motivating some banks to engage in tax-oriented leases to reduce their tax liability.

Non-Tax-Oriented Asset Funds or Income Funds Now Engage in Equipment Leasing

Asset funds or so-called income funds to engage in non-tax-oriented equipment leasing have been formed by brokers and investment banks to satisfy the appetite of individual investors who formerly invested in tax shelters. Leases deposited in such funds have large residual assumptions and expectancies that are necessary to achieve the advertised yields and pay the large retail broker commissions while at the same time remaining competitive.

New Lessee Prospects as a Result of AMT

Due to the AMT, some companies are finding leasing new equipment to be attractive even though they may not have leased equipment in the past. Other companies are using sale-and-leasebacks of used equipment as a method of managing their AMT liability. Companies are motivated to make their regular corporate tax equal to their AMT. A company subject to AMT can deduct the full amount of its rental payments even though it cannot efficiently use tax depreciation deductions due to lower depreciation rates, longer class lives, a lower tax rate, and taxation of book depreciation.

Leases May Be Used to Help Manage Foreign Tax Credit

Management of foreign tax credit is more difficult for many multinational companies as a result of the new lower corporate tax rates. Leases are being used to increase taxable net income to make better use of or to avoid loss of foreign tax credits.

Public Utilities

Public utilities were singled out for especially rough treatment under the new tax law. (However, they may benefit from repaying deferred tax recognized for rate-making purposes at a higher tax rate.) Most public utility equipment is classified as 15-year (or 20-year) property. Utilities subject to large tax liability will be motivated to act as lessors.

Portfolio Sales

As companies drop out of the lease market or become subject to the alternative minimum tax, they will be inclined to sell off their leasing companies or their lease portfolios. A burgeoning market in recycling these lease portfolios is developing.

Co-Generation Equipment Made Less Attractive

Co-generation equipment is more expensive to finance due to its being classified as 15-year class property under the TRA rather than as five-year property as under the old law.

Less Construction Equipment Is Leased

The lengthening of depreciation lives for commercial buildings from 19 years using the 150 percent declining-balance method to 31.5 years using the straight-line depreciation method is discouraging construction of new commercial buildings. Consequently, the construction industry is simply not purchasing much new equipment.

Leasing Will Be Hurt by General Decline in Capital Spending

Equipment leasing will be adversely affected by any general decline in capital spending and movement of manufacturing activities overseas which may result from the new tax law.

Used Equipment Values Will Rise

The elimination of ITC effectively increases the cost of purchasing new equipment by the amount of ITC which would have been available under the old tax law (6 percent in some cases and 10 percent in most cases). Higher cost replacement of old equipment is causing many companies to defer or eliminate some new equipment acquisitions. Consequently, used equipment values are increasing, existing leases are being renewed at somewhat higher rentals than in the past, and existing equipment lease portfolios have increased in value.

More Difficulty in Meeting 90 Percent Test for an Operating Lease in Some Cases

The reduction in tax rates is making it more difficult to qualify some leases as operating leases under the 90 percent present value rule of *FAS* 13.

Greater Reliance on Residual Values by Lessors

Lessors are encouraged to take larger residual risks in order to make lease pricing more attractive to lessees and in order to qualify leases as operating leases under the 90 percent test for lessees.

Longer Lease Terms

Lessors are offering longer lease terms to make pricing more attractive to lessees as an alternative to shorter term leases with larger residual assumptions.

Residual Insurance and Guarantees Will Be More Frequently Used

Residual insurance is being used to bolster residual risk by lessors seeking to qualify leases as operating leases for lessees as well as to reduce lease rates. Manufacturers are under pressure to provide guarantees on the residual value of their products as a means of promoting sales by reducing lease pricing for their products. (This raises a tax issue if the lessor is not at risk to some extent.)

Fixed-Price Purchase Options and Renewal Options

Lessors are under competitive pressure to grant fixed-price purchase options, midterm purchase options, evergreen renewals, and wintergreen renewal options under the guise of estimating the residual value at the outset of the lease.

Short-Term Leases

More lessors are offering aggressive short-term (less than full payout) leases in an effort to compete. In 1987 the National Banking Act was amended to permit subsidiaries of national banks to engage in short-term leasing.

Leveraged Leases Have Higher Leverage

The debt-to-equity ratio in a leveraged lease under the new law is generally in the range of 80 percent debt and 20 percent equity. Transactions are more debt driven than in the past.

Increase in Volume and Size of Direct Leases

Some companies who were almost exclusively engaged in leveraged leasing in the past now find direct leasing attractive because of the larger cash returns on the larger investments. As a consequence, direct leases are being written for larger amounts.

Forty Percent of Equipment Placed in Service during the Fourth-Quarter Rule Is Motivating Companies to Lease

A company that is in danger of having more than 40 percent of all its property eligible for ACRS being placed in service during the fourth quarter of its taxable year and thus being required to use mid-quarter convention for all its property in that taxable year is inclined to lease equipment to avoid becoming subject to the 40 percent mid-quarter convention rule.

Forty Percent Rule May Result in Higher Pricing for Lessees for Equipment Placed in Service during the Fourth Quarter

The 40 percent mid-quarter convention rule affects both lessees and lessors. Since most lessors report federal income tax on a calendar year basis, this may result in premium lease pricing for equipment placed in service during the fourth quarter.

Transitional Property

The Tax Reform Act contains 25 pages of transitional rules and exempts a great many pending equipment acquisition transactions from loss of ITC or less favorable depreciation deductions than available under the TRA. Tax benefits on transitional property can be claimed by lessors, and such transactions are especially attractive to lessors.

Foreign Source Income Definition Expanded

The definition of foreign source income was expanded by the TRA so as to make certain aircraft and ship leases that were not considered to be sources of foreign source income under the old law to now fall within the scope of the definition. Foreign source income is undesirable for some lessors because such income reduces the amount of foreign tax credit the lessor or its parent can claim by reducing both the numerator and denominator in computing the fraction of U.S. taxable income that can be offset.

State Income Tax

Lessors with the ability to shelter state income tax, such as in New York and California, are able to offer more competitive rates than lessors without the ability to shield significant state tax liability.

Tax Indemnities for Future Tax Rate Changes

The possibility of future upward movement of the corporate tax rate is an issue between lessees and lessors as to which will bear the risk. This issue should be settled early in lease negotiations.

FOREIGN TAX CREDIT MANAGEMENT THROUGH LEASING UNDER TRA

U.S. corporations pay income tax on their worldwide income. Since some of this income is generated in foreign countries it is also subject to income tax in those countries. In order to reduce the burden of double taxation of the same income, the Internal Revenue Code allows a credit against U.S. income tax for foreign income tax paid on the same income, subject to a limitation measured by the amount of U.S. tax attributable to "foreign source."

Foreign Tax Credit Limit

This limitation is expressed in the following formula:

$$\text{Foreign tax credit limit} = \frac{\text{Foreign source income}}{\text{Worldwide income}} \times \text{U.S. tax on worldwide income}$$

Any increase in expense allocated to foreign source income reduces the numerator of the fraction and, therefore, reduces the limit. Conversely, allocating rental expense or other expenses against U.S. source income reduces the denominator (worldwide income) of the fraction without impacting its numerator and thus increases the limit and the capacity to absorb foreign tax credits against the U.S. tax liability.

Tax Credit Limit Computation prior to TRA

Prior to the TRA, expenses such as interest expense that were definitely allocable to either U.S. or foreign source income were so allocated. For example, mortgage interest on a building generating U.S. source income would be allocated to the United States. However, interest expense not definitely allocable to either U.S. or foreign source income, from general borrowings, for example, were allocated to the subsidiary doing the borrowing, and U.S. or foreign status of the interest expense was determined by the character of the income (U.S. or foreign) generated by that subsidiary. Therefore, prior to the TRA a multinational company seeking to improve its foreign tax credit simply did its general borrowing through one of its subsidiaries with limited or no foreign assets generating foreign source income to ensure that virtually all interest paid was characterized as a U.S. source expense. As a result, foreign source income (numerator in fraction) increased while worldwide income (denominator in the fraction) decreased. Thus, multinational corporations were easily able to maximize their foreign source income and increase their foreign tax credit limit.

Tax Credit Limit Computation under the TRA

The Tax Reform Act of 1986 changed this formula to require all members of U.S. affiliated subsidiaries filing a consolidated income tax return to allocate interest expense on a consolidated group basis. The effect of these changes is to reduce the foreign tax credit limitation of any corporation that formerly had taken advantage of the separate company-by-company treatment that allowed them to characterize virtually all interest paid as a U.S. source expense.

For purposes of this formula, interest expenses on general borrowing are generally allocated between foreign and U.S. sources in the same proportion as the location of the corporation's assets that generate U.S. and foreign source income. That is, if 65 percent of the company's assets generate U.S. source income, 65 percent of its interest expense is considered U.S. sourced.

However, the old rules regarding specifically allocable expense still apply under the TRA. Interest specifically allocated to financing a particular asset is sourced in conformity with the income generated by the asset financed and is not subject to the newly modified indirect allocation rules.[11] Therefore, a company undertaking significant capital expenditures in the United States should, to the extent feasible,

---

[11] To specifically allocate interest expense to a given asset, *all* of the following requirements must be met:

1. The indebtedness on which the interest is paid must have been specifically incurred for the purposes of purchasing, maintaining, or approving those specific properties.
2. Proceeds of the borrowing must have actually been applied to the specified purposes.
3. The creditor must be able to look only to the specific property (or any lease or other interest therein) as security for payment of the principal and interest of the loan, that is, nonrecourse.
4. It must be a reasonable assumption that the return (cash flow) on or from the property will suffice to fulfill the terms and conditions of the loan agreement principal and interest.
5. There must be restrictions in the loan agreement on the disposal or use of the property consistent with the assumptions described in 3 and 4 above.
6. Even if 1 through 5 are satisfied, the motive for structuring the transaction in the manner described must have economic significance.

finance such assets with a lease rather than relying on the proceeds of a general borrowing program for such financing.

Use of Leases to Increase Foreign Tax Credit Limit

Leasing equipment provides a method for increasing the allowable foreign tax credit under the new law. As noted above, this is because the allocation of rental expense is based upon the location of the rented property. Lease rentals paid on equipment located in the United States are characterized as a U.S. source expense, irrespective of the location of the company's other assets. Consequently, multinational companies should consider leasing as an alternative vehicle to company-by-company borrowing as a means of characterizing financing costs as U.S. source expense.

For example, a U.S. company that enters into a sale-leaseback of equipment located in the United States financed with general borrowings may use the proceeds from the sale to reduce its general borrowings and related interest expense. In effect, it substitutes a rental expense (U.S. source) for an interest expense (allocated between foreign and U.S. sources). In the foreign tax credit limit formula, the numerator increases (less foreign expense) and the denominator decreases (more U.S. expense). The result is that the fraction increases and consequently increases the company's foreign tax credit limit.

CONCLUSION

Although the tax benefits associated with equipment ownership have changed significantly in recent years, tax-oriented leasing continues to be an attractive method for financing the acquisition of equipment for lessees unable to currently claim tax benefits. Tax-oriented leasing also continues to be an attractive business for lessors currently able to claim tax benefits associated with equipment ownership.

5

Federal Income Tax Requirements for True Lease Transactions

The Internal Revenue Code distinguishes among three general categories of leases, which are as follows:

1. Non-tax-oriented leases, called leases intended as security, conditional sale leases, hire-purchase leases, or money-over-money leases.
2. Tax-oriented true leases, which in turn fall into two subcategories:
   a. Single-investor leases (also called direct leases).
   b. Leveraged leases.
3. TRAC leases containing terminal rental adjustment clauses.

The major characteristic differentiating these three types of leases is the type of purchase options available to the lessee. True leases have fair-market-value types of purchase options. Conditional sale leases have nominal fixed-price purchase options or automatically pass title to the lessee at the end of the lease. TRAC leases are a special category of leases that retain the characteristics of a true lease even though they contain the equivalent of fixed-price purchase options for the lessee and a put option for the lessor.

Although most of this chapter will be devoted to a discussion of true leases, a brief review of these three categories of leases is appropriate in order to get true leases in perspective.

THE NON-TAX-ORIENTED LEASE, OR THE LEASE INTENDED AS SECURITY

This type of transaction is regarded by the IRS as a conditional sale or a secured loan, not a true lease. Such a transaction, therefore, transfers all the tax effects of ownership to the lessee and does not generate the lowered lease payments associated with true leases in which the lessor claims the tax benefits. A non-tax-oriented lease (or lease intended as security) usually either gives the lessee a bargain purchase option or renewal option not based on fair market value at the time of exercise, or requires the lessee to purchase the equipment for a fixed price at the conclusion of the lease.

Generally, the lessee in a non-tax-oriented lease is considered to have legal title as well as being considered to be the owner for tax purposes. However, this is not always the case since the test for a true lease for legal purposes has been held by some courts to be more liberal than the test for a true lease for tax purposes. For example, conditional sale leases for tax purposes include leases for a term that is more than 80 percent of the original useful life of the leased property or leases in which the estimated fair market value of the leased property at the end of the lease term is less than 20 percent of the original cost. In some instances the lessor under such circumstances might be considered to be the owner for legal purposes.[1]

The lessee under a conditional sale lease treats the property as owned, depreciates the property for tax purposes, and deducts the interest portion of "rental" payments for tax purposes. The lessor under a conditional sale lease treats the transaction as a loan and cannot offer the low lease rates associated with a true lease since the lessor is not the owner and cannot claim depreciation deductions.

THE TRUE LEASE

The true lease offers all of the primary benefits commonly attributed to leasing, including low-cost rentals. It is a tax-oriented lease in which

---

[1] True lease status for legal purposes is determined by state courts, and there is no uniformity in state court decisions on this subject. Generally, the state courts will treat the lessee as legal owner if the lessee has a purchase option of 10 percent or less at the end of the lease term and treat the lessor as legal owner if the lessee has a purchase option at the end of the lease term of 20 percent or more. Cases involving leases with purchase options between 10 and 20 percent sometimes hold the lessor to be legal owner and sometimes hold the lessee to be legal owner.

the lessor claims the tax benefits of ownership but passes through most of those benefits to the lessee in the form of reduced rentals. The lessor claims the depreciation deductions, and the lessee deducts the full lease rental payments as an expense. The lessor owns the leased equipment at the end of the lease term.

The intent of the parties as evidenced by the facts is the key test for determining whether a transaction constitutes a true lease, on the one hand, or a conditional sale or loan, on the other hand. As indicated previously, a purchase option based on fair market value rather than a nominal purchase option is a strong indication of intent to create a lease rather than a conditional sale or lease. The test is whether the interest of the lessor in the leased property is a proprietory interest with attributes of ownership rather than a mere creditor's security interest in the leased property.

A lease generally qualifies as a true lease if all of the following criteria are met:

1. At the start of the lease, the fair market value of the leased property projected for the end of the lease term equals or exceeds 20 percent of the original cost of the leased property (excluding front-end fees, inflation, and any cost to the lessor for removal).
2. At the start of the lease, the leased property is projected to retain at the end of the initial term a useful life that (a) exceeds 20 percent of the original estimated useful life of the equipment and (b) is at least one year.
3. The lessee does not have a right to purchase or release the leased property at a price that is less than its then fair market value.
4. The lessor does not have a right to cause the lessee to purchase the leased property at a fixed price.
5. At all times during the lease term, the lessor has a minimum unconditional "at-risk" investment equal to at least 20 percent of the cost of the leased property.
6. The lessor can show that the transaction was entered into for profit, apart from tax benefits resulting from the transaction.
7. The lessee does not furnish any part of the purchase price of the leased property and has not loaned or guaranteed any indebtedness created in connection with the acquisition of the leased property by the lessor.

Additional criteria and guidelines for true leases are described in Revenue Ruling 55–540 and Revenue Procedures 75–21, 75–28, and 76–30, which are discussed in detail later in this chapter.

The lower cost of leasing realized by a lessee throughout the lease term in a true lease must be weighed against the loss of the leased asset's residual value at the end of the term. Since that loss does not occur until the end of the lease, its present value must be compared on an after-tax basis with the present value of the ongoing cash flow benefits from the low rental payments under a true lease. To make the comparison a rational one, both are calculated using a discounted cash flow method of analysis to evaluate the tax and timing efforts. Typically, the residual value given up is of small significance as long as the lease term constitutes a substantial portion of the economic life of the asset, and renewal options permit continuity of control for the asset's economic life. Further discussion of considerations involved in a lease or purchase decision is contained in Chapter 6 and Appendix C.

TRAC LEASES

The Deficit Reduction Act of 1984 authorized a new type of lease for motor vehicles, called a "TRAC lease," that combines the benefits of a true lease and conditional sale. The Tax Reform Act of 1986 did not change the law authorizing TRAC leases. The name "TRAC lease" is derived from the fact that such a lease contains a "terminal rental adjustment clause." Properly structured, a TRAC lease can be used to provide a lessee with true tax-oriented lease rates even though the lease contains a TRAC.

Equipment Eligible for TRAC Leases

TRAC leases can be used to finance motor vehicles used in a trade or business. While the statute is not entirely clear on the subject, the term *motor vehicles* most likely includes only motor vehicles licensed for highway use. Under this definition, motor vehicles such as trucks, truck tractor and trailer rigs, automobiles, and buses are eligible for TRAC leases. On the other hand, vehicles such as farm tractors, construction equipment, and forklifts probably are not eligible for TRAC leases.

Terminal Rental Adjustment Clause Defined

A terminal rental adjustment clause permits or requires an upward or downward adjustment of rent to make up any difference between the projected value and the actual value of a leased motor vehicle upon the sale or disposition of the vehicle.

How a TRAC Lease Works

At the time a typical TRAC lease is signed, the lessee and lessor agree on a monthly rental and a table of projected residual values for the leased motor vehicles at various agreed dates on which the lease may be terminated. When the lessee terminates the lease, the value of the terminated motor vehicles is determined either by an arm's-length resale to a third party, by agreement between the lessee and the lessor, or by an independent appraisal. If the value at termination is less than the agreed projected value, the lessee pays the lessor the difference. If the value of the equipment at termination is more than the agreed projected value, the lessee may keep all or part of the difference, depending on the terms of the lease agreement.

TRAC leases are sometimes called "open-end leases" because the liability of the lessee at the end of the lease is open-ended. However, as noted above, the lessee has upside potential if the leased equipment is worth more than the projected residual value.

Except for TRAC Clause, a TRAC Lease Must Qualify as a True Lease

A TRAC lease must meet the usual Internal Revenue Service requirements for a true lease. The projected termination value cannot be less than 20 percent of the acquisition cost.

Other IRS Requirements

A TRAC lease cannot be structured as a leveraged lease.

Also, in order to qualify under the Internal Revenue Code a separate written statement separately signed by the lessee must be included in the lease agreement. The statement (1) must contain the lessee's certification (under penalty of perjury) that it intends more than 50 percent of the use of the leased vehicles to be in a trade or business of the lessee, (2) must clearly specify that the lessee has been advised it will not be treated as the owner of the leased vehicle for federal income tax purposes, and (3) must not be known by the lessor to be false.

Advantage of TRAC Leases

TRAC leases provide lessees of vehicles with the benefits of true lease rental rates while at the same time protecting lessees against the loss of potential upside residual value. TRAC leases also encourage lessors to take substantial residual values into consideration in pricing rents since lessors are protected against downside risk by the terminal rental adjustment clause. TRAC leases consequently provide lessees with a very attractive cost for the use of leased over-the-road vehicles.

INTERNAL REVENUE CODE REQUIREMENTS
FOR A TRUE LEASE

The Internal Revenue Service rulings distinguish between transactions that are true leases and transactions that are conditional sales. Revenue Ruling 55–540 (1955–2 Cum. Bull. 39) states:

> Whether an agreement, which in form is a lease, is in substance a conditional sales contract depends upon the intent of the parties as evidenced by the provisions of the agreement, read in light of the facts and circumstances existing at the time the agreement was executed. In ascertaining such intent no single test, nor special combination of tests, is absolutely determinative. No general rule, applicable in all cases, can be laid down. *Each case must be decided in the light of its particular facts.* [Emphasis added.]

Revenue Ruling 55–540 has been largely superseded and refined by Revenue Procedure 75–21 and subsequent procedures. However, the six factors outlined in Revenue Ruling 55–540 to indicate that a transaction is a conditional sale rather than a true lease are of interest from a historical standpoint and should be noted:

1. Portions of the periodic payments are specifically applicable to an equity interest in the leased asset to be acquired by the lessee.
2. The lessee will acquire title to the leased asset upon payment of a stated amount of "rentals" that the lessee is required to make under the contract.
3. The total amount that the lessee is required to pay for a relatively short period of use of the leased asset constitutes an inordinately large proportion of the total sum required to be paid to secure transfer of title.
4. The agreed "rental" payments materially exceed the current fair rental value. This may indicate that the lease payments include an element other than compensation for the current use of property.
5. The leased property may be acquired by the lessee under a purchase option at a price that is nominal in relation to the fair market value of the property at the time when the option may be exercised, as determined at the time of entering into the original agreement, or that is a relatively small amount when compared with the total payments required to be made.
6. Some portion of the periodic payment is specifically designated as interest or is otherwise recognizable as the equivalent of interest.

The above were the only official Internal Revenue criteria for determining whether a transaction was a true lease until 1975, when the Internal Revenue Service issued guidelines in Revenue Procedure 75–21 for obtaining favorable private revenue rulings on leveraged true lease transactions. While these guidelines are defined as applicable to ruling requests for leveraged leases and are stricter than substantive law relating to true lease requirements, many tax counsel are of the opinion that the Internal Revenue Service will use these guidelines on audit in determining whether either a leveraged lease or a direct lease qualifies as a true lease. Indeed, true leases are sometimes referred to as "guideline leases."

The guidelines contained in Revenue Procedure 75–21 for qualifying a lease transaction as a true lease are summarized below.

Twenty Percent Minimum At-Risk Investment

The lessor is required to make or to be unconditionally obligated to make a 20 percent minimum at-risk equity investment at the beginning of the lease when the equipment is placed in service and is required to maintain a minimum at-risk equity investment throughout the lease term. The lessor's investment can be provided with funds borrowed on a recourse basis as well as with the lessor's own funds.

The lessor's minimum 20 percent at-risk investment required under Revenue Procedure 75–21 will be satisfied if the excess of (a) the rents required to be made by the lessee to or on behalf of the lessor over (b) the cumulative disbursements required to be made by or for the lessor in connection with the ownership of the property (debt service), but not including the initial equity investment, is never greater than the sum of the excess, if any, of the lessor's initial equity investment over the 20 percent minimum investment and the cumulative pro rata portion of the projected profit from the transaction, excluding tax benefits. Generally, compliance with the 20 percent minimum investment requirement is not a problem since optimum debt-to-equity ratios usually result in equity in the range of 20 to 25 percent.

The lessor must not be entitled to a return of any portion of its investment through any arrangement with the lessee or any member of the lessee group.[2] This requirement prohibits "unwind" agreements if the transaction is closed and some event that is a condition of the agreement and is to be satisfied after closing does not take place. The condition might, for example, relate to the productive capacity of a facility, the obtaining of an environmental permit, or even the obtain-

---

[2] The "lessee group" includes the lessee, any shareholder of the lessee, or any related party. See Section 318 of the IRC.

ing of a tax ruling. It makes no difference that the event is beyond the control of the lessor. Prior to Revenue Procedure 75–21, unwind agreements were commonly used. The lessor in such a situation can protect itself from performance failures by means of construction bonds, holdbacks, or rental adjustments tied to performance. Bonds or political risk insurance may be available to protect against a failure to obtain environmental permits. The lessor may have a right to recover its investment from a person not a member of the lessee group, such as the contractor or the manufacturer of the facility or equipment.

There is case law to the effect that an investment of 13 percent or 14 percent is satisfactory in an equipment lease. Real estate leveraged leases are commonly done with an equity investment of 5 percent or even less than 5 percent. As noted above, as a practical matter, since the debt must be paid from lease payments, most leveraged equipment leases today will have an investment of about 20 percent.

Twenty Percent Residual Value

A reasonable estimate of the expected fair market value of the leased equipment at the end of the lease term must be equal to at least 20 percent of the original cost of the equipment without taking into account inflation or deflation during the lease term and net of the lessor's cost of removal and delivery of possession of the leased equipment at termination. However, the lease may require the lessee to dismantle and transport the equipment to some location.

At the time the lease commences the lessor should either obtain one or more independent appraisals confirming the estimated residual value of 20 percent or more of original cost at the end of the lease term or create a contemporaneous record which shows its rationale for reaching the conclusion the residual value would equal at least 20 percent of original cost at the end of the lease term. This appraisal or rationale should be retained for safekeeping with the original documentation. The fact that the lessor (or equity participants) have used an estimated residual value of zero or much less than 20 percent is not controlling as to the actual value for tax purposes.[3] The lessee may provide appraisals to the lessor supporting a 20 percent residual value and may provide a representation that it believes the appraisal is correct, but the lessee will usually not indemnify the lessor as to the correctness of the appraisal and will shift the burden of accepting or verifying the appraisal to the lessor.

---

[3] The estimated value for pricing is usually a "quick sale" price, while the estimated value for tax purposes is a "retail" price.

There is case law supporting residual values in the range of 14 and 15 percent of original cost. Prior to Revenue Procedure 75–21 an estimated residual value of 15 percent or more was thought to be adequate for a true lease.

Twenty Percent Remaining Useful Life

A reasonable estimate of the remaining useful life of the leased equipment at the end of the lease term must be at least one year or at least 20 percent of the originally estimated useful life of the leased equipment, whichever is longer. The "useful life" of equipment means the period of time during which the equipment can be useful to either the lessee or a third party; useful life is not limited to the period of time during which the equipment is useful to the lessee.

The contemporaneous appraisal of estimated fair market value at the end of the lease term discussed above should also include an appraisal that the remaining useful life of the leased equipment at the end of the lease term will be at least equal to 20 percent or more of the originally estimated useful life of the leased equipment. The relationship between the parties regarding this appraisal is the same as for the residual value appraisal.

Lease Term Includes Renewal Periods

The lease term for purposes of the foregoing tests of residual value and remaining useful life includes all fixed and optional renewal periods, except renewal periods that are at the option of the lessee at fair-market-value rental.

No Purchase Option except at Fair Market Value

Neither the lessee nor any member of the lessee group may have any contractual right to purchase the property from the lessor at a price less than the fair market value at the time such right may be exercised. Fixed-price purchase options are prohibited by Revenue Procedure 75–21[4] even if they are based on an estimate of the expected fair market value at the time such purchase options may be exercised, although purchase options based on the higher of a fixed price or the fair market value at the time of exercise are permitted.

As a practical matter most tax counsel have no difficulty giving favorable opinions that a leveraged lease qualifies as a true lease even

---

[4] However, as discussed later in this chapter, many tax counsel are of the opinion that Revenue Procedure 75–21 does not correctly reflect the case law with regard to prohibiting all fixed-price purchase options.

though the lease contains a fixed price purchase option which is based on a reasonable estimate of fair market value, at the conclusion of the lease, taking estimated currency inflation factors into account. There is case law to support this. Typically such options will be in the range of 40 percent of original cost and higher. They should be supported by an independent appraisal. Also, favorable letter rulings have been issued for nonleveraged leases containing fixed-price purchase options that were based on an estimated fair market value.[5]

Lessor Put Prohibited

The lessor must not have any contractual right to require the lessor or any party to purchase the property at any price, including the fair market value, except under default or casualty loss provisions. The lessor must not have any right to abandon the property but, as noted earlier, may require the lessee to dismantle and transport the equipment to some location at the lessee's expense. The lessee cannot be economically compelled to purchase the leased asset because of difficulty in removal or contractual obligation to a third party of which the lessor is aware.

The prohibition against puts apparently does not prohibit residual value insurance running to the benefit of the lessor.

Lessee May Not Provide Any Part of Cost of Leased Equipment

The lessee or any related party may not provide any part of the original cost of the leased equipment. The lessee is also prohibited from paying any part of the cost of improvements or additions to the leased equipment, other than severable improvements, which are defined to be improvements to leased equipment that are owned by a member of the lessee group and are readily removable without causing material damage to the leased equipment. All other improvements are considered to be nonseverable improvements.

Expenses related to the transaction, such as legal expenses of the equity participants and lenders, debt placement fees, and printing expense, are regarded as part of the cost of the leased equipment and must be capitalized and financed as part of the lease and not paid directly by the lessee.

If material nonseverable improvements to the equipment are made and paid for by the lessee during the lease term, the Internal Revenue Service may require that the lessor agree to recognize the cost of any such improvements as taxable income. Revenue Procedure 79–48 sets

---

[5] See Letter Rulings 8120024 and 8130087.

out instances where the IRS will not require the lessor to take such nonseverable improvements into income and permits the lessee or a member of the lessee group to pay for a nonseverable improvement under the following circumstances:

1. The improvement is not needed to complete the equipment for its intended use by the lessee.
2. The lessee or members of the lessee group do not acquire an equity interest in the leased equipment as a result of paying for the improvement.
3. The improvement does not cause the equipment to become limited-use property.

In addition, at least one of the following conditions must be met:

1. The improvement must be required by certain governmental standards.
2. The improvement must not substantially increase the capacity or productivity of the leased property or modify the leased property so that it can be employed for a materially different use.
3. The cost of the improvement is less than 10 percent of the original cost of the leased property (adjusted for inflation).

The requirements of Revenue Procedure 79–48 prohibiting the lessee from paying for the cost of improvements are contrary to established precedents, and tax counsel may be willing to provide opinions to the contrary where a ruling is not sought.

Lessee May Not Lend or Guarantee Indebtedness

All members of the lessee group are prohibited from lending the lessor any of the funds necessary to acquire the leased equipment or from guaranteeing any indebtedness (including the leveraged debt) created in connection with the acquisition by the lessor of the leased equipment.

On the other hand, members of the lessee group are permitted to guarantee the lessee's obligations to pay rent, to maintain the leased equipment, to pay insurance premiums, and to meet other conventional obligations of a net lease. This seems inconsistent, since guaranteeing the lessee's lease obligations is the equivalent of guaranteeing the leveraged debt, except in certain bankruptcy situations.

The guidelines as published appear to permit third-party guarantees of the debt and of the lessee's lease obligations. These guarantees may be in the form of letters of credit, residual insurance guarantees, and government agency guarantees, although the IRS has been reluctant to rule on guarantees of these kinds.

The IRS has ruled favorably where government guarantees were involved or where letters of credit were issued for the lessor's account and for the lender's benefit and gave the issuer no rights against the lessee.[6]

Lessor Must Have Profit Motive

The lessor must represent and demonstrate that it expects to receive a profit from the transaction apart from any tax benefits but including the residual value of the equipment. The profit test is intended to prove that the lease transaction will produce at least a modest profit for the lessor apart from the tax benefits. The profit test is satisfied if the aggregate rents and payments required by the lessee over the lease term plus the anticipated residual value at the end of the lease term exceed the total disbursements the lessor must make to finance the purchase of the leased equipment and its equity investment in the leased equipment, including any costs directly incurred to finance such equity investment.[7] The costs of general borrowings used to finance the lessor's equity investment are not included.

Transaction Must Generate Positive Cash Flow for Lessor

The lessor must represent and demonstrate that its aggregate cash receipts under the lease will exceed its aggregate cash disbursements during the lease by a reasonable minimum amount. The Internal Revenue Service has informally indicated that this test will be satisfied by an average annual return of 2 percent on the equity investment. Disbursements include any costs incurred to directly finance the lessor's equity investment.

Uneven Rents Limited or Prohibited

While uneven rent will not affect the status of the lease as a true lease, if the rent for any year is more than 10 percent above or below the average rental level, a ruling must be requested as to whether any of the uneven rent is prepaid or deferred rent. If the test is not satisfied and rent is in effect prepaid, the prepaid rent is not currently deductible by the lessee, and if rent is deferred, the deferred rent is currently includable in the lessor's income.[8]

---

[6] See Letter Rulings 8024066 and 8006023.

[7] As a practical matter the lessor can always satisfy the profit test by using an aggressive (but not ridiculous) residual assumption.

[8] Section 467 of the Internal Revenue Code, which was added by the Deficit Reduction Act of 1984, requires level rents under some circumstances. Current IRS regulations should be consulted to ascertain any changes in this portion of Revenue Procedure 75–21. Section 467 is discussed in more detail later in this chapter.

REVENUE PROCEDURE 75–28

Revenue Procedure 75–28 elaborated on the application of the guidelines set forth in Revenue Procedure 75–21 and on the information required to be filed in connection with applications to the IRS for rulings. It is specifically mentioned here because it should be consulted if the reader contemplates applying for a ruling.

LIMITED-USE PROPERTY; REVENUE PROCEDURE 76–30

In order to obtain an advance ruling in a leveraged lease transaction, it is necessary to establish to the satisfaction of the IRS that "the use of the property at the end of the lease term by the lessor or some other person, other than a member of the lessee group, who could lease or purchase the property from the lessor, is commercially feasible on the basis of present knowledge and generally accepted engineering standards." In other words the leased property must not be "limited-use property" valuable only to the lessee. Examples of limited-use property include custom-made pollution control equipment, smokestacks, and nonmovable equipment with no access for supplies of feedstock, raw material, energy, or fuel or no easements or means of egress for production.

Revenue Procedure 76–30 amplified Revenue Procedures 75–21 and 75–28 on the definition of limited-use property. Six examples of different kinds of equipment that either does or does not constitute limited-use property are contained in Revenue Procedure 76–30. Because of the importance and complexity of this issue, these examples are reproduced below in their entirety.

(1) X builds a masonry smokestack attached to a masonry warehouse building owned by Y, and leases the smokestack to Y for use as an addition to the heating system of the warehouse. The lease term is 15 years; the smokestack has a useful life of 25 years; and the warehouse has a remaining useful life of 25 years.

It would not be commercially feasible to disassemble the smokestack at the end of the lease term and reconstruct it at a new location. The smokestack is considered to be limited use property.

(2) X builds a complete chemical production facility on land owned by Y and leases the facility to Y, a manufacturer of chemicals. The lease term is 24 years, and the facility has a useful life of 30 years. The land is leased to X pursuant to a ground lease for a term of 30 years.

The technical "know-how" and trade secrets Y possesses are necessary elements in the commercial operation of the facility. At the time the lease is entered into, no person who is not a member of the lessee group possesses the technical "know-how" and trade secrets necessary for the commercial operation of the facility.

The taxpayers submit to the Service the written opinion of a qualified expert stating it is probable that by the expiration of the lease term of the facility third parties who are potential purchasers or lessees of the facility will have independently developed such "know-how" and trade secrets.

The facility is considered to be limited use property. In reaching this conclusion, the Service will not take into account such expert opinion because such opinions are too speculative for advance ruling purposes.

(3) The facts are the same as in the example set forth in subsection (2) except X has an option, exercisable at the end of the lease term of the facility, to purchase from Y the "know-how" and trade secrets necessary for the commercial operation of the facility, and it would be commercially feasible at the end of such lease term for X to exercise the option and operate the facility itself. The facility is not considered to be limited use property.

(4) The facts are the same as in the example set forth in subsection (2) except it would be commercially feasible for the lessor at the end of the lease term to make certain structural modifications of the facility that would make the facility capable of being used by persons not possessing any special technical "know-how" or trade secrets.

Furthermore, if such modifications were made, it would be commercially feasible, at the end of the lease term, for a person who is not a member of the lessee group to purchase or lease the facility from X. The facility is not considered to be limited use property.

(5) X builds an electrical generating plant on land owned by Y and leases the plant to Y. The lease term is 40 years, and the plant has an estimated useful life of 50 years. The land is leased to X pursuant to a ground lease for a term of 50 years. The plant is adjacent to a fuel source that it is estimated will last for at least 50 years.

Access to this fuel source is necessary for the commercial operation of the plant, and Y has recently obtained the contractual right to acquire all fuel produced from the source for 50 years. Y will use the plant to produce and generate electrical power for sale to a city located 50 miles away. The plant is synchronized into a power grid that makes the sale of electrical power to a number of potential markets commercially feasible.

It would not be commercially feasible to disassemble the plant and reconstruct it at a new location. The electrical generating plant is considered to be limited use property because access to this fuel source held exclusively by Y is necessary for the commercial operation of the plant.

(6) The facts are the same as in the example set forth in subsection (5) except X has an option, exercisable at the end of the lease term of the plant, to acquire from Y the contractual right to acquire all fuel produced from the fuel source for the 10-year period commencing at the end of such lease term.

It would be commercially feasible at the end of such lease term for X to exercise this option. Furthermore, it would be commercially feasible, at the end of such lease term, for a person who is not a member of the lessee group to purchase the contractual right to the fuel from X for an amount equal to the option price and purchase or lease the plant from X. The plant is not considered to be limited use property.

SHARING RESIDUALS WITH BROKERS

Another issue that has arisen in the application of Revenue Procedure 75–21 in obtaining advance rulings from the IRS relates to the treatment of residual-sharing agreements with brokers.

The IRS now seems willing to rule that residual-sharing agreements with lease brokers that are applicable only to amounts in excess of 20 percent of the original cost of the equipment will not affect the status of the transaction as a lease so long as the broker gets no more than a portion of the residual above the 20 percent floor.

METHODS USED TO MINIMIZE RESIDUAL VALUE RISK BY LESSEES

Although Revenue Procedure 75–21 indicates that a Revenue Ruling will not be given if a lease contains a fixed-price purchase option, as previously discussed, many tax counsel are of the opinion that a fixed-price purchase option that reflects the expected fair market value at the conclusion of the lease is permissible under case law. Since another provision of Revenue Procedure 75–21 states that the minimum expected residual value permissible is 20 percent of the original cost without regard to inflation, the minimum fixed-price purchase option which tax counsel are generally willing to approve is at a price that is equal to at least 20 percent of original cost plus an inflation factor for the term of the lease. As a practical matter, fixed-price purchase options under this approach are rarely less than 40 percent of the original cost of the leased equipment.

In view of the fact true leases cannot contain fixed-price purchase options (except as discussed above), lessees and lessors have attempted to minimize risk to the lessee in a number of ways that sometimes skirt the edges of Revenue Procedure 75–21. Some of these methods (which should be reviewed with tax counsel before use) are as follows:

1. A fixed-rate renewal option at 50 percent of the original base period rental rate, so long as the sum of the base term and renewal term does not exceed the useful life requirement or the 20 percent residual value requirement.

2. Evergreen renewal options, which involve renewals based on

new appraisals of estimated remaining useful life at the end of each renewal period.

3. Insurance coverage from a third party that the value of the residual will not exceed a certain amount.
4. Arbitration clauses to arrive at fair market value.
5. Right of first refusal on sale of residual running to the benefit of the lessee. A variation of this couples a right of first refusal to the lessee with the right to not have the equipment sold to certain named parties such as competitors. These kinds of provisions discourage third-party bidders. They may also raise legal and tax problems and should be reviewed based on the facts in a particular case.
6. Negotiation of provisions regarding removal expenses and place of delivery can put a burden on the lessor that will lower the value of the equipment to the lessor.

Obviously the 20 percent residual requirement and 80 percent useful life requirement and other requirements of Revenue Procedure 75–21 must be carefully considered and usually met. Nevertheless, the bargaining position of the lessee can be improved in many situations.

THREE-MONTH WINDOW

The Internal Revenue Code provides that within three months of the time a taxpayer places equipment in service,[9] the taxpayer can arrange a sale-and-leaseback of the property on a basis whereby the lessor can treat the property as new property for federal income tax purposes and consequently can claim ACRS (and ITC, if any) on the leased equipment as if it were new equipment.

Prior to this change in the law, equipment was not considered new and was not eligible for the ITC unless the lessor clearly owned it at the time it was originally placed in service. Consequently, lessees and lessors had to be especially careful to see that equipment was not placed in service by the lessee or anyone else before the lessor acquired title. This resulted in inefficiencies and needless administration expense for lessees and lessors. One method used to prove compliance was to create a record of a purchase order assignment and invoices naming the lessor as purchaser. The three-month window remedied some of the admin-

---

[9] Care must be taken in ascertaining the date equipment is deemed to be "placed in service." For example, equipment delivered, ready, and available for use by the lessee may be considered to have been placed in service even though it is not used.

istrative problems, but it also raised sales and use tax questions as well as legal lien problems, discussed later in this chapter.

The three-month window does not permit warehousing a lease transaction by a broker for resale or assignment to another lessor within three months.

With the repeal of ITC, the importance of the three-month window has declined, but it may still be useful in certain situations involving ACRS or transitional property eligible for ITC.

SALE-AND-LEASEBACK TRANSACTIONS

Any sale-and-leaseback transactions of used property under state law, including transactions under the three-month window provision described above, should be concerned with liability for state sales or use tax. Three potential taxable transactions occur: the initial purchase by the user; the sale to the lessor; and the leaseback to the user. Many states take the position that lease rentals are taxable on a sale-and-leaseback transaction even though the lessee paid a sales tax on the original purchase.

Sale-and-leaseback transactions must be approached cautiously in any event. Careful title lien searches should be made. State statutes should be researched to assure compliance with usury laws, creditor notification laws, and bulk sales laws. The lessee's loan agreements should be checked to make sure that sale-and-leasebacks are not prohibited or do not result in the violation of ratio restrictions. While sale-and-leasebacks are very legitimate commercial transactions, they are sometimes used by companies as last-resort financing, so credit analysis should be especially stringent in such cases.

PRACTICALITY OF OBTAINING A RULING

One of the effects of Revenue Procedure 75–21 has been to reduce sharply the number of requests for Revenue Rulings. The voluminous data required for ruling requests had discouraged structures that do not meet the strict requirements of Revenue Procedure 75–21. Furthermore, if the requirements of 75–21 are clearly met, there is little point in obtaining a ruling. If the requirements of 75–21 are not met, an unfavorable ruling flags the transaction for tax audit. Under these circumstances, lessors and lessees now tend to rely on the opinion of tax counsel rather than obtaining a tax ruling when entering into an equipment lease transaction that is not in strict conformity with Revenue Procedure 75–21.

CONGRESSIONAL ENDORSEMENT OF REVENUE PROCEDURES

The legislative history contained in the congressional reports relating to the Economic Recovery Tax Act of 1981, the Tax Equity and Fiscal Responsibility Act of 1982, and the Deficit Reduction Act of 1984 reviewed Revenue Procedures 75–21, 75–28, and 76–30 in some detail. It can be argued that this discussion shows that Congress was on notice and understood those guidelines. It can further be argued that the failure of Congress to change them amounted to an endorsement of the guidelines. Certainly, the Internal Revenue Service will be inclined to take that view and will be encouraged to use Revenue Procedures 75–21, 75–28, and 76–30 as audit guidelines, even though they have not been particularly successful when specific guidelines have been challenged in the courts.

BOOT TRANSACTIONS

In boot transactions, the lessor pays a fair market value for new property to be leased that is higher than the lessee is obligated to pay or would be able to include in its tax basis. Typically, the lessor purchases from the lessee the lessee's right to acquire the equipment for a price (that is, the boot). The lessee pockets this amount as profit. The lessor's tax basis is the total purchase price of the equipment plus the amount paid to the lessee. The lessor claims ACRS on this tax basis. The rents paid by the lessee are calculated on the basis of the total cost to the lessor of acquiring the leased equipment, including, of course, the boot.

Boot transactions arise where for inflationary or other reasons the fair market value of equipment at the time of delivery is significantly higher than the contract price the lessee is obligated to pay. Boot transactions have occurred in recent years in the case of commercial aircraft, executive aircraft, and satellites.

A major risk in a boot transaction is whether the lessor's tax basis is correct. This depends on whether the lessor's tax basis reflects the actual fair market value of the property at the time of its acquisition by the lessor. The lessor's basis should be supported by independent appraisals of qualified appraisers.[10] If any question exists, the lessor should seek indemnification of the price from the lessee.

---

[10] In the event of challenge by the IRS and litigation on this issue, the IRS is at a disadvantage where the taxpayer has a contemporaneous appraisal from a reputable appraiser and the IRS has only a hindsight opinion or appraisal. However, in one recent situation involving a large boot payment on a lease of a satellite, the IRS is rumored to have learned of the transaction at the time it was consummated and employed an independent appraiser to obtain a contemporaneous appraisal of its own.

UNEVEN RENT UNDER SECTION 467 OF THE INTERNAL REVENUE CODE

Prior to the Deficit Reduction Act of 1984, the IRS permitted uneven rents if the annual rent for any year was no more than 10 percent above or below the average annual rents for the initial period and, during the remainder of the lease term, was no more than the highest annual rent for any year during the initial period of the lease term and no less than one half of the average annual rent during that period. However, Section 467 of the Internal Revenue Code, added by the Deficit Reduction Act of 1984, has raised serious questions regarding the permissibility of uneven rents, and these questions require clarification by IRS regulation.

If the rentals are too high in the early years and too low in the later years, the excess rentals constitute prepaid rent, so that the lessee will be required to defer its deduction for excess rentals in the early years until later years, while the lessor may be required to recognize the full rental payments in the early years. On the other hand, if the rentals are low in the early years and high in the later years, the excess rentals in later years may constitute deferred rent, so that the lessee may receive higher rental deductions in the early years while the lessor may be required to recognize rental income on a level basis, resulting in reduced tax losses in the early years.

Rental adjustments that are based on fluctuations in the interest rate charged on debt will not cause an uneven rent problem, and rentals that fluctuate in proportion to some recognized interest rate index should present no problem.

Uneven rents generally do not affect the true lease status of a transaction unless such rents prevent satisfying other requirements for a true lease.

In view of the uncertainties regarding uneven rents, a closer look at Section 467 is appropriate.

Section 467 Level Rent Requirement

A lessor or lessee that is party to a "Section 467 rental agreement" must report rental income or deductions using the accrual method of accounting.

A Section 467 rental agreement includes a lease of equipment in which either:

1. Some amount allocable to the use of property during a year is to be paid after the close of the calendar year in which such use occurs.
2. The rent payments increase over the lease term under the lease agreement.

In other words, where rents increase the lessor must report rental income and deductions using the accrual method of accounting.

So long as no tax-avoidance motive is deemed to exist, the modified accrual method is used to reallocate rents. Under this method the amount of rent accruing during any taxable year is determined by:

1. Allocating rents in accordance with the lease agreement.
2. Taking into account on a present value basis any rent to be paid after the close of the taxable year.

At this time, in the absence of regulations, it is not clear how expenses related to rent required to be accrued will be treated by a cash basis taxpayer. The open question is whether such expenses may be claimed when they are paid or when they are accrued.

A Section 467 rental agreement can also be a "disqualified leaseback or disqualified long-term agreement." In such case a special method of accrual of rents, called "normalization," is prescribed. A disqualified leaseback or long-term agreement is defined as an agreement in which the principal purpose of increasing rents is the avoidance of tax and in which the property is leased to either:

1. A person who had an interest in the property within the past two years.
2. For a term in excess of 75 percent of the specified statutory recovery period (that is, the applicable ACRS period) for such property.

The Internal Revenue Code provides that tax avoidance will not result where:

1. Rents increase by reference to some economic or interest rate index beyond the control of the parties.
2. Rents are based on a percentage of the lessor receipts (common in real estate leases to retail stores).
3. There are changes in the amounts paid to third parties (floating interest rate debt in a leveraged lease, insurance charges, or property taxes, for example).
4. There are reasonable rent holidays. (This apparently refers to interim rents.)

Normalization Accrual

The normalization method of accrual is the amount that, if paid at the conclusion of each lease rental period, would result in a stream of rental payments whose present value, discounted at 110 percent of the applicable federal rate—under Section 1274(d)—would equal all payments due under the lease. The excess of rents allocated to periods in which they were not paid is taxed as imputed interest income.

At this writing, the Internal Revenue Service has not issued regulations clarifying Section 467. Numerous questions remain to be resolved, including questions involving interim rents.

TAX INDEMNITIES

Lease agreements generally provide for an indemnity against the possible loss by the lessor of the income tax benefits the lessor expects to receive. This is true even though a tax ruling is obtained.

From the lessor's standpoint, the lease rate contemplates that the lessor will be able to claim certain tax benefits, and the lease rate should be adjusted upward or a cash settlement made if such tax benefits are not available. The lessor regards its risk as a lending risk, not as a speculative risk on the availability of tax benefits. In the event the tax benefits are unavailable and the lease rate is adjusted accordingly, the lessor regards the lessee as being no worse off than the lessee would have been if the lessee had borrowed instead of leased.

The tax events against which equity participants seek protection include the following:

1. Loss of true lease status.
2. Disallowance of ACRS deductions because of method, recovery period, basis, or change in the law.
3. Recapture of ACRS deductions.
4. Disallowance or recapture of investment tax credit, if applicable.
5. Change in the federal income tax rate.
6. Inclusion in taxable income of the lessor of any item other than rent, including indemnity payments and insurance payments.
7. Disallowance of the lessor's tax basis, particularly where it is based on fair market value in a boot transaction that is above the lessee's original contracted price for the equipment.
8. Changes in the law affecting the availability to the lessor of ITC, ACRS deductions, or interest deductions.

The lessee, on the other hand, may regard the lease rate as including some risk factor for changes in tax consequences to the lessor, including changes in tax law or tax rates after the lease commences. Usually the lessee wishes to assume responsibility only for its own acts or omissions that may affect the tax benefits available to the lessor. However, since the lessor passes a substantial part of the tax benefits to the lessee and the lessee receives a substantial reduction from the cost of conventional long-term debt financing, the lessee may provide some additional degree of tax indemnification.

Needless to say, negotiations over tax indemnities can become lengthy and difficult in proportion to the risk of adverse tax consequences that either the lessee or the lessor perceives to be present in the transaction.

As a practical matter, smaller leases contain broad tax indemnities protecting the lessor in the "boilerplate" language, which lessees often do not challenge. Disputes and lengthy negotiations occur in connection with larger leases, and in the final analysis may become pricing issues.

Where the lessor does suffer a loss as a result of some event covered by the tax indemnities provisions, the method for computing the indemnity payment is spelled out in the lease agreement. While a variety of methods are used to compute the indemnity payment due under various circumstances, the objective is always to pay the equity participants amounts sufficient to compensate them for loss of the expected tax benefits. This includes a gross up computation so that the equity participants are paid amounts sufficient to pay additional income tax that may be due by reason of the indemnity payment. The lessee is entitled to a repayment from the equity participant for subsequent refunds or for any recovery of tax benefits arising from the initial loss.

Sometimes a lessee will seek the right to contest the loss of tax benefits. The equity participant rarely gives such a right to the lessee but may be willing to permit the lessee the right to approve any settlements and may be willing to litigate the issue at the lessee's request. In such event, the equity participant retains the right to determine the court since the choice of forum may affect the contest of other tax issues unrelated to the leasing transaction. The cost of such litigation may be paid by either the lessee or the lessor or may be shared by both.

Tax indemnities are discussed further in Chapter 14.

WRAP LEASES

Wrap leases are sometimes used by brokers and leasing companies to finance equipment purchases. They are controversial because the Internal Revenue Service takes the position that some wrap lease structures lack economic substance and do not qualify as true leases. Typically, wrap leases are used in connection with single purchases of items of equipment costing in excess of $1 million per unit.

Exhibit 1 illustrates a typical wrap lease structure used for equipment such as IBM computers. The steps in structuring a wrap lease identified in Exhibit 1 are as follows:

1. The originating leasing company enters into a lease agreement to lease equipment costing $4 million to a lessee/user for a term of 60 months at a rent of $80,000 per month (sometimes called the "user lease" in a wrap lease structure). The lessor assumes that the equipment will generate lease rentals for 84 months and have a 15 percent residual after 84 months.

2. The originating leasing company finances the $4 million purchase price by arranging a 60-month bank loan of $3.6 million

EXHIBIT 1   Wrap Lease

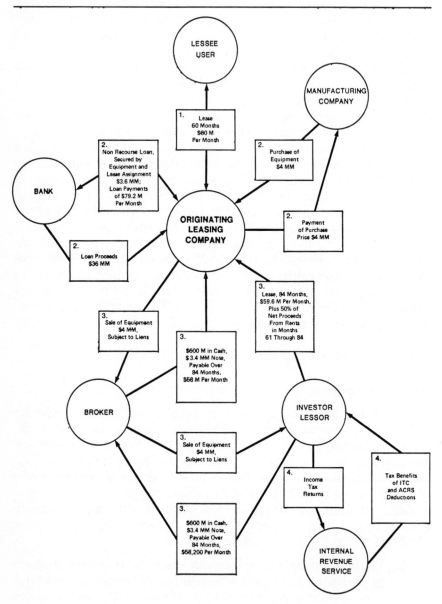

secured by the equipment and an assignment of the lease and the lease payments; the loan payments would be $79,200 per month.

At this point, the transaction is a simple lease transaction in which the lessor has financed most of the cost of the equipment with a loan secured by the equipment and lease. The wrap lease results from the addition of the next step.

3. A broker locates an investor/lessor with tax shelter objectives. The broker then purchases the equipment from the originating leasing company for $4 million, subject to liens, and pays the purchase price with $600,000 in cash and $3.4 million in a note payable over 84 months in monthly installments of $58,000. Simultaneously, the broker sells the equipment, subject to liens, to the investor/lessor for $4 million payable $600,000 in cash with the balance payable over 84 months in installments of $58,200 per month. And also simultaneously, the originating leasing company enters as lessee into a lease with the investor/lessor for 84 months at a rent of $59,600 per month plus 50 percent of the net proceeds from lease rentals realized from subleases in months 61 through 84 plus the residual value of the equipment (sometimes called the "head lease" in a wrap lease structure).

4. The investor/lessor treats the transaction as a true lease and claims ACRS deductions, providing additional cash flow sufficient in the first year to cover the $600,000 cash payment.

After rights of offset, the net effect is that the originating company has sold its $400,000 equity for $600,000. The broker is compensated by the difference between the loan payments paid to the originating leasing company and the loan payments received from the investor. The investor/lessor realizes a positive cash flow measured by the difference between the lease payments received and the monthly payments paid the broker. The investor/lessor also realizes a one half share of the rents in months 61 through 84, the residual value net of selling expenses and tax benefits. The originating lessor stands to gain a one half share of the rents during months 61 through 84 plus fees for remarketing the equipment when it is no longer rented.

In a competitive situation, the driving force for the ultimate pricing of rents under the lease to the lessee user is the price the wrap lessor charges the originating lease company.

Wrap lease structures have also been used to strip off ITC to one investor and ACRS to another investor.

The problem with wrap leases is that the Internal Revenue Service may not recognize that the lessor investor has enough of the benefits and burdens of ownership in a given transaction to be considered the owner and lessor of the leased property.[11] Wrap leases are particularly vulnerable to Internal Revenue requirements for useful life and residual values.

REQUIREMENT FOR REGISTRATION OF EQUIPMENT LEASE TAX SHELTERS BY BROKERS

Section 6111 of the Internal Revenue Code requires any "tax shelter organizer" to register a "tax shelter" with the Internal Revenue Service not later than the day on which the "first offering for sale of interests" in the shelter occurs. The term *tax shelter organizer* is defined broadly and should be assumed to include most lease brokers if the tax shelter definition is otherwise satisfied. The day on which the first offering for sale of interests in a lease transaction occurs is the day of the first contact with a prospective equity source.

A "tax shelter" is defined as any investment:

1. With respect to which any person could reasonably infer from the representations made, or to be made, in connection with the offering for sale of an interest in the investment that the "tax shelter ratio" for any investor as of the close of any of the first five years ending after the date on which such investment is offered for sale may be greater than 2 to 1.
2. Which is
   a. Required to be registered under a federal or state law regulating securities.
   b. Sold pursuant to an exemption from registration requiring the filing of a notice with a federal or state agency regulating the offering or sale of securities.
   c. A substantial investment (that is, the amount of equipment exceeds $250,000, and there are expected to be five or more investors).

The "tax shelter ratio" is defined as the ratio that (1) the aggregate amount of the gross deductions and 200 percent of the credits that are or will be represented as potentially allowable to any investor bear to (2) the investment base (generally the amount of money contributed by the investor as of the close of the year, subject to certain exclusions). For example, a traditional direct lease with no leveraged financing

---

[11] See National Office Technical Memorandums LTR 8118010, dated January 23, 1981, and LTR 8219005, dated January 23, 1982. Also see *Rice's Toyota World* v. *Commissioner* (1983), 81 T.C. 184 (1983), affirmed in part and reversed in part 752 F. 2d. 89 (1985); *Coleman* v. *Commissioner* 87 T.C. No. 12 (1987); *Mukerji* v. *Commissioner* 87 T.C. No. 37 (1987); *Bussing* v. *Commissioner* 88 T.C. No 21 (1987); and *Torres* v. *Commissioner* 88 T.C. No. 40 (1987).

would result in a tax shelter ratio of 1.2 to 1 (for example, $100 ACRS deductions and $20 adjusted credits for a $100 cash investment). A leveraged lease with 60 percent debt would yield a tax shelter ratio of greater than 3 to 1 (depending on the amount of tax benefits for interest deductions on the leveraged debt) and thus meets one of the characteristics for a tax shelter.

For a tax shelter to exist, however, five or more investors in leased equipment costing more than $250,000 (that is, a substantial investment) must be expected.

Since lease syndication activities are conducted under the private placement exemption from securities registration, there is no registration requirement.

Therefore, in situations where it is expected that there will be five or more investors in a leveraged lease with a tax shelter ratio of greater than 2 to 1, registration will be required not later than the day that equity sources are first contacted. In such situations, a lease syndicator or broker should immediately file IRS Form 8264 for registration of tax shelters. Substantial penalties will result for failure to make a timely filing of the registration form unless such failure is due to reasonable cause. The penalty for any one tax shelter is the greater of (1) $500 or (2) 1 percent of the equipment cost, the total penalty being limited to $10,000 in any event. (However, there is no limitation if the registration requirements are intentionally disregarded.)

SPECIAL RULES FOR INDIVIDUAL LESSORS AND CLOSELY HELD CORPORATIONS

This chapter has been concerned with corporate lessors that are not closely held.

The tax rules applicable to individuals and closely held corporations are different from the general rules applicable to corporations. Individual lessors may have special problems relating to the amount of investment interest they can deduct under the Internal Revenue Code. They may also have tax preference problems resulting from ACRS deductions that would result in imposition of an alternative minimum tax under Section 55 of the Code. Individuals investing as limited partners are, of course, subject to these limitations.

Even more important for both individuals and closely held corporations is the applicability of at-risk limitations under Section 465 of the Code.

Under Section 465 of the Code, individuals and certain closely held corporations cannot deduct losses in excess of the amount they have at risk at year-end with respect to a particular lease transaction. If ITC is available, an individual cannot claim investment tax credit in excess of the investment actually at risk.

The net effect of the at-risk limitations on an individual or a closely held corporation lessor is that to gain the full benefit of the anticipated tax consequences of a leveraged lease transaction, the individual lessor or the closely held corporate lessor will be required to assume personal liability for some or all of the leveraged debt. In other words, the economics of nonrecourse leverage are simply not available.

The at-risk limitations generally apply to any closely held corporation of which 50 percent or more of the stock is owned directly or indirectly by five or fewer individuals, after taking into account certain attribution rules.[12]

Furthermore, Section 469 of the Internal Revenue Code, added by the Tax Reform Act of 1986, provides that losses from an active business such as equipment leasing in which the individual is a passive participant can only be deducted against income from such activities in the case of an individual taxpayer, and against such income and active business activities for a closely held nonservice corporation.

The net result of these limitations is to make equipment leasing unattractive for most individual investors.

CONCLUSION

Revenue Procedure 75–21 is controversial among lessees, lessors, and their respective tax counsel. The rules are not perfect. Relaxing certain requirements with changes that would result in little loss of tax revenue would make it easier to document lease transactions.

On the other hand, the Revenue Procedure 75–21 guidelines can provide many lessees and lessors with a great deal of comfort so long as they adhere strictly to those requirements.

The IRS guidelines have not proved to be a serious deterrent to doing business. As a matter of fact, leasing has flourished and grown since the guidelines were enacted in 1975.

The tax laws applicable to equipment leasing are dynamic.[13] Significant changes occur from time to time as a result of legislation, regulations, and rulings. The reader is therefore cautioned to check the current status of the tax laws before proceeding with an equipment leasing transaction.

---

[12] A closely held corporation is not subject to these limitations if it is "actively engaged in equipment leasing," that is, if 50 percent or more of its gross receipts are attributable to equipment leasing activities.

[13] The Practicing Law Institute has published a number of books on equipment leasing and leveraged leasing over the years, including: *Equipment Leasing 1987*, edited by Ian Shrank and William Flowers; *Equipment Leasing 1986*, edited by Ronald M. Bayer and Ian Shrank; and *Leveraged Leasing 1984*, edited by Bruce E. Fritch. These symposiums contain excellent articles on tax aspects of equipment leasing. The most recent tax articles by William Flowers, Richard Bronstein, and Stuart Odell are especially noteworthy.

6

Economics of Lease versus Purchase Decisions

The after-tax cost of either leasing or purchasing equipment has increased as a result of the passage of the Tax Reform Act of 1986 (TRA). This chapter illustrates the increased cost and the fact that the cost of leasing equipment is attractive compared to purchasing equipment where the lessee cannot currently claim ACRS deductions or is subject to alternative minimum tax. A general framework that a lessee can employ to analyze the lease versus purchase decision is provided in Appendix C.

NET PRESENT VALUE COST OF LEASING
OR PURCHASING

Based on certain assumptions set forth in Exhibit 1, the following table illustrates how the after-tax net present value cost[1] of leasing or purchasing automobiles, computers, manufacturing machines, and

---

[1] The net present value (NPV) is generally a dollar amount. In this chapter we show the NPV as a percentage of the original cost. The concepts of present value and net present value are discussed in Appendix B.

EXHIBIT 1   Lease versus Purchase Analysis Assumptions

Equipment	Automobiles	Computer	Manufacturing	Commercial aircraft
Term	4 years	5 years	10 years	15 years
Leverage	None on lease; 90/10 debt to down payment on loan	78.3517% for old and new law analyses; 90/10 debt to down payment on purchase loan	66.3508% for old law analysis; 80.0000% for new law analysis; 90/10 debt to down payment on purchase loan	59.4629% for old law analysis; 78.7160% for new law analysis; 90/10 debt to down payment on purchase loan
Purchase loan payment schedule	48 level monthly in-arrears payments	60 level monthly in-arrears payment	40 level quarterly in-arrears payments	30 level semiannual in-arrears payments
Lease payment schedule	48 monthly in-advance payments of 1.6501% for old law analysis; 48 payments of 1.8211% for new law analysis	60 monthly in-advance payments of 1.7164% for old law analysis; 60 payments of 1.9679% for new law analysis	20 quarterly in-arrears payments of 2.6386% and 20 at 3.2249% for old law analysis; 20 payments at 3.1411% followed by 20 at 3.8392% for new law analysis	15 semiannual in-arrears payments of 3.8713% and 15 at 4.7316% for old law analysis; 15 payments at 4.7178% followed by 15 at 5.7662% for new law analysis
Placed in service	April 1, 1985, for old law analysis; April 1, 1988, for new law analysis	April 1, 1985, for old law analysis; April 1, 1988, for new law analysis	April 1, 1985, for old law analysis; April 1, 1988, for new law analysis	April 1, 1985, for old law analysis;. April 1, 1988, for new law analysis

Depreciation	3-year ACRS for old law analysis; 5-year ACRS for new law analysis	5-year ACRS for old law analysis; 5-year ACRS for new law analysis	5-year ACRS for old law analysis; 7-year ACRS for new law analysis	5-year ACRS for old law analysis; 7-year ACRS for new law analysis
ITC	6% for old law analysis; none for new law analysis	10% for old law analysis; none for new law analysis	10% for old law analysis; none for new law analysis	10% for old law analysis; none for new law analysis
Residual	35% guaranteed residual	5% for lessor pricing and 5% for purchase	10% for lessor pricing and 10% for purchase	20% for lessor pricing and 20% for purchase
Debt interest rate	9.0%	9.0%	9.0%	9.0%
ADR midpoint	3 years	6 years	10 years	12 years
Tax rate for old law (1985) analyses	46%	46%	46%	46%
Tax rate for new law (1988) analysis	34% (20% for AMT analyses)	34% (20% for AMT analyses)	34% (20% for AMT analyses)	34% (20% for AMT analyses)
Discount rate for NPV	9.0% (pre-tax)	9.0% (pre-tax)	9.0% (pre-tax)	9.0% (pre-tax)
Implicit interest rate in lease	(11.4051%) under old law and (6.6969%) under new law	1.2020% under old law and 6.9840% under new law	3.0465% under old law and 6.5914% under new law	3.2871% under old law and 6.0738% under new law
Lessor yield in lease	6.0% (nominal, after-tax)	7.0% (nominal, after-tax)	7.0% (nominal, after-tax)	7.0% (nominal, after-tax)

commercial aircraft has changed under the new law for a current corporate taxpayer.

Equipment	Term	Old tax law @ 46% tax rate			New tax law @ 34% tax rate		
		NPV (AT) purchase	NPV (AT) lease	Spread	NPV (AT) purchase	NPV (AT) lease	Spread
Automobiles	4 years	36.7924%	39.2124%	2.4200%	51.4946%	51.7405%	0.2459%
Computer	5 years	49.2296	49.8073	0.5777	67.5353	67.9383	0.4030
Manufacturing	10 years	47.9389	49.3059	1.3670	67.5819	68.0724	0.4905
Commercial aircraft	15 years	45.7962	47.9376	2.1414	65.5635	66.3361	0.7726

The table below illustrates how the implicit cost of leasing has increased for the same equipment under the new tax law and compares the implicit cost to a debt interest rate for a comparable lessee/owner.

Equipment	Term	Implicit lease rates		Debt interest rate for a comparable company
		Old tax law @ 46% tax rate	New tax law @ 34% tax rate	
Automobiles	4 years	(11.4051)%	(6.6969)%	9%
Computer	5 years	1.2020	6.9840	9
Manufacturing	10 years	3.0465	6.5914	9
Commercial aircraft	15 years	3.2871	6.0738	9

The above analyses assume that the lessor and lessee have the same borrowing rates, debt-to-equity ratios, required return on equity, and residual value assumptions.[2] The aircraft, computer, and manufacturing equipment leases used for comparison purposes are leveraged leases, and the automobile lease is a single-investor TRAC lease. After-tax cash flows are discounted at 9 percent, which is the same rate of interest assumed for leveraged debt.

The increase in the after-tax cost of leasing or purchasing equipment under the TRA as compared to the old law is due to three causes: loss of ITC, change in depreciation deductions, and lower tax rates. The following table shows the relative value of each of these factors to a purchaser.

---

[2] The reader is reminded that, as noted previously in the text, other assumptions are shown in Exhibit 1.

Equipment	Term	ITC	Depreciation	Tax rate	Total
Automobiles	4 years	4.61%	1.21%	8.88%	14.70%
Computer	5 years	7.78	−0.64	11.16	18.30
Manufacturing equipment	10 years	7.78	0.89	10.98	19.64
Commercial aircraft	15 years	7.78	0.88	11.11	19.77

The largest element of the increased after-tax cost in all cases is the decrease in the corporate tax rate, which lessens the value of the tax benefits of depreciation deductions, interest expense, and rental expense.

The loss of ITC and changes in depreciation deductions represent a real net increase in the cost of acquiring equipment. The loss of ITC is net of the gains due to the higher depreciable base (100 percent versus 97 percent or 95 percent). Changes in depreciation deductions alone result in cost increases in the aircraft, manufacturing equipment, and automobile examples despite the higher rate of depreciation (that is, 150 double-declining balance to 200 double-declining balance) because the class lives are lengthened to seven, seven, and five years, respectively. The computer example shows a lower cost because the class life remains the same and the more aggressive 200 percent declining-balance method of depreciation is available under the TRA.

The relative difference in cost of purchasing versus leasing remains about the same under the old law and TRA for the computer example. However, the difference is much smaller in the case of the aircraft, automobile, and manufacturing equipment. For example, in the case of the aircraft, using old ACRS and ITC with a 46 percent tax rate results in a net present value spread of 214 basis points in favor of purchasing if the user is currently able to use tax benefits. Under the TRA, that difference is reduced to 77 basis points.

Leverage Is Constrained under the New Law

Nonrecourse leverage is constrained by the pre-tax present value of rentals. With ACRS and ITC under the old law, the pre-tax present value of rents for the manufacturing equipment and aircraft were about 66 and 60 percent of equipment cost, respectively, resulting in nonrecourse leverage in that range. In the TRA examples the pre-tax present value of rents is about 80 percent, resulting in nonrecourse leverage in that amount. On the purchase side the leverage is arbitrarily fixed at 90 percent of the asset value for all cases. Since the after-tax cost of debt is less than the after-tax cost of equity, the cost of leasing increased relatively less than the cost of purchasing under the new law as compared to the old law.

Lease versus Purchase Economics for a Company in a Tax Carryforward Position

Tax-oriented leasing is especially attractive for a company with tax benefits that are delayed or unused due to net operating loss (NOL) carryforwards. Exhibits 2, 3, 4, and 5, illustrate the after-tax present value costs of purchasing versus leasing for the four example cases (automobile, computer, manufacturing equipment, and aircraft), assuming NOL carryforwards from zero years through five years. The overall after-tax costs of both purchasing and leasing increase for all four cases under the TRA as compared to the old law. However, despite the loss of ITC, the inability of the lessee/purchaser to use tax benefits

---

EXHIBIT 2   Lease Purchase Analysis (Four-year automobile TRAC
lease—regular corporate tax rate)

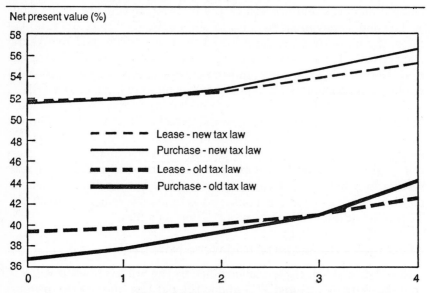

Net present value (%)

Years of delay to receive tax benefits

Years of delay	Old tax law at 46%		New tax law at 34%	
	NPV purchase	NPV lease	NPV purchase	NPV lease
0	36.7924%	39.2124%	51.4946%	51.7405%
1	37.7109	39.5301	51.9853	52.0542
2	39.4581	40.2362	53.1322	52.7439
3	41.8966	41.2933	54.6071	53.7654
4	44.2536	42.6666	56.2111	55.0783
5	45.8841	44.0620	57.4568	56.3980

EXHIBIT 3   Lease Purchase Analysis (Five-year computer lease—regular corporate rate)

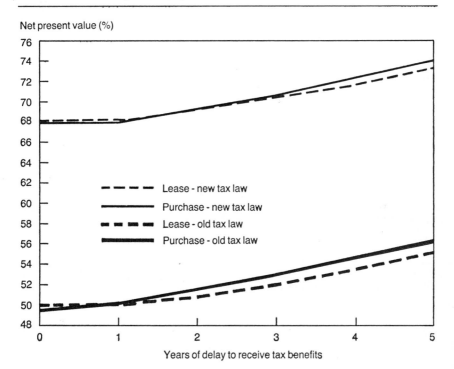

Net present value (%)

Years of delay to receive tax benefits

	Old tax law at 46%		New tax law at 34%	
Years of delay	NPV purchase	NPV lease	NPV purchase	NPV lease
0	49.2296%	49.8073%	67.5353%	67.9383%
1	50.1223	50.1377	68.0280	68.2772
2	51.5303	50.8722	69.1859	69.0226
3	53.3551	51.9718	70.6879	70.1264
4	55.5239	53.4002	72.3412	71.5451
5	57.9684	55.1239	74.0964	73.2386

remains an important factor in all four cases and especially in the cases of the manufacturing equipment and aircraft.

The taxes saved by purchasing still exceed those of leasing in the first years, but the difference is not nearly as great as under the pre-TRA law. A delay in receipt of those benefits of only two to three years is large enough to make leasing less costly than purchasing.

These examples assume that the residual value used by the lessor for pricing is the same value the lessee/purchaser will use in a lease/purchase analysis. Obviously, this will seldom be the case, and

---

EXHIBIT 4   Lease Purchase Analysis (Ten-year manufacturing equipment
lease—regular corporate rate)

Net present value (%)

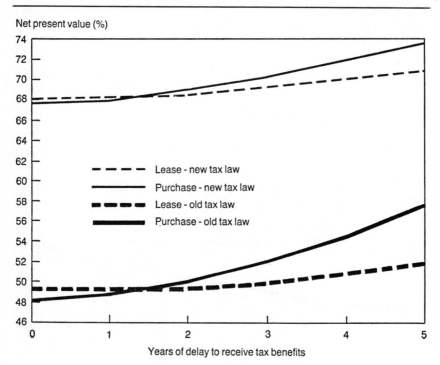

Years of delay to receive tax benefits

Years of delay	Old tax law at 46%		New tax law at 34%	
	NPV purchase	NPV lease	NPV purchase	NPV lease
0	47.9389%	49.3059%	67.5819%	68.0724%
1	48.8331	49.4746	67.9679	68.2519
2	50.2619	49.8496	68.9063	68.6468
3	52.1432	50.4111	70.2043	69.2317
4	54.4194	51.1407	71.7277	69.9836
5	57.0369	52.0212	73.3824	70.8816

a real-life subjective analysis would have to be adjusted accordingly.
However, realistic residual assumptions used by both of the parties
will not significantly change the outcome in these examples. Break-
even residual analysis is discussed later in this chapter.

Lease versus Purchase Analysis Where a Company Is Subject to the Alternate Minimum Tax

The alternate minimum tax (AMT) requires companies to compute
their income tax twice—once under the standard corporate income tax

EXHIBIT 5   Lease/Purchase Analysis (Fifteen-year airplane lease—regular corporate rate)

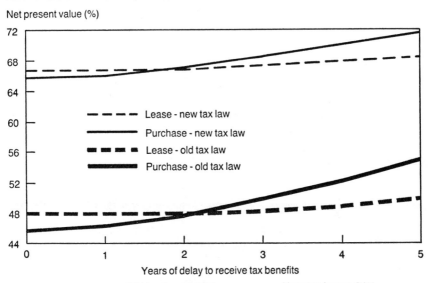

Net present value (%)

Years of delay to receive tax benefits

| | Old tax law at 46% | | New tax law at 34% | |
Years of delay	NPV purchase	NPV lease	NPV purchase	NPV lease
0	45.7962%	47.9376%	65.5635%	66.3361%
1	46.6867	48.0606	65.9480	66.4700
2	48.1155	48.3342	66.8872	66.7646
3	50.0062	48.7440	68.1940	67.2012
4	52.3064	49.2766	69.7373	67.7627
5	54.9674	49.9197	71.4328	68.4335

and again under the AMT provisions. Companies pay whichever method results in the higher amount of tax. The AMT liability is computed at a 20 percent rate applied to minimum taxable income.

AMT income is equal to the sum of the taxpayer's regular taxable income or loss plus items of tax preference. Among the items of tax preference are ACRS depreciation deductions and 50 percent of the difference between taxable income and profits reported for book accounting purposes.

Depreciation deductions for equipment are recomputed under the AMT using the 150 percent declining-balance method over the ADR midpoint lives, with special rules for selected assets. The book income preference is determined by consolidating the book income of those corporations that are consolidated for tax purposes; 50 percent of the excess of a taxpayer's pre-tax book profit over taxable income is a perference item.

In terms of a purchase versus lease decision, the key AMT preference item is ACRS depreciation under the TRA. For the years in which an owner of equipment is an alternative minimum taxpayer, the owner only realizes depreciation deductions of 150 percent declining balance to straight line over the ADR midpoint life of the equipment as compared to 200 percent declining balance to straight line over the often shorter ACRS class life under the TRA.

Since lessors will conduct their business so as not to be subject to AMT, they will gain the benefits of larger depreciation deductions and be able to offer lease pricing that will compare favorably with purchase costs on an after-tax basis, particularly for a company which is subject to AMT.

The examples shown in Exhibits 6, 7, 8, and 9 illustrate the after-tax present value cost of purchasing as compared to leasing for the

---

EXHIBIT 6   Lease/Purchase Analysis (Four-year automobile TRAC
lease—lessee subject to AMT)

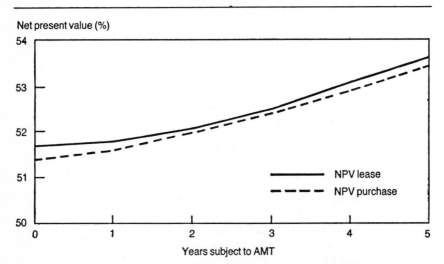

Net present value (%)

Years subject to AMT	Four-year automobile lease	
	NPV purchase	NPV lease
0	51.4946%	51.7405%
1	51.6404	51.8697
2	52.0012	52.1537
3	52.4456	52.5743
4	52.9432	53.1149
5	53.4561	53.6583

EXHIBIT 7   Lease/Purchase Analysis (Five-year computer lease—lessee subject to AMT)

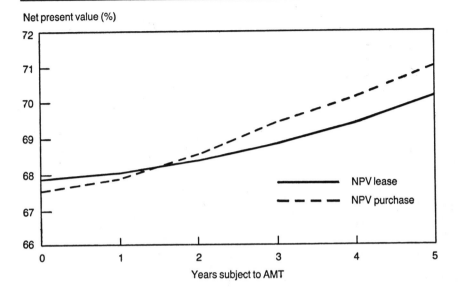

Net present value (%)

Years subject to AMT	Five-year computer lease	
	NPV purchase	*NPV lease*
0	67.5353%	67.9383%
1	67.8226	68.0779
2	68.4864	68.3848
3	69.3090	68.8393
4	70.1582	69.4234
5	71.0172	70.1208

four sample cases plotted against the years in which the lessee/owner is subject to AMT.[3]

In the automobile case (Exhibit 6) leasing becomes less expensive than purchasing after one year. The difference is never very great because the ADR midpoint (five years for minimum tax purposes) is equal to the class life.

In the computer example shown in Exhibit 7, the ADR midpoint is six years, and the ACRS class life is five years. Leasing becomes less expensive after only one year of minimum tax and remains that way

---

[3] It should also be noted that these examples reflect only the longer depreciation life and lower depreciation rates and do not show the further adverse effect of book income preference.

EXHIBIT 8   Lease/Purchase Analysis (Ten-year manufacturing equipment lease—lessee subject to AMT)

Net present value (%)

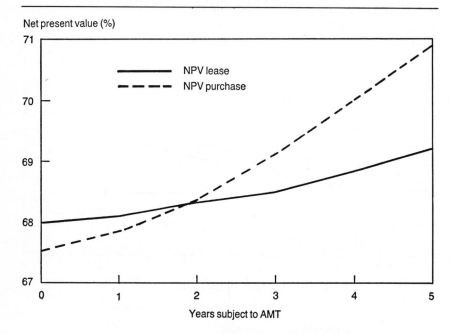

Years subject to AMT	Ten-year manufacturing lease	
	NPV purchase	NPV lease
0	67.5819%	68.0724%
1	67.8168	68.1463
2	68.3870	68.3088
3	69.1515	68.5497
4	70.0189	68.8593
5	70.9281	69.2291

---

during the entire lease. This reflects the low 5 percent resale value/residual which does not benefit from the 20 percent AMT tax rate.

In the manufacturing equipment example shown in Exhibit 8, the ADR midpoint is 10 years and the ACRS class life is 7 years. Leasing becomes less expensive during the first year and significantly less expensive in a relatively short period of time.

In the aircraft example (Exhibit 9) a wide differential immediately arises between leasing and purchasing. This is because the ADR midpoint of 12 years is considerably greater than the class life of 7 years.

EXHIBIT 9   Lease/Purchase Analysis (Fifteen-year aircraft lease—lessee
subject to AMT)

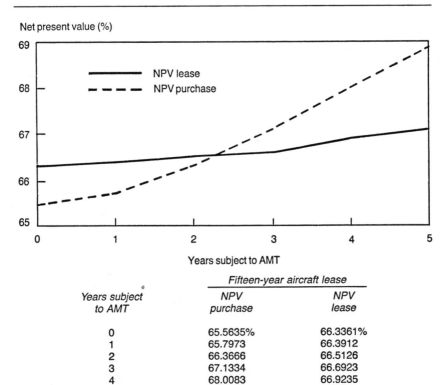

Net present value (%)

Years subject to AMT

Years subject to AMT	Fifteen-year aircraft lease	
	NPV purchase	NPV lease
0	65.5635%	66.3361%
1	65.7973	66.3912
2	66.3666	66.5126
3	67.1334	66.6923
4	68.0083	66.9235
5	68.9324	67.1998

Consequently, there is a significant difference in depreciation benefits
available to the lessor as compared to the user. The present value costs
get closer after year 8 as the cost of purchasing levels off. This is due
to the fact the depreciation is fully exhausted, and the asset begins to
generate "negative preferences" as book depreciation exceeds tax depreciation. At the end of 15 years, there is a decrease in the cost of
purchasing for a permanent alternative minimum taxpayer because
the 20 percent resale price is taxed at the 20 percent minimum tax
rate. This results in only a minor change in present value because the
resale date is 15 years out in the future.

Additional minimum tax not reflected in the above analysis will be
incurred by the owner of equipment as a result of the difference between
taxable income and book pre-tax net profit, which is increased if book
depreciation is straight line and tax depreciation accelerated. This will

make leasing all the more attractive as compared to purchasing equipment.

Break-Even Residual Analysis

The examples discussed above do not take into consideration different residual value assumptions the lessor might use for pricing or the lessee might use for evaluation of a lease or purchase, although such subjective appraisals should not significantly affect the outcome if they are within a realistic range.

If the lessee/purchaser is a current taxpayer, the break-even value of the residual (that is, the residual value expressed as a percent of original cost at which an economic lease or purchase decision is indifferent) is as follows for the examples previously discussed:

	Residual assumed for pricing	Break-even residuals as a percent of original cost	
		Old tax law	New tax law
Automobiles	35%	29.6403%	34.5329%
Computer	5	3.6569	4.1879
Manufacturing	10	5.9574	8.6746
Aircraft	20	11.9713	17.2139

For example, under the new law for a purchase of an aircraft to make economic sense, the residual value at the end of the lease would have to exceed 17.2139 percent of original cost.

If the lessee/purchaser expects to be in a loss carryforward position for one or more years and is subject only to the regular corporate tax rate, the break-even residual value which the lessee/purchaser must realize for a purchase to make economic sense rises as indicated in Exhibits 10, 11, 12, and 13. This effect is magnified by the AMT. Exhibits 10, 11, 12, and 13 also show break-even residual values a taxpayer subject to AMT must realize in making a lease/purchase decision where it expects to be subject to AMT for various numbers of years.

THE EFFECT OF FUTURE TAX RATE CHANGES

Another concern of lessees and lessors is the effect of future tax rate increases on the economics of lease or purchase decisions. If the lessor assumes a tax rate of 34 percent in calculating its lease rate, the lessor's economics will be adversely affected if the tax rate has increased at the time the deferred taxes resulting from ACRS become payable.

EXHIBIT 10   Break-even (Indifferent) Residual Values (Four-year automobile TRAC lease/purchase financing decision for a company subject to AMT or to NOL carryforward)

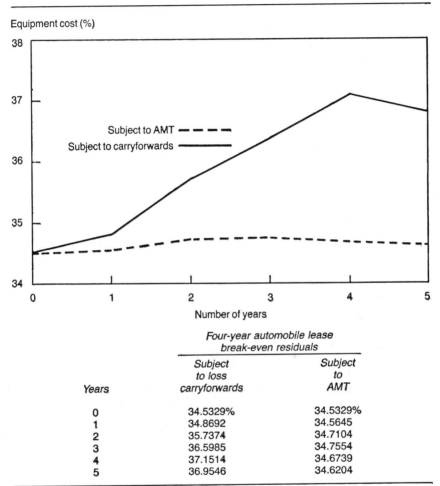

Equipment cost (%)

Number of years

Years	Four-year automobile lease break-even residuals	
	Subject to loss carryforwards	Subject to AMT
0	34.5329%	34.5329%
1	34.8692	34.5645
2	35.7374	34.7104
3	36.5985	34.7554
4	37.1514	34.6739
5	36.9546	34.6204

Usually the lessor will seek to shift this risk to the lessee by requiring the lessee through a tax indemnity clause to assume the risk of future tax rate and tax law changes that adversely affect its yield on the theory that the lessee is no worse off than it would have been had the lessee purchased the equipment. Not surprisingly, the lessee will resist assuming liability for any tax indemnity payments beyond those resulting from its own "acts or omissions." In the final analysis competitive conditions of the marketplace and the pricing of the lease

EXHIBIT 11 Break-even (Indifferent) Residual Values (Five-year computer lease/purchase financing decision for a company subject to AMT or to NOL carryforward)

Equipment cost (%)

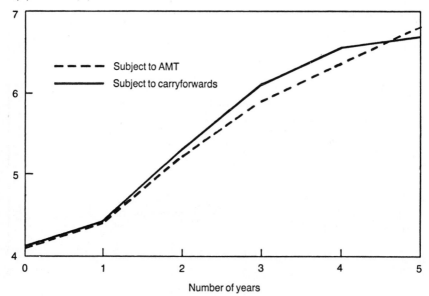

Number of years

	Five-year computer lease break-even residuals	
Years	*Subject to loss carryforwards*	*Subject to AMT*
0	4.1879%	4.1879%
1	4.4978	4.4857
2	5.3292	5.2048
3	6.1315	5.9465
4	6.6043	6.4807
5	6.7285	6.8063

will be factors both the lessee and lessor will consider in reaching agreement on tax indemnity liability to be assumed by the lessee.

Where the parties do agree that the lessee will indemnify the lessor for future changes in tax law such as rate increases, the measure of damages and method of payment must also be agreed upon. There are various ways of doing this, including preserving the lessor's assumed yield and/or cash flow through either a lump-sum payment or increased rents during the remainder of the lease.

EXHIBIT 12 Break-even (Indifferent) Residual Values (Ten-year manufacturing equipment lease/purchase decision for a company subject to AMT or to NOL carryforward)

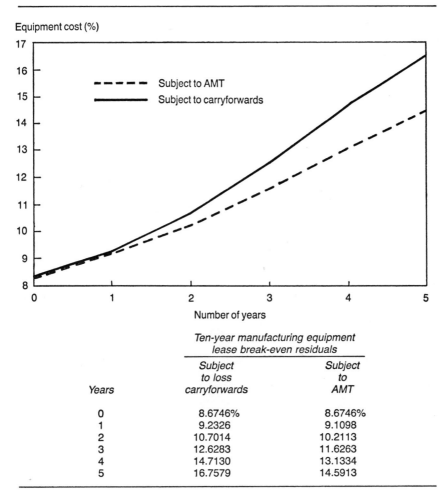

Equipment cost (%)

- - - - - Subject to AMT
——————— Subject to carryforwards

Number of years

Ten-year manufacturing equipment
lease break-even residuals

Years	Subject to loss carryforwards	Subject to AMT
0	8.6746%	8.6746%
1	9.2326	9.1098
2	10.7014	10.2113
3	12.6283	11.6263
4	14.7130	13.1334
5	16.7579	14.5913

Exhibit 14 illustrates the effect of a tax rate change from 34 percent in 1988 to 40 percent in 1990 for the example leases that are assumed to commence in 1988. Exhibit 14 also shows the effect of a lump-sum indemnity payment by the lessee sufficient to maintain the lessor's yield/cash flow in 1990. Exhibits 15 and 16 show the impact on the lessor's yield and cash flow, respectively, of changes in the tax rate from 34 percent to 40 percent or 45 percent after various elapsed periods of time for the 10-year lease of a manufacturing facility example.

EXHIBIT 13   Break-even (Indifferent) Residual Values (Fifteen-year aircraft lease/purchase financing decision for a company subject to AMT or to NOL carryforward)

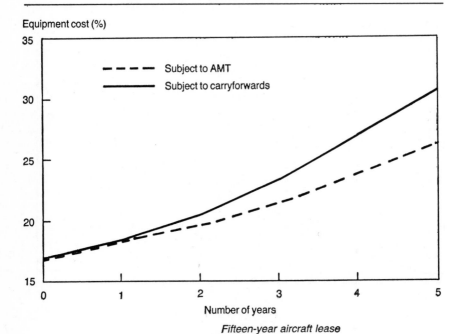

Equipment cost (%)

	Fifteen-year aircraft lease break-even residuals	
Years	Subject to loss carryforwards	Subject to AMT
0	17.2139%	17.2139%
1	18.1177	17.8583
2	20.4421	19.4739
3	23.5801	21.5904
4	27.1271	23.9116
5	30.8147	26.2477

EXHIBIT 14   Impact of a Tax Rate Change from 34 Percent to 40 Percent in 1990, for Leases Commencing in 1988

	4-year automobile		5-year computer		10-year manufacturing		15-year aircraft	
	34% constant	34% switching to 40% in 1990	34% constant	34% switching to 40% in 1990	34% constant	34% switching to 40% in 1990	34% constant	34% switching to 40% in 1990
Nominal after-tax yield	6.0000%	5.2099%	7.0000%	3.4413%	7.0000%	3.0608%	7.0000%	4.9142%
NPV (after-tax) purchase	51.4946	50.4423	67.5353	65.2442	67.5819	64.5902	65.5635	62.3020
NPV (after-tax) lease (with no indemnity payment)	51.7405	49.4106	67.9383	64.5019	68.0724	64.1713	66.3361	62.6836
Break-even residual (with no indemnity payment)	34.5329	37.1241	4.1879	6.6131	8.6746	11.1917	17.2139	18.5787
NPV (after-tax) lease (with indemnity payment)		51.2734		65.7775		65.8355		64.6310
Break-even residual (with indemnity payment)		33.2887		3.8411		6.4575		11.3263

EXHIBIT 15   Impact on After-Tax Yield of Change in Tax Rate (For ten-year lease of manufacturing facility from 34% in year 1)

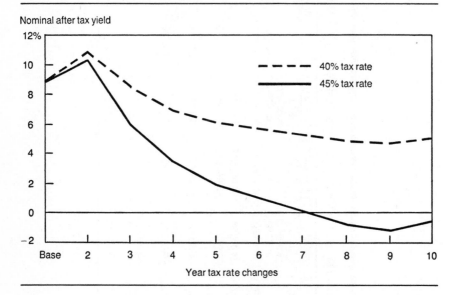

EXHIBIT 16   Impact on After-Tax Cash of Change in Tax Rate (For ten-year lease of manufacturing facility from 34% in year 1)

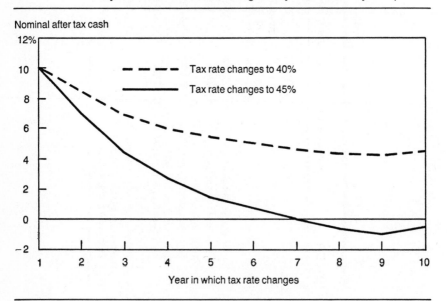

SECTION II

Operating a Leasing Company

7

Considerations in Establishing and Operating a Leasing Company

As noted at the beginning of this book, more equipment is financed today using equipment leases than using commercial bank loans or any other method of financing. The growth in the annual volume of leasing has been accompanied by growth in the number of companies engaged in leasing. These include subsidiaries of banks and bank holding companies, captive finance companies of industrial corporations, independent finance companies, and manufacturers and dealers providing financing for their products. Banks have discovered that leasing is a profitable, efficient use of tax shelter that provides a service demanded by their customers, protects their customer base, and is useful as a competitive product in penetrating new accounts. Industrial companies have found leases attractive as investments and as a profitable method for deferring income tax. Manufacturers and dealers use leasing as a competitive and profitable method for financing their products. Many industrial companies have expanded their captive leasing companies' operations to lease equipment in addition to their own products.

Establishing an equipment leasing subsidiary to engage in tax-oriented leasing is attractive for many companies because of the low entry cost, the tax shelter that can be generated, and the attractive profit potential. No investment in capital equipment (except as part of the portfolio) is required in establishing a leasing company. Borrowings and capital contributions are offset by receivables.

Until recently an industrial company was only required to report its equity investment in a financial subsidiary on its balance sheet. The liabilities of a leasing subsidiary were not required to be shown on its parent's balance sheet. A balance sheet for the financial subsidiary was shown in the footnotes to the parent's balance sheet. As this book goes to press, the Financial Accounting Standards Board is considering, and is expected to adopt, a new accounting standard that would require most financial subsidiaries to be consolidated with their parents for financial accounting purposes, beginning in 1989. If this rule or some variant of it is adopted, as appears likely, companies with financial subsidiaries will break out the results of their financial subsidiaries and other operations separately in footnotes.

The purpose of this chapter is to discuss some of the considerations in planning, funding, and administering an equipment leasing company. In Chapter 10, we shall focus on the concerns of manufacturers/vendors in establishing a product sales financing program, which may include the formation of a leasing company or a finance company for that purpose.

LEASES ARE PART OF THE LARGER EQUIPMENT FINANCE MARKET

In planning a company to engage in equipment leasing, it is important to understand that the market for lease products is part of a much broader market for equipment financing. The lease product is but one of a number of alternative products available to companies that seek to finance equipment.

Products in addition to conventional leases and loans that are used to finance equipment include:

1. Various kinds of conventional bank financing and finance company financing.
2. Chattel mortgages.
3. Secured loans.
4. Installment loans.
5. Vendor financing.
6. Industrial revenue bonds.
7. Export agency financing.
8. Equipment trust certificates and public offerings related to specific equipment.

9. Preferred stock related to specific equipment.
10. Special purpose corporations using public or private debt.
11. Conditional sales types of cross border leases.

Lease products must also compete against the alternative of using internally generated funds for financing equipment that might otherwise be leased.

A strategy for marketing equipment lease products must be concerned with competing against these financing alternatives that are available to prospective lessees.

DETERMINE TAX CAPACITY

In determining the feasibility of a proposed equipment leasing operation, the first step a bank or company should take is to ascertain the amount of tax liability that will be available to the leasing company for the next several years. The products to be offered, the marketing strategies to be employed, and the ability to compete in various market segments are dependent on the availability of regular corporate tax liability for the tax deductions and credits that are to be generated by the proposed leasing operation. Tax deductions will be significant for several years after a lease is booked.

This is not to say that a company cannot engage in equipment leasing without tax liability. Rather, it means that there is no point in designing a marketing organization and strategy in the expectation of offering true leases only to discover at a later date that such products cannot be offered because little or no tax liability is available for lease products to shelter.

Surprising as it may seem, many companies interested in engaging in equipment leasing as lessors have proceeded far down the road in setting up leasing operations before seriously ascertaining the extent to which tax liability will be made available to the proposed leasing company. Often, tax availability is incorrectly assumed on the basis of a cursory review of income taxes paid in prior years, which may not reflect the true status of the future available tax shelter.

Sometimes informal talks with company tax accountants are taken more seriously by the proposer of the leasing operation than by the tax accountants and simply do not focus sufficiently on the tax shelter that is available as a basis for an equipment leasing operation.

A company currently or prospectively subject to alternative minimum tax is not a good candidate for engaging in tax-oriented leasing as a lessor because the AMT seriously reduces the value of depreciation deductions.

Consequently, at the outset of the planning for any proposed leasing operation it is essential that an in-depth study of the tax liability that will be available for the next several years be conducted in conjunction with the company's senior tax advisers and its outside public accounting firm. The conclusions reached should be reduced to writing and circulated to all of the concerned parties so as to prevent any future misunderstanding. This simple procedure can save time and cost and prevent embarrassment.

LEASE PRODUCTS

General Classification

Leasing companies generally concentrate on one or more of the following lease products to penetrate the market for equipment leasing:

1. Conditional sales, which are called leases.
2. Money-over-money leases (single-investor or direct leases with nominal purchase options).
3. Single-investor or direct leases that are true leases.
4. Leveraged leases.
5. TRAC leases.
6. Operating leases (short term).[1]
7. Vendor leases, which may be any of the above.
8. Loans to leasing companies.
9. Discounting of lease receivables.
10. Loans secured by chattel mortgages.
11. Leases to municipalities or governmental agencies.
12. Cross border leases.

Except for short-term operating leases and some kinds of municipal leases, all of the above are designed to provide the lessor with a full recovery of its investment, interest expense on its investment, and profit from a combination of firmly committed rent payments, residual value, and tax benefits.

Short-term operating leases are written for a fraction of the life of the leased asset. (A one-year lease of an IBM computer is an example of an operating lease.) In such operating leases the lessor assumes a substantial risk of failure to recover its investment from release or sale of the property. Knowledge of used equipment values and technical obsolescence risks is essential for a lessor that offers short-term operating leases.

Each of the above lease products might be offered at an interest rate that is fixed for the term of the lease or at an interest rate that floats

---

[1] The term *operating lease* is used in this context as the term is used in the industry to describe a relatively short-term lease for a fraction of the life of the asset, as contrasted to the accounting definition which may include payout type leases for up to 75 percent of the useful life of an asset.

for the term of the lease, with the offering party acting in one of the following capacities:

1. A direct or leveraged *investor*.
2. An *underwriter* guaranteeing to either arrange or take the investment for its own account.
3. A *broker*.

Lease Products Classified by Term

Merely defining lease products by general categories is not very precise. Greater precision can be gained by segmenting the length of time each lease product will be offered. For example, a lessor might prepare a chart similar to that shown as Exhibit 1 as an aid to defining its products. Placing an *x* in the appropriate boxes opposite the products to be offered will disclose a pattern of leasing products. The chart can be reviewed and revised as the target market is further defined.

START-UP OF AN EQUIPMENT LEASING COMPANY

A newly established leasing subsidiary or company will generally start with a small staff and concentrate on one or two lease products with a view to expanding into additional products after its initial products have generated profits.

A bank subsidiary, an industrial company, or a finance company, for example, might choose to concentrate initially on investments in leveraged leases. This could be accomplished with a staff of one or two persons who are knowledgeable about leveraged leasing. These persons could rely on brokers as sources for lease investments. As an alternative strategy, they might enter into a management contract or a joint venture arrangement with an established leasing company as a means of generating business and gaining experience in administering a lease portfolio. Credit advice and counsel could be obtained from parent company personnel. Under normal circumstances and prudent management, acceptable lease investments will present themselves so that within a year or so the leasing subsidiary could be generating revenues sufficient to produce a profit after meeting overhead expense associated with its initial staff and any additional staff necessary to service the leases. Once such a leasing subsidiary has been firmly established as a profitable operation, it is in a position to add to its staff and to incur the overhead expense necessary to expand its operations into marketing additional lease products.

The foregoing scenario assumes, of course, that the parent company has tax liability available for such an activity. It also assumes that the key personnel of the subsidiary are able to correctly analyze the

EXHIBIT 1   Planning Chart for Lease Products

	Up to 3 yrs.	3–5 yrs.	5–8 yrs.	8–10 yrs.	10–15 yrs.	15–20 yrs.	20–25 yrs.
Conditional sales, fixed rate							
Conditional sales, floating rate							
Money-over-money leases, fixed rate							
Money-over-money leases, floating rate							
Direct leases, true leases, fixed rate							
Direct leases, true leases, floating rate							
Leveraged leases, fixed rate							
Leveraged leases, floating rate							
TRAC leases, fixed rate							
Vendor leases, fixed rate							
Vendor leases, floating rate							
Loans to leasing companies, fixed rate							
Loans to leasing companies, floating rate							
Discounting lease receivables							
Loans secured by chattel mortgages, fixed							
Loans secured by chattel mortgages, floating							

true profitability and risks inherent in prospective lease transactions presented by brokers. In addition it assumes a commitment to administer the leases throughout their terms.

ACQUISITION OF AN EXISTING LEASING COMPANY

Another method of entering the leasing business is through the acquisition of an existing leasing company. Such an acquisition requires considerable skill. A partial checklist of the many factors to be considered in acquiring a leasing company includes the following:

1. As a practical matter, all that is being acquired is a portfolio of receivables and personnel. There is little goodwill.
2. The earnings history or net worth of a leasing company can be very misleading since lease accounting permits early recognition of anticipated income, and this can be abused.
3. Leasing personnel are highly mobile. They can be hired without acquiring a company. Unless rewarded, they will not stay with a company that is being acquired.
4. The value of receivables, including any expected residuals, can be ascertained only by examining each credit and document individually. Equipment may have to be inspected and appraised. This is a lengthy and painstaking process.
5. Existing tax benefits and tax indemnities attributable to a lease portfolio are not easily transferred.

Three methods are commonly used to evaluate a leasing company for purchase. They are the liquidating-value method, the price-earnings method, and the return-on-investment method. A goodwill factor can be added to a valuation arrived at by any of these methods if the market position and continuity of the company justify any goodwill value.

The starting place for any negotiation is the liquidating value of the company. This is arrived at by determining the cash flow to be generated by the portfolio over its remaining life, less payments for interest and principal on debt used to fund the portfolio and the costs of administering the portfolio to liquidation. Applying a present value factor to these projected after-tax cash flows results in the liquidating value. This assumes, of course, that all documentation and credits have been carefully reviewed to make sure the cash flows are real and assignable. Add a realistic goodwill factor, and a realistic price results.

The problem with trying to arrive at a price-earnings value is the difficulty in determining the earnings. Since the earning of a leasing company can be accelerated and adjusted in many ways, a past earnings history is suspect unless past earnings are carefully audited and dissected.

The return-on-investment method can be used subjectively by the purchaser to arrive at a price that is attractive to it as an investor. This is a subjective decision because there are no well-established industry standards and because each portfolio is different. Also the investor may be able to enhance the earnings by lowering borrowing costs or providing tax liability to shield.

This is not to say that acquisition of an existing leasing company is not a feasible method of entering the lease business. However, such an acquisition must be accomplished in a prudent and cautious manner so that key personnel are retained and the anticipated revenue is realistic and protected.[2]

Chapter 9 discusses the analysis of financial statements of leasing companies.

MARKET SEGMENTS

Market analysis and market understanding can best be achieved by segmentation of the entire market universe into parts and groups. Using a systematic approach permits and encourages a leasing company to concentrate on the most important market segments and to design marketing strategies, methods, and products that will penetrate those market segments. Segmentation simplifies the establishment of marketing objectives.

By design or otherwise, some companies try to offer a wide variety of lease products to all market segments. However, this "all things to all people" approach rarely works very efficiently. Most companies do not have the resources to serve most of the market universe. When they try to do so, their efforts are diluted, with the result that no part of the market is served very well.

At the other extreme are companies that confine themselves to narrow market segments and aim to serve such markets more effectively by concentrated, focused marketing efforts. A leasing company with high borrowing costs may choose this strategy with a view to offsetting its pricing disadvantage with equipment expertise, highly tailored products, service, and close customer relationships.

Most leasing companies prefer to adopt a marketing strategy that is somewhere between these two extremes. This allows flexibility to shift to new products and new markets as old markets fade or new opportunities present themselves. Market segmentation is in various ways the key to formulating such a marketing strategy.

---

[2] The purchaser of a successful leasing company as a going concern will have two sets of negotiations—one with the seller and another with the key personnel to induce them to stay. This involves careful research to determine the identity of the key personnel.

Classification of Lease Market Segments by Cost of Equipment Leased

Market segments for lease products may be classified by the cost of the equipment or the groups of equipment that are being financed, as described below.

Consumer Leases. The consumer market segment consists of leases to individuals. Automobile leases, private aircraft leases, and pleasure boat leases for nonbusiness use are examples of consumer leases. This market segment is identified in order to distinguish consumer leases from retail leases.

Retail Leases. The retail market segment covers leases for business equipment costing $500 to $50,000. The terms for such leases are generally two to five years. The word *retail* is used to describe the size of the lease rather than the ultimate consumer. Retail leases include leases for such equipment as typewriters, personal computers, office equipment, furniture, and vehicles. Retail leases tend to be less price sensitive than larger leases. Administrative costs and credit approval costs are high as a percentage of equipment costs. Good systems are required for volume. Documentation must be standard. If equipment is leased to small companies, credit approval is time-consuming.

Small Middle-Market Leases. This market segment covers leases for equipment costing $50,000 to $500,000. Typical terms for such leases are three to eight years. Equipment in this category includes construction equipment, agricultural equipment, computer peripherals, minicomputers, small machine tools, telephone interconnect equipment, and small aircraft. Leases in this category are less price sensitive than larger leases. Administrative costs and credit approval costs are high as a percentage of equipment cost, but the percentage is lower than that of retail leases. Good systems and standard documentation are required for volume.

Middle-Market Leases. The middle-market segment includes leases for equipment costing $500,000 to $5 million. The terms for such leases range from 5 to 12 years. Equipment in this market includes executive aircraft, mining equipment, drilling rigs, computers, and groups of equipment such as trucks, forklifts, construction equipment, railroad cars, barges, and containers. These leases are much more price sensitive than small middle-market leases. The transactions tend to be more tailored to the lessee's needs.

Big-Ticket Market. This segment covers leases for equipment costing over $5 million. Generally, a "big-ticket lease" will be a leveraged lease. The terms for big-ticket leases will be 5 to 25 years in most cases. This market includes leases of commercial aircraft, ships, large computer processing units, quantities of railroad cars, large quantities of production equipment, and energy facilities. These leases are very price sensitive. They are individually negotiated.

Matching Lease Market Segments to Lease Products

The matrix shown as Exhibit 2 can be used to match lease market segments to lease products. This type of matrix can also be used to match lease products to various market segments. For example, industry market segments or equipment market segments might be substituted for market segments by dollar size in the left-hand column.[3]

Geographic Market Segments

Markets for lease products are often segmented by geographic territory—for example, by city, county, state, region, the United States, designated foreign countries, and continents. Different products can be offered to different geographic market segments. Geographic market segments can be further segmented by size of company, type of industry, type of equipment, and so forth.

Market Segments by Size and Net Worth

The lease market can be segmented by prospective lessee companies with certain common size characteristics, such as sales or net worth, or by prospective lessee companies with a combination of such characteristics. Companies that specialize in marketing services can quickly identify and describe companies in particular geographic areas segmented by size and net worth criteria.

Market Segments by Characteristics of the Prospective Lessee

A prospective lessee will probably have some of the following characteristics:

1. The company is not paying income tax currently or has little available ability to claim tax benefits associated with equip-

---

[3] The marketing matrixes shown in this chapter are intended as conceptual starting places for the reader to structure his own matrixes for market analysis.

EXHIBIT 2   Matrix for Matching Lease Market Segments to Lease Products

Market segment by size	Lease products	Length of lease term	Range of equipment cost
Consumer			
Retail, $500 to $50,000			
Small middle market, $50,000 to $500,000			
Middle market $500,000 to $5,000,000			
Big ticket, $5 million and larger			

ment ownership. (Inability to pay tax is often due to factors that may not affect credit standing, such as a recent large write-off, a large capital expenditure program, being subject to alternative minimum tax, or depletion allowances.)

2. The company has been or is a lessee.
3. The company has large planned equipment requirements in relation to internally generated funds.
4. The company needs working capital to meet other operational needs.
5. Numerous opportunities exist for the profitable investment of earnings and working capital in new products, acquisitions, and so forth.
6. New conventional financing will impose certain restrictions, will be costly to arrange, or is not timely for one reason or another.
7. Off-balance sheet financing is desirable (if an operating lease under *FASB 13* can be arranged).

8. Technological changes create the need for up-to-date equipment.
9. The company's current progress and profits are limited by depreciation guidelines. It cannot use accelerated depreciation benefits.
10. After closing its capital budget, the company or a division thereof has a sudden equipment need.
11. The company is "on the way up"; that is, it is a growing concern that needs its cash and wants to take quick advantage of alternative investment opportunities.
12. The company's stock is selling for less than book value, making raising capital by equity or equity-related securities unattractive.

Equipment

The market may be segmented by equipment users such as the following:

1. Barge operators.
2. Computer mainframe users.
3. Computer peripheral equipment users.
4. Container companies and shipping companies using containers.
5. Executive jet users.
6. Machine tool users.
7. Oil drilling equipment operators.
8. Packaging machine users.
9. Railroad car users.
10. Truck fleet users.
11. Automobile fleet users.
12. Electric generator users.
13. Communication equipment users.

Markets of this kind can often be identified by vendors of equipment who are anxious that their equipment be financed.

Market Segments by Industry

Market segmentation by industry is important since each industry has characteristics that are peculiar to it. Certain industries, for example, may present better credit risks, may tend to use equipment with upside potential on residual values, or may present more long-range potential for developing a customer base. On the other hand, certain industries may have undesirable characteristics associated with long-term growth potential or a tendency to lease undesirable equipment. Overconcentration of credit exposure in one industry may result in a need to cease pursuing business in that market segment.

Marketing services such as Dun & Bradstreet categorize industries into hundreds of classifications. However, industry markets might generally be segmented as follows:

Airlines	Mining (other than coal)
Agriculture related	Municipal or state government
Auto dealers	Ocean shipping
Catalog sales	Petrochemicals
Coal mining	Railroads
Construction	Restaurants
Container companies	Retail sales
Electronic manufacturing	Steel manufacturing
Food processing	Trucking
General manufacturing	Utilities

Channels of Business

Channels used to generate equipment lease business include the following:

1. The marketing staff of the leasing company.
2. Brokers.
3. Commercial banks.
4. Investment banks.
5. Existing customers.
6. Other departments of the leasing company (contract administration, equipment inspection, and so forth).
7. Advertising.
8. Loan officers of an affiliated bank.
9. Officers of affiliated companies offering financial services.
10. Correspondent banks.
11. Other lessors.
12. Vendors such as dealers or manufacturers.
13. Referrals by customers.
14. Law firms.
15. Accounting firms.

Many leasing companies seek to avoid the expense of a marketing staff by relying on channels outside the company for new lease business. These outside channels might consist of brokers, banks, or the sales force of a manufacturer seeking financing for its products.

The use of lease brokers has the attraction of providing a rapid method for building a portfolio. There are a great many reputable lease brokers who are anxious to satisfy this need. However, a broker always has an inherent conflict of interest since the broker's fee is dependent on selling the transaction to the investor. In many situations a broker will have been retained by the prospective lessee to arrange the lease and act as the lessee's financial advisor.[4] This conflict must be rationalized.

One difficulty in dealing extensively with some brokers is the lack of control over their conduct. Some brokers will hold themselves out to the market as the leasing company's agent despite being told not to do so. Credit quality assurances and representations made to prospective lessees by brokers or their employees anxious to earn a quick commission can also be problems. Some brokers will indicate they have a mandate from a lessee to arrange a transaction when that is not the case.

The deciding factors in developing or relying on a particular channel of lease business are the cost, the quality, and the profitability of the lease business generated from that channel.

Competition for Equipment Financing

Products that compete in the market for equipment financing are offered by various lending institutions and agencies, including the following:

1. Domestic banks.
2. Foreign banks.
3. Finance companies.
4. Investment bankers.
5. Individual investors.
6. Dealers.
7. Manufacturers.
8. Government financing, export agencies, and so forth.
9. Independent leasing companies.
10. Lease brokers.
11. Insurance companies.
12. Foreign leasing companies.
13. Asset funds.
14. Income funds.

All these sources of funds compete for segments of the market for equipment financing.

---

[4] In the parlance of the trade, the broker will have a "mandate" for the transaction.

There are no very reliable statistics regarding the volume of lease financing or equipment financing over the years. Estimates of total lease financing in recent years are about $100 billion annually, and this amount is estimated to be one fourth to one half of the potential equipment financing market. Of the $100 billion annual volume, approximately $25 to $30 billion is tax oriented. In the absence of reliable statistics, however, it is not possible to measure the market share of equipment financing that leasing enjoys or the market share of equipment leasing that a particular company enjoys.

Exhibit 3 shows some of the products offered by various participants in the equipment financing market and estimates the degree of participation among those competitors. This same type of chart can be used to illustrate market participation by individual participants or more narrowly defined groups of participants.

PRICING

A leasing company should establish pre-tax and after-tax target rates of return on its equity and assets. Such targets must compare favorably with rates of return available to the parent company from other uses of funding and tax shelter resources. Pricing strategies are then formulated to achieve these objectives.

The pricing of a lease should take the following factors into consideration:

1. The cost of funds.
2. The expected residual value, if any.
3. The current and future federal and state income tax rates and liability of the lessor.
4. The timing of the delivery of the leased equipment.
5. The timing of actual receipt of cash flows attributable to tax benefits.
6. The timing of the payment of the purchase price.
7. The general overhead expense attributable to the leasing operations.
8. The cost of booking the transaction.
9. The servicing costs during the lease, for billing, collecting, inspecting, insuring, and answering inquiries regarding the lessee or the equipment.
10. The cost of disposition of the equipment (if a true lease) at the end of the lease.
11. The special expenses attributable to the transaction.
12. The risk or loss reserve on the portfolio.
13. The special risk or loss reserve attributable to the transaction.

EXHIBIT 3   Competition in Equipment Financing Market

| | Banks | | | | Participants | |
Product	Money center	Regional	Country	Foreign	Finance companies	Investment bank
Single-investor true lease, retail, $500–$50,000	o	O	O	o	O	°
Small middle market, $50,000–$500,000	o	O	**O**	o	O	°
Middle market, $500,000–$5 million	**O**	O	o	o	**O**	o
Big ticket, $5 million and over	**O**	o	°	°	O	**O**
Leveraged true lease investor	**O**	O	O	o	**O**	o
Underwriter and broker	o	o	°	°	o	o
Broker	o	o	°	°	o	**O**
Direct conditional sale leases, retail, $500–$50,000	**O**	O	O	o	**O**	°
Small middle market, $50,000–$500,000	**O**	**O**	o	o	**O**	°
Middle market, $500,000–$5 million	**O**	o	°	o	o	°
Big ticket, $5 million and over	**O**	o	°	°	o	o
Equipment loans	**O**	**O**	O	O	O	o
Loans to leasing companies	**O**	**O**	O	O	O	°
Purchase of manufacturers' receivables	**O**	o	°	°	**O**	°
Purchase of dealers' receivables	**O**	O	o	°	**O**	°
Purchase of leasing company receivables	**O**	O	o	°	**O**	°

Insignificant participation = °   Participation = O
Some participation = o   A major player = **O**

EXHIBIT 3   (*concluded*)

		Participants				
Independent lessors	Insurance companies	Manufacturers' and dealers' vendor programs	Industrial captive finance companies	Individuals	Government revenue bonds	Foreign government
o	o	o	o	O	o	o
O	o	O	o	O	o	o
O	o	O	o	o	o	o
o	o	o	o	o	o	o
o	o	o	O	O	o	o
o	o	o	o	o	o	o
O	o	o	o	o	o	o
O	o	O	o	o	o	o
O	o	O	o	o	o	o
O	o	o	o	o	o	O
o	o	o	o	o	o	O
o	o	O	o	o	O	O
o	o	o	o	o	o	O
o	o	o	o	o	o	o
o	o	o	o	o	o	o
o	o	o	o	o	o	o

The pricing of a lease is usually expressed as a "yield." In a non-tax-oriented lease (sometimes called a money-over-money lease), the yield is similar to the yield on a loan, as illustrated in Appendix B, and standard yield measurements of ROA (return on assets) and ROE (return on equity) behave fairly similarly to a loan. In a tax-oriented lease, the yield is often expressed on a pre-tax basis after taking tax benefits into consideration. This is an ROI (return on investment) measurement, which may differ from an ROA or ROE measurement on either a transaction or portfolio basis.[5]

The sales and general administrative costs incurred in connection with the closing of a large transaction may not be different from such costs for a small transaction. For this reason, these costs should be considered for pricing purposes as a reduction of yield measured as a percentage of the investment in the equipment. Companies sometimes make the mistake of charging a flat percentage of the cost of the leased equipment to each lease transaction for general administrative and sales expenses. This penalizes larger transactions and shows smaller transactions in a more favorable light than is warranted. Exhibit 4 illustrates the reduction of yield for lease transactions of various dollar amounts for particular types of equipment. Leases of different types of equipment have different administrative costs. However, the yield-size relationship will usually resemble the relationship shown in Exhibit 4. Using standard documentation for large volumes of leases that are repetitious in nature can result in greater efficiencies and lower costs. Such standardization is essential for small leases.

The pricing of either a tax-oriented or a non-tax-oriented lease can be dramatically affected if the lessor takes a residual value into consideration in pricing. Of course, this raises considerable downside risk for the lessor if any residual assumed for pricing purposes is not realized. Estimating anticipated residual values is an inexact science at best. The "expert opinions" of lease brokers and their appraisers must be viewed in light of their desire to sell transactions.

The administrative costs associated with a true lease are generally higher than the administrative costs associated with a money-over-money transaction. Extra care is required in the documentation and closing of a true lease to preserve its tax status. Extra expense is incurred in disposing of the equipment at the conclusion of a true lease.

Special expenses that will be incurred in connection with a particular transaction should be taken into account in pricing. Factors such as multiple deliveries, large numbers of units, wide disbursal of equipment, and licensing and registration requirements can dramatically raise the administrative costs of a transaction.

---

[5] For an excellent explanation of lease pricing, see James M. Johnson, *Fundamentals of Finance for Equipment Lessor* (Association of Equipment Lessors, 1986).

EXHIBIT 4   General Sales and Administration Expenses Expressed as a
Reduction in Yield for Equipment with Various Initial Costs

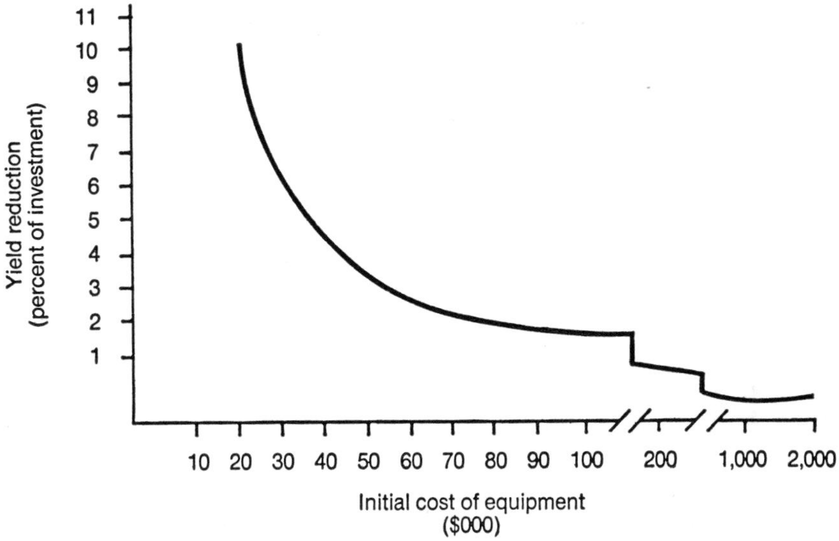

Special loss risk exposures due to such factors as unusual credit, tax, or residual problems should be taken into consideration in pricing. The longer the term of the lease, the greater is the credit risk exposure.

The funding of fixed-rate leases is a risk that must be considered in pricing where the lessor cannot match-fund the lease with fixed-rate borrowing for a similar term. Interest rate swaps or rate futures can be used to hedge the risk of short-term borrowings to fund fixed-rate leases. The lessee can assume the funding risk by agreeing to a floating rate lease. Funding is discussed in more detail later in this chapter.

The marketing force will tend to regard every prospect as either a valued customer or a target account. Consequently, pricing discipline is necessary to maintain a consistent and objective pricing strategy that will achieve the target rate of return for the portfolio and the company.

FUNDING A LEASING COMPANY

A leasing company may be funded in the same manner as a finance company, using a great variety of sources and instruments. Its sources of funds may include domestic and foreign banks, other domestic and foreign leasing companies, institutional lenders, vendors, export agencies, and corporate and individual investors in notes and commercial paper.

The instruments used by leasing companies include bank loans, notes, debentures, bonds, subordinated debt instruments, and commercial paper. Interest rate risk can be covered by using interest rate futures and swaps. Also, rent receivables and leases may be laid off or sold with or without recourse to a variety of investors or lenders. Debt may be floating or fixed. If floating, it may be tied to a number of indexes, including the prime interest rate and the London Interbank Offered Rate (LIBOR). If fixed to be set (or reset) at some date in the future, it may be tied to U.S. Treasury bonds of similar maturity or some published private sector bond index for similar maturities such as those published by Salomon Brothers.

LEVERAGE

A leasing company engaged in writing operating leases is typically leveraged two (or possibly three) parts debt to one part equity. A leasing company engaged in writing payout leases with little or no residual risk is typically leveraged 5 or 6 to 1 and sometimes as high as 10 to 1.[6] However, these general guidelines for the leverage of a leasing company's equity can legitimately vary under different circumstances. Debt that is truly subordinated to conventional borrowings is often considered to be the equivalent of additional capital, thus increasing the leasing company's overall debt-to-equity ratio. The ITC that has vested but has not as yet been recognized into income is sometimes recognized as additional capital. If a leasing company sells its leases and lease paper to banks at regular intervals, its leverage and debt-to-equity ratios may vary a great deal as it warehouses transactions for sale and later sells them.

From the lender's standpoint, a careful analysis of the equity a leasing company seeks to leverage is warranted. The apparent equity may be unrealistically increased, for example, by the anticipated realization of residual values. Senior positions in leases and lease receivables may have already been sold or encumbered. Paper profits must be carefully analyzed to determine the true net worth. When examining an unfamiliar leasing company credit, many lenders prefer to look closely at the quantity and quality of the unencumbered receivables as compared with the borrowings to support those receivables. The existence of direct, indirect, or contingent guarantees must be determined. The rules and practices of lease accounting are very different from the accounting rules and practices followed by banks, finance companies, or industrial companies.

---

[6] General Electric Credit Corporation is currently leveraged 10 to 1. Japanese leasing companies are typically leveraged 15 to 1 or higher.

LIABILITY MANAGEMENT

The structure of a leasing company's liabilities should, of course, match the asset side of the balance sheet to the maximum extent possible.

If leases are written at fixed rates, borrowings should also be at fixed rates. In addition, borrowings should match the maturities of the assets. Foreign exchange risk should be covered to the maximum extent possible.

In managing the liability side of the true lease portfolio, the funding exposure is far different from that for a term loan or money-over-money (non-tax-oriented) lease portfolio because of the early positive cash flows from tax benefits.

Due to market conditions, it is not always possible to ideally match the maturities and other characteristics of assets and liabilities. Most leasing companies have a variety of short-term, medium-term, and long-term debt and follow a strategy of restoring a certain balance to their liabilities when borrowing conditions permit. Successful leasing companies (like successful finance companies) discipline themselves to borrow term funds at regular intervals, even though the rates may sometimes seem high, on the theory that these borrowings average out over time. Interest rate futures and interest rate swaps can be used in conjunction with floating debt or commercial paper to hedge fixed-rate lending or leasing risk.

CREDIT CONTROLS, PORTFOLIO ADMINISTRATION, AND COLLECTIONS

A leasing company must have well-thought-out strategies and procedures for credit controls, portfolio administration, and collections. These subjects are discussed in Chapter 8.

BANK AND BANK HOLDING COMPANY LEASING COMPANIES

When a bank holding company considers entry into the leasing business, the determining factor in deciding whether to establish the leasing operation as a subsidiary of the bank or as a direct subsidiary of the bank holding company is often the relative advantages and disadvantages of the different methods of funding available to those two types of subsidiaries.

Leasing companies that are subsidiaries of banks usually depend on borrowing funds for their leasing operations from their associated bank. The bank, in turn, obtains funds from deposits or other conventional sources of bank funding. The bank may also borrow from its holding company if it has one.

Leasing companies that are direct subsidiaries of bank holding companies are prohibited from borrowing from their associated bank under Section 23A of the Federal Reserve Act. They may, however, borrow from their parent holding company, which, in turn, may borrow using commercial paper and notes. A direct subsidiary of a bank holding company may also borrow directly from third-party sources, utilizing bank loans and commercial paper, either with or without the guarantees of its holding company.

Leasing subsidiaries of either banks or bank holding companies may sell off or discount leases or lease receivables as a means of raising capital.

CONCLUSION

The equipment leasing business can be a good business if it is properly managed.[7] The entry costs are low and profit opportunities are high compared to those of other finance businesses, particularly where the lessor has tax liability to shelter.

Generally speaking, the profits from a leasing company will come from pricing correctly, borrowing at the lowest possible cost, realizing any residual values, and administering the market force and lease portfolio so as to protect those profit elements.

The success or failure of the lease business, like that of all businesses, depends on good management and well-thought-out strategies. Hopefully, this chapter has offered a few ideas that will be helpful in developing such strategies and in achieving such management.

---

[7] No leasing company reference library should be without this book, the latest Practicing Law Institute books, Terry A. Isom and Sudher Amembal, *Handbook of Leasing* (Petrocelli Books, 1982), and James M. Johnson's book referred to in footnote 5.

8

Credit Policies and Lease Portfolio Administration

Extending credit to lessees involves a term commitment that is usually at a fixed interest rate. Typically 100 percent of equipment cost is financed in a lease. Consequently, the credit analysis and judgment in extending credit to lessees is similar to the credit decision process in making a 100 percent secured term loan at a fixed rate of interest. In this chapter we discuss credit considerations and policies in extending credit to lessees.

PROSPECTIVE CREDIT CRITERIA

The primary consideration for extending credit to any prospective lessee is the ability of the prospective lessee to meet its payment obligations under the lease.

Credit decisions start with screening prospects for lease business from a credit standpoint. Companies with the following characteristics are good prospects:

1. The prospective customer has a reasonably low business failure for the type of business in which it is engaged.

2.   The prospective customer has been operating successfully for a reasonable period of time (three or more years) and has shown sound growth, financial stability, and profits.
3.   The prospect has excellent prospects for continued profitable operations together with cash flow sufficient to meet its obligations.
4.   The net worth of the prospective lessee is substantial in relation to debt with sufficient liquid assets to support the credit.
5.   The prospective lessee is an established business. Lease payments should not be contingent on the success of an unproven or speculative venture.

REPAYMENT SOURCES

At the time a credit is approved, the lease must have a well-defined primary payment source as well as a secondary or "worst case" source of payment. The payment sources should be well understood by both the lessee and the lessor. This should be detailed in the lessor's credit files in order to reduce misunderstanding should the lease subsequently become a credit problem.

Two principles set the stage for future creditors' rights and should be followed in all lease transactions:

1.   The leasing company must have a first right of ownership or first lien on the leased equipment, except in the case of a leveraged lease.
2.   Apart from the lease collateral, the leasing company should be a senior creditor of the lessee and not be subordinate to other lenders. If the lessor is not a senior creditor, the credit decision should reflect this exception and the rationale for extending credit.

In basic terms, there are only three sources for lease repayment:

1.   The leased asset.
2.   The balance sheet of the lessee.
3.   The earnings or cash flow of the lessee.

The leased asset is the primary source for repayment of a lease. It represents collateral in which the lessor has perfected legal title in true leases and in most conditional sale types of leases. The right of the lessor to the leased property is consequently superior to a lender with a security interest in collateral that must be perfected. However, in either case the resale value of used equipment is usually not sufficient to satisfy the outstanding balance on a lease. Consequently, lease credit analysis requires identification of alternative sources of payment.

The lessee's balance sheet as a source of lease or loan repayment requires the liquidation or conversion of an asset. As such the balance sheet represents an important but last resort source of payment.

The cash flow of the lessee will typically be the major source of lease payments for credit analysis purposes. Cash flow can be defined as net after-tax earnings plus depreciation and other noncash charges. Depreciation is available as a source of cash flow to the extent it represents a noncash charge. Reported net earnings are, after all, expenses, including depreciation and other noncash items. In order to determine the total cash flow available it is necessary to add back depreciation and any other noncash charges to the reported net after-tax figure.

Refinancing might be considered a fourth source of lease payment. Refinancing is a balance sheet source although it does not require liquidation of an asset. Refinancing can involve moving a loan to an unsecured lender or obtaining credit elsewhere that better meets the lessee's needs.

ANALYSIS OF FINANCIAL STATEMENTS

A lessee that constitutes an acceptable credit must show an ability to meet its obligations under the proposed transaction as a result of a detailed review and analysis of its financial statements.

Balance Sheet Analysis

Credit analysis of the balance sheet as a source of lease or loan repayment requires detailed study of each major asset and liability item along the following lines:

Cash. Is the cash shown on the balance sheet free to be applied on the lease or debt?

Investments. Are the investments liquid assets that are readily marketable?

Accounts receivable. Are the accounts current? What is their aging? Is the borrower dependent on a few customers? What is the borrower's historic bad debt expense? Is the reserve for bad debts adequate?

Fixed assets. Fixed assets may represent a significant part of the borrower's or lessee's net worth but have little market value.

Inventory. Is inventory marketable? How often does inventory "turn"? How is inventory valued for financial statement purposes, and if on the LIFO method, what are the LIFO reserves? What is the condition of the inventory? Are work in process, obsolete goods, or damaged goods included?

Intangibles. In liquidation, intangible assets may not have value as a source of funds for loan repayment.

Understanding of the lessee's liabilities is as important as understanding the lessee's assets. Other creditors may have claim on the borrower's or lessee's assets and cash flow.

Accounts payable. Is trade debt current, and what is the accounts payable aging? Is trade debt concentrated, with one or two suppliers?

Notes payable to banks. Does the lessee have credit available from banks?

Commercial paper. If the lessee issues commercial paper, unused bank lines of credit may have to be used to cover outstanding commercial paper in the event the paper cannot be rolled over. In such an event, the lessee may have little flexibility to conduct business or meet its lease obligations.

Restrictive covenants limiting leasing. Some bank loan agreements or long-term debt agreements contain covenants that restrict the volume of equipment leasing.

Long-term debt. Term loans may contain numerous covenants that create a risk of events of default that may accelerate the maturity of the entire loan balance or trigger cross-default clauses in other loan agreements.

Leases. Other leases are disclosed either on the face of the balance sheet or in the footnotes. These obligations are equivalent to senior debt and may control key assets of the lessee.

Subordinated debt. The mere fact debt is labeled subordinated or is, in fact, subordinated to bank debt and/or long-term debt does not mean it is necessarily subordinate to leases or the transaction under consideration. A lessee cannot view subordinated debt as tantamount to "equity" unless such debt is specifically subordinated to leases.

Net worth. Is the net worth "real," or does the net worth include fictitious paper-retained earnings.

Contingent and indirect liabilities. Contingent liabilities such as guarantees and take-and-pay contracts can have a material effect on the creditworthiness of the borrower or lessee. These are contained in footnotes to the balance sheet.

Tax deferrals. If income tax deferrals are large, the likelihood and effect of a future tax rate increase should be considered.

A number of key ratios such as the current ratio and the debt-to-equity ratio should be considered in reaching a credit decision. However, no single ratio or no single calculation is conclusive. The key ratios should be compared with those in previous financial statements in order to identify trends and compare the borrower's statements with those of others in the same industry. Industry financial ratios are available from a number of sources, including Robert Morris Associates.

Cash Flow Analysis

The prospective lessee's cash flow represents the primary source of lease payments. The ability to service lease and debt payments is based not only on the total amount of cash flow but also on the timing of the receipt of those funds.

While depreciation is taken into consideration in computing cash flow, depreciation can be an uncertain source of funds for debt repayment since lessees will find it necessary to reinvest an amount at least equal to annual depreciation expense in order to maintain modern and competitive plant and production equipment.

Most audited financial statements will include a statement called the Consolidated Statement of Changes in Financial Position or Source and Application of Funds Statement. This statement provides much of the data required to determine cash flow and will usually include the following items:

> Funds provided by operations:
> Net earnings.
> Non-cash changes.
> Depreciation and expense.
> Deferred income taxes.
>
> Total cash from operations.
>
> Cash used:
> Increase (or decrease) in short-term debt.
> Increase (or decrease) in long-term debt.
> Additions to property and equipment.
> Dividend payments.
> Stock redemptions or purchases.

Since net earnings represent the major source of cash, it is important to determine the quality of those earnings, which can be affected by some of the following factors:

> An item of extraordinary income or expense. The nonrecurring sale of a business unit or major piece of real estate, for example.
>
> The company's market position compared to competitors'. Is it gaining or losing market share?
>
> The company's products. Which products are the "cash cows"? What is the outlook for future sales of those products?

Inventory pricing methods, such as LIFO, which may significantly understate the current market value of inventory with corresponding effect on earnings and net worth.

Pending litigation that may result in a large claim.

Unfunded pension expenses that may have a priority in case of bankruptcy.

Special tax elections that permit the deferral of the payment of taxes that eventually must be paid.

While past performance provides an indication of future expectations, future lease payments will be generated from future cash flows rather than from historic earnings. In order to properly analyze the projected future earnings of a prospective lessee, pro forma income statements and balance sheets are required for several years in the future. Exhibits 1, 2, 3, 4, 5, and 6 consist of forms that can be used as a starting place for credit analysis.

A complete description of the equipment to be leased is, of course, necessary. If the lessor is unfamiliar with the equipment, it should be inspected. If the equipment is used, it should be inspected and carefully appraised. No more than "market price" plus closing costs should be financed for new or used equipment.

If the lease represents a significant financial undertaking for either the lessee or the lessor, the lessor may wish to make an on-site visit to the lessee in order to meet and evaluate management of the lessee and to examine the workplace for orderliness, work flow, and general housekeeping.

Equipment as Collateral

As in a secured loan, the primary source for payment of a lease in event of default is the equipment that has been leased. However, since equipment leasing typically involves financing of the entire purchase price and since the resale value of used equipment is usually substantially less than original cost, the collateral value of equipment is generally not sufficient to cover the outstanding balance of payments due on the lease even on a present value basis. Some equipment, of course, tends to have greater collateral value than other equipment. Characteristics of equipment that is particularly suitable for leasing are as follows:

New. The equipment will require little maintenance. Clear title is assured.

High potential residual value. The equipment has high upside potential residual value.

EXHIBIT 1 Historical (Projected) Consolidated Balance Sheets

	19___	19___	19___	19___	19___
Assets					
Current assets					
Investments					
Property, plant, and equipment (gross)					
Accumulated depreciation	—	—	—	—	—
Property, plant, and equipment (net)					
Other tangible assets					
Intangible assets (list by type)	═	═	═	═	═
Total assets	═	═	═	═	═
Liabilities and Stockholders' Equity					
Current liabilities					
Long-term debt (less current portion)					
Other liabilities					
Deferred taxes					
Stockholders' equity	—	—	—	—	—
Total liabilities and stockholders' equity	═	═	═	═	═
Quick ratio					
Current ratio					
Receivables turnover					
Inventory turnover					
Short-term debt/current assets					
Working capital ratio					

EXHIBIT 2   Historical (Projected) Consolidated Income Statements

	19____	19____	19____	19____	19____
Sales					
Cost of goods sold	____	____	____	____	____
Gross margin					
Selling and advertising expense					
Depreciation					
General and administrative expenses					
Research and development expenses					
Rent expense					
Interest on long-term debt					
Interest on short-term debt					
Other expenses					
State and federal taxes	____	____	____	____	____
Income before federal income taxes and extraordinary items					
Federal income taxes	____	____	____	____	____
Income before extraordinary items					
Extraordinary items (describe each item)	____	____	____	____	____
Net income	═══	═══	═══	═══	═══
Number of shares used for per-share calculations					
Earnings per share					
Dividends per share					
Return on total assets					
Return on long-term capital					
Return on equity					

(Footnote to explain income tax, current and deferred, and tax loss carryback or carryforward credit, if applicable.)

Essential to the lessee. In the event of financial problems, the lessee will be strongly motivated to pay rent to retain possession.

Marketable. A market exists for resale of equipment after it is used.

Portable. The equipment can be easily transported at the end of the lease.

Special protection in the event of bankruptcy. Federal statutes provide special protection for lessors in the case of aircraft and railroad rolling stock.

Economic life of 5 to 15 years. This enables vesting of the tax depreciation and matches the funding objectives and capabilities of most leasing companies.

Fungible. The equipment is useful to many users. It is interchangeable with other units of the same equipment. It does not

EXHIBIT 3   Breakdown of Sales and Profits

	Net sales				
	19____	19____	19____	19____	19____
(List by product showing dollar amount and percent)					
Total	$ 100%	$ 100%	$ 100%	$ 100%	$ 100%
	Before-tax profit contribution				
	19____	19____	19____	19____	19____
(List by product showing dollar amount and percent)					
Total	$ 100%	$ 100%	$ 100%	$ 100%	$ 100%

have unique characteristics that make it of limited value to other users.

Discrete. The equipment is readily identifiable by description and can be used alone without other pieces of equipment or real estate controlled by the lessee or a third party.

Identifiable. The equipment has serial numbers or characteristics that make the equipment readily identifiable when mixed with other similar equipment of the lessee. Consequently, the equipment can more easily be located for inspection, identified for lien recording, repossessed, or identified at the end of the lease.

Low maintenance cost. The equipment will tend to be returned in good condition if maintenance costs are low.

EXHIBIT 4   Historical (Projected) Consolidated Sources and Uses of
Funds Statements

	December 31,				
	19____	19____	19____	19____	19____
Sources of funds: (List items)					
Total					
Uses of funds: (List items)					
Total					
Required projected financing					

High unit costs. A lease of a single unit or a few large pieces of
equipment is preferable to a lease of many pieces of equipment
because of the administration costs in delivering, booking, inspecting, and disposing of the equipment.

Low rate of obsolescence. The equipment will continue to have
value for the lessee and will have high residual value at the end
of the lease term.

State of the art equipment. Equipment at the start of a new model
cycle will tend to have a higher residual than equipment in use
for many years. For example, a new generation of computers or
aircraft is more desirable than models that have been in use for
many years.

EXHIBIT 5   Schedule of Long-Term Debt

Long-term debt	Year-end before proposed lease	Repayments 19___	19___	19___	19___	19___
List and describe existing debt (bank loans, term notes and so forth)						
Sub-Total						
Proposed lease						
Total						
Ending current portion of debt						
Ending long-term debt						
Lease payments						
Interest expense:						
Short-term debt						
Long-term debt						
Total						

Footnote long-term debt obligations to show:
Interest rate and final maturity.
Source of the financing.
Major financial covenants.

As noted above, a leasing company should not rely upon the collateral value of the leased equipment as the source of repayment. In some cases the collateral value may buttress the credit. However, a lessor should look to the general credit of the lessee for payment as well as any collateral value of the leased equipment.

CREDIT DECISION-MAKING PROCESS

A leasing company must design its credit review process so as to ensure a fast response time. At the same time, the credit review must be thorough and professional. Excessive credit losses will, of course, destroy a leasing company.

A centralized credit review process offers the advantages of control, consistency, and independence from the perceived pressures of the marketing force. On the other hand, a leasing company with widely dispersed offices may choose to decentralize the credit authority for smaller transactions in order to provide a fast response to the requests of the marketing representatives.

In entering into a lease agreement, a leasing company must conduct the same type of credit examination as is conducted by a medium-term

EXHIBIT 6 Schedule of Lease Obligations

	Minimum annual rental payments						Present value (percent)
	19__	19__	19__	19__	19__	Next five-year period	Next five-year period	

	19__	19__	19__	19__	19__	Next five-year period	Next five-year period	Present value (percent)
Capital leases								
Assets:								
(List assets leased)	—	—	—	—	—	—	—	—
Total assets	═	═	═	═	═	═	═	═
Present value of capital leases								
Average interest rate used to compute present value								
Operating leases								
Assets:								
(List assets leased)	—	—	—	—	—	—	—	—
Total assets	═	═	═	═	═	═	═	═
Total rental Payments	═	═	═	═	═	═	═	═

lender. If the leased equipment has value, its collateral value may provide some credit support for the transaction. However, conservative leasing companies are generally concerned with the lessee's ability to pay the lease rentals from future cash flows without reliance on the collateral value of the leased equipment. As noted earlier in this chapter, this involves a comprehensive analysis of the historical performance, current trends, and long-term outlook of the lessee and the lessee's industry. Most lessors simply do not want to enter into a lease in which a credit examination indicates a possible repossession of the leased asset.

Some leasing companies are "asset lenders." In making a credit decision, they rely not only on the credit of the lessee but on the collateral value of the leased equipment and on their ability to resell or re-lease the equipment as sources of the funds from which they will be repaid. Typically, such lessors have considerable expertise in the remarketing of such equipment, and they may also have the facilities or the ability to rebuild or refurbish the equipment. They are familiar with the obsolescence risk involved in the equipment. Vendors are often asset lenders for their own equipment.

Leasing companies with high funding costs sometimes choose to deal with lessees that constitute high credit risks in order to obtain the high lease rates necessary to maintain spreads.

Warrants and conversion features are sometimes used to increase the upside potential of a lessor leasing to a marginal credit.

Lessors that rely on collateral for repayment may improve their credit exposure by demanding security deposits equal to one or more month's rent. Cross-collateralization with other equipment may also be used to improve an otherwise marginal credit. Sinking funds from income generated by the leased asset can be established with trustees to cover lease payments.

Steps in Credit Decision Making

In this section, we will discuss the organization of a credit approval function for a lessor.

The credit decision-making process involves a number of steps:

First, credit information is obtained regarding the prospective borrower or lessee. If the prospect is a public company, this information is readily available. Otherwise, it should be obtained from the prospective lessee as early as practical in the marketing process.

Second, the information is analyzed as discussed previously. A judgment is made regarding the lessee's repayment capability.

Third, the terms and conditions of the lease are discussed and negotiated with the lessee. This part of the credit decision-making process can be critical. Whereas one structure may not be acceptable to the lessor another may be. The questions of collateral, guarantees, and covenants should be discussed and negotiated.

Fourth, the credit analysis together with the terms of the credit are presented to the credit decision-making body as outlined below.

Credit Committee Approval Process

The formal approval process will vary with the size of the transaction. Senior officers of the lessor should have credit authority commensurate with the size of the institution and their respective credit experience. Above a certain exposure level, the credit decision should be made by credit committees following practices consistent with the lessor's parent organization. Also, the credit committee should review credit approvals by officers of the lessor acting within their credit authority.

Procedure

The recommending leasing officer is responsible for preparing an appropriate report recommending the transaction. This report should be prepared in a standard format that is consistent with the general method of presentation used by the parent.

Among other things, the report might include:

1. A descriptive summary of the proposed transaction indicating the lease term, pricing, yield, and ROA. Some lessors also use ROI as an investment criteria.
2. The amount proposed to be advanced and the lease repayment schedule.
3. A summary of present outstandings to the lessee by the lessor and its parent.
4. A summary of the lessee's balance sheet before and after the proposed lease if significantly different as a result of the booked transaction.
5. A description of the lessee, its financial history and outlook, and a similar discussion of the industry of the lessee.
6. Financial statements of the lessee.
7. An analysis indicating the ability of the lessee to meet its obligations from primary and secondary sources.

8. Any special covenants, conditions, guarantees, collateral, and so on, which would influence the credit decision.

Approval of the credit should be formal and in writing. Responsibility for approving the credit should be clear. The purpose of this is to be able to assess responsibility at a later date and to make sure people are assuming responsibility when the credit decision is made.

Meetings of the credit committees should be formal meetings. Minutes of the meetings should be written and circulated. The minutes must indicate the matters considered and the action taken. Attendance by telephone can be permitted.

In lieu of a formal committee meeting, action can be taken by written approval of a formal circulated resolution, although meetings are much more effective in providing exchange of ideas.

Board of Directors

All credit approvals and credit committee actions and minutes should be submitted to the board of directors of the lessor for inclusion as an informational matter in the minutes of the board. The board may formally ratify all credit decisions. However, board members may balk at such blanket ratification of actions that have already been taken. Consequently, a report included in the minutes as a matter of information may be more acceptable and practical.

LEASE PORTFOLIO ADMINISTRATION

Lease administration follows after the credit decision is made. In effect, this function executes the credit decisions that have just been made. The transaction is closed, and the funds are disbursed in accordance with the formal recorded credit decision and authority granted. All original documents relating to the transaction are maintained by the loan and lease administration function. Rents are collected and recorded. UCC filings are made. Lease collateral is inspected upon delivery and periodically thereafter. Any covenants are monitored.

The lease administration function maintains customer credit files that contain all correspondence, resolutions and corporate/partnership documents, credit information, appraisals, loan approval documents, landlord waivers, and UCC filings. Periodic reports are made by the lease administration function on the status of the lease, including any delinquencies in payments.

Lease administration also plays a vital quality control role in lease structure and handling. Lease structure, term, agreements, and documentation should be consistent with the lessor's policies and closely monitored for compliance by lease administration. Exceptions to policy can be made, but should be documented and approved by applicable lessor authorities.

The lease administration function (called "lease administration") should actively take part in the credit decision-making process to make sure that:

- The lessor's policies are sound and competitive.
- The lessor's policies are consistently followed.
- Financial and economic analysis in support of lending recommendations is thorough, applicable, and timely.
- The pricing is adequate and appropriate in relation to the cost of funds and credit risk.

In some cases, leases that originally met the standards established by the credit policy may deteriorate after they are made. If leases are not handled as agreed or renegotiated on a timely basis in a satisfactory manner, they become problem credits. If administered properly, a problem lease need not result in a loss. A certain number of problem leases can be expected in even the highest quality portfolios. The challenge of lease administration is not to avoid risk but rather to manage a credit risk in a business-like manner that will mitigate any loss. Effective administration of a lease portfolio requires early detection of problems and immediate corrective action.

PERIODIC REVIEWS AND REPORTS

A leasing company should have in place a system that provides for periodic reviews of its entire portfolio. To be effective such reviews should be timely, realistic, and coordinated with other areas of the leasing company. A necessary feature of such reviews are devices for taking appropriate action if problems are identified. Examples of periodic review activities include:

Annual review of all lease payment receivable accounts. This includes documentation as well as accounts receivable. It includes compliance with any covenants such as furnishing financial information.

Internal audits and a review after audit. The lessor should have a separate internal audit function for documentation and systems. (This is discussed later in this chapter.) Technical exceptions must then be reviewed by loan administration and corrected within a specific time period.

Internal portfolio quality review. Internal quality assessments of the lease portfolio should be performed by loan administration at specific intervals. This is a critical function of loan administration. It should be required at least once yearly and include firsthand examination of all leases. These reviews should be specific, objective, and require risk grading of leases as discussed below. The quality review will provide the basis for any leases to be charged off and the identification of candidates for the credit-watch list.

A *formal credit-watch list should be established and revised quarterly.* This list highlights problem credits and will result in a plan of action for problem accounts.

A *report of doubtful lease credits.* These leases will be potential or actual charge-offs. This list will be reviewed monthly by executive management, and the status of such should be reviewed with the credit committee and board of directors of the leasing company.

LEASES SHOULD BE GRADED INTO SEVERAL CATEGORIES OF CREDIT STRENGTH IN PERIODIC REPORTS

An internal lease grading program should be adopted as part of the lease review system. Such a grading system, if used properly with objectivity and uniformity, can be a constructive tool in reducing lease losses. A grading system for leases is similar to bank loan grading systems and for consistency should follow the definitions of the leasing company parent. A lease grading system might, for example, be based on the following categories of leases.

Excellent leases. Leases to business borrowers who have a record of five consecutive years of strong earnings, a strong and liquid financial condition, and good cash flow. Lease payments are timely, and performance is in accordance with the lease.

Good leases. Leases to business borrowers who have a record of at least three consecutive years of strong earnings, adequate financial condition and cash flow, and timely lease payments.

Special-mention leases. Leases with potential problems that may, if not corrected, weaken the credit at some future date. The lessee's competitive position may be determining. While the financial condition has not reached the point where lease payments are in arrears, the situation requires monitoring.

Substandard leases. Leases to lessees with unprofitable operations. The collateral value is less than the lease termination value. Lease payments are slow.

Doubtful leases. Rent payments are consistently late, and there exists a possibility of full or partial loss. A serious financial problem exists, and the leasing company must take action to minimize loss.

The frequency of lease grading depends on the quality of the lease. Leases graded excellent need to be reviewed only once a year, usually following receipt of the annual financial statement, unless a drastic change in circumstances requires a more frequent review. Leases graded special mention or substandard should be reviewed at least quarterly.

AUDIT AND REVIEW FUNCTION

An audit and review function is important for effective credit and portfolio controls. The principal purpose of this function will be to audit the credit status and value of the leases on the leasing company's books and compliance with credit policies and procedures. This function can be performed in coordination with the external audit of the financial statements of the leasing company.

Initially, a newly formed leasing company might choose to employ an outside consultant to conduct this review. As the leasing company grows, it can organize an internal credit audit and review function. The credit audit and review function also will provide management with an ability to monitor continuously the performance of the leasing company.

The audit and review function is an after-the-fact evaluation of a credit. Lessees and leases should be rated by their degree of risk using the same grades as lease administration and should include an estimate of risk of any loss with the credit. The review function also should generally evaluate the completeness of the credit files since a lack of documentation or information regarding the credit may in itself impose additional risks on the credit control and leasing process.

The credit audit and review function is as critic and evaluator of the credit decision-making and loan administration functions. For this reason it is important to keep the audit and review function separate from the loan and lease administration function. The audit and review function must also be independent of those areas measured by loan and customer profitability.

The audit and review function should report to the senior management and submit its reports to the board of directors for their information and action if appropriate.

COLLECTION PROCEDURES

Collection problems are, of course, best controlled in the credit approval process and the lease administration process. However, even the best-managed leasing and finance companies have collection problems from time to time and must deal effectively with such situations to maintain yields.

Proper lease administration requires a formal program to monitor lease collections. Monitoring lease receivables serves two purposes:

1. Early identification of lessees that may be in financial difficulty.
2. Identification of lessees that habitually pay late to improve their cash position.

If a lessee is in financial difficulty, the leasing company needs to know about that difficulty as soon as possible in order to plan defensive moves to protect the lease collateral, to encourage the timely payment of rents, and to consider its options.

Dealing with a lessee that habitually pays its rents many days or even weeks after rents are due presents a different type of problem. A lease yield is obviously figured on the basis of prompt payment of the rent. If the rent is not paid promptly, the lessor loses the use of the expected cash flow and its yield suffers accordingly. Most lessors seek to control this problem by including a provision in the lease agreement calling for interest charges on late payments at as high an interest rate as is permitted by law. The enforcement of this provision must be balanced in some instances against the need to maintain the lessee's goodwill. For example, some Fortune 500 companies that are excellent credits have a reputation among suppliers and lessors as being consistently slow payers, and dealing with such companies requires either the collection of the late charges or adjustment of the initial rental rate to take into account the expected delay in the stream of rental payments.

Leasing companies that elect to deal with marginal credits as a conscious strategy become collection agencies. Most of such a company's energies are spent on collection matters.

A leasing company should maintain appropriate reports of delinquent accounts that will inform the management of the leasing company at least on a weekly basis as to the status of all delinquent receivables. When any account is two business days overdue, the customer should be telephoned by a collection officer to determine the reason for the delay. Follow-up calls should be made by both the collection officer and the originations officer until payment is received. If the explanation for late payment or the response is unsatisfactory, the leasing company management should be alerted and additional action taken to collect the account as may be appropriate.

Appropriate general and individual reports regarding delinquent accounts must be provided to senior management of the leasing company on a timely basis.

9

Analysis of Financial Statements of Leasing Companies for Purposes of Lending to or Investing in Leasing Companies

---

A company considering purchasing a leasing company or lending to a leasing company must understand the intricacies of lessor accounting as well as the basic characteristics of a well run equipment leasing business. Lessor accounting is different from that of other types of service businesses or even finance businesses. A potential purchaser of a leasing company or lender to a leasing company that does not appreciate and understand these differences can be misled as to the profitability and creditworthiness of the equipment leasing company.

Earlier we indicated that one method of entering the leasing business was through the acquisition of an existing company and that three methods are commonly used to arrive at a value for a leasing company when considering a purchase. These methods are: (1) the liquidating value method, (2) the price-earnings method, and (3) the return-on-investment method. All of these methods are dependent upon determining the quality of the earnings and balance sheet. While in the final analysis the value of the assets of a leasing company (which consist of the receivables) can only be determined by carefully examining and appraising each credit and document, the starting place for evaluating a leasing company is its financial statements.

In this chapter we attempt to provide some guidelines for gaining a quick overview of a company's financial condition and value through examining its financial statements. Leasing companies like finance companies are highly leveraged as compared to other businesses. This creates opportunities for lenders (including leasing companies) to fund the operations of leasing companies.

Equipment leasing companies use three distinctly different methods to raise funds:

Some leasing companies write leases that they then assign or discount without recourse to a lender that purchases the transactions based on the credit of the lessee. In such situations the lender makes its credit decision on the basis of the lessee's credit standing and the documents describing the lessee's obligations.

In other instances, leasing companies directly borrow the funds used to finance their leases. The loan is secured by a lien on the leases.

Other situations exist in which leases are discounted by a leasing company with recourse to the leasing company in the event the lessee or lessees do not meet their obligations.

PAYOUT LEASING AND NON-PAYOUT LEASING

Leasing companies generally fall into two categories: leasing companies specializing in payout leases or direct financing leases,[1] on the one hand, and leasing companies specializing in short-term non-payout leases, on the other hand. Some leasing companies offer both types of leases.

There are two types of payout leases (or direct financing leases).

One type of payout lease is a true lease in which the lessor claims and retains tax benefits associated with equipment ownership consisting of accelerated tax depreciation (or possibly ITC on transitional property or energy tax credit). In a true lease the lessor owns the equipment at the end of the lease term. This ownership of the equipment at the end of the lease term adds a new dimension to the receivables column in that the lessor usually estimates a value for the equipment at the end of the lease term that it will include as a receivable in its accounting for the lease. In a true lease the lessor expects to recover its investment, its financing costs, and its administrative

---

[1] The term *direct financing lease* is precisely defined in *FAS 13*. The term *payout lease* is often used in the trade to describe a direct financing lease. See David P. Dekker, Nick S. Cyprus and M. Lyman Bates, "Accounting for Initial Direct Costs and Bad Debts under Accounting Standards No. 91," *Journal of Equipment Leasing*, vol. 5, no. 3, Fall 1987.

costs from the lease receivables, the value of any tax benefits, and the value of the equipment at the end of the lease term.

Another type of payout lease is a "conditional sale lease" or "lease intended as security" which is a non-tax-oriented lease in which the lessor expects to recover its investment, its financing costs, and its administrative costs over the lease term from the lease rentals plus any nominal amount the lessee is required to pay for the equipment at the end of the lease term. This type of lease is also called a "money-over-money lease." Ordinarily, one does not think of a conditional sale lease as having any contingent residual receivable for accounting purposes. However, it should be noted that some non-tax-oriented leases are written on a basis whereby the purchase option at the end of the lease may not be so much of a bargain that the lessee is economically motivated or compelled to buy the equipment. In such cases the lessor has only a contingent receivable.

ACCOUNTING METHODS

Under *Statement of Financial Accounting Standards No. 13 (FAS 13)*, "Accounting for Leases," there are two methods by which a leasing company may record leases. One is the finance lease method, and the other is the operating lease method. Briefly stated, the finance method is used for payout leases in which the lessor expects to recover its investment and cost of funds from the lease payments, from any tax benefits associated with ownership of the leased equipment, and from a fairly nominal residual value. The operating method is used for short-term nonpayout leases with substantial residual exposure.

Finance Lease Method

Under the finance lease method the net value of a lease is recorded at the time of closing and consists of the sum of all minimum lease payments to be received and the estimated residual value of the leased equipment. Under FAS 13 and FAS 17 the difference between the cost of the leased equipment and the sum of the receivables is called "unearned income," and a portion of the unearned income plus an amount equal to the provision for doubtful receivables was taken into current income at the time of booking the lease to offset expenses associated with consummating the lease. The remainder of the unearned lease income was taken into income over the term of the lease, commencing with the month the lease is executed, so as to produce a constant periodic rate of return on the net investment in the lease. The expenses associated with consummating the lease are called initial direct costs or, in the parlance of the trade, "front-end load." Under FAS No. 91

issued in 1987, the front loading of revenues to match expensed initial direct costs is not allowed.

Costs which are determined to qualify as initial direct costs are required to be capitalized on the balance sheet as a deferred asset and included as part of the net investment in the lease. This asset is amortized to income over the lease term so as to produce a constant periodic rate of return on the net investment in the lease.

The theory behind either capitalizing or recognizing into income immediately an amount sufficient to offset the expenses associated with consummating the lease is that the sales and administrative costs of originating and booking a lease are largely incurred around the time the transaction is actually booked. If the leasing company is burdened with those costs with no offsetting revenue, its profits will be unfairly penalized in the year in which the lease is originated.

Not all leasing companies that write direct financing leases or payout leases use a front-end load in recording income. A seasoned leasing company with an existing large portfolio may not be adversely affected by failing to capitalize or offset sales and front-end administration expense in the year in which a lease is booked. On the other hand, a growing leasing company would tend to operate at a loss during its growth years if it did not capitalize or offset its sales and front-end administration expenses with a front-end-load charge.

Where a company has charged or is capitalizing direct sales and administration front-end expenses at the time it books a lease, an important question is whether the charge is reasonable. Using the front-end-load charge as a pretext, it is possible for a leasing company engaged in writing direct finance leases to, in effect, report almost its entire expected profit from the lease in the first year of the lease using a high front-end-load charge. Furthermore, if the leasing company has booked a substantial residual value, it can use the front-end load to help flow through to earnings its expected residual value. Obviously, in analyzing the financial statements of a leasing company using the finance method of accounting, an early question is to determine the amount and the reasonableness of the front-end load. This will, in turn, determine the quality of unearned income yet to be booked.

A leasing company that writes non-tax-oriented conditional sale types of leases (also called leases intended as security or money-over-money leases) may recognize interest income on an accrual basis. Alternatively, some leasing companies report such leases as direct financing leases with a front-end load.

Operating Lease Method

Where a leasing company is primarily engaged in writing less than full payout leases, the leases are accounted for as "operating leases" as defined by *FAS 13*. Under this accounting method, the leased property is recorded at cost. This cost less the estimated residual value is typically depreciated over the estimated useful life of the equipment on a straight-line basis. Gains and losses arising from disposition of operating lease equipment are included in operating lease revenues. Rentals are recognized in income over the lease terms as they become receivable according to provisions of the lease agreements.

Where a leasing company engages in both payout (direct financing) leasing and less than full payout operating leasing in a significant way, the portfolios are broken out separately in the financial statements.

ANALYZING THE FINANCIAL STATEMENTS OF A LEASING COMPANY THAT USES THE FINANCE METHOD OF ACCOUNTING

The best way to discuss analysis of the financial statements of a leasing company is to review the highlights of a sample set of financial statements. With this in mind, Exhibit 1 and Exhibit 2 are the balance sheet and profit statement of a hypothetical leasing company called the ABC Payout Leasing Company that is engaged in the business of writing direct financing leases or payout leases. Exhibits 3 and 4 represent the balance sheet and finance statement of a hypothetical leasing company called the Short-Term Leasing Company that is engaged in the business of writing short-term (less than full payout) operating leases. We will review each of these statements.[2]

In Exhibit 1, the balance sheet of the ABC Payout Leasing Company indicates the leasing company is engaged in two types of financing transactions: direct financing leases and extensions of credit in the form of notes. The primary business of ABC Payout Leasing Company is writing direct financing leases most of which are tax-oriented true leases.

Portfolio Maturities

Since the bulk of the assets of the ABC Payout Leasing Company are composed of lease receivables, the footnotes should be consulted to determine additional information regarding the makeup of the lease portfolio. Usually the footnotes will show the receivables broken out by year for the ensuing five years and thereafter. Sometimes the footnotes will actually break out the leases for longer than five years. In

---

[2] The purpose of the financial statements in Exhibits 1, 2, 3, and 4 is to provide a point of reference for discussion purposes. These statements do not include the footnotes that would contain important detailed information regarding the companies under discussion.

EXHIBIT 1

ABC PAYOUT LEASING COMPANY
Balance Sheet
December 31, 19_____
(in thousands)

Assets

Cash	$ 10
Short-term investments	100
Investment in finance receivables:	
Direct financing leases:	
Minimum lease payments	15,000
Estimated residual values	1,500
Less: Unearned income...........................	(3,000)
	13,500
Notes receivable:	
Principal	6,000
Accrued interest	600
Less: Unamortized discount	(500)
	6,100
Groross finance receivables.........................	19,600
Less: Allowance for doubtful receivables............	(400)
Net investment in finance receivables	19,200
Net investment...................................	19,310
Other assets:	
Deferred expense...............................	20
Equipment held for sale or lease..................	1,290
	1,310
Total assets	$18,000

Liabilities and Stockholder Equity

Liabilities:	
Short-term notes................................	$ 4,000
Accounts payable and accrued expense	200
Deferred federal income tax.......................	1,500
Long-term debt:	
Senior	8,300
Subordinated	1,000
Total liabilities..............................	15,000
Stockholders equity:	
Common stock..................................	300
Retained earnings...............................	2,700
Total liabilities and stockholder equity.............	$18,000

any event, this information gives the lender a feel for the type of business done by the company, the credit exposure, and the funding exposure. Some of the most important information regarding the ABC Payout Leasing Company's business will be contained in footnotes to its balance sheet.

EXHIBIT 2

ABC PAYOUT LEASING COMPANY
Statement of Earnings
For the Year Ended December 31, 19_____
(in thousands)

Operating income:	
Earned interest and discount on notes receivable...................	$ 800
Income from leases:	
Direct financing leases	2,000
Gain on disposal of leased equipment...........................	300
Other (late charges, commitment fees, etc.).......................	100
Total operating income	3,200
Costs and expenses:	
Interest and debt expense	1,500
Provision for doubtful receivables...............................	200
Operating expenses...	1,000
Total costs and expenses.....................................	2,700
Earnings before taxes..	500
Provision for taxes on income	150
Net earnings	$ 350

Short- and Long-Term Debt

The liabilities on the balance sheet indicate the breakdown between short-term and long-term debt. The footnotes usually will provide additional information with regard to these maturities.

It is the nature of the leasing business that leases are fixed rate. A conservatively run leasing company will consequently fund its leases with a significant amount of long-term debt. Some leasing companies in the past have made a lot of money by mismatch funding of their leases and relying heavily on short-term borrowings to finance long-term fixed-rate leases. Leasing companies have also lost substantial funds by writing long-term leases and funding short.

In view of the interest rate fluctuations experienced since the late 1970s and early 1980s, one would suppose that leasing companies would be conservative in providing match funding for their payout lease investments. However, greed is a strong motivator, and the profits possible from funding with short-term debt so long as those rates do not climb may cause a leasing company to engage in undue interest rate speculation.

Some conservatively run leasing companies will speculate to some extent with short-term funding of long-term payout lease investments. However, this is generally done on a temporary basis with the leasing company replacing its short-term funding with long-term debt at regular intervals. At no time should a payout leasing company be funded less than 50 percent with long-term debt. In view of the experience since the late 1970s and early 1980s the matched funding will preferably never drop below 60 or 70 percent of assets funded, and at least once a year long-term debt should constitute at least 80 percent (and ideally near 100 percent) of the funding needs for the portfolio.

Of course there is nothing inherently wrong with interest rate speculating by funding payout leases with short-term debt. In such circumstances, however, the lessor and its lenders should recognize that the leasing company is engaged in some other business than just acting as a leasing company formed to make profits from fixed-interest rate spread. It is also an interest rate speculator and lending decisions should be made with that fact in mind.

Debt-to-Equity Ratio

Another question with regard to the debt of a payout leasing company is the debt-to-equity ratio. While the American Association of Equipment Lessors publishes statistics on this type of ratio and other ratios from time to time, these ratios are not benchmark ratios because the sampling used is not necessarily representative of the industry or of the type of leasing company that may be under review. Generally, a leasing company in the business of writing payout type leases will have a debt-to-equity ratio in the range of about five parts debt to one part equity.

This debt-to-equity ratio may be increased by a layer of subordinated debt that is clearly subordinated to the senior debt of a leasing company. Under such circumstances the ratio of senior debt to subordinated debt and capital remains at about 5 or 6 to 1, but the overall debt-to-equity ratio may be based on equity plus subordinated debt.

Some very successful leasing companies are very highly leveraged. General Electric Credit Corporation, for example, is leveraged about 10 to 1, as are some large bank leasing subsidiaries and captive leasing companies. The Japanese leasing companies are typically leveraged 15 to 1 or higher. However, those are unusual situations, and a 5 or 6 to 1 debt-to-equity ratio (or less) is more in line with customary practice in the United States for companies engaged in writing payout leases without a strong parent able and willing to back them.

Residual Values

An unrealistic policy regarding booking residual value can badly distort the earnings, the apparent performance, and the real net worth of a leasing company. Since the investment in finance lease receivables in the example balance sheet for ABC Payout Leasing Company indicates a portion of the receivables is represented by estimated residual values, a question arises as to whether the company is conservative or aggressive in its approach to establishing residual values. The company's policy with regard to residual values used in booking leases should be explained in footnotes to the balance sheet.

Competition for lease business is severe, and in recent years leasing companies have found themselves under increasing pressure to be aggressive in their residual value assumptions for pricing and for booking leases in order to be competitive. Current and future earnings and net worth will be overstated if realistic residual values are not used in booking leases.

The policy followed by a number of the leading leasing companies such as General Electric Credit Corporation and BankAmeriLease Companies is to book a residual value on true leases equal to no more than 50 percent of the estimated quick-sale price of the equipment at the end of the lease term. In the event the estimated quick-sale residual value is higher than 20 percent, these companies then might book a residual somewhat higher than 50 percent of the estimated residual value but never higher than an amount equal to 10 percent of the original equipment cost less than the estimated quick-sale price. For example, if the estimated residual value of an asset was 25 percent of original cost, a conservative leasing company in such a case might book an amount equal to 15 percent of original cost as the estimated (and expected) residual value.

Until the passage of the "Competitive Equality Banking Act of 1987," leasing companies that were subsidiaries of banks could not book a residual higher than an amount equal to 25 percent of the original equipment cost. As this book goes to press leasing companies that are subsidiaries of bank holding companies cannot book a residual higher than 20 percent of the original cost of the leased asset, although this may change in view of the change in the law with regard to subsidiaries of national banks. The general principle under bank regulations is that a lease by a bank or bank holding company subsidiary must be "essentially equivalent to an extension of credit." The regulations recognize that payout leases are similar to extensions of credit and, therefore, a permissible activity. Until the recent change in law, the regulations indicated that non-payout short-term leases were a different type of business not permissible for banks and bank holding companies and their subsidiaries.[3]

[3] For a discussion of bank and bank holding company regulations, see Chapter 10 of Peter K. Nevitt, Frank J. Fabozzi, and Edmond J. Seifried, *Equipment Leasing for Commercial Bankers* (Robert Morris Associates, Philadelphia, PA, 1987).

Leasing companies engaged in tax-oriented true leases will tend to have leases in which they have booked a residual value since under Internal Revenue Service requirements for a true lease, the lessee cannot have a fixed-price nominal purchase option and the equipment must have an estimated fair market value of at least 20 percent of original cost.[4]

Some lessors engaged in non-tax-oriented leasing assume residual values for pricing purposes in order to improve their pricing and competitive position.

Reserve for Losses

Since the ABC Payout Leasing Company is using the finance method of recording its leases, it has established a reserve for losses which is shown as a reduction in the total receivables. This reserve is usually set up at the time the lease is booked. Future lease losses are charged to the reserve. In reviewing the financial statements the question arises as to whether this reserve is adequate. This in turn depends upon the loss experience of the leasing company over a number of years. If the leasing company has only been in business a few years, the loss experience may be misleadingly low.

Some leasing companies that purposely book expected residual values at a very low price may regard and treat the unrealized and unrecognized residuals as assets that may be used as a backup for a loss reserve. If the reserve for doubtful accounts is inadequate, it is possible the leasing company may have hidden assets that provide a contingency reserve for such purpose. However, this should be verified.

Deferred Taxes

Deferred taxes appear on the liability side of the balance sheet. In true leases the yield of the lessor is based in part upon the cash flow expected from claiming and retaining tax benefits associated with equipment ownership, which under current tax laws would consist of depreciation deductions. Since tax depreciation is accelerated, a timing difference results between income for tax purposes and income for book purposes. This is reflected in the deferred tax account. Consequently, the deferred tax account can be viewed as a borrowing from the government at no cost. The larger the deferred tax account the larger the

---

[4] Rev Proc 75–21 is discussed in Chapter 5. The fact the leasing company books a residual value less than 20 percent is not inconsistent with this requirement since the IRS requirement is more or less gauged against a retail value, while a lessor books a "fire sale" or quick liquidation value.

free borrowings. Eventually, however, the taxes must be paid at the tax rate then in effect. If the tax rate increases over the rate assumed at the time the lease was written or after adjustment to a current lower tax rate during the life of the lease, the leasing company will face a larger liability than assumed at the time it wrote the lease or used for book purposes.

Equipment Held for Sale or Lease

The nature and amount of equipment held for sale or lease shown in the asset account should be fully understood. If the leasing company is writing true leases, it will have an inventory of equipment returned at the end of its leases and held for resale. The account will also include leased assets that have been repossessed.

In the case of the ABC Payout Leasing Company a lender or potential investor would want to understand fully the nature of the equipment held for sale or lease. Since the amount shown is high for a full payout leasing company, questions arise as to whether the ABC Payout Leasing Company is taking extraordinary risk in writing leases and having to repossess equipment. Is the equipment off rent realistically valued? How long has the equipment been off rent and what does the company plan to do with it?

A company primarily engaged in the payout lease business does not want to hold inventory for very long. Most well managed leasing companies will make every effort to either sell or release equipment to the original lessee. If the lessee does not want the equipment, the leasing company will dispose of it at a quick-sale price. When a leasing company starts hanging on to equipment hoping for higher prices, it is in the used equipment business rather than in the leasing business. Most of the assets of a payout type leasing company should be either in equipment on lease or in cash—not in inventory sitting in a warehouse.

ANALYZING THE FINANCIAL STATEMENTS OF A LEASING COMPANY ENGAGED IN LESS THAN FULL PAYOUT LEASING

Leasing companies engaged in less than full payout leasing use the operating lease method of accounting. Under the operating lease method of accounting as defined by *FAS 13*, property acquired for lease is recorded at cost. The cost, less an estimated residual value, is then depreciated over the estimated life of the equipment on a straight-line accelerated basis. Rentals are recognized into income over the lease term as they become receivable according to provisions of the lease agreement.

Operating Leases

As noted earlier, the term *operating lease* has different meanings under different circumstances. From the standpoint of a lessor engaged in the payout lease business the term means "less than full payout lease." This usually means that a substantial portion of the lessor's investment will not be repaid from the receivables of the *initial* lease of the equipment.

Payout lessors prefer the finance method of accounting because lease payments under a payout type lease are less than under an operating lease, and the operating lease method of accounting would result in lower reported income during the first years of the lease.

Lessees, on the other hand, have a different view of operating leases. Lessees prefer to characterize leases as operating leases in order to keep them from being capitalized as debt on their balance sheets. Consequently, lessees often characterize *payout* type leases as operating leases.

Thus, under present accounting rules it is quite usual and common for the same lease to be treated as a capital lease or financing lease by a lessor and as an operating lease by a lessee.[5]

This confusion between lessee and lessor accounting definitions can lead to confusion in analyzing leasing companies' financial statements. The point to remember in such analysis is that payout type leasing companies use the finance method of accounting and less than full payout leasing companies use the operating method of accounting.

Where a leasing company is engaged in writing both full payout leases and short-term non-payout leases, the portfolio should be broken down into two separate portfolios using the appropriate accounting method for each portfolio.

The Short-Term Leasing Company

The financials for the Short-Term Leasing Company are shown in Exhibits 3 and 4. Assume that for purpose of this discussion the Short-Term Leasing Company is engaged in the business of writing less than full payout leases and has been in business for a little over three years. Assume it is primarily engaged in writing leases for 24 months for a particular item of equipment in which there is some risk of obsolescence. In order to recover the cost of the equipment and its estimated administrative expenses after claiming any tax benefits of depreciation on the equipment, the Short-Term Leasing Company needs to keep the equipment on lease for at least 40 months at the rentals it is receiving for the first 24 months. Obviously, it can break even by accepting

---

[5] See Chapter 3 for a discussion of accounting for leases.

EXHIBIT 3

SHORT-TERM LEASING COMPANY
Balance Sheet
December 31, 19___
(in thousands)
Assets

Cash..	$ 10
Short-term investment...	90
Investment in operating leases:	
Equipment cost..	12,000
Less: Accumulated depreciation..................................	(3,000)
Net investment in operating leases.............................	9,000
Equipment held for sale or lease	3,000
Total assets...	$12,100

Liabilities and Stockholder Equity

Liabilities:	
Short-term notes..	$ 3,100
Three-year revolver	6,500
Total liabilities	9,600
Stockholder's equity	
Common stock	100
Retained earnings	2,400
Total stockholder equity......................................	2,500
Total liabilities and stockholder equity	$12,100

EXHIBIT 4

SHORT-TERM LEASING COMPANY
Statement of Earnings
For the Year ended December 31, 19___
(in thousands)

Operating income:	
Income from leases:	
Operating leases, net of depreciation.........................	$3,200
Gain (loss) on disposal of leased equipment	(200)
Other (late charges, etc.)....................................	100
Total operating income.......................................	3,100
Costs and expenses:	
Interest and debt expense......................................	1,000
Provision for doubtful receivables	100
Operating expenses..	600
Total costs and expenses	1,700
Earnings before taxes	1,400
Provision for taxes on income	400
Net earnings..	$1,000

smaller rentals over a longer period of time. For purposes of the example, we will assume that the leased equipment will have a useful life of about 60 months although the equipment will not be able to demand the same rents toward the end of the 60-month period as at the beginning. Also assume the leading manufacturer of the particular type of equipment leased by the Short-Term Leasing Company has followed a policy in the past of reducing rentals and the purchase price of its equipment during the third, fourth, and fifth years of the equipment life.

At first glance, the Short-Term Leasing Company seems to be doing very well. It has been in business a little over three years. During that time it has increased its net worth to $2 million, and its net earnings for its most recent year are $1 million. However, on closer examination, a number of factors are disturbing about the Short-Term Leasing Company.

Debt-to-Equity Ratio

To begin with, the debt-to-equity ratio is almost 4 to 1. A company engaged in the business of writing short-term leases is not entitled to the same leverage as a company writing payout leases. Obviously, the risk of renewal of the leases and realization of residual values is much greater. This type of company should be operating with a debt-to-equity ratio of about 2 to 1 rather than 4 to 1. Simply stated, the Short-Term Leasing Company is highly leveraged for an operating lease company.

Equipment Held for Sale or Lease

Another item that raises immediate questions is the amount of equipment held for sale or lease—$3 million or one fourth of the total assets of the company. Although it is not unusual for companies engaged in the business of writing operating leases to hold equipment for release since that is the nature of their business, a question arises as to whether the amount of $3 million worth of equipment off lease early in the fourth year of operations is reasonable. The sales support of the manufacturer should be reviewed.[6] The experience of similar leasing companies should be compared. The condition of the equipment should be investigated. Its location and state of repair should be verified. (A visit to the warehouse may be appropriate.) The plans of the company to get the equipment out on lease should be reviewed. As a matter of fact, in view of the relatively short life of this leasing com-

---

[6] Many manufacturers are long on remarketing promises and short on results. Taking a short-term view, they (or their salesmen) do not make money marketing used equipment.

pany, a question arises as to its ability to release or sell equipment once it comes off lease. Its experience and strategies in that regard should be thoroughly investigated.

A relatively new short-term operating lease company is made to order for a misleading (and not necessarily intentional) pyramiding scheme. Revenues look great so long as ever-increasing amounts of new equipment go on lease. Rents from new equipment pay interest on loans to finance early equipment that is off rent. Until, of course, the house of cards collapses with lenders holding an empty bag. If a short-term operating lease company cannot keep its equipment on rent, it is in real trouble and so are its lenders. Consequently, such companies need to be closely monitored.

Depreciation Policy

A very key consideration is the depreciation policy of the Short-Term Leasing Company. The rents are reported into income as they are received, and it has been assumed depreciation is taken on a straight-line basis over the estimated useful life of the equipment. The policy of the Short-Term Leasing Company in claiming depreciation should be ascertained. Since rents will be higher earlier in the life of the equipment, accelerated depreciation may be more appropriate than straight-line depreciation. Over what term is the company claiming depreciation? Obviously, if it is claiming straight-line depreciation over a longer period of time than most people would accept as the useful life of the equipment, it is inflating its earnings. This is exactly what a great many computer leasing companies did in the early 1970s. Consequently, they reported magnificent earnings by depreciating IBM equipment straight-line over 10 years. When the equipment turned out to have a life of about five years, most of those companies either went bankrupt or became workout situations in which their lenders gained an expensive education regarding the operating method of accounting for short-term leases.

If, in fact, the depreciation claimed is not realistic, then the retained earnings in the stockholder's equity account is incorrect, and the stockholder's equity account merely reflects "soft dollar" book income improperly recorded. If the stockholder's equity account is overstated, the debt-to-equity ratio is much higher than indicated.

OTHER FACTORS

Several other factors common to both payout and non-payout leasing companies should be considered in analyzing leasing companies.

Accounts Receivable

In the case of both the ABC Payout Leasing Company and the Short-Term Leasing Company, the quality of earnings is going to be affected by the quality of the accounts receivable. If leases are being written to poor credits, the earnings of the leasing company will be adversely affected. This is particularly true in the case of the ABC Payout Leasing Company. It is of less concern to a well managed short-term operating lease type of company that has the ability to quickly repossess and release equipment coming off rent.

The most common method of measuring delinquencies is to compare the total balances past due to the total portfolio. An alternative method is to simply compare the amount of rents past due to the total amounts billed for a particular rental period. However, the total portfolio approach provides a better early warning as to the quality of the total portfolio.

The economic return to a leasing company is based upon timely receipt of rental payments. Apart from early warning of credit problems, control of delinquencies is essential to the success of a leasing company. The lease administration function of a leasing company should follow up immediately on delinquencies and track and report those delinquencies to management in accordance with a set policy.[7]

Charge-Offs

As discussed in Chapter 8, leasing companies should have a credit grading system and should periodically review and grade each lease in its portfolio. Leases should be partially or entirely written off as their collectibility warrants. When an account becomes more than 90 days past due, income should no longer be accrued. When an account becomes six months past due, it should be written down to the amount the leasing company can reasonably expect to realize from the sale or release of the asset. Exceptions to these types of policies can be made by the credit committee under special circumstances. However, a leasing company should not allow exceptions to become the rule in writing down its assets.

Lease Administration

Also as discussed in Chapter 8, the lease administration should be conducted in a businesslike manner. The lessor or lender should make appropriate UCC filings and equipment inspections to protect the collateral.

---

[7] See Chapter 8 for a discussion of lease administration.

ROI and ROA

The question frequently arises to quantify what constitutes an acceptable return on investment (ROI) and return on assets (ROA) for a leasing company. This varies a great deal with the type of leasing company, the type of equipment being leased, the objectives of the owners, the conservative or aggressive nature of its accounting practices, and the amount of equity employed.

An after-tax of a ROI of 12 to 15 percent will usually indicate a well managed leasing company provided the accounting practices are reasonably conservative. The ROA of a leasing subsidiary engaged in tax-oriented leasing and dependent upon its parent for tax shelter should exceed the ROA of the parent.

Deferred Tax Liability

In view of the low corporate tax rates provided by the Tax Reduction Act of 1986, a lender or potential purchaser must be concerned regarding the deferred tax liability of the leasing company. If the deferred tax liability is significant, the possibility of a tax rate increase in the future that would increase deferred tax liability, the timing of such an increase, and the ability of the company to pay the tax liability, must be carefully considered.

CONCLUSION

Entering or expanding a leasing business through acquisition of a leasing company can be successfully accomplished by a careful analysis of the financial statements of the target company and an examination of the underlying documents and assets.

Lending to leasing companies can be an attractive activity for a bank or other lender, provided its lending officers are willing and able to spend the time necessary to understand the financial statements of leasing companies. Lenders that have had unpleasant experiences in lending to leasing companies usually have not made that kind of a commitment.

10

Concerns of Manufacturers/Vendors in Establishing a Product Sales Financing Program

---

The importance of having manufacturers provide financing for the sale of new equipment has grown dramatically in recent years. Providing customers with financing packages for purchasing or leasing equipment is viewed as an important marketing strategy for selling products. Purchasers of equipment have become more demanding in seeking financing as a condition to the completion of sales transactions. The lack of financing programs often means lost sales. This is particularly true if competitors offer programs to finance their products.

A manufacturer can provide financing for its customers in many ways. Some manufacturers offer financing directly to their customers. Others have established captive finance companies to achieve greater efficiency in financing their products. Many companies supplement their own sales financing by taking advantage of vendor leasing programs offered by third-party leasing companies.

The purpose of this chapter is to discuss and examine some of the major factors and alternatives a manufacturer (vendor) should consider in providing equipment financing for its customers.

OBJECTIVES OF PRODUCT SALES
FINANCING PROGRAMS

In order to formulate a program for financing its products a vendor must first identify, review, consider, and weigh the objectives and desired results to be achieved by such a program. These objectives generally include as many of the following results as possible:

1. The ability to provide medium- and long-term financing to its customers without carrying a receivable on its balance sheet.
2. The ability to report the transaction as a current sale for financial accounting purposes, thus immediately recognizing the profit on the sale.
3. The generation of maximum cash from the transaction as quickly as possible.
4. The generation of cash without recording a liability.
5. The deferral of federal and state income tax on the sale as long as possible.
6. The ability to claim ACRS depreciation on as much of the retail sale price as possible.
7. Where a cash sale is not possible, the recovery of the entire retail price of the product over the life of the lease or installment sale, plus interest, from the lessee's unconditional obligation to make payments plus the value of any residual that the lessee can reasonably expect to receive.
8. Where the lessee does not own the property at the conclusion of any lease or conditional sale, the realization by the vendor of the maximum residual value.
9. An assignment of any stream of receivable payments for cash on a nonrecourse or limited recourse basis and at a minimum discount.
10. The management of earnings over several years.
11. A structure that will *not* require the lessee/purchaser to account for the transaction as one or more of the following:
    a. A liability on its balance sheet.
    b. A liability prohibited or limited by its loan agreements.
    c. A capital expenditure for budgetary purposes.
12. A 100 percent financing package that is attractive to the lessee/purchaser from the standpoint of term and cost.
13. Isolation of financing profit from the profit on the sale of the product so as to achieve an accurate measure of product profitability.
14. Avoidance of overhead expense involved in billing, collecting, and accounting for receivables.
15. Control of the aftermarket for financed or leased equipment.

16. The ability to finance large amounts of equipment year after year without exceeding borrowing capacity.
17. The programs offered by the vendor should not be so inexpensive and efficient that its products will not attract outside sources of financing.

It is not possible to achieve all of these objectives in a given situation. Some of the objectives are inconsistent with others. An arrangement that permits a vendor to report the sale as currently completed for financial accounting purposes, while at the same time claiming ACRS deductions, challenges the imagination. However, financial executives (spurred on by their operating and marketing departments, that are anxious to achieve sales goals) devote considerable effort to achieve such results.

In the remainder of this chapter, we shall explore a number of the instruments, structures, and vehicles that are used in product sales financing in an attempt to offer vendors some suggestions for balancing their objectives and for achieving the maximum favorable results possible in a given situation.

INSTRUMENTS USED TO FINANCE EQUIPMENT

Instruments used by manufacturers, their captive finance companies, dealers, and third-party leasing companies to finance equipment sales and accomplish their objectives include the following:

Installment sale contracts, in which title passes to the purchaser immediately and the sale price is paid in installments, usually at a fixed rate, for a term that approximates the conservative estimated economic life of the equipment to be financed.

Leases intended as security, in which title passes to the lessee at the conclusion of the lease (*a*) when the last payment is made, (*b*) upon exercise of a bargain purchase option by the lessee, or (*c*) upon exercise of a put by the lessor. As noted in earlier chapters, this type of instrument is called a conditional sale lease, a money-over-money lease, or a hire-purchase agreement.

Tax-oriented true leases, in which the lessee either has no purchase option or the lessee may acquire title at the conclusion of the lease by exercise of a fair-market-value purchase option. True leases include short-term operating leases.

TRAC leases, in which the lessee can purchase a motor vehicle at the end of the lease or during the lease under a terminal rental adjustment clause.

The choice of a particular method of financing may depend on the vendor's federal income tax situation. The federal income tax attributes of the various instruments used to finance equipment are as follows:

Instrument	Entity entitled to ACRS deductions
Installment sale	Purchaser
Leases intended as security	Lessee
True leases (include short-term operating leases and leveraged leases)	Lessor
TRAC leases	Lessor

Another important tax consideration, applicable when the purchase price is paid over a period of time, is the ability of a vendor to elect the installment method of reporting profits on the sale of its products and thus defer income tax on the sale.[1]

ACCOUNTING FOR LEASES AND SALES FINANCED BY LEASES

Product sales reported for financial accounting purposes are the lifeblood of most manufacturers because of the immediate impact of such sales on revenues and earnings. Consequently, it is very important that leases used to finance products will qualify such transactions as sales under *FAS 13*.

Lease Accounting Generally

In a full-payout lease, the lessor recovers substantially all of the normal sale value of the equipment plus interest over the lease term from firmly committed rental payments, any tax benefits, and a conservative residual value.

In an operating lease the lease term is short compared to the useful life of the equipment, and the firmly committed rental payments are for only a fraction of the normal sale value of the equipment. The lessor has a substantial residual risk exposure after taking any tax benefit into account.[2]

---

[1] The Tax Reform Act of 1986 and the alternative minimum tax contain provisions limiting tax deferrals on installment sales under certain circumstances. See Chapter 4.

[2] The term *operating lease* as used in the trade in a vendor financing context generally refers to a relatively short-term lease. The accounting definition is much broader but, of course, includes vendor-type operating leases.

The distinction is important for lessors for financial reporting purposes because full-payout leases generally qualify as sales-type leases under *FAS 13* and result in immediate recognition of earnings on the sale equipment. Full-payout leases may be either leases intended as security or true leases. Operating leases, on the other hand, do not qualify as sales-type leases under *FAS 13*, do not result in a sale for book purposes, and require income from the "sale" (rental) of the equipment to be spread over the life of such leases as it is received. Operating leases are true leases for tax purposes.

Most vendor leases are structured as full-payout leases so far as the lessor is concerned. Industry statistics indicate that less than 10 percent of all equipment leases are other than full-payout leases.

From the standpoint of the lessee, the characterization of a lease as an operating lease is significant because the lessee does not have to capitalize operating leases, whereas *FAS 13* requires lessees to capitalize capital leases or financing leases. Under *FAS 13*, the same lease may be an operating lease for the lessee and a full-payout lease for the lessor. Consequently, careful consideration of the accounting rules of *FAS 13* is appropriate in formulating a vendor financing strategy.

Lessor Accounting under *FAS 13*

On a lessor's books a lease of equipment is classified for accounting purposes under *FAS 13* as either a direct financing lease or a sales-type lease (if manufacturing or dealer profits are involved), provided the lease meets *any one* of the following criteria:

1. The lease transfers ownership of the leased equipment to the lessee by the end of the lease term.
2. The lease contains an option to purchase the leased equipment at a bargain price.
3. The lease term is equal to 75 percent or more of the estimated economic life of the leased equipment (this requirement is applicable only to new property; different rules pertain for used property).
4. The present value of the rentals and the other minimum lease payments is equal to 90 percent or more of the fair market value of the leased equipment (less any related investment tax credit retained by the lessor).

and *both* of the following criteria:

1. Collectibility of the minimum lease payments is reasonably predictable.
2. No important uncertainties surround the amount of unreimbursable costs yet to be incurred by the lessor under the lease.

Lessors recognize interest income from sales-type leases by amortizing unearned income over the lease term so as to produce a constant periodic rate of return on the net lease investment. The net lease investment is the gross investment less unearned income. The gross investment consists of the minimum lease payments (net of any executory costs paid by the lessor) plus unguaranteed residual value accruing to the benefit of the lessor.

A manufacturer records the sales price of products sold and financed under a sales-type lease as the present value of the minimum lease payments (net of executory costs including profit thereon), computed at the interest rate implicit in the lease.[3] A lease that does not meet the criteria for a direct financing lease or a sales-type lease is classified as and must be accounted for as an operating lease. Rents are reported as income over the lease term as they are earned according to the provisions of the lease. For convenience, lessors often refer to direct financing leases or sales-type leases as capital leases.[4]

Conflict between the Lessee and the Lessor as to Classification of a Lease

In a situation where the lessee wants to record a lease as an operating lease so as to keep the lease off its balance sheet and/or out of its income statement except as rental expense, a potential conflict as to classification of the lease exists between the lessee and the lessor, with the lessor, in nearly all cases, wanting to record the lease as a capital lease.

There is, however, no requirement that a lease classified as an operating lease for the lessee must also be classified as an operating lease for the lessor. A lessor and lessee may report the same lease as a capital lease and an operating lease, respectively, for example, by using different interest rates in determining the present value of minimum lease payments: the lessor uses the rate of interest implicit in the lease, and the lessee uses its incremental borrowing rate. The lessee's higher discount rate results in a present value of rentals that is less than that of the 90 percent FASB test, while the lessor's lower interest rate, implicit in the lease, results in a present value greater than that of the 90 percent present value test. Furthermore, the lessor and lessee may arrive at different conclusions on judgmental issues such as the

---

[3] See Chapter 3.

[4] In order to avoid confusion it is important to understand that the term *direct financing lease* is an accounting term used in *FAS 13* and is not the same as a "finance lease" under the tax laws.

estimated economic life, lease terms, bargain purchase options, and so on. Also, the guarantees of residual values may affect the classification.

Leases between Related Parties

Leases between related parties are classified in the same way as similar leases between unrelated parties, except in cases where it is clear that the terms of the transaction have been significantly affected by the fact that the lessee and lessor are related. In cases that fall within the scope of the exception, the classification and accounting must be modified to recognize the economic substance of the transaction. Related parties include a parent and its subsidiaries, an owner company and its joint venturers (corporate and otherwise) and partnerships, and an investor and its investees. Significant influence may be exercised through guarantees of indebtedness, extension of credit, or ownership of warrants, debt obligations, or securities.

Captive Finance Companies

Any vendor engaged in providing extensive product financing for its customers must consider the advantages and disadvantages of providing such financing through a wholly owned finance company. Among the advantages cited as favoring the formation of a captive finance company to provide product financing are the following:

Reduction of borrowing by the parent. Borrowing funds for financing products through a captive finance company will reduce direct borrowings that the parent might otherwise have to make, thus preserving the borrowing capacity of the parent for other needs.

Increase in the overall borrowing capacity. A captive finance company can borrow significant funds on the basis of its own balance sheet. Finance companies generally enjoy a much higher degree of leverage with their lenders than do industrial companies. This makes it possible to use a captive finance company to enhance the total borrowing capacity of the parent corporation.

Access to new sources of funds. The captive finance company may be able to obtain access to long-term fixed-rate borrowings not available to the parent due to other borrowings of the parent, restrictive covenants, regulatory problems, or industry borrowing practices.

Off-balance sheet debt. As this book goes to press, the borrowings of a properly structured captive finance company do not have to be reflected on the balance sheet of its parent company. Rather, the parent company's balance sheet shows only its equity investment in the captive finance company. The balance sheet of the captive finance company is shown in a footnote to the parent's balance sheet. However, the FASB has issued an exposure draft, "Consolidation of all Majority-Owned Subsidiaries," which would require consolidation of all majority-owned financial subsidiaries.[5] In such event companies will still break out the financial statements of their finance subsidiaries and other operations separately in footnotes. Rating services will still rate the debt on financial subsidiaries where appropriate, and such finance subsidiaries will still raise funds separately from the parent.[6]

Debt rating of parent. The debt rating of the parent may not be affected by finance company borrowings within normal debt-to-equity and debt-coverage ratios. Even if the FASB requires consolidation of financial subsidiaries, the rating services will likely separate the parent and financial subsidiary for rating purposes. However, in rating the parent's debt the rating agencies will review the borrowings and operations of the captive finance company to make sure its borrowings, leverage, and operations are

---

[5] Consolidation of the subsidiary would be required even if it has "nonhomogeneous" operations, a large minority interest, or a foreign location. Subsidiaries most commonly excluded from consolidation on the basis of nonhomogeneous operations have been finance, insurance, real estate, and leasing subsidiaries of manufacturing and merchandising enterprises.

Summarized information about the assets, liabilities, and results of operations, or separate financial statements, of previously unconsolidated majority-owned subsidiaries would continue to be provided after those subsidiaries are consolidated. For majority-owned subsidiaries that remain unconsolidated, the use of the equity method would no longer be appropriate and those subsidiaries would be accounted for by the cost method.

The proposed statement would be effective for financial statements for years ending after December 15, 1987. Restatement of comparative financial statements for earlier years would be required.

[6] Under present accounting rules, for a captive finance company to be entitled to treatment as a finance company on its parent's balance sheet, so that the parent will merely report and show the equity investment in the finance company on its balance sheet, the captive finance company must be organized and operated in a manner that establishes its legal, economic, and operating independence to the satisfaction of its outside auditor.

The finance company should be a separate corporation with its own officers and directors, who may also be officers or directors of the parent company. The company should have some employees whose primary duties are to administer the affairs of the finance company. The relationship between the parent company and the captive finance company is typically spelled out in an operating agreement that sets forth the kinds of leases, loans, and other investments that the finance subsidiary is to make. Since the primary function of most captive finance subsidiaries is to finance leases and installment receivables arising from the sale of the parent company's products, the operating agreement typically spells out the obligation of the parent company to tender such leases and receivables to the finance company, as well as the terms and conditions upon which such receivables are to be purchased by the finance company.

reasonable under the circumstances. Also, any guarantees will be taken into account.

Reporting a sale for financial accounting purposes. Financing operating leases through a captive finance company may enable a parent manufacturer to report such transactions as sales for financial accounting purposes rather than as operating leases. Profits on such sales can be reported immediately, whereas profits on operating leases by the manufacturers are measured by manufacturing costs and must be taken in over the life of such leases.[7]

Tax benefits retained. Since captive finance companies are typically more than 80 percent owned, a parent company can claim tax benefits generated by its captive finance company on its consolidated income tax return. Such tax benefits include ACRS depreciation deductions on equipment purchased in connection with leases written by the captive finance company as well as deductions for interest expense on debt.

Tax deferral. Where the parent sells products to the captive that are leased by the captive to customers, the parent may provide installment sale financing to its captive and elect to defer tax by reporting such sales on the installment basis.[8]

Cost accounting and profitability measurement. A manufacturer can more easily determine the performance and profitability of its operations and products by isolating financing revenues from sales revenues.

Increased sales. Where a manufacturer would not otherwise provide financing for its products, there are various marketing-related reasons for financing products that favor the establishment of such a subsidiary. These reasons include customer needs, possible incremental sales to marginal credits if financing is provided, ease in handling trade-ins, and less complicated financing of improvements and upgrades. Many manufacturers confine the activities of their captive finance companies to financing products sold to customers that are unable to obtain financing from conventional sources and to being lenders of last resort for such purchases. Such manufacturers rely on third-party leasing companies and other financing sources to provide any needed financing to their creditworthy customers.

---

[7] However, if a finance company is used fairly exclusively for financing operating leases, the parent will not be able to report the transactions as sales.

[8] See footnote 1.

Control of equipment aftermarket. A captive finance company can be used to maintain better control over the equipment aftermarket than is possible if reliance is placed on outside sources for financing. This can also be a source of substantial profits.

Customer contact. A manufacturer can maintain better customer communication and interface through financing provided by a captive finance company than through financing provided by outside sources.

Qualification to do business. A manufacturer providing direct financing to its customers might have to qualify to do business in states in which it finances or owns equipment under lease, thus subjecting it to state and local income tax, including unitary tax and franchise taxes. Such tax consequences may be less onerous if a captive finance company is used.

Credit control. Removing the approval of credit from the manufacturer and placing it (at least to a greater extent) under executives not directly charged with producing sales results in more rational credit decisions.

Collections. Collections can be pursued more effectively by an independent unit that is less aggressively concerned with future sales than the parent company.

Efficiency. Where a company has several manufacturing units requiring product financing, such service can be provided more efficiently through a single finance subsidiary.

Profitability. A finance subsidiary can earn substantial profits for its parent.

Other finance-related activities. A finance subsidiary can be used as a platform for launching other finance-related activities of the parent.

Control of sales force. Better discipline and control of the sales force may be possible using a captive finance company.

Image. The perception of the stockholders, directors, and the financial community is that the company is doing everything possible to promote sales and earn profits while utilizing the prudent controls inherent in an arm's-length captive financing structure.

On the other hand, there are significant disadvantages and concerns connected with the formation of a captive financing subsidiary. These must be considered and addressed by a manufacturer that is contemplating such a move. Some of them are as follows:

High administrative costs. The administrative and overhead costs of setting up and operating a finance subsidiary may be high enough to outweigh the benefits. This is subjective and must be weighed on a case-by-case basis.

Control by marketing department. The finance subsidiary (or any sales financing by the vendor) will be unduly influenced by the marketing department and may be used as an excuse to provide large discounts and subsidies to promote sales at inadequate margins. This obviously can be controlled by management.

Credit controls. It will be easier for a third party to turn down credits or take a hard line on collections than for the vendor or its captive. Again, this is a matter of control.

An unfamiliar business. A manufacturing company should know what business it is in (manufacturing rather than finance) and stick to it. A manufacturer may have to be in the finance business to meet the needs of customers. It may be in the finance business even though management is reluctant to recognize or admit that it is.

Possible adverse effect on parent's debt rating. Higher leverage is fictitious since analysts and rating services will include debt of the captive with the parent. Debt of the finance subsidiary, however, can have a minimum impact on the parent if the captive is set up and operated correctly and if this is explained to analysts and rating services.

State income tax problems. The state income tax consequences may be adverse. The finance subsidiary tax losses may not be available for tax consolidation with the parent for state income tax purposes. The state unitary income tax theory employed by some states might subject the parent's worldwide income to state income tax in a state even though the finance subsidiary and not the parent is doing business in a particular state. However, these are questions for tax counsel. The effect may be minor.

Similar services may be provided more efficiently by some third-party lessors. As discussed in the next section, the essential objectives can be accomplished more efficiently by using third-party vendor leasing and financing programs. Even if that is done, however, a finance subsidiary may still make sense to take care of unusual transactions or difficult credits.

The ability of a finance subsidiary to leverage its equity capital is based on characteristics that are typical of finance companies, including such characteristics as high liquidity of assets, stable earning power, and diversity of assets and debtors. Therefore, if the captive finance company is to achieve the high leverage of 5 to 1, or as high a leverage as 10 to 1 on the basis of the leverage permitted some well-managed independent finance companies, its portfolio of assets must have similar characteristics. For example, heavy investment in operating leases with a large speculation on residual values will result in low leverage. Also, heavy investment in loans that are long term and illiquid in nature will have a material effect on the ability of the captive finance company to borrow on its own merit. The ability of the captive finance company to borrow from outside sources can, of course, be enhanced by keep-well letters and undertakings by a strong parent company. Furthermore, the parent may even guarantee the debt of the captive finance company, although this is another factor that the outside auditors and rating agencies must take into consideration in determining whether the captive finance company qualifies for off–balance sheet treatment of its debt.

The degree of leverage that a captive finance company may achieve is largely a matter for negotiation between the finance company, its parent, its lenders, and rating services, taking all the factors affecting the debt into consideration. Captive finance companies may have layers of subordinated debt and even junior subordinated debt to support senior debt.

If the captive finance company expects to borrow long-term debt from insurance companies, it should be operated so that interest on debt obligations and other fixed charges are covered by income to the extent currently required to meet the legal requirements for insurance company investment under New York law and the rating requirements of the rating agencies. This may limit borrowings by newly established captive finance companies to short-term debt obligations during the early years of operation, or it may cause term debt to be recourse to the parent. These requirements can sometimes be satisfied by using an existing subsidiary of the parent with a satisfactory operating profit history to house a newly established finance subsidiary.

The independent character and security used to back the borrowings of finance subsidiaries has led some lenders to the conclusion that lending to a finance subsidiary may be less risky in some instances than lending to its parent. Indeed, some lenders may regard the possible bankruptcy of the parent as not necessarily posing a threat to the finance subsidiary. However, recent experience with celebrated credit problems involving manufacturers in the computer, automobile, and farm equipment businesses, among others, has had a sobering effect on those who previously believed that there was a strong likelihood of being able to separate a parent's credit problems from those of its finance subsidiary.

THIRD-PARTY VENDOR LEASE FINANCING PROGRAMS

Product sales financing can be provided directly or indirectly through third-party vendor lease programs. Many companies rely entirely on such third-party vendor programs to provide product sales financing. Some companies utilize such programs to supplement their own product sales financing programs. In any event, a strategy for providing product financing must carefully consider the use of third-party vendor finance programs as an efficient method for achieving product financing objectives.

Third-party vendor finance programs fall into the following four general categories:

Discounting receivables. Discounting receivables of installment sales, full-payout leases, and short-term operating leases is the most commonly used method for financing product sales. Most vendor lease programs fall into this category, and such programs often include partial recourse to the vendor and a best-efforts remarketing agreement by the vendor. Discounting can be done on either a notification (to the lessee) basis or a nonnotification basis and as either a sale of or loan against the receivables.[9]

Non-tax-oriented leases. These transactions consist of non-tax-oriented conditional sale leases or installment sales on a full-payout basis. The lessee is the legal owner and claims the tax deductions for the interest portion of rent payments and ACRS depreciation. These are sometimes called money-over-money leases. (Money-over-money leases may, in turn, be discounted.)

True tax-oriented leases. In true leases, the lessor is the legal owner and claims the tax benefits of the ACRS depreciation. Although such tax-oriented programs are difficult to administer, they have come into increasing use in recent years.

ELSAs. In Equipment Loan Security Agreements (ELSAs), the leases are operating leases and the lendor assumes considerable residual risk.[10] Although ELSAs have been used sparingly, they have attracted attention because of their potential tax and accounting benefits to the vendor. However, the accounting profession does not always agree with the accounting benefits claimed for ELSA programs.

---

[9] Public offerings of securities that are backed by leases on equipment are a new development in vendor financing, which was pioneered in February 1985 by a $200 million offering by Sperry Rand. Automobile lease receivables (CARS) and credit card receivables (CARDS) also have been used to collateralize public offerings of securities. At this time it is not clear whether such a transaction constitutes a sale or a loan for financial accounting reporting purposes. However, if the issuer gives up control and any future benefits from the collateralized receivable, a good argument can be made that a sale occurs except to the extent the receivable is guaranteed.

[10] The lender is dependent on future uncommitted rentals or residual values as well as the base term rentals for recovery of its investment and realization of its spread. Many lessors wrote these types of leases for Storage Technology with disastrous results.

Each of these categories of programs is discussed in more detail later in this chapter.

In third-party vendor finance programs, the manufacturer's objectives continue to be the same as its objectives under its own programs, with particular emphasis on raising cash and being able to report a sale for book purposes. Third-party vendor leasing programs often offer the best avenue for achieving these objectives.

Reasons Vendors Use Third-Party Lessors for Financing Products

Manufacturers use and rely on third-party vendor lease and finance programs for many reasons, including the following:

Balance sheet benefit. Third-party finance programs permit vendors to remove receivables and debt from their balance sheets.

Reporting a sale. Third-party leases and discounting programs permit a vendor to report a transaction as a completed sale for financial accounting purposes, with immediate recognition of profits on the sale.

Cash flow. The vendor realizes immediate cash where a third-party lessor provides financing. The cash realized may exceed 100 percent of the sales price if there is an interest rate differential. Marketing the discount rate variables to the underlying receivables assures both the vendor and the lessor of a limited rate risk.

Tax deferral. Where the vendor finances the sale to the third-party lessor, the vendor can usually defer income tax by electing the installment method, while at the same time reporting the sale for financial accounting purposes. However, the Tax Reform Act of 1986 provides certain limits on tax deferrals resulting from installment sales as discussed in Chapter 4.

Improved tax benefits. By having the vendor's captive finance company enter into a partnership with the third party and the vendor financing the sale price to the partnership, the vendor can claim its partnership share of benefits of ACRS on the retail price, while at the same time using the installment method for tax purposes in reporting the sale. Tax counsel do not agree on the proportion of the partnership permitted the vendor, but 50 percent is generally viewed as safe.

Long-term strategy. Third-party finance programs allow a consistent strategy for providing large amounts of financing for products year after year without exceeding borrowing capacity.

Customer interface. The financing can be arranged so that vendor/customer interface is maintained and the third party is invisible to the customer. Leases assignable to a transparent lender can be written in the manufacturer's name.

Low lease rates. Where the vendor cannot claim tax benefits associated with equipment ownership, a third-party lessor offering true leases can provide low-cost competitive financing for the vendor's products.

Strategy for vendor claiming ITC on retail price. Where the vendor can claim tax benefits but the normal selling price of the equipment is much higher than its manufactured cost, a third-party lender/lessor able to claim ITC on the selling price can offer lower rentals under a lease than can be offered by a manufacturer that can only claim ITC on the manufactured cost.

Reduces debt. Use of a third-party lessor eliminates or lessens the need for the vendor to provide debt for financing its products and the resulting adverse effect on the vendor's financial statements.

Reduces need for a captive finance company. Third-party lessor financing obviates some or all of the need for forming, administering, and arranging debt for a captive finance company.

Preserves resources for incremental sales. Third-party lessor financing preserves a manufacturer's financial resources and may provide extra cash flow for entering into less creditworthy leases and unusually structured leases.

Reduces staffing needs. Reliance on a third-party lessor for product financing lessens the need for staffing that would otherwise be required for direct vendor financing. Third-party lessors can sometimes provide training to the vendor's sales force and assist with customer calls, promotional advertising, and brochures.

Qualification to do business and tax exposure. Third-party financing may eliminate the need to qualify to do business and exposure to state income and franchise tax in states in which equipment is financed.

Lessor administers lease. In the case of a full-service vendor lease program, the lessor relieves the vendor from documentation, billing, collecting, accounting, and other administrative costs.

Image. Using a well-known third-party leasing company with a nationwide presence for financing enhances the image and marketability of the vendor's products.

Training and education. A third-party lessor can be used initially when instituting a vendor financing program, with a view to eventually taking over the program after the vendor's employees gain some experience in lease financing.

Leverage through portfolio rollover. Through discounting existing accumulating portfolios at regular intervals as those portfolios achieve certain investment levels, capital can be raised to finance additional sales. Such a strategy permits a modest amount of capital to be used and to be rolled forward to finance a large volume of sales.

Credit Concerns of a Third-Party Lessor

The credit of lessees is of major concern to a third-party lessor in discounting lease receivables or in directly providing vendor leasing. This is especially true where the lessor has limited or little control over the credit quality of the lessees. Unless the vendor guarantees the credit of its discounted receivables or its lessees, the discount rates or the lease rates of the lessor will necessarily reflect the credit losses expected. Since the third-party lessor will tend to be conservative in assessing the risk of potential credit losses, it is often in the best interests of the vendor to assume some of the credit risk.

Credit support can be provided by the vendor in a variety of ways as discussed below. Where credit support is provided, the vendor may not be able to report a sale, at least to the extent of the guaranteed amount.[11]

Full guaranty. A full guaranty by the vendor that the lessees will make all payments and perform all obligations under the leases it originates or discounts. Such a guaranty might take the form of a guaranteed return or profit on the transaction as well as a guaranty of rentals.

Limited guaranty. A guaranty limited as to amount—for example, a guaranty with total portfolio exposure limited to some dollar amount or some percentage of the transferred receivables or leases. Under this arrangement, the total loss under a particular lease is covered, provided total credit losses do not exceed the dollar or percentage-of-portfolio limitation. This type of arrangement is called a deficiency guaranty, a first-loss guaranty, or an ultimate net loss guaranty. Such a guaranty can be further refined by an assigned credit ranking of the lessee in which "A" credits might have a five percentage first-loss guaranty, while "B" credits would be covered by a larger percentage first-loss

---

[11] Discussed later in this chapter.

guaranty. The percentage first-loss guaranty reflects the true overall creditworthiness of the lessee's leases in the portfolio and allows the vendor to control the recourse liability assumed by controlling the customers accepted for financing.

Remarketing agreement. In a remarketing agreement, the vendor agrees to remarket or assist in remarketing any equipment that comes off lease or is repossessed. These arrangements may provide that the lessor's equipment will be remarketed (*a*) on an equal basis, (*b*) on a priority basis, or (*c*) on a best-efforts basis with similar new and used equipment of the manufacturer that the manufacturer is also seeking to remarket. Such arrangements often spell out in some detail the obligations and incentives inherent in remarketing. Remarketing agreements go hand in hand with limited guarantees to protect the vendor and the third-party lessor from excessive loss.

Right of substitution. An agreement that provides that in the event of a default by the lessee under a lease, the lease can be transferred by the lessor back to the vendor, which will substitute a similar lease.

Cross-collateralization and/or pooling. In cross-collateralization and pooling with other leases, the lessor can look to other leases owned by the vendor as a source of funds for repayment in the event the proceeds from assigned or discounted leases is less than the same specified amount.

Holdback. In a holdback agreement, the transferee of leases retains a portion of the transfer price that is released to the manufacturer on a pro rata basis as the receivables are collected.

A third-party lessor will be inclined to assume greater credit risk if it has an opportunity to participate in the credit decision. Another approach used by lessors and vendors to solve the credit exposure problem is a credit grading system whereby the lessor agrees to accept credits that meet certain standards and takes expected credit losses into consideration in its lease pricing, based on such standards.

Residual Value Concerns

Third-party lessors are sometimes asked to assume considerable risk regarding the residual value of equipment leased under vendor programs utilizing true leases and operating leases. Residual risk and pricing go hand in hand. The greater the residual risk assumed, the lower rentals will be and the more attractive the lease will be to the vendor's customers.

Where a third-party lessor is unwilling to assume the residual risk requested, the vendor may provide residual value support in a variety of ways, including the following kinds of undertakings:

Guaranty of residual value by the vendor. A guaranty that certain residual values will be realized by the lessor is the simple solution. This might be done on a lease-by-lease basis or on a portfolio basis. It might be measured by a dollar amount or in terms of a guaranteed return or profit on the transaction. However, as discussed later, such a guaranty will adversely affect the ability of the vendor to report a sale.

Third-party guaranty. A guaranty by a third party, such as an insurance company, that certain residual values will be realized can be used. This is discussed further below and in Chapter 11.

A pledge of other residuals. A pledge or assignment by the vendor of residual values on additional equipment that the vendor has on lease. The assignment may be exercised in the event that and to the extent that the residuals realized by the third party are less than the amount assumed for pricing purposes.

Pooling residuals. Under a pooling arrangement, the proceeds from sales of equipment residuals in excess of expected residual value by the guarantor and/or the guaranteed party are set aside in a "pool" that is to be used to cover losses where residuals are sold for less than the amount expected.

Remarketing agreement. Under a remarketing agreement, the manufacturer agrees to remarket the lessor's equipment at the end of the lease on either a priority or a best-efforts basis. This might be coupled with a residual sharing arrangement to give the manufacturer a strong motive to perform and obtain the best price available.

Where a true lease is used to finance the vendor's equipment, care must be taken to see that any guaranty of residual does not destroy the true lease character of the transaction.

Adverse Effects on Sales Resulting from Vendor Assuming Risks

Closely connected with any consideration of credit support or residual value support by the vendor is the effect of such support on the vendor's ability to report a completed sale. Under *FAS 5* and *FAS 77*, where the vendor obligates itself to provide credit support or residual value support in excess of an amount equal to 10 percent of the sales price, the estimated loss to be incurred as a result of providing such support is accounted for as a charge to profit and loss. Assume that a vendor is obligated to a third-party vendor lessor under a credit or residual deficiency guarantee for an amount equal to 20 percent of the sales prices financed by the lessor, and assume further that the vendor estimates that its actual loss exposure will amount to 12 percent of the sales prices. The sale would be recorded as follows:

Sales amount	100
Less: Provision for recourse obligation	12
Adjusted sales amount	88

However, if the estimated loss exposure was less than 10 percent, the entire sales price could be taken into income.

Leap of Faith

Sometimes a vendor will ask a third-party lessor to take a "leap of faith" in assuming credit risk or residual risk in lease transactions involving its products on the supposition that without any formal or legal obligation the vendor will make sure that the lessor realizes its credit and/or residual objectives. Usually the lessor is reminded of past satisfactory relationships and favorable experiences with the vendor. In such situations, the vendor wants to be in a position to look its auditor in the eye and assert that it has no legal, binding obligation to support credits or residual values. Since this may not be very comforting to the lessor, a "leap of faith" is required for the lessor to do business on such a basis.

Such arrangements are difficult to characterize. Often, a strong moral obligation exists for the vendor to provide support if called upon to do so. Sometimes existing banking relationships and a reputation for acting in an ethical manner are at stake. Sometimes the very ability to continue in business without third-party financing, in the event of a breach of such a moral understanding, is involved. In the final analysis, an auditor may conclude that the vendor is at risk to support credits or residuals even though a formal legal obligation does not exist.

RESIDUAL VALUE INSURANCE

In some instances, residual value insurance can be used to achieve certain accounting and tax objectives of vendors, lessors, and lessees. However, residual value insurance is expensive. Typically, premiums of up to 10 percent of the amount to be guaranteed are charged at the inception of the lease.

In any event, residual value insurance must constitute an unconditional obligation for the insurer to pay under certain circumstances in order to meet the accounting and tax requirements necessary to achieve the desired results. Policies are not uniform and should be carefully reviewed to make sure the benefits conform to the needs of the parties. The strength of the insurer should be subjected to a credit review, and the exposure of the insurer to particular classes of equipment should be determined.

Another approach to enable the vendor to report a completed sale is to combine a vendor guarantee of up to 10 percent with credit or residual insurance containing a 10 percent deductible. In the above example, the vendor could take the entire sales price into income if it provided a deficiency guarantee for an amount equal to 10 percent of the sales price and protected itself (or the third-party lessor) from additional loss by credit insurance (sometimes called stop-loss credit insurance) or residual value insurance covering the second 10 percent (or perhaps only 2 percent if the vendor's auditors were satisfied with that amount of coverage).

CONCERNS OF LESSEES IN CHOOSING A METHOD FOR FINANCING EQUIPMENT

Lessee concerns in selecting a method for financing equipment involve cost, residual value, and tax consequences. Exhibit 1 summarizes these concerns with respect to four methods of equipment financing—installment sales, conditional sale leases, true leases (full payout), and operating leases.

CONCERNS OF VENDOR/MANUFACTURER WHERE VENDOR/MANUFACTURER IS THE LENDER OR LESSOR

Exhibit 2 summarizes the concerns of the vendor/manufacturer where the vendor/manufacturer is the lender or lessor with respect to six financing methods: installment sales, conditional sale leases, true leases (full payout), operating leases (less than full payout), discounting lease receivables, and equipment loan and security agreements (ELSAs).

CONCERNS OF THIRD-PARTY LESSORS IN PROVIDING VENDOR LEASING PROGRAMS

Exhibit 3 summarizes the concerns of third-party lessors with respect to the same six methods of vendor financing: installment sales, conditional sales, true leases (full payout), operating leases (less than full payout), discounting lease receivables, and equipment loan and security agreements (ELSAs).

WRAP LEASES

As we discussed in Chapter 5, wrap leases are sometimes used by brokers and leasing companies to finance equipment purchases. Typically, wrap leases are used in connection with single purchases of items of equipment costing in excess of $1 million per unit. While wrap leases are not usually vendor leases, manufacturers should be familiar with this structure and its advantages and shortcomings.

Exhibit 1 of Chapter 5 illustrates the steps in structuring a wrap lease that might be used for equipment. As we noted in Chapter 5, the problem with wrap leases is that the Internal Revenue Service may not recognize that the lessor investor has enough of the benefits and burdens of ownership in a given transaction to be considered the owner and lessor of the leased property. Wrap leases are particularly vulnerable in being able to meet Internal Revenue requirements for useful life and residual values.

A manufacturer of equipment has little choice except to be indifferent as to whether wrap leases are used by third parties in financing equipment for its customers. However, manufacturers should be aware of wrap-type structures. If the IRS disallows a large number of wrap leases, litigation between investors and brokers may adversely affect the lessees, and the ripple effect may affect the manufacturer.

EXHIBIT 1 Concerns of Lessees in Choosing a Method for Financing Equipment

Concern	Installment sales	Conditional sale leases	True lease (full payout)	Operating lease
Cost to lessee	The cost reflects the cost of funds to the lessor, and the credit of the lessee, reduced by any subsidy that the manufacturer provides.	The cost reflects the cost of funds to the lessor, and the credit of the lessee, reduced by any subsidy that the manufacturer provides.	The cost is determined by the cost of funds to the lessor, reduced by any tax benefits that the lessor can claim and elects to reflect in the financing cost and by any residual value that the lessor expects to receive and elects to reflect in the price.	The cost is determined by the cost of funds to the lessor, reduced by any tax benefits that the lessor can claim and elects to reflect in the financing cost and by any residual value that the lessor expects to receive (up to any fixed-purchase option) and elects to reflect in the price.
Cost comparison	More expensive than tax-oriented leases. About the same as conditional sale leases.	More expensive than tax-oriented leases. About the same as an installment sale, unless the lease reflects a residual value speculation by the lessor.	The least expensive if the residual has little value to the lessee.	The least expensive where the lessee wants to use the equipment for a short period of time and the lessor expects to realize a higher residual value than the lessee could reasonably expect to realize.

Residual value	The purchaser retains the residual value.	The lessee retains the residual value.	The lessor retains the residual value, except that in certain cases the lessee may control the residual through a purchase option in the range of 40 percent of the original cost.	The lessor retains the residual value and assumes the residual risk in almost all cases. It is possible to give the lessee a purchase option that is not a ''bargain'' purchase option and still have an operating lease.
Tax consequences	The lessee is entitled to the ITC, ACRS depreciation, and interest deductions.	The lessee is entitled to the ITC, ACRS depreciation, and interest deductions.	The lessee is entitled to deduct lease payments. By agreement with the lessor, the lessee can claim the ITC.	The lessee is entitled to deduct lease payments. By agreement with the lessor, the lessee can claim the ITC.
Accounting treatment under FAS 13	A loan liability.	Capitalized as a loan on the balance sheet.	May be capitalized as a loan or treated as an operating lease if structured carefully to meet the requirements of *FAS 13* for an operating lease.	Not capitalized as a loan.

EXHIBIT 2   Concerns of Vendor/Manufacturer Where Vendor/Manufacturer Is the Lender or Lessor

Concern	Installment sales	Conditional sale leases	True lease (full payout)	Operating lease (less than full payout)	Discounting lease receivables	Equipment loan and security agreement (ELSA)
Revenue; maximum cash generation as quickly as possible	Typically, recovery of principal and interest in level payments over the term of the agreement.	Typically, recovery of principal and interest in level payments over the term of the agreement.	Recovery the same as under installment sales or conditional sale lease except that tax benefits are recovered earlier, and residual income, if any, is recovered later.	Lease payments are typically higher than for payout leases or installment sales. However, recovery of manufacturing cost or retail sale price is contingent upon the equipment being kept on rent beyond the initial lease term.	Cash and revenue equal to the present value of lease receivables discounted at an appropriate interest rate taking into consideration the credit risk of the transaction.	Cash and revenue equal to the present value of a lease rent multiple, discounted at an appropriate interest rate. The "multiple" includes firm lease receivables and expected lease residuals.

Attractive to customer from a cost standpoint	More expensive than tax-oriented leases. About the same as a conditional sale lease.	More expensive than tax-oriented leases. About the same as an installment sale.	The least expensive if the residual value has little value to the lessee. (Especially attractive if the lessee cannot claim the tax benefits of the ACRS currently.)	The least expensive where the lessee wants to use the equipment for a short period of time and the lessor expects to realize a higher residual value than the lessee could reasonably expect to realize.	The customer is indifferent since the transaction is between the vendor and the lessor. However, a low discount rate will enable the vendor to offer attractive rates.	The customer is indifferent, except to the extent that attractive financing enables the lessor to offer a low rate.
Tax consequences	The lessee is entitled to the ACRS depreciation and interest deductions. The manufacturer (vendor) can defer income tax by reporting the transaction as an installment sale.	The lessee is entitled to the ACRS depreciation and interest deductions. The manufacturer (vendor) can defer income tax by reporting the transaction as an installment sale.	The manufacturer is entitled to the ACRS depreciation. (However, the manufacturer can only claim the ACRS on the manufactured cost.) The lessee is entitled to deduct lease payments.	The manufacturer is entitled to the ACRS depreciation. (However, the manufacturer can only claim the ACRS on the manufactured cost.) The lessee is entitled to deduct lease payments.	Discounting conditional sales or installment sales and contracts may create tax sales. (But it may not if these are properly structured.) Discounting receivables under true leases does not usually create sales tax.	The ELSA structure is designed to prevent a tax sale by the vendor. Vendors can deduct interest on the "loan."

EXHIBIT 2   (continued)

Concern	Installment sales	Conditional sale leases	True lease (full payout)	Operating lease (less than full payout)	Discounting lease receivables	Equipment loan and security agreement (ELSA)
Accounting: Reporting a sale and profit where the manufacturer is the seller or lessor	Reported as a sale based on the retail sale price.	Reported as a sales-type lease. Profit on the sale based on the present value of the lease payments reported in the year of sale.	Reported as a sales-type lease. Profit on the sale based on the present value of the lease payments reported in the year of sale.	Reported as an operating lease. Profit on the sale reported over the total period of time that the equipment is expected to be on rent.	A sale for accounting purposes, provided the vendor does not retain substantial ownership risks. If the risk can be quantified (through a deficiency guarantee, loan loss experience, etc.), the sales price may be reduced by that amount.	The ELSA structure is intended to create a sale for accounting purposes. However, the accounting profession is far from unanimous that a sale occurs, and another widely accepted view is that the ELSA structure constitutes a loan to the vendor.
Accounting: Reporting a sale and profit where a captive finance company of the manufacturer is the lessor and purchases the asset from the parent.	The vendor reports a sale. The captive reports the installment purchase as a loan. The captive is a borrower rather than a lessee.	The vendor reports a sale. The captive reports the lease as a direct financing lease.	The vendor reports a sale. The captive reports the lease as a direct financing lease.	The vendor reports a sale. The captive reports the lease as an operating lease.	A sale for accounting purposes, provided the vendor does not retain substantial ownership risks.	The ELSA structure is intended to result in a sale for accounting purposes. However, the accounting profession does not agree on this result, and another widely accepted view is that a loan occurs.

Residual exposure by the vendor (or captive) where the vendor (or captive) acts as the lessor	No residual exposure.	No residual exposure, unless the lease contains a purchase option and the lessor assumes a residual value in pricing rents.	Residual exposure to the extent that the lessor assumes a residual value in pricing rents.	Considerable exposure that the residual value will not be realized. However, if rents are based on the retail price and the wholesale price is much less than the retail price, the manufacturer may have little residual exposure in order to recover its cost.	Residual retained by the vendor and residual exposure retained by vendor.	The vendor shifts the residual risk to the lender. However, a vendor is usually obligated to remarket the equipment on a nonpriority basis. Such remarketing arrangements often provide residual value sharing after a target yield has been realized by the lender in order to provide an incentive to the vendor to realize maximum residual values.
How are lease or loan receivables financed?	May be financed with conventional financing or by discounting receivables. A captive finance company may be used as the financing entity.	May be financed with conventional financing or by discounting receivables. A captive finance company may be used as the financing entity.	May be financed with conventional financing or by discounting receivables. A captive finance company may be used as the financing entity.	May be financed with conventional financing or by discounting receivables. A captive finance company may be used as the financing entity.	Conventional financing.	Conventional financing.

EXHIBIT 2 *(concluded)*

Concern	Installment sales	Conditional sale leases	True lease (full payout)	Operating lease (less than full payout)	Discounting lease receivables	Equipment loan and security agreement (ELSA)
Earnings management	Earnings can be managed by moving profits on sales from one year to another by emphasizing outright sales, third-party leases, or installment sales.	Earnings can be managed by moving profits on sales from one year to another by emphasizing outright sales, third-party leases, or installment sales.	Earnings can be managed by moving profits on sales from one year to another by emphasizing outright sales, third-party leases, or installment sales.	Earnings can be managed by moving profits on sales from one year to another by emphasizing outright sales, third-party leases, or installment sales.	Earnings can be managed by discounting conditional sales and installment sales to a third party.	Earnings management by creating a sale, subject to the comments above.
Residual value insurance	Not needed except as additional collateral value for the loan.	Can be used to protect residual value and profits where the residual value is taken into consideration in pricing to strengthen the borrowing base.	Can be used to protect residual value and profits where the residual value is taken into consideration in pricing to strengthen the borrowing base.	Can be used by a vendor to protect the assumption of residual risk and thus offer an operating lease to a lessee (with attendant accounting, budgeting, ratio advantages) while at the same time permitting the vendor to report the sale and protecting its residual exposure.	Can be used as described under other columns to improve the position of the lessee and the lessor. Can be used to protect the lender to the extent that the lender is relying on the residual as a discounted receivable.	Can be used by a vendor to protect the assumption of residual risk in an ELSA and thus to offer an operating lease to a lessee, with attendant accounting, budgeting, and ratio advantages.

EXHIBIT 2 (concluded)

Concern	Installment sales	Conditional sale leases	True lease (full payout)	Finance lease (full payout)	Operating lease (less than full payout)	Discounting lease receivables	Equipment loan and security agreement (ELSA)
Lease documentation	Vendor controls.	Vendor controls.	Vendor controls.	Vendor controls.	Vendor controls.	Vendor controls.	Vendor controls.
Customer interface and origination	By the vendor.	By the vendor.	By the vendor.	By the vendor.	By the vendor.	By the vendor.	By the vendor.
Administration of portfolio (billing, collecting, accounting)	Vendor.	Vendor.	Vendor.	Vendor.	Vendor.	Vendor.	Vendor.
Sale of residual	Not applicable.	Vendor subject to purchase option.	Vendor.	Vendor subject to purchase option.	Vendor.	Vendor.	Vendor subject to residual sharing agreement.
Equipment tracking	Vendor.	Vendor.	Vendor.	Vendor.	Vendor.	Vendor.	Vendor.

EXHIBIT 3 Concerns of Third-Party Lessors in Providing Leasing Programs

Concern	Installment sales	Conditional sale leases	True lease (full payout)	Operating lease (less than full payout)	Discounting lease receivables	Equipment loan and security agreement (ELSA)
Credit coverage	The lender may assume credit responsibility if it approves credits. If the lender does not approve credits, the lender may require the manufacturer to support the credit through guarantees and remarketing agreements.	The lessor may assume credit responsibility if it approves credits. If the lessor does not approve credits, the lessor may require the manufacturer to support the credit through guarantees and remarketing agreements.	The lessor may assume credit responsibility if it approves credits. If the lessor does not approve credits, the lessor may require the manufacturer to support the credit through guarantees and remarketing agreements.	The lessor may assume some or all credit responsibility if it approves credits. If the lessor does not approve credits, the manufacturer is to support the credit through guarantees and remarketing agreements.	The lender may assume some or all credit responsibility if it approves credits. If the lender does not approve credits, the lender may require the manufacturer to support the credit through guarantees and remarketing agreements.	The lender may assume some or all credit responsibility if it approves credits. If the lender does not approve credits, the lender may require the manufacturer to support the credit through guarantees and remarketing agreements.

Residual exposure	No residual exposure.	No residual exposure, unless the lessor speculates on the lessee exercising a purchase option.	Residual exposure to the extent that the lessor assumes a residual value in pricing rents. A remarketing agreement or residual guarantee from the manufacturer may be required.	Considerable exposure that the residual value will not be realized. A remarketing agreement or residual guarantee from the manufacturer may be required. Residual insurance may be required, particularly by a bank holding company subject to regulations limiting residual exposure.	No residual exposure. Investor avoids residual risk.	Considerable exposure that the residual value will not be realized. Residual insurance may be required, particularly by a bank holding company subject to regulations limiting residual exposure. The vendor is usually obligated to remarket equipment on a nonpriority basis. Such remarketing arrangements often provide for sharing residual values after a target yield has been realized by the lender in order to provide an incentive to the vendor.
Funding	Conventional financing or discounting receivables.	Conventional financing or discounting receivables.	Conventional financing, discounting receivables, and/or syndicating to third-party investors interested in tax benefits.	Conventional financing, discounting receivables, and/or syndicating to third-party investors interested in tax benefits.	Conventional financing. Syndication to other vendor lessors.	Conventional financing. Syndication to other vendor lessors.

EXHIBIT 3 (concluded)

Concern	Installment sales	Conditional sale leases	True lease (full payout)	Operating lease (less than full payout)	Discounting lease receivables	Equipment loan and security agreement (ELSA)
Tax consequences	The lessee is entitled to the ACRS depreciation and interest deductions. The inability of the lender to utilize tax benefits is not a limiting factor.	The lessee is entitled to the ACRS depreciation and interest deductions. The inability of the lender to utilize tax benefits is not a limiting factor.	The lessor is entitled to claim the ACRS depreciation and interest deductions. The lessee is entitled to deduct lease payments.	The lessor is entitled to claim the ACRS depreciation and interest deductions. The lessee is entitled to deduct lease payments.	No tax benefits to the lender providing the discounting facility. On the other hand, the inability of the lender to utilize tax benefits is not a limiting factor.	This structure is designed to permit the vendor to claim the ACRS depreciation. However, such a result requires careful structuring.
Lease documentation	Satisfactory to both the vendor and the lessor.	Satisfactory to both the vendor and the lessor.	Satisfactory to both the vendor and the lessor.	Satisfactory to both the vendor and the lessor.	The original lessor provides all lease documentation.	The vendor provides all lease documentation.
Customer interface and origination	By the vendor; third-party involvement is transparent to the customer if assignable.	By the vendor; third-party involvement is transparent to the customer if assignable.	By the vendor; third-party involvement is transparent to the customer. However, the lessor's name appears as the owner unless it is assigned prior to commencement.	By the vendor; third-party involvement is transparent to the customer. However, the lessor's name appears as the owner unless it is assigned prior to commencement.	By the vendor; third-party involvement is transparent to the customer if assignable.	By the vendor; third-party involvement is transparent to the customer if assignable.

Administration of portfolio (billing, collecting, accounting)	Usually by the vendor; however, the lessor performs this function in "full-service vendor leases."	Usually by the vendor; however, the lessor performs this function in "full-service vendor leases."	Usually by the vendor; however, the lessor performs this function in "full-service vendor leases."	Usually by the vendor; however, the lessor performs this function in "full-service vendor leases."	The vendor performs this service; however, the lessor performs this function in some "full-service leases."	Usually by the vendor; however, the lessor performs this in some "full-service vendor leases."
Sale of residual	Not applicable.	Not applicable.	The vendor may assist for a fee.	The vendor will typically be required to assist on a nonpriority and nondiscriminatory basis.	The vendor will typically be required to assist on a nonpriority and nondiscriminatory basis.	The vendor will typically be required to assist on a nonpriority and nondiscriminatory basis.
Equipment tracking	By the vendor.	Usually by the vendor.	By the vendor or the lessor.	By the vendor; but audited by the third-party lessor.	By the vendor but subject to audit.	By the vendor but audited by the lessor.
Residual value insurance	Not needed except as additional collateral value for the loan.	Expensive, but can be used to protect residual value and profits where the residual value is taken into consideration in pricing. Can be used to strengthen the borrowing base.	Expensive, but can be used to protect residual value and profits where the residual value is taken into consideration in pricing. Can be used to strengthen the borrowing base.	Can be used to provide an operating lease to a lessee (with attendant accounting, budgeting, and ratio advantages), while at the same time protecting the lessor's residual risk. (May be expensive.) Can enable a bank to meet regulatory requirements regarding residual exposure.	Can be used as described under other columns to improve the position of the lessee or the lessor. Can be used to protect the lender to the extent that the lender is relying on the residual as a discounted receivable. Can enable a bank lender to meet regulatory requirements regarding residual exposure.	Can be used to offer an operating lease to a lessee with attendant accounting, budgeting, and ratio requirements, while at the same time protecting the lessor's residual risk. (May be expensive.) Can enable a bank to meet regulatory requirements regarding residual exposure.

11

Lessor Concerns with Disposition of Residuals

In a true lease, the lessor is entitled to possession of the leased equipment at the end of the lease term. Many lessors, faced with the return of such equipment for the first time, are understandably apprehensive about taking possession of it and selling it, but if a lease transaction has been well planned from the beginning, the lessor that has booked a conservative expected residual value in pricing its product should be in a position to take advantage of additional opportunities. This chapter addresses some of the concerns a lessor may face and identifies opportunities that arise in connection with the disposition of residuals. This chapter will also aid lessees in negotiating with lessors regarding residual values of leased equipment.

EXAMINATION OF LEASE DOCUMENTATION

The first step a lessor should take when faced with the prospect of the return and disposition of equipment under lease is to examine the lease documentation to determine the rights and obligations of the parties. The following checklist may be helpful in this regard:

1. *Purchase options.* The Internal Revenue Service in Revenue Procedure 75-21 generally takes the position that a fixed-price purchase option at less than fair market value jeopardizes the true lease status of a lease. However, some true leases may contain such options since many tax counsel think fixed price purchase options at estimated fair market value are permissable. The appropriate questions are:
   a. Does the lessee have an option to purchase equipment at the conclusion of the lease for a fair-market-value price?
   b. Does the lessee have an option to purchase equipment at the conclusion of the lease at a fixed price?
   c. Does the lessee have a right of first refusal on a sale of the property?

2. *Puts.* The Internal Revenue Service frowns on puts to the lessee or most third parties. However, such provisions were not uncommon in older leases predating the IRS rules setting such standards. The appropriate questions are:
   a. Does the lease contain a "put" for the lessor?
   b. Does the lessor have the right to require the lessee to purchase the equipment at some price?
   c. Does the lessor have the right to require some third party to purchase the equipment at some price?

3. *Renewal options.* The appropriate questions are:
   a. Does the lessee have an option to renew the lease at the conclusion of the initial term?
   b. For a set rent for a set term?
   c. For a "fair rent"? (The purpose of a fair rent renewal option or a fair-market-value purchase option is to protect the lessee by keeping the equipment from being sold out from under it.)

4. *Notice requirements.* Careful review and attention are necessary to ensure compliance with notice requirements. The appropriate questions are:
   a. Under any of the above circumstances, what steps must be taken by the lessor and the lessee to protect their respective rights?
   b. What notices must be given?
   c. What are the consequences of failure to give notice?
   d. If both the lessee and the lessor are given options, which option overrides the other?

5. *Termination date.* Leases may contain many schedules with different termination dates. Notices may be required for each schedule. The appropriate questions are:
   a. Does all equipment under a lease terminate simultaneously?

    b. Do lease schedules vary the lease terms?

6. *Obligation to return.* The provisions on this matter may strengthen the lessor's bargaining position. The appropriate questions are:

    a. What is the lessee's obligation to return the equipment?

    b. Must the equipment be returned to one location by the lessee?

    c. Must the lessor pick up the equipment?

7. *Maintenance obligation.* Failure by the lessee to properly maintain the equipment in accordance with the terms of the lease may strengthen the bargaining position of the lessor. The appropriate questions are:

    a. What was the lessee's obligation to maintain the equipment in good working order?

    b. What are the consequences or the measures of damages if the lessee failed to maintain the equipment?

8. *Side documentation.* While no ethical leasing company writes secret side letters with true lease or operating lease implications, there are sometimes side documents containing purchase options or other provisions affecting the lessor's rights to equipment under lease. The appropriate questions are:

    a. Does the lessor have all the lease documentation regarding the leased asset?

    b. Are there any side letter agreements or understandings?

9. *Rights of third parties.* At one time, brokers were fairly successful in negotiating a share of the residual value as part of their fee arrangements. Also, manufacturers sometimes retain remarketing rights as part of their price for referrals or credit support to lease transactions involving their products. The appropriate questions are:

    a. Does anyone other than the lessee or lessor have a right to the residual?

    b. Did the lessor ever transfer the residual?

    c. If a broker or packager put the deal together, did the lessor assign to him a part of the residual as a portion of his fee?

    d. If so, does the broker or packager have any obligation or right to take charge of the equipment and dispose of it at the end of the lease term?

10. *Automatic renewal.* If the equipment has little value and the lease automatically renews in the absence of notice by the lessee to the lessor, the best strategy for the lessor may be to do nothing in the hope that the automatic renewal will occur. The appropriate questions are:

    a. Does the lease renew automatically if neither party terminates, either under the lease terms or by law?

    b. If so, at what rent?

11. *Guarantors.* Guarantors often cease to be bound by their guarantees if the lessor and lessee change the underlying contract without the consent of the guarantor. Consequently, guarantors should receive copies of notices sent to the lessee that affect the guarantors' obligations. The appropriate questions are:

    a. Is there a guarantor of the lessee's obligations under the lease?

    b. What notices are required to the guarantor to protect the lessor's rights to assert a claim against the guarantor?

12. *Was the ITC claimed on the transaction, and is it vested?* If claimed ITC is not vested due to the fact that the equipment has been owned for less than the period of time required for vesting, the lessor will probably want to continue ownership until the ITC is vested by releasing the equipment or by holding the equipment for release.

NOTICES

After a lessor has determined the rights and obligations of the parties under the lease, it should take whatever steps, such as notification, as are necessary to protect its rights, and it should be aware of changes in its rights that may result from actions or inactions of the lessee. The lessor may wish to remind the lessee of the lessee's rights as a matter of courtesy and good business relations.

IDENTIFICATION OF EQUIPMENT

In order to sell leased equipment to a third party or in order to obtain an appraisal of the value of the equipment, it is necessary to have a complete and exact inventory describing the leased equipment. In the case of equipment such as trucks, construction equipment, machine tools, material handling equipment, aircraft, and computers, for example, the description should include the name of the manufacturer, the serial number, the model number, the model name, the year of manufacture, a list of all special features and accessories, and the location. In the case of leases of furniture and fixtures or numerous small items of equipment, a complete inventory should be prepared of each and every item of equipment, with the name of the manufacturer, the year of manufacture, the serial number (if any), and the location.

(Photographs of the equipment are also helpful for purposes of identification.)

Such detailed information can usually be obtained from the invoices. Additional information can be obtained from manufacturers' brochures and catalogs.

This information can also be used as a checklist to make sure that the correct equipment and all of the leased equipment will be returned at the conclusion of the lease.

PRELIMINARY APPRAISAL

After determining exactly which equipment is to be returned, the lessor should determine the current fair market value of that equipment.

Knowledge of how the equipment has been used is important in appraising its value. The questions that should be asked include the following:

1. Has the equipment been used 24 hours a day, or has it been used sparingly?
2. Has it been used in a manner that would quickly exhaust its useful life?
3. In the case of a truck, what is the mileage?
4. In the case of a machine or an airplane, what are the hours of use?
5. Has the equipment been well maintained?
6. Is the lessee currently using the equipment?
7. How essential is the equipment to the lessee?

A well-managed leasing company will have conducted periodic inspections of equipment during the lease term to inventory and determine the location and condition of equipment. Its inspection reports will provide valuable information regarding the location, description, and condition of equipment.

Large lessors employ full-time appraisers to determine property values. Most lessors will want to use an appraiser for any sizable transaction. However, quick appraisals can often be made by consulting published reference works that set values for many kinds of typically leased equipment. Examples of such publications for cars, trucks, construction equipment, material handling equipment, and aircraft include the following:

- Cars (*Red Book*), trucks (*Blue Book*), and farm tractors and equipment: National Market Reports, Inc., 900 South Wabash Avenue, Chicago, IL 60605.
- Executive aircraft, commercial aircraft: AVMARK, Inc., 1911 N. Fort Myer Drive, Arlington, VA 22209. Aircraft: *Aircraft Price*

Digest, Aircraft Appraisal Association of America, Inc., Box 59985, Oklahoma City, OK 73159.
● Construction equipment, material handling equipment, trucks, and trailers: *Green Guide,* Equipment Guide Book Company, 3980 Fabian Way, Palo Alto, CA 94303.
● Farm tractors and equipment: *Official Guide: Tractors and Farm Equipment,* Far West Equipment Dealers Association, 1601 N. Main Street #204, Walnut Creek, CA 94596.
● Forklifts: *Green Guide,* Equipment Guide Book Company, 2800 West Bayshore Road, Palo Alto, CA 94303.

The reliability of these publications is attested to by their widespread use. The valuations are based on an assumed state of repair that is usually specified.

Franchised dealers and manufacturers of the equipment to be appraised are often a good source of information. Used equipment dealers are another source of information.

Where reliable sources are not available, the counsel of a reputable independent appraiser should be sought. The cost of consultation with an independent appraiser is well worth the advice in most cases. A lessor may be pleasantly surprised at the value of the equipment or may save time and effort by determining that the value of the equipment is much less than was imagined.

A full-fledged on-site appraisal by the appraiser may be necessary and desirable. However, a consultation will often suffice at this stage of preparing for the negotiations.

ARRIVING AT TARGET PRICE FOR RESALE

"Fair market value" is usually defined as the price at which a willing buyer would agree to purchase an item from a willing seller in a perfect marketplace. The current fair market value of the equipment must be adjusted to arrive at a target sales price that is realistic in view of the expenses and inconveniences the lessor or the lessee will incur.

Plus factors from the lessor's point of view are as follows:

1. The lessee's need for the equipment and the replacement cost.
2. The lessee's obligation (if required by the lease) to return the equipment to the lessor at a designated location at its expense.
3. The lessee's ability (or inability) to return the equipment (as in the case of furniture and fixtures or small items).
4. Dismantling expense the lessee is obligated to pay.
5. The lessee's obligation to have properly maintained the equipment; the lessee's expense of bringing the equipment to the state of working order and maintenance required by the lease.

Negative factors from the lessor's point of view are as follows:

1. Expense in selling the equipment, such as advertising expense and broker's fees.
2. The expense or cost of storage, transportation to storage, and transportation to purchaser.
3. Reconditioning expense.
4. Executive time in handling the sale of equipment.
5. Customer's ill will incurred by insisting on a strict adherence to lease terms.
6. The tax consequences of a sale or lease to a third party.
7. Negative residual, where the equipment has no value and the lessor must dispose of it.

Appraisers generally think in terms of three pricing target zones:

1. Retail price.
2. Wholesale price.
3. Fire-sale or quick-sale price.

In seeking an opinion from an appraiser, all three prices should be sought, and the appraiser should be requested to give an opinion of the value that in his opinion fits the language of the lease.

Although a lessor would naturally prefer to receive a retail price, a wholesale price is a much more realistic target for net proceeds from a sale if the equipment has to be sold to a third party. Such a price opens the door to a broad spectrum of potential buyers. The wholesale price approximates the net price the lessor would receive if a commission were paid to a dealer or an auctioneer employed to complete a sale. The wholesale price permits a sale to a dealer, who can then realize a profit on resale.

With these factors in mind, the lessor should determine an acceptable sales price for the equipment.

If the lessor is willing to renew the lease or obligated to renew the lease at a fair rental value, the lessor should determine:

1. An acceptable renewal term.
2. An acceptable rent.
3. Whether to offer a renewal option.
4. Whether to finance the purchase and, if so, over what term.

NEGOTIATIONS

After the lessor has prepared itself by researching the lease documentation, reviewing the value of the equipment, and determining its negotiating objectives, the lessor is ready to negotiate with its best prospect, the lessee.

If the lessee has any need for the equipment, continued use of the leased equipment at a reduced rent may be much more desirable than immediate replacement. If the lessee does not need the equipment, its obligation under most lease agreements to return equipment to the lessor at some designated location in like-new condition, normal wear and tear expected, can place a considerable burden, and in some cases an impossible burden, on the lessee.

The lessor should commence negotiations by giving the lessee such timely written notice as is required by the lease documentation. In some instances, the lease documentation may require an estimate of the value of the equipment. Care must, of course, be exercised in stating this value.

After appropriate notice, the lessor should commence a dialogue with the lessee on the subject of renewal or return of the equipment. If the lessee desires to renew the lease or to purchase the equipment, negotiations on the terms for such purchase or renewal can commence. So long as the lessor is armed with facts and knowledge of its legal rights, the outcome of such negotiations is a measure of its negotiating skill.

If the parties agree that their mutual negotiating objective is a purchase at fair market value or a renewal at fair rental value, or if such purchase or renewal is called for by the original lease, each party may call in an independent outside appraiser to buttress its respective position. The lessor, being in many cases less familiar than the lessee with the value of the equipment, may seek the help of an appraiser fairly early in such negotiations. This has the added advantage of setting a good tone for the negotiations. It indicates to the lessee that the lessor is serious, knowledgeable, and not willing to settle for a nominal purchase price.

Sometimes lessees expect the lessor to sell or release the equipment at a bargain price. The use of an appraiser aids the lessor in getting the lessee into a frame of mind to pay a realistic price. Most lessees understand that a leasing company cannot sell its assets at unrealistic prices.

Also, lessors should be concerned regarding criticism by shareholders as to whether due diligence was exercised in selling assets acquired at the termination of leases. A sales price that reflects a reasonable relationship to an appraised value guards against such second guessing.

The fee for a written appraisal of the value of used equipment may range from $50 to $500 or more per item, depending on the time the appraiser must spend on the assignment and on whether an inspection is necessary. Fees can run much higher in appraisals of facilities or very large assets. In most cases, the appraisal is based on an assumed state of repair, and an inspection is not necessary. The appraisal fee should be settled with the appraiser prior to performance of the appraisal and after a brief discussion as to the probable result.

The lessee may seek a month-to-month renewal. This should be resisted by the lessor unless the minimum renewal term is sufficient to cover the expected residual. Otherwise, the lessor may compromise its advantageous bargaining position while the lessee satisfies an immediate need or shops for new equipment.

As a negotiating stance adopted with a view to driving a good bargain on a purchase or release, many lessees that need and want to retain leased equipment initially contend they do not need or want the equipment. As in any negotiation, the lessor must determine whether the lessee is "negotiating" or is serious when it declines interest in the equipment. If the lessor is properly prepared going into the negotiations, knows its rights, knows the approximate value of the equipment, and knows its alternatives, the lessor is in a good position to stand pat and smoke out the real intentions of the lessee. Arrangements to have a prospective buyer or two inspect the equipment prior to the end of the lease, while it is still in the lessee's hands, may hasten a decision by the lessee as to its interest in renewing the lease or purchasing the equipment.

The most difficult negotiations involve equipment with little resale value. Furniture and fixture leases are examples. The equipment has low resale value and must be stored and insured pending a sale. The leased equipment may include signs, carpeting, light fixtures, shelving, and custom furniture with practically a negative residual. Typically, the lessee is a retailer that is a fairly skilled negotiator.

The negotiation strength of the lessor centers on the value of the equipment to the lessee, on the lessee's ability to identify and return the equipment, on the cost to the lessee of assembling and returning the equipment if this is required by the lease, and on the lessor's ability to convince the lessee that it can resell the equipment if the equipment is returned.

Negotiations over items such as store fixtures can sometimes become quite spirited and may not be settled until the 11th hour, when the lessor's truck is parked at the loading dock. The ability of the lessor to offer a short-term renewal lease with a purchase option usually provides an equitable and face-saving solution to both parties. It is reasonable to expect some residual on store fixtures.

RETURN OF EQUIPMENT

If the lessee does not want the equipment, arrangements should be made for an orderly delivery from the lessee in accordance with the lease provisions.

The equipment should be in working order. If the lessee has added accessories or units to the leased equipment, the lessor may be entitled to such units.

If the lessee cannot return the equipment, or if the equipment returned has not been kept in good working order, the lessor may be able to declare a breach of the lease agreement whereby the lessee is liable for the fair market value of similar used equipment in good working order. A casualty loss might also be declared under such circumstances if the casualty loss schedule of the lease supports a reasonable recovery.

DISPOSITION OF RETURNED EQUIPMENT

The lessor can undertake the sale or disposition of returned equipment in a number of ways. The most usual way of disposing of used equipment is through an honest used equipment dealer or auctioneer specializing in sales of the particular equipment involved. Generally, such dealers work on commission plus out-of-pocket expenses. Commissions are on a sliding scale based on the size of the deal. Such dealers are often equipped to arrange for the pickup and storage of equipment pending a resale. They can also arrange for the rehabilitation of equipment if that will enhance its value. The reputation of a prospective dealer or auctioneer can usually be checked through banks or leasing companies that have used such services.

If the leased units are fairly standard, a franchised "new equipment" dealer for that brand of equipment probably also sells used equipment taken as trade-ins and may be a good prospect for a purchase or a good agent for resale. Such a dealer can sometimes substantially increase the value of used equipment by rehabilitating the equipment in his own shop as fill-in work. The best arrangement with a franchised dealer is a percentage arrangement. If the dealer is willing to purchase the equipment for cash, he probably expects a quick turnover at a much higher markup than the commission. On the other hand, a cash offer anywhere in the lessor's target price range should be accepted.

Some kinds of equipment, such as cars, trucks, construction equipment, and even private aircraft, are sold at regularly scheduled and well-attended auctions.

The lessor can undertake the sale of the returned equipment itself by advertising the equipment and contacting prospective buyers. There are publications that specialize in advertisements for used machinery and equipment. *Surplus Record* (20 North Wacker Drive, Chicago, IL 60606) consists of a carefully indexed, exhaustive list of used machinery and construction equipment available for sale throughout the United States and is widely consulted by users and dealers seeking secondhand equipment. In addition, various trade publications, magazines, and newspapers are good advertising media for used equipment.

Large established leasing companies have found it economical to have a person or staff engaged full time in the disposition of used equipment. Some leasing companies undertake the rehabilitation of equipment on their own as an aid to resale.

12

Guidelines for Obtaining and Maintaining Adequate Insurance Coverage

Lessees are generally liable for loss of the leased equipment and are generally required to indemnify the lessor from any claims arising out of their use or custody of the leased equipment. Generally, lessees are required to provide insurance against such losses.

A lessor must have a well-administered insurance program to make sure that its lessees provide the insurance they are required to provide and thereby to protect its collateral, to bolster the credit of its lessees in the event of a casualty loss or a personal injury claim, and to protect itself from personal injury or damage claims. Rather surprisingly, such an insurance program is a contract administration item that many lessors tend to neglect. While this chapter is not intended to serve as an exhaustive discussion of the complex subject of insurance, it is intended to provide lessors and lessees with some general guidelines for obtaining and maintaining adequate insurance coverage.

INTRODUCTION

Many types of insurance are available to a lessor, including the following:

1. Property or physical damage insurance (also called hazard insurance).
2. Personal liability insurance (also called public liability, casualty liability, or comprehensive general liability insurance).
3. Product liability insurance.
4. Oil spill insurance.
5. Residual insurance.
6. Political risk insurance.
7. Credit insurance.

This chapter is for the most part limited to a discussion of property insurance (or physical damage insurance) and personal liability insurance. Property or physical damage insurance insures against loss of the leased property from certain named perils or casualties. Personal liability insurance insures against claims arising out of damage or injury to third parties.

In a long-term true lease or payout lease, the lease agreement generally provides that the lessee will provide, maintain, and pay for insurance coverage in certain agreed-upon amounts insuring against physical damage to the leased asset and personal liability claims arising out of the use, ownership, and operation of the leased asset. The extent of property damage liability for which the lessee is liable throughout the lease term is usually set forth in a stipulated loss schedule or casualty loss schedule attached to the lease. (These schedules will be discussed in Section III of this book.) However, it is up to the lessor to make sure that the lessee provides the insurance coverage required by the lease agreement.

The lessor should be identified as "additional insured" in the policies of insurance provided by the lessee. In the case of the physical damage insurance, the lessor should also be named as "loss payee." It is not satisfactory for a lessee to merely furnish evidence that it carries such insurance. At the risk of some repetition, these points will be reiterated throughout this chapter.

Insurance coverage does not remove the lessee's primary liability to the lessor for any property loss or indemnification of any claims against the lessor arising out of or in connection with the lessee's use or custody of the leased equipment.

A lessor or its parent should carry large "safety net" public liability policies to protect the lessor from possible claims arising out of the ownership or use of leased equipment. However, it should be borne in mind that these kinds of policies may not offer continuing protection since a large claim may result in the cancellation of such policies or in the raising of premiums to an uneconomic level.

GENERAL REQUIREMENTS

This chapter features checklists that provide some general standards for the insurance coverage required by a personal property lease. However, the following general requirements should be observed with regard to all insurance provided by a lessee:

1. The insurance should be evidenced by a certificate signed by an authorized officer or an authorized agent of the insurer.
2. Where the required insurance coverage is provided by the lessee's insurance, the lessor should be covered as an "additional insured." In the case of property damage insurance, the lessor should also be a "loss payee." Mere evidence of insurance in force in the lessee's name is insufficient.
3. The lessor should be entitled to the same notice from the insurance company as the lessee in the event of material change in or cancellation of a policy.
4. The limits of the lessee's insurance will generally be adequate for the lessor. Where any question exists as to adequacy of coverage, the help of an insurance consultant should be sought. Aicraft and ship coverage should be discussed with a consultant in all cases.
5. Understanding insurance coverage is dependent on understanding the definitions and terms used. These are not always entirely consistent in the insurance industry. Consequently, the definitions of terms in a particular policy should be carefully read in all cases.

ACCEPTABLE FORM OF EVIDENCE OF INSURANCE

Acceptable evidence of insurance coverage may take the following forms:

1. Duplicate *certificate of insurance, policy,* or *memorandum of insurance,* dated and signed by the appropriate agent, broker, or underwriter. In the alternative, a copy of the *underlying policy* (or excerpts from the policy giving the lessee's interest and the master policy number plus applicable endorsements).
2. All endorsements to the lessor should be indicated on the above-described certificate or policy. Either the insurance company's

preprinted endorsements or the forms suggested later in this chapter can be used. (See Exhibits 1, 2, and 3.)

3. If none of the above are available when equipment is to be purchased, an insurance binder confirmed in writing by an agent or broker can be issued pending receipt of a certificate or policy.

The types of information that should be included in the evidence of insurance are described in the following sections.

PHYSICAL DAMAGE INSURANCE

Property damage insurance is also called "physical damage insurance" and "hazard insurance."

1. *Fire and all risk insurance.* Property at a fixed location is often insured under a *fire insurance policy.* This type of contract is designed to insure property against certain "named perils" at a specific location clearly identified in the policy. Coverage for "all-risk" perils is preferable since only the hazards of flood and earthquake are usually excluded from "all perils." The conditions of these policies are basically dictated by the laws of the various states.

2. *Inland marine floater.* Equipment that is not used at a fixed location and is mobile in nature and equipment that is associated with transportation in some form may be insured on an inland marine floater policy. This form of policy might be used to insure locomotives, shipping containers, pipelines, railroad cars, contractors' equipment, mining equipment, and so forth. This type of policy is more flexible in form than a fire insurance policy and can cover a wider range of perils.

3. *Boiler and machinery.* Certain perils are specifically excluded from either of the above policies. For example, the exposure of any of the leased equipment to explosion of boilers or pressure vessels or to mechanical breakdown and electrical arcing is written only by boiler and machinery underwriters that specialize in assuming these types of risk. In particular, such coverage should be considered in connection with leases of generators, ammonia plants, and steam-generating facilities.

4. *Other transportation.* Property damage to equipment that is licensed for highway use may be written under a *casualty insurance policy.* Automobiles are covered by an *automobile basic policy.* Physical damage on aircraft or on waterborne property is covered by special insurance policies discussed later in this chapter.

5. *Coinsurance.* Coinsurance is physical damage insurance that covers a percentage of the value of the property. Unless a conscious decision is made to permit self-insurance, the lessor should require coinsurance to be 80 to 90 percent of the value. In such a case, on any loss, partial or complete, the insurance will cover only 80 to 90 percent of the value of the equipment.

Checklist for Physical Damage Insurance

The *evidence of insurance* for physical damage insurance (see Exhibit 1 for a typical form) should cover the following points and include the following information:

1. *The underwriting company should meet minimum financial standards.* The most widely accepted method of determining the financial stability of the underwriting company is to refer to the latest volume of *Best's.*[1] A rating of B + BBBB + should be satisfactory as a minimum requirement for properties in the United States.

2. *The lessee is the named insured; the lessor is an additional insured and a loss payee.* The *evidence of insurance* should clearly show that the "named insured" is the lessee and that the lessor is an "additional insured" and a "loss payee." If the lessor can be named only as one of the foregoing, the lessor should probably be identified as an "additional insured." The lessor does not want to be identified as "named additional insured" since that definition imposes additional obligations on the lessor.

3. *Notice of cancellation or material change.* There should be specific reference in the evidence of insurance to the fact that the underwriter assumes the obligation to furnish the lessor written notice of any cancellation of or material change in the policy. For this reason, the lessor's mailing address for notice should be stated.

4. *The policy number and expiration date should be specified.* The policy number and expiration date should be clearly identified. In some instances, policies are written on an "until canceled" basis. This is acceptable if provision is made for adequate notice to the lessor.

5. *Description of property insured.* The description of property insured should specifically describe or encompass the leased

---

[1] *Best's Insurance Reports, Property Liability,* AM Best Company, Park Avenue, Morristown, NJ 07960.

EXHIBIT 1   Form of Physical Damage Insurance Endorsement

PHYSICAL DAMAGE INSURANCE ENDORSEMENT

LESSEE (Named Insured):   LESSOR (Additional Insured and Loss Payable):

_____   _____

Address   Address

_____   _____

_____   _____

It is understood and agreed that at all times no less than $_____ shall be reserved for payment of the interest of the above lessor for any loss or damage to Lessor's property insured under this policy regardless of any other insured interests.

It is understood and agreed that this is a true copy of the original policy as of the date appeearing on this endorsement and, subject to the terms of the loss payable endorsement, no material change will be made in the coverage or conditions in the policy as it pertains to property at _____

_____, without 10 days prior written notice to the lessor, or as provided in said loss payable endorsements, whichever is applicable.

Attached to and hereby made a part of Policy No. _____

OF _____
                                 (Insurance Company)

Effective date of this Endorsement: _____

_____
                                 (Authorized Signature)

Date signed _____

---

item of equipment. In most instances, coverage will not be written to apply solely to the item of equipment that is leased. Instead, the value of the leased item will merely be incorporated with existing insurance on other property owned by the lessee.

The following terms may be found in a fire or inland marine policy describing the property insured:

> *Machinery and equipment; furniture and fixtures; stock.* Coverage is limited to apply only to the particular property falling within these descriptions.
>
> *Contents.* A broader term incorporating the above three items at a named location.
>
> *All personal property.* A very broad term in which coverage *may* extend beyond the confines of a building to include property in the open or elsewhere.
>
> *Improvements and betterments.* Fixed improvements to realty made by a tenant. Under the terms of the lease, the landlord may acquire title to this property.

> *Buildings.* This applies to real property only and will not include any contents.
>
> *Real property.* This is a broader term than *buildings* and may incorporate other structures on the described premises.

6. *Location of property insured.* The location of the insured leased equipment should be specific and should agree with the location shown in the lease. The description and location of property are vital portions of a *fire insurance contract.* If an incorrect address is given or if the property is moved to another location without an amending endorsement, insurance coverage may not exist.

7. *Amount of insurance.* If the amount of insurance is not in excess of the *casualty loss value* in the lease, a judgment must be made as to its adequacy.

   The endorsement should state the amount of physical damage insurance for the leased equipment. In some instances the lessee may not be able to provide insurance in an amount sufficient to pay the casualty loss value in the event of loss. Policies will ordinarily be written on a *replacement-cost basis* (the cost of replacing the item with new equipment of a similar nature at the time and place of loss) or on an *actual-cash-value basis* (the replacement cost less physical depreciation).

   When property owned by the lessor is insured along with other property owned by the lessee, it may not be possible to fully determine whether the amount of coverage is adequate. This will often be complicated by a coinsurance clause. Under this policy condition, the insured lessee agrees to maintain insured coverage for not less than an agreed percentage of the value of all the property insured. If the lessee fails to do so, the lessee participates in the loss to the same extent that the lessee fails to meet its commitment. This can mean that if a lessee has actually purchased one half of the insurance that it agreed to maintain and a loss occurs, the insurance pays only one half of the value of the insured equipment that has been determined to be destroyed. As a result of the above-mentioned conditions, the lessee self-insures and the lessor assumes some degree of financial risk as a creditor.

8. *Mortgages.* If a mortgage is shown in either the certificate or an attached *mortgage clause,* any interest of the mortgage in the *lessor's items of equipment* should be specifically excluded.

   It is not uncommon to find that a mortgage is shown to have an interest in the property of the lessee. Sometimes this interest arises by operation of law.

9. *Perils insured.* The perils of *fire and extended coverage* include fire, lightning, windstorm, hail, smoke, explosion, riot, aircraft, and vehicles. Insurance coverage against these perils should be considered as a minimum requirement. Exposure to loss from other causes could cause the lessor to look for additional coverage. A chemical plant, for example, should have boiler and machinery coverage; a plant located on a floodplain should have flood insurance; and so forth.

10. *Deductible.* If the deductible under a policy is unusually high, a credit judgment must be made by the lessor as to whether it is excessive. In making such a judgment, it should be borne in mind that such losses may have to be assumed at unpredictable periods of time and with unpredictable frequency.

11. *Multiple policies.* In order to obtain an adequate amount of insurance, it may be necessary for a lessee to purchase more than one fire insurance policy. If so, these policies should have concurrent conditions respecting perils, deductibles, coinsurance, and so on. (This applies only to policies intending to cover the *same* perils.)

    Policies providing coverage for *different* perils may apply to the same property and, obviously, will not be concurrent. For example, a *fire and extended coverage policy* may be complemented by a *different in conditions* (DIC) *policy* that extends coverage from a "named-peril" basis to an "all-risk" basis.

CHECKLIST FOR PUBLIC LIABILITY INSURANCE OR COMPREHENSIVE GENERAL LIABILITY INSURANCE COVERAGE

The evidence of insurance for public liability insurance or comprehensive general liability insurance should cover the following points and include the following information:

1. *General requirements for endorsements on certificate.* Public liability insurance endorsements should be included in one document (see Exhibit 2 for a typical form) and should include *all* of the following endorsements:

    a. *Additional insured endorsement.* Note the distinction between "additional insured" and "additional named insured." As in the case of physical damage insurance, the former is the preferred identification and adds the lessor as an additional insured under the liability policy. The latter (or merely "named insured") obligates the lessor beyond the lessor's desire or need.

EXHIBIT 2   Form of Liability Insurance Endorsement

LIABILITY INSURANCE ENDORSEMENT

LESSEE (Named Insured):   LESSOR (Additional Insured)

_____   _____

Address   Address

_____   _____

_____   _____

It is understood and agreed that the above LESSOR is named as an Additional Insured as respects bodily injury and property damage liability arising out of the ownership, maintenance, existence, or use of the properties while leased to the LESSEE the Named Insured, except while such properties are in custody of the LESSOR.

This insurance shall be primary to and non-contributing with any insurance effected by the above additional insured, and the Insurance Company shall be liable to the full extent of those policy limits as set forth in the declarations with respect to the policy obtained by the Named Insured.

The Insurance Company shall give ten (10) days prior written notice to the designated Additional Insured of any cancellation or change in the policy affecting the interest of the Additional Insured. Such notice shall be mailed to the address of the Additional Insured as shown above.

If there is more than one corporation, person, organization, firm, or entity insured under this policy, this policy shall protect each such corporation, person, organization, firm, or entity in the same manner as though a separate policy had been issued to each, but nothing contained herein shall operate to increase the Insurance Company's limits of liability.

All other terms and conditions of this policy remain unchanged. This Endorsement is attached to and hereby made a part of Policy No. _____

OF _____
                        (Insurance Company)

Effective date of this Endorsement: _____

                        _____
                              (Authorized Signature)

            Date signed _____

---

b. Primary insurance endorsement. This endorsement states that the policy to which the lessor has been added as an additional insured will compensate the lessor without regard to excess or umbrella policies that the lessor may have on its own behalf.

    c. *Severability of interest endorsement.* This endorsement states that in the event that more than one entity is named as an insured under the policy, each will be wholly insured as if each had a separate policy. However, nothing contained therein shall operate to increase the insurance company's limits of liability.

    d. *Certification and material change.* The insurer should agree to give the lessor 10 to 30 days' notice of any cancellation or material change.

2. *Named insured and address.* The name and address of the lessee as shown on the insurance policy should be verified to be sure that they coincide with the name and address on the lease agreement. In many cases, the lessee may be a subsidiary company and the parent will be named in the *certificate of insured.* This is satisfactory if it can be verified that the lessee is a subsidiary company and that the policy provides coverage for the parent and *all* subsidiary companies.

3. *Certificate holder and address.* The name of the lessor should be placed in the blank space provided for *certificate holder* or *certificate issued to.*

4. *Name of insurance company.* The name of the insurer should be noted carefully and then reviewed in *Best's.* The insurance company should have a rating of at least B + BBBB + .

5. *Policy number.* The policy number should be shown in the certificate of insurance.

6. *Coverage.*

    a. *Limits of liability.* The limits of liability should conform to those required in the specific lease. The minimum requirement ought to be $1 million combined single limit bodily injury and property damage. However, if the leased equipment is licensed for the road, the minimum limit of liability might be raised to $3 million or even $5 million. Larger leases might require minimum limits of $10 million or $20 million, such as in the case of an entire plant site.

    b. *Policy period.* The policy period should be checked to be sure that the policy is in force at the time the certificate is issued. A suspense file should be set up to notify the lessee approximately 30 days prior to the expiration date that the certificate needs to be renewed.

    c. In some cases, the expiration date will show "until canceled." In such instances, the lessee should be requested to confirm that the coverage is still in force.

7. *Insurance deductible.* Self-insurance to some amount such as $100,000 is not unusual in an insurance policy furnished by a lessee with an adequate net worth of, say, $10 million. Higher

deductibles may be appropriate for larger lessees with larger resources. Self-insurance should be approved by appropriate credit procedures. The lessor should receive the lessee's written confirmation of responsibility for self-insurance.

8. *Comprehensive general liability.* A typical lease agreement provides that the lessee will hold the lessor harmless for all liabilities arising out of the use or custody of the leased equipment. While "all liabilities" may not be subject of insurance, many are. If the lessee has comprehensive general liability insurance, evidence of this coverage should be indicated on the certificate of insurance.

9. *Contractual liability insurance. Blanket contractual liability insurance* provides coverage for all written agreements in which the insured is assuming liability of others. If "blanket contractual" is shown on the certificate, the insured probably has coverage for the "hold harmless agreement" in the lease. However, the insured may sometimes provide contractual liability insurance only for specific lease agreements. If this is the case, contractual liability for the agreement between the lessee and the lessor should be indicated on the certificate.

10. *Notice of cancellation.* The lease agreement should provide that insurance coverage will not be canceled or materially altered unless the certificate holder has been notified 10 to 30 days prior to the cancellation or material change. This condition should be noted on the certificate.

11. *Additional insured.* As noted earlier, the lessor should be shown on the certificate as an "additional insured" for the policies involved. It is also satisfactory if the certificate shows the lessor as an "additional insured" only for the equipment leased under the agreement. The lessor should not be shown as a "named additional insured" since that imposes additional liabilities on the lessor, although it is better to be a "named additional insured" than nothing.

   A mere certificate showing that the insurance is in effect is unsatisfactory.

   The lessor is not a "loss payee" on public liability insurance since any insurance proceeds will be paid to the injured party.

12. *Summary.* It should be noted that the type of equipment subject to the lease should be reviewed carefully. If it is equipment of a permanent nature designed for use on land and not licensed for the road, coverage should be provided under a comprehensive general liability policy. If it is equipment licensed for use on public highways (either self-propelled or trailer type), coverage should be provided under a comprehensive

automobile liability policy. If it is equipment other than these two types, such as aircraft or marine equipment, the help of an insurance consultant should be sought.

AIRCRAFT LIABILITY INSURANCE

The lessee's evidence of aircraft liability insurance should include the following:

1. *Insured.* The lessor should be stated as an additional insured on the policies that are evidenced in the certificate.
2. *Period of insurance.* The time period for which the insurance policies are in effect should be shown.
3. *Geographical limit.* Ideally, the insurance coverage should be on a worldwide basis. In any case, however, the insurance should at least cover all flight routes of the lessee's aircraft, including all possible charter operations. If the coverage is not worldwide, all excluded territories should be listed.
4. *Description of aircraft insured and leased.* The leased aircraft should be described by registration number, and a description of the specific lease agreement should be stated. At the same time it would be helpful to have a statement that the underwriters acknowledge the existence of the (lease) agreement and the other related agreements.
5. *Coverages.* The coverage should include bodily injury and property damage, including passenger liability. These are the major coverages for aircraft liability insurance, excluding ground exposures. Other derivative coverages might also be evidenced. For example, cargo legal liability, although not specifically mentioned in the lease provisions, should be carried by the lessee if it is a commercial airline.
6. *Limit of liability.* Liability coverage for small aircraft is a matter of judgment, although it is desirable for the lessor to have as much coverage as possible.
   The amount of existing liability coverage varies considerably among the major airlines. The limits for world carriers range from $75 million to upwards of $200 million. The adequacy of total limits depends on, but is not limited to, the following factors:
   a. *Seating capacity of aircraft.* An aircraft whose maximum seating capacity is in the range of 150 passengers needs a smaller total limit of liability than does an aircraft that can carry up to 350 passengers.
   b. *Geographic territory over which the aircraft flies.* The proportion of international versus domestic flights is a crucial

factor in determining adequate limits of liability since otherwise only the minimum limits requested may be shown rather than the full limits of liability that are carried by the airline. The amount of liability can be written as a combined single limit or on a per person, per occurrence basis. Ground liability coverages might have an aggregate limitation.

7. *Contractual liability clause.* The certificate should contain a provision indicating that the insurance afforded the lessee in the policies described in the certificate applies specifically to the liability assumed by the lessee under the lease.

8. *Insured.* Both domestic and London aircraft liability policies contain definitions of "named insured" and "insured." The lessor's interests are sufficiently protected when the lessor is included as an "insured" or "additional insured" under the lessee's liability insurance policy with respect to the leased aircraft while it is leased to the lessee. Underwriters of commercial aviation insurance usually do not wish to include the lessor as a "named insured" since this usually involves an automatic provision to cover newly acquired aircraft as well as all aircraft owned or operated by the "named insured."

9. *Severability of interest clause.* The certificate should contain a provision specifying that each of the several "insureds" will have the same protection as would have been available had liability policies been issued individually to each of them.

10. *Breach of warranty.* If possible, the evidence of insurance should stipulate that the insurance provided the lessor will not be invalidated by any act or neglect of the lessee that is a "named insured," whether or not such act or neglect is a breach or violation of any warranties, declarations, or conditions of the policies.

11. *Notice of cancellation.* A 30-day notification by the insurer in case of cancellation has become a fairly standard provision in the insurance policies for large commercial airlines and is also the minimum time necessary to place the insurance elsewhere. This 30-day notification by underwriters should be evidenced on the certificate. The maximum time for notification of cancellation for war risk and allied coverages is about seven days.

12. *Evidence of insurance.* Evidence of insurance may be provided by:
    a. A certified copy of the insurance policy.
    b. Certificates of insurance issued by the insurer.
    c. Certificates of insurance issued by independent aircraft insurance brokers.

d. For noncommercial aircraft, such evidences should consist of a certified copy of the policy or a certificate of insurance issued by the insurer.

In the case of commercial aircraft, there is a practical advantage to the lessor in relying on a broker's certificate of insurance since it is much less complex than the multiple certificates provided by insurers. However, a broker's certificate often contains a disclaimer to the effect that the broker is not an insurer and has no liability of any sort under the policies evidenced or as a result of its certification.

AIRCRAFT HULL INSURANCE

The essential elements to be contained in the lessee's aircraft hull insurance are as follows:

1. *Description of insurance.* Many of the terms and provisions for hull insurance are similar to those for aircraft liability insurance. The details on the insured, the term of insurance, the geographic limits, and the description of the aircraft are all essentially the same as those that have been presented in the preceding section.

2. *Coverage.* The coverage of hull insurance should be "all risk" or "physical loss" or "damage to the aircraft."

3. *Amount of insurance.* An aviation hull policy is usually an agreed-value contract. In case of total loss or constructive total loss, the insurer pays a fixed, agreed-upon sum of money rather than the actual cost value, which includes depreciation, as under most insurance contracts. This "agreed" or "insured value" is probably the most important component of all the certificates. Under this description of insured value, the following information should be included:

    a. *The leased aircraft and their respective insured values.* With this knowledge of the insured values, the lessor can determine whether the insured values of the aircraft are at least equal to the *stipulated loss value* specified in the lease agreement.

    b. *Self-insurance.* A description of deductibles, if any, as well as of all other types of self-insurance or coinsurance that may be applicable to the leased aircraft, should be clearly set forth. There may be different deductibles for "in motion," "not in motion," and "ingestion" losses. It is important that all types of deductibles and coinsurance agreements be evidenced so that the lessor can be assured that the lessee is keeping within the self-insurance limitations of the lease.

4. *Identification of the lessor as the "insured."* The lessor should be identified as an "insured" and/or a "loss payee." The lessor should also receive a waiver of subrogation from the lessee. Legal counsel should review the designations of the "insureds" or "loss payees" to determine whether all appropriate parties are covered.

5. *Loss payable clause.* The loss payable provision, which specifies that all losses will be adjusted with the lessee and payable (depending on the size of the loss) to the lessee or the lessor for the account of all concerned, should be evidenced on the lessor's certificate (see Exhibit 3). In addition, the amount of the insured loss should be stated since the size of this figure determines to whom the money is paid. The lessor can then determine whether this figure is the same as that contained in the lease agreement.

6. *Breach of warranty.* This provision in the hull policy functions similarly to the breach of warranty provision in the liability policy. However, since the hull policy is an agreed-value, first-party contract, underwriters are not as reluctant to provide this provision in the hull policy as they are to provide it in the liability policy.

7. *Notice of cancellation.* Refer to the previous section, "Aircraft Liability Insurance."

8. *Evidence of insurance.* The evidence of insurance should be essentially the same as that described in the previous section, "Aircraft Liability Insurance."

9. *War and allied risks.* Due to social unrest, hijackings, and irregular warfare, the war risk exclusion and war risk coverage for both hull and liability insurance have changed considerably in the past few years. Airline policies contain the common North American War Risk Exclusion, which eliminates coverage for the following five areas:

   a. War and related acts.

   b. Detonation of atomic or nuclear weapons.

   c. Unlawful seizure, diversion, or exercise of control of aircraft.

   d. Strikes, riots, civil commotion, and so forth.

   e. Vandalism, sabotage, and so forth.

Generally, most exclusions except war risk can be suspended for an additional premium.

MARINE INSURANCE

Marine insurance takes two forms: protection of the physical entity itself through *hull insurance* and protection against the liabilities aris-

EXHIBIT 3   Form of Loss Payable Endorsement

LESSOR'S LOSS PAYABLE ENDORSEMENT

With respect to the interest of   , its successors and assigns (hereinafter called the Lessor), in its capacity as Owner and Lessor of the Property insured under this policy, the Company hereby agrees as follows:

1. Amounts due under this policy shall be payable to the Lessor.

2. The insurance under this policy, as to the interest only of the Lessor, shall not be impaired in any way by any change in the interest of the Lessee in the property described in this policy, or the transfer of possession thereof without the consent of the Lessor, or by any breach of warranty or condition of the policy, or by any omission or neglect, or by the performance of any act in violation of any terms or conditions of the policy or because of the failure to perform any act required by the terms or conditions of the policy or because of the subjection of the property to any conditions, use or operation which would cause the policy not to be in effect, or not permitted by the policy or because of any false statement concerning this policy or the subject thereof, by the Lessee or the Lessee's employees, agents or representatives; whether occurring before or after the attachment of this agreement, or whether before or after the loss or damage. It is understood, however, that the wrongful conversion, embezzlement or secretion by the Lessee is not covered under this policy, unless specifically insured against and premium paid therefor.

3. In the event of failure of the Lessee to pay any premium or additional premium which shall be or become due under the terms of this policy, the Company agrees to give written notice to the Lessor of such nonpayment of premium and it is a condition of the continuance of the rights of the Lessor hereunder that the Lessor when so notified in writing by the Company of the failure of the Lessee to pay such premium shall pay or cause to be paid the premium due within ten (10) days following receipt of the Company demand in writing therefor. If the Lessor shall decline to pay said premium or additional premium, the rights of the Lessor under this Lessor's Loss Payable Endorsement shall not be terminated before ten (10) days after receipt of said written notice by Lessor.

4. If the Company elects to cancel this policy in whole or in part for nonpayment of premium or for any other reason, the Company will forward a copy of the cancellation notice to the Lessor at its office specified hereinafter concurrently with the sending of notice to the Lessee but in such case this policy shall continue in force for the benefit of the Lessor only for ten (10) days after written notice of such cancellation is received by the Lessor. In no event, as to the interest only of the Lessor, shall cancellation of any insurance under this policy covering the property described in the policy be effected at the request of the Lessee before ten (10) days after written notice of request or cancellation shall have been given to the Lessor by the Company. In the event of cancellation of this policy the unearned premium shall be paid to the Lessor, provided the Lessor has advanced the premium.

5. If there be any other insurance upon the property described in this policy, the Company shall be liable under this policy as to the Lessor only for the proportion of such loss or damage that the sum hereby insured bears to the whole amount of valid and collectible insurance of similar character on said property under policies held by, payable to and expressly consented to by the Lessor, and to the extent of payment so made the Company shall be subrogated (pro rata with all other insurers contributing to said payment) to all of the Lessor's rights of contribution under said other insurance.

6. Whenever the Company shall pay to the Lessor any sum for loss or damage under this policy and shall claim that as to the Lessee no liability therefor exists, the Company at its option may pay to the Lessor all obligations due or to become due from the Lessee to the Lessor under the terms of the Lease between the Lessor and Lessee and the Company shall thereupon receive a full assignment and transfer, without warranty or recourse, of the Lessor's rights under the Lease covering the property that is the subject of the insurance and of the property itself, but no subrogation shall impair the right of the Lessor to recover the full amount of its claim.

7. The coverage granted under this policy shall continue in full force and effect as to the interest of the Lessor only, and the Lessee agrees to pay premium therefor, for a period of ten (10) days after expiration of said policy unless an acceptable policy in renewal thereof with loss thereunder payable to the Lessor in accordance with the terms of this Lessor's Loss Payable Endorsement shall have been issued by some insurance company and accepted by the Lessor. In the event of a loss not otherwise covered during the extended ten (10) day period herein referred to, an annual policy covering the same hazards to the property insured under the original policy shall be issued and accepted by the Lessor.

8. Should the Lessor or its agent take possession of the property covered by this policy, insurance under this policy shall continue for the term thereof for the benefit of the Lessor, but in such event any privileges granted by this Lessor's Loss Payable Endorsement which are not also granted to the Lessee under the terms and conditions of this policy, or under other riders and endorsements attached thereto shall not apply to the insurance hereunder as respects such property.

9. All notices herein provided to be given by the Company to the Lessor in connection with this policy and this Lessor's Loss Payable Endorsement shall be mailed to or delivered to the Lessor at its office at
            Nothing herein contained shall be held to vary, alter, waive or extend any of the terms, conditions, agreements or limitations of the policy, other than as above stated.

For attachment to and forming part of Policy No. _____ of the _____

_____
(INSURANCE COMPANY)

Countersigned on this _____ day of _____, 19 ___, at _____

                                        By _____
                                                (AUTHORIZED REPRESENTATIVE)

ing out of the use and ownership of the vessel through *protection and indemnity insurance.* Marine insurance is a specialized type of insurance and is best handled by a competent marine insurance broker. It is generally tailored to suit the needs of the individual vessel charterer.

Sometimes the U.S. government, through the Maritime Administration, is involved in marine insurance because of the guarantee of loans issued under Title XI of the Merchant Marine Act of 1936, as amended. Most contracts provide that the U.S. government must approve any form used for hull and liability insurance coverage. This has resulted in an accepted format in the wording and insurance requirements of sections of leases and bareboat charters where the U.S. government is involved.

Evidence of insurance should be as discussed earlier in this chapter.

The following is a checklist for the insurance requirements of vessels under construction (*builder's risk insurance*) or vessels completed and navigating (*navigating insurance*):

1. *Insured assured.* The lessor should be identified in the evidence of insurance as an insured. All interests, financial or otherwise, should be named.
2. *Loss payee.* The lessor should be named as a loss payee up to a certain amount, which should match the amount stated in the lease agreement.
3. *Types of insurance.*
    a. Builder's risk insurance should be provided up to the ultimate completed contract value.
    b. Navigation insurance should provide an agreed amount during operation (not less than the stipulated loss value).
4. *Limits of coverage.* The limits of coverage should be adequate to protect the lessor and should be consistent with the lease.
5. *Term of insurance.* The term that the insurance is in force should be stated.
6. *Name of insurance company.* The name of the insurer should be noted carefully and reviewed in *Best's.* The insurance company should have a rating of B+BBBB+.
7. *Navigation limits.* The navigation limits should be broad enough to encompass all of the areas in which a vessel might operate.
8. *Waiver of subrogation.* The evidence of insurance should provide a waiver of subrogation against the lessor.
9. *Material changes.* No material change should be made without 30 days' prior written notification to the lessor.
10. *Cancellation.* The lessor should receive 30 days' prior written notice of cancellation.

11. *Expiration.* The lessor should receive adequate prior notification of expiration.

PRODUCT LIABILITY INSURANCE

Generally, perils resulting from product liability will be covered by the lessee's personal liability policy. Moreover, holding a finance lessor liable for a product that it did not sell, select for lease, or manufacture is extending liability far beyond a party that could have been responsible for some product defect.

However, in this era of consumerism and the desire of some to require others to provide a risk-free world, the risk of product liability for a lessor requires attention. This is particularly true where a lessor sells or re-leases property coming off lease to third parties. Consequently, a lessor should consider product liability insurance coverage.

ADMINISTRATION AND FOLLOW-UP

A leasing company must set up adequate procedures to provide follow-up for the lessee's insurance.

The time to make sure that the correct insurance is in force is at the outset of the lease, prior to delivery of and payment for the equipment. The lessee's legal department and financial officers negotiating the lease will place a high priority on obtaining the required insurance when it is a condition for closing. Once the closing has been completed, however, the priority becomes much less important to the lessee's legal and financial people, and the lessee's insurance department or agent may become much less responsive in providing the lessor with evidence of insurance.

The insurance departments of lessee companies that do a great deal of leasing are set up to provide required insurance certificates to lessors with a minimum of time and effort on the lessors' part. Not surprisingly, it tends to be more difficult for lessors to deal with and obtain needed information from lessees that do not lease extensively or that employ insurance agents with little experience in leasing.

In all cases, however, it is essential for the lessor to make provision for follow-up procedures to make sure that the required insurance is obtained and remains in effect. The lessor should also be aware that the liability of the lessee for property damage throughout the term of the lease is limited to the amounts set forth in the stipulated loss or casualty loss schedule of the lease. If the residual value of the leased equipment exceeds the residual value contemplated in the stipulated loss or casualty loss schedule, the lessor may have an uninsured property loss exposure.

SECTION III

Lease Documentation for a Nonleveraged Lease Transaction

13

Terms of a Typical
Nonleveraged Lease

This chapter and the two that follow contain an overview of the subject of lease drafting. They highlight some of the concerns and objectives of both lessees and lessors. Generally speaking, there is no mystery about lease documentation. Lease language should be arranged in a logical order and written in plain language that a concerned party can understand and interpret.

In 95 percent of all equipment lease transactions, the lease documents are rarely looked at (except for routine lease administration) after they are signed and the transaction is originally closed. Disputes or misunderstandings between the parties occur in the remaining 5 percent of all lease transactions. It is in these transactions where lease documents are of great importance in determining the relative rights and obligations of the parties.

Since there is no way to initially determine which transactions will constitute the critical 5 percent, all leases have to be drawn and negotiated on the basis that a precise clear understanding of the rights and obligations of the parties may be necessary at some future date.

Note: The authors acknowledge extensive help and review by attorney Cheryl A. Knowles in preparation of this chapter and the two that follow.

OVERVIEW OF LEASE DOCUMENTATION

The lease documents set forth and discussed in these three chapters include the following:

1. Lease.
2. Schedule attached to and incorporated into the lease, that describes the equipment to be leased as well as the term and rental for each unit.
3. Purchase agreement assignment.
4. Request to purchase.
5. Acceptance supplement.
6. Guaranty.
7. Consent to removal of personal property.
8. Financing statement.

The lease and the schedule are the key documents. The lease is discussed in this chapter and the schedule in the next chapter. The other seven documents are discussed in Chapter 15.

The example lease used as a basis for discussion is not presented as the ideal lease from the standpoint of either the lessor or the lessee. Rather, it is a fairly typical lease upon which either the lessor or the lessee may build, depending on the facts and circumstances of a particular transaction and possibly also on the parties' negotiating skills.

The example lease analyzed has been drafted as a nonleveraged "true lease" of equipment designed for equipment costing $50,000 to $5 million. The lease document for a leveraged lease would contain nearly all of the same provisions. Although the example lease is a true lease, most of its provisions would be the same in a lease with a nominal purchase option (sometimes called a "money-over-money lease") treated for tax purposes as a conditional sale (see Chapter 5).

The concept of drafting the lease and schedule separately is based on the supposition that the lease will cover several units of equipment with different depreciable lives, different lease terms, and different delivery dates. The lease constitutes the master document with provisions that are applicable to most kinds of equipment. The schedule supplements the lease and sets forth the particulars regarding the lease of specific units of equipment such as the description of the equipment, the purchase price, the lease term, the rental rate, the location, the casualty loss value, and any additional provisions applicable to the particular equipment described in the schedule. A schedule can pertain to one unit of equipment or to a variety of equipment, depending on what is convenient for the lessee and lessor. The schedule can be amended to add equipment, or completely new schedules can be added to the lease. Later schedules can incorporate the terms of the master lease by reference even if this was not originally contemplated by the master lease. An arrangement utilizing a master lease and schedules saves both the lessee and the lessor time and legal expense once the master lease is in place.

The treatment of each section of the lease and schedule is broken down, where applicable, into the following parts:

1. The actual language of the section in the example lease.
2. A summary of the points covered in the section.
3. A discussion of the section, with consideration given to possible points of contention and alternatives available to the parties.

THE LEASE

The lease agreement is the basic lease document. Provisions in the lease agreement typically cover the following subjects which are numbered for easy reference to correspond to the example lease sections discussed in this chapter.

Introduction: Identification of lessor and lessee.
Introduction: Agreement between lessor and lessee.
1. Procurement, delivery, and acceptance.
2. Term, rent, and payment.
3. Warranties.
4. Possession, use, and maintenance.
5. Taxes.
6. Risk of loss; waiver and indemnity.
7. Insurance.
8. Default.
9. Return of units.
10. Assignment.
11. Further assurance.
12. Late payments.
13. Effect of waiver.
14. Survival of covenants.
15. Applicable law; merger of prior agreements.
16. Financial information.
17. Notices.
18. Counterparts.

Each of these provisions is discussed below.

IDENTIFICATION OF LESSOR AND LESSEE

Lease Language

This lease agreement ("Lease") dated as of _____, 19___, is between _____, a _____ corporation, with its principal office at _____("Lessor"), and _____, a _____ corporation, with its principal office at _____("Lessee").

Discussion

The purpose of this paragraph is to clearly identify the names of the lessor and lessee. The correct corporate names of the lessee and lessor, the state in which each company is incorporated, and the address of the company in that state should be inserted. The lessee may not be a "division" of a company unless the company of which it is a division is named too. The lessor must rely on the credit of the company identified as the lessee. Proper identification of the lessee will correct any misunderstandings as to which member of an affiliated group of companies will actually be liable as lessee. Proper identification is also important for preparing and filing financing statements under the Uniform Commercial Code.

For corporations operating multiple leasing subsidiaries, proper identification of the correct lessor subsidiary is essential to assure ownership of the equipment by the proper subsidiary and to assure that tax benefits are claimed by the appropriate subsidiary and that the expected first-year depreciation will be realized. Many lease transactions are priced on the assumption that a particular subsidiary will be the lessor. Incorrect identification of the lessor in these circumstances can severely affect the anticipated yield on the transaction.

AGREEMENT BETWEEN LESSOR AND LESSEE

Lease Language

Lessor agrees to acquire and lease to Lessee and Lessee agrees to lease from Lessor certain personal property (the "Units" and individually a "Unit") described in the Schedule (the "Schedule") attached hereto and made a part hereof, upon the terms and conditions hereinafter set forth.

Discussion

This paragraph sets forth the basic premise that the lessor will acquire certain personal property described in the schedule for the lessee and then lease that property to the lessee. For bank holding companies, banks, and bank subsidiaries, this type of provision meets the requirements set forth in Comptroller's Ruling 7.3400 and Regulation Y of the Board of Governors of the Federal Reserve System, which state that national banks and bank holding companies, respectively, or their subsidiaries can acquire property only at the specific request of the lessee and cannot stockpile equipment or maintain an equipment leasing "inventory." The basic reason for this limitation is that banks and bank holding companies can only engage in leasing activities that are alternative financings functionally equivalent to extensions of credit. Leasing companies that are not affiliates of banks or bank holding companies are not concerned with these requirements.

Regardless of the type of lessor company, the language of the paragraph puts the lessee on notice that the lessor is going to acquire the property for lease to the lessee and obligates[1] the lessee to then lease the property from the lessor.

Although this paragraph and Section 1 below assume that the lessor will take title to the equipment directly from a third-party vendor, sometimes this is not possible. In such an instance (and sometimes merely for the convenience of the parties), the transaction may be structured as a sale to the lessee followed by a sale to the lessor and a leaseback to the lessee before the asset is placed in service. Care must be taken to avoid a double sales tax or use tax in such a transaction.

The language references the schedule and incorporates the schedule as part of the lease. As discussed earlier, the concept of the separate lease and schedule is that the lease agreement constitutes a master document with provisions applicable to many types of equipment and that the schedule supplements the lease by setting forth particulars regarding the lease of specific units of equipment. While the language in the example lease contemplates one schedule, that language can be modified to permit multiple schedules, or later schedules can incorporate the lease language by reference.

1. PROCUREMENT, DELIVERY, AND ACCEPTANCE

Lease Language

Section 1. Procurement, Delivery, and Acceptance.
    1.1 *Purchase Agreement Assignment.*
    Lessee either has ordered or shall order the Units pursuant to one or more purchase orders or other contracts of sale ("Purchase Agreements" and individually a "Purchase Agreement") from one or more vendors

---

[1] The obligation to lease arises when the lessor actually orders the equipment at the request of the lessee or accepts an assignment of the lessee's purchase agreement. Prior to such time, as long as there is no commitment fee, the lessee generally incurs no obligation to the lessor.

("Vendors" and individually a "Vendor"). Prior to the earlier of the time that title to any Unit has been transferred by the applicable Vendor or the Delivery Date (as hereinafter defined), Lessee shall assign to Lessor all the right, title, and interest of the Lessee in and to the applicable Purchase Agreement insofar as it relates to such Unit in a manner satisfactory to Lessor.

The Delivery Date of each Unit shall be the date on which such Unit is physically delivered by the Vendor. Lessor agrees to accept the assignment and assume the obligations of the Lessee under the Purchase Agreement to purchase and pay for such Unit, but no other duties or obligations of the Lessee thereunder; provided, however, that Lessee shall remain liable to the Vendor in respect of its duties and obligations in accordance with the Purchase Agreement, and provided further that Lessee shall bear the risk of loss with respect to and shall hold Lessor harmless from any loss or claim (including strict liability in fact) relating to any Unit covered by any purchase agreement so assigned from the date of such assignment and whether or not such Unit ever is leased hereunder. Lessee represents and warrants in connection with the assignment of any Purchase Agreement that (a) the Lessee has the right to assign the Purchase Agreement as set forth herein; (b) the right, title, and interest of the Lessee in the Purchase Agreement so assigned shall be free from all claims, liens, security interests, and encumbrances; (c) the Lessee will warrant and defend the assignment against lawful claims and demands of all persons; and (d) the Purchase Agreement contains no conditions under which Vendor may reclaim title to any Unit after delivery, acceptance, and payment therefor.

1.2 *Obligation to Pay for Units.*

The obligation of Lessor to pay for each Unit is subject to the following conditions:

(a) Lessee shall have accepted the Unit on the Delivery Date, whereupon the Unit shall immediately become subject to and governed by all the provisions of this Lease. All Delivery Dates shall be on or before the Availability Date set forth in the schedule.

(b) There shall exist no Event of Default or any condition, event, or act which with notice or lapse of time, or both, would become an Event of Default which has not been remedied or waived.

If either of the foregoing conditions has not been met with respect to any Unit, Lessee shall be deemed to have assumed the obligation of Lessor to pay the purchase price in accordance with the Purchase Agreement, and upon such payment, Lessor shall assign, transfer, and set over unto the Lessee all the right, title, and interest of Lessor in and to such Unit and the Purchase Agreement insofar as it relates to such Unit.

1.3 *Acceptance Supplements.*

For each Unit, Lessee shall execute and deliver to Lessor within fifteen (15) days of the Delivery Date of that Unit an executed Acceptance Supplement in the form of Exhibit ___ hereto, confirming the Delivery Date. Each Acceptance Supplement shall be accompanied by the related invoice if it has been received by that time. If the invoice has not been received, Lessee shall within five (5) days of its receipt forward it to Lessor.

 1.4 *Delivery of Documents and Security Deposit.*

On or before the first Delivery Date hereunder, Lessee shall deliver to Lessor the following, in form and substance satisfactory to Lessor:

 (*a*) Evidence of the authority of Lessee to execute and deliver this Lease and all documents required hereunder and to perform its obligations hereunder or relating thereto.

 (*b*) A certificate of insurance indicating that insurance coverage for the Units is in accordance with Section 7 of this Lease.

 (*c*) Waivers from owners or lienholders with respect to the real property in which or upon which the Units will be located, assuring Lessor's ownership and right to remove the Units free from any lien, encumbrance, or right of distraint.

 (*d*) A cash security deposit in the amount of _____.

 (*e*) A guaranty agreement of _____ guaranteeing payment of rent and performance by the Lessee of its obligations under this lease.

Summary

Section 1 indicates the following:

1. The lessee is responsible for ordering the units.
2. The lessor agrees to purchase and pay for the units but is not responsible for anything else that the lessee and vendor may have agreed to when the lessee ordered the units.
3. The lessor must be assigned the right to purchase the units prior to the earlier of the time that title passes to the lessee or the units are physically delivered to the lessee.
4. The lessee bears the risk of loss and holds the lessor harmless from all claims with respect to units that are ordered and assigned to the lessor.
5. The lessor will not pay for a unit unless:
    a. The lessee accepts the unit on its "delivery date."
    b. The delivery date for the unit is on or prior to a specified date.
    c. The lessee is in compliance with the terms of the lease.
6. The lessee will have to purchase the units itself if it fails to comply with the provisions indicated in (5) above.
7. Within 15 days of the delivery date of a unit, the lessee will execute and deliver an "acceptance supplement" to the lessor, confirming the acceptance of the leased unit and specifying the delivery date.
8. The lessee agrees to deliver the following to the lessor prior to the first delivery date:

    a. Evidence of the lessee's authority to lease.
    b. Evidence of insurance.
    c. Waivers of landlord's or mortgagee's liens.
    d. A cash security deposit of _____.
    e. A guaranty agreement of _____ guaranteeing perfor-
    mance of the lease by the lessee.

Discussion

Section 1.1. Purchase Agreement Assignment. Key items to note in Section 1.1 are:

    1. The definition and concept of the delivery date.
    2. The concept of the purchase agreement assignment.

In most prospective lease transactions, the lessee will have already entered into a purchase agreement with a vendor. The lessor wants the lessee to assign its right to purchase the units to the lessor *prior to the time that the lessee would otherwise acquire title to the units.* The lessor will generally have a standard form that it will require for this assignment. Frequently, the required form will be attached to the lease as an exhibit. A fairly typical purchase agreement assignment form is discussed in Chapter 15.

The assignment must take place prior to title passage, principally to avoid any intervening liens and having to do a sale-and-leaseback of the units. Another reason is to protect the lessor's "first-user" status for income tax and sales tax purposes. Unless the lessor can be considered the "first user," it will not be able to claim any investment tax credit which may be available[2] or to depreciate the equipment as new property. Since federal tax law permits a lessor to treat property as new if acquired by the lessor within three months of being placed in service, the first-user status of the lessor is not a difficult test. However, the lease should usually begin as close to delivery and acceptance as possible in order to avoid the possibility of a double sales tax.

The law is sometimes unclear as to the date on which title passes. However, the purchase agreement between the lessee and the vendor may specify the date of title passage, as may the shipping documents. If the purchase agreement or shipping terms are silent on title passage, title can generally be assumed to pass to a purchaser of equipment on the date the equipment is received by the purchaser, as that is the date on which the seller will usually have completed performance. However,

---

[2] The investment tax credit was repealed by the Tax Reform Act of 1986. However, some equipment continues eligible for ITC under transitional rules. See Chapter 4.

it is always advisable to check the shipping terms and the purchase agreement to make sure that a particular date other than the physical delivery date has not been specified as the date on which title passes.

As noted above, the assignment must take place within three months of the time that the equipment is "placed in service" for federal income tax purposes in order for the lessor to preserve its first-user status. Passage of title is one factor that may be considered in determining whether equipment has been placed in service, but it is not the determinative factor. If it were, the parties could contractually agree that title was to pass on a particular date without regard to when the equipment was delivered or used.[3] The Internal Revenue Service takes the position that actual use of the equipment is not necessary for it to be considered "placed in service." According to the IRS, the equipment need only be "in a condition or state of readiness" for use.

The example lease requires the assignment to take place prior to the time of title passage and the delivery date, defined as the date on which the lessee gets physical possession of the equipment. In many cases, the latter date will be the placed-in-service date because the equipment will be available for use on such date. Some types of equipment require extensive installation and assembly, and for such equipment the term *delivery date* may be redefined as the date on which such installation and assembly are complete.

As noted earlier, in most transactions, the lessee will have already entered into a purchase agreement with a vendor by the time the lease is signed. Rather than canceling that arrangement and entering into a purchase agreement directly with the vendor, the lessor typically requests that the lessee assign to the lessor the right to purchase the unit under its purchase agreement by means of a purchase agreement assignment form (discussed in Chapter 15). The lessor usually wants the vendor to acknowledge the assignment.

The main reason for using the assignment approach is that many standard purchase agreements simply do not fit the reality of the lease transaction. They may place obligations on the purchaser-owner over which the lessor has no control. For example, computer purchase agreements may require the purchaser to provide adequate space for installation, assistance in installation, and so forth. The lessee is the appropriate party to handle such matters. By using an assignment, the lessor can contractually agree to assume only the obligation to purchase and pay for the equipment, leaving intact installation and other obligations agreed to between the lessee and the vendor.

---

[3] In addition, if title were the determinative factor, there could never be any sale-and-leaseback true leases.

It is also possible for the lessor to order directly from the manufacturer, but as a rule lessors prefer to use the assignment procedure.

The following factors should be kept in mind in connection with assignments of purchase agreements:

1. Not all purchase agreements are assignable. If such an agreement turns out to be absolutely unassignable, a sale-and-lease-back transaction may have to be structured.
2. Not all vendors will agree to sign a lessor's assignment form. The vendor may simply want the lessor to sign its own form, or it may want to structure a different sort of "consent to assignment" form. No matter whose form is used, the two basic factors of importance to the lessor are that:
   a. The vendor acknowledge that the lessor will purchase the equipment and that payment will come from the lessor.
   b. The lessor is generally not responsible for any other obligations in the purchase agreement, and the vendor and the lessee still have rights and duties to each other.
3. It is important for the lessee to send a copy of the purchase agreement assignment form to the vendor as early as possible before the delivery date.
4. The lessor should review the terms of the purchase agreement at as early a date as possible.
5. Considerable time can be spent negotiating with a vendor over the terms of the vendor's consent to the assignment.

Section 1.2. Obligation to Pay for Units. In order for the lessor to be considered the "first user" of a particular piece of equipment for purposes of the federal income tax laws, the lessor must be unconditionally obligated to pay for the equipment within three months of the date on which it is placed in service.

The example lease contemplates that the lessor will take title and the lease will begin when the equipment is delivered to and accepted by the lessee. Under the example lease, the lessor is not unconditionally obligated to pay until the provisions of Section 1.2 have been met. These provisions require acceptance of the equipment on the delivery date, which is defined, as noted earlier, as either the date on which the lessee takes physical possession or the date on which installation and assembly of the equipment are complete. This acceptance "triggers" the lease for that particular piece of equipment.

Section 1.2 also requires that all delivery dates occur on or before the "availability date." The availability date is the last date on which equipment may be placed under the lease. Usually this date will correspond to the date up to which the line of credit has been approved. The availability date is important because the lessee must have made use of the credit extended prior to that date. Under Section 1.2 the lessor is not obligated to purchase the unit (and thereby, in effect, extend credit to the lessee) unless the lessee accepts the unit on or before the availability date. If the lessee accepts a unit after the availability date, the lessee will not have used the line of credit within the proper time limit. This is a matter of conforming the lease terms to the lessor's internal procedures for an extension of credit.

In addition to requiring acceptance on the delivery date and prior to a specified cutoff date, Section 1.2 also makes clear that the lessor is not obligated to buy equipment and lease it to the lessee if the lessee is or would thereby be in default. Obviously, this is an important credit requirement for the lessor.

The last paragraph of Section 1.2 spells out the lessee's obligation to assume the lessor's obligations to the vendor to pay for the equipment already ordered and possibly delivered if the other requirements of Section 1.2 are not met by the lessee. This is called an unwind provision because it prescribes a method for the entire transaction to be unwound if the transaction does not work out for one reason or another. Unwinds can cause tax problems. The Internal Revenue Service may claim that the lessor was never really unconditionally obligated to pay and never the owner with all the risks of ownership if the lease contains an unwind. However, unwinds that can occur only prior to or simultaneously with the placed-in-service date of equipment are not generally considered fatal. Post-placed-in-service unwinds, on the other hand, can destroy the true lease status of a transaction. Lessors and lessees must evaluate all unwinds with this risk in mind.

Section 1.3. Acceptance Supplements. Section 1.3 requires the lessee to deliver both an acceptance supplement and the vendor's invoice for each piece of equipment. The acceptance supplement (sometimes called a certificate of acceptance) serves as written confirmation that the equipment was received on a particular date and accepted by the lessee. It should contain a complete description of the equipment since the schedule will normally describe the equipment only by general type. It should also specify the full purchase price, including any sales, use, or similar front-end taxes and any installation or freight charges that the lessor has agreed to pay and capitalize. Since this is the only document signed by the lessee that specifically identifies the individual pieces of equipment that are under the lease, it is essential that all of the information requested be listed in detail and with great accuracy.

The example lease calls for delivery of acceptance supplements within 15 days of the delivery date of the equipment. Many lessees want this time period extended. Depending on the practices of the individual lessor, as long as the acceptance supplement merely confirms acceptance and does not serve as an operative document, it is generally possible to extend the period of its delivery for at least a few days. However, lessees should be aware that this document is normally considered a "pay" document by lessors. That is, a lessor will not pay the vendor until it receives a properly executed acceptance supplement. Thus, extension of the period for delivery of the acceptance supplement may disrupt relations with vendors or cause late charges to be incurred.

The requirement for delivery of the vendor invoice assures that the lessor will pay the amount billed by the vendor. As a rule lessors will also require lessees to approve each vendor invoice for payment. For this reason many lessors request that the vendor continue to send all invoices directly to lessees. Once the lessee has approved the invoice, it is forwarded to the lessor for payment.

Section 1.4. Delivery of Documents and Security Deposit. This section lists the items that the lessor expects to receive from the lessee on or prior to the date on which the first piece of equipment is delivered and accepted for leasing. The list will expand or contract depending on the size and complexity of the transaction.

Because of standard audit and regulatory examination requirements in the banking industry, most bank-affiliated leasing companies will require corporate lessees to deliver a corporate resolution authorizing either the specific lease transaction or lease transactions in general. Sometimes an opinion of the lessee's counsel addressing the issue of authorization will be accepted in lieu of a resolution. Sometimes, in large transactions, an opinion of counsel will be required in addition to the corporate resolution. Similar requirements are imposed on partnership lessees so that the lessor has some independent evidence of the authority of the lessee to enter into the lease. Non-bank-affiliated lessors may rely more frequently on the legal concepts of apparent authority of partners or corporate officers. However, the practice of requiring corporate resolutions or their partnership equivalent is fairly prevalent among all types of lessors.

As with the acceptance supplement, most lessors will consider the documents listed in Section 1.4 as "pay" documents and will not disburse funds to the vendor until the documents have been duly and properly delivered to the lessor.

2. TERM, RENT, AND PAYMENT

Lease Language

Section 2. Term, Rent, and Payment.

2.1 The term of this Lease as to each Unit shall commence on the Delivery Date in respect thereto and continue as specified in the Schedule.

2.2 The rent for each Unit shall be in the amounts, and shall be payable at the time set forth, in the Schedule.

2.3 Rent and all other sums due Lessor hereunder shall be paid at the principal office of Lessor set forth above.

2.4 This Lease is a net lease, and Lessee shall not be entitled to any abatement or reduction of rent or any setoff against rent, whether arising by reason of any past, present, or future claims of any nature by Lessee against Lessor or otherwise. Except as otherwise expressly provided herein, this Lease shall not terminate, nor shall the obligations of Lessor or Lessee be otherwise affected by reason of any defect in, damage to, loss of possession or use, or destruction of any of the Units however caused, by the attachment of any lien, encumbrance, security interest, or other right or claim of any third party to any Unit, by any prohibition or restriction of or interference with Lessee's use of the Unit by any person or entity, or by the insolvency of or the commencement by or against Lessee of any bankruptcy, reorganization, or similar proceeding, or for any other cause, whether similar or dissimilar to the foregoing, any present or future law to the contrary notwithstanding. It is the intention of the parties that all rent and other amount payable by Lessee hereunder shall be payable in all events in the manner and at the times herein provided unless Lessee's obligations in respect thereof have been terminated pursuant to the express provisions of this Lease.

Summary

This section indicates that:

1. The term of the lease and the amount of rental and the timing of payments are set forth in the schedule.
2. Rental is payable at a particular office of the lessor.
3. The lease is a "net" lease, and rental must be paid without setoff "come hell or high water."

Discussion

Section 2.1. Term; Section 2.2. Rent; Section 2.3. Place of Payment. These sections are largely self-explanatory. Sections 2.1 and 2.2 refer to the schedule, in which the specifics will be listed for each type of equipment to be leased. If a lease-schedule concept were not used, or if only one piece of equipment were to be placed under the lease, these sections could be expanded to include those specifics. This is not generally the industry practice, however.

Section 2.3 specifies the place of payment. Even for lessors with multiple office locations, payments are frequently consolidated at one location, usually the home office. Lessees may prefer to deal solely with the local or regional office of the lessor, but legal, tax, and operational constraints will generally make the place of payment a nonnegotiable item.

Section 2.4. Net Lease. Section 2.4 states that rental must be paid no matter what happens, regardless of whether the lease is terminated by operation of law or otherwise. This type of provision is commonly referred to as a "hell or high water" or "net lease" provision. Its effect is to require payment of rent even if the equipment fails to perform and to make clear that the lessor has no obligation to the lessee except to finance the equipment. For bank-affiliated lessors and bank holding company–affiliated lessors, this type of provision is required by the Comptroller's Regulation and by Regulation Y of the Board of Governors of the Federal Reserve System to ensure that the lease will be functionally equivalent to an extension of credit. Other types of leasing companies require this type of provision in order to make clear what type of leasing product they are offering. Some lessees confuse the concept of net lease with a service lease or a vendor's financing arrangement and take the position that a provision such as Section 2.4 is unfair. This position indicates a fundamental misunderstanding of the leasing product being offered.

When the lease transaction is required by law or company policy to be a net lease transaction, or when the transaction has been priced on the basis that the lease will be a net lease, lessees should not expect to be able to negotiate substantial changes in the wording of the net lease provision. Nonetheless, some lessors may be willing to give the lessee a carefully worded, specific "right of quiet enjoyment"[4] clause either in this section or in later sections dealing with the use and possession of the equipment. Other lessors may be willing to grant the lessee what amounts to a right of quiet enjoyment by altering the language of Section 2.4 in selected places. For example, the phrase "interference with Lessee's use of the Unit by any person or entity" might be modified by the addition of the phrase "other than Lessor" after the word *entity*. Lessees should still keep in mind, however, that the basic concept of Section 2.4 cannot be altered if the transaction is to remain a net lease.

3. WARRANTIES

Lease Language

Section 3. Warranties.
    LESSEE ACKNOWLEDGES AND AGREES (*a*) THAT EACH UNIT IS OF A SIZE, DESIGN, CAPACITY, AND MANUFACTURE SELECTED BY LESSEE; (*b*) THAT LESSEE IS SATISFIED THAT THE

---

[4] A right of quiet enjoyment means that the lessor will not interfere with the lessee's use or operation of the leased equipment so long as there is no event of default under the lease.

SAME IS SUITABLE FOR ITS PURPOSES; (c) THAT LESSOR IS NOT
A MANUFACTURER THEREOF NOR A DEALER IN PROPERTY OF
SUCH KIND; AND (d) THAT LESSOR HAS NOT MADE, AND DOES
NOT HEREBY MAKE, ANY REPRESENTATION OR WARRANTY OR
COVENANT WITH RESPECT TO THE MERCHANTABILITY, CON-
DITION, QUALITY, DESCRIPTION, DURABILITY, OR SUITABILITY
OF ANY SUCH UNIT IN ANY RESPECT OR IN CONNECTION WITH
OR FOR THE PURPOSES AND USES OF LESSEE. Lessor hereby as-
signsns to Lessee, to the extent assignable, any warranties, covenants, and
representations of the Vendor with respect to any Unit, provided that
any action taken by Lessee by reason thereof shall be at the sole expense
of Lessee and shall be consistent with Lessee's obligations pursuant to
Section 2 hereunder.

Summary

This section provides that:

1. The lessor makes absolutely no warranties of any kind with
   respect to the equipment.
2. The lessor passes any warranties received from the vendor on
   to the lessee to the extent that the lessor can do so.
3. Action by the lessee to recover under the warranties will be at
   the lessee's expense.

Discussion

In many lease transactions, the lessor is not the vendor or manufacturer of the leased equipment. Rather, it is a "third-party lessor"
providing funds to enable the lessee to lease rather than buy the equipment of its choice. The third-party lessor will typically have little or
no expertise in selection of the equipment, and it will have no involvement in the process. Frequently, in fact, the lessee will have already
placed an order for the equipment prior to entering into lease financing
discussions with the lessor. Thus, third-party lessors will always want
the lessee to acknowledge that the lessor had no involvement with the
selection of the equipment and that the lessor has made no warranties
that the equipment may be merchantable or fit for any particular
purpose. As in all commercial transactions, this acknowledgment or
disclaimer should be clear and conspicuous, in type of a different size
or in bold-faced print, so that it stands out from other provisions in
the lease.

In the absence of such an acknowledgment or disclaimer, the implied
warranty provisions of Sections 314 and 315 of Article 2 of the Uniform
Commercial Code may be held to be applicable despite the fact that
the warranty provisions of Uniform Commercial Code Article 2 are

only supposed to be applicable to a merchant lessor when the lease is in the nature of a security interest rather than a true lease. Unfortunately, the holdings of the courts are inconsistent regarding the status of leases under the Uniform Commercial Code. It is possible to find cases standing for almost any proposition that a lessee or lessor may wish to advocate.[5]

As the consequences of a breach of an implied warranty of merchantability are severe (a lessee may recover consequential damages in addition to recovering lease payments previously paid), lessees are unlikely to find lessors willing to alter the language of their warranty provisions substantially.

Whether the warranty section is written as an acknowledgment of the lessee or as a disclaimer by the lessor may be a point of discussion between lessors and lessees. Lessees sometimes prefer to have the language of this section written as a disclaimer by the lessor for these reasons:

1. The lessee may not wish to make any statement as to whether or not the lessor is a manufacturer or a dealer in the type of equipment leased.
2. The lessee may be concerned that a paragraph written in the form of an acknowledgment, especially with clauses similar to clauses (*a*) and (*b*), will have an adverse effect on the lessee's ability to proceed against the vendor on its warranties.

With respect to the first problem, many lessees are willing to accept insertion of the language "agree for the purposes of this Lease" before the phrase "that Lessor is not a manufacturer thereof nor a dealer." Others insist that the paragraph be rewritten as the lessor's disclaimer. With respect to the second problem, the addition of the words "as between Lessee and Lessor" before clause (*a*) is usually a satisfactory solution.

Sometimes the lessee desires the language to be clarified to require the lessor to render "reasonable assistance" in pursuing any warranty remedy. A lessor agreeing to such assistance will almost always require

---

[5] Merchant lessors have been held to have made implied warranties of fitness and merchantability under the Uniform Commercial Code, even though a true lease was involved rather than a conditional sale or a secured loan. Implied warranties will probably not be extended to third-party lessors that only occasionally lease the type of equipment involved in a questioned lease transaction. The distinction between implied warranties for a merchant lessor and those for a third-party lessor is based on the fact that the lessee in a finance lease selects the equipment and does not rely on the lessor's expertise. On the other hand, the lessee dealing with a merchant lessor might claim to rely on the lessor's expertise. However, where a third-party lessor has entered into a vendor lease arrangement in which it regularly deals with the type of equipment being leased, the implied warranties of a merchant might be imputed to the third-party lessor.

that such assistance be at "lessee's expense." Other lessors may be reluctant to agree to give any assistance, fearing this would jeopardize the net lease status of the lease.

4. POSSESSION, USE, AND MAINTENANCE

Lease Language

Section 4. Possession, Use, and Maintenance.

    4.1 *Use of Units.*

Lessee shall not (*a*) use, operate, maintain, or store any Unit improperly, carelessly, or in violation of any applicable law or regulation of any governmental authority; (*b*) sublease any Unit or permit the use thereof by anyone other than Lessee without the prior written consent of Lessor, which consent shall not be unreasonably withheld; (*c*) permit any Unit to be removed from the location specified in the Schedule without the prior written consent of Lessor; (*d*) affix or install any Unit to or in any other personal property or to or on any real property without first obtaining and delivering to Lessor such waivers as may be necessary to assure Lessor's ownership and right to remove such Unit free from any lien, encumbrance, or right of distraint, or any other claim which may be asserted by any third party; or (*e*) sell, assign, or transfer, or directly or indirectly create or incur or suffer to be created or incurred or to exist any lien, claim, security interest, or encumbrance of any kind on any of its rights under this Lease or in any Unit.

    4.2 *Maintenance of Units.*

Lessee shall at its sole expense at all times during the term of this Lease maintain the Units in good operating order, repair, condition, and appearance.

    4.3 *Repairs and Additions.*

Lessee shall not alter any Unit or affix or install any accessory, equipment, or device on any Unit, if such alteration or addition will impair the originally intended function or use or reduce the value of any such Unit. All repairs, parts, supplies, accessories, equipment, and devices furnished, affixed, or installed to or on any Unit shall thereupon become the property of Lessor. If no Event of Default has occurred and is continuing, Lessee may remove at its expense any such accessories, equipment, and devices at the expiration of the term with respect to such Unit, provided that such accessories, equipment, and devices are readily removable and that such removal will not impair the originally intended function or use of such Unit.

    4.4 *Labeling and Inspection.*

If Lessor supplies Lessee with labels, plates, or other markings, stating that the Units are owned by Lessor, Lessee shall affix and keep the same upon a prominent place on the Units during the term of this Lease. Upon prior notice to Lessee, Lessor shall have the right at all reasonable times to inspect any Unit and observe its use.

Summary

This section provides that:

1. The equipment must be used carefully by the lessee and used in accordance with applicable law.
2. The equipment may not be moved from the location originally agreed upon without the lessor's consent.
3. The equipment may not be subleased to or used by third parties without the lessor's consent.
4. The equipment cannot be made a part of other personal property or affixed to any real property unless the lessee obtains a consent to removal from the owner of such real or personal property.
5. The lessee will not encumber either the equipment or its leasehold interest.
6. The equipment must be properly maintained by the lessee.
7. The lessee may not make changes in or additions to the equipment that will impair its originally intended function.
8. Repair parts and accessories added to the equipment become the property of the lessor, although easily removable additions that do not affect the operating condition of the leased equipment may be removed by the lessee at the end of the lease, provided the lessee is not in default to the lessor.
9. The lessee must identify the equipment with labels indicating the lessor's ownership if requested to do so by the lessor.
10. The equipment may be inspected by the lessor during the lease.

Discussion

Section 4.1. Use of Units. This section is designed to protect the lessor's ownership interest in the leased equipment, including expected residual value, and to assure that the lessee's use of the equipment will not jeopardize that ownership interest, reduce the residual value of the equipment, or subject the lessor to potential legal liability.

Some lessees may be concerned that a prohibition on violating "any applicable law" is too sweeping. A lessor may be willing to reduce the standards to require compliance with "all laws of which Lessee has or should have knowledge" since compliance with any and all laws may be too high a standard, given the wide variety of laws, rules, and regulations in existence. As a rule, however, lessors will be less willing to revise the standard to require lessees to "comply in all material respects with all laws." This second variation is less acceptable since a "nonmaterial" violation of a given law may still jeopardize the lessor's ownership of the equipment.

In negotiating lease language similar to that of this section, the lessor must keep in mind that the lessee's actions can jeopardize the lessor's ownership interest and the residual value of the leased equipment, even though the owner has no knowledge of particular laws or regulations nor knowledge of the lessee's compliance (or lack thereof) with such laws or regulations. Furthermore, both the lessee and the lessor should remember that the lessee is in a much better position than the lessor to know of and to comply with rules and regulations that apply to the particular types of equipment being leased.

Section 4.1(*b*) limiting subleasing is important to protect the title to the equipment, its use during the lease, and its condition at the conclusion of the lease.

If the lessor is willing to allow use or subleasing by another party, the lessor will usually want to exercise control over the form of arrangement entered into by the lessee and the other party. For example, the lessor would not want the sublease to contain provisions inconsistent with the main lease (particularly any provision, such as a fixed-price purchase option, that might jeopardize the true lease status of the main lease). Any sublease should also be subordinate to the main lease, it should not relieve the lessee of its obligations to the lessor, and it should make clear that the lessor's rights may be exercised despite the terms of the sublease (remedies of lessee's/sublessor's default, right to inspect the equipment, and so forth). Most lessors also want the sublessee to be made aware of the fact that the lessor and not the lessee/sublessor is the owner of the equipment. Many lessors will want to take a security interest in any sublease.

If the lessor and lessee contemplate at the outset that subleasing is to be permitted, language similar to that in Section 4.1(*b*) of the example lease is no longer appropriate. A new provision specifying the terms on which subleasing will be permitted will have to be negotiated. The existence of clause (*b*) ensures that the subject will be raised if the lessee intends to sublease the equipment.

Section 4.1(*c*) of the example lease restricts the lessee's right to move the equipment from a particular location, and that location is specified in the schedule. The location may be a particular street address, in which case the lessee may feel it necessary to negotiate with the lessor for greater flexibility. In many cases, however, the lessor will consent "up front" to movement of the equipment within a single state or between states. There are numerous important issues concerning the right to movement of the equipment that must be considered by the parties in structuring a provision such as Section 4.1(*c*):

1. The equipment must be located in the United States if the ACRS depreciation and any applicable investment tax credit are to be claimed. (There are certain exceptions for rolling stock and aircraft and other mobile equipment.)
2. Moving the equipment may damage it (and possibly reduce its residual value).
3. The lessor will usually file precautionary UCC financing statements covering the leased equipment. These must be filed in the state (or, in some cases, the county) in which the equipment is located. If the equipment is moved, a new financing statement must be filed. If the locations specified in the schedule include more than one state (or county), the lessor should at a minimum require *notice* of changes in location, even if the lessor does not have to consent to the change. (Note that, as drafted, Section 4.1(c) does not refer to such notice.)
4. There may be tax disadvantages to having certain types of equipment located in certain states. State tax depreciation deductions may be lost. The new state may have a unitary income tax. New use tax or property taxes may arise. While the lessee is responsible for use tax or property taxes in a net lease, the lessor wants to be sure they are paid. Otherwise, the lessor may be liable or liens may attach to the leased asset.
5. The lessor may not be qualified to do business in a particular state. If qualification becomes advisable or necessary, a franchise tax can be incurred that was not factored into the lease pricing.
6. There may be other laws—laws affecting title or usury laws, for example—that may have a negative impact on the lessor of certain types of personal property located in a given state.
7. If the lessee can use equipment in only one or two states, the lessor has a much easier time evaluating state law risks in the transaction. The lessor cannot be expected to research the laws of all 50 states for each lease.
8. The lessor needs to know where its equipment is located in order to exercise its inspection rights effectively or in order to be able to repossess quickly in default situations.

Section 4.1(d) is largely self-explanatory. A lessor must have reasonable access to its equipment. Lessors do not wish to become involved in arguments with landlords or owners of other pieces of property to which the lessee may have attached the lessor's equipment. If the lease involves large, stationary pieces of equipment that might be considered fixtures, the lessor should determine whether the lessee is leasing the real estate on which or in which the leased equipment will be located. If so, the lessee should be made aware of the need for the landlord or mortgagee to sign a "consent to removal." It will almost always be the lessee's responsibility to obtain such consent, and it should be obtained prior to delivery and installation of the equipment. Unfortunately, "consents to removal" are not always easy to obtain. Landlords and mortgagees may want to negotiate their terms. Considerable time can elapse before a signed consent is obtained even when no negotiation takes place.[6]

Note that Section 4.1(e) covers both liens on the equipment and liens on the leasehold interest. With respect to the equipment, in a true lease situation the lessee should not be able to encumber it except for mechanics' or materialmen's liens that might arise in fulfilling its obligations to maintain the equipment. Some lessees want such liens carved out of this section since they arise as a matter of law. A lessor can usually agree to this, provided the lease is clear that any such lien must be discharged by the lessee before it becomes "delinquent."

Section 4.2. Maintenance of Units. Lessees frequently ask that "ordinary wear and tear excepted" be added to language similar to that of Section 4.2. This is ordinarily a reasonable qualification, provided the lessee understands that the equipment is not to be returned to the lessor in a state that requires the lessor to spend time and money on "restoration" to good working condition. Care must be taken in drafting this type of provision when certain types of equipment, such as aircraft and computers, are involved. Many leases will contain special maintenance provisions that fit particular equipment—for example, midtime hours on aircraft engines and maintenance contracts with vendors for computer equipment—and it is important not to dilute the requirements of these provisions if the residual value of the equipment is to be adequately protected.

Some lessees may object to the word *appearance* in maintenance provisions, fearing that the lessor may impose unreasonable repainting requirements. Railroad lessees are particularly concerned about this.

Section 4.3. Repairs and Additions. The key items to note in Section 4.3 are:

1. The lessee may make alterations or additions to the equipment as long as such alterations or additions do not impair its original function or value.

---

[6] If the equipment being leased can be characterized as a fixture, most lessors will want to file a precautionary fixture filing as well as a regular financing statement. If the equipment itself might be characterized as "real property" (e.g., sheds to house machinery), national bank-affiliated lessors, limited by the Comptroller's Regulation to leasing only personal property, will normally insist that the lease contain language indicating the "intent" of the parties that the property be treated as "personal property" and in addition may require that this statement of intent be recorded in the real estate records.

2. Any additions and any replacement parts are considered property of the lessor during the lease. (Not all lessors will require this.)

3. At the conclusion of the lease, the lessee is allowed to remove any additions, if such removal will not impair the equipment and if there is no default.

Lessees, particularly lessees of computers, frequently take issue with items similar to (2) and (3). Obviously, replacement parts and repairs should become the property of the lessor. However, many lessees want easily removable features or modifications that have been added to equipment to remain their property. Other lessees want the right to remove such accessions at the conclusion of the lease, or they want the lessor to compensate them for the increased residual value resulting from the accessions. Lessors are not inclined to agree to compensation.

Arguably, allowing ownership of accession to be in the lease could indicate that the lessee has an ownership interest in the resulting combined piece of equipment or that there is an intent to transfer title in the original piece of equipment to the lessee. To avoid such implications, the lessor should be the owner during the lease period. Furthermore, ownership of the accessions by the lessor gives the lessor more control over what can be added to or removed from the equipment. In the event of a default, the lessor does not have to argue with the lessee about what is the lessor's property and what is the lessee's property when the lessor seeks to repossess equipment.

Lessees that are leasing accessions from other lessors will object strongly to language similar to that of the example lease. While a lessor may ultimately agree to give a lessee the right to add leased accessions, most lessors will usually attempt to restrict this right, and many will require the lessor of the accessions to sign an acknowledgment that the basic equipment is under lease and that the lessor of the basic equipment may request immediate removal of the accessions in default situations.

From a tax standpoint, readily removable accessions added by the lessee are not generally considered income to the lessor at the time they are added, although if left on the equipment, they will be income to the lessor at the end of the lease term or upon disposal of the equipment. Thus, insisting on actual title to accessions may raise an "income to lessor" issue where it would not arise otherwise. However, many lessors do not feel that this risk is significant enough to change the fairly standard practice of requiring title to be vested in the lessor during the lease term.

In leveraged lease transactions, the Internal Revenue Service has taken the position that accessions not readily removable constitute income to the lessor when they are added. Title to such accessions should always be in the lessor because of the likelihood of the income characterization.

Where the lease allows removal of accessions that are readily removable at the end of the term, care should be used to distinguish between repairs and the like, permanent accessions, and readily removable accessions.

Section 4.4. Labeling and Inspection. The purpose of labeling is to give actual notice of the lessor's ownership of the equipment to third parties such as landlords, creditors of the lessee, and purchasers from the lessee. Labeling also aids in locating equipment for inventory and inspections during the lease.

A provision similar to Section 4.4 is included in most leases, as this type of provision gives the lessor the right to label the leased equipment. Not all lessors will exercise this right at the outset. However, even lessors that do not generally label equipment feel that such a provision is extremely important since the labeling of equipment may forestall prolonged arguments with creditors or a bankruptcy trustee if the lessee gets into financial difficulty.

Most lessees do not question the lessor's right to label, but the question of what form of label will be required is a frequent point of discussion. Lessees usually want the labeling to be as unobtrusive as possible, usually for aesthetic reasons but sometimes for operational reasons. For example, certain lessees of trucks may object to the labeling requirement because of fear that weight station operators will be confused by the label and will hold up the trucks to make inquiries into the terms of the lease. Usually some accommodation can be reached by agreeing to label unobtrusively or by labeling the trucks as leased, but without mentioning the lessor. It should be noted that vehicle licensing and titling regulations, particularly for interstate carriers, frequently require that the equipment be identified on the registration form as under long-term lease, so a truck lessee's argument against labeling is not very strong.

With some types of equipment, such as railroad cars, labeling of the equipment is important to protect the lessor's title. Lessors must use the form prescribed by the ICC.

A right of inspection is necessary in order to verify the existence, location, and condition of the equipment and to make sure that the lessee is complying with the provisions of the lease. Lessees may wish to have such inspections limited to times when the equipment is located on property of the lessee. They may also wish to have the inspections conducted when this will not materially interfere with production. Ordinarily, these limitations are acceptable. However, if the equipment is located on leased property, if it is highly mobile and not likely to be returned to the lessee on a regular basis (as, for example, is frequently the case with containers or vehicles), or if it will be subleased, the lessee must obtain inspection rights for the lessor from the other users, or the lessor or owner of the premises where the equipment is located must make some arrangement to enable the lessor to exercise its inspection rights.

5. TAXES

Lease Language

Section 5. Taxes.

    5.1 *Taxes and Fees.*

    All payments to be made by Lessee hereunder will be free of expense to Lessor with respect to the amount of any local, state, or federal taxes (other than any federal, state, or city net income taxes or franchise taxes measured by net income based on such receipts, except any such tax which is in substitution for or relieves Lessee from the payment of taxes which it would otherwise be obligated to pay or reimburse as herein provided) or license fees, assessments, charges, fines, or penalties (all such expenses, taxes, license fees, assessments, charges, fines, and penalties, together with any interest payable with respect thereto being hereinafter called "Impositions") hereafter levied or imposed upon or in connection with or measured by this Lease or any sale, rental, use, payment, shipment, delivery, or transfer of title under the terms hereof, all of which Impositions Lessee assumes and agrees to pay on demand in addition to the payments to be made by it provided for herein. Lessee will also pay promptly all Impositions which may be imposed upon any Unit or for the use or operation thereof or upon the earnings arising therefrom (except as provided above) or upon Lessor solely by reason of its ownership thereof and will keep at all times all and every part of such Unit free and clear of all Impositions which might in any way affect the title of Lessor or result in a lien upon any such Unit; provided, however, that Lessee shall be under no obligation to pay any Impositions of any kind so long as it is contesting in good faith and by appropriate legal proceedings such Impositions and the nonpayment thereof does not, in the opinion of Lessor, adversely affect the title, property, or rights of Lessor hereunder. If any Impositions shall have been charged or levied against Lessor directly and paid by Lessor, Lessee shall reimburse Lessor on presentation of an invoice therefor.

    5.2 *Reports.*

    In the event that any reports with respect to Impositions are required to be made, Lessee shall make such reports in such manner as shall be satisfactory to Lessor.

Summary

This section provides that:

1. The lessee is responsible for all local, state, and federal taxes in connection with the lease transaction and ownership of the property except for the lessor's income taxes or franchise taxes based on net income of the lessor (unless such income or franchise taxes are in lieu of a tax that the lessee would otherwise pay, in which case the lessee pays the tax).
2. The lessee is responsible for all local, state, and federal government fees or charges.
3. If the lessor pays any tax or fee directly, reimbursement for such payment is "on demand" by the lessor.
4. The lessee is obligated to keep the equipment free of tax liens, although it may contest taxes and charges that have been imposed in connection with the transaction or equipment, provided such contest:
   a. Is in good faith.
   b. Does not affect the lessor's title.
   c. Is at the expense of the lessee.
5. The lessor can require the lessee to make any necessary reports that taxing or other authorities may require in connection with the taxes or other charges that have been imposed.

Discussion

Section 5.1. Taxes and Fees. Section 5.1 covers the responsibility for payment of sales, use, property, and all other taxes.[7] In a net lease the lessee is responsible for all such taxes, except net income taxes of the lessor, and lessees cannot expect to negotiate on this point. However, there may be some room for negotiation in the matter of whether property taxes will be paid directly by the lessee or paid initially by the lessor, with the lessee then reimbursing the lessor upon presentation of a bill. Individual lessors will have different practices in this area. Some lessors will not allow the lessee to pay these taxes directly

---

[7] In some cases sales or use taxes paid by the lessor at the outset of the lease are capitalized and added to the lessee's rental payments. In other cases such taxes are billed separately, as the lessor pays the taxes. Capitalizing a sales or use tax and adding it to the rent is possible only when the tax is levied "up front" on the sales price of the equipment. In some states the tax is based on the rental stream to the lessor rather than the sales price, and this tax must be paid periodically rather than up front. In some states the taxpayer has the option of paying the tax at the time of purchase or as rent is paid.

because the property taxes are imposed on the lessor as purchaser and owner of the equipment, and the lessors want to ensure that such taxes are in fact paid. Other lessors are willing to let lessees pay all of these taxes directly so long as the lessees keep adequate records, including receipts, evidencing that proper payment has been made. As a practical matter administration of property tax payments by a lessor is time-consuming and expensive and leads to needless disputes with lessees.

Licensing, titling, and registration fees are also the responsibility of the lessee. In contrast to taxes, these fees are usually paid directly by the lessees.[8]

The question of whether the lessee pays a tax or fee directly or reimburses the lessor will have an impact on the contest rights of the lessee. When the lessee pays the tax or fee directly, it can decide prior to payment whether or not to contest a particular tax or fee. When the lessor pays the tax or fee directly, the lessee may be forced to contest after the fact in a suit for a refund. With property taxes the assessment is often what must be contested, and once the time for contesting assessments has passed, there is no ability to contest the tax itself. If the lessee pays the tax directly, it may feel that it can convince the taxing authorities to send it the notice of assessment and that it will thus be in a position to protest the assessment if necessary. On the other hand, if the lessor pays the tax, the notice of assessment will always be sent to it in the first instance, so the lessee will be dependent on the lessor to forward the notice in a timely manner to it. While most lessors are sympathetic to lessees' requests for a prepayment right to contest taxes or fees imposed on the equipment or its use, lessees need to be aware of the administrative burden that must be borne by the lessor if it grants them such a right. For example, lessors may not have adequate staff to ensure that notices of assessment are in fact sent to lessees. Lessees and lessors may see this as a persuasive argument for having the lessee pay all taxes and fees directly, but as noted earlier, this may no longer be a viable alternative for some types of taxes.

Section 5.2. Reports. The need for a provision such as Section 5.2 should be self-evident. The lessee has possession of the equipment and monitors its use on a daily basis. It also knows the exact location of the equipment. The lessor, which only occasionally inspects the equip-

---

[8] In the case of banks and bank holding companies and their affiliates, the Comptroller's Ruling and Regulation of the Board of Governors of the Federal Reserve System requires renewal of licenses to be handled by the lessee, except in particular instances in which the lessor's ownership or security interest would be jeopardized by this practice. Such renewals are regarded as characteristic of a service lease and are functions that a bank or bank holding company cannot provide. Banks sometimes contract out this service.

ment, is dependent on the lessee for much of the information that tax authorities are likely to request. It must therefore have the right to obtain all necessary information from the lessee. Some lessees insist that provisions such as Section 5.2 be reciprocal, although as a practical matter it is usually the lessee that will have the types of information needed.

6. RISK OF LOSS; WAIVER AND INDEMNITY

Lease Language

Section 6. Risk of Loss; Waiver and Indemnity.

6.1 Casualty Occurrences.

In the event that any Unit shall be or become worn out, lost, stolen, destroyed, or irreparably damaged, from any cause whatsoever, or taken or requisitioned by condemnation or otherwise (any such occurrence being hereinafter called a "Casualty Occurrence"), Lessee shall promptly and fully notify Lessor with respect thereto. On the rental payment date next succeeding such notice, or if there be no such date within thirty (30) days of such notice, Lessee shall pay to Lessor an amount equal to the rental payment or payments in respect of such Unit due and payable on such date plus a sum equal to the Casualty Value (as defined in the Schedule) of such Unit as of the date of such payment as set forth in the Schedule. Upon the making of such payment by Lessee in respect of any Unit, the rental for such Unit shall cease to accrue, the term of this Lease as to such Unit shall terminate, and Lessor shall be entitled to recover possession of such Unit. Provided that Lessor has received the Casualty Value for any Unit, Lessee shall be entitled to the proceeds of any recovery in respect of such Unit from insurance or otherwise to the extent that they do not exceed the Casualty Value of such Unit, and any excess shall be retained by Lessor. Except as otherwise expressly provided in this Lease, Lessee shall not be released from its obligations hereunder in the event of, and shall bear the risk of, any Casualty Occurrence to any Unit.

6.2 Indemnity.

Lessee hereby waives and releases any claim now or hereafter existing against Lessor on account of, and agrees to indemnify, reimburse, and hold Lessor harmless from, any and all claims (including, but not limited to, claims relating to patent infringement and claims based upon strict liability in tort), losses, liabilities, demands, suits, judgments, or causes of action, and all legal proceedings, and any costs or expenses in connection therewith, including attorneys' fees and expenses which may result from or arise in any manner out of the condition, use, or operation of any Unit prior to or during the term thereof, or which may be attributable to any defect in any Unit, arising from the material or any article used therein or from the design, testing, or use thereof, or from any maintenance, service, repair, overhaul, or testing of any Unit, regardless of when such defect shall be discovered, whether or not such Unit is in the possession of Lessee, and no matter where it is located.

Summary

Section 6 provides that:

1. If the equipment should be lost, worn out, stolen, destroyed, damaged beyond repair, or taken by condemnation, the lessee must notify the lessor and pay the lessor the casualty value of the equipment (which is specified in Section 6 of the schedule to the lease).
2. Once the casualty value has been paid for a unit of equipment, the lease ceases as to that piece of equipment.
3. The lessor is entitled to recover the equipment, if there is anything left to recover.
4. If the lessor has been paid the casualty value of the equipment by the lessee and the lessor then receives insurance or salvage proceeds covering the loss, these proceeds up to the amount of the casualty value paid will be turned over to the lessee (insurance and salvage proceeds in excess of the casualty value are retained by the lessor).
5. The lessee bears the risk of loss (beginning on the date that the purchase agreement covering the equipment is assigned to the lessor pursuant to Section 1.1).
6. The lessee cannot make any claim against the lessor with respect to use or operation, maintenance or repair of, or defects in the equipment.
7. The lessee will indemnify the lessor against third-party claims relating to use, operation, maintenance, or repair of or defects in the equipment.

Discussion

Section 6.1. Casualty Occurrences. This section calls for the lessee to pay the lessor an amount equal to the casualty value (frequently referred to as the "stipulated loss value") of the leased equipment upon the happening of certain stated events resulting in the loss or destruction of the equipment.[9] Under Section 2.4, the lease imposes the obligation on the lessee to continue paying rent regardless of the status

---

[9] In leases of computer equipment, the vendor's exercise of its rights to reclaim or substitute equipment under a patent indemnity agreement should also be considered a casualty occurrence.

or condition of the equipment. Section 6.1 is not inconsistent with this requirement since one element of the casualty value is discounted future rentals on the equipment (from the time of the casualty until what would have been the expected end of the lease). In addition to compensation for loss of rental, payment of the casualty value will compensate the lessor for:

1. Loss of tax benefits (since the lessor is not only unable to claim further depreciation after a casualty but may also lose some or all of the ACRS depreciation deductions and investment tax credit (if applicable) previously claimed inasmuch as the events listed are "recapture events" for tax purposes and depending on when the casualty occurs).

2. Loss of expected residual value, discounted to present value (since the lessor will not have a functioning unit to sell at the end of the lease).

Casualty value is not necessarily the same as "termination value," the amount that the lessee must pay if it terminates the lease early for reasons other than loss or destruction of the equipment.[10] In most cases, in fact, casualty value will be significantly higher than termination value since, as noted above, casualty value compensates the lessor for loss of expected residual (the equipment being destroyed or lost), whereas termination value generally does not include a lost residual component much in excess of the residual value used in pricing the lease, on the theory the equipment is still in existence and can be returned to the lessor. Individual lessors will have different methods of calculating casualty values and termination values. In some cases, these figures are negotiable. (Casualty values for the leased equipment are listed in the schedule[11] rather than the lease; casualty values will vary for different types of equipment depending on expected tax benefits, residual value, and profit.)

The timing of the casualty value payment and the decision as to whether casualty value is to be paid in addition to rent or in lieu of rent will vary with the practices of individual lessors. These items are usually negotiable, although in some cases the limits of the lessor's computer programs may restrict flexibility on them.

In a casualty situation, the lessor is entitled to recover possession of whatever is left of the equipment. Salvage value does not belong to the lessee because it is a "benefit" and attribute to ownership that belongs to the lessor in a true lease. In the example lease, however, if

---

[10] Not all leases permit early termination for reasons other than a casualty to the equipment.

[11] See Chapter 4.

the lessee pays the casualty value and then the lessor receives proceeds from the sale of the scrap, the lessee will be given the benefit of those proceeds up to the amount of the casualty value paid. The same is true with respect to insurance proceeds. If the lessee pays the casualty value and the lessor then receives insurance proceeds relating to the loss, those proceeds are turned over to the lessee up to the amount of the casualty value paid. Many lessees argue that all insurance proceeds, even those in excess of the casualty value, should be turned over to the lessee. However, most lessors take the position that the lessee is not entitled to insurance proceeds in excess of the casualty value because the lessor is the owner and therefore has the insurable interest in the equipment. Permitting the lessee to share in the excess insurance proceeds might be interpreted as an indication that the lessee has an ownership interest in the equipment, thereby casting a shadow on the true lease status of the lease. If the proceeds in excess of the casualty value can somehow be related to the lessee's insurable interest (business interruption, replacement, loss of use, and so forth), however, then the lessee can argue that the portion of the insurance that can be so related may be returned to the lessee without jeopardizing the true lease status of the lease.

The final sentence of Section 6.1 makes clear that the lessee bears the risk of all casualty occurrences. This is an essential part of the net lease concept, and the only possible exception that lessors might be willing to carve out would be casualty occurrences caused solely by the gross negligence or willful misconduct of the lessor.

Section 6.2. Indemnity. This section is the general indemnity section of the example lease. It protects the lessor against claims relating to defects in the equipment or its use, operation, or maintenance. As finance lessors do not maintain the equipment or actively supervise its use or operation and have no part in the selection of the equipment, they are unwilling to assume liability for these risks. Thus, provisions such as Section 6.2 are usually drafted quite broadly, with the purpose of protecting the lessor as fully as possible. While there may be some room for negotiation with respect to general indemnity provisions, most lessors will be unwilling to accept responsibility for anything other than their own active gross negligence or willful misconduct. From the lessor's perspective, extreme care must be observed in negotiating the terms of any general indemnity. If the lessor is not clearly indemnified by the express terms of such a provision, the lessor cannot presume to be adequately protected. For example, an express reference to indemnification against claims based on strict liability in tort should always be included in a general indemnity, as indemnities do not normally cover such claims unless they are expressly mentioned. Care must also be taken to ensure that the indemnity survives the termination of the lease. Otherwise, the lessor might find itself responsible for causes of action that arose during the lease but were not discovered or pursued until after its expiration.

As a rule, the general indemnity section of a lease will not cover tax-related matters specifically. Indemnities for loss of tax benefits are usually separate provisions of either the lease or the schedule, depending on the practices of the individual lessor.[12]

7. INSURANCE

Lease Language

Section 7. Insurance.

Lessee, at its own cost and expense, shall keep the Units insured against all risks for the value of such Units and in no event for less than the Casualty Value of such Units as specified in the Schedule, and shall maintain public liability and property damage insurance against such risks and for such amounts as Lessor may require. All such insurance shall be in such form and with such companies as Lessor shall approve, shall name Lessee as insured and Lessor as additional insured, and shall provide that such insurance may not be canceled as to Lessor or altered without at least ten (10) days' prior written notice to Lessor. All liability insurance shall be primary and without right of contribution from any other insurance carried by Lessor. All insurance covering loss or damage to the Units shall contain a "breach of warranty" clause satisfactory to Lessor and shall provide that all amounts payable by reason of loss or damage to the Units shall be payable solely to Lessor. Lessee shall deliver to Lessor on or before the Delivery Date of each Unit evidence satisfactory to Lessor of all such insurance.

Summary

This section provides that:

1. The lessee must insure the equipment.
2. Property damage insurance coverage must be for the actual value, but not less than the casualty value, of the equipment.
3. The amount of public liability insurance must be acceptable to the lessor.

---

[12] In the example lease, the lessee's obligation to pay taxes relating to the equipment or its use is covered in Section 5 above and the lessee's obligation to indemnify the lessor against losses for tax benefits is covered in Section 7 of the Schedule discussed in Chapter 14.

4. The types of risks insured against must be acceptable to the lessor.
5. The insurance carrier must be acceptable to the lessor.
6. The lessor must be an "additional insured."
7. The insurance policy must provide for 10 days' notice to the lessor prior to any modification or cancellation.
8. The insurance policy cannot require "contribution" from any insurance held by the lessor.
9. The insurance policy must provide for coverage and payment to the lessor even if the lessee breaches some obligation to the insurance company that might otherwise let the insurance company off the hook (breach of warranty clause).
10. The lessor must be the sole loss payee under property damage insurance.
11. Evidence of insurance must be delivered to the lessor on or before the delivery date.

Discussion

Section 6 of the example lease sets forth the obligation of the lessee to pay for loss of the equipment due to casualty and to indemnify the lessor for liabilities resulting from the use or operation of the equipment. Section 7 sets forth the obligation of the lessee to arrange and maintain insurance that will protect the lessor and lessee against such claims or such losses, including losses in excess of the casualty value set forth in Section 6, thus assuring the lessor that if there is damage to the equipment or if injury to people or property occurs as a result of use of the equipment, insurance proceeds will be available to aid the lessee in meeting its obligations to the lessor under Section 6. In the absence of insurance, the lessee might not be able to pay the lessor the casualty value when the lessee is obligated by the lease to do so.

In the example lease, the equipment must be insured for the value of the equipment and for not less than the casualty value of the equipment (set forth in the schedule). At the beginning of the lease, the casualty value may exceed 100 percent of the original cost of the equipment, because the casualty value is usually made up of components relating to the lessor's loss of tax benefits, future rents, residual value, and expected profits. If the lessor was able to claim investment tax credit, the loss of investment tax credit by the lessor is "grossed up" to the pretax amount necessary for the lessor to receive in order to recover ITC on an after-tax basis. In such situations, lessees may have difficulty in obtaining insurance up to the casualty value. Insurance in excess of original cost can be obtained in many cases, however, as long as the insurance covers a specified monetary obligation of the lessee with respect to the equipment (that is, to pay the casualty value). This point may involve negotiations with the lessee's insurance carrier that may significantly increase the time needed to negotiate final documentation.

Not all lessors require insurance to equal casualty value when casualty value exceeds the actual value of the equipment. The decision as to whether to require such insurance is basically founded on credit considerations, since without such insurance only the lessee's resources are available to pay the casualty value.

As the lease continues, the actual value of the leased equipment may become much higher than the casualty value. Lessors, as owners of the equipment, want their equipment fully insured. In a true lease, this includes protection against loss of their "upside" potential,[13] a benefit that is clearly part of their ownership interest.[14] Thus, during a lease, lessors will normally review the insurance coverage being provided by the lessee to make sure it is adequate in view of the current value of the equipment and will periodically remind lessees of their obligation to keep the equipment insured to its full value at all times during the lease, even if that value exceeds the casualty value.

The dollar amount of liability insurance required will depend on the lessee, the equipment and its use, and the custom of the lessee's industry. Since for certain types of equipment many leasing companies have preestablished insurance guidelines based on industry norms, and since lessees frequently have substantial insurance coverage that can be made available to cover the lessee's obligations under the lease, the amount of insurance coverage is rarely the subject of considerable negotiation in most lease transactions. However, if the amount of insurance coverage becomes the subject of negotiations, insurance consultants may have to be called in, a fact that can lengthen the negotiation process.

In addition to requiring insurance coverage in a specified amount, most lease insurance provisions, as in the example lease, require the following:

1. The lessor must be listed as an insured and for property damage insurance must be listed as a loss payee. Some lessors are more specific, as in the example lease, and want to be listed as an "additional insured" since the insurance carrier has an obligation to defend the additional

---

[13] The possibility that the equipment will increase in value.

[14] Failure to require protection against this loss might be an indication that the lessor has given away this benefit of ownership, thus jeopardizing its status as owner for true lease purposes. While this argument is not particularly persuasive in and of itself, it may carry more weight in situations in which the lessee is permitted to keep insurance proceeds in excess of the casualty value.

insured against liability claims, yet the additional insured has no obligation to the carrier, as would be the case for a "named insured" or an "additional named insured." Many lessors want to be the sole loss payee to avoid having to obtain the lessee's endorsement on insurance checks. Lessees may seek to negotiate an insurance provision that merely requires the lessee to maintain insurance and to provide the lessor with proof that the insurance is in force, without listing the lessor as an additional insured or a loss payee. This type of provision is usually unsatisfactory to the lessor since the lessor then has no control over the insurance proceeds and no direct rights against the insurance company. In such instances, the lessor must treat the lessee as essentially self-insured.

2. The insurance may not be canceled without prior notice to the lessor. Since the lessor relies on insurance to aid the lessee in meeting its obligations to the lessor, the lessor obviously has a continuing interest in the status of the insurance policies. Without a requirement of prior notice of changes or cancellation, the requirements of insurance provisions similar to those of Section 7 would essentially become meaningless.

3. The insurance must not require contribution from any insurance carried separately by the lessor. Lessors want the full insurance responsibility to be on the lessee and do not wish to be in the middle of disputes between insurance carriers as to which of them is responsible.

4. The insurance must cover the lessor, even if the lessee breaches some obligation or warranty to the carrier. All insurance policies place certain requirements on the insured. If the lessee fails to comply with those requirements, the lessor does not want that failure to affect its right to be paid or protected under the policy. Provisions that permit payment to third parties despite the insured's breach of the policy are generally referred to as "breach of warranty" clauses.

5. Proof of insurance must be given to the lessor before the equipment is delivered. Most lessors will consider proof of insurance as a condition precedent to making payment to the vendor. Once the equipment is delivered and paid for, furnishing proof of insurance may be fairly low on the lessee's list of priorities.

Self-Insurance. The example lease does not contemplate or allow for self-insurance by the lessee. In recent years, however, the right to self-insure has become increasingly important to lessees due to the fact certain kinds of insurance have become difficult to obtain except at exorbitant prices.

The decision to permit self-insurance is based on credit considerations and generally requires a formal credit determination by the lessor that the lessee is strong enough financially to meet its obligations under the casualty occurrence provisions of the lease and, if applicable, the general indemnity provisions.

Many lessees have property damage insurance policies with deductibles that are in excess of the value of the equipment. Such lessees, in effect, self-insure to the extent of the deductibles. Lessees desiring this type of self-insurance also have to meet lessors' credit standards for self-insurance. Usually this is a reasonable request by the lessee that the lessor should permit.

Lessees that refuse to make the lessor an additional insured or a loss payee should be considered "self-insurers" insofar as the lessor is concerned, since the lessor has no rights under any policies carried by the lessee. Lessees that are not creditworthy enough to meet the lessor's self-insurance credit standards should not be allowed to deviate from the practice of naming the lessor an insured and a loss payee.

In drafting self-insurance provisions, consideration should be given to the following:

1. Is self-insurance merely for the deductible portion of an existing policy? If so, are there limits on the size of the deductible?
2. Is self-insurance allowed for both property damage and public liability?
3. Is the right to self-insure granted for the whole term of the lease or on a yearly basis depending, for example, on the net worth of the lessee?
4. Can the lessee lose the right to self-insure upon the happening of certain events?
5. Does the lessee have to escrow or reserve funds to help cover losses that may occur?
6. Does the lessee's self-insurance program have to meet certain standards common in the lessee's industry?

8. DEFAULT

Lease Language

Section 8. Default.

8.1 If one or more of the following events ("Events of Default") shall occur:

(a) Default shall be made by Lessee in the making of any payments to Lessor when due hereunder;

(b) Any representation or warranty of Lessee contained herein or in any document furnished to Lessor in connection herewith shall be untrue or incorrect in any material respect when made;

(c) Default shall be made in the observance or performance of any of the other covenants, conditions, agreements, or warranties made by

Lessee hereunder and such default shall continue for ___ days after written notice thereof to Lessee;

(*d*) Lessee shall file any petition or action under any bankruptcy, reorganization, insolvency, or moratorium law or any other law or laws for the relief of, or relating to, debtors; or

(*e*) Any involuntary petition shall be filed under any bankruptcy statute against Lessee, or any receiver, trustee, or custodian shall be appointed to take possession of the properties of Lessee, unless such petition or appointment is set aside or withdrawn or ceases to be in effect within sixty (60) days from the date of said filing or appointment; then, in any such case, Lessor, at its option, may:

(*aa*) proceed by appropriate court action or actions, either at law or in equity, to enforce performance by Lessee of the applicable covenants of this Lease or to recover damages for the breach thereof; or

(*bb*) by notice in writing to Lessee terminate this Lease, whereupon all rights of Lessee to the use of the Units shall absolutely cease and terminate, but Lessee shall remain liable as hereinafter provided; and thereupon Lessor may by its agents enter upon the premises of Lessee or other premises where any of the Units may be and take possession of all or any of such Units and thenceforth hold the same free from any right of Lessee, its successors, or assigns, but Lessor shall, nevertheless, have a right to recover from Lessee any and all amounts which under the terms of this Lease may be then due or which may have accrued to the date of such termination (computing the rental for any number of days less than a full rental period by multiplying the rental for such full rental period by a fraction of which the numerator is such number of days and the denominator is the total number of days in such full rental period) and also to recover forthwith from Lessee (*i*) as damages for loss of the bargain and not as a penalty, a sum, with respect to each Unit, which represents the excess of (*x*), the present value, at the time of such termination, of the entire unpaid balance of all rental for such Unit which would otherwise have accrued hereunder from the date of such termination to the end of the term of this Lease as to such Unit, over (*y*), the then present value of the rentals which Lessor reasonably estimates to be obtainable for the Unit during such period, such present value to be computed in each case by discounting at a rate equal to the then judgment rate of interest fixed under the law of the State of _____, compounded at the same frequency as rentals are paid hereunder, from the respective dates upon which rentals would have been payable hereunder had the Lease not been terminated, and (*ii*) any damages and expenses in addition thereto which the Lessor shall have sustained by reason of the breach of any covenant, representation, or warranty contained in this Lease other than for the payment of rental.

8.2 Lessee shall pay to Lessor a reasonable sum for its attorneys' fees and all other costs and expenses of Lessor in enforcing this Lease.

8.3 The remedies hereunder provided in favor of Lessor shall not be deemed exclusive, but shall be cumulative and shall be in addition to all other remedies in its favor existing at law or in equity. Lessee hereby waives any mandatory requirements of law, now or hereafter in effect, which might limit or modify the remedies herein provided, to the extent that such waiver is permitted by law.

Summary

Section 8 provides that:

1. The lessee will be in default in the event of any of the following:
   a. The lessee fails to pay rent when due.
   b. Any material representation or warranty by the lessee proves to be untrue when made.
   c. The lessee fails to comply with the covenants of the lease after the lessor has given notice of a specified amount of time to cure the default.
   d. The lessee files a petition in bankruptcy.
   e. A petition for "involuntary bankruptcy" is filed against the lessee and remains undismissed after a period of 60 days.
2. If any event of default occurs, the lessor has two options under the lease:
   a. Continue the lease in force, but sue for damages and specific performance.
   b. Notify the lessee that the lease is terminated, repossess the equipment, and collect (sue for) all rental due to the date of such termination plus (1) the present value of all future rentals minus the present value of what the lessor can reasonably expect to receive in releasing the equipment to another lessee for a period equal to the remainder of the original term and (2) any damages or expenses incurred that relate to the lessee's breach.
3. The lessee pays the lessor's attorneys' fees in enforcing the lease.
4. The remedies under this section are not exclusive but are in addition to all other remedies available to the lessee at law (and in equity).
5. The lessee waives to the extent permitted by law the benefit of any laws that might otherwise limit or modify the remedies set forth in the lease.

Discussion

Section 8.1. Events of Default. The events of default in the example lease are very basic. Many leases contain additional provisions, commonly covering matters such as defaults under other leases or under borrowing agreements, failure to maintain certain financial standards, or failure of certain other documents to be in effect (for example, guaranties and security agreements).

Exactly what will trigger default, and when, can be the subject of considerable discussion during lease negotiations. One of the principal areas of discussion is that of grace periods. Lessees frequently want 5 or 10 days' grace before nonpayment is a default, and sometimes up to 30 days' grace before other failures to comply with the express terms of the lease become defaults. Another area of discussion is whether the lessor should be required to give notice and a cure or grace period to the lessee before certain events become defaults.

From the lessee's perspective, the issue is usually one of "technical default" and whether missing a payment by one day will subject it to possible loss of the equipment. Grace periods, particularly when combined with notice, "buy" extra time for the lessee. Although this fear of technical default may be real, it is not entirely convincing. In a true situation involving technical default, the last thing that the lessor is likely to be interested in is repossession with all its attendant difficulties. However, some kind of notice requirement and cure period before a lessor can repossess equipment is a fairly reasonable request by the lessee.

From the lessor's perspective, the issue is to maintain the maximum ability to move quickly in serious default situations in which fast action may be necessary to protect its interests. Grace periods, particularly those combined with notice, drastically reduce the lessor's ability to move quickly. Having the ability to move quickly may become even more important to lessors under the Bankruptcy Code[15] since many lessors may feel that in potential bankruptcy situations they would be better off to terminate the lease effectively and repossess before a bankruptcy petition can be filed, rather than risk the trustee's assumption and possible assignment of the lease.

Another factor from the lessor's standpoint is that the lessor's yield is calculated on the basis that rentals will be paid on time. Strict provisions with regard to rent payment help to achieve that objective.

Regardless of the arguments on either side, flexibility on the issue of notice and grace periods may ultimately be a matter of company policy to the point that the issue becomes a "deal" point. (This is frequently the case when the party in question has had a bad experience centering on the issue.) In other cases, flexibility (or the lack thereof) may be influenced by the type of lessor company involved. Bank and finance company lessors usually take a hard line on both notice and grace period issues, generally refusing to give notice with respect to

---

[15] 11 U.S.C. 101 et seq.

nonpayment and keeping grace periods short, if these are granted at all. This practice is consistent with that used in most loan transactions and is simply carried over into lease transactions. Merchant lessors, on the other hand, may take a more flexible stand. Bank and finance company lessors tend to be more liberal on larger transactions to creditworthy lessees.

As noted above, the Bankruptcy Code now gives the trustee the ability to assume and assign unexpired leases. The Bankruptcy Code also invalidates ipso facto bankruptcy clauses similar to Sections 8.1d and 8.1e of the example lease[16] (at least with respect to equipment already under lease). Because of these two "facts of life" under the recently enacted Bankruptcy Code, lessors' attorneys are redesigning and redrafting events of default clauses for leases. Many more "bright line," "early warning" types of defaults may be included so as to permit the lessor to terminate the lease in advance of the filing of a petition. Also, references to the lessee being "generally unable to pay its debts as they become due" are likely to be added, as are other references that track the language of the new Bankruptcy Code.[17]

Section 8.1. Remedies.   The remedies afforded to the lessor in any lease should be designed to compensate the lessor without penalizing the lessee, as attempts to penalize the lessee will probably be unenforceable and might jeopardize the lessor's legitimate recovery rights.

Under Section 8.1 of the example lease, the lessor has two basic remedies. Under Section 8.1(*aa*), the lease continues in force, and the lessor sues for actual damages caused by the lessee's default and then, if applicable, for specific performance of the terms of the lease.

Under Section 8.1(*bb*), the lease is terminated by the lessor (written notice is given by the lessor in this case) and the lessor becomes entitled to immediate possession of the equipment.[18] In addition, the lessor is

---

[16] 11 U.S.C. 541(c)(1). However, the lessor may still wish to include these provisions in the lease as a statement of intent. Also, many equipment lease forms predate the new Bankruptcy Code, and these types of provisions still commonly appear in lease documents.

[17] For a succinct discussion of leasing and the Bankruptcy Code, see "Structuring and Documenting Business Financing Transactions under the Federal Bankruptcy Code of 1978," *Business Law* 35 (July 1980) pp. 1645, 1699–1707. See also Glenn S. Gerstell and Katryn Hoff-Patrinas, "The Bankruptcy Code and Equipment Leasing," in *Equipment Leasing*, ed. Ian Shrank and William E. Flowers (New York: Practicing Law Institute, Fall 1987), pp. 659–689.

[18] Even though true leases are not directly governed by Article 9 of the Uniform Commercial Code, peaceful self-help must be utilized in the repossession. Court assistance is necessary in situations in which peaceful self-help is not possible. Care should also be taken to draft the remedies provision with Article 9 in mind, as a court may apply certain of its provisions by analogy. See *Equipment Leasing 1987*, ed. Ronald M. Bayer and Ian Shrank (New York: Practicing Law Institute). See especially the articles therein by Steven Harris, pp. 177–254 and Ronald Bayer pp. 255–94.

entitled to all past-due and accrued rentals. Future rentals are not "accelerated," as would be the case if the transaction were a loan.[19] Instead, the example lease provides for liquidated damages based on (1) the present value of the future rentals less (2) the present value of estimated reasonable rentals obtainable for the remainder of the original term. The present value is obtained by discounting the two rental amounts by the state court judgment rate of interest (so as to comply with state usury laws) at the time of the default. In addition to the amount obtained in accordance with this formula, the lease also provides for recovery of actual damages and expenses incurred as a result of the default.

Provisions similar to those in the example lease are unlikely to be construed as penalty provisions. So long as the lease contains no unconscionable provisions, specific performance simply forces the lessee to abide by the provisions that it agreed to, and presumably understood, from the outset. On the other hand, if the lessor elects to terminate the lease because of the default, it is still entitled to receive the benefit of its bargain with the lessee. Provisions similar to those of Section 8.1(*bb*) are designed to do just that. In addition to past-due rentals and actual damages and expenses, the lessor receives damages based on a formula tied to leasing rather than sale of the equipment, leasing being the transaction that both parties contemplated for the entire term. In the example lease, the rental figures are discounted to present value to account for the time value of money. The discount rate is tied to the state court judgment rate. This rate would normally be expected to be fairly low, which is a benefit to the lessor, but not so low as to be a penalty for the lessee.[20]

Some leases will have an alternative measure of damages provision based on the difference between the casualty value of the unit and the sales proceeds received upon sale of the unit on default. As the casualty value usually contains a factor to compensate the lessor for loss of expected residual, this type of provision may act as a penalty in situations in which the sales proceeds received are minimal. Lessors are usually wary, therefore, of using such a formula as the sole method of determining damages on default. Aside from the possible penalty aspects of such a provision, most lessors are also reluctant to measure damages solely in relation to sales proceeds since at the time of default

---

[19] Rent acceleration clauses are extremely controversial. Courts may consider them a penalty, or they may consider them evidence that a loan rather than a true lease was intended by the parties.

[20] Case law in California, for example, upholds the judgment interest rate as a reasonable discount factor in determining charges.

there may be important reasons, such as possible recapture of any applicable investment tax credit, that make an immediate sale inadvisable.

In drafting and negotiating remedies provisions, extreme care must be taken to ensure that the remedies are and remain enforceable under the governing law of the lease. In multistate transactions, enforceability under the law of the lessee's principal place of business should also be considered, unless one can be reasonably sure that a court in such a state would honor the choice of law clause in the lease.

Section 8.2. Attorneys' Fees. Provisions similar to Section 8.2 are found in most net leases. Some lessees want this provision narrowed to cover only litigation expense. However, many lessors are unwilling to agree to such a limitation since attorneys' fees in negotiation and "workout" proceedings (short of actually filing suit) can be considerable. Lessors that agree to limit payment of attorneys' fees to litigation situations should avoid making payment of those fees by the lessee contingent upon the lessor prevailing in the suit. Courts may, in certain circumstances, be unable to decide which party clearly prevailed and refuse to enforce such a provision.

Section 8.3. Cumulative Remedies. Section 8.3 is a fairly standard "boilerplate" type of provision designed to maximize the lessor's remedies. Such provisions are usually not the subject of negotiation, although some lessees may object to language that requires them to waive unknowns and may request at least a partial history of the types of waivers that the lessor has in mind (for example, waiver of statute of limitations).

9. RETURN OF UNITS

Lease Language

Section 9. Return of Units.
Upon expiration of the term in respect of each Unit, or if Lessor shall rightfully demand possession of such Unit pursuant to this Lease or otherwise, Lessee, at its expense, shall forthwith deliver possession of such Unit to Lessor either (*a*) by delivering such Unit appropriately protected to Lessor at such place within the location set forth in the Schedule as may be specified by Lessor or (*b*) by loading such Unit appropriately protected on board such carrier as Lessor shall specify and shipping the same, freight collect, to the destination designated by Lessor at the option of Lessor.

Summary

This section stipulates that:

1. The lessee must pay for return of the equipment.
2. The lessee must properly protect the equipment being returned.
3. The lessee bears the full cost of returning the equipment to the lessor if the lessor designates a place within the location specified in the schedule.
4. The lessee may send the equipment freight collect if the lessor designates a place outside the location specified in the schedule.

Discussion

Return provisions are especially important in true leases as the lessor cannot have the right to abandon the equipment without jeopardizing the true lease status of the transaction. Thus, all true leases should contain provisions making clear that at the end of the lease term the property is to be returned to the lessor and not simply abandoned on the spot.

Return provisions can also help the lessor protect the realization of the maximum residual value at the conclusion of the lease by making clear the lessee's obligation (1) to protect the equipment in transit and (2) to deliver the equipment promptly to whatever location is specified by the lessor.

The return provision in the example lease is very basic. Many leases will contain far more elaborate provisions, particularly if the equipment involved is likely to be at many locations (for example, rail cars, motor vehicles, containers). Provisions for "holding over" so that equipment may be gathered in and for delivering equipment to multiple locations are not uncommon. Many return provisions (particularly in leases of aircraft and high-technology equipment) also specify operating conditions or maintenance requirements the equipment must meet upon return.

In drafting and negotiating return provisions, the following key concepts should be kept in mind:

1. The lessee in a true lease will always be responsible for returning the equipment to the lessor.
2. The equipment must be properly prepared for movement by the lessee in order to protect against losses in the residual value.
3. In net leases, the expense of returning the equipment to a nearby warehouse, shipping depot, rail siding, or subsequent lessee or buyer is always borne by the lessee.

4. In order to maximize their ability to sell the equipment in many different markets, lessors want maximum flexibility in specifying the location of redelivery. Except in unusual circumstances, however, lessees will not generally be required to pay for shipping the equipment to faraway locations but will be permitted to ship it "freight collect" to locations outside the area in which they could reasonably be expected to return it. (Freight collect is normally specified because the risk of loss stays with the shipper until the shipment reaches its destination.)

In some leases, lessors or lessees will seek to obtain some future advantage in negotiating for the sale or purchase of the leased equipment at the end of the lease term by imposing conditions on the return of the equipment as to delivery or condition that will encourage the lessee or lessor, as the case may be, to purchase or sell the equipment at a reasonable price. Care must be taken in such situations that the lessor or lessee is not compelled by economics to sell or purchase the leased asset at a price that bears no relation to its fair market value lest the Internal Revenue Service take the position that the lease does not constitute a true lease for tax purposes.

10. ASSIGNMENT

Lease Language

Section 10. Assignment.
All or any of the right, title, or interest of Lessor in and to this Lease, and the rights, benefits, and advantages of Lessor hereunder, including the rights to receive payment of rental or any other payment hereunder, and title to the Units, may be assigned or transferred by Lessor at any time. Any such assignment or transfer shall be subject and subordinate to the terms and provisions of this Lease and the rights and interests of Lessee hereunder. No assignment of this Lease or any right or obligation hereunder whatsoever may be made by Lessee or any assignee of Lessee without the prior written consent of Lessor.

Summary

This section provides that:

1. The lessor may assign the lease, any portion of its rights or obligations under the lease, or title to the equipment to any other party at any time without the consent of the lessee.
2. Any assignment by the lessor must recognize the rights of the lessee under the lease.

3. The lessee may not assign its rights or obligations under the lease without the prior written consent of the lessor.

Discussion

Assignment provisions of the type in the example lease are very common in "finance" leases. The lessor may assign freely; the lessee may not. Generally, the first half of provisions of this type is not the subject of much discussion. Since the finance lessor's basic obligation is to provide funds for the purchase of the equipment, and since that obligation is fulfilled at the outset, lessees have little reason to object to an assignment that as a practical matter only alters the recipient of the rent. Some lessees may, however, be uneasy about the possibility of assignments to their direct competitors. Since a lessor's interest in assigning the lease is usually based on considerations of financial flexibility, as long as its rights to assign the lease to recognized financial institutions or other finance lessors are assured, the lessor usually has no objection to restrictions on its ability to assign the lease to a competitor of the lessee, provided the term *competitor* can be adequately defined under the circumstances.

Lessees seeking to limit the right of a lessor to assign the lease paper or to sell the lease receivables should be aware that many lessors fully intend to assign the lease or the receivables to a financial institution, frequently even prior to the date on which the equipment is delivered to the lessee. These lessors will be considerably less flexible in negotiating limitations on their rights to assign than will lessors that simply want to preserve those rights in case at some future point business considerations might make assignments attractive. Lessees must also be sensitive to the fact that a lessor company that is a member of a large corporate family will almost always insist on the right to assign the lease freely within that corporate family.

The second half of an assignment provision such as Section 10 can lead to considerable negotiation. Many lessees want to be able to transfer their obligations under the lease, usually as a hedge against the possibility that the equipment might not be useful to them for the entire term, and sometimes because they expect to merge with or be acquired by another entity at some point during the lease and wish to avoid the lessor's involvement in that transaction. As in a loan transaction, however, credit considerations will usually make lessors unwilling to permit such transfers without their prior consent. Occasionally, lessors will permit transfers "with recourse" to the original lessee without the need for the prior consent of the lessor, although even in this circumstance most will require that the assignment take a particular form and that the assignee meet certain specified standards.

11. FURTHER ASSURANCE

Lease Language

Section 11. Further Assurance.
Lessee will, at its expense, do and perform any other act and will execute, acknowledge, deliver, file, register, and record any further instruments which Lessor may reasonably request in order to protect Lessor's title to the Units, this Lease, and the rights and benefits thereof.

Summary

This section provides that the lessee may be asked to execute additional documents or to perform further acts that the lessor may consider necessary to protect its title to the equipment and its rights under the lease.

Discussion

Almost all leases will have this sort of catchall provision. When the provision is drafted broadly, as in the example lease, lessees may request an explanation of what is intended. Usually the lessor will have in mind such things as precautionary financing statements,[21] the registration and titling of motor vehicles, or the registration of filing of the lease with the necessary governmental authorities.[22] Lessees may prefer to have such items listed specifically in the lease. While lessors may agree to such a listing, as a rule there will still be a catchall referring to "such other documents or such other acts as Lessor may require," so that the lessor has the right to ask the lessee to take further actions should these be warranted by the circumstances of a particular transaction. Lessees can be expressly protected by drafting in a standard of reasonableness if they feel that such a standard is necessary.

12. LATE PAYMENTS

Lease Language

Section 12. Late Payments.
Lessee shall pay to Lessor, on demand, interest at the rate of fourteen percent (14%) per annum on the amount of any payment not made when due hereunder from the date thereof until payment is made.

---

[21] Precautionary financing statements are filed by many lessors in true leases in order to protect against the possibility that the lease might be held to be a lease intended for security.

[22] Leases of railroad cars and aircraft must be filed with the Interstate Commerce Commission and the Federal Aviation Authority, respectively. Certain ship leases must also be filed with governmental authorities.

Summary

This section indicates that the lessee will be penalized for paying late, at a specified rate of interest per annum.

Discussion

Since the lessor's yield on the lease transaction is dependent on rental payments being made on time, many, if not most, leases contain provisions similar to Section 12 to encourage prompt payment of rental. The interest rate specified in these provisions may or may not be negotiable. Many lessors have a standardized rate built into a computerized billing system, so that use of a rate other than the one built into the system would require "hand" billing of all late charges. Changing the date on which late charges begin to accrue may cause the same problem. Thus, many lessors are unwilling to negotiate on either of these points.

As a practical matter, the interest rate specified in late payment provisions is unlikely to be troublesome to most lessees, as the lessor must be very careful that the interest rate specified does not exceed the rate permitted by applicable law. In multistate transactions, however, it may be difficult to tell whether the rate specified is permissible, since usury rates vary so widely from state to state. Potentially, the law of three or more states may have to be considered in determining the interest rate that may be lawfully charged: the law of the lessor's home state (usually the governing law of the lease), the law of the state of the lessee's principal place of business, and the law of the state or states in which the equipment is located. National bank lessors will have the benefit of the *Marquette National Bank* case in determining what interest rate they may charge, but other lessors will have to go through a choice of law analysis in order to determine the appropriate rate.[23]

13. EFFECT OF WAIVER

Lease Language

Section 13. Effect of Waiver.

No delay or omission to exercise any right, power, or remedy accruing to Lessor upon any breach or default of Lessee hereunder shall impair any such right, power, or remedy nor shall it be construed to be a waiver of any such breach or default, or an acquiescence therein of or in any

---

[23] Some states treat late charges as liquidated damages rather than interest. In such states the charge must be reasonably related to the damage caused by the late payment.

similar breach or default thereafter occurring, nor shall any waiver of any single breach or default be deemed a waiver of any other breach or default theretofore or thereafter occurring. Any waiver, permit, consent, or approval of any kind or character on the part of Lessor of any breach or default under this Lease must be in writing specifically set forth. No variation notification or amendment of this Lease shall be valid unless in writing.

Summary

This section provides that:

1. The failure of the lessor to take action or exercise its rights on any single occasion does not limit its right to take action or exercise its rights.
2. The lessor's inaction cannot be construed as a waiver or acquiescence.
3. All waivers and consents must be in writing.
4. All amendments must be in writing.

Discussion

Provisions such as Section 13 are rarely controversial; however, lessors, of course, cannot place undue reliance upon them. In spite of the absolute statement to the contrary, inaction can be construed as a waiver, and leases can be amended by the "custom and practice" of the parties. Nonetheless, almost all lease agreements contain "no waiver" and "modifications in writing" provisions for whatever limited protection these offer to the lessor.

14. SURVIVAL OF COVENANTS

Lease Language

Section 14. Survival of Covenants.
All covenants of Lessee under Sections 1, 2, 4, 5, 6, 8, 9, and 12 shall survive the expiration or termination of this lease to the extent required for their full observance and performance.

Summary

This section indicates that certain obligations of the lessee do not expire with the lease.

Discussion

The purpose of a "survival clause" such as Section 14 of the example lease is to extend certain of the lessee's obligations beyond the lease term because:

1. The lessee may not have fulfilled all of its obligations under the lease when the term has ended.
2. The lessor still needs the right to enforce certain provisions of the lease against the lessee.
3. Some obligations, for example, those in Section 9, "Return of Units," do not arise until the lease has been terminated.

Since the provisions of each section mentioned in a survival clause can be of potential importance to the lessor after the lease has ended, most lessors will not permit variations in the substance of such clauses.

15. APPLICABLE LAW; MERGER OF PRIOR AGREEMENTS

Lease Language

Section 15. Applicable Law.
    15.1 This Lease shall be governed by, and construed under, the laws of the State of _____.
    15.2 This Lease exclusively and completely states the rights of Lessor and Lessee with respect to the leasing of the Units and supersedes all prior agreements, oral or written, with respect thereto.

Summary

This section specifies that:

1. The law of a particular state will be used to interpret the lease.
2. Any previous agreements with respect to leasing the equipment terminate upon execution of the lease.

Discussion

Section 15.1. Governing Law. Most lessors select the law of a particular state as the governing law for all of their direct leases in order to:

1. Avoid "conflict of law" questions should a dispute arise.
2. Maintain consistency of interpretation for their standard lease document.

3. Ensure that the lease is drafted to comply with that state's law.[24]

Section 15.2. Merger of Prior Agreements. Section 15.2 is typical of the integration provisions found in most leases. The importance of such a provision in negotiations is to raise the question of whether the lease in fact represents the prior negotiated understanding of the parties and reflects the lessee's bid letter, if any, and the lessor's answer proposal and/or commitment letter. All points of difference should be discussed so that the lease clearly represents the understanding of the parties.

16. FINANCIAL INFORMATION

Lease Language

Section 16. Financial Information.
    Lessee shall keep its books and records in accordance with generally accepted accounting principles and practices consistently applied and shall deliver to Lessor its annual audited financial statements and such other unaudited financial statements as may be reasonably requested by Lessor.

Summary

This section states that:

1. The lessee must keep its records in accordance with generally accepted accounting principles.
2. The lessee must deliver its annual audited financial statements to the lessor.
3. The lessor can request unaudited financial statements as well.

---

[24] Bank leasing companies may also select their home state's law in an effort to tie their activities closely to their home states so as to avoid "branch banking" issues.

Lessees may wish to have the laws of some other state control. However, most leasing companies typically reserve the right to name the state law that will control the lease transactions. If the lessor agrees to a choice of law other than that of its home state, the law of a state with well-developed commercial legal precedents, such as New York, California, or Illinois, will usually be chosen if there are sufficient legal contacts to justify such a choice.

Changes in governing law are usually consented to only in extreme cases, and such a change can cause documentation delays as the lessor may not have enough information about the laws of the chosen state to know what effect a switch in governing law would have on the enforceability of the lease, thus necessitating the involvement of local counsel in reviewing the documentation for enforceability.

Discussion

A nonleveraged lease of personal property does not usually contain financial covenants, except for one requiring adherence to accounting norms and delivery of unaudited financial information each quarter and audited financial information each year.[25] This type of provision is rarely the subject of negotiation, except in instances where generally accepted accounting principles do not apply to a particular lessee or where the lessee does not have audited financial statements of its own (usually because of consolidation of financial information with its parent). In negotiating provisions relating to delivery of financial information, the key points to remember are:

1. The lessor must have financial information:
   a. To make the initial credit decisions.
   b. To be informed of the lessee's financial status or to be in a position to take steps to protect the leased equipment against claims of third-party creditors.

2. The lessee must be required to adhere to some readily understandable standard in maintaining its records, or those records will be of little or no value to the lessor.

3. The lessor may want more than audited statements and, at the very least, the right to ask for additional information. Usually lessees have no objection to furnishing various financial reports that would be prepared in the usual course of business.

4. If specialized reporting requirements are negotiated, the lessee should review those requirements with the personnel in its organization responsible for providing such reports to make sure that compliance is feasible without undue expense.

17. NOTICES

Lease Language

Section 17. Notices.

All demands, notices, and other communications hereunder shall be in writing and shall be deemed to have been duly given when personally delivered or when deposited in the mail, first-class postage prepaid, or delivered to a telegraph office, charges prepaid, addressed as follows:

To Lessor:

_____

_____

Attention: Vice President Contract Administration

---

[25] A large single investor lease or a leveraged lease might include a restriction on the merger of the lessee or a sale of assets by the lessee.

To Lessee:

_____

_____

_____

Attention: Vice President Finance

or at such other address as may hereafter be furnished in writing by either party to the other.

Summary

This section provides that:

1. Notices must be written.
2. Notices are deemed effective when addressed to the appropriate party and (*a*) delivered personally, (*b*) deposited in the mail (with a stamp), or (*c*) delivered to a telegraph office (and prepaid).
3. Either party may specify an address for notices different from the one listed in the lease.

Discussion

Some lessees request that notices be sent by registered mail, return receipt requested. However, most lessors will resist this type of provision as it is expensive and time-consuming and forces the lessor to wait for and track the return receipt. Registered mail is also often slower than regular mail. Furthermore, unless the use of registered mail for this purpose is standard procedure for operational departments, clerks in documentation and accounting may forget to send the right kind of notice. Computerized and mechanized mailing procedures are utilized by many lessors, and this will limit the flexibility of lessors on this point. Lessors that have agreed to give lessees notice of nonpayment before a default is triggered will be particularly reluctant to agree to sending notices by registered mail with return receipt.

With respect to the lessor's address, always use the headquarters office of the lessor, rather than a branch office, because:

1. The lessor wants the transaction tied as closely as possible to the home state.
2. The headquarters office is set up to administer the lease.

To avoid confusion, the street address in the first paragraph of the lease and the street address in Section 17 should be consistent when the lease is originally signed.

The lessor and the lessee should have notices sent to the attention of an officer or supervisor to make sure that any notice receives prompt attention.

18. COUNTERPARTS

Lease Language

Section 18. Counterparts.

Two counterparts of this Lease have been executed by the parties hereto. One counterpart has been prominently marked "Lessor's Copy." One counterpart has been prominently marked "Lessee's Copy." Only the counterpart marked "Lessor's Copy" shall evidence a monetary obligation of Lessee.

Summary

This section provides that:

1. A specified number of counterparts of the lease have been executed.
2. One copy is marked "Lessee's Copy," and one is marked "Lessor's Copy."
3. Only one of these copies is to be treated as chattel paper.

Discussion

Ordinarily, only the lessor and lessee need executed copies of the lease. In railroad car and aircraft leases, however, an executed copy of the lease must be filed with the ICC or FAA, respectively. In other cases, the lessee or lessor may wish additional executed copies for some particular reason. The number of copies actually executed should be reflected in the lease document.

The principal reason for keeping track of the number of executed copies of the lease is to enable the lessor to sell the lease as chattel paper if it so desires. Any potential buyer would want to know whether other executed copies exist that might already have been sold as chattel paper. The last sentence of this section is an attempt to limit the number of executed leases that evidence a monetary obligation of the lessee and thus constitute chattel paper. If it is clear that only one document (the lessor's copy in the example lease) evidences a monetary obligation of the lessee, the ability of the lessor to sell the lease receivable is facilitated since the purchaser need not require that all executed copies be surrendered. The purchaser only has to hold the "Lessor's Copy."[26] Some leases may provide for the numbering of each executed counterpart, with only "Counterpart 1" evidencing the monetary obligation of the lessee.

---

[26] When the lessee is allowed to sublease the equipment, the lessor may require that language similar to that contained in this section be inserted in the sublease in order to restrict the number of sublease counterparts that can be treated as chattel paper.

14

A Typical Lease Schedule

In this chapter, we shall provide an overview of the "schedule" attached to and incorporated into the "lease." The format we used in the previous chapter to discuss the lease agreement will be used to discuss the provisions of the schedule; that is, the treatment of each provision of the schedule will be broken down, as far as possible, into three parts: (*a*) schedule language, (*b*) summary, and (*c*) discussion.

THE SCHEDULE

The provisions typically included in the schedule are as follows:

1. Description of units and maximum purchase price.
2. Term of the lease for each unit.
3. Rental for each unit.
4. Availability date for commitment.
5. Location of leased equipment.
6. Casualty value.
7. Tax indemnification.
8. Early termination.
9. Purchase and renewal options.
10. Commitment fees.

In tax-oriented leases, the structuring of certain provisions in both the lease and the schedule is dominated by the potential implications for tax treatment.

Each of the 10 typical schedule provisions is discussed below.

DESCRIPTION OF UNITS AND MAXIMUM PURCHASE PRICE

Schedule Language

> *Section 1. Description of Units and Maximum Purchase Price.*
> A description of the Units to be leased is as follows:
>
> (Describe the units including the estimated Purchase Price.)
>
> The aggregate actual Purchase Price (as hereinafter defined) of all Units shall not exceed _____ without the prior written consent of Lessor. Purchase Price shall mean the full amount paid by Lessor for each Unit, including any applicable front-end tax, freight, or installation charges.

Summary

This section contains:

1. A description of the equipment to be leased.
2. The estimated purchase price of the equipment.
3. The maximum amount the lessor is committed to pay for the equipment to be leased, which can be exceeded only with the prior written consent of the lessor.

Discussion

The purpose of this section is to provide the lessor with an adequate description of the equipment to be leased for purposes of collateral value, tax depreciation, and residual assumption. The lessor has entered into the lease and calculated its yield on the basis that certain equipment would be leased. An inadequate description permitting the lessee to substitute less desirable equipment, with different tax depreciation, less collateral value, or less potential residual value, would have an adverse effect on the credit risk and economics of the transaction.

The purpose of the section is not necessarily to provide such a complete description as to permit identification of a particular unit at a later date. Identification by serial numbers, for example, may not be possible until the equipment is delivered. Thus, such specific information would normally be listed on the acceptance supplement rather than in the schedule. There may be circumstances in which a more specific description of equipment is appropriate in the schedule, however. In leases of aircraft, the serial numbers of the plane, engines, and propellers are normally listed, as are the specific model and type of aircraft. Without such a detailed description in the schedule, proper registration of the aircraft may be delayed.

The limitation on the purchase price in the next to last sentence of Section 1 of the example lease schedule defines the overall credit exposure of the lessor. In multiple-lease situations, lessors will frequently place an aggregate limit on the purchase price of equipment under all leases—for example, "The aggregate purchase price of all Units under this lease and all equipment leased pursuant to the Lease dated _____ between Lessee and Lessor [or perhaps the lessee and some other affiliated lessor] shall not exceed $_____ without the prior written consent of Lessor." While limiting the lessor's overall credit exposure, this type of limit also gives the lessee maximum flexibility in determining exactly how much equipment to place under each lease. The lessee can use the maximum amount under one lease or divide that amount up as it chooses.

TERM OF THE LEASE FOR EACH UNIT

Schedule Language

Section 2. Lease Term.
The lease term for each Unit shall be comprised of an interim term followed immediately by a base term. The interim term for each Unit shall commence on the Delivery Date in respect thereto and shall continue until the applicable Scheduling Date (as hereinafter defined) for such Unit. The base term for each Unit shall commence on the Scheduling Date for each Unit and continue for the number of months specified below. The Scheduling Date for each Unit shall be the _____ day of the calendar month following the Delivery Date of such Unit.

No. of Months of Base Term: _____

Summary

This section specifies the length of the lease term and divides the lease term into two parts.

Discussion

Most lessors will require that the lease term commence on the delivery date of the equipment. This might be defined as either the date on which the equipment is physically delivered to the lessee or the installation date, if assembly and installation are necessary.[1] The reason for this requirement is not only to protect first-user rights but also to make sure that the lessee is required to use the equipment in accordance with all the provisions of the lease, since if the start of the lease term for a particular unit is delayed to a date beyond the delivery date, certain provisions of the lease may not be operative with respect to that unit.

However, beginning the lease term for each unit on its delivery date may cause administrative confusion for both the lessor and the lessee, particularly in multiple-delivery situations. For example, lease terms will expire on different dates, lease rental payments will be due on different dates, and the billing cycle or lease term may not match the lessee's payment cycle or its need for the use of the equipment over a particular period.

This problem is solved in the example lease schedule by use of an interim term that runs from the delivery date until a specified date when the base term commences. That date can be selected with the particular needs of the lessee in mind. In the example lease schedule the date selected is a date falling in the calendar month following the delivery date of each unit. Thus, for all units delivered in May, for example, the base term and base rental payments would commence on the same date in June. If deliveries over several months are expected and the lessee wants the lease terms for all equipment to end on the same date, the scheduling date can be redefined to accomplish that goal (for example, "The Scheduling Date for all Units delivered and accepted between and including May and June 30, shall be July 1").

Whenever an interim term is used, however, lessors need to remember that the interim term must be considered in determining whether 20 percent residual value and useful life tests of the true lease can be met. Care must also be taken that a long rent holiday or period of interim rents does not violate uneven rent restrictions of the Internal Revenue Service.

RENTAL FOR EACH UNIT

Schedule Language

Section 3. Rental.
   3.1 *Supplemental Rent.*
   If Lessor is required to advance funds for the purchase of any Unit prior to the Delivery Date for such Unit, Supplemental Rent shall accrue

---

[1] Lessors defining the delivery date as the latter date should make sure that the lessee or vendor bears the risk of loss between the time the equipment is delivered and the time it is installed and becomes subject to the lease.

on the funds so advanced at a rate per annum (calculated on the basis of a year of 360 days and actual days elapsed) equal to ____% of the published prime rate of ____, as such rate may change from time to time, with any change effective as to Lessee on the publicly announced effective date of such change; Supplemental Rent shall be computed from the date funds are so advanced by Lessor to, but not including, the Delivery Date for such Unit and shall be payable when Lessee is billed therefor by Lessor. If Lessee should fail to lease any Unit for which Lessor has advanced funds pursuant to this paragraph, Lessee shall, on demand of Lessor, purchase any such Unit from Lessor for the amount paid by Lessor or which Lessor is obligated to pay for such Unit, plus rentals at the rate specified above from the date of such demand to the date of purchase by Lessee from Lessor.

3.2 *Interim Rent.*

Interim Rent for each Unit shall accrue during the Interim Term with respect thereto and shall be computed from the Delivery Date for such Unit to, but not including, the Scheduling Date for such Unit, at the daily equivalent of the Base Rent for such Unit. Interim Rent for each unit shall be payable on the Scheduling Date for such Unit.

3.3 *Base Rent.*

Base Rent for each Unit shall accrue from the Scheduling Date in respect thereto and shall be payable in the number of consecutive monthly payments in the dollar amount per thousand dollars of the Purchase Price specified below, with the first such payment due and payable one month following the Scheduling Date for such Unit.

No. of Payments: ____

Dollars per $1,000 of Purchase Price: ____

Summary

This section of the schedule enumerates the three types of rental that may be applicable in a given transaction: predelivery rent (interest); rent for use of the equipment during the gathering period or interim term; and rent for use of the equipment during the major portion of the lease term.

Discussion

Lessors may sometimes use terms different from those in the example lease to describe the various types of rental or payments that might be applicable throughout the lease. However, the underlying concepts will be the same.

If the lessor is required to advance funds for the equipment prior to the time the lessee accepts it, the lessor will inevitably want two things: interest on the funds disbursed and protection against the possibility that the lessee may refuse to accept equipment for which funds were advanced. Lessors should remember that since predelivery rent is a charge for the use of money rather than the use of equipment, all predelivery rent will be subject to state usury laws. Lessors should also remember to specify the per annum basis (360 or 365/366) on which interest is calculated. As a general rule, the 360-day basis cannot be safely used unless it is specified in the document. Care should also be taken to clearly define "prime rate" or "base corporate rate" or whatever basic interest rate term is utilized. Definitions that refer to the "best rate" of interest should be avoided unless it is very clear that the rate in question is in fact the best rate available.

Unlike supplemental rent, interim rent and base rent are charges for the use of the equipment and are not subject to usury laws when the transaction is a true lease. Some lessees may want to delay the start of base or interim rent until the lessor has actually paid for the equipment. However, since the lessee has the use of the equipment regardless of whether the lessor has paid the vendor, most lessors insist that rental be paid from the delivery date.

AVAILABILITY DATE FOR COMMITMENT

Schedule Language

> *Section 4. Availability Date.*
> No Units may be accepted for leasing and placed in service under this Lease after _____.

Discussion

This section of the example schedule specifies a "cutoff" date, the last day on which equipment can be placed under the lease. Acceptance supplements may be delivered after this date under the provisions of Section 1.2 of the example lease in Chapter 13, but those acceptance supplements must confirm that actual acceptance of the units took place on or prior to the availability date. Some lessors require confirmations of acceptance to be received prior to the cutoff date. This may cause operational problems and may effectively reduce the period of time that the lessee has to place equipment under lease since the lessee will have to allow time to deliver the acceptance documents to the lessor. If the acceptance documents are merely confirmatory and do not trigger the obligation of the lessor to pay for equipment, lessees may be able to negotiate any requirement that the documents be delivered prior to the cutoff date. If, however, the acceptance documents trigger the lessor's obligation to pay, there will be little room for negotiation on this point.

The length of time that lessors are willing to hold themselves open to purchase equipment is generally less than a year. The difficulty in fixing rates in periods of extreme fluctuations in interest rates and the cost of funds may make lessors reluctant to extend availability dates more than two to three months from the date of the lease unless they reserve the right to readjust rental rates every so often with respect to equipment not yet accepted and under lease. Such adjustments might, for example, be tied to some regularly published interest rate index.

LOCATION OF LEASED EQUIPMENT

Schedule Language

Section 5. Location.
    States of _____, _____, and _____; provided, however, Lessee shall, within thirty (30) days of the Delivery Date of each Unit, give Lessor notice of the state and county in which such Unit is to be principally located (the "Base Location") and shall give Lessor written notice of any permanent change in such Base Location within thirty (30) days after such permanent change.

Discussion

Section 5 of the example lease schedule is drafted to permit the lessee the option of locating and moving the equipment within a three-state area. Not all lessors are willing to permit this flexibility, and some may specify a single street address as the location where the leased equipment must be kept unless the lessor gives its prior written consent to a change. Ordinarily, unless the equipment is particularly sensitive to movement or the creditworthiness of the lessee is extremely tenuous, lessees can bargain for increased flexibility in this type of provision. However, as discussed in connection with Section 4 of the lease in Chapter 13, lessors must know the location of equipment for tax purposes and in order to exercise inspection rights and to move quickly to repossess in default situations. Therefore, most lessors will insist on notice of the principal location of the equipment and at least after-the-fact notice of changes in locations.

With some kinds of highly mobile equipment, provisions similar to Section 5 of the example schedule may be unworkable and require redrafting. Containers, for example, may be shipped cross-country and never kept in a particular location long enough for one to say that they have a principal location. In such cases, the lessor may require periodic reports showing the expected location of the units on particular dates or access to the lessee's records that keep track of the equipment.

CASUALTY VALUE

Schedule Language

Section 6. Casualty Value.
The Casualty Value of each Unit as of each rental payment date in respect thereto shall be that percentage of the Purchase Price of such Unit as is set forth in Exhibit _____ opposite the number of rental payments in respect of such Unit which would have become due to and including such date.

Discussion

The actual casualty value numbers could be and frequently are listed in the lease schedule itself. The choice between listing them in the schedule and listing them in an exhibit is usually based on clerical convenience and nothing more. For a discussion of the components that make up the specific casualty values, see Section 7 of the example lease in Chapter 13.

TAX INDEMNIFICATION

Schedule Language

Section 7. Tax Indemnification.
7.1 This Lease has been entered into on the basis that Lessor shall be subject to a federal corporate tax rate of _____% and shall be entitled to such credits and deductions as are provided by federal, state, and local law to an owner of new property ("Tax Benefits"), including,
(a) The investment credit allowed by Section 38 and related sections of the Internal Revenue Code of 1986, as amended ("Code"), in an amount equal to _____% of the Purchase Price of the Units;[2] and
(b) The deduction for ACRS tax depreciation on the Units under various sections of the Code and related depreciation provisions of California state tax law based upon a useful life of _____ years.
7.2 If Lessor not be subject to a corporate tax rate of _____% or shall lose, shall not have, or shall lose the right to claim, or if there shall be

---

[2] For purposes of illustration, the example lease is assumed to be of equipment eligible for ITC. As noted throughout this book, the investment tax credit was repealed by the Tax Reform Act of 1986, except for certain "transitional" property. The Internal Revenue Code of 1954 has been renamed the Internal Revenue Code of 1986, although the section numbers remain the same.

disallowed or recaptured with respect to Lessor, all or any portion of the Tax Benefits as are provided to an owner of property with respect to any Unit ("Loss"), then on the next succeeding rental payment date after written notice to Lessee by Lessor that a Loss has occurred, or if there be no such date, thirty (30) days following such notice, Lessee shall pay Lessor an amount which, in the reasonable opinion of the Lessor and after deduction of all taxes required to be paid by Lessor with respect to the receipt of such amount, will cause Lessor's net after-tax return over the term of the Lease in respect of such Unit to equal the net after-tax return that would have been available if Lessor had been entitled to the utilization of all of the Tax Benefits.

7.3 For purposes of this Section 7, a Loss shall occur upon the earliest of (*a*) the happening of any event (such as disposition or change in use of any Unit) which may cause such Loss, (*b*) the payment by Lessor to the Internal Revenue Service of the tax increase resulting from such Loss, or (*c*) the adjustment of the tax return of Lessor to reflect such Loss.

7.4 Lessor shall not be entitled to a payment under this Section 7 on account of any Loss due solely to one or more of the following events: (*a*) a disqualifying disposition due to sale of the Unit by Lessor prior to any default by Lessee; (*b*) a failure of Lessor to claim timely or properly the Tax Benefits for the Unit in the tax return of Lessor; (*c*) a disqualifying change in the nature of Lessor's business or liquidation thereof; (*d*) a foreclosure by any person holding through Lessor of a lien on the Unit, which foreclosure results solely from an act of Lessor; (*e*) any event which by the terms of this Lease requires payment by the Lessee of the Casualty Value, if such Casualty Value is thereafter actually paid by lessee; or (*f*) the failure of Lessor to have sufficient taxable income or tax liability to utilize such Tax Benefits.

7.5 All of Lessor's rights and privileges arising from the indemnities contained in this Section shall survive the expiration or other termination of this Lease.

7.6 For purposes of this Section, the term "Lessor" shall include any affiliated group (within the meaning of Section 1504 of the Code) of which Lessor is a member for any year in which a consolidated income tax return is filed for such affiliated group.

Summary

This section provides that:

1. The lessor has assumed that, in entering into the lease (and setting the lease rentals), it will be subject throughout the lease term to a corporate tax rate of ____%, and certain tax benefits will be available to it relating to the equipment the lessor will own and lease to the lessee under a true lease. Briefly stated, the tax benefits consist of the following:

    a. The investment tax credit which for purposes of this example lease is assumed to be 10 percent.[3]

    b. ACRS tax depreciation deductions.

    c. State tax benefits consisting of any available credits or depreciation under applicable state tax law.

2. The lessor's assumed value of the tax benefits under the Internal Revenue Code is dependent upon the federal tax rate being ____% throughout the lease term. If, for example, the tax rate rises after the deferred tax resulting from ACRS becomes payable, the lessor's expected yield and cash will decrease. If the lessor loses those tax benefits, the lessee must pay the lessor enough dollars to compensate it for the loss.

3. The amount owed is "grossed up" to cover any taxes that the lessor must pay in connection with its receipt of the tax indemnity payment.

4. The tax indemnity payment is due, in a lump sum, on the next rental payment date following notice by the lessor that a loss of tax benefits has occurred, or, if rental is no longer due, within 30 days of such notice.

5. A loss of tax benefits is deemed to occur upon the *earliest* of any of the following:

    a. The happening of any event that may cause a loss.

    b. The lessor's payment of any tax that results from a loss.

    c. The adjustment of the lessor's tax return to reflect a loss.

6. The lessee is not required to make any payment under this section if a loss occurs solely because of any of the following events:

    a. The lessor sells the unit prior to default by the lessee (such a sale would automatically result in a "loss" if it occurred before the end of the vesting period for any available ITC or before the equipment had been fully depreciated under ACRS).

    b. The lessor does not file its tax return on time, or it fails to properly prepare its tax return.

---

[3] As noted in Footnote 2, the ITC was repealed by the Tax Reform Act of 1986, except for certain transitional property. In some cases, the lessor may agree to pass the investment tax credit directly to the lessee. Such transactions are referred to as "PIC" transactions as opposed to "RIC" transactions, in which the lessor retains the ITC. In PIC transactions references to the ITC would be deleted in the indemnity, and a new provision covering the "pass-through" of the ITC would be added as a separate section of the schedule. For a discussion of the "pass-through" certificate, see Chapter 15. ITC claimed after the tax rate is reduced from 46% in 1986 to approximately 40% in 1987 and 34% in 1988 is subject to a reduction to 82.5% of full ITC in 1987 and 65% of full ITC in 1988.

    c. The lessor ceases to be a taxpayer eligible to claim the tax benefits, or it liquidates.

    d. The lessor acts in a manner that entitles a third party to foreclose on the equipment.

    e. There is a casualty occurrence, and the lessee pays the lessor the casualty value of the affected equipment. (The casualty value includes loss of tax benefits.)

    f. The lessor does not have sufficient income or tax liability to utilize any available ITC or to benefit from accelerated depreciation.

7. The lessee's obligations under Section 7 extend beyond the termination or expiration of the lease.

8. The lessor, under this section, is defined broadly to include any affiliated group filing a consolidated return with the lessor.

Discussion

Lessors in most tax-oriented true leases take the position that the lease transaction is essentially a financial transaction in which they assume the "credit risk" that the lessee may not be able to meet its lease obligations, and the "residual risk" that the equipment may not be valuable at the end of the lease term, but not the "tax risk" that the tax benefits available to owners of property will be unavailable or disallowed. Lessees that have been given most of the tax benefits (ACRS depreciation deductions and ITC, if available) through low lease rates are generally asked by lessors to assume the risk of loss of those benefits.

The provision that addresses the question of who bears the risk of loss of tax benefits and to what extent is normally referred to as the special tax indemnity. As in the example lease, this provision usually does not address any other tax or indemnity matters. (In the example lease, the definition of and risk of loss of tax benefits are covered in Section 7 of the schedule. Section 5 of the lease covers all other tax matters, and Section 6 of the lease covers the lessee's obligation to indemnify the lessor for matters unrelated to the loss of tax benefits.)

Almost all special tax indemnities provide for the lessor to "be made whole" for any loss of tax benefits on an after-tax basis. This means that to the extent any reimbursements by the lessee to the lessor would constitute taxable income to the lessor, such reimbursements must be increased to take into account the tax due on the indemnity payment. Generally, this means that the lessee's payments must be approximately double the amount of the increase in the lessor's taxes resulting from the loss of the tax benefits.

Because of the potential for significant monetary liability for the lessee under the special tax indemnity provision and the potential for significant losses to the lessor if the tax benefits are denied and the lessor is not adequately indemnified (or the lessee for some reason can't meet its obligations under the indemnity provision), lessees and lessors must be concerned both that the transaction be structured correctly for tax purposes and that the scope of the indemnity be realistic. Discussions on this latter point can be time-consuming and sometimes quite heated. Most special tax indemnity provisions in single investor leases are drafted quite broadly, requiring the lessee to pay an indemnity if tax benefits are lost for any reason (including circumstances beyond the actual control of the lessee) other than a reason related solely to certain specified circumstances that are "carved out" of the indemnity provision. This type of special indemnity provision is normally called an all-events indemnity. Lessees frequently want to expand the list of events that are carved out. Within limits, that approach may be acceptable to lessors. At least it is usually more acceptable to lessors than redrafting the entire provision to provide for an indemnity obligation that arises only upon the occurrence of certain specified events. This narrower type of indemnity is generally known as an "errors and omissions" or "acts and omissions" indemnity because it is usually triggered only if the loss occurs due to an act, error, or omission of the lessee. Some lessors simply will not consider such an indemnity as a matter of company policy. Others will be more flexible, but many will require an increase in rate to compensate for the increased risk being assumed in the transaction, or extra documentation or representations from the lessee or third-party appraisers or experts with respect to the expected residual value of the equipment and the contemplated depreciation method and schedule, before agreeing to other than an all-events indemnity.

It is difficult to generalize as to what is customary and fair in drafting tax indemnity provisions. In single-investor leases and smaller leveraged leases, lessors include all-events indemnities in the "boiler plate" language of their leases and take a fairly firm negotiating stance on retaining that language. In large leveraged leases involving fairly standard items of equipment, lessees are often successful in insisting on indemnities that limit their liability to their acts and omissions.

Lessees frequently request the right to contest any determination of a loss of tax benefits. Right of contest provisions may be as heatedly debated as the scope of the indemnity itself. Commonly, lessees want full control of the contest procedure, including any litigation. Just as commonly, lessors are unwilling to allow such control to be given to the lessee, as to do so would mean loss of control of the audit and contest of their total tax return, of which the lease issue in question would normally be only a minor portion. A "middle ground" that is sometimes acceptable to both parties is for the lessor to grant the lessee the right, in certain specified circumstances, to force the lessor to contest the disallowance of the tax benefits, leaving full control to compromise and settle with the lessor but providing that settlements adverse to the lessee and without its consent will not give rise to an indemnity obligation. In single-investor leases and smaller leveraged leases, lessors are generally successful in resisting lessee demands to participate in contesting federal income tax determinations. However, lessees usually gain participation rights to challenge adverse tax determinations in larger leveraged leases.

Other matters that are frequently the subject of negotiation with respect to the special tax indemnity are:

1. Changes in the federal corporate tax rate.
2. Manner of payment—over time or in a lump sum.
3. Lessee or third-party review of the lessor's determination of the amount of the indemnity.
4. Provision for giving the lessee the benefit of any favorable changes in tax laws.

As a result of the passage of the Tax Reform Act of 1986, the federal corporate tax rate was reduced to 34 percent commencing in 1988. In view of the rising federal deficit, most lessors and lessees are concerned that the tax rate may rise in subsequent years. If the tax rate rises in the early years of a lease, the value of the ACRS tax benefits to the lessor increases. If the tax rate rises in the later years of the lease, the deferred tax liability resulting from ACRS reductions will be larger than assumed and adversely affect the lessor's yield and cash flow. Consequently, lessors have become very concerned that lessees indemnify them from loss of yield or cash flow resulting from an increase in the tax rate. In smaller single-investor leases the lessor will usually assume this risk, but in larger single-investor and leveraged leases this is a difficult issue. Lessees that are asked to indemnify the lessor against changes in tax rate usually request that they be given the benefit of any favorable changes in tax rate.

With respect to the manner of payment of an indemnity, many indemnities, as in the example lease, call for a lump-sum payment. Some leases provide for an adjustment to the rental rate. However, since the loss of tax benefits may not occur until well after the lease has been terminated (since the IRS audit of the lessor's books may be several years in arrears), most lessors will normally insist on a provision for lump-sum settlements once the lease has ended.

Lessee review of the lessor's determination of the amount of the indemnity liability is a very sensitive issue with lessors, as certain of the information used in that determination relates to the lessor's profit and yield, which lessors may consider to be "privileged" information.

Lessors are sometimes unwilling to provide all assumptions and computations directly to the lessee. Presentation of the same information to an independent accounting firm for review may be an acceptable solution in such cases, although most lessors are unwilling to agree that the findings of the third party should be binding on the lessor except in cases of manifest error in the lessor's determination of the indemnity amount.

EARLY TERMINATION

Schedule Language

Section 8. Early Termination.

Provided that this Lease has not been earlier terminated and Lessee is not in default hereunder, Lessee shall have the right at its option at any time during the initial term of any Unit, on at least sixty (60) days' prior written notice to Lessor, to terminate this Lease with respect to such Unit on a day or days when a rental payment in respect of such Unit is due (hereinafter for purposes of this paragraph called with respect to such Unit the "Termination Date"), specified in such notice, provided that Lessee shall have made a good faith determination that the Unit is obsolete or surplus to Lessee's requirements and further provided that each such Termination Date shall not be a date before the _____ rental payment date with respect to such Unit. During the period from the giving of such notice until the Termination Date, Lessee as agent for Lessor shall use its best efforts to obtain bids for the purchase of such obsolete or surplus Unit described in such notice. Lessee shall certify to Lessor in writing the amount and terms of each bid received by Lessee and the name and address of the party (who shall not be Lessee or any person, firm, or corporation affiliated with or a shareholder of Lessee) submitting such bid. On each such Termination Date, Lessor shall, without recourse or warranty, sell such Unit for cash to the bidder who shall have submitted the highest bid prior to such date. The total sales price realized at such sale shall be retained by Lessor and, in addition, on each such Termination Date, Lessee shall pay to Lessor the excess, if any, of the Termination Value, for the Unit computed as of such date, over the sale proceeds of the Unit received by Lessor after all expenses incurred by Lessor in connection with such sale. The Termination Value with respect to the Unit as of each rental payment date in respect thereto shall be that percentage of the Purchase Price of such Unit as is set forth in Exhibit _____ opposite the number of rental payments which would have become due to and including such date. If no sale shall have occurred on or as of the Termination Date, this Lease shall continue in full force and effect as to the Unit; provided, however, that Lessee may subsequently terminate, or attempt to terminate, this Lease in respect of such Unit pursuant to this paragraph during the remaining term. In the event of any such sale and upon compliance by Lessee with the provisions of this paragraph, the obligation of Lessee to pay rent hereunder with respect to such Unit after the Termination Date shall cease and the term for such Unit shall end on the Termination Date.

Summary

This section provides that:

1. The lessee may terminate the lease with respect to a particular unit before its scheduled expiry date *if* that unit is obsolete or excess to the lessee's requirements.
2. No such early termination may take place before a specified rental payment date.
3. The lessee must look for buyers not affiliated with the lessee for the units it wishes to terminate early.
4. The lessor will sell the units to the highest bidder, without recourse or warranty.
5. The lessor is entitled to the sales price, and, *in addition,* the lessee must pay the lessor the excess, if any, of the early termination value (listed in an exhibit) over the sales price received (after deducting from such sales price any expenses incurred in the sale).
6. If the lessee cannot find a buyer for the units, the lease may not be terminated with respect to those units.
7. The lessee may keep trying to find buyers for the excess or obsolete units so that it can terminate the lease in accordance with the procedure outlined in this section.
8. Once the lease has been terminated under this section, the lessee has no further rental obligation with respect to the units so terminated.

This section does not permit the lessee or its affiliates to buy the units for their early termination value. This would be equivalent to a fixed-price purchase option and might seriously jeopardize the status of the lease as a true lease for income tax purposes.

Discussion

Many direct leases do not provide for early termination for reasons of economic obsolescence of the equipment or for any other reason, and many lessors regard the inclusion of such a provision as a concession on their part. However, if the lessor is willing to give the lessee the right to terminate the lease early, lessors and lessees should consider the following important matters in drafting and negotiating the early termination provision.

Care must be taken to structure the early termination provision in a way that will not jeopardize the true lease status of the transaction. The Internal Revenue Service takes the position that if the lessee has a bargain purchase option, the economic incentive to exercise that option will be so great that the lessee should be considered to have purchased the equipment from the outset. Thus, the parties will, despite the form of their agreement, be deemed to have entered into a sale, not a lease, and the lessor will be denied any tax benefits based on ownership of the equipment. The IRS also takes the position that any fixed-price option, regardless of the amount, will adversely affect the true lease status of the transaction.[4] Many tax counsel disagree with this somewhat extreme position if the fixed price is a reasonable estimate of what the fair market value of the equipment will be at the time the lessee exercises the option. However, most lessors and lessees prefer not to risk the challenge and, consequently, avoid fixed-price purchase options as well as more obvious bargain options.

Lessors will generally want to minimize the ability and incentive of the lessee to use the early termination provision to acquire the leased equipment for purposes of speculating in its residual value. As lessees are generally more knowledgeable than most finance lessors with respect to fluctuations in the market value of equipment, lessors are fearful of the possibility that lessees will seize the opportunity to purchase the equipment when the fair market value is low, knowing that in the near future its value will substantially increase.

Finally, lessors subject to the Comptroller of the Currency's Ruling 7.3400 or Regulation Y of the Board of Governors of the Federal Reserve System will require payment of a minimum termination value in order to ensure that the full-payout provisions of the ruling or regulation, as the case may be, are met. Reliance simply on payment of the fair market value of the equipment would not ensure that those provisions are met, since the fair market value at any given time might be substantially lower than the lessor's initial investment and insufficient, even when added to the rentals and tax benefits already received, to assure the necessary return of its investment plus reasonable profit. Accordingly, these lessors require payment of a minimum termination value that would normally be the amount necessary to compensate the lessor for loss of future rentals (discounted to present value) and any loss or recapture of tax benefits. In some cases the "booked residual" amount will also be included, as protection against "downside" residual

---

[4] Revenue Procedure 75–21.

risk, and in many cases, a penalty amount, to discourage terminations, may also be added.[5]

In the example provision, these three considerations are handled by permitting the lessee to terminate only if:

1. The equipment is excess or obsolete for its needs.
2. A sale to an unaffiliated third party can be arranged.
3. The lessee makes up any difference between the sale proceeds received and the specified termination value (when such value is higher than the sales price).

In some circumstances, however, the lessee may have a particular need to be able to purchase the equipment itself before the end of the lease, so a provision such as the example one will be unacceptably limiting. In such a situation, the lessor may be willing to allow the lessee to terminate and purchase. However, to avoid the problems noted earlier, such a provision would normally require that the lessee purchase the equipment for the higher of fair market value or a specified value, usually the casualty value or stipulated loss value, as that value is generally higher than the termination value. The lessee is thus forced to pay a larger premium to acquire the equipment in circumstances in which the fair market value is depressed.

PURCHASE AND RENEWAL OPTIONS

Schedule Language

Section 9. Purchase and Renewal Options.

If no Event of Default shall have occurred and be continuing and this Lease has not been earlier terminated, Lessee may by written notice delivered to Lessor not more than nine (9) months and not less than six (6) months prior to the end of the original term or any extended term of this Lease, as the case may be, in respect of any Unit (*a*) elect to extend the term of this Lease in respect of all, but not less than all, Units for which this Lease is then expiring, for such number of years as is designated in said notice, at a "Fair Rental Value" payable in monthly payments, or (*b*) elect to purchase all, but not less than all, the Units for which this Lease is then expiring for a purchase price equal to the "Fair Market Value" of such Units as of the end of the original or extended term of this Lease, as the case may be.

---

[5] As noted in the discussion of Section 6 of the example lease in Chapter 13, casualty values and termination values are usually different, with the former being higher; termination values may be negotiable, depending on the individual lessor's method of computing the values.

Fair Rental Value shall be determined on the basis of, and shall be equal in amount to, the value which would obtain in an arm's-length transaction between an informed and willing lessee (other than a lessee currently in possession) and an informed and willing lessor under no compulsion to lease, and, in such determination, costs of removal from the location of current use shall not be a deduction from such value. If four (4) months prior to the end of the term of this Lease in respect of any Unit, Lessor and Lessee have not agreed upon the Fair Rental Value of the Units, an appraiser shall be appointed upon application of either party by the American Arbitration Association and instructed to determine the Fair Rental Value of the Units within thirty (30) days after appointment and promptly communicate such determination in writing to Lessor and Lessee. The determination so made shall be conclusively binding upon both Lessor and Lessee. The expenses and fees of the appraiser shall be borne by Lessee.

Fair Market Value shall be determined on the basis of, and shall be equal in amount to, the value which would obtain in an arm's-length transaction between an informed and willing buyer (other than a buyer currently in possession) and an informed and willing seller under no compulsion to sell, and, in such determination, costs of removal from the location of current use shall not be a deduction from such value. If four (4) months prior to the end of the term of this Lease in respect of any Unit, Lessor and Lessee have not agreed upon the Fair Market Value of the Unit, an appraiser shall be appointed upon application of either party by the American Arbitration Association and instructed to determine the Fair Market Value of the Units within thirty (30) days after appointment and promptly communicate such determination in writing to Lessor and Lessee. The determination so made shall be conclusively binding upon both Lessor and Lessee. The expenses and fees of the appraiser shall be borne by Lessee.

Upon payment of the purchase price, Lessor shall execute and deliver to Lessee a bill of sale (without representations or warranties except that such Units are free and clear of all claims, liens, security interests, and other encumbrances by or in favor of any person claiming by, through, or under Lessor) for the Units.

Summary

This section provides that:

1. Upon written notice delivered between the sixth and ninth month prior to the end of the lease in respect to any unit, the lessee may elect to do one of the following:
   a. Extend the lease for all units for which the lease term would otherwise end for additional periods at a fair market rental value.
   b. Purchase the units for which the lease term would otherwise end for the fair market value of such units.

2. The fair market and fair rental value are to be determined in a specified manner based on the concept of arm's-length negotiation.

3. An appraiser will be used to determine the fair rental or fair market value if the lessor and lessee cannot agree on such values, and the appraiser's decision will bind the lessor and lessee.

4. The expenses of the appraiser are to be borne by the lessee.

5. If the lessee exercises its purchase option, the lessor will sell the units to the lessee "as is" and execute a bill of sale.

Discussion

The purpose of provisions such as Section 9 of the example lease schedule is to provide an orderly procedure whereby at the end of the lease term for the equipment, the lessee may elect to either purchase the equipment at its fair market value or renew the lease at a fair rental value. As discussed in Chapter 5, in a true lease transaction a lessee cannot have a purchase option at a bargain fixed price without jeopardizing the lessor's ability to claim tax benefits for the leased equipment. Only a fair-market-value option will pass muster with the IRS. As an extra precaution, the definition of fair market value in the example lease is based on the IRS definition.[6]

Many leases also provide the lessee with a right to renew the lease at a fair rental value. Lessees usually want this kind of provision in order to ensure that they can retain the equipment if needed at the end of the lease term. Sometimes a lease may provide for a number of renewals at fixed rentals. However, lessees and lessors must both remember that when fixed-rate renewals are offered, the fixed-rate renewal periods must be included as part of the initial term for purposes of meeting the IRS true lease requirements of 20 percent value and 20 percent remaining economic life at the end of the initial term.

The example lease provides for no less than six months' and no more than nine months' notice by the lessee of its intention to exercise its option to renew the lease or purchase the equipment. This type of provision gives the parties plenty of time to negotiate an acceptable price and to make arrangements in the event that an agreement on fair rental or fair market value is difficult to reach. It also forces the determination of those values to be made fairly close to the end of the lease term, so that the determination is an accurate one when the renewal or purchase actually takes place.

---

[6] Rev. Proc. 75–21. As noted previously, not all tax counsel agree that a true lease cannot contain a fixed price purchase option based on expected fair market value.

Normally, neither option may be exercised if an event of default has occurred and is continuing. Lessors simply do not want to have to talk about fair-market-value or fair-rental-value options if the rent has not been paid!

The example section contains a provision for arbitration as a safety valve for the parties in the event they cannot come to an agreement. As a practical matter, most lessees and lessors rarely fall back on arbitration as a means of settling disputes under this type of provision.

The example section also contains a provision that requires a lessee to exercise its option as to either all of the equipment or none of the equipment for which the lease is expiring at a particular time. This prevents "cherry picking" of the equipment by the lessee. Such a requirement is normally negotiable.

In some transactions, the lessee may be granted a right of first refusal rather than a purchase option. With a right of first refusal, the lessee may buy *only* if the *lessor* decides it wants to sell.

A right of first refusal might operate as follows:

1. The lessee notifies the lessor six months prior to the end of the lease that it wishes to retain its right of first refusal.
2. If the lessor is so notified, the lessor agrees not to sell the equipment during a specified period after the end of the lease (normally 30 days) without first (*a*) giving notice to the lessee of its intent to sell and (*b*) allowing the lessee the opportunity to meet the highest bid for the equipment that the lessor is considering.
3. Within the right of first refusal period, the lessee may elect to meet the highest bid and purchase the unit (but it may never purchase for less than fair market value, so if for some reason the highest bid is less than fair market value, it must pay the latter; this situation is rare since a bona fide bid is usually the best evidence of fair market value).
4. During the right of first refusal period, the lessor may require that the lessee store the equipment at its expense and allow the lessor and possible purchasers access to the equipment.
5. At the end of the right of first refusal period (or before, if the lessee has decided not to exercise its right and has notified the lessor to that effect), the equipment is returned to the lessor in accordance with other provisions of the lease (in the example lease, Section 9, Return of Units).
6. At the end of the right of first refusal period, if the lessee has not exercised its option to meet the highest bid, the lessor is free to sell the unit to anyone.

The lessor's decision to grant a right of first refusal rather than a purchase option will depend on the particulars of the transaction or the equipment. For example, transactions are occasionally structured with two sequential lessees. Obviously, the first lessee cannot be granted a purchase option at the end of its lease since the second lessee has the right to lease and use the equipment at the end of the first lease term. The first lessee might be granted a carefully structured right of first refusal, however, without interfering with the right of the subsequent lessee.

COMMITMENT FEES

Schedule Language

Section 10. Commitment Fees.
10.1 Lessee has paid Lessor a commitment fee in an amount equal to one percent (1%) of Lessor's commitment described in Section 1 of this Schedule. Said fee shall be credited against the first month's rent of any Unit leased hereunder in an amount equal to one percent (1%) of the Purchase Price of each such Unit. If the aggregate Purchase Price of all Units leased hereunder on or before _____ is insufficient for the full amount of the commitment fee to be credited as set forth above, any remainder shall be retained by Lessor.
10.2 On _____, Lessee shall pay to Lessor a nonutilization fee in an amount equal to two percent (2%) of the difference between _____ Dollars ($_____) and the Purchase Price of all Units delivered to Lessee on or before _____.

Summary

1. The lease acknowledges the payment by the lessee to the lessor of a commitment fee of 1 percent of the total amount committed by the lessor.
2. A portion of the commitment fee is credited against the first month's rent for each item of equipment.
3. A nonutilization fee is to be charged equal to 2 percent of any part of the commitment (or some minimum amount which is less than the commitment) not used by the lessee.

Discussion

The purpose of commitment fees is to compensate the lessor for committing funds to the transaction and thus forgoing other leasing or lending opportunities. There are two types of commitment fees in the example lease:

1. A refundable commitment fee, which would usually be paid at the time a commitment letter is signed and is "refunded" in

whole or in part by crediting a portion of the amount paid against the first month's rent for each unit as the commitment is used. (Some leases or commitment letters include totally nonrefundable fees, particularly where more than two or three months elapse before initial takedown of the commitment.)

2. The nonutilization fee, which is paid at the end of the commitment period as a percentage of all or part of the commitment that is not used. This type of fee is frequently more acceptable to lessees, many of which do not like to pay up-front fees as a matter of principle.

The amounts and nature of fees will vary with the volatility of the money markets at the time of the lease commitment. A fee of 1 percent may be inexpensive for a lessee if it permits the lessee to refinance if rates go down. In times of tight money, refundable fees of 5 percent or higher may be appropriate. In the alternative, a nonutilization fee of 5 percent or higher may be easier to sell yet achieve the desired result.

Some lessees are, of course, unwilling to pay commitment fees. Lessors then must decide whether the circumstances (such as the profitability of the transaction and the likelihood the lease will go forward) warrant making a commitment without any compensation.

15

Other Lease Documents

This chapter provides an overview of the following seven ancillary lease documents:

1. Purchase agreement assignment.
2. Request to purchase.
3. Acceptance supplement.
4. Guaranty.
5. Consent to removal of personal property.
6. Financing statement.
7. Election of lessor of new Section 38 property to treat lessee as purchaser for purposes of ITC, if available.

PURCHASE AGREEMENT ASSIGNMENT

Form

An example of a *purchase agreement assignment* is shown as Exhibit 1.

EXHIBIT 1   Purchase Agreement Assignment

THIS PURCHASE AGREEMENT ASSIGNMENT, dated _____, 19__, is between _____, a _____, corporation ("Assignor"), and _____, a _____, corporation ("Assignee").

WHEREAS, Assignor has entered into a purchase agreement or purchase order No. _____, dated _____, 19__ ("Purchase Agreement"), between Assignor and _____ ("Vendor"), a copy of which Purchase Agreement is attached hereto, providing for the sale to Assignor of _____, the "Units."

WHEREAS, Assignor desires that Assignee acquire the Units and lease the Units to Assignor.

NOW, THEREFORE, the parties hereto agree as follows;

1.   Assignor does hereby sell, assign, transfer, and set unto Assignee all of Assignor's right, title, and interest in, under, and to the Purchase Agreement and in and to the Units. Assignee hereby accepts such assignment.

2.   Assignor may not amend, modify, rescind, or terminate the Purchase Agreement without the prior express written consent of Assignee, which consent shall not be unreasonably withheld.

3.   It is agreed that, anything herein contained to the contrary notwithstanding: (a) Assignor shall at all times remain liable to Vendor under the Purchase Agreement to perform all the duties and obligations of the purchaser thereunder to the same extent as if this Agreement had not been executed, and Assignee does not assume and shall not be obligated to perform any of these duties and obligations; (b) the exercise by Assignee of any of the rights assigned hereunder shall not release Assignor from its duties or obligations to Vendor under the Purchase Agreement; (c) the Assignee accepts only the obligation to purchase the Units for an amount equal to the purchase price as described in the Purchase Agreement; and (d) the obligation of the Assignee to purchase each Unit is conditioned upon acceptance of such Unit by the Assignor.

4.   Assignor agrees at any time and from time to time upon written request of Assignee to promptly and duly execute and deliver any and all such further instruments and documents and take such further actions as Assignee may reasonably request in order to obtain the full benefits of this agreement and of the rights and powers granted herein.

5.   Assignor does hereby represent and warrant that: (a) the Purchase Agreement is in full force and effect and enforceable in accordance with its terms and Assignor is not in default thereunder; (b) Assignor has the legal right to enter into this Agreement; (c) the Purchase Agreement is free from all claims, security interests, liens, and encumbrances, except for the interest being conveyed hereunder and the interest of Assignor therein.

IN WITNESS WHEREOF, the parties hereto have caused this Agreement to be executed as of the day and year first written above.

(ASSIGNEE)	(ASSIGNOR)
By _____	_____
(SIGNATURE) (TITLE)	(SIGNATURE) (TITLE)
By _____	_____
(SIGNATURE) (TITLE)	(SIGNATURE) (TITLE)

EXHIBIT 1   (*concluded*)

ACCEPTED AND AGREED TO:

                        (VENDOR)

BY _____
         (SIGNATURE)   (TITLE)

This _____ day of _____, 19___.

Summary

The introductory paragraphs of this purchase agreement assignment form provide a reference to the following:

1. The date of the assignment.
2. The parties to the assignment, the assignor-lessee, and the assignee-lessor.
3. The assignor-lessee remains responsible to the vendor as if the assignment had not been executed.
4. The assignee-lessor is not liable to the vendor except to pay the purchase price; no other duties are assumed by the assignee-lessor.
5. Payment of the purchase price by the assignee-lessor is conditioned on acceptance of the equipment by the assignor-lessee.
6. The assignor-lessee is obligated to execute whatever documents may prove necessary to fully implement the provisions of the assignment.
7. The assignor-lessee represents that it can make the assignment, that it is not in default under the purchase agreement, and that there are no liens or encumbrances on the purchase agreement or any rights thereunder.

Discussion

As noted in the discussion of the lease in Chapter 13, in many, if not most, lease transactions, the lessee will have entered into a purchase agreement directly with the vendor and thus will need to assign that agreement to the lessor. In the example lease the assignment is accomplished by means of the purchase agreement assignment form set forth above, which is intended to be attached to the lease as an exhibit.

The virtue of an assignment form such as the example form is that it causes minimal interference with the underlying contractual relationship between the vendor and the lessee. The lessee "remains on the hook" as far as the vendor is concerned, but the lessor agrees to pay for the equipment if the lessee accepts it for leasing (giving the vendor an additional party to look to for payment and relieving the lessee of the payment responsibility once it accepts the unit). All other aspects of the underlying agreement are untouched.

The example form contains a provision for the vendor to acknowledge the assignment. While such a provision is not legally necessary as long as the underlying agreement is assignable without the vendor's consent and the assignment doesn't attempt to alter the vendor's basic rights, having the vendor acknowledge the assignment can avoid potential misunderstandings as to which party is responsible for or entitled to what. For example, a vendor that is unaware of an assignment may be confused as to why payment is being received from a third-party lessor rather than the customer it contracted with. Nonetheless, requiring the vendor to acknowledge an assignment can cause time delays and perhaps negotiation problems if the vendor doesn't want to sign the form "as is." Of course, if the underlying agreement is not assignable, or if it is assignable only with the prior consent of the vendor, some sort of written vendor acknowledgment will have to be obtained.

In any event, care must be taken to obtain an executed assignment well in advance of the date on which the equipment is placed in service. For this reason, the form of assignment (or, if applicable, the procedure for directly ordering the equipment) should be thoroughly discussed by the lessor and lessee in the early stages of negotiations, and the documents that will be required to accomplish the assignment (or direct order from the vendor) should be attached to the lease as exhibits whenever possible to facilitate this process.

REQUEST TO PURCHASE

Form

An example of a *request to purchase* is shown in Exhibit 2.

Discussion

In some situations, the lessee may not have entered into a purchase agreement at the time the lease was executed, and the lessee may prefer to have the lessor deal directly with the vendor. Certain types of lessors (captive finance companies, for example, or lessors dealing

EXHIBIT 2   Request to Purchase

TO:

Request To Purchase

Gentlemen:

The undersigned _____ _____ requests that you as Lessor
purchase equipment of the type and quantity hereinafter described, from the supplier(s) designated.

Name and Address of Supplier	Quantity	COMPLETE DESCRIPTION OF EQUIPMENT (New, unless otherwise specified) ☐ See Schedule Attached (Check if Applicable)	Cost
			$
		TOTAL PRICE	$_____
		FEDERAL EXCISE TAX (IF ANY)	$_____
		TRANSPORTATION (IF ANY) *	$_____
		INSTALLATION (IF ANY)	$_____
		OTHER	$_____
	* Shipping Instructions to be as specified by Lessee to Shipper	TOTAL COST	$

SHIP TO LESSEE AT:
Street Address _____
City _____ County_____ State_____

Lessee agrees upon written acceptance hereof, by you as Lessor, to lease said equipment from you on the terms
and conditions of a lease to be executed by and between you as Lessor and the undersigned as Lessee.

Lessee agrees to hold Lessor harmless and bear all risk of loss of any kind or character that may occur prior
to date of execution of lease, or prior to receipt and acceptance by Lessee of property, which is subject of the
lease, whichever event occurs last, at which time the provisions of the lease shall become applicable.

Date delivery expected: _____   _____
                                                                                 Lessee

Dated: By _____
                                                                                 Title

Accepted:

By _____
              Title

in one specific product) may have excellent working relationships with particular vendors and may even have specific procedures and forms in place to expedite the purchase and delivery of equipment from such vendors. In such cases, the lessor will normally expect to order equipment directly from the vendor at the request of the lessee. Rather than an assignment, the lessee will execute a requisition or request to purchase form, specifying the type and quantity of equipment desired and the approximate cost. In order to protect the lessor, such forms, as in the example form, may contain some sort of hold harmless language as well as other terms that make clear that the lessor is purchasing the equipment for the lessee's use and at the lessee's request. Once the lessor has received the request to purchase, it issues a purchase order or enters into a purchase agreement with the vendor.[1]

Not all lessors are willing to deal directly with vendors on behalf of the lessee. Many do not have the staff to process all of the necessary paperwork or to follow through on a huge volume of orders. Delays and disruption of vendor relationships can be the result. Thus, the requisition or request to purchase procedure may be less desirable from the lessee's standpoint in certain situations. Many lessors find the request to purchase method less desirable as well, not only from an operational-administrative standpoint, but also because direct agreements with vendors may contain provisions that simply do not work well in lease situations (for example, responsibility for assistance in installation).

ACCEPTANCE SUPPLEMENT

Form

An example of an *acceptance supplement* is shown as Exhibit 3.

Discussion

Although the form of acceptance document may vary widely among lessors, its purpose is to provide the lessor with the lessee's written confirmation that specific items of equipment were delivered[2] to the lessee on a stated date and that the lessee accepted those items for lease on such date.

In a lease such as the example lease, in which the equipment is described only in general terms in the lease and schedule, the accep-

---

[1] The example lease would have to be redrafted if a request to purchase procedure were utilized in lieu of the purchase agreement assignment procedure.

[2] If installation and assembly are required, the acceptance supplement would usually confirm, not the date of delivery, but the date on which installation and assembly were complete.

EXHIBIT 3   Acceptance Supplement

Reference is made to the Lease Agreement dated as of _____
between _____ , as Lessor, and _____ ,
as Lessee. The terms used herein shall have the same meaning as such terms have
in such Lease Agreement.

The undersigned confirms that the following Units have been accepted by Lessee
for leasing under the Lease, that such Units have become subject to and governed
by the provisions of the Lease, and that Lessee is obligated to pay the rentals and
all other sums provided for in the Lease with respect to such Units.

Specific Description of Units   *Purchase Price*
(include serial number, if
applicable)

Total Purchase Price $

The Delivery Date in respect of such Units is _____ .

IN WITNESS WHEREOF, the undersigned has executed this Acceptance Supplement as of the Delivery Date set forth above.

By _____

---

tance supplement (or certificate, as it is sometimes called) should contain as complete a description of the equipment as possible either on
the acceptance supplement itself or by reference to invoices accom-
panying and preferably attached to the acceptance supplement. When
the description of the equipment in the lease itself is quite detailed,
the acceptance document may simply acknowledge receipt.

As the acceptance supplement may contain terms that are defined
in the lease document (for example, "Delivery Date"), lessees and lessors need to make sure that employees responsible for processing these
forms thoroughly understand the relevant lease terms. Misunderstandings can cause significant delays in properly administering the lease.

GUARANTY

Form

Exhibit 4 contains an example of a *guaranty.*

EXHIBIT 4   Guaranty

THIS AGREEMENT made and entered into by and between _____,
hereinafter called Guarantors, and _____
_____, hereinafter called Lessor.

WITNESSETH:

WHEREAS, _____,
hereinafter called Lessee, has requested that Lessor and Lessee enter into a lease agreement under and by virtue of which Lessor will purchase and may from time to time in the future purchase, at the request of Lessee, personal property to be leased by Lessor to Lessee pursuant to the terms of said lease agreement, and

WHEREAS, Lessor as a condition precedent to entering into said lease agreement has requested that Guarantors unconditionally guarantee payment to Lessor of all rental and monies due and to become due to Lessor from Lessee under said lease agreement, and under any other lease agreement entered into between Lessor and Lessee, and of all other monies due or to become due to Lessor from Lessee under the terms of any purchase agreement, agreement to repay advances, or any other monies due or to become due to Lessor from Lessee in connection with any of the transactions referred to above, hereinafter called the Obligations,

NOW, THEREFORE, the Guarantors, and each of them, unconditionally guarantee and promise to pay Lessor, on demand, all of the Obligations; provided, however, that this Guaranty shall not apply to any Obligation incurred after actual receipt by Lessor of written notice of its revocation as to future Obligations.

The liabilities of Guarantors and each of them hereunder are joint and several and separate and independent of the Obligations, and a separate action may be brought and prosecuted against Guarantors or any of them whether action is brought against Lessee or whether Lessee is joined in any such action; and Guarantors waive the benefit of any Statute of Limitations affecting their liability hereunder or the enforcement thereof.

Guarantors authorize Lessor, without notice or demand and without affecting their liability hereunder, from time to time, to:

(a)   renew, compromise, extend, accelerate, or otherwise change the time for payment of or otherwise change the terms of the Obligations or any part thereof;

(b)   take and hold security for the payment of this Guaranty or the Obligations, and exchange, enforce, waive, and release any such security; and

(c)   apply such security and direct the order and manner of sale thereof as Lessor in its discretion may determine. Lessor may, without notice, assign this Guaranty in whole or in part.

Guarantors waive any right to require Lessor to (a) proceed against Lessee, (b) proceed against or exhaust any security held from Lessee, or (c) pursue any other remedy in Lessor's power whatsoever. Guarantors waive any defense arising by reason of any disability or other defense of Lessee or by reason of the cessation from any cause whatsoever of the liability of Lessee. Until all the Obligations shall have been paid in full, Guarantors shall have no right of subrogation, and waive any right to enforce any remedy which Lessor now has or may hereafter have against Lessee, and waive any interest in the property leased and any benefit of and any right to participate in any security now or hereafter held by Lessor. Guarantors waive all presentments, demands for performance, notices of nonperformance, protests, notices of protests, notices of dishonor, and notices of acceptance of this Guaranty.

EXHIBIT 4 *(concluded)*

In addition to all liens upon and rights of setoff against the monies, securities, or to the property of Guarantors given to Lessor by law, Lessor shall have a lien upon and a right of setoff against all monies, securities, and other property of Guarantors now or hereafter in the possession of Lessor, whether held in a general or special account or for safekeeping or otherwise, and every such lien and right of setoff may be exercised without demand upon or notice to Guarantors. No lien or right of setoff shall be deemed to have been waived by any act or conduct on the part of Lessor, or by any neglect to exercise such right of setoff or to enforce such lien, or by any delay in so doing, and every right of setoff and lien shall continue in full force and effect until such right of setoff or lien is specifically waived or released by an instrument in writing executed by Lessor.

Any indebtedness of Lessee now or hereafter held by Guarantors is hereby subordinated to the Obligations and any other indebtedness of Lessee to Lessor; and the indebtedness of Lessee to Guarantors, if Lessor shall so request, shall be collected, enforced, and received by Guarantors as trustees for Lessor and shall be paid over to Lessor on account of the Obligations and any other indebtedness of Lessee to Lessor, but without reducing or affecting the liability of Guarantors under the other provisions of this Guaranty.

Guarantors agree to pay reasonable attorneys' fees and all other costs and expenses which may be incurred by Lessor in the enforcement of this Guaranty.

Where a single Guarantor executes this Guaranty, then all words used herein in the plural shall be deemed to have been used in the singular where the context and construction so require, and when this Guaranty is executed by more than one Guarantor, the word Guarantor shall mean all and any one or more of them.

Guarantors shall deliver to Lessor financial statements in such form and at such times as Lessor may require.

If Lessee is a corporation or a partnership, Lessor shall have no duty to inquire into the powers of Lessee or the officers, directors, partners, or agents acting or purporting to act on its behalf, and any lease agreement entered into in reliance upon the professed exercise of such powers shall be guaranteed hereunder.

IN WITNESS WHEREOF, the undersigned Guarantors have executed this Guaranty this _____ day of _____, 19___.

_____

_____

_____

Summary

This guaranty provides that:

1. The guarantor guarantees all lease obligations of the lessee to the lessor under existing and future leases.
2. The guarantor may revoke the guaranty at any time, but the revocation is effective only with respect to lease obligations incurred after the lessor has received notice of the revocation.

3. The guarantor may be sued separately from the lessee.
4. The guarantor can be sued even after the time that state law might otherwise protect it from suit.
5. The underlying lease can be changed without notice to the guarantor.
6. The lessor can take security for the lease obligations or the guaranty obligations without affecting the guaranty.
7. The lessor doesn't have to account to the guarantor if it disposes of any collateral.
8. The lessor doesn't have to proceed first against the lessee, or against any collateral, or take any other step before calling on the guarantor.
9. Even if the lessee's obligation becomes unenforceable for some reason, the guarantor will still pay.
10. Until the lessor has been paid in full, the guarantor cannot proceed against the lessee to collect whatever monies it has paid out on behalf of the lessee.
11. The lessor doesn't have to give the guarantor notice of lessee defaults.
12. The lessor has a right to set off against the guaranty obligation any money or other security held by the lessor and belonging to the guarantor.
13. If the lessee owes the guarantor money, that debt is subordinated to the lessee's debt to the lessor (that is, the lessor gets its money first).
14. The guarantor is liable for attorneys' fees if the guarantor does not pay voluntarily and the lessor incurs costs in enforcing the guaranty.
15. The guarantor will deliver information on its financial condition at the request of the lessor.

Discussion

If the creditworthiness of the lessee does not measure up to the lessor's standards, the lessor may require a guaranty from some creditworthy third party of the rental and other obligations of the lessee.[3] As guarantors have traditionally been "favorites of the law," lessors must be extremely careful in drafting and negotiating the form of guaranty. The example form is designed to maximize the protection given the lessor and to minimize the possibility that the guarantor might be "let off the hook" because of some action or inaction on the

---

[3] Guaranties of the lease rental obligations do not jeopardize the true lease status of a lease. Unless provided by an insurance company, guaranties of the residual value of the equipment may destroy true lease status.

lessor's part. Specifically, the example form attempts to prevent discharge of the guarantor as a result of:

1. A change (favorable or unfavorable) in the terms of the underlying lease transaction.
2. A grant to the lessor of a security interest in property of the lessee or the guarantor.
3. Disposition of collateral without consultation with the guarantor.
4. Failure to proceed first or jointly against the lessee or other guarantors.
5. Failure to dispose of collateral.
6. Failure to exercise any remedy.
7. Failure to give the guarantor notice of lessee defaults.

Failure to address these points specifically in the guaranty may make the guaranty unenforceable under certain circumstances. For example, if the guaranty is silent on whether the terms of the underlying lease may be modified without the consent of the guarantor, the lessor will have to make extraordinary efforts to continually inform the guarantor of proposed changes and obtain its consent to each and every one or risk the discharge of the guarantor for even small changes made without its consent.

Other matters that ought to be addressed in the drafting and negotiating of guaranties are as follows:

1. Should the guaranty be for a single transaction, or should it be a continuing guaranty covering future transactions as well as the current one? Continuing guaranties may seem overreaching to guarantors. Single-transaction guaranties have to be worded carefully so that they are not inadvertently superseded by later guaranties covering different transactions.
2. Should the guaranty be a guaranty of payment or a guaranty of collection? The latter is usually unacceptable to lessors as it essentially requires the lessor to exhaust its remedies against the lessee before calling on the guarantor. The example guaranty is a guaranty of payment. The lessor may proceed directly against the guarantor.
3. Should the indebtedness of the lessee to the guarantor be subordinated to the indebtedness of the lessee to the lessor? Should subrogation of the guarantor to the lessor be limited to the situation in which the lessor has been paid in full? Without such provisions the lessor and the guarantor may be in direct competition for funds of the lessee.
4. How and when may the guarantor terminate the guaranty? How will termination affect existing obligations? Termination

should generally be effective only as to future obligations, or the guaranty will be essentially meaningless.

5. What kinds of financial information does the lessor need from the guarantor, and how often must that information be presented and in what form? What if the guarantor's financial condition deteriorates during the lease term? A noncreditworthy guarantor is of little help to the lessor!

A word of caution regarding guaranties is very appropriate. No matter how well drafted, a guaranty is never easy to enforce. It is especially difficult to collect from individuals. Where more than one guarantor is involved, the guarantors commence arguing with each other and involving the lessor in their dispute if collection efforts are made. Lessors should understand that guaranties can give a false sense of security in appraising the creditworthiness of a transaction. Unless the guarantor is a strong corporation with a good reputation, do not count on being able to rely on a guaranty for payment. A guaranty is better than nothing, but it is not a substitute for the creditworthiness of the lessee in many situations.

CONSENT TO REMOVAL OF PERSONAL PROPERTY

Form

Exhibit 5 contains an example of a *consent to removal* form.

Discussion

When personal property that is leased by a lessor will be attached to real property owned by a party other than the lessee or subject to a mortgage or deed of trust held by a mortgagee or beneficiary other than the lessee, a consent to removal form should be obtained. The purpose of forms of this type is twofold. They are a statement of the intention of the parties that the property is and shall remain the personal property of the lessor, regardless of whether it is affixed or installed on any real property and might otherwise be characterized as a fixture, and regardless of whether local law might give the landlord or mortgagee an interest in such property by virtue of its placement on the property. Such forms also give the lessor the clear right to enter the premises and remove the property.

Except in states with peculiar right of distraint laws, most lessors will not require the execution of a consent to removal form unless the leased property is actually affixed to the real property or is so big and cumbersome that it could not be removed easily. In states with highly developed trade fixture law, it may not be necessary to obtain a consent

EXHIBIT 5   Consent to Removal

RECORDING REQUESTED BY:

AND WHEN RECORDED, MAIL TO:

_____

(Space above This Line for Recorder's Use)

CONSENT TO REMOVAL OF PERSONAL
PROPERTY AFFIXED TO REAL PROPERTY

KNOW ALL MEN BY THESE PRESENTS:

(*i*)   The undersigned has an interest either as owner, mortgage holder, trust deed holder, lessor, or seller under a conditional contract of purchase and sale in the following described real property (the "Real Property"):

That certain real property in the County of _____, State of _____, described as:

(*ii*)   _____ ("Customer") has or will enter into a Lease Agreement in which _____ Corporation is the Lessor and Customer is the Lessee; which Lease Agreement or Security Agreement (the "Agreement") covers certain personal property (the "Personal Property"), which is or will be located upon the Real Property, which Personal Property is described as follows:

(*iii*)   Lessor, as a condition to entering into the Agreement, requires that the undersigned consent to the removal by Lessor of the Personal Property from the Real Property, no matter how it is affixed thereto, and to the other matters set forth below.

NOW, THEREFORE, for a good and sufficient consideration, receipt of which is hereby acknowledged, and to induce Lessor to enter into the Agreement, the undersigned consents to the placing of the Personal Property on the Real Property, and agrees with Lessor as follows:

1. The Personal Property shall be considered to be personal property and shall not be considered part of the Real Property regardless of whether or by what means it is or may become attached or affixed to the Real Property.
2. The undersigned has not and will not claim any interest in the Personal Property. The undersigned hereby acknowledges that the Personal Property is owned by Lessor.

EXHIBIT 5 *(continued)*

3. The undersigned will permit Lessor to enter upon the Real Property during normal business hours for the purpose of exercising any right it may have under the terms of the Agreement, or otherwise including, without limitation, the right to remove the Personal Property from the Real Property.
4. In the event that Lessor or agent or assignee of Lessor removes the Personal Property from the Leased Property, there shall be no obligation on such person so removing the Personal Property to restore the Real Property to its former condition, *provided that* nothing herein contained shall relieve Customer of any responsibility under the Agreement or otherwise to so restore the Real Property.
5. This Consent shall be binding upon the heirs, successors, and assigns of the undersigned.

IN WITNESS WHEREOF, the undersigned has executed this Consent at
_____ this _____ day of _____, 19___.

The foregoing Consent must be
acknowledged before a Notary
Public and returned to:

By _____

By _____

By _____

INDIVIDUAL ACKNOWLEDGMENT

STATE OF _____)
)SS.
COUNTY OF _____)

On _____ before me, the undersigned, a Notary Public in and for said County and State, personally appeared _____, known to me to be the person _____, whose name _____ subscribed to the within instrument and acknowledged that _____ executed the same.

WITNESS my hand and official seal.

_____
Notary Public in and for said
County of _____,
State of _____.
My commission expires _____, 19___.   (This Area for Official Notarial Seal)

EXHIBIT 5   (*concluded*)

CORPORATE ACKNOWLEDGMENT

STATE OF _____)
) SS.
COUNTY OF _____)

On this ___ day of _____, 19___, before me _____,
a Notary Public in and for said County and State, personally appeared _____

known to me to be the _____, and _____,
known to me to be the _____ of the _____,
the Corporation that executed the within instrument, and also known to me to be
the person who executed the within instrument, on behalf of the Corporation herein
named, and acknowledged to me that such Corporation executed same, and further
acknowledged to me that such Corporation executed the within instrument pursuant
to its bylaws or a resolution of its Board of Directors.

WITNESS my hand and official seal.

_____
Notary Public in and for said
County of _____,
State of _____.
My commission expires _____, 19___.   (This Area for Official Notarial Seal)

PARTNERSHIP ACKNOWLEDGMENT

STATE OF _____)
) SS.
COUNTY OF _____)

On this ___ day of _____, in the year ___, before me, _____
_____, a Notary Public in and for said County and State, person-
ally appeared _____, known to me to be one of the partners of
the partnership that executed the within instrument, and acknowledged to me that
such partnership executed the same.

WITNESS my hand and official seal.

_____
Notary Public in and for said
County of _____,
State of _____:
My commission expires _____, 19___.   (This Area for Official Notarial Seal)

in order to ensure that the property will remain personal property (rather than become real property), but the administrative burden and cost of doing in-depth research on such matters on a state-by-state basis has led many lessors to require consents of this type, regardless of the favorable law in particular states.

FINANCING STATEMENT

Form

An example of a *financing statement* is shown as Exhibit 6.

Discussion

A lessor's security interest in a conditional sale type of lease (lease intended as security) is perfected by filing a "financing statement" with the appropriate public office designated by the Uniform Commercial Code for the state in which the equipment is located. Usually this will be the county court or recorder for the county in which the equipment is located, but sometimes this will be the Secretary of State for the state in which the equipment is located.[4]

The financing statement must contain the following information:

1. Name of the lessor.
2. Name of the lessee.
3. Address of the lessor (not a post-office box).
4. Mailing address of the lessee (post-office box is permissable).
5. A complete description of the equipment.
6. Signature of the lessee.

Perfection of a lessor's security interest in a true lease accomplishes nothing since the lessor is already the owner of the equipment. However, most lessors in true lease transactions nevertheless file precautionary financing statements. The purpose of filing such statements is to protect the lessor against the possibility that the lease might be held to be a lease intended for security. In such a situation if the lessor had not filed a financing statement, its interest in the equipment would be "unperfected," and other creditors of the lessee that filed financing statements covering the leased property (a blanket filing covering equipment, for example) would have an interest in the leased property superior to that of the lessor. It is obviously important to file a financing statement promptly so as to avoid an intervening lien by some other creditors.

---

[4] UCC Section 9–302 and 9–401.

EXHIBIT 6   Financing Statement

UNIFORM COMMERCIAL CODE — FINANCING STATEMENT — FORM UCC-1

INSTRUCTIONS
1. PLEASE TYPE this form. Fold only along perforation for mailing.
2. Remove Secured Party and Debtor Copies and send other 3 copies to the filing officer. Enclose filing fee.
3. When filing is to be with more than one office, Form UCC-2 may be placed over this set to avoid double typing.
4. If the space provided for any item(s) on the form is inadequate the item(s) should be continued on additional sheets, preferably 5" x 8" or 8" x 10". Only one copy of such additional sheets need be presented to the filing officer with a set of three copies of the financing statement. Long schedules of collateral, indentures, etc. may be on any size paper that is convenient for the secured party.
5. If collateral is crops or goods which are or are to become fixtures, describe generally the real estate and give name of record owner.
6. When a copy of the security agreement is used as a financing statement, it is requested that it be accompanied by a completed but unsigned set of these forms, without extra fee.
7. At the time of original filing, filing officer should return third copy as an acknowledgment. At a later time, secured party may date and sign termination legend and use third copy as a Termination Statement.

This FINANCING STATEMENT is presented to a filing officer for filing pursuant to the Uniform Commercial Code | 3 Maturity date (if any):

1 Debtor(s) (Last Name First) and address(es)	2 Secured Party(ies) and address(es)	For Filing Officer (Date, Time, Number, and Filing Office)

4 This financing statement covers the following types (or items) of property:

Check ☒ if covered: ☐ Proceeds of Collateral are also covered   ☐ Products of Collateral are also covered. No. of additional sheets presented

Filed with:

By:...   By:...
  Signature(s) of Debtor(s)   Signature(s) of Secured Party(ies)

STANDARD FORM — UNIFORM COMMERCIAL CODE — FORM UCC-1

A precautionary financing statement is filled out and filed in exactly the same way as a regular financing statement, except that additional language is added at the end of the description of the leased property to make clear that the parties believe the transaction to be a true lease. An example of such a statement would be: "The foregoing property is leased to debtor pursuant to a lease dated as of September 10, 1987. This is a precautionary financing statement, not to be deemed an admission by the parties that the lease transaction referred to above is other than a true lease."[5]

In some states, the words *lessor* and *lessee* may be substituted for the words *debtor* and *secured party* on the form.

---

[5] Excellent discussions of the rights of lessors as creditors are contained in *Equipment Leasing 1987,* ed. Ronald M. Bayer and Ian Shrank (New York: Practicing Law Institute). See especially the articles therein by Steven Harris, pp. 177–254, and by Ronald M. Bayer, pp. 255–294.

ASSIGNMENTS OF EQUIPMENT LEASES

Related problems arise where conditional sale types of leases or true leases are assigned by a lessor to a third party either as a sale of chattel paper or as security for a loan by the assignee. An assignment should contain the following representations and warranties.

1. The assignor owns the lease free and clear of all liens, claims, or encumbrances.
2. In a true lease assignment, the assignor owns the leased equipment free and clear of all liens, claims, and encumbrances except the lease.
3. The assignor has power and authority to assign.
4. The assigned lease is the only document executed by the lessee and lessor.
5. The lease is genuine, and the signatures are correct.
6. The lease complies with all applicable regulations and laws.
7. The lease is and will continue to be free from rights of offset, counter claims, and defenses.
8. The lease constitutes a valid perfected first lien on the equipment or reserved title to the equipment.

An assignment of an equipment lease is perfected by the assignee taking possession of the original lease or by filing a UCC financing statement containing the names and addresses of the assignee and assignor as described above.[6]

ELECTION OF LESSOR OF NEW SECTION 38 PROPERTY TO TREAT LESSEE AS PURCHASER FOR PURPOSES OF ITC

Form

Exhibit 7 is a *Section 38 election* to treat the lessee as owner for purposes of ITC.

Discussion

In a true lease of equipment eligible for ITC,[7] either the lessee or the lessor may claim the investment tax credit. As noted in Chapter 14, transactions in which the lessor retains the investment tax credit

---

[6] UCC Section 9–304(1).

[7] As discussed previously, ITC was repealed by the Tax Reform Act of 1986 except for certain "transitional property."

EXHIBIT 7 Election of Lessor of New Section 38 Property to Treat
Lessee as Purchaser for Purposes of Investment Tax Credit

**ELECTION OF LESSOR OF NEW SECTION 38 PROPERTY
TO TREAT LESSEE AS PURCHASER FOR PURPOSES OF
INVESTMENT TAX CREDIT**

(Name)

(Address)

(City and State)   _(Taxpayer Account No.)_

as Lessor
and

(Name)

(Address)

(City and State)   _(Taxpayer Account No.)_

as Lessee,
of the property described below, hereby agree that Lessee may claim the investment tax credit thereon.

Income tax returns are filed at the District Director's office indicated:

(Lessor — City and State)   _(Lessee — City and State)_

Possession of property transferred to lessee on _____ _(Date)_

Description of property:	ESTIMATED USEFUL (DEPRECIABLE) LIFE TO LESSOR	FAIR MARKET VALUE OF PROPERTY ON DATE OF TRANSFER

Lessor: ACCEPTED
Lessee:

By _____ _(Title)_   By _____ _(Title)_

Date _____   Date _____

are known as RIC transactions. If the investment tax credit is to be claimed by the lessee, it must be "passed" to the lessee by the lessor, and the transaction is then called a PIC transaction. Whether the transaction will be PIC or RIC is determined by the parties in structuring the lease based on their tax positions and on their ability to use the investment tax credit directly.

If, at the request of the lessee, a PIC transaction is structured, the lessor will execute and deliver a pass-through certificate that is substantially similar to the example form in Exhibit 7. The useful life and fair-market-value information on the form must be utilized by the lessee in determining the amount of investment tax credit to claim.

SECTION IV

Leveraged Leases

16

Leveraged Lease Fundamentals

The leveraged form of a true lease is the ultimate form of lease financing. The most attractive feature of a leveraged lease from the standpoint of a lessee is its low cost as compared to that of alternative methods of financing. Leveraged leasing also satisfies a need for lease financing of especially large capital equipment projects with economic lives of up to 25 or more years, although leveraged leases are also used where the life of the equipment is considerably shorter. The leveraged lease can be a most advantageous financing device when used for the right kinds of projects and structured correctly.

Single-investor nonleveraged leases are simple two-party transactions involving a lessee and a lessor. In single-investor leases (sometimes called nonleveraged leases or direct leases), the lessor provides all of the funds necessary to purchase the leased asset from its own resources. While the lessor may borrow some or all of these funds, it does so on a full-recourse basis to its lenders, and it is at risk for all of the capital employed.

A leveraged lease is conceptually similar to a single-investor lease. The lessee selects the equipment and negotiates the lease in much the same manner. Also, the terms for rentals, options, and responsibility for taxes, insurance, and maintenance are similar. However, a leveraged lease is appreciably more complex in size, documentation, legal involvement, and, most importantly, the number of parties involved and the unique advantages that each party gains.

Leveraged leases are generally offered only by corporations acting as lessors. This is because in a leveraged lease the tax benefits available to individual lessors are much more limited than those available to a corporation. This chapter is devoted to leveraged leases offered by corporations.

The lessor in a leveraged lease becomes the owner of the leased equipment by providing only a percentage (20–30 percent) of the capital necessary to purchase the equipment.[1] The remainder of the capital (70–80 percent) is borrowed from institutional investors on a nonrecourse basis to the lessor. This loan is secured by a first lien on the equipment, an assignment of the lease, and an assignment of the lease rental payments. The cost of the nonrecourse borrowing is a function of the credit standing of the lessee.[2] The lease rate varies with the debt rate and with the risk of the transaction.

A leveraged lease is always a true lease. The lessor in a leveraged lease can claim all of the tax benefits incidental to ownership of the leased asset even though the lessor provides only 20 to 30 percent of the capital needed to purchase the equipment. This ability to claim the tax benefits attributable to the entire cost of the leased equipment while providing and being at risk for only a portion of the cost of the leased equipment is the "leverage" in a leveraged lease. This leverage enables the lessor in a leveraged lease to offer the lessee much lower lease rates than the lessor could provide under a direct lease.

The legal expenses and closing costs associated with leveraged leases are larger than those for single-investor nonleveraged leases and usually confine the use of leveraged leases to financing relatively large capital equipment acquisitions. However, leveraged leases are also used for smaller lease transactions that are repetitive in nature and use standardized documentation so as to hold down legal and closing costs.

Several parties may be involved in a leveraged lease. Direct or single-investor nonleveraged leases are basically two-party transactions with a lessee and a lessor. However, leveraged leases by their nature

---

[1] The exact amount is a function of the economic result the lessor seeks to achieve. If investment tax credit is available to the lessor under a transition rule, the equity investment may be a larger amount up to 40 or 50 percent. ITC was repealed by the Deficit Reduction Act of 1986 except for certain property excepted under transition rules usually relating to a firm contract to acquire such equipment entered into prior to December 31, 1985.

[2] If the credit of the lessee is insufficient to support the transaction, a guarantor of the lessee obligations under the lease including payment of rents may be necessary. This guarantor may, for example, be the parent or sister company of the lessee, an interested third party, or a government agency. As discussed elsewhere, leveraged debt can not usually be directly guaranteed under the tax requirements of the IRS.

involve a minimum of three parties with diverse interests: a lessee, a lessor, and a nonrecourse lender. Indeed, leveraged leases are sometimes called three-party transactions.

Several owners and lenders may be involved in a leveraged lease. In such a case, an owner trustee is generally named to hold title to the equipment and represent the owners or equity participants, and an indenture trustee is usually named to hold the security interest or mortgage on the property for the benefit of the lenders or loan participants. Sometimes a single trustee may be appointed to perform both of these functions.

In order to provide a better understanding of leveraged leasing, in this chapter we will review the rights, obligations, functions, and characteristics of the various parties that may be involved; the structure of a leveraged lease; the cash flows; and the debt arrangements possible. Tax requirements for leveraged leases are discussed in Chapter 5.

PARTIES TO A LEVERAGED LEASE

The Lessee

The lessee selects the equipment to be leased, negotiates the price and warranties, and hires the use of the equipment by entering into a lease agreement. The lessee accepts, uses, operates, and receives all revenue from the equipment. The lessee makes rental payments. The credit standing of the lessee supports the rent obligation, the credit exposure of the lenders of leveraged debt, and the credit exposure of the equity participants.

Equity Participants

The equity participants (sometimes called owner participants) provide the equity contributions (20 to 30 percent of the purchase price) needed to purchase the leased equipment. They receive the rental payments remaining after the payment of debt service and any trustee fees. They claim the tax benefits incidental to the ownership of the leased equipment, consisting of ACRS (tax depreciation) deductions and deductions for interest used to fund their investment.[3] The equity participants are sometimes referred to as the lessors. Actually, in most cases they are the beneficial owners by way of an owner trust that is the lessor. Equity participants are also sometimes referred to as equity investors, owner participants, or trustors.

---

[3] An equity participant in rare instances may also be able to claim investment tax credit (ITC) if the property qualifies as transition property.

Loan Participants or Lenders

The loan participants or lenders are typically banks, finance companies, insurance companies, trusts, pension funds, and foundations. The funds provided by the loan participants, together with the equity contributions, make up the full purchase price of the asset to be leased. The loan participants provide 70 to 80 percent of the purchase price on a nonrecouse basis to the equity participants. As noted earlier, these loans are secured by a first lien on the leased equipment, an assignment of the lease, an assignment of rents under the lease, and an assignment of any ancillary agreements such as easements and supply contracts. Principal and interest payments that are due the loan participants (or lenders) from the indenture trustee are paid by the lessee to the indenture trustee, which then pays the loan participants.

Owner Trustee

The owner trustee represents the equity participants, acts as the lessor, and executes the lease and all of the basic documents that the lessor would normally sign in a lease. The owner trustee records and holds title to the leased asset for the benefit of the equity participants, subject to the mortgage or security agreement to the indenture trustee. The owner trustee issues trust certificates to the equity holders evidencing their beneficial interest as owners of the assets of the trust, issues bonds or notes to loan participants evidencing the leveraged debt, grants to the indenture trustee the security interests that secure repayment of the bonds (that is, the lease, the lease rentals and a first mortgage on the leased asset), receives distributions from the indenture trustee, distributes earnings to the equity participants, and receives and distributes any information or notices regarding the transaction that are required to be provided to the parties. The owner trustee has little discretionary power beyond that specifically granted in the trust agreement and has no affirmative duties.

The owner participants indemnify the owner trustee against costs and liabilities arising out of the transaction, except for willful misconduct or negligence. From the standpoint of the equity participants, additional practical reasons often cited for having an owner trustee are as follows:

1. An owner trust is a simple and convenient way to hold title to the equipment where there are two or more equity participants.
2. The lessee and loan participants have the practical convenience of dealing with one entity where there is an owner trustee.

3. The existence of the owner trustee helps justify keeping the nonrecourse leveraged debt off the balance sheet of the equity investor.

4. Equity participants may avoid the need to qualify to do business in the state in which the equipment is located.

5. Loan participants (lenders) want an owner trustee in order to prevent a trustee in bankruptcy for an equity participant from disavowing the lease or delaying payments due under the lease.

6. The owner trustee may provide the equity participant with a shield against tort liability.

7. Bank equity investors avoid the possible application of Regulation Q.

8. In an aircraft lease involving foreign beneficiaries, if the owner trustee is a U.S. citizen, the transaction and security interest may be recorded with the FAA.

9. Under the Internal Revenue Code, the owner participants share ratably in the tax benefits. The tax advantages of a partnership are gained without the need for a formal partnership agreement.[4]

These reasons have various degrees of merit. It can be argued that an owner trustee is unnecessary. Where a leveraged lease has a single equity investor, the parties may conclude that an owner trustee is not needed and that the equity investor may act as the lessor. However, the modest cost of an owner trustee as compared with the apparent and possible benefits usually justifies the use of an owner trustee in a leveraged lease unless the transaction is extremely simple and straightforward.

Indenture Trustee

The indenture trustee (sometimes called the security trustee) is appointed by and represents the lenders or loan participants. The owner trustee and the indenture trustee enter into a trust indenture whereby the owner trustee assigns to the indenture trustee, for the benefit of the loan participants and as security for the leveraged debt and any other obligations, all of the owner trustee's interest as lessor in:

1. The equipment to be leased and the lessor's rights under manufacturer's or contractor's warranties related to the equipment.

---

[4] In order to achieve these tax objectives, under Treasury Regulation 301.7701-2 the trust must be a "pass-through" or "grantor trust" and have not more than two of the following four corporate characteristics: continuity of life, limited liability, central management, and free transferability of interests. This is discussed later in this chapter.

2. The lease agreement.
3. The lessor's right to receive rents (including all payments) owed by the lessee (subject to such exceptions as the lessor and lessee agree to).
4. The lessor's rights to receive any payments under any guarantee agreements (subject to the same exceptions as the payments due the lessor).
5. The lessor's rights under any ancillary facility support agreements such as easements, service contracts, supply contracts, and sales contracts.

The indenture agreement sets forth the form of the notes or loan agreements, the events of defaults, and the instructions and priorities for distributions of funds to the loan participants and other parties.

The indenture trustee receives funds from the loan participants (lenders) and the equity participants when the transaction is about to close, pays the manufacturer or contractor the purchase price of the equipment to be leased, and records and holds the senior security interest in the leased equipment, the lease, any ancillary facility support contracts, and the rents for the benefit of the loan participants. The indenture trustee collects rents and other sums due under the lease from the lessee. Upon the receipt of rental payments, the indenture trustee pays debt payments of principal and interest due on the leveraged debt to the loan participants and distributes revenues not needed for debt service to the owner trustee. In the event of default, the indenture trustee can foreclose on the leased equipment and take other appropriate actions to protect the security interests of the loan participants.

Single Trustee Acting as Both an Indenture Trustee and an Owner Trustee

A single trustee may assume the duties of both an owner trustee and an indenture trustee in a leveraged lease. Where a single trustee is used, the trustee is referred to as the owner trustee. Those who favor using a single trustee in a leveraged lease transaction argue that such an arrangement is simpler and reduces the costs of the transaction.

Although the use of a single trustee in a leveraged lease has become an increasingly common arrangement, serious conflicts of interest may arise between the equity participants and the loan participants in the event of a default by the lessee. Such potential conflicts make the use of a single trustee unattractive if there is any question regarding the lessee's credit.

In the event the lessee defaults, the trustee is faced with conflicting choices. For example, if the trustee repossesses and sells the equipment quickly for cash at a price that is only sufficient to return the loan participants' debt balance, the equity participants are left with nothing. On the other hand, if a higher price can be obtained by selling the leased equipment using an installment sale, the equity participants might recover part or all of their investment. In the installment sale alternative, however, the loan participants are subject to additional risk, so that the use of an installment sale to achieve the objectives of the equity participants might result in a breach of the fiduciary duties of the trustee to the loan participants.

A possible solution is to permit the trustee to resign one or both of the trusteeships in the event of a default. However, this begs the questions since a successor trusteeship under such circumstances would be difficult to arrange, and the loan participants or the equity participants, or both, would be left in a difficult position to pursue their respective claims.

Manufacturer or Contractor

The manufacturer or contractor manufactures or constructs the equipment to be leased. The manufacturer or contractor (or supplier) receives the purchase price upon acceptance of the equipment by the lessee and delivers the equipment to the lessee at the beginning of the lease. The warranties of the manufacturer, contractor, or supplier as to the quality, capabilities, and efficiencies of the leased equipment are important to the lessee, the equity participants, and the loan participants.

Packager or Broker

The packager or broker is the leasing company arranging the transaction. In many instances, the packager is purely a broker and not an investor. From the standpoint of the lessee, it may be desirable that the packager also be an equity participant. The packager may, in fact, be the sole equity participant.

Guarantor

A guarantor of the lessee's credit may be present in some leveraged lease transactions. Although a member of the lessee group may not guarantee the leveraged debt under Internal Revenue rules, a member of the lessee group may guarantee the lessee's obligation to pay rent.[5]

A party unrelated to the lessee may guarantee either rents or debt. Such a guarantor might be a third party such as a bank under a letter

---

[5] See Chapter 15 for a discussion of guarantees.

of credit agreement, an insurer of residual value, or a government guarantor. Where rents are guaranteed by a third party, a controversy may arise under Revenue Procedure 75–21 that relates to whether the lessor is at risk for an amount equal to 20 percent of the cost of the equipment.[6] It can be strongly argued that such a guarantee is merely the equivalent of a second credit exposure and does not alter the fact that the lessor is "at risk."

STRUCTURE OF A LEVERAGED LEASE

A leveraged lease transaction is usually structured as follows where a broker or a third-party leasing company arranges the transaction.

The leasing company arranging the lease, "the packager," enters into a commitment letter with the prospective lessee (obtains a mandate) that outlines the terms for the lease of the equipment, including the timing and amount of rental payments. Since the exact rental payment cannot be determined until the debt has been sold and the equipment delivered, rents are agreed upon based on certain variables, including assumed debt rates and the delivery dates of the equipment to be leased.

After the commitment letter has been signed, the packager prepares a summary of terms for the proposed lease and contacts potential equity participants to arrange for firm commitments to invest equity in the proposed lease to the extent that the packager does not intend to provide the total amount of the required equity funds from its own resources. Contacts with potential equity sources may be fairly informal or may be accomplished through a bidding process. Typical equity participants include banks, independent finance companies, captive finance companies, and corporate investors that have tax liability to shelter, have funds to invest, and understand the economics of tax-oriented leasing. The packager may also arrange the debt either directly or in conjunction with the capital markets group of a bank or an investment banker selected by the lessee or the lessor. If the equipment is not to be delivered and the lease is not to commence for a considerable period of time, the debt arrangements may be deferred until close to the date of delivery.

The packager may agree at the outset to "bid firm" or underwrite the transaction on the mandated terms and may then "syndicate" its bid to potential equity participants. However, the lessee may prefer to use a bidding procedure without an underwritten price on the theory that more favorable terms can be arranged using this approach.

---

[6] Revenue Procedure 75–21 is discussed in Chapter 5.

In some instances the lessee may prefer to prepare its own bid request and solicit bids directly from potential lessors without using a packager or broker to underwrite or arrange the transaction. This might be the case, for example, where the lessee has considerable experience in leveraged leasing and the transaction is repetitious of previous leases of similar equipment that the lessee has leased, such as computers or computer systems.

If an owner trustee is to be used, a bank or trust company mutually agreeable to the equity participants and the lessee is selected to act as owner trustee. If an indenture trustee is to be used, another bank or trust company acceptable to the loan participants is selected to act as indenture trustee. As discussed previously, a single trustee may act as both owner trustee and indenture trustee.

Exhibit 1 illustrates the parties, cash flows, and agreements among the parties in a simple leveraged lease.

If the leveraged lease is arranged by sponsors of a project who want to be the equity participants, the structure and procedures are essentially the same as those for a leveraged lease by a third-party equity participant. In such circumstances, the sponsors are the equity investors. If some of the sponsors can use tax benefits and some cannot, the equity participants may include a combination of sponsors and one or more third-party leasing companies. This arrangement is more complex, but the structure and procedures are essentially the same as those for a leveraged lease by a third-party equity participant.

CLOSING THE TRANSACTION

Participation Agreement

The key document in a leveraged lease transaction is the participation agreement (sometimes called the financing agreement). This document is, in effect, a script for closing the transaction.

When the parties to a leveraged lease transaction are identified, all of them except the indenture trustee enter into a participation agreement that spells out in detail the various undertakings, obligations, mechanics, timing, conditions precedent, and responsibilities of the parties with respect to providing funds and purchasing, leasing, and securing or mortgaging the equipment to be leased. More specifically: The equity participants agree to provide their investment or equity contribution; the loan participants agree to make their loans; the owner trustee agrees to purchase and lease the equipment; and the lessee agrees to lease the equipment. The substance of the required opinions of counsel is described in the participation agreement. The representations of the parties are detailed. Tax indemnities and other general

EXHIBIT 1   Leveraged Lease

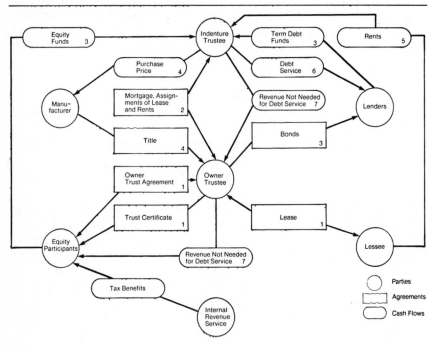

Summary:
1. An owner trust is established by the equity participants, trust certificates are issued, and a lease agreement is signed by the owner trustee as lessor and the lessee.
2. A security agreement is signed by the owner trustee and the indenture trustee, a mortgage is granted on the leased asset, and the lease and rentals are assigned as security to the indenture trustee.
3. Notes or bonds are issued by the owner trustee to the lenders, term debt funds are paid by the lenders (loan participants) to the indenture trustee, and equity funds are paid by the equity participants to the indenture trustee.
4. The purchase price is paid, and title is assigned to the owner trustee, subject to the mortgage.
5. The lease commences; rents are paid by the lessee to the indenture trustee.
6. Debt service is paid by the indenture trustee to the lenders (loan participants).
7. Revenue not required for debt service or trustees' fees is paid to the owner trustee and, in turn, to the equity participants.

indemnities are often set forth in the participation agreement rather than the lease agreement. The exact form of agreements to be signed, the opinions to be given, and the representations to be made by the parties are usually attached as exhibits to the participation agreement.

Key Documents

The key documents in a leveraged lease transaction that are in addition to the participation agreement are: the lease agreement, the owner trust agreement, and the indenture trust agreement.

The lease agreement is between the lessee and owner trustee. The lease is for a term of years and may contain renewal options and fair-market-value purchase options. Rents and all payments due under the lease are net to the lessor, and the lessee waives defenses and offsets to rents under a "hell or high water clause."

The owner trust agreement creates the owner trust and sets forth the relationships between the owner trustee and the equity participants that it represents. The owner trust agreement spells out the duties of the trustee, the documents the trustee is to execute, the distribution to be made of funds it receives from equity participants, lenders, and the lessee. The owner trustee has little or no authority to take discretionary or independent action.

The owner trust grants a lien or security interest on the leased equipment and assigns the lease agreement, any ancillary facility support agreements and right to receive rents under the lease to the indenture trustee (which may also be the owner trustee). It spells out the obligations of the indenture trustee to the lenders.

Indemnities by the Lessee

Lessee indemnities fall into three general categories:

1. A general indemnity which protects all of the other parties to the transaction from any claims of third parties arising from the lease or the use of the leased equipment.
2. A general tax indemnity which protects all of the other parties to the transaction from all federal, state, or local taxes arising out of or in connection with the transaction except for certain income tax or income-related taxes.
3. Special tax indemnities by the lessee which protect the owner participants from the loss of expected income tax benefits as a result of the acts and omissions of the lessee and certain other events.

The coverage of the special tax indemnities beyond the acts and omissions of the lessee is a matter of significant negotiation between the lessee and lessor. Special tax indemnities are discussed in more detail in Chapter 13.

Closing Procedure

When the transaction is about to close, the equity participants pay the amount of their equity investments to the indenture trustee. As noted earlier, IRS takes the position this investment must be at least 20 percent of the cost of the equipment to qualify as a true lease for federal tax purposes. Usually the equity participants' investment will be in the range of 20 to 30 percent of the acquisition cost of the leased equipment, including the expenses incurred in connection with the acquisition of the equipment and the closing of the lease transaction, such as legal costs, printing expense, and brokers' fees. The loan participants pay the balance of the acquisition cost of the leased equipment to the indenture trustee. The owner trustee simultaneously issues equity participation certificates to the equity participants, and promissory notes, bonds, or debt certificates to the loan participants. The debt evidenced by the notes, bonds, or debt certificates is without recourse to either the owner trustee or the equity participants.

In the meantime, a lease agreement for the equipment has been signed by the owner trustee (as lessor) and the lessee.[7] The indenture trustee has recorded a security interest or mortgage on the equipment to be leased. The owner trustee assigns the lease agreement and the right to receive rents under the lease to the indenture trustee as security for the benefit of the loan participants under a security agreement between the owner trustee and the indenture trustee. The loan participants agree to look exclusively to lease rentals for repayment or, in the event of default by the lessee, to their security interest in the lease, the rentals, and their mortgage or security interest in the leased equipment.[8]

In most lease transactions, the lessee has already contracted to purchase the equipment at the time the lessee seeks to arrange the lease financing. Where these circumstances exist, the lessee assigns the purchase contract or the construction agreement to the owner trustee (as lessor). This assignment conveys to the owner trustee all of the lessee's rights, title, and interest to receive delivery, to be transferred title, and to be protected by warranties. The lessee also obtains the consent of the manufacturer or contractor to the foregoing assignment.[9]

At the closing of the purchase of the equipment, the lessee signifies its acceptance of the equipment by signing an acceptance certificate. The indenture trustee pays the purchase price for the equipment to the manufacturer, contractor, or any construction lenders and also pays

---

[7] Most of the terms of this type of lease agreement are very similar to a typical single-investor lease, which is discussed in Chapter 13. Special provisions relate to the rights of the lessor as compared to the leveraged debt participants and are discussed later in this chapter.

[8] If the parties elect to use a single trustee, rather than both an indenture trustee and an owner trustee, the single trustee performs the functions, outlined above, of both the indenture trustee and the owner trustee.

[9] However, neither the owner trustee nor the owner participants assume the lessee's liabilities to the manufacturer or the contractor.

any expenses (legal fees, printing fees, brokerage fees, and so forth) being financed as part of the transaction. The indenture trustee uses funds collected from the loan participants and the equity participants for that purpose. Title is then conveyed to the owner trustee, subject to the previously recorded security agreement and mortgage. The equipment is then delivered to the lessee, and the lease commences.

CASH FLOWS DURING THE LEASE

The equity participants receive cash flow from three sources: rents after the payment of debt service and trustee fees, tax benefits, and proceeds from the sale of the equipment at the conclusion of the lease.

The lessee pays periodic rents to the indenture trustee, which uses such funds to pay currently due principal and interest payments to the loan participants and to pay trustee fees for its services. The balance of the rental payments is paid to the owner trustee. After the payment of any trustee fees due the owner trustee and any administrative or other expenses, the owner trustee pays the remainder of the rental payments to the equity participants.

The equity participants also realize cash flow from tax benefits as quickly as they can claim such benefits on their quarterly tax estimates and tax returns.

The leveraged debt is usually amortized over a period of time identical to the lease term, with payments of principal and interest due on or shortly after the due date of the rental payments. These payments may be monthly, quarterly, semiannual, or annual. Where "optimized debt" structures are used for competitive reasons, the rental payments approximately equal the debt service payments plus deferred income tax. This has the effect of reducing the leveraged debt payments in the later years of the lease. Rental payments are usually level but (subject to Internal Revenue Service limitations discussed in Chapter 5) may vary upward or downward (sawtooth rents) to achieve a maximum yield for the lessor. Also, debt payments may be concluded entirely before the lease term ends in order to generate additional cash for the lessor.

When the lease terminates the equipment is returned to the owner trustee, who sells or releases the property at the direction of the owner participants.

The lease agreement usually requires the lessee to furnish the owner trustee and the indenture trustee with financial statements, evidence of insurance, and other similar information. The trustees distribute this information to all parties to the transaction.

INCOME TAX TREATMENT OF AN OWNER TRUST ACTING AS A LESSOR

Single Equity Participant Grantor Trust

Where a single equity participant is the equity investor in a leveraged lease, an owner trust is not necessary but nevertheless may be desirable for one or more of the reasons discussed earlier in this chapter. An owner trust for the benefit of a single equity participant will generally be treated as a grantor trust for tax purposes since all items of income, gain, loss, deductions, and credits relating to the property held by the owner trustee will flow through to the equity participant. The tax consequences to the equity participant under a grantor trust are generally the same as they would be if the equity participant owned the leased property directly.

Owner Trust for Two or More Equity Participants

An owner trust established for the benefit of two or more equity participants is taxed as a partnership for federal income tax purposes. The owner trust is not taxable as a corporation so long as the trust agreement has both of the following provisions:

1. Each of the equity participants is prohibited from transferring its interest in the owner trust without the consent of the other equity participants.
2. The owner trustee cannot take any action except as provided in the trust agreement or as specifically instructed by the equity participants.

These provisions prevent the owner trust from possessing two of the four criteria of the Internal Revenue Service for a corporation, namely free transferability of ownership and centralized management.[10] If the trust were taxed as a corporation, the equity participants (with less than 80 percent control) would not be entitled to claim tax benefits attributable to the transaction on their income tax returns.

When the owner trust is treated as a partnership for federal income tax purposes, each equity participant (partner) takes into account its separate proportional distributive share of the partnership's income, gain, loss, tax deductions, and tax credits. The owner trust (partnership) makes tax elections that determine the tax benefits available to the equity participants. The owner trust (partnership) may have a taxable year different from the taxable year of one or all of the equity

---

[10] Treasury Regulation 301.7701-2. The owner trust qualifies as a pass-through or grantor trust.

participants. If the partnership's taxable year in the year in which property is placed in service is less than 12 months, the first-year ACRS deduction will be proportionately reduced.

Ownership of leased property by equity participants as tenants in common has been used as a device to avoid the adverse consequences of either a short taxable year or equity investors having different tax years. Tenancies in common can be structured as partnerships for tax purposes. From a legal and tax standpoint, however, the documentation of a leveraged lease with equity participants as tenants in common is generally much more complex than that of an owner trust.

Other entities that are used to hold title to leased equipment under a leveraged lease include general partnerships, limited partnerships, and contractual joint ventures, all of which can be structured to file partnership tax returns.

DEBT FOR LEVERAGED LEASES

Debt for leveraged leases is usually at a fixed rate of interest although it may be at a floating rate of interest. Such debt is available from a variety of sources. The lead equity source or packager may arrange the debt. Sometimes the lessee may prefer to have the debt arranged by its commercial bank, the capital markets group of its commercial bank, or its investment bank. Most leveraged lease debt is raised in the private placement market at little or no premium over what the lessee would expect to pay directly for such debt. The sources include:

- Insurance companies.
- Pension plans.
- Profit-sharing plans.
- Commercial banks.
- Finance companies.
- Savings banks.
- Domestic leasing companies.
- Foreign banks.
- Foreign leasing companies.
- Foreign investors.
- Institutional investors.

Other less frequently used instruments and sources of debt that may be useful in special circumstances include the following:

Commercial Paper Investors. Commercial paper has sometimes been used for leveraged debt for short (five to seven years) leveraged leases. The major risks in using commercial paper are the floating interest rates and the inability to roll over the commercial paper. Such debt may require a backup line of credit. Interest rate risk can be hedged to some extent by using interest rate futures or interest rate swaps.

Public Debt Markets. It is possible, but not very practical, to use the public debt markets for leveraged debt. Public debt is expensive since it must be registered under the Securities Act unless it is guaranteed by an agency of the United States. Also, amending the lease is difficult when public debt is used.

Government Financing. If government financing is available, it can sometimes be used as leveraged debt.

Industrial Revenue Bonds. Industrial revenue bonds, including bonds in which interest is tax free, can usually be used as leveraged debt.

Supplier Financing. Supplier financing can be an excellent source of leveraged debt (shipyard financing for a ship, for example). Export-Import Bank financing offers such opportunities. One difficulty in using this source is matching the debt maturities to the lease maturities. Where the lease is for a longer term than that of the supplier financing, wraparound debt is difficult to arrange, particularly if the security interest of such debt must usually be subordinate to the supplier financing.

Multicurrency Financing. Where the lessee generates more than one currency from the sale of its product or service, it may prefer the leveraged debt to be in one or more matching currencies. Debt and rents can be arranged to satisfy this need. Currency swaps can be used to hedge the foreign exchange risk of foreign currency debt.

Eurodollar and Eurobond Markets. The attractive interest rates available in the Eurodollar and Eurobond markets will probably bring these markets into use in the future. Floating rate notes (FRNs) with interest rate hedges or futures may also be used.

Bridge Financing. If interest rates on fixed long-term debt are, in the opinion of the lessee, unusually high, the lessee may arrange bridge financing on a floating-interest-rate basis with a view to refinancing term debt at a more favorable fixed-interest rate at a later time. The floating debt might, for example, have a term of 15 years identical to the lease term, float at one percent over LIBOR (London Interbank

Offered Rate) for five years, three over in the sixth year, four over in the seventh year, and so on. Such an arrangement enables the lessee to arrange financing with a commercial bank, which feels assured under these circumstances that it will be taken out (have its loan paid off) at the end of five years.

FACILITY LEASES

Leveraged leases have been used increasingly in recent years to finance the use of equipment that is impractical to move, such as electric generating plants, mining equipment, refineries, and chemical facilities. The equipment's lack of portability does not make it limited-use property for tax purposes so long as the facility is reasonably expected to have a fair market value equal to 20 percent of its original cost at the conclusion of the lease.[11] The 20 percent useful life tests of Revenue Procedure 75–21 are met if at the conclusion of the lease the facility can continue to be used at its original location for a period of time equal to 20 percent or more of the base lease term plus any fixed-rate renewal terms.

Facility Support Agreements

A series of facility support agreements are needed in order to provide the lessor with rights to the leased equipment upon the conclusion of the original lease.

The lessor will want either to own the land on which the facility is located or to have a leasehold interest in the land that is at least 20 percent longer than the base lease term and any fixed-rate renewal lease terms available to the lessee. The lessor will also want easement and access rights to the property on which the facility is located. If supply contracts for raw material, fuel, or energy are necessary for successful operation of the facility, these must be assigned by the lessee to the lessor at the conclusion of the initial lease. Rights-of-way for power lines, rail lines, pipelines, and roads may be necessary, as may access rights to adjoining port, rail, or pipeline facilities. The leased equipment facility may be part of a large complex of similar facilities in some cases, and in such a case the lessor should have rights to service, fuel, energy, and so forth, shared in common with the other facilities owned by the lessee or other parties.

Exhibit 2 is a diagram of a leveraged lease of an electric coal-fired generating facility that illustrates the parties, the cash flows, and the agreements involved in a facility lease transaction in which the owner

---

[11] See chapter 5.

EXHIBIT 2   Leveraged Lease of an Electric Generating Facility

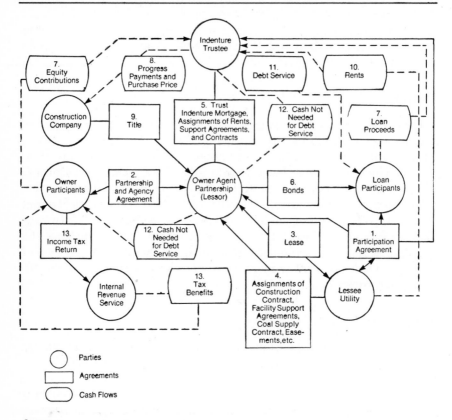

○ Parties

▭ Agreements

▱ Cash Flows

Summary:

1. A participation agreement is entered into between the owner agent, the lessee, the loan partic-ipants, and the indenture trustee. This agreement constitutes the master agreement for the leveraged lease and spells out the general rights and obligations of the parties.
2. A partnership and agency agreement is entered into between the owner participants and a bank or trust company acting as the owner agent and lessor.
3. A lease agreement is entered into between the partnership and the lessee for a term of 20 years. Rents are net to the lessor. The lessee assumes all obligations and risk that relate to the leased equipment. The lessee agrees to pay all rent and monetary obligations "come hell or high water" and waives defenses and offsets to such payments.
4. The lessee assigns to the partnership its interest in the construction contract, facility support agreements, coal supply contracts, easements, and so forth.
5. The owner agent, on behalf of the partnership, enters into a trust indenture and mortgage with the indenture trustee and assigns to the indenture trustee all rents and other payments to be received under the lease, the construction contract for the facility to be leased, the facility support agreements, coal supply contracts, easements, and so forth, all as security for bonds (leveraged debt) that are to be sold by the owner agent.
6. Bonds are issued to the bondholders.
7. Loan proceeds and equity contributions are paid to the indenture trustee.
8. The purchase price is paid to the construction company.
9. Title to the leased facility is conveyed by the construction company to the partnership.
10. The lease commences, and rental payments commence to be paid by the lessee to the indenture trustee.
11. The indenture trustee services the debt to the loan participants; cash not needed for debt services is distributed to the owner participants.
12. In the meantime the owner participants file income tax returns and receive tax benefits associated with equipment ownership.

trustee takes title during construction. This transaction contemplates the assignment of the facility support agreements.

In this example the purpose of the facility support agreements between the lessee and the owner trustee is to provide the owner trustee with access to all properties and things necessary or desirable to allow the owner trustee (acting on behalf of the equity participants) to operate the electric generating facility as an independent commercial electric generating unit and to sell electricity generated by the facility into a grid. The agreements stipulate that maintenance services, fuel supply, power transmission and/or distribution, and other things are to be provided by the lessee (for which the lessee will be reimbursed), while a third party is operating the facility on behalf of the lessor or on lease from the lessor. Without facility support agreements the assets of the project have little value as collateral. The facility support agreements are assigned to the indenture trustee as support for the leveraged debt. They remain in effect throughout the interim lease term, the base lease term, and any renewal lease terms, and for at least long enough thereafter to meet the useful life tests of the Internal Revenue Service. Another purpose of the facility support agreements is to ensure that the facility will have value to someone other than the lessee at the end of the lease so as to satisfy the true lease requirements of the Internal Revenue Service.

For example, the mere ownership of the facility by the owner trustee, without the underlying supply contracts for coal to be used as fuel for the facility, might seriously undermine the value of the facility for collateral security purposes and residual value purposes. To protect the interests of the equity participants and the loan participants, it is necessary for the lessee to assign to the owner trustee any coal supply contracts that might be advantageous or valuable to it. The owner trustee, in turn, assigns its interest in such contracts to the indenture trustee for the benefit of the loan participants.

The supplier to the facility must consent to the assignment, and the form of consent is usually included as part of the coal supply agreement.

Construction Contract Assignment

The participation agreement and the lease agreement (as in Exhibit 2) may contemplate that the title to the property to be leased will be transferred to the owner trustee (lessor) while the facility is still in early stages of construction. In this situation the construction contract is assigned by the lessee to the owner trustee, and construction financing is arranged as described later in this chapter.

Although the facility will usually be constructed by a third-party contractor, the utility may wish to supervise the performance of the construction contract with the third-party contractor. In this situation a construction supervision agreement is entered into between the lessee and the owner trustee. The purpose of this agreement is to arrange for and require the owner trustee to use the services of the utility in the capacity of construction supervisor to oversee the construction testing, delivery, and acceptance of the facility.

CONSTRUCTION FINANCING

In the usual leveraged lease transaction the equity participants pay in their equity funds simultaneously with the receipt of leveraged debt funds from the loan participants at the closing, when the leased equipment is accepted by the lessee and the lease begins.

However, where the construction period extends over a considerable time the contractor may require progress payments during construction. In such a situation the parties may agree that the owner trust will take title to the facility during construction, so that the lease involves an interim lease term during construction that precedes the base lease term. Where this type of arrangement is made, a separate interim loan (construction loan) agreement is entered into by the lessee, the owner trustee, and the construction lenders, who are usually not also to be loan participants during the base term lease. The lessor's equity investment and short-term construction loan financing is used until the completion of construction, acceptance by the lessee, drawdown of the long-term financing (leveraged debt), and commencement of the base lease term. The lessee pays interim rents to the owner trustee in an amount sufficient to cover interest on the construction loan and an adequate yield to the equity participants. In the alternative, construction loan interest may be capitalized into the cost of the facility and included in the total cost of the facility which is to be financed by the lease.

Construction financing is usually provided by commercial banks. Such financing is secured by an assignment of interim rents and by the lessee's obligation to pay off the principal of the loan if the long-term lenders fail to provide the financing or if the facility is not constructed or completed by a certain date. In such a situation, the equity participants will also look to the lessee's guarantee to recover their investments plus an adequate yield. All of the lessee's guarantees of construction loans are eliminated on or before completion and acceptance of the leased equipment and commencement of the base term of the lease. Eliminating lessee guarantees of the owner trust debt obligations is necessary in order to comply with the Internal Revenue guidelines set forth in Revenue Procedure 75–21 and discussed in Chapter 5.

CREDIT EXPOSURE OF EQUITY PARTICIPANTS

As noted earlier, equity participants realize their yields from the following sources:

1. The interest rate spread between their yield on investment and their cost of funds.
2. Tax benefits from ACRS (tax depreciation) deductions.
3. The residual value of the equipment at the conclusion of the lease.

Although equity participants sometimes like to view their credit exposure as being limited to their original equity investment, most of which may be recovered in the first few years of the lease term of a leveraged lease, this is not the case if a "forgiveness" of the leveraged debt occurs in the later years of the lease. In such a situation the lessor may be deemed to realize taxable income from the forgiveness. A forgiveness might occur, for example, where the lessee defaults and the indenture trustee (on behalf of the loan participants) repossesses and sells the equipment for less than the outstanding principal of the leveraged debt.

For these reasons, leveraged leases are available only to lessees that present no apparent credit risk. Lenders and equity sources must be confident regarding the lessee's ability to meet all of its obligations under the lease, both for rental payments and for maintenance of the leased equipment.

POINTS OF CONTENTION BETWEEN LENDERS AND EQUITY PARTICIPANTS

Since the indenture trustee has an assignment of the rental payments, an assignment of the lease, and a first lien on the equipment, and since the lien position of the equity participants is junior to that of the loan participants unless otherwise provided, points of contention can arise between the equity participants and the lenders as each group seeks to protect its respective interest in the transaction.

Indenture Defaults Which Are Not Lease Defaults

The equity participants must be sure that any event of indenture default that does not constitute a lease default is controlled by the equity participants or by the owner trustee acting on their behalf. In the absence of such protection, the equity participants could find themselves in default under the indenture and lose their interest in the equipment even though the lessee might continue to possess and use the equipment.

Control of Sale of Leased Property in the Event of Default

The equity participants in a leveraged lease should have some protection against the sale of the leased property to satisfy lenders in the event of a default by the lessee. Since the loan participants have a first lien on the leased property, they are interested in selling the property at a price that approximates their exposure, whereas the equity participants want to follow a strategy for realizing the maximum amount obtainable from a continuation of the lease, a release of the leased equipment, or a sale of the leased equipment. Also, if tax benefits have not vested, the equity participants will suffer a further loss if the leased equipment is sold to a third party.

Cure Rights of Equity Participants

The equity participants will want to negotiate the right to cure defaults of the lessee so as to prevent the indenture trustee (on behalf of the loan participants) from foreclosing and selling the leased property at a fire-sale price. The lenders, on the other hand, may resist this approach because it limits their ability to seize the equipment at an opportune time for resale, and because the value of the equipment may deteriorate in the hands of a lessee that is in financial difficulties and unable to properly maintain the equipment. This conflict can usually be resolved by permitting the equity participants to take action to prevent or cure a default on a basis whereby the equity participants have the right to purchase the notes evidencing the leveraged debt as they come due or the right to make up a certain number of consecutive rental payments to cover some or all future debt payments.

Fish or Cut Bait Provision

Another point of contention may arise where a technical default occurs that may be impractical or impossible to remedy and the indenture trustee begins to withhold payments otherwise due the equity participants in order to build an unofficial security deposit for the lenders. In order to provide equity participants with protection against such an occurrence, "fish or cut bait" provisions are negotiated that require the indenture trustee under such circumstances either to accelerate the entire loan within some time limit or to pay the equity participants.

Tax Indemnity Payments

Tax indemnity payments that may be due the equity participants are another possible area of disagreement. Since tax payments and indemnifications by the lessee against their loss are the lifeblood of the equity participants' yields and return of their investments, the equity participants argue that they should receive any tax indemnity payment to which they are entitled ahead of the lenders. Loan participants, of course, argue that their claim against the lessee and the leased equipment arising out of the leveraged debt is ahead of any claim of the equity participants. The trend has been for equity participants to prevail on this issue. The equity participants' rights to tax indemnity payments are "carved out" of the lessee's obligations assigned to the loan participants.

Payments by the lessee under general indemnities and liability insurance proceeds are also frequently carved out for the benefit of the equity participants.

In arranging a leveraged lease the equity participants and the lessee should have a clear understanding with the loan participants on these points at the time of arranging, pricing, and obtaining a commitment for the leveraged debt so as to avoid misunderstandings at a later date, particularly where interest rates may have moved upward between the time of commitment and the time of closing.

TAX INDEMNIFICATION FOR FUTURE CHANGES IN TAX LAW

Where a company requiring equipment intends to use a true lease to finance its equipment acquisitions, the lessee and lessor must agree as to which of them will bear the burden of future tax changes. In the past this issue was not much of a problem because historically corporate tax rate changes were very rare and, when they occurred, had been in the range of 2 percent. However, in view of the extraordinary reductions in corporate tax rates included in the Tax Reform Act of 1986 (from 46 percent in 1986 to 39.95 percent in 1987 to 34 percent in 1988) and the mounting federal deficit, the risk of future tax rate increases has assumed new dimensions that lessees and lessors simply cannot ignore.

Under the TRA, the tax benefits available to a lessor usually consist of accelerated depreciation deductions. During the early years of a lease, tax deductions attributable to accelerated depreciation equal all or part of taxable rental income. This results in deferral of taxable income attributable to the lease rentals until the later years of the lease when depreciation deductions decline or are exhausted. If in the early years of a lease the tax rate rises above that assumed by the lessor for pricing, the lessor's cash flows and yield will rise during the years in which the lessor claims depreciation deductions. On the other hand, if the tax rate is higher than assumed by the lessor for pricing during the years in which the rental income exceeds the depreciation deductions, the lessor's cash flow and yield will decline or even disappear.[12]

Lessors generally take the position that they should be held harmless by the lessee in the event of any tax law changes or tax rate changes adversely affecting their contemplated yield or cash flow. Lessors argue that the lessee is no worse off under such an indemnification than the lessee would have been had the lessee purchased the leased equipment and directly claimed tax benefits associated with equipment ownership. Lessees, on the other hand, generally take the position that after delivery of the leased equipment, lessors should assume the risk of loss of tax benefits for any reason except as a result of acts or omissions of the lessee.

The problem facing both lessees and lessors is how to engage in equipment leasing and protect themselves in view of the future tax rate uncertainties. A significant tax rate change can have disastrous consequences for a lessor, and the possibility of such a change is very real.

Initial questions facing lessors and lessees include the following:

1. What is the definition of the tax covered by the indemnity?
2. What is the risk of tax rate change that is to be covered?
3. What event or events will trigger a tax indemnity?
4. For what period of time will tax indemnities apply? For the entire lease? Or for a limited number of months or years?
5. How will the loss (or gain) resulting from indemnified tax rate risks be computed?
6. How will the indemnified party be compensated?
7. Under what circumstances can the lessee or lessor terminate the lease?

Definition of the Tax to Be Covered by the Tax Rate Change Indemnity

This discussion is directed at tax indemnities that relate to changes in the regular U.S. federal corporate income tax rate, since that is the rate with which lessees and lessors will be most concerned.

Other corporate income and excise taxes may affect the lessors' yield and cash flow, and lessors may seek indemnity protection against

---

[12] See the sensitivity analysis of tax rate change in Chapter 18.

changes in those tax rates. These other corporate income tax and excise taxes include the following:

1. State or city income tax.
2. The federal alternative minimum tax.
3. Federal income or excise surtax based on the regular federal income tax or the alternative minimum tax such as the so-called superfund tax.

The definition of the tax which is to be covered by a tax rate change indemnity should, consequently, be precise.

Lessees inclined to provide some degree of protection to lessors with regard to the regular federal corporate tax rate are generally going to be reluctant to provide further protection for various other potential corporate taxes based upon income.

A lessor that may be subject to the alternative minimum tax is going to be hard-pressed to convince a lessee to provide indemnity protection against such an occurrence. Competition from lessors with no risk of being subject to alternative minimum tax will force most lessors to assume that risk. In any event, a corporation's liability for alternative minimum tax may take several years to determine, which makes such an indemnity very impractical to administer.

The Risk of Tax Rate Change to Be Covered by an Indemnity

An early question to be addressed is to define what risk of tax rate change is to be covered by the tax indemnity. These, of course, range from none to the entire risk of change. However, there are methods of limiting or sharing the risk that the parties may wish to consider. These may be expressed in terms of the number of months or years in which the indemnity is to be in effect.The limits may also be expressed in terms of dollar caps or limits on the compensation to the indemnified party. A lessee providing an indemnity will also want a "two-way-street clause" which will provide the lessee with the benefits of tax rate changes that improve the lessor's cash flow or yield.

Dimensions of the Problem; The Triggers

The trigger for activation of a tax indemnity covering a change in the corporate tax rate will usually be related to one or more of the following events:

1. A defined amount of percentage change such as, for example, from 34 percent to 36 percent or higher.

2. The cumulative effect of the tax rate change measured by some stated amount of yield or cash flow.
3. The cumulative effect of the tax rate change and any other tax law changes measured by some stated amount of yield or cash flow.

It is often impractical and uneconomical and not in either party's best interests to trigger indemnity clauses for small changes in the tax rate or tax law that have a relatively minor effect on yield or cash flow, particularly in the case of smaller leases.

Time Limits on Tax Indemnity

Some of the various possibilities for defining the time limits during which tax indemnities or lease rate adjustments will apply include any changes in tax rates that become effective and/or are actually enacted into law by Congress, on or before:

1. The date the lease commences (this traditionally has been the lessee's risk with right of cancellation of the lease).
2. Some date in the future between the lease commencement date and the date the base lease term terminates.
3. The date the base lease term terminates.
4. Some date in the future after the termination of the base lease term.

One possibility for compromise in an otherwise satisfactory lease arrangement is presented by the lessee assuming the risk of tax rate change for a period of time that is somewhat less than the entire lease term and also gaining the benefits of a tax rate change during the same time period that would otherwise improve the lessor's yield or cash flow.

Basic Remedies for an Indemnified Party

In the event a tax indemnity is triggered, the parties have two basic remedies:

1. They may continue the lease with a lump sum payment and/or certain adjustments to rents or term; or
2. They may terminate the lease on some agreed basis which will usually involve a payment or payments by the lessee to the lessor ("burdensome buyout price").

Usually the lessee will want the right to terminate the lease if certain events occur, such as the rent adjustments, etc., being above a certain level if the lease is continued. The lessor will usually wish to have a right to avoid the buyout by waiving some (or all) of the tax indemnity rental adjustments. (This right may be needed in any event to avoid running afoul of Revenue Procedure 75-21, 1975-1 C.B. 715.)

Computation of the Loss or Benefit

Lessees will seek the benefit of any "windfall" to the lessor resulting from a tax rate change. This benefit may take the form of future decreased rents.

Lessors will seek to gear any adjustment to which they are entitled as a result of a tax rate change so as to preserve both their cash flow and yield (a "double-barrelled indemnity").

Lessees will usually prefer indemnities to the lessor limited to maintaining the lessor's yield. The computation of any loss or benefit to a lessor's yield as a result of tax legislation may be somewhat sensitive for lessors since they may not care to disclose how they arrived at their yield. However, since lease yield timeshare plans are available to everyone, a defined formula of input to serve as a basis for yield maintenance offers one avenue for agreement. Typically, the lessor might compute the adjustment, submit it to the lessee for approval, and the two parties either agree or then sort out any differences. Another approach is to use an independent third party such as a CPA firm to compute the appropriate adjustment where the parties are unable to agree.

A further question the parties must face is whether the lessor after-tax yield is to be preserved under the old law or the new law. Another question is what will constitute the target yield under the new tax law or under a matrix of new tax rates.

Lessors may be more concerned with maintaining a certain cash flow than maintaining a certain yield. The so-called double-barreled indemnity mentioned earlier whereby the lessor maintains both a certain yield and cash flow has not been unusual in the past.

There is also the question of recovery of lessee and lessor costs in originally entering into the transaction. Usually each party will bear its own costs.

Specific Remedies of the Indemnified Party

The remedies available to the indemnified party or to the party subject to liability for an indemnity payment include the following:

1. Cancellation of the lease with each party bearing its expense.
2. Cancellation of the lease with some stated amount of dollar compensation by one party to the other party to the lease.
3. Adjustment of the lease rentals over the term of the lease.

4. Adjustment of the lease rentals over some shorter period than the entire term of the lease (resulting in high/low rentals, for example).
5. Extension of the term of the lease with the same rents or higher rents.
6. Payment of a lump sum.

The parties might predetermine a rental adjustment or a term adjustment by a matrix formula in the lease documentation. So-called unwind provisions to terminate the lease if certain events occur run counter to IRS true-lease guidelines. Tax lawyers will have to rationalize their way around such guidelines in light of the special circumstances involved. So-called burdensome buyouts may be unacceptable to lessees if unduly burdensome.

Leveraged Debt Provisions Should Contemplate Possible Tax Indemnity

Lessors and lessees should be careful in arranging debt for leveraged leases to obtain the agreement of debt participants in the event of a tax indemnity event to either prepay the debt or terminate the lease while leaving the debt in place. Failure to obtain such consent will undermine the tax indemnity remedies and options of the lessee. Obviously, this type of consent should be obtained at the outset of lease negotiations and included in the debt participant's commitment letter. Such a provision cannot be left until late in the lease negotiations as a routine request.

Risk of Future Rate Change Is Significant

The risk of a change in the future corporate tax rate that will adversely affect the yields and cash flows of lessors is significant.

Lessors and lessees must consequently be concerned with the new dimensions of this risk in future lease documentation. Lessors must be satisfied that a proposed lease transaction makes economic sense on a worst-case basis. In the final analysis adjustments in the original lease rate pricing may be the key to resolving negotiation disputes regarding who will bear the risk of future corporate tax rate changes.

LEVERAGED LEASES WITH INDIVIDUAL INVESTORS

Leveraged leases of equipment can be structured with individual investors acting as equity participants. Usually these are structured as partnerships. The income tax requirements and consequences for individual equity participants in a leveraged lease are very different from those for corporations. At-risk rules prevent effective leveraging and lease periods are limited if ITC is to be claimed. Interest deductions and depreciation deductions are severely limited by income tax preference limitations. In any event, a discussion of leveraged leases by individuals acting as lessors is beyond the scope of this chapter.

CONCLUSION

Although the total volume of documentation involved in a leveraged lease is formidable, the individual documents are straightforward and not particularly complex. Consequently, leveraged leasing is a practical financing alternative for lessees that are willing to take the time to understand and negotiate such a transaction. In the right situations the rewards for such an exercise are extremely attractive financing costs.

Leveraged leases can also be attractive tax-oriented investments for corporations. However, such leases are not passive investments. Professional expertise and technical skill are needed in pricing, negotiating, closing, and administering leveraged lease transactions. For the lessor the leverage in a leveraged lease is like a two-edged sword. Both the benefits and the risks are magnified by leverage.[13]

---

[13] Over the years the best legal technical discussions on leveraged leasing have been contained in the publication *Leveraged Leasing* by the New York Practicing Law Institute published in 1977, 1980, and 1984 and edited by Bruce Fritch. See particularly the articles by Mr. Fritch and Mr. Shrank. *Equipment Leasing 1987* edited by Ian Shrank and William E. Flower (Practicing Law Institute) contains excellent discussions of leveraged leasing.

17

Arranging and Documenting a Leveraged Lease

In Chapter 16 we discussed the parties, structures, cash flows, and some of the issues that arise in arranging a leveraged lease. In this chapter we will be concerned with the practical aspects of arranging and documenting a leveraged lease from the standpoint of a lessee.

NEED FOR A FINANCIAL ADVISER

An initial question for a company considering a leveraged lease is to determine its need for a financial adviser or broker.[1] Basically, this question boils down to whether the services performed by a financial adviser will be cost-effective as compared to the expenditure for the financial adviser's fee.

---

[1] Generally the lessee's financial adviser will locate the equity and/or debt investors and thus perform the brokerage function. From the standpoint of the investor and in the parlance of the trade, the lessee's financial adviser is a broker.

The services to be performed by a financial adviser include some or all of the following:

1. Advise the company in structuring financing of the planned equipment acquisition:
   a. Understand the company's objectives, priorities, and constraints.
   b. Analyze the tax, legal, accounting, and economic consequences for the company as well as the potential market acceptance of alternative approaches.
   c. Meet and work with the company's legal and tax counsel with regard to the proposed financing.
   d. Consider alternative methods of financing and compare their advantages and disadvantages with lease financing.
   e. If leasing is the best alternative, recommend the optimal lease financing strategy.
2. Assist the company in establishing a realistic transaction timetable, ensuring that all aspects of the financing progress in a timely and systematic fashion.
3. Assist the company in preparing an equity offering memorandum describing the transaction for distribution to prospective equity sources.
4. Identify the most appropriate equity investors for the transaction.
5. Solicit commitments on a consistent basis from prospective equity participants so as to ensure a complete underwriting of the equity investment in the transaction. Arrange meetings and make face-to-face presentations with priority prospects to explain the transaction.
6. Arrange meetings between the company's key executives and priority prospects where that is advisable.
7. Review, rank, and clarify the equity responses for the company. Evaluate the economics of the equity commitments, including all relevant terms and conditions. Assist the company in selecting the best equity investor(s).
8. Assist the company in negotiating and completing the commitment letter and any pricing adjustments with the equity participants.
9. Arrange for the private placement of the leveraged debt or assist in doing so. Advise the company with regard to structuring the leveraged debt to achieve optimal pricing, amortization, and flexibility, as well as favorable terms and conditions.
10. In conjunction with company and its counsel, negotiate and document the terms and conditions of the various leveraged lease documents.

   11. Assist in the closing of the transaction.

In order to proceed without a financial adviser, a prospective lessee must be satisfied that:

   1. It has the technical and professional expertise to perform the above services with its own staff.
   2. Those persons on its staff with the technical ability and expertise to arrange a lease can devote the time necessary to arrange, negotiate, and complete the transaction as successfully as a financial adviser would do.
   3. It can gain access to the lease equity and/or debt placement markets as effectively and competitively as the financial adviser.

Some companies that have regularly used leveraged leases to finance equipment feel comfortable with arranging additional leveraged leases themselves, particularly when the additional leases are repetitious and very similar to what they have done in the past. While such companies undoubtedly have the expertise to structure and negotiate leveraged leases, the questions they must address are whether they are familiar enough with changing lease equity markets to be up-to-date with regard to the latest innovative developments in those markets and whether they will be able to identify the full range of potential investors. Oftentimes the newest entrants are the most aggressive bidders as they seek to quickly build their portfolios.

Financial Adviser Fees for a Completed Transaction

The fees charged by a financial adviser for assisting in structuring a transaction and arranging placement of debt and equity vary with the size and complexity of the transaction. The all-in transaction fees, including debt and equity placement fees and attorneys' fees for debt and equity (but not for the lessee) will usually run in the range of 1½ to 2 percent of the capitalized cost for a leveraged lease financing in the range of $75 to $100 million. It is difficult to generalize regarding fees because complex facility-type leases to story credits require more time and effort and are more expensive. On the other hand, repetitious plain vanilla leases to investment-grade credits are less expensive. The fees on smaller transactions run higher as a percentage of cost because they involve the same amount of work as a larger transaction. A $10 or $15 million leveraged lease might involve all-in fees and closing costs of 4 or 5 percent of capitalized cost, for example.

Leveraged leases sold to individuals through limited partnerships may have all-in fees and closing costs of as high as 20 percent.

In the final analysis a lessee should be concerned with the cost of lease financing the equipment after taking fees into consideration, as compared to the cost of alternative methods of financing including fees, measured on a present-value basis and/or by the implicit interest rate.

Financial Adviser Fees Where No Lease Is Completed

When the lessee elects not to proceed with a lease, the formally retained financial adviser is paid a fee, usually figured on an hourly basis. This may be in addition to or an offset to a retainer fee. In the alternative the lessee may indirectly compensate the adviser at a later date with an award of some other business.

Controlling Costs

While financial advisers will estimate the total cost in arranging and closing a leveraged lease to the best of their ability, they are reluctant to guarantee or underwrite such costs, and equity investors are reluctant to guarantee a cap on such costs. The reason for the reluctance of financial advisers to guarantee or cap closing costs is because the lessee itself is the party in the best position to either control the costs or by its actions to run up the arranging and closing costs of a transaction.

A lessee can hold down its costs by closely supervising and giving direction to its attorneys during the documentation and negotiation process. The lessee should consult with its attorneys to separate the legal and tax issues from business decisions and to identify what is important and what is not. The lessee should promptly make business decisions when the need arises. Without such supervision the lessee's attorneys may, with the best of intentions, feel constrained to leave no stone unturned in negotiating every legal, tax, and business issue that may arise in order to protect the interests of its client.[2] Needless to say, the equity participants should provide the same restraints and direction to their counsel.

THE STEPS IN STRUCTURING, NEGOTIATING, AND CLOSING A LEVERAGED LEASE

Various steps and milestones in structuring, negotiating and closing a leveraged lease are as follows:

1. Review of the transaction by the lessee and its counsel.
2. Preparation of drafts of the equity and debt-placement memos.
3. Preparation of the equity and debt-placement offering memorandums with the lessee and its counsel.

---

[2] The occasional suggestion that some lawyers would redraft the Lord's Prayer if given the chance is probably an exaggeration.

4. Preparation of equity and debt solicitation lists.
5. Completion of the equity solicitation and receipt of firm commitments from selected equity sources.
6. Completion and execution of the equity commitment letter.
7. Completion of a draft of all documents to be required.
8. Completion of debt solicitation and receipt of firm commitments from debt participants.
9. Review of debt documents by the lessee and equity participants.
10. Completion and execution of the debt commitment letter.
11. Completion of negotiations and agreement as to documents by the lessee and equity participants.
12. Review of documents by the debt participants.
13. Completion of negotiations and agreement as to debt documents by the equity participants, the lessee, and the debt participants.
14. Completion of final documents and signatures on all documents by all parties.
15. Delivery of the leased equipment and acceptance by the lessee.

The timetable for accomplishing those steps varies with each transaction depending upon the complexity of the structure, the strength of the lessee's credit, and the time remaining before the property to be leased is expected to be placed in service. While the placed-in-service date cannot in and of itself result in a rapid time schedule, it can motivate the parties to move with a greater sense of urgency than might otherwise be the case. As noted earlier the lessee and the lessor can speed the process and hold down the costs by closely supervising their attorneys, segregating business decisions from legal decisions, and making business decisions promptly so that the documentation can move forward.

While it is possible to arrange a facility lease in a fairly short time, the financial planning for a large facility is complex and may involve a lead time extending over several months. Exhibit 1 is a flowchart for a facility leveraged lease transaction showing the decisions that will be made and the events that will take place from the inception to the completion of such a transaction.

THE COMMITMENT LETTER

After the equity investor has been identified, the initial written document between the lessee and the lessor is the commitment letter. If more than one equity participant is to invest in the lease transaction, all participants should sign the commitment letter. If one participant is willing to commit to a substantial portion of the total equity investment required, the commitment letter may simply be executed with that investor as the lead equity investor; other investors will then be required to agree to the same terms.

Leveraged leases may be arranged privately on a negotiated basis with one or more equity investors located by the lessee or financial adviser. This is in contrast to a leveraged lease in which the equity participants are selected on the basis of competitive bidding. Either method is technically a "private placement" for SEC purposes[3] so long as SEC rules for private placements are followed.

The advantages of using the negotiated method are as follows:

1. Speed in closing where time is a factor.
2. Confidentiality of financial information where confidentiality is important to the lessor.
3. Where previous transactions have been negotiated with the same investor, the same documentation can be utilized, and the lessee is assured of a good working relationship with the investor and its counsel if that has been its past experience with the investor.
4. Where a special relationship exists between the lessee and the investor, the lessee may feel the goodwill from that relationship will extend to the lease negotiations.

The main disadvantages of proceeding on a negotiated basis are the distinct possibilities of not obtaining the best price and the loss of bargaining position with the investor during negotiations since there is not a backup equity source ready to proceed with the transaction if negotiations break down over some issue.

In a bid transaction (which is discussed later in this chapter) the commitment letter covers the provisions contained in the *offering memorandum* or agreed to as a result of the offering memorandum, which serves as a ready-made checklist.

In a negotiated transaction, while the parties start out in general agreement, they usually have not reached an understanding anywhere near as precise as laid out in an offering memorandum for bids.

Briefly stated, the commitment letter should cover the following points:

1. Identification of the lessee of the equipment and the equity participant.
2. Identification of any guarantor and description of the guaranty.
3. A specific description of the facility and its estimated cost.

---

[3] As opposed to a public offering.

EXHIBIT 1 Critical Path Chart of Leveraged Lease Financing for an Electric Generating Unit

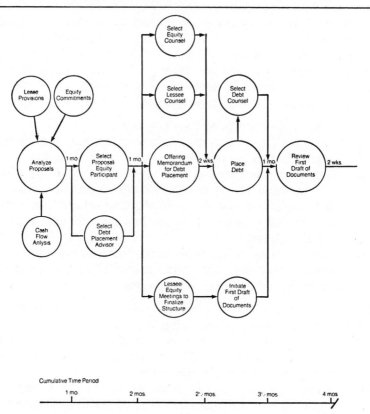

4. The funding and mechanics of the transaction including the in-service date.
5. The breakdown of the debt and equity funds to be provided for the lease and the conditions underlying the nonrecourse, long-term debt.
6. Specifications with regard to the lease term and any renewal options.
7. The lease rate and payment frequency, the leveraged debt rate assumed, and the tax benefits upon which the lease rate is predicated.
8. The net lease provisions, which require the lessee to maintain, insure, and assume responsibility for taxes and expenses related to the operation of the facility.

EXHIBIT 1 (*concluded*)

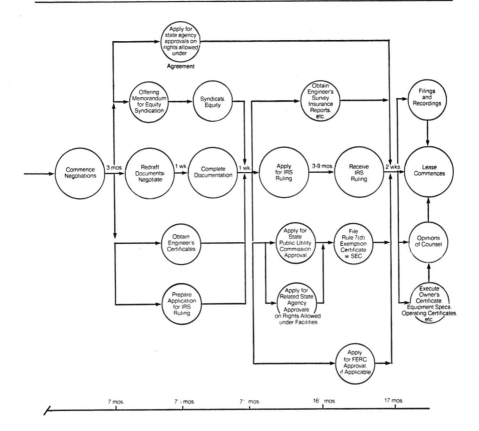

9. A general description of the tax and any special indemnities to be provided by the lessee.
10. A description of the lessee's general indemnity obligations, which covers liabilities arising out of ownership or operation of the facility.
11. The provisions relating to early termination of the lease due to casualty loss or economic obsolescence.
12. A description of any ancillary facility support contracts to be assigned in connection with the transaction such as site leases, facilities agreements and, perhaps, fuel-supply contracts.
13. A description of the rights, options, and obligations of the respective parties at the maturity of the lease.

More precisely stated, the commitment letter should cover as many of the points contained in the offering memorandum (which is discussed next in this chapter) as is possible. Once the commitment letter is negotiated and accepted by the lessee, it serves as the basis for preparing first drafts of the operative documents.

A great deal of time may be spent in negotiating a commitment letter. It is a common complaint of parties to a proposed lease that "we are spending too much time on the commitment letter." As a practical matter, however, a properly drawn commitment letter can be a great time saver in the long run. If the commitment letter spells out the substantive terms in understandable language, the attorneys for both parties are provided with clear guidelines for drafting the operative legal documents.[4] If the parties cannot agree, the time to reach that conclusion is at the commitment letter stage of negotiations.

The Offering Memorandum

An offering memorandum (request for bids) by the lessee should usually be prepared in either a negotiated or bid transaction. In a negotiated transaction the offering memorandum will probably not have been agreed to prior to the parties sitting down to negotiate the commitment letter. In such a case it will nevertheless serve as a checklist for negotiations.

In a bid transaction the winning equity participant has pretty well agreed to the terms of the offering memorandum except where it has specifically registered its objection. The commitment letter will simply reflect the terms of the offering memorandum. Also, the successful bidder knows (or imagines) there are backup bidders familiar with and eager to step into the transaction if the negotiations break down.

Exceptions to Use of Commitment Letter

In some situations the relationship of the lessee and the equity participant may be such that they can go directly to documentation

---

[4] The primary function of the operative agreements is to describe the business elements of the transaction and the commitments of the respective parties. The agreements include a participation agreement, a lease agreement, a facilities and site lease agreement, and an indenture trust agreement. The participation agreement (sometimes referred to as the financing agreement) is the central document containing the obligations of all principal parties to the transaction [the lessee, the owner trustee (as lessor), the equity participants, the loan participants, the vendor, and guarantors, if applicable] necessary to effect the purchase financing and lease of the facility. All other documents are exhibits to the participation agreement and are executed only by the respective parties in interest. The lease is executed between the lessee and owner trustee, as lessor; the purchase agreement between the owner trustee, as lessor and the vendor; and the trust indenture between the owner trustee, as lessor and indenture trustee. Opinions and representations are provided by the parties and their attorneys.

without a commitment letter. Custom and practice as a result of repetitious transactions for documenting certain kinds of equipment in certain industries may make a detailed commitment letter unnecessary except for term and price (railroad rolling stock and computer processing units, for example). In such situations the lessee may simply attach a set of documents that the equity participant is to accept as a condition of its bid.

Form of Offering Memorandum or Request for Bids from Equity Investors

Exhibit 2 is a sample "Offering Memorandum" or "Request for Bids" for a hypothetical company that plans to construct and lease a manufacturing plant facility expected to cost about $50 million. For purposes of illustration, this bid request is very detailed and would discourage all but very serious bidders. A financial adviser or broker might adopt a different strategy by using a less strict bid request in hope of attracting more bidders.[5] This would be the case, for example, where the lessee is a "story credit."[6] On the other hand, a very creditworthy lessee might go even a step further than the example in Exhibit 2 by also attaching a fairly one-sided lease agreement and demanding complete acceptance of its terms subject only to specified exceptions.

DEBT TERM SHEET AND COMMITMENT LETTER

Arranging leveraged debt for a leveraged lease is usually accomplished through direct negotiations with prospective lenders rather than through a bidding process. However, the transaction may be discussed with a number of prospective lenders in order to obtain the best terms. The lease typically seeks a single lender or a lender who will take a significant debt participation and assume the role of a lead lender.

The lessee should prepare a "debt term sheet" outlining the transaction to provide a basis for discussion with prospective lenders. This term sheet should incorporate the equity bid request that outlines the transaction and puts the debt participants on notice regarding those terms. In order to avoid future disputes and misunderstandings, this bid sheet should include any special provisions the lessee or possibly the equity participants will want included in the documentation.

---

[5] An aggressive detailed bid request by a prospective lessee may discourage some lessees from considering a transaction, particularly where they have alternative investments available. A very formal detailed bid request may be interpreted by some investors as also indicating time-consuming negotiations will be required. Any serious reply to a bid request requires a considerable investment of time by an investor.

[6] Marginally investment grade credit.

EXHIBIT 2   Request for Bids (Summary of principal terms and conditions)

LOW TECH CORPORATION
Offering Memorandum
Leveraged Lease of a
$50,000,000 Manufacturing Facility

Lessee:	Low Tech Corporation
Guarantor:	_____(insert name)_____ will unconditionally guarantee the obligations of the Lessee under the lease and supporting documents.
Financial Adviser:	_____(insert name of financial adviser)_____.
Lessor:	An Owner Trust established for the benefit of the Owner Participant(s).
Owner Trustee:	To be selected by Owner Participant(s) and to be acceptable to the Lessee.
Debt Participants:	Debt Participants (for permanent and possibly for interim debt) will be arranged by Financial Adviser and will be acceptable to the Lessee and the Owner Participant.
Indenture Trustee:	To be selected by the Lessee and acceptable to the Lessor and Loan Participants.
Owner Participant(s):	One or more institutions to be arranged by Financial Adviser and acceptable to the Lessee. If there is more than one Owner Participant, all of the Owner Participants will be required to use the same legal counsel and the same documentation. The term Owner Participant herein refers to all the Owner Participants if there is more than one Owner Participant.
Equipment:	An undivided interest in a ___(describe the type of plant)___ plant (herein sometimes called "Facility") to be located ___(insert location)___.
Lease:	The Lease will be absolutely net. The Lessee will be obligated to pay all costs, charges, fees, and expenses associated with use, possession, control, and operation of the Equipment, and to indemnify the parties with respect to such liabilities.
Facility Cost:	Approximately $50,000,000 (plus or minus 10%).
In-Service Date:	Presently scheduled for July 1, 1988.
Lease Commencement Date:	On the In-Service Date.
Basic Lease Term:	The Base Lease Term will commence on the In-Service Date and end 20 years thereafter.

EXHIBIT 2   *(continued)*

Basic Rent/ Basic Rental Factors:	Basic Rent will consist of 40 payments, payable semiannually in arrears, beginning six months after the commencement of the Basic Lease Term, determined by applying the Basic Rental Factors to the Lessor's Cost.
Interim Lease Term:	The Interim Lease Term will commence on the Closing Date and will extend to the commencement of the Basic Lease Term.
Lease Term:	The Interim Lease Term plus the Basic Lease Term shall be the "Lease Term."
Alternative Rent Structures:	The Lessee wishes to minimize the present value of all rental payments when discounted at 9% per annum. Alternative rental structures will be analyzed. However, the Lessee will not accept any tax indemnification risk arising out of these alternative structures.
Basic Lease Term Rental Adjustment:	The Basic Rental Factors are subject to increase or decrease to reflect: (*i*) any change in the Internal Revenue Code of 1986 (the "Code") which is enacted and effective after _____(insert current date)_____ and prior to the Closing Date provided that notice is given to the Lessee prior to the Closing Date, (*ii*) a rate of interest on the Secured Notes which is greater or less than the Assumed Interest Rate, (*iii*) the Closing Date occurring on a date other than _____(insert date)_____ , (*iv*) the actual In-Service Date, (*v*) the actual Transaction Expenses, and (*vi*) the actual Lease Term.

The adjustments to Basic Rental Factors will be calculated to preserve the Owner Participant's net after-tax yield and total after-tax cash flow (the "Lessor's Return"). Each such adjustment and corresponding adjustments to Termination and Casualty Values shall be computed by the Owner Participant on the same basis that was used in the calculation of the original Basic Rental Factors and Termination and Casualty Values. All adjustments will be subject to confirmation by the Lessee and its Financial Adviser.

If as a result of an adjustment to the Basic Rental Factors by reason of a change in the Code prior to the Closing Date the Lease becomes uneconomic to the Lessee, the Lessee shall have the right to terminate its commitment with respect to the Lease.

EXHIBIT 2   *(continued)*

Support Agreements:

Lessee will enter into certain agreements with Lessor relating to the ownership and operation of the Facility. These agreements will be designed to assure the Lessor's continued use and operation of the Facility for its useful life, will be in effect for a term extending to the end of a period equal to the originally estimated useful life of the Facility, and will provide for fair market value compensation to Lessee for such rights after the termination of the Facility Lease. The Support Agreements will include major agreements and provisions such as the following:

(*a*) Additional Facilities. Lessee will make available to Lessor the use of additional facilities, if any, necessary for the operation of the Facility which Lessee has at the site.

(*b*) Site Access. Lessee will ensure Lessor has access to the site, the Facility, and to any common facilities.

Action of Lessor on the In-Service Date:

On the In-Service Date the Lessor will: (*i*) accept a full warranty deed of sale from Lessee and pay the Facility Cost, (*ii*) lease the Facility to Lessee under the Lease, and (*iii*) issue Debt under a trust indenture or other debt instrument. The Lessor will assign the Lease to the Indenture Trustee or the Debt Participant(s), as the case may be.

Purchase Options:

At any time after the 10th anniversary of the In-Service Date, Lessee will have the right to purchase the Facility for an amount equal to the greater of the termination value referred to below or the then appraised fair market value.

In addition, in the event that tax indemnities become payable and, on a pro forma basis, such indemnities would result, in the opinion of the Lessee, in a burdensome increase in Lessee's Lease rentals, Lessee will have the right at any time to purchase the Facility for an amount equal to the greater of the termination value or the then appraised fair market value, plus, as an indemnity payment, any amount required to maintain the Lessor's Return to the date of purchase.

Furthermore, at the expiration of the Lease Term or at the expiration of any renewal lease term, Lessee will have an option to purchase the Facility for its then appraised fair market value.

EXHIBIT 2   (*continued*)

Renewal Options:	Fixed-Rental Renewal: At the end of the Lease Term, Lessee will have the right to extend the term of the Lease for two additional periods of five years each.

At the end of the Fixed-Rental Renewal term, Lessee will have a one-time right to have the remaining useful life of the Facility determined by independent appraisal. If at that time such appraisal shall show a remaining estimated life of more than _____ years, Lessee shall have the right to renew the Lease for a period of not less than one year nor more than that number of years which, when added to the Lease Term and the Fixed-Rental Renewal Terms, shall not exceed 80 percent of the estimated useful life of the Facility under such appraisal. Final determination of this period will depend upon an assessment of original useful life of the facility.

All renewal terms hereunder shall be at Fixed Lease Rentals equal to one half of the average of the Lease Rentals over the Base Lease Term.

Fair Market Rental Renewal: At the end of any renewal term, Lessee will have the right to extend the term for additional periods of from one to five years each, for Lease Rentals equal to the then fair rental value of the Facility.

Lessors' Return: The after-tax return on investment for the Owner Participant(s), computed using a method agreed upon by the Owner Participant(s) and Lessee.

Early Termination: If the Facility becomes uneconomic or surplus to Lessee at any time after the 10th anniversary of the In-Service Date, Lessee may effect an early termination of the Lease. Upon such early termination, the Facility will be sold and Lessee will be required to pay to the Lessor an amount equal to the difference, to the extent such difference is positive, between the Termination Value ("Termination Value") as of such date of termination and the net proceeds of such sale. Termination Value will be calculated to return to the Lessor its unrecovered investment and to preserve the Lessor's Return to the date of payment.

EXHIBIT 2 *(continued)*

Casualty Value:

Casualty Value will be calculated so as to return to the Lessor its unrecovered investment and to preserve the Lessor's Return to the date of payment. Casualty Value will include an amount which takes into account a maximum of a 20 percent residual value for the Facility.

Event of Loss:

In the event that the Facility shall be substantially destroyed or rendered unfit for its intended use or taken by any governmental authority for a period extending beyond the Lease Term, or any renewal lease term, Lessee shall be required to pay to the Lessor the Casualty Value of the Facility. Upon such payment Lessee will be entitled to all awards and insurance or other proceeds in respect of such loss.

Additions and
Improvements:

The Lessor will finance both severable and non-severable improvements requested by Lessee or mandated by government regulations, provided that the Lease Rentals are adjusted to cover the repaying of 100% debt financing employed to finance such addition. Subject to there having occurred no material adverse change in Lessee's creditworthiness and the availability of sufficient tax liability and funds on the part of the Owner Participant(s), the Owner Participant(s) will agree to negotiate in good faith additional equity contributions to finance such additions and improvements at the lowest cost to Lessee, consistent with a reasonable rate of return to the Owner Participant(s). Lessee also reserves the right to finance severable and non-severable additions on its own, subject to the restrictions of Revenue Procedure 79–48 or any amendment or superseding law or administrative guidance.

Transaction Expenses:

The Lessor will pay third-party costs and expenses of documenting and closing the transaction ("Transaction Expenses") including, but not limited to, printing and other reproduction costs, courier and delivery costs, accounting and appraisal fees, investment banking fees, and all initial Trustee's fees, and fees and expenses of counsel to the Debt Participants, the Owner Participant, and the Indenture Trustee, but ex-

EXHIBIT 2   *(continued)*

cluding fees and expenses of counsel for the Lessee (other than document preparation, reproduction, courier, and related charges). Each Owner Participant should assume Transaction Expenses equal to 0 percent of Lessor's Cost in its assumptions for pricing. If there is more than one Owner Participant, each Owner Participant will pay its proportionate share of such Transaction Expenses.

The Lessee shall pay all reasonable fees and expenses of counsel to the parties, all printing costs, and all other reasonable out-of-pocket expenses of the parties and their counsel if the transaction shall be terminated by the Lessee after commitments have been obtained and agreed to in writing, and the termination is not as a result of the Owner Participant's actions.

TAX MATTERS:

Tax Assumptions:
The Basic Rental Factors should be calculated by the Owner Participant based on the assumption that the Owner Participant will be entitled, for federal income tax purposes, to the following:

1. Lessor's basis for depreciation will be equal to 100 percent of Capitalized Lessor's Cost.
2. 7-year ACRS deductions will be available to Lessor.
3. Lessor will be entitled to interest deductions with respect to the Secured Loan Certificates.

IRS Revenue Ruling:
No rulings will be requested from the Internal Revenue Service.

Indemnification:
The Lessee will pay all fees, state and local taxes, and other charges imposed in the United States upon the Equipment or in respect of the transactions contemplated herein, except that the Lessee will not be required to pay franchise taxes and taxes on doing business, capital stock taxes, or any fees, taxes, and other charges on, or measured by, gross or net income or receipts (including minimum taxes, alternative minimum taxes, withholding taxes, and taxes on or measured by items of tax prefer-

EXHIBIT 2   *(continued)*

ence) of any indemnified party, taxes resulting from a voluntary transfer by or a bankruptcy of an indemnified party, taxes to the extent such taxes would not have been imposed if an indemnified party had not engaged in activities in the jurisdiction imposing such taxes which activities are unrelated to the transactions contemplated hereby, any interest and penalties resulting from an indemnified party's failure to file returns that are timely and proper, and certain other taxes.

Lessee will provide a limited indemnity to the Owner Participant for the additional amount (on a grossed-up basis) of Federal income taxes payable by the Owner Participant as a result of diminution, loss or recapture of any of the assumed tax benefits (as described above) used in computing the final Basic Rental Factors, resulting directly from an act or omission of the Lessee. The terms and conditions of the documents will not be deemed to constitute an act or omission of the Lessee. The Lessee is not required to indemnify if the loss results from an act or omission of the Owner Participant.

Events or occurrences for which the Lessee will *not* indemnify the Owner Participant include:

(*i*)   failure of the transaction to constitute a "true lease" for Federal income tax purposes;

(*ii*)   any tax law changes or tax rate changes occurring on or after the Closing Date;

(*iii*)   any acts or omissions which are required or contemplated by the agreements, instruments, and documents used in connection with the overall transaction and the execution of such agreements, instruments, and documents;

(*iv*)   the timing of the receipt of the rent under section 467 of the Code; and

(*v*)   the existence of an Owner Trust.

Contest Rights: Subject to providing an opinion of counsel that there is reasonable basis for a contest, the Lessee will have the right to require the Owner Participant to contest (and not to settle) any claim that might give rise to an indemnity payment

EXHIBIT 2   *(continued)*

and to appeal any determination. Lessee shall have the right to participate with the Owner Participant concerning the conduct of any such contest or appeal.

Right to Cure:

The Lessor will have the right to cure a payment default of the Lessee. Cure rights will be negotiated by the Lessor and Debt Participants.

Assignment;
Sublease:

The Lease shall not be assigned by Lessee without the prior written consent of Lessor. Lessee shall not sublease the Facility without the prior written consent of Lessor.

Closing Conditions:

The conditions precedent to providing equity on a date immediately prior to the In-Service Date will be specified in documentation satisfactory to the parties and will include certificates, documents, and opinions normally associated with lease transactions and any regulatory or environmental approvals and permits which must be obtained for the assembly and operation of the facility.

Events of Default:

The following shall constitute the Events of Default under the Lease: (*a*) failure by the Lessee and the Guarantor to make rental or indemnity payments when due and the continuation of such failure for 10 days after demand, (*b*) failure to perform any other material term, condition, or covenant in the Lease, the Guaranty Agreement, or any related agreement and the continuation thereof for a period of 30 days after receipt of notice thereof, (*c*) any material warranty or representation in the Lease, the Guaranty Agreement, or any related agreement or any certificate or document furnished pursuant thereto made by the Lessee, shall prove to have been false in any material respect when made, (*d*) insolvency, bankruptcy, appointment of a trustee or receiver, and like events with respect to the Lessee or the Guarantor. Upon the occurrence of an Event of Default, the Lessor may terminate the Lease and require the Lessee to pay the higher of the excess of Termination Value over fair market value or fair market rental.

EXHIBIT 2 *(continued)*

DEBT MATTERS:

Assumed Interest Rate:	Basic Rental Factors should be calculated based upon an Assumed Interest Rate of 9 percent on the Secured Loan Certificates.
Secured Notes:	The Secured Notes shall be nonrecourse to the Lessor and shall be secured by: (*i*) an assignment of the Lease and all rents payable thereunder, (*ii*) an assignment of the Guaranty Agreement between the Guarantor and the Lessor, (*iii*) an assignment of the Support Agreements, and (*iv*) a security interest in the Equipment (Facility). Neither the tax nor general indemnities in favor of the Owner participant will be assigned to or otherwise benefit the Loan Participants.

Although fixed-rate debt is anticipated to be used, the Lessee reserves the right to use interim debt and variable rate debt in the transaction.

Although it is anticipated the Secured Notes will be payable in U.S. Dollars, the Lessee reserves the right to make such notes payable in Japanese Yen or other appropriate currency at Lessee's direction.

ASSUMPTIONS:

All proposals should be based on the foregoing terms with any exceptions noted and should include the following pricing assumptions:

Funding and Closing Date:	July 1, 1988.
In-Service Date:	July 1, 1988.
Lessor's Cost:	A total Lessor's Cost of $50,000,000.
ACRS Recovery Period:	The ACRS recovery period is 7 years.
Debt Parameters:	It should be assumed that the Secured Loan Certificates will bear interest at 9 percent per annum and will be amortized by semiannual payments on an optimized basis.
Interim Lease Term:	Interim Lease Term will commence on ___(To be stated by Lessee)___ and end on ___(To be stated by Lessee)___.
Interim Rent:	Any Interim Rent payable on the In-Service Date will be equal to Interim Debt Service.

EXHIBIT 2   *(concluded)*

Basic Lease Term:	Basic Lease Term will be 20 years commencing on the In-Service Date.
Lease Rental Frequency:	During the Basic Lease Term, Basic Rent will be payable semiannually in arrears commencing six months after the In-Service Date.
Transaction Expenses:	Transaction Expenses shall be assumed to be 0 percent of Lessor's Cost.

The Lessee desires operating lease treatment under *FAS 13* and wishes to minimize the net present value cost of the lease rentals utilizing a discount rate of 9 percent. Proposals containing unique or unusual rental structures will be acceptable. However, the Lessee will not accept any tax indemnification risk arising out of these alternative structures.

ALL PROPOSALS SHOULD INCLUDE THE FOLLOWING ADDITIONAL INFORMATION:

1. The amount and expiration date of the equity commitment by the Owner Participant.
2. What portion, if any, of the Owner Participant's equity commitment is not contemplated to be retained for the Owner Participant's account and the identity of any other Owner Participant.
3. The name of the proposed Owner Trustee, if an Owner Trustee is to be used.
4. The name of Owner Participant's counsel.
5. The implicit lease rate.
6. The Basic Rental Factors.
7. The debt-to-equity ratio of the lease structure.
8. The debt amortization schedule.
9. The Casualty Loss (or Stipulated Loss) Value.
10. The Termination Value Schedule.
11. The tax rate assumptions used in the above calculations.
12. The dates on which the Owner Participant's first tax year commences and concludes.
13. Any exceptions to the terms and conditions outlined in the Summary of Principal Terms.
14. The Lessor's Rental Factors assuming a July 1, 1988, in-service date.

In Chapter 16 a number of points of possible contention between the equity participants and debt are discussed that the lessee may wish to include in the debt term sheet. Note particularly that the equity participants will probably insist on certain cure rights and the right to receive tax indemnity payments ahead of the debt participants.

Another point of concern to the lessee will be the right to refinance the debt in the event the lessee can obtain better terms (that is, rate) for some reason at a later date. The debt participants will usually give on this point for some kind of prepayment premium.

After selection of the debt participant(s) an appropriate commitment letter should be signed to avoid any disputes or misunderstandings arising at the closing.

Lessees and their attorneys spend most of their time negotiating with the equity participants. Sometimes they tend to take the debt participants a little too much for granted, fail to button up the debt commitment, and consequently are surprised when problems arise with the debt participants over "details" at the closing.

THE LEASE DOCUMENT IN A LEVERAGED LEASE

The lease document specifies the rights, liabilities, and duties of the lessee and the lessor (the owner trustee representing the equity participants) for the term of the agreement. Many of the provisions in the lease document for a leveraged lease are similar to those contained in a nonleveraged lease document such as discussed in Chapter 13, and the reader interested in leveraged lease documentation should review that chapter for a detailed discussion of provisions common to both leveraged and nonleveraged leases. However, certain aspects of the lease document in a leveraged lease are different and more complex due to the number of parties involved.

While the participation agreement identifies the general requirements of each party entering the transaction, the lease specifies the rights, liabilities, and duties of the two principals—the lessee and owner participants—for the term of the agreement. The format of the lease agreement generally will follow that of the offering memorandum and the commitment letter. The following is a brief summary of the lease provisions that are contemplated by the offering memorandum previously presented.

1. Lease Term. A description of the length of the lease term, including the commencement date of the lease and the maturity of the lease.

2. Definitions. Definitions of all necessarily defined terms in the lease.

3. Lease Rental Payments. The amount of each lease rental payment, its periodicity, and any penalties for delinquent lease rental payments are detailed either in the lease or in a schedule attached to the lease and incorporated by reference. The section may also deal with various methods for adjusting lease rental payments based on indemnities or occurrences after the start of the lease term. Interim and supplemental rent under the lease will be described, and the place and time of such payments are stated.

4. Net Lease Provision. This section of the lease agreement describes the lease as a net noncancelable agreement. It describes the burdens of ownership passed on to the lessee with respect to maintenance, costs, expenses, and taxes, such as personal property taxes. This may include license arrangements to operate a particular kind of equipment, registration fees, franchise taxes, sales taxes, use taxes, and any other levies, imposts, duties, or charges that may be imposed upon the equipment or facility being leased. This section also describes the logistics of how the tax indemnities operate in conjunction with the lease itself.

5. Right to Inspect and Lessee Reporting. The lessor retains the right to reasonably inspect the facility and certain records of the lessee that pertain to the leased equipment. The lessee is required to (*a*) maintain reports and records, some of which will be periodically distributed to the lessor, that describe the normal and regular maintenance being performed on the facility (equipment); (*b*) report any lawsuits, claims, or actions against the facility or the lessee in operating the facility that may reasonably be of concern to the lessor; (*c*) notify the lessor in the event any liens or tax liens are assessed against the facility; and (*d*) deliver to the lessor and to the senior note holders certain periodic financial information.

6. Insurance. This section describes the insurance coverages the lessee is required to maintain and the manner in which their coverages are extended to the lessor.

The lessee is required to maintain insurance to cover loss or damage to the facility. The lessee is required to maintain insurance throughout the term of the lease, basically in amounts and under the same terms and conditions that the lessee would maintain for similar or like facilities it presently owns. As a minimum the insurance coverages must be for an amount sufficient to cover the stipulated loss value described in the casualty section of the lease. Lessees generally are permitted to self-insure to the same extent they would self-insure for like facilities they own.

The lessee is required to maintain insurance against public liability and property damage. Here again the lessee is required to maintain the insurance coverage in amounts that are not less than the amounts in force for like or similar facilities owned by the lessee.

A compliance provision is also a part of this section whereby the lessee is required to provide a certificate showing that the insurance provision has been complied with prior to the payment for the equipment and is further required to provide certificates or evidence of renewal from time to time before the expiration dates.

See Chapter 12 for a discussion of insurance coverage.

7. Modifications and Alterations. Any and all modifications made to the facility or equipment, that are made an integral part of the facility, become the property of the lessor. The test commonly used to decide upon severable or nonseverable modifications is whether the equipment or the attachment can be separated without any loss of value or loss of usability to the leased asset. Under the maintenance section the lessee is, of course, required to make all alterations and modifications and normal maintenance necessary to keep the facility in good operating condition. Further, the lessee is required under this section to make any alterations such as pollution-control modifications that are required by law in order to keep the facility in good operating condition and in compliance with all laws and regulations. In addition, there may be instances where the lessee desires to make modifications that will increase the efficiency and productivity of the plant.

Provisions for these alterations can be made in the lease. However, loss of equity in the alteration and the possible tax implications should be considered.

8. Possession and Use. The lessee agrees not to assign the lease and use of the facility without the express written permission of the lessor, to use the facility for the purpose that it was intended, and to clearly mark the equipment as being the property of the lessor.

9. Warranties of Equipment. Typically, in a lease financing of a facility the lessee has contracted for the building of the facility and the delivery and installation of the related equipment. The lessor as owner takes an assignment of the construction contract and the purchase orders and purchases the facility and equipment under terms, conditions, and prices negotiated by the lessee. Therefore, the lessee indemnifies the lessor against any and all failures of the equipment to perform as represented by the builder and agrees to lease the facility without any warranties or representations by the lessor except for the passing through of only those warranties that are available from the builder to the lessee. The lessee agrees to waive the right of nonpayment of rent in the event the equipment does not perform as contemplated.

10. Events of Default. This section describes the events or circumstances under which the lessor may declare an event of default under the lease. These events of default give rise to remedies (discussed next) that allow the lessor to pursue certain rights in order to recapture its investment. The events of default section is important because it describes the circumstances under which the lessor may, for instance, claim its equipment and proceed in a timely manner to sell or release the equipment.

Typical events of default are as follows:

a. The lessee's failure to make any payment of a rent within a reasonable period of time or payment of stipulated loss value or termination value when due under the lease.

b. Any lessee failure to perform any other covenant in the lease agreement or participation agreement for a reasonable period of time.

c. Any failure on the part of the lessee to uphold a representation or warranty made by the lessee in the participation agreement or lease.

d. The failure of the lessee to make any payments or indebtedness when due for any other mortgage indenture.

e. Any insolvency or bankruptcy on the part of the lessee or written admittance that it has an inability to pay its debts as they mature.

f. Any appointment of a trustee or receiver for the lessee not discharged within a reasonable period of time.

g. Any outstanding judgments against the lessee not paid within a reasonable period of time.

h. Any material misrepresentation of authority or material fact in the documents of agreements as represented by lessee.

11. Remedies. This section describes the various courses of action that may be taken by the lessor in the event an event of default exists under the previous section. Typical remedies for the lessor include:

a. Immediate possession of the leased property.

b. Public or private sale or lease of the property to a third party.

c. The right to recover all rents and additional sums (supplemental rent) accrued and unpaid from the time of termination to the date of sale.

d. Reasonable liquidated damages.

e. The right on the part of the lessor to pursue any other rights it may have under the applicable laws in a court of law or equity.

12. Economic Obsolescence and Early Termination. Most lease agreements provide for the lessee to be able to voluntarily terminate the lease if there is a representation in good faith that the facility or equipment is obsolete or is uneconomical for the lessee to operate. Such a right is usually granted after a period of years. In order to effect this option, the lessee must identify and transact the sale of the facility to an independent third party. All proceeds from the sale would flow to the lessor. If such proceeds are less than the amount set forth in the termination schedule, then the lessee would be responsible for the difference. The termination schedule is calculated in such a way as to return to the lessor an amount that will (a) retire the senior notes, (b) pay off the lessor's remaining investment, and (c) gross up lost tax benefits. (This schedule should be spelled out in the bidding process.)

13. Stipulated Loss Value. This section deals with the loss or destruction of the leased property to such a degree that it is no longer serviceable. The lessee is provided with a schedule called Stipulated Loss Value or Casualty Loss Value. This value is typically the minimum amount that is insured and includes everything in early termination value plus an amount that represents the lessor's anticipated residual return on the equipment. (This schedule should be spelled out in the bidding process.)

14. Purchase Option. This section sets forth the circumstances under which the lessee may purchase the equipment at the conclusion of the lease term. Whether this option is granted after a certain number of renewals or at the maturity of the basic lease term, the purchase option will usually be at fair market value at that time. In such instances, the lease will describe the method to be employed in determining fair market value. In the alternative, the lease may provide a fixed-price purchase option at an estimated fair market value that will usually be in the range of 40 percent or higher.

15. Renewal Options. The lessee may be given a right to renew the lease at a fixed rental for a fixed term or at a fair market renewal rate to be negotiated between the lessee and lessor in a manner similar to the purchase option.

16. Return of Asset. If at the end of the lease the lessee does not elect to renew the lease or purchase the equipment, this section describes the manner in which the equipment is to be returned to the lessor. This section may, for example, require the lessee to dismantle the property in such a manner that it would be in condition to transport on a common carrier to a location specified by the lessor. It might require the lessee to deliver the equipment to a common carrier for transport to said location. The nature of the burdens and requirements placed on the lessee or lessor obviously influence negotiations for sale of the property at the conclusion of the lease.

CONCLUSION

Arranging a leveraged lease is not for amateurs. Unless a prospective lessee has people with current experience in leveraged leasing and those people have the necessary time to devote to arranging the transaction, the prospective lessee is well advised to seek professional help from a financial adviser (broker) in arranging its lease.

18

Pricing and Analysis of
Leveraged Leases

In the preceding chapter we presented an example of a request for a leveraged lease proposal on behalf of a prospective lessee. In this chapter we shall analyze and price a proposal by a lessor for the leveraged lease requested by the lessee in the preceding chapter.

The first portion of this chapter is devoted to a general discussion of methodology used in lease analysis and pricing. Later we discuss the assumptions used, the pricing, and the analysis of the example lease.

The initial discussion on methodology is somewhat technical. Fortunately, several user-friendly timeshare programs incorporating that technology are available to lessees and lessors.

LEASE ANALYSIS IN GENERAL

The usual method of analyzing a lease transaction is to determine a "yield" or "return on investment." The investment is the initial dollar amount invested to purchase the leased asset, including all fees and expenses paid by the lessor. This investment is expected to provide a periodic net cash flow to the lessor resulting from several sources and uses of funds, including the following:

- Lease payments.
- Debt service (leveraged lease only).
- Deferred taxes and tax credits.
- Income from funds set aside to cover future tax liabilities (leveraged lease only).
- Proceeds from sale of the asset at the end of the lease.
- Any other miscellaneous obligations (rights) of lessor to pay (receive) cash (for example, fees to trustees).

The "yield" calculation is simply the internal rate of return (IRR) of the after-tax cash flows.[1]

Since the cash flows are different in each year and the yield is calculated on a present value basis, computation of the yield is complex and would require significant time if done by hand. However, by computer, the yield can be calculated very rapidly by a directed search method.

In contrast to term loan yields, which are calculated on an annual pre-tax basis, lease yields are calculated on an annual after-tax basis and then converted to a more easily interpreted pre-tax equivalent and expressed as an annual pre-tax rate.

LEVERAGED LEASE ANALYSIS

Leveraged leases utilize the principle of financial leverage to increase the return to the equity participants. By funding part of an investment at an interest cost less than the yield on the investment, it is always possible to increase the return on equity. Because the debt is nonrecourse to the equity participant, it is analytically correct to include the debt service in the economic analysis.

Mixed Cash Flows Problem in Lease Analysis

As leverage is increased, the net cash flows in the latter part of the lease term turn negative. This occurs because the rental payment is insufficient to pay both the debt service and the taxes due. The result is an investment with mixed cash flows. The term *mixed cash flows* refers to an investment with more than one sign change (positive/negative) in the net cash flows. A simple investment, such as the term loan or nonleveraged lease, has one sign change: the initial investment as a negative outflow followed by a series of positive inflows.

---

[1] The calculation of a yield is presented in Appendix B.

Nonsimple investments with mixed cash flows create theoretical problems when the internal rate of return is used as a measure of profitability.

Discussion of Mathematics of Internal Rate of Return (IRR)

To understand these theoretical problems it is necessary to understand the mathematics of the internal rate of return (IRR). The IRR of an n period investment is the solution to an nth degree polynominal. The Fundamental Theorem of Algebra states that a polynominal of the nth degree always has exactly n real or complex roots, which are not necessarily unique. Complex roots always occur in pairs. The only roots of economic interest are those that are greater than -100 percent. A mathematical theorem called Descartes' Rule of Signs says that the number of such roots, which may not all be unique, either equals the number of sign changes in the polynominal or is less by a multiple of two. A simple investment with one sign change will have one IRR greater than -100 percent and this can be used as a measure of profitability. An investment with two sign changes will have either two distinct internal rates of return, one repeated rate, or no rates greater than -100 percent.

When an investment has multiple internal rates of return, none of the IRRs is a correct measure of profitability. Moreover, for an investment with mixed cash flows, even when the rate of return is unique, the IRR may not be an appropriate measure of profitability because when measured at the rate of return, the investment may be a use of funds in some periods and a source of funds in others. The only time it is correct to use an internal rate of return of an investment with mixed cash flows as a measure of profitability is when the investment is not recovered until the final cash flow, that is, the investment is always in an investment, or use of funds, phase.

To overcome the problems associated with mixed cash flows, several different "adjusted yield methods" have come into use. The purpose of these methods is to compute a unique yield that can be used in evaluating leveraged leases. All of these methods require the specification of an interest earning rate for funds put into a sinking fund to cover later liabilities.

STANDARD SINKING FUND METHOD OF LEASE ANALYSIS

One of the first widely used adjusted yield methods of lease analysis is the standard sinking fund method (SSFM), also called the traditional sinking fund method. The standard sinking fund method of lease analysis assumes that all negative cash flows occurring after the initial investment will be paid from the proceeds of a hypothetical sinking fund which earns interest at the sinking fund reinvestment rate. The yield is computed on the cash flows remaining after the sinking fund is set up. Since the cash flows after the initial investment are all positive or zero, there is only one sign change in the cash flows, and the yield computed is unique.

MULTIPLE INVESTMENT SINKING FUND METHOD OF LEASE ANALYSIS

The most widely used yield method today is the multiple investment sinking fund method (MISF) or separate phases method of lease analysis. The multiple investment or separate phases method of recognizing income is the accounting method prescribed by the Financial Accounting Standards Board in *FAS 13* for leveraged leases (see *FAS 13*, Par. 109c).

This method recognizes multiple investment phases in a leveraged lease. Typically, the cumulative cash flow during the early years of a leveraged lease exceeds the investment, producing a negative investment balance during the middle years of the lease. The investment returns to a positive balance again during the later years of the lease as funds are "reinvested" in anticipation of the subsequent investment recovery related to residual receipt. This pattern of cash flows results from the fact that income tax reductions from ACRS depreciation and interest are replaced by additional income tax payments in later years as tax benefits from depreciation and interest expense diminish. At the termination of the lease, the investment balance becomes zero with the realization of the residual value.

This method may also have sinking funds set up but it differs from the standard sinking fund method of lease analysis in the calculation of the yield. The calculation breaks the net cash flows into nonoverlapping investment and sinking fund phases such that each investment phase earns the yield rate. An investment phase may contain a sequence of mixed cash flows, but this does not create a problem since, by definition, the investment is not recovered until the last net cash flow is allocated to the investment phase.

The multiple investment method of reporting income recognizes income at a level after-tax rate of return on net investment in the years in which the net investment is positive. Generally, the lessor's investment balance becomes negative in the middle years of the lease which indicates the lessor has not only recovered its initial investment but also has temporary use of funds which for economic analysis purposes will be reinvested in the later years of the lease. Earnings on such funds are reflected in income at such time as they actually occur (in years in which the lessor's investment is negative) and are not reportable with income from the lease itself. According to *FAS 13*, the multiple investment method of reporting income associates income with the unrecovered balance of the earning asset in a manner most consistent with the investor's view of the transaction.

When structuring a leveraged lease, the lessor calculates rental payments and debt repayment schedules that meet its profitability objectives and satisfy legal, tax, and accounting constraints while either minimizing the present value of rentals or the cost to lessee (internal rate of return of the rentals). Whether the present value of rentals or the cost to lessee are minimized depends on the lessee's method of lease-versus-buy analysis. The profitability objectives are usually stated as a specified target yield (book or economic) and a minimum net cash flow (either as a percent of cost or of equity). Today most leases are priced using the MISF yield method. The MISF method with a zero sinking fund reinvestment rate is used to calculate the book yield, and the MISF method with a conservative sinking fund reinvestment rate is used to calculate the economic return.

MULTIPLE INVESTMENT METHOD COMPARED TO STANDARD SINKING FUND METHOD

Generally, where a residual value is assumed, use of the multiple investment method of analysis will produce a higher yield than the standard sinking fund method. This results because, for yield computation purposes under the multiple investment method, the effect of the positive cash flows that actually occur during the later years of the lease (primarily the realization of the residual value) is included in the excess cash flows used to compute yield as if such positive cash flow had occurred earlier in the lease.

To accomplish this, the lessor assumes that future tax liabilities are paid out of general corporate funds as those liabilities become due (that is, it reinvests) instead of providing for them through a sinking fund. This additional lessor investment is ultimately repaid (with interest at the yield rate) when the residual value is realized. The effect, of course, is to make available in the early years of the lease more positive cash flows (relative to the standard sinking fund method) to discount against the lessor's initial investment, thus increasing yield.

On the other hand, the standard sinking fund method includes the residual value in the yield computation at the time it is actually realized. Thus, the yield computation uses positive cash flows net of those set aside in the sinking fund with the positive cash flow of the anticipated residual discounted back from the time it is actually to be realized.

OPTIMAL DEBT-TO-EQUITY RATIO

In general, each leveraged lease has an optimal debt-to-equity ratio. A number of variables are involved in the computation of that figure, most of which are subject to either IRS, administrative, or other practical constraints. Factors that affect the computation include the lease term, the method of depreciation and the depreciable life, the availability of investment tax credit, the debt rate, the lessor's book yield requirements, and whether the debt is payable in level payments or can fluctuate.

For purposes of internal rate of return, beyond the optimal point, as the amount of debt is increased in a leveraged lease, economic yield increases while book yield decreases. This occurs because with a fixed amount of rent being paid by the lessee, more debt results in more interest expense throughout the term of the lease, and this results in less cash from rentals available to lessor. While it is generally true that the yield in an economic sense (assuming a time value benefit on the sinking fund) is increased as the amount of the debt is increased, less "hard" cash accrues to the lessor and book yield decreases. Thus, the trade-off between book yield and economic yield is a very important constraint on the amount of debt in a leveraged lease.

Another way of illustrating the constraint inherent in the interaction of the book yield and leverage is that with a given amount of rent being paid by the lessee (assuming a competitive lease rate), there is a limit to the amount of periodic debt service that can be derived from rent, assuming that some cash must go to the lessor in order to achieve a satisfactory book yield. For example, using a lease rate of 6 percent per annum (simple interest equivalent assuming ITC is claimed by the lessor) and assuming only 15 percent of the periodic rent is allocated to the lessor over the entire term of the lease, the amount of debt at a 12 percent annual interest rate that can be serviced by the remainder of the rent is limited to approximately 59.61 percent of the equipment cost.

The most advantageous debt-to-equity ratio will, of course, vary as a function of such factors as the debt rate, the amortization schedule of the debt, and the amount of tax benefits available. Under IRS guidelines the lessor must invest at least 20 percent of the equipment cost in the form of equity. Thus, according to the IRS guidelines, 80 percent of equipment cost is the maximum amount of debt that can be used in a leveraged lease.

When the standard sinking fund method of yield analysis was the most commonly used method, optimized debt consisted of "sinking fund minimization." This meant that leverage was increased, and negative net cash flows were created, only up to that point where the effective cost of repaying the increased leverage, considering the necessity of creating a sinking fund, equaled the after-tax yield rate. This usually resulted in the debt repayment being structured so that the net cash flows in the latter part of the lease were zero or positive.

Now that the MISF yield method is widely used, many leases are structured with an optimized debt method that, while still minimizing uneconomic sinking funds, creates negative net cash flows that are put into secondary investment. This secondary investment is recovered by the positive net cash flows that come from either an ending residual or, in some cases where shortened debt is used, the rentals. When this debt structure is used, it is important for the lessor to realize that the MISF yield is the return on both a primary and secondary investment. The secondary investment may be substantial and occur far in the future. Optimized debt, when used with the MISF yield method, is capable of producing a deceivingly attractive combination of high yield and high cash flow. The lessor should be aware of when the lease will generate its earnings and, perhaps using present value techniques, determine their value to the lessor today. The use of the more conservative standard sinking fund yield method can also be useful in evaluating the true benefit to the lessor.

Lease analysis programs are now appearing that structure leases using the technique of linear programming. This powerful mathematical algorithm gives the lessor the ability to generate optimal bids. As linear programming guarantees that the solution is a "global optimum," there will be no combination of rent and debt payments that satisfy the lessor's profitability requirements and that produce a lower cost to lessee or present value of rentals (depending on what the lessor wishes to minimize).

OPTIMIZED DEBT

The lessor has most flexibility in the determination of the amount of leverage and the repayment schedule of the nonrecourse loan. Early leveraged leases were usually structured with level debt service payments, perhaps with some interest-only periods. This debt structure produced the mixed cash flows previously discussed and created a controversy over which adjusted yield method was the "correct" one to use for leveraged lease analysis. It was observed that with the yield method and the sinking fund reinvestment rate specified, there often was an optimal amount of debt beyond which the yield would begin to decline. It became apparent that increase in leverage, creating later negative net cash flows (covered by earlier positive net flows into a sinking fund) were beneficial only up to the point where the "effective" after-tax cost of the increase in leverage was equal to the after-tax yield on the equity investment. The effective cost of debt considers when cash flows must be allocated to provide for negative cash flows created by increased leverage. Since most lessors are only willing to use conservative sinking fund reinvestment rates, the effective cost of increasing leverage grows rapidly once sinking funds must be set up. Therefore, what has come to be called optimized debt evolved.

LESSOR ANALYSIS TO PRICE EXAMPLE LEASE

In the previous chapter we considered and discussed a request for bids for a 20-year leveraged lease by a hypothetical company, Low Tech Corporation, for a manufacturing facility. We will now consider a financial analysis by an equity participant (called lessor in this chapter) to arrive at pricing for a leveraged lease in response to that bid request.

Lessor's Objectives and Assumptions

In calculating a rental rate for a proposed leveraged lease, the lessor must first define its yield objectives. For purposes of this pricing example we have assumed the lessor will wish to achieve a pre-tax yield of 15 percent. We also assume that the lessor will wish to receive some positive cash return.

Most of the basic assumptions required for a yield calculation have already been established by the lessee.

Therefore, as a starting point for calculating a lease bid, the lessee's specifications and the lessor's yield objectives are summarized below together with a few other basic factual assumptions:

Lessee's specifications:

Total cost:	$50,000,000.
In-service date:	7-1-88.
Lease commencement date:	7-1-88.
ACRS:	7-year class.
ADR midpoint:	12 years.
Lease term:	20 years.
Rentals:	Payable semiannual in arrears.
Debt payments:	Payable semiannual in arrears.
Debt rate:	9% per annum.
Accounting objective:	Operating lease treatment.
ITC:	None.

Lessor's assumptions and objectives:

Yield analysis method:	Multiple investment sinking fund.
Yield target:	15 percent pre-tax.
Residual value for pricing:	5 percent of original equipment cost.
Taxable year:	Calendar year.
Federal tax rate:	34 percent throughout.
State tax rate:	None assumed.
Rent structure:	Low present value objective; low to high within 90 to 110 percent rule.
Debt structure:	Optimize debt payments.
Debt-to-equity ratio:	Optimize debt to equity.
Tax recognition:	Accrual basis.
Sinking fund earnings:	Zero.
Investment tax credit:	None.

Based on these assumptions, the lessor instructs its lease analysis program to provide the following information:

Schedule of rent payments.

Schedule of debt payments.

Casualty value schedule and termination value schedule.

Investment, tax liability, and cash flow statement.

Tax accounting statement.

Annual cash flow and proof of yield analysis.

Balance sheet analysis.

Earnings statement analysis.

Some lessor's have their own in-house leveraged lease analysis programs. However, the burden of designing and keeping a leveraged lease analysis program current is more than most lessors want to or can afford to maintain. Consequently, most leveraged lease lessors (and lessees) rely upon one or more of a number of very sophisticated (and user-friendly) timeshare programs for leveraged lease analysis.[2]

---

[2] The four state-of-the-art timeshare programs for leveraged lease analysis in widest use at the time this book goes to press in the experience of the authors are:

Clease (Chase Bank)	212-552-7132
Interet	201-763-1200
LAS (Warren & Selbert)	805-963-0776
TIP (TXL Corporation)	415-434-0850

Accordingly, the lessor in the instant case has relied upon a time-share program to obtain the information needed.[3]

Briefly stated this analysis results in the following information for lessor's bid request.

Lessor's yield:	15 percent pre-tax.
Debt-to-equity ratio:	78.0929 percent debt and 21.9071 percent equity.
Rent payments:	18 rent payments of $2,173,760.53, followed by 22 rent payments of $2,656,818.43, payable semiannual in arrears.
Implicit cost to lessee:	7.0888 percent.
Present value cost to lessee:	86.0314 percent.
Casualty loss schedule:	See Exhibit 13.
Termination value schedule:	See Exhibit 13.

The leveraged lease analysis provided by the timeshare program is usually in the form of a summary analysis with various supporting schedules and calculations. Exhibits 1 through 7 consist of supporting schedules for the proposed bid to Low Tech Corporation and are summarized below:

Schedule	Exhibit
Debt Service	1
Investment, Taxability, and Cash Flow Statement	2
Annual Tax Accounting	3
Annual Cash Flow and Proof of Yield Analysis	4
Pro Forma Annual Assets Statement under *FAS 13*	5
Pro Forma Annual Liabilities Statement under *FAS 13*	6
Pro Forma Annual Results Under *FAS 13*	7

Timeshare programs are expensive to use for training, experimentation, or indiscriminate structuring. With the rapid development in power, memory, and capability of IBM Personal Computers and their many clones, leveraged lease analysis programs with many features of the timeshare programs will eventually become available. At present Ivory Consulting Corporation (415-486-0690) has a leveraged lease program that produces practical results for sizing and preliminary structuring a competitive transaction. The Association of Equipment Lessors (703-527-8655) publishes a leasing software catalog that lists and describes a number of programs for lease analysis and administration.

[3] The TIP timeshare program was used for this example.

EXHIBIT 1   Debt Service

Equipment cost: $50,000,000
Equity investment: $10,953,525
Debt rate: 9 percent
Payment: Semiannual arrears
Lease term: 20 years

Payment number	Date	Principal outstanding	Interest	Principal recovery	Debt service
	7/1/88	$39,046,474.63			
1	1/1/89	38,629,805.46	$ 1,757,091.36	$ 416,669.17	$ 2,173,760.53
2	7/1/89	38,194,386.18	1,738,341.25	435,419.28	2,173,760.53
3	1/1/90	37,739,373.03	1,718,747.38	455,013.15	2,173,760.53
4	7/1/90	37,263,884.29	1,698,271.79	475,488.74	2,173,760.53
5	1/1/91	36,766,998.55	1,676,874.79	496,885.74	2,173,760.53
6	7/1/91	36,247,752.95	1,654,514.93	519,245.60	2,173,760.53
7	1/1/92	35,705,141.30	1,631,148.88	542,611.65	2,173,760.53
8	7/1/92	35,138,112.13	1,606,731.36	567,029.17	2,173,760.53
9	1/1/93	34,545,566.65	1,581,215.05	592,545.48	2,173,760.53
10	7/1/93	33,926,356.62	1,554,550.50	619,210.03	2,173,760.53
11	1/1/94	33,279,282.14	1,526,686.05	647,074.48	2,173,760.53
12	7/1/94	32,603,089.31	1,497,567.70	676,192.83	2,173,760.53
13	1/1/95	31,896,467.80	1,467,139.02	706,621.51	2,173,760.53
14	7/1/95	31,158,048.32	1,435,341.05	738,419.48	2,173,760.53
15	1/1/96	30,386,399.96	1,402,112.17	771,648.36	2,173,760.53
16	7/1/96	29,580,027.43	1,367,388.00	806,372.53	2,173,760.53
17	1/1/97	28,737,368.13	1,331,101.23	842,659.30	2,173,760.53
18	7/1/97	28,267,086.83	1,293,181.57	470,281.30	1,763,462.87
19	1/1/98	27,236,110.07	1,272,018.91	1,030,976.76	2,302,995.67
20	7/1/98	26,336,028.92	1,225,624.95	900,081.15	2,125,706.10
21	1/1/99	25,317,725.68	1,185,121.30	1,018,303.24	2,203,424.54
22	7/1/99	24,380,829.24	1,139,297.65	936,896.44	2,076,194.09
23	1/1/00	23,301,767.17	1,097,137.31	1,079,062.07	2,176,199.38
24	7/1/00	22,308,889.65	1,048,579.52	992,877.52	2,041,457.04
25	1/1/01	21,165,321.75	1,003,900.03	1,143,567.90	2,147,467.93
26	7/1/01	20,113,090.35	952,439.48	1,052,231.40	2,004,670.88
27	1/1/02	18,901,160.31	905,089.07	1,211,930.04	2,117,019.11
28	7/1/02	17,786,026.83	850,552.21	1,115,133.48	1,965,685.69
29	1/1/03	15,992,033.77	800,371.21	1,793,993.06	2,594,364.27
30	7/1/03	14,054,856.86	719,641.52	1,937,176.91	2,656,818.43
31	1/1/04	12,030,506.99	632,468.56	2,024,349.87	2,656,818.43
32	7/1/04	9,915,061.37	541,372.81	2,115,445.62	2,656,818.43
33	1/1/05	7,704,420.70	446,177.76	2,210,640.67	2,656,818.43
34	7/1/05	5,394,301.20	346,698.93	2,310,119.50	2,656,818.43
35	1/1/06	2,980,226.32	242,743.55	2,414,074.88	2,656,818.43
36	7/1/06	457,518.08	134,110.19	2,522,708.24	2,656,818.43
37	1/1/07	.00	20,588.30	457,518.08	478,106.38
			$42,501,937.34	$39,046,474.63	$81,548,411.97

EXHIBIT 2 Investment, Tax Liability, and Cash Flow Statement

Equipment cost: $50,000,000
Equity investment: $10,953,525

Tax year 12/31	Cash investment	Free cash and taxes saved	Cumulative cash balance	Cash flow				
				Rentals and residuals	–	Debt	=	Free cash
1988	$ –10,953,525	$ 2,058,214	$ –8,895,312	$ 0		$ 0		$ 0
1989	0	3,703,157	–5,192,155	4,347,521		4,347,521		0
1990	0	2,764,890	–2,427,265	4,347,521		4,347,521		0
1991	0	1,851,091	–576,174	4,347,521		4,347,521		0
1992	0	1,186,981	610,807	4,347,521		4,347,521		0
1993	0	1,090,316	1,701,123	4,347,521		4,347,521		0
1994	0	1,051,030	2,752,153	4,347,521		4,347,521		0
1995	0	325,377	3,097,530	4,347,521		4,347,521		0
1996	0	–480,085	2,597,445	4,347,521		4,347,521		0
1997	0	–338,975	2,258,470	4,347,521		3,937,223		410,298
1998	0	–80,372	2,178,098	5,313,637		4,428,702		884,935
1999	0	–6,304	2,171,794	5,313,637		4,279,619		1,034,018
2000	0	–6,559	2,165,236	5,313,637		4,217,656		1,095,980
2001	0	–6,950	2,158,285	5,313,637		4,152,139		1,161,498
2002	0	–7,366	2,150,919	5,313,637		4,082,705		1,230,932
2003	0	–1,274,305	876,614	5,313,637		5,251,183		62,454
2004	0	–1,458,474	–581,860	5,313,637		5,313,637		0
2005	0	–1,592,690	–2,174,551	5,313,637		5,313,637		0
2006	0	–1,739,258	–3,913,809	5,313,637		5,313,637		0
2007	0	3,034,154	–879,655	5,313,637		478,106		4,835,530
2008	0	6,054,987	5,175,332	7,813,637		0		7,813,637
2009	0	–175,332	5,000,000	0		0		0
Total	$ –10,953,525	$15,953,525	$ 5,000,000	$100,077,695		$81,548,412		$18,529,283

EXHIBIT 2   (concluded)

Equipment cost: $50,000,000
Equity Investment: $10,953,525

			Federal tax liability		
Tax year 12/31	Gross income	Depreciation	Interest, fees, misc. expenses	Taxable income	Total taxes saved
1988	$ 2,173,761	$ 7,142,857	$ 1,757,091	$ − 6,726,188	$ 2,058,214
1989	4,347,521	12,244,898	3,457,089	− 11,354,466	3,703,157
1990	4,347,521	8,746,356	3,375,147	− 7,773,981	2,764,890
1991	4,347,521	6,247,397	3,285,664	− 5,185,540	1,851,091
1992	4,347,521	4,462,426	3,187,946	− 3,302,852	1,186,981
1993	4,347,521	4,462,426	3,081,237	− 3,196,142	1,090,316
1994	4,347,521	4,462,426	2,964,707	− 3,079,612	1,051,030
1995	4,347,521	2,231,213	2,837,453	− 721,145	325,377
1996	4,347,521	0	2,698,489	1,649,032	− 480,085
1997	4,830,579	0	2,565,200	2,265,378	− 749,273
1998	5,313,637	0	2,410,746	2,902,891	− 965,307
1999	5,313,637	0	2,236,435	3,077,202	− 1,040,322
2000	5,313,637	0	2,052,480	3,261,157	− 1,102,539
2001	5,313,637	0	1,857,529	3,456,108	− 1,168,448
2002	5,313,637	0	1,650,923	3,662,713	− 1,238,298
2003	5,313,637	0	1,352,110	3,961,527	− 1,336,759
2004	5,313,637	0	987,551	4,326,086	− 1,458,474
2005	5,313,637	0	589,442	4,724,194	− 1,592,690
2006	5,313,637	0	154,698	5,158,938	− 1,739,258
2007	5,313,637	0	0	5,313,637	− 1,801,377
2008	5,156,818	0	0	5,156,818	− 1,758,650
2009	0	0	0	0	− 175,332
Total	$100,077,695	$50,000,000	$42,501,937	$ 7,575,758	$ − 2,575,758

EXHIBIT 3   Annual Tax Accounting

Equipment cost: $50,000,000
Equity investment: $10,953,525
Federal tax rate: 34 percent
State tax rate: None

Tax year 12/31	Gross income	Federal tax depre- ciation	Interest expense	Taxable income	Federal tax liability
1988	$ 2,173,761	$ 7,142,857	$ 1,757,091	$ −6,726,188	$−2,286,904
1989	4,347,521	12,244,898	3,457,089	−11,354,466	−3,860,518
1990	4,347,521	8,746,356	3,375,147	−7,773,981	−2,643,154
1991	4,347,521	6,247,397	3,285,664	−5,185,540	−1,763,083
1992	4,347,521	4,462,426	3,187,946	−3,302,852	−1,122,970
1993	4,347,521	4,462,426	3,081,237	−3,196,142	−1,086,688
1994	4,347,521	4,462,426	2,964,707	−3,079,612	−1,047,068
1995	4,347,521	2,231,213	2,837,453	−721,145	−245,189
1996	4,347,521	0	2,698,489	1,649,032	560,671
1997	4,830,579	0	2,565,200	2,265,378	770,229
1998	5,313,637	0	2,410,746	2,902,891	986,983
1999	5,313,637	0	2,236,435	3,077,202	1,046,249
2000	5,313,637	0	2,052,480	3,261,157	1,108,793
2001	5,313,637	0	1,857,529	3,456,108	1,175,077
2002	5,313,637	0	1,650,923	3,662,713	1,245,323
2003	5,313,637	0	1,352,110	3,961,527	1,346,919
2004	5,313,637	0	987,551	4,326,086	1,470,869
2005	5,313,637	0	589,442	4,724,194	1,606,226
2006	5,313,637	0	154,698	5,158,938	1,754,039
2007	5,313,637	0	0	5,313,637	1,806,637
2008	5,156,818	0	0	5,156,818	1,753,318
Total	$100,077,695	$50,000,000	$42,501,937	$ 7,575,758	$ 2,575,758

The best way (and perhaps the only way) to gain an understanding regarding the mathematics of leveraged leasing is to review schedules such as presented in Exhibits 1 through 7.

Also attached as Exhibits 8 through 12 are a series of five charts

Description of charts	Exhibit
Net Pre-Tax Cash Flow	8
Federal Taxable Income and Taxes Paid	9
Net After-Tax Cash Flow	10
Net After-Tax Cash Compared to Investment	11
Investment Book Earnings Compared to Investment	12

EXHIBIT 4   Annual Cash Flow and Proof of Yield Analysis

Equipment cost: $50,000,000
Equity investment: $10,953,525

Tax year 12/31	Lease receipts	Debt service			To lessor	Cash flows	
		Interest expense	Principal payment	Unpaid balance		Taxes saved	Total
1988	$ 0	$ 0	$ 0	$39,046,475	$ -10,953,525	$ 2,058,214	$ -8,895,312
1989	4,347,521	3,495,433	852,088	38,194,386	0	3,703,157	3,703,157
1990	4,347,521	3,417,019	930,502	37,263,884	0	2,764,890	2,764,890
1991	4,347,521	3,331,390	1,016,131	36,247,753	0	1,851,091	1,851,091
1992	4,347,521	3,237,880	1,109,641	35,138,112	0	1,186,981	1,186,981
1993	4,347,521	3,135,766	1,211,756	33,926,357	0	1,090,316	1,090,316
1994	4,347,521	3,024,254	1,323,267	32,603,089	0	1,051,030	1,051,030
1995	4,347,521	2,902,480	1,445,041	31,158,048	0	325,377	325,377
1996	4,347,521	2,769,500	1,578,021	29,580,027	0	-480,085	-480,085
1997	4,347,521	2,624,283	1,312,941	28,267,087	410,298	-749,273	-338,975
1998	5,313,637	2,497,644	1,931,058	26,336,029	884,935	-965,307	-80,372
1999	5,313,637	2,324,419	1,955,200	24,380,829	1,034,018	-1,040,322	-6,304
2000	5,313,637	2,145,717	2,071,940	22,308,890	1,095,980	-1,102,539	-6,559
2001	5,313,637	1,956,340	2,195,799	20,113,090	1,161,498	-1,168,448	-6,950
2002	5,313,637	1,755,641	2,327,064	17,786,027	1,230,932	-1,238,298	-7,366
2003	5,313,637	1,520,013	3,731,170	14,054,857	62,454	-1,336,759	-1,274,305
2004	5,313,637	1,173,841	4,139,795	9,915,061	0	-1,458,474	-1,458,474
2005	5,313,637	792,877	4,520,760	5,394,301	0	-1,592,690	-1,592,690
2006	5,313,637	376,854	4,936,783	457,518	0	-1,739,258	-1,739,258
2007	5,313,637	20,588	457,518	0	4,835,530	-1,801,377	3,034,154
2008	7,813,637	0	0	0	7,813,637	-1,758,650	6,054,987
2009	0	0	0	0	0	-175,332	-175,332
Total	$100,077,696	$42,501,939	$39,046,475		$ 7,575,758	$ -2,575,758	$ 5,000,000

Equipment cost: $50,000,000
Equity investment: $10,953,525

| Tax year 12/31 | Allocation of cash flows | | | | Tax reserve Sinking fund | |
| | To investment | | To tax | Unrecovered investment balance | | |
	Earnings	Recovery	Sinking fund		Earnings	Balance
1988	$ 433,669	$ -9,328,981	$ 0	$9,328,981	$ 0	$ 0
1989	824,518	2,878,639	0	6,450,342	0	0
1990	553,447	2,211,443	0	4,238,898	0	0
1991	362,045	1,489,046	0	2,749,852	0	0
1992	235,164	951,817	0	1,798,036	0	0
1993	142,622	947,694	154,708	850,341	0	0
1994	45,981	850,341	325,377	0	0	154,708
1995	0	0	-480,085	0	0	480,085
1996	0	0	0	0	0	0
1997	7,628	-346,603	0	350,928	0	0
1998	17,167	-97,539	0	449,684	0	0
1999	20,366	-26,670	0	476,686	0	0
2000	21,587	-28,145	0	505,183	0	0
2001	22,877	-29,828	0	535,382	0	0
2002	24,245	-31,611	0	567,387	0	0
2003	11,673	-1,285,978	0	1,947,600	0	0
2004	0	-1,458,474	0	3,665,684	0	0
2005	0	-1,592,690	0	5,701,328	0	0
2006	0	-1,739,258	0	8,100,277	0	0
2007	1,852,272	-1,181,881	0	5,659,724	0	0
2008	424,740	5,454,915	175,332	0	0	175,332
2009	0	0	-175,332	0	0	0
Total	$5,000,000	$ 0	$ 0		$ 0	$ 0

EXHIBIT 5 Pro Forma Annual Assets Statement—Balance Sheet/Income Statement (Using leveraged lease accounting under FAS 13)

Equipment cost: $50,000,000
Equity investment: $10,953,525

Taxable year 12/31	Lease cash flow	Cash balance	ITC	Rentals receivable	Residual value	Unearned deferred income	Total assets/ liabilities	Net investment
1988	$−8,895,312	$−8,895,312	$0	$16,029,283	$2,500,000	$−6,918,684	$2,715,287	$9,328,981
1989	3,703,157	−5,192,155	0	16,029,283	2,500,000	−5,669,414	7,667,714	6,450,342
1990	2,764,890	−2,427,265	0	16,029,283	2,500,000	−4,830,859	11,271,159	4,238,898
1991	1,851,091	−576,174	0	16,029,283	2,500,000	−4,282,306	13,670,803	2,749,852
1992	1,186,981	610,807	0	16,029,283	2,500,000	−3,925,997	15,214,093	1,798,036
1993	1,090,316	1,701,123	0	16,029,283	2,500,000	−3,709,902	16,520,503	850,341
1994	1,051,030	2,752,153	0	16,029,283	2,500,000	−3,640,234	17,641,202	−154,708
1995	325,377	3,077,530	0	16,029,283	2,500,000	−3,640,234	17,966,579	−480,085
1996	−480,085	2,597,445	0	16,029,283	2,500,000	−3,640,234	17,486,494	0
1997	−338,975	2,258,470	0	15,618,985	2,500,000	−3,622,124	16,755,331	350,928
1998	−80,372	2,178,098	0	14,734,050	2,500,000	−3,594,270	15,817,878	449,684
1999	−6,304	2,171,794	0	13,700,032	2,500,000	−3,562,908	14,808,918	476,686
2000	−6,559	2,165,236	0	12,604,052	2,500,000	−3,529,669	13,739,618	505,183
2001	−6,950	2,158,285	0	11,442,554	2,500,000	−3,494,443	12,606,395	535,382
2002	−7,366	2,150,919	0	10,211,621	2,500,000	−3,457,111	11,405,429	567,387
2003	−1,274,305	876,614	0	10,149,167	2,500,000	−3,296,645	10,229,136	1,947,600
2004	−1,458,474	−581,860	0	10,149,167	2,500,000	−2,903,298	9,164,009	3,665,684
2005	−1,592,690	−2,174,551	0	10,149,167	2,500,000	−2,232,157	8,242,460	5,701,328
2006	−1,739,258	−3,913,809	0	10,149,167	2,500,000	−1,232,624	7,502,734	8,100,277
2007	3,034,154	−879,655	0	5,313,637	2,500,000	−333,229	6,600,753	5,659,724
2008	6,054,987	5,175,332	0	0	0	0	5,175,332	−175,332
2009	−175,332	5,000,000	0	0	0	0	5,000,000	0
Total	$ 5,000,000							

EXHIBIT 6   Pro Forma Annual Liabilities Statement—Balance Sheet/Income Statement (Using leveraged lease accounting under *FAS 13*)

Equipment cost: $50,000,000
Equity investment: $10,953,525

Tax year 12/31	Lease cash flow	Reserve for taxes		Pretax Earnings	Provision for taxes (Liabilities)		A/T income	Periodic net income	Retained earnings
		Current	Deferred		Current	Net deferred			
1988	$−8,895,312	$−228,690	$ 2,510,309	$ 657,074	$ 2,286,904	$−2,510,309	$ 433,669	$433,669	$ 433,669
1989	3,703,157	−386,052	6,795,579	1,249,269	3,860,518	−4,285,270	824,518	824,518	1,258,187
1990	2,764,890	−264,315	9,723,841	838,556	2,643,154	−2,928,263	553,447	553,447	1,811,633
1991	1,851,091	−176,308	11,673,433	548,553	1,763,083	−1,949,591	362,045	362,045	2,173,678
1992	1,186,981	−112,297	12,917,548	356,309	1,122,970	−1,244,115	235,164	235,164	2,408,842
1993	1,090,316	−108,669	14,077,708	216,094	1,086,688	−1,160,160	142,622	142,622	2,551,464
1994	1,051,030	−104,707	15,148,463	69,668	1,047,068	−1,070,755	45,981	45,981	2,597,445
1995	325,377	−24,519	15,393,653	0	245,189	−245,189	0	0	2,597,445
1996	−480,085	56,067	14,832,982	0	−560,671	560,671	0	0	2,597,445
1997	−338,975	77,023	14,068,910	18,110	−770,229	764,071	11,952	11,952	2,609,398
1998	−80,372	98,698	13,091,398	27,855	−986,983	977,512	18,384	18,384	2,627,782
1999	−6,304	104,625	12,055,812	31,361	−1,046,249	1,035,586	20,699	20,699	2,648,480
2000	−6,559	110,879	10,958,320	33,239	−1,108,793	1,097,492	21,938	21,938	2,670,418
2001	−6,950	117,508	9,795,220	35,226	−1,175,077	1,163,100	23,249	23,249	2,693,668
2002	−7,366	124,532	8,562,591	37,332	−1,245,323	1,232,630	24,639	24,639	2,718,307
2003	−1,274,305	134,692	7,270,230	160,466	−1,346,919	1,292,361	105,908	105,908	2,824,214
2004	−1,458,474	147,087	5,933,099	393,348	−1,470,869	1,337,131	259,609	259,609	3,083,824
2005	−1,592,690	160,623	4,555,061	671,141	−1,606,226	1,378,038	442,953	442,953	3,526,777
2006	−1,739,258	175,404	3,140,863	999,532	−1,754,039	1,414,198	659,691	659,691	4,186,468
2007	3,034,154	180,664	1,640,020	899,396	−1,806,637	1,500,842	593,601	593,601	4,780,069
2008	6,054,987	175,332	0	333,229	−1,753,318	1,640,020	219,931	219,931	5,000,000
2009	−175,332	0	0	0	0	0	0	0	5,000,000
Total	$ 5,000,000	0	0	$7,575,758	$−2,575,758	$ 0	$5,000,000		5,000,000

EXHIBIT 7   Pro Forma Annual Results—Earnings Analysis (Using leveraged lease accounting under *FAS 13*)

Equipment cost: $50,000,000
Equity investment: $10,953,525
Tax rate: 34 percent

Taxable year 12/31	Lease cash flow	Allocation of cash flow		Net investment	Pretax income	Tax effect of pretax income
		To investment recovery	To earnings			
1988	$ -8,895,312	$ -9,328,981	$ 433,669	$9,328,981	$ 657,074	$ -223,405
1989	3,703,157	2,878,639	824,518	6,450,342	1,249,269	-424,752
1990	2,764,890	2,211,443	553,447	4,238,898	838,556	-285,109
1991	1,851,091	1,489,046	362,045	2,749,852	548,553	-186,508
1992	1,186,981	951,817	235,164	1,798,036	356,309	-121,145
1993	1,090,316	947,694	142,622	850,341	216,094	-73,472
1994	1,051,030	1,005,049	45,981	-154,708	69,668	-23,687
1995	325,377	325,377	0	-480,085	0	0
1996	-480,085	-480,085	0	0	0	0
1997	-338,975	-350,928	11,952	350,928	18,110	-6,157
1998	-80,372	-98,756	18,384	449,684	27,855	-9,471
1999	-6,304	-27,002	20,699	476,686	31,361	-10,663
2000	-6,559	-28,496	21,938	505,183	33,239	-11,301
2001	-6,950	-30,200	23,249	535,382	35,226	-11,977
2002	-7,366	-32,005	24,639	567,387	37,332	-12,693
2003	-1,274,305	-1,380,213	105,908	1,947,600	160,466	-54,558
2004	-1,458,474	-1,718,084	259,609	3,665,684	393,348	-133,738
2005	-1,592,690	-2,035,644	442,953	5,701,328	671,141	-228,188
2006	-1,739,258	-2,398,949	659,691	8,100,277	999,532	-339,841
2007	3,034,154	2,440,553	593,601	5,659,724	899,396	-305,794
2008	6,054,987	5,835,056	219,931	-175,332	333,229	-113,298
2009	-175,332	-175,332	0	0	0	0
Total	$ 5,000,000	$ 0	$5,000,000		$7,575,758	$-2,575,758

---

that illustrate and compare certain of the key cash flows and economic and accounting results reflected in Exhibits 1 through 7.

The casualty loss schedule and termination value schedule for the proposed response to the bid request are shown in Exhibit 13. The components of termination value are illustrated in Exhibit 14, and the tax bill is reconciled from termination value in Exhibit 15. Exposure of the lessor in the event of default by the lessee is shown in Exhibit 16. The casualty value, termination value, and unrecovered book investment are charted in Exhibit 17.

Further comment on particular aspects of the lease analysis is appropriate.

Multiple Investment Sinking Fund (MISF) Analysis

As noted earlier, the multiple investment sinking fund (MISF) method of lease analysis is generally used today by lessors in pricing lease transactions. Under this method of lease analysis, the structure alternates between the investment phase and the sinking fund phase. During the initial investment phase, all positive net cash flows from the transaction are used to reduce the investment balance plus earnings on the balance. After the investment balance is entirely paid off, later positive cash flows are allocated to a sinking fund to pay future deferred federal income tax. Since the sinking fund is typically not sufficient to pay all future deferred taxes as they become due, the lessor is required to make additional investment in anticipation of (and which is expected to be recovered from) future positive cash flows. Hence the term *multiple investment* literally means the lessor is required to make additional investment during the lease.

Exhibits 4, 5, 11, and 12 illustrate the two investment phases in the example lease pricing proposal.

Optimum Debt-to-Equity Ratio

The optimum debt-to-equity ratio is a function of the rent payments available to service debt while providing sufficient positive cash to support the lessor's yield and cash objectives. Also, the rent payments are constrained by the 90 percent to 110 percent variation in rent that is allowable under Section 467 of the Internal Revenue Code as discussed in Chapter 5. Exhibits 4 and 5 illustrate the optimum debt-to-equity ratio. The timeshare programs force the calculation to comply with Section 467 and will provide a printout proof of that calculation if one is desired.

Termination Value Schedule

Leveraged leases usually provide the lessee with an option, usually after a minimum period of time has passed, to terminate the lease by payment of termination value if the equipment becomes obsolete and surplus to its needs. The termination schedule in the lease specifies the "termination values" which are the amounts of the required payments on each allowable termination date. If the equipment is disposed of for less than the applicable termination value, the lessee must make

EXHIBIT 8   Net Pretax Cash Flow ($50 million capitalized equipment cost)

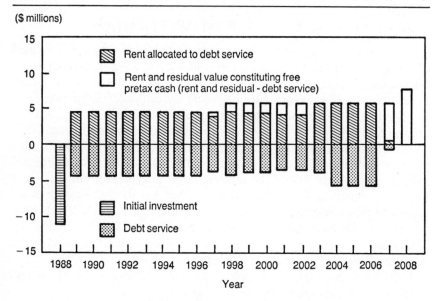

EXHIBIT 9   Federal Taxable Income and Taxes Paid ($50 million capitalized equipment cost)

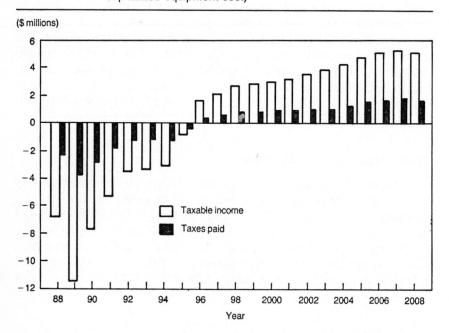

EXHIBIT 10   Net Aftertax Cash Flow ($50 million capitalized equipment cost)

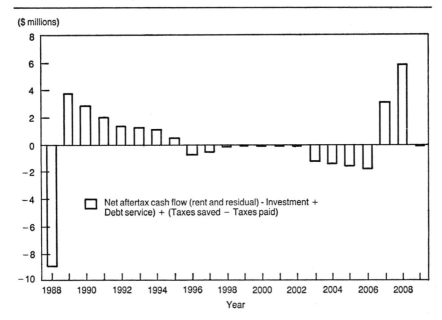

EXHIBIT 11   Net Aftertax Cash Compared to Investment ($50 million capitalized equipment cost)

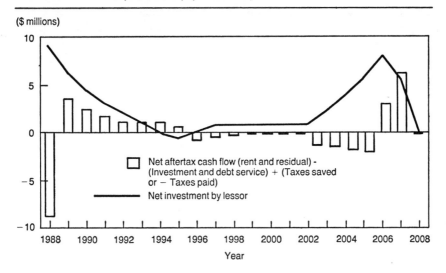

EXHIBIT 12   Investment Book Earnings Compared to Investment (Per $ million capitalized equipment cost)

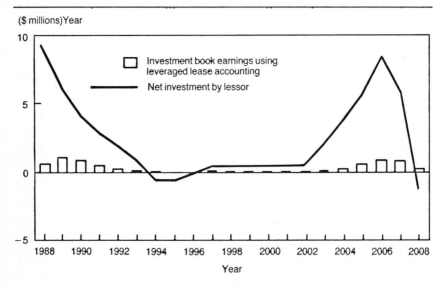

up the difference. Sale proceeds greater than the applicable termination value are retained by the lessor.

The termination value is calculated so that it is sufficient to pay off the lessor's unrecovered investment, the loan balance on the nonrecourse debt, and all taxes due. The unrecovered investment and the loan balance are known quantities at each point in the lease term. The calculation of the taxes due is more complex because the receipt of the termination amount is, itself, a taxable event. In addition, if ITC was claimed by the lessor, the termination may cause ITC recapture to occur.

The termination values can be calculated using either the booking or pricing assumptions. The booking analysis must use the multiple investment yield method of analysis with a zero reinvestment rate. The pricing analysis will usually use the multiple investment yield method and a conservative sinking fund reinvestment rate. The residual value used for booking may be less than the residual value used for pricing, and both are less than the expected residual value at the end of the lease term. This provides the lessor with some upside potential in both book profits and economic yield. The unrecovered investment balance depends on the yield calculation method, sinking fund reinvestment rate (if any), and residual value. The termination values protect, on a present value basis, the residual used in the calculation. Ideally, the lessor wants to use the higher of its book or economic investment balance in the termination value calculation to ensure that it will not realize either a book or economic loss. The lessee would prefer that the termination values be calculated using a zero residual assumption and that the lessor assume all residual risk due to obsolescence. Usually the termination schedule will at least protect the lessor's book investment. The example termination value calculation in Exhibit 13 protects the lessor's book yield.

Casualty Loss Schedule

Every lease also includes a casualty loss value schedule (also called "stipulated loss value" or "insured value"). This schedule establishes the liability of the lessee to the lessor if the equipment is lost or rendered unusable at various times during the lease term due to a casualty. The casualty loss values must compensate the lessor for the loss of the anticipated residual at the end of the lease term. The most common method of calculating casualty loss values is to add the present value of the unprotected residual value to the termination values. The unprotected residual is the difference between the expected residual value at the end of the lease term and any booked residual value that is already protected in the termination value calculations. As a practical matter the 20 percent residual value necessary to qualify the transaction as a true lease is sometimes used in lieu of the actual residual value estimate when calculating the stipulated loss values (assuming that the residual value protected in the termination schedules is less than 20 percent).

The discount rate used is an after-tax rate since it is really the after-tax unprotected residual value that is present valued and then pretaxed (producing the same result as taking the present value of the unprotected residual). The discount rate used may be a subject of negotiation. The lessor will want to use a conservative rate, while the lessee will want to use a more aggressive rate such as the after-tax economic return to the lessor in the transaction. In the example transaction shown in Exhibit 13 a discount rate of 9 percent was used which is equivalent to the debt rate. Exhibit 17 shows the casualty value and termination value in graph form.

Credit Exposure to Equity Participants in the Event of Repossession and Resale of the Leased Asset

If the lessee defaults, the equipment may be repossessed and sold to a third party. Since the leveraged debt participants have a first lien on the equipment, they are entitled to receive the outstanding loan

EXHIBIT 13 Casualty Loss Schedule (20% residual) and Termination
Value Schedule (5% residual)

Payment date	Casualty loss value	Termination value
7-1-88	102.4962	100.0000
1-1-89	103.3247	100.7140
7-1-89	103.9033	101.1730
1-1-90	104.2153	101.3597
7-1-90	104.2922	101.3057
1-1-91	104.1602	101.0368
7-1-91	103.8527	100.5861
1-1-92	103.3894	99.9730
7-1-92	102.7933	99.2202
1-1-93	102.0796	98.3427
7-1-93	101.2541	97.3459
1-1-94	100.3060	96.2186
7-1-94	99.2376	94.9628
1-1-95	98.0419	93.5710
7-1-95	96.7701	92.0942
1-1-96	95.4412	90.5509
7-1-96	94.0527	88.9382
1-1-97	92.6018	87.2528
7-1-97	91.1091	85.5148
1-1-98	88.6179	82.7671
7-1-98	86.0539	79.9348
1-1-99	83.4191	77.0195
7-1-99	80.7112	74.0181
1-1-00	77.9284	70.9285
7-1-00	75.0686	67.7477
1-1-01	72.1299	64.4733
7-1-01	69.1101	61.1024
1-1-02	66.0072	57.6323
7-1-02	62.8187	54.0599
1-1-03	59.5428	50.3824
7-1-03	56.2096	46.6291
1-1-04	52.8345	42.8147
7-1-04	49.4107	38.9315
1-1-05	45.9519	34.9922
7-1-05	42.4514	30.9892
1-1-06	38.9248	26.9370
7-1-06	35.3653	22.8278
1-1-07	31.7905	18.6782
7-1-07	28.0538	14.3402
1-1-08	24.1310	9.7887
7-1-08	20.0000	.0000

EXHIBIT 14   Components of Termination Value

Payment date	Termination value	Unrecovered investment book	Loan balance	Tax
7-1-88	100.0000	21.9071	78.0929	.0000
1-1-89	100.7140	18.8119	77.2596	4.6425
7-1-89	101.1730	15.7577	76.3888	9.0265
1-1-90	101.3597	13.0071	75.4787	12.8739
7-1-90	101.3057	10.4482	74.5278	16.3298
1-1-91	101.0368	8.5477	73.5340	18.9551
7-1-91	100.5861	6.8203	72.4955	21.2703
1-1-92	99.9730	5.5451	71.4103	23.0176
7-1-92	99.2202	4.4334	70.2762	24.5105
1-1-93	98.3427	3.6257	69.0911	25.6258
7-1-93	97.3459	2.5826	67.8527	26.9106
1-1-94	96.2186	1.7147	66.5586	27.9453
7-1-94	94.9628	.6188	65.2062	29.1378
1-1-95	93.5710	−.3094	63.7929	30.0875
7-1-95	92.0942	−.7395	62.3161	30.5176
1-1-96	90.5509	−.9062	60.7728	30.7383
7-1-96	88.9382	−.5046	59.1601	30.2827
1-1-97	87.2528	.0000	57.4747	29.7781
7-1-97	85.5148	.0000	56.5342	28.9806
1-1-98	82.7671	.0000	54.4722	28.2948
7-1-98	79.9348	.0000	52.6721	27.2628
1-1-99	77.0195	.0000	50.6355	26.3840
7-1-99	74.0181	.0000	48.7617	25.2564
1-1-00	70.9285	.0000	46.6035	24.3249
7-1-00	67.7477	.0000	44.6178	23.1299
1-1-01	64.4733	.0000	42.3306	22.1427
7-1-01	61.1024	.0000	40.2262	20.8762
1-1-02	57.6323	.0000	37.8023	19.8300
7-1-02	54.0599	.0000	335.5721	18.4878
1-1-03	50.3824	1.0192	31.9841	17.3791
7-1-03	46.6291	2.5605	28.1097	15.9590
1-1-04	42.8147	3.9273	24.0610	14.8264
7-1-04	38.9315	5.7499	19.8301	13.3514
1-1-05	34.9922	7.3919	15.4088	12.1915
7-1-05	30.9892	9.5390	10.7886	10.6616
1-1-06	26.9370	11.4967	5.9605	9.4798
7-1-06	22.8278	14.0145	.9150	7.8983
1-1-07	18.6782	11.9768	.0000	6.7014
7-1-07	14.3402	9.2839	.0000	5.0563
1-1-08	9.7887	6.0992	.0000	3.6895
7-1-08	.0000	−1.9287	.0000	1.9287

EXHIBIT 15   Reconciliation of Tax Bill from Termination Payment

Payment date	(1) + Termination value	(2) − Rent YTD	(3) − Interest YTD	(4) = Book value	(5) Taxable income	(6) − Tax due at 34%	(7) Cumulative tax
7-1-88	100.0000	.0000	.0000	100.0000	−.0000	−.0000	−.0000
1-1-89	100.7140	.0000	.0000	85.7143	14.9997	5.0999	.4574
7-1-89	101.1730	4.3475	3.4767	85.7143	16.3295	5.5520	−3.4745
1-1-90	101.3597	.0000	.0000	61.2245	40.1353	13.6460	.7721
7-1-90	101.3057	4.3475	3.3965	61.2245	41.0322	13.9509	−2.3788
1-1-91	101.0368	.0000	−.0000	43.7318	57.3050	19.4837	.5286
7-1-91	100.5861	4.3475	3.3090	43.7318	57.8928	19.6836	−1.5868
1-1-92	99.9730	.0000	−.0000	31.2370	68.7360	23.3702	.3526
7-1-92	99.2202	4.3475	3.2135	31.2370	69.1173	23.4999	−1.0107
1-1-93	98.3427	.0000	−.0000	22.3121	76.0305	25.8504	.2246
7-1-93	97.3459	4.3475	3.1091	22.3121	76.2722	25.9325	−.9780
1-1-94	96.2186	.0000	−.0000	13.3873	82.8313	28.1626	.2173
7-1-94	94.9628	4.3475	2.9951	13.3873	82.9279	28.1955	−.9424
1-1-95	93.5710	.0000	.0000	4.4624	89.1086	30.2969	.2094
7-1-95	92.0942	4.3475	2.8707	4.4624	89.1086	20.2969	−.2207
1-1-96	90.5509	.0000	.0000	.0000	90.5509	30.7873	.0490
7-1-96	88.9382	4.3475	2.7348	.0000	90.5509	30.7873	.5046
1-1-97	87.2528	.0000	.0000	.0000	87.2528	29.6660	−.1121
7-1-97	85.5148	4.3475	2.5864	.0000	87.2529	29.6738	.6932
1-1-98	82.7671	.0000	.0000	.0000	82.7671	28.1408	−.1540
7-1-98	79.9348	5.3136	2.4512	.0000	82.7672	28.1511	.8883
1-1-99	77.0195	.0000	.0000	.0000	77.0195	26.1866	−.1974
7-1-99	74.0181	5.3136	2.2786	.0000	77.0531	26.1981	.9416
1-1-00	70.9285	.0000	.0000	.0000	70.9285	24.1157	−.2092
7-1-00	67.7477	5.3136	2.0972	.0000	70.9642	24.1278	.9979
1-1-01	64.4733	.0000	.0000	.0000	64.4733	21.9209	−.2218
7-1-01	61.1024	5.3136	1.9049	.0000	64.5112	21.9338	1.0576
1-1-02	57.6323	.0000	.0000	.0000	57.6323	19.5950	1.1208
1-1-03	50.3824	.0000	.0000	.0000	50.3824	17.1300	−.2491
7-1-03	46.6291	5.3136	1.4393	.0000	50.5035	17.1712	1.2122
1-1-04	42.8147	.0000	.0000	.0000	42.8147	14.5570	−.2694
7-1-04	38.9315	5.3136	1.0827	.0000	43.1624	14.6752	1.3238
1-1-05	34.9922	.0000	.0000	.0000	34.9922	11.8974	−.2942
7-1-05	30.9892	5.3136	.6934	.0000	35.6094	12.1072	1.4456
1-1-06	26.9370	.0000	.0000	.0000	26.9370	9.1586	−.3212
7-1-06	22.8278	5.3136	.2682	.0000	27.8732	9.4769	1.5786
1-1-07	18.6782	.0000	.0000	.0000	18.6782	6.3506	−.3508
7-1-07	14.3402	5.3136	.0000	.0000	19.6538	6.6823	1.6260
1-1-08	9.7887	.0000	.0000	.0000	9.7887	3.3281	−.3613
7-1-08	.0000	10.3136	.0000	.0000	10.3136	3.5066	1.5780

EXHIBIT 16   Default Exposure Schedule (Percentage of equipment cost)

Equipment cost: $50,000,000
Equity investment: $10,953,525
Assumed residual value: 5 percent

Tax-able year 12/31	Default exposure (after tax)	Required market value	Components of required market value			Reconciliation of tax bill from sale at required market value						
			Unrecovered cash balance	Loan balance	Tax bill	Sale price +	Rent (YTD) −	Interest (YTD) −	Book value =	Taxable income	Tax due at 34%	Accrued tax credit
1988												
7/88	14.4587	100.0000	21.9071	78.0929	.0000	100.0000	.0000	.0000	100.0000	−.0000	−.0000	−.0000
1989												
1/89	14.4587	103.5142	17.7906	81.6071	4.1164	103.5142	−4.3475	.0000	85.7143	13.4524	4.5738	.4574
7/89	14.4587	102.6433	13.8588	80.7363	8.0483	102.6433	.0000	3.4767	85.7143	13.4524	4.5738	−3.4745
1990												
1/90	14.4587	101.7333	10.3843	79.8263	11.5227	101.7333	−4.3475	.0000	61.2245	36.1613	12.2948	.7721
7/90	14.4587	100.7823	7.2334	78.8753	14.6737	100.7823	.0000	3.3965	61.2245	36.1613	12.2948	−2.3788
1991												
1/91	14.4587	99.7886	4.8545	77.8815	17.0525	99.7886	−4.3475	−.0000	43.7318	51.7093	17.5812	.5286
7/91	14.4587	98.7501	2.7391	76.8430	19.1679	98.7501	.0000	3.3090	43.7318	51.7093	17.5812	−1.5868
1992												
1/92	14.4587	97.6649	1.1523	75.7578	20.7547	97.6649	−4.3475	−.0000	31.2370	62.0803	21.1073	.3526
7/92	14.4587	96.5308	−.2109	74.6237	22.1180	96.5308	.0000	3.2135	31.2370	62.0803	21.1073	−1.0107
1993												
1/93	14.4587	95.3457	−1.2216	73.4387	23.1287	95.3457	−4.3475	−.0000	22.3121	68.6861	23.3533	.2246
7/93	14.4587	94.1073	−2.4242	72.2002	24.3313	94.1073	.0000	3.1091	22.3121	68.6861	23.3533	−.9780
1994												
1/94	14.4587	92.8131	−3.4022	70.9061	25.3093	92.8131	−4.3475	−.0000	13.3873	75.0783	25.5266	.2173
7/94	14.4587	91.4608	−4.5619	69.5537	26.4690	91.4608	.0000	2.9951	13.3873	75.0783	25.5266	−.9424
1995												
1/95	14.4587	90.0475	−5.5043	68.1405	27.4114	90.0475	−4.3475	−.0000	4.4624	81.2376	27.6208	.2094
7/95	14.4587	88.5707	−5.9344	66.6636	27.8414	88.5707	.0000	2.8707	4.4624	81.2376	27.6208	−.2207

EXHIBIT 16   (concluded)

Equipment cost: $50,000,000
Equity investment: $10,953,525
Assumed residual value: 5 percent

Taxable year 12/31	Default exposure (after tax)	Components of required market value				Reconciliation of tax bill from sale at required market value							
		Required market value	Unrecovered cash balance	Loan balance	Tax bill	Sale price +	Rent (YTD) –	Interest (YTD) –	Book value =	Taxable income	Tax due at 34%	Accrued tax credit
1996												
1/96	14.4587	87.0274	−6.1551	65.1203	28.0621	87.0274	−4.3475	.0000	.0000	82.6799	28.1111	.0490
7/96	14.4587	85.4146	−5.6995	63.5076	27.6065	85.4146	.0000	2.7348	.0000	82.6799	28.1111	.5046
1997												
1/97	14.4587	83.7293	−5.1949	61.8223	27.1019	83.7293	−4.3475	.0000	.0000	79.3818	26.9898	−.1121
7/97	14.4587	81.9682	−4.3896	60.0611	26.2966	81.9682	.0000	2.5864	.0000	79.3818	26.9898	.6932
1998												
1/98	13.9171	80.1647	−4.5169	59.0782	25.6034	80.1647	−5.3136	.0000	.0000	74.8510	25.4494	−.1540
7/98	13.4500	77.3023	−4.1823	56.9235	24.5611	77.3023	.0000	2.4512	.0000	74.8510	25.4494	.8883
1999												
1/99	12.7489	74.3589	−4.3562	55.0423	23.6728	74.3589	−5.3136	.0000	.0000	69.0452	23.4754	−.1974
7/99	12.1505	71.3238	−4.1240	52.9140	22.5338	71.3238	.0000	2.2786	.0000	69.0452	23.4754	.9416
2000												
1/00	11.3840	68.2045	−4.3436	50.9559	21.5921	68.2045	−5.3136	.0000	.0000	62.8908	21.3829	−.2092
7/00	10.7496	64.9880	−4.0977	48.7007	20.3850	64.9880	.0000	2.0972	.0000	62.8908	21.3829	.9979
2001												
1/01	9.9373	61.6822	−4.3305	46.6256	19.3871	61.6822	−5.3136	.0000	.0000	56.3685	19.1653	−.2218
7/01	9.2650	58.2734	−4.0698	44.2355	18.1077	58.2734	.0000	1.9049	.0000	56.3685	19.1653	1.0576
2002												
1/02	8.4042	54.7700	−4.3166	42.0364	17.0502	54.7700	−5.3136	.0000	.0000	49.4563	16.8151	−.2350
7/02	7.6916	51.1574	−4.0404	39.5034	15.6944	51.1574	.0000	1.7011	.0000	49.4563	16.8151	1.1208

2003												
1/03	6.7793	47.4445	−4.3018	37.1728	14.5736	47.4445	−5.3136	.0000	.0000	42.1309	14.3245	−.2491
7/03	6.6969	43.5702	−2.9655	33.4234	13.1123	43.5702	.0000	1.4393	.0000	42.1309	14.3245	1.2122
2004												
1/04	6.6969	39.5215	−1.7532	29.3747	11.9000	39.5215	−5.3136	.0000	.0000	34.2078	11.6307	−.2694
7/04	6.6969	35.2906	−.1601	25.1438	10.3069	35.2906	.0000	1.0827	.0000	34.2078	11.6307	1.3238
2005												
1/05	6.6969	30.8693	1.1637	20.7225	8.9831	30.8693	−5.3136	.0000	.0000	25.5557	8.6889	−.2942
7/05	6.6969	26.2491	2.9035	16.1022	7.2433	26.2491	.0000	.6934	.0000	25.5557	8.6889	1.4456
2006												
1/06	6.6969	21.4209	4.3491	11.2741	5.7977	21.4209	−5.3136	.0000	.0000	16.1073	5.4765	−.3212
7/06	6.6969	16.3755	6.2490	6.2287	3.8978	16.3755	.0000	.2682	.0000	16.1073	5.4765	1.5786
2007												
1/07	6.6969	11.1030	7.8276	.9562	2.3192	11.1030	−5.3136	.0000	.0000	5.7894	1.9684	−.3508
7/07	3.8210	5.7894	5.4470	.0000	.3424	5.7894	.0000	.0000	.0000	5.7894	1.9684	1.6260
2008												
1/08	.3140	.4758	1.7593	.0000	−1.2836	.4758	−5.3136	.0000	.0000	−4.8379	−1.6449	−.3613
7/08	−6.4930	−9.8379	−6.6150	.0000	−3.2229	−9.8379	5.0000	.0000	.0000	−4.8379	−1.6449	1.5780

EXHIBIT 17   Casualty Value and Termination Value Schedules (Percent of capitalized cost)

Percent of capitalized cost

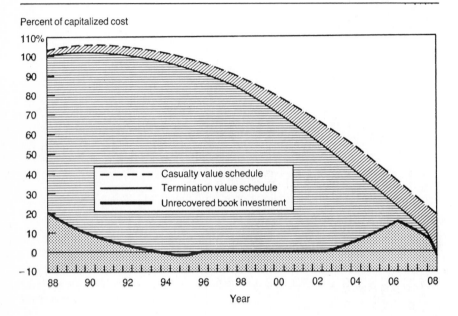

Year

balance before the lessor (equity participants) can receive any of the sale proceeds. If the sale proceeds are less than or equal to the loan balance, the lessor (equity participants) receives nothing. Nevertheless, the sale produces taxable income equal to the loan balance. First there is the taxable income due to the sale, then the "forgiveness of debt" equal to the difference between the loan balance and the sale proceeds.

A measure of credit risk is the "maximum exposure value." This is the pre-tax amount that the lessor would have to receive, in the event of a forced sale that netted an amount less than or equal to the loan balance, to pay off its unrecovered investment and all taxes payable. Intuitively, it can be seen that this amount will be equal to the termination value minus the loan balance since the termination value includes both the loan balance and the taxes on the loan balance. (See Exhibits 16 and 17.)

Sensitivity to Tax Rate Change

In view of the recent tax rate reductions from 46 percent to 34 percent, the lessor in the instant case will be very concerned regarding future tax rate increases after the transaction has turned taxable.

The effect of an increase in tax rate in later years of the lease upon the lessor's after-tax book yield and after-tax cash are as follows compared to a base case 9 percent after-tax yield and 10 percent after-tax cash.

40 percent tax rate			45 percent tax rate		
Rate change in year	Nominal after-tax yield	After-tax cash	Rate change in year	Nominal after-tax yield	After-tax cash
2	10.66%	8.28%	2	10.34%	6.85%
3	8.44	6.92	3	6.04	4.35
4	7.13	5.98	4	3.53	2.64
5	6.33	5.36	5	1.98	1.50
6	5.85	4.96	6	1.02	0.77
7	5.41	4.58	7	0.09	−0.07
8	4.98	4.21	8	−0.78	−0.60
9	4.88	4.13	9	−0.99	−0.76
10	5.11	4.32	10	−0.52	−0.39

See Exhibits 18 and 19 for a graphic illustration of the above table.

Since the lessee in the instant case has indicated a reluctance to indemnify the lessor for tax rate increases, the lessor might wish to achieve a higher yield assuming a constant 34 percent tax rate and adjust its bid accordingly in view of any perceived risk in a tax rate increase. The lessor might, for example, assume the tax rate will rise to 40 percent in the third or fourth year and price accordingly.

Sensitivity to Residual Value

The lessor in the instant case might be concerned regarding the effect a lower residual value would have on its yield. Since the lessor has only assumed a 5 percent yield for pricing and the residual is not to be realized for 20 years, the effect of a zero residual is negligible.

Sawtooth Structure

The lessor can slightly improve the lessee's implicit cost by adopting a sawtooth rent structure in which both the rents and debt service fluctuate throughout the lease term. This fluctuation makes it possible to more closely match cash inflows from rents with cash outflows needed to service debt and pay deferred taxes during the later years of the lease. This further curtails the need for a sinking fund to pay deferred taxes.

The implicit cost to the lessee declines from 7.0888 percent to 7.0371 percent under this structure, and the present value cost is reduced

EXHIBIT 18   Impact on Aftertax Yield of Change in Tax Rate

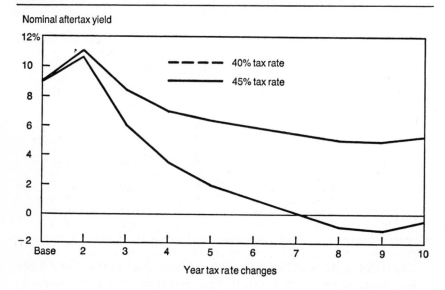

Nominal aftertax yield

— — — — 40% tax rate

———— 45% tax rate

Year tax rate changes

EXHIBIT 19   Impact on Aftertax Cash of Change in Tax Rate (From 34% in year 1)

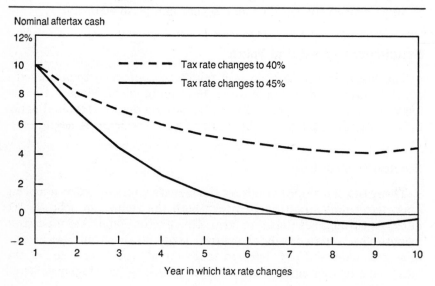

Nominal aftertax cash

— — — — Tax rate changes to 40%

———— Tax rate changes to 45%

Year in which tax rate changes

from 86.0314 percent to 85.5258 percent. The lessor's investment is increased from 21.9071 percent to 22.3139 percent. These are small changes, but some transactions are won or lost as a result of basis point differences in yield, implicit rate, and/or present value.

Exhibit 20 is a table showing the sawtooth rents including the annual cash flow and proof of yield analysis.

Other Techniques to Reduce the Present Value of Rents

Where the lessee's objective is to reduce the present value of rents, there are a number of methods used by lessors to reduce the lessee's present value of rents while maintaining the lessor's target yield. These methods are based upon the difference in the discount rates used by the lessee and the lessor in valuing the cash disbursements and cash receipts, respectively. The lessee's discount rate is typically its medium- to long-term debt rate, and the lessor's discount rate is generally the lessor's after-tax yield rate. Since the rate used by the lessee is typically higher than the rate used by the lessor, the difference in measuring the time value of money can be used to decrease the present value of rents to the lessee while holding the yield constant. Furthermore, in a leveraged lease in which the lessor is using the multiple investment sinking fund method of lease analysis, the lessor only uses the after-tax yield as a measurement during the investment phase and switches to zero or a lower rate during the sinking fund phase.

Some of the methods used are as follows:

1. *Variable Rents Weighted toward End of the Lease.* Variable rents coupled with step rents weighted to the end of the lease as much as possible while still meeting the 90–110 percent constraints of Revenue Procedure 75–28 and Section 467 of the Internal Revenue Code. (See preceding section on sawtooth rent structure.)

2. *Staged or Delayed Equity Contributions.* In this situation the early rents are actually less than the amount needed for debt service. The lessor makes additional delayed equity payments to fund the debt service in excess of rents. If payments are semiannual in arrears, the first payment in a year may be very low, so long as the annual payments meet the IRS 90–110 percent requirements. Care must also be used to meet the 20 percent initial equity contribution requirement of Revenue Procedure 75-21.

3. *Rents Paid in Arrears Switching to Rents Paid in Advance.* This method may reduce the lessee's net present value by switching from rents paid in arrears to rents paid in advance at the time the lease enters the sinking fund phase.

EXHIBIT 20   Periodic Cash Flow and Proof of Yield Analysis (Sawtooth rent structure

Equipment cost: $50,000,000
Equity investment: $11,156,965
Debt rate: 9 percent
Payment: Semiannual arrears
Lease term: 20 years

| Taxable year per month | Lease receipts | Debt service | | | Cash flows | |
		Interest expense	Principal payment	Unpaid balance	To Lessor	Taxes saved
1988						
6 Dec.	$ 0	$ 0	$ 0	$38,843,035	$ −11,156,965	$ 2,185,714
	$ 0	$ 0	$ 0		$ −11,156,965	$ 2,185,714
1989						
12 June	$1,747,937	$1,747,937	$ 0	38,843,035	$ 0	$ 1,983,480
18 Dec.	2,616,215	1,747,937	868,279	37,974,756	0	1,740,623
	$4,364,152	$3,495,873	$ 868,279		$ 0	$ 3,724,103
1990						
24 June	$1,708,864	$1,708,864	$ 0	37,974,756	$ 0	$ 1,580,195
30 Dec.	2,655,288	1,708,864	946,424	37,028,332	0	1,193,390
	$4,364,152	$3,417,728	$ 946,424		$ 0	$ 2,773,584
1991						
36 June	$1,666,275	$1,666,275	$ 0	37,028,332	$ 0	$ 1,063,214
42 Dec.	2,697,877	1,666,275	1,031,602	35,996,730	0	798,017
	$4,364,152	$3,332,550	$ 1,031,602		$ 0	$ 1,861,231
1992						
48 June	$1,619,853	$1,619,853	$ 0	35,996,730	$ 0	$ 688,048
54 Dec.	2,744,299	1,619,853	1,124,446	34,872,284	0	510,711
	$4,364,152	$3,239,706	$ 1,124,446		$ 0	$ 1,198,759
1993						
60 June	$1,569,253	$1,569,253	$ 0	34,872,284	$ 0	$ 608,719
66 Dec.	2,794,899	1,569,253	1,225,646	33,646,638	0	495,227
	$4,364,152	$3,138,506	$ 1,225,646		$ 0	$ 1,103,946
1994						
72 June	$1,514,099	$1,514,099	$ 0	33,646,638	$ 0	$ 588,401
78 Dec.	2,850,053	1,514,099	1,335,955	32,310,683	0	478,350
	$4,364,152	$3,028,197	$ 1,335,955		$ 0	$ 1,066,751
1995						
84 June	$1,453,981	$1,453,981	$ 0	32,310,683	$ 0	$ 224,879
90 Dec.	2,910,171	1,453,981	1,456,191	30,854,492	0	118,578
	$4,364,152	$2,907,961	$ 1,456,191		$ 0	$ 343,457
1996						
96 June	$1,388,452	$1,388,452	$ 0	30,854,492	$ 0	$ −216,498
102 Dec.	2,975,700	1,388,452	1,587,248	29,267,245	0	−242,849
	$4,364,152	$2,776,904	$ 1,587,248		$ 0	$ −459,347
1997						
108 June	$1,317,026	$1,317,026	$ 0	29,267,245	$ 0	$ −318,672
114 Dec.	3,047,126	1,317,026	1,272,878	27,994,367	457,222	−264,705
	$4,364,152	$2,634,052	$ 1,272,878		$ 457,222	$ −583,377
1998						
120 June	$1,259,747	$1,259,747	$ 0	27,994,367	$ 0	$ −489,437
126 Dec.	4,074,217	1,259,747	1,960,424	26,033,943	854,047	−430,614
	$5,333,964	$2,519,493	$ 1,960,424		$ 854,047	$ −920,051
1999						
132 June	$1,171,527	$1,171,527	$ 0	26,033,943	$ 0	$ −553,301
138 Dec.	4,162,436	1,171,527	2,198,760	23,835,183	792,149	−457,609
	$5,333,964	$2,343,055	$ 2,198,760		$ 792,149	$ −1,010,910

Total	To investment Earnings	To investment Recovery	To tax Sinking fund	Unrecovered investment balance	Tax reserve sinking fund Earnings	Tax reserve sinking fund Balance
$ −8,971,251	$ 440,609	$ −9,411,860	$ 0	$9,411,860	$ 0	$ 0
$ −8,971,251	$ 440,609	$ −9,411,860	$ 0		$ 0	
$ 1,983,480	$ 455,123	$ 1,528,357	$ 0	7,883,503	$ 0	0
1,740,623	376,653	1,363,970	0	6,519,533	0	0
$ 3,724,103	$ 831,775	$ 2,892,327	$ 0		$ 0	
$ 1,580,195	$ 309,908	$ 1,270,287	$ 0	5,249,246	$ 0	0
1,193,390	250,366	943,024	0	4,306,222	0	0
$ 2,773,584	$ 560,274	$ 2,213,311	$ 0		$ 0	
$ 1,063,214	$ 204,374	$ 858,840	$ 0	3,447,382	$ 0	0
798,017	164,247	633,770	0	2,813,612	0	0
$ 1,861,231	$ 368,621	$ 1,492,610	$ 0		$ 0	
$ 688,048	$ 133,522	$ 554,526	$ 0	2,259,086	$ 0	0
510,711	107,784	402,927	0	1,856,160	0	0
$ 1,198,759	$ 241,306	$ 957,453	$ 0		$ 0	
$ 608,719	$ 86,861	$ 521,857	$ 0	1,334,302	$ 0	0
495,227	61,246	433,981	0	900,321	0	0
$ 1,103,946	$ 148,107	$ 955,839	$ 0		$ 0	
$ 588,401	$ 38,786	$ 549,614	$ 0	350,707	$ 0	0
478,350	11,753	350,707	115,890	0	0	115,890
$ 1,066,751	$ 50,540	$ 900,321	$ 115,890		$ 0	
$ 224,879	$ 0	$ 0	$ 224,879	0	$ 0	340,769
118,578	0	0	118,578	0	0	459,347
$ 343,457	$ 0	$ 0	$ 343,457		$ 0	
$ −216,498	$ 0	$ 0	$ −216,498	0	$ 0	242,849
−242,849	0	0	−242,849	0	0	0
$ −459,347	$ 0	$ 0	$ −459,347		$ 0	
$ −318,672	$ 0	$ −318,672	$ 0	322,211	$ 0	0
192,517	6,198	186,319	0	132,353	0	0
$ −126,155	$ 6,198	$ −132,353	$ 0		$ 0	
$ −489,437	$ 0	$ −489,437	$ 0	633,513	$ 0	0
−1,423,433	16,950	406,483	0	215,307	0	0
$ −66,005	$ 16,950	$ −82,954	$ 0		$ 0	
$ −553,301	$ 0	$ −553,301	$ 0	785,667	$ 0	0
334,540	23,541	310,999	0	463,319	0	0
$ −218,762	$ 23,541	$ −242,302	$ 0		$ 0	

EXHIBIT 20 (concluded)

Equipment cost: $50,000,000
Equity investment: $11,156,965
Debt rate: 9 percent
Payment: Semiannual arrears
Lease term: 20 years

Taxable year per month	Lease receipts	Debt service			Cash flows	
		Interest expense	Principal payment	Unpaid balance	To Lessor	Taxes saved
2000						
144 June	$1,072,583	$1,072,583	$ 0	23,835,183	$ 0	$ −589,577
150 Dec.	4,261,380	1,072,583	2,096,976	21,738,207	1,091,821	−487,886
	$5,333,964	$2,145,166	$ 2,096,976		$ 1,091,821	$−1,077,463
2001						
156 June	$ 978,219	$ 978,219	$ 0	21,738,207	$ 0	$ −625,180
162 Dec.	4,355,744	978,219	2,216,926	19,521,281	1,160,599	−516,761
	$5,333,964	$1,956,439	$ 2,216,926		$ 1,160,599	$−1,141,942
2002						
168 June	$ 878,458	$ 878,458	$ 0	19,521,281	$ 0	$ −662,124
174 Dec.	4,455,506	878,458	2,347,818	17,173,462	1,229,230	−547,288
	$5,333,964	$1,756,915	$ 2,347,818		$ 1,229,230	$−1,209,413
2003						
180 June	$ 772,806	$ 772,806	$ 0	17,173,462	$ 0	$ −701,237
186 Dec.	4,561,158	772,806	3,338,778	13,834,684	449,574	−579,618
	$5,333,964	$1,545,612	$ 3,338,778		$ 449,574	$−1,280,855
2004						
192 June	$ 622,561	$ 622,561	$ 0	13,834,684	$ 0	$ −754,397
198 Dec.	4,711,403	622,561	4,088,842	9,745,842	0	−625,593
	$5,333,964	$1,245,122	$ 4,088,842		$ 0	$−1,379,990
2005						
204 June	$ 438,563	$ 438,563	$ 0	9,745,842	$ 0	$ −820,917
210 Dec.	4,895,401	438,563	4,456,838	5,289,004	0	−681,896
	$5,333,964	$ 877,126	$ 4,456,838		$ 0	$−1,502,813
2006						
216 June	$ 238,005	$ 238,005	$ 0	5,289,004	$ 0	$ −894,799
222 Dec.	5,095,958	238,005	4,857,953	431,051	0	−743,267
	$5,333,964	$ 476,010	$ 4,857,953		$ 0	$−1,638,066
2007						
228 June	$ 19,397	$ 19,397	$ 0	431,051	$ 0	$ −975,331
234 Dec.	5,314,566	19,397	431,051	0	4,864,118	−810,161
	$5,333,964	$ 38,795	$ 431,051		$ 4,864,118	$−1,785,492
2008						
240 June	$ 0	$ 0	$ 0	0	$ 0	$−1,378,632
246 Dec.	7,833,964	0	0	0	7,833,964	−1,198,596
	$7,833,964	$ 0	$ 0		$ 7,833,964	$−2,577,229
2009						
252 June	$ 0	$ 0	$ 0	0	$ 0	$ −266,355
258 Dec.	0	0	0	0	0	0
	$ 0	$ 0	$ 0		$ 0	$ −266,355
Total	$1.0045E8	$ 4.287E7	$38,843,035		$ 7,575,758	$−2,575,758

| | Allocation of cash flows | | | | Tax reserve sinking fund | |
| | To investment | | To tax | Unrecovered | | |
Total	Earnings	Recovery	Sinking fund	investment balance	Earnings	Balance
$ −589,577	$ 0	$ −589,577	$ 0	$ 1,062,888	$ 0	$ 0
603,935	44,635	559,300	0	493,973	0	0
$ 14,359	$ 44,635	$ −30,277	$ 0		$ 0	
$ −625,180	$ 0	$ −625,180	$ 0	1,151,102	$ 0	0
643,837	47,532	596,305	0	523,209	0	0
$ 18,657	$ 47,532	$ −28,875	$ 0		$ 0	
$ −662,124	$ 0	$ −662,124	$ 0	1,219,172	$ 0	0
681,942	50,344	631,597	0	554,117	0	0
$ 19,817	$ 50,344	$ −30,527	$ 0		$ 0	
$ −701,237	$ 0	$ −701,237	$ 0	1,291,192	$ 0	0
− 130,044	53,318	− 183,362	0	1,474,861	0	0
$ −831,282	$ 53,318	$ −884,600	$ 0		$ 0	
$ −754,397	$ 0	$ −754,397	$ 0	2,312,183	0	0
− 625,593	0	− 625,593	0	3,062,421	$ 0	0
$−1,379,990	$ 0	$−1,379,990	$ 0		$ 0	
$ −820,917	$ 0	$ −820,917	$ 0	4,047,207	0	0
− 681,896	0	− 681,896	0	4,942,126	$ 0	0
$−1,502,813	$ 0	$−1,502,813	$ 0		$ 0	
$ −894,799	$ 0	$ −894,799	$ 0	6,096,601	$ 0	0
− 743,267	0	− 743,267	0	7,157,217	0	0
$−1,638,066	$ 0	$−1,638,066	$ 0		$ 0	
$ −975,331	$ 0	$ −975,331	$ 0	8,505,051	$ 0	0
4,053,957	1,647,130	2,406,827	0	4,686,999	0	0
$ 3,078,626	$1,647,130	$ 1,431,496	$ 0		$ 0	
$−1,378,632	$ 0	$−1,378,632	$ 0	6,316,898	$ 0	0
6,635,367	469,119	5,899,893	266,355	0	0	266,355
$ 5,256,735	$ 469,119	$ 4,521,261	$ 266,355		$ 0	
$ −266,355	$ 0	$ 0	$−266,355	0	$ 0	0
0	0	0	0	0	0	0
$ −266,355	$ 0	$ 0	$−266,355		$ 0	
$ 5,000,000	$5,000,000	$ 0	$ 0		$ 0	

4. *Serial Debt.* Serial debt consists of several tranches of debt with different interest rates for different final maturities. If the later maturities of serial debt are significantly higher than shorter maturities, a lower overall cost of debt may be achieved, and rents may be reduced accordingly.

5. *Zero Coupon Notes.* By using a zero coupon bond as the last tranche in serialized debt, debt service can be lowered in the early years of a lease although tax deductions are preserved for accrued but unpaid interest.

CONCLUSION

Lessees and lessors have truly remarkable timeshare programs available to them to aid in the analysis of lease transactions.

However, a mistake some lessor analysts make in using these programs is to lose track of and to forget the true objective of the exercise, which is to produce free cash and actual dollars of return as a percentage of dollars of risk and the value of tax benefits utilized. A yield figure by itself may look attractive but be extremely misleading as to the relative merits of a transaction.

A mistake some lessees sometimes make is to overly rely upon lease programs to squeeze the last basis point out of a lessor while losing sight of the character and credibility of the lessor and the ability to deal with the lessor over a period of years on a professional basis. In other words, the lowest implicit cost or present value of lease payments may not be the best deal for the lessee.

Glossary

Acres   Pronounced "ay-kers," a short way of saying ACRS.

ACRS   Accelerated cost recovery system. The portion of the Internal Revenue Code that sets forth tax depreciation deductions.

ACRS Deductions   Tax depreciation deductions allowed under Section 168(a) of the Internal Revenue Code. Equipment falls into one of eight asset classes ranging from 3 to 31.5 years. Most equipment falls into 3-, 5-, 7-, and 10-year classes and uses 200 percent declining-balance method switching to straight line.

Accrual Accounting   A method of accounting in which revenue is recognized when earned and expenses are recognized when incurred without regard to the timing of cash receipts and expenditures (cf. cash accounting). The TRA generally requires accrual accounting.

Accrued Interest   Interest earned but not collected. Interest earned but not paid since the latest payment date.

Additions   Features and enhancements that may be installed on leased equipment, usually subject to removal by the lessee. However, the lessor owns additions subject to the right of removal.

ADR   Asset depreciation range method of depreciation under regulations implementing Internal Revenue Code Section 167(m), which under most circumstances requires longer equipment life to be used for tax depreciation than ACRS. Generally, ACRS tax depreciation has replaced depreciation using ADR, except where alternative minimum tax is applicable.

Advance Rent   A general term to describe any rent that precedes the base lease term and the base lease rent.

Alterations   Modifications to leased equipment, generally subject to restoration at the conclusion of the lease.

Alternative Minimum Tax See AMT.

AMT An acronym for alternative minimum tax, which is a separate federal income tax imposed on corporations where their alternative minimum tax exceeds their regular corporate tax. Alternative minimum tax is computed after adjustments to regular corporate taxable income.

AMTI Alternative minimum taxable income. The amount of income used to compute alternative minimum tax.

Amortization The gradual reduction of any amount over a period of time. A general term which includes various specific practices such as depreciation, depletion, write-off of intangibles, prepaid expenses, and deferred charges; or general reduction of loan principal. Gradual repayment of a debt over time, for example, through the operation of a sinking or purchase fund.

Antichurning Rules These rules prevent ACRS deductions being available on sale-and-leasebacks of property acquired before 1981.

Arbitrage General term for transactions involving moving capital from one market to another, from one security to another, or from one maturity to another in the hope of realizing a higher yield or capital gain.

Assignment A transfer of legal title. In leasing, a transfer of the lessor's interest in a lease and the leased equipment to a transferree such as a financial institution or any entity assuming the lessor's position. A lessee is usually prohibited from assigning its interest in a lease without the lessor's consent. The term is also used in leveraged leasing to describe transfers of the first security interest in a lease and lease rentals to a security trustee for leveraged debt holders.

At-Risk Rules Federal tax laws that prohibit individuals (and some corporations) from deducting tax losses from equipment leases in excess of the amount they have at risk.

Bailment An archaic term for a lease of personal property.

Bailment for Hire Same as Bailment.

Bargain Purchase Option A provision that allows the lessee, at its option, to purchase the leased asset during or at the conclusion of a lease for a price that is sufficiently lower than the expected fair market value at the time such option becomes exercisable so the exercise of the option appears, at the inception of the lease, to be reasonably assured.

Bargain Renewal Option A provision that allows the lessee, at its option, to renew the lease for a rental sufficiently lower than the expected fair rental for the property at the time such option becomes exercisable so that the exercise of the option appears, at the inception of the lease, to be reasonably assured.

Base Rate Floating interest rates on bank loans in the United States are quoted on the basis of the prime rate or the base rate of the lender.

Base Rent Rental paid during the base term of the lease.

Base Term   The basic term of the lease used by the lessor in computing payout and relied on by the lessee as the minimum time period during which the lessee will have the use and custody of the equipment.

Base Term Commencement Date   The date on which the base term of the lease commences.

Basic Rent   Same as Base Rent.

Basis Points   Used as a measurement of a fraction of a percentage for figuring interest. There are 100 basis points in 1 percent.

Bonds   As used in leasing the term *bonds* refers to notes or loan certificates issued by the owner trustee evidencing indebtedness in a leveraged lease.

Boot   An amount (which may not exceed fair market value) that a lessor is willing to pay a lessee in excess of the lessee's tax basis for equipment to be leased to the lessee. Boot may not be included in a lessor's tax basis in a finance lease but may be included in a true lease.

Broker   A company or person that arranges lease transactions between lessees and lessors for a fee.

Burdensome Buyout   Provision in a lease allowing the lessee to purchase the leased equipment at a value to be determined in some fashion when the buyout is exercised in the event that payments under the general indemnity clauses are deemed by the lessee to be unduly burdensome. Care must be taken to see that the existence of such a provision does not invalidate the true lease nature of the transaction and thus make the lessee liable under the tax indemnity clause.

Call   An option to purchase an asset at a set price at some particular time in the future. Care must be used in negotiating a purchase option or call in a lease agreement. If this is done improperly, many of the advantages of a true lease (such as tax savings) may be disallowed by the Internal Revenue Service.

Capital Cost Recovery Allowances   Tax depreciation deductions.

Capital Lease   Under *FAS 13,* a lease is classified and accounted for by a lessee as a "capital lease" if it meets any of the following criteria: (*a*) the lease transfers ownership to the lessee at the end of the lease term; (*b*) the lease contains an option to purchase property at a bargain price; (*c*) the lease term is equal to 75 percent or more of the estimated economic life of the property (except for used property leased toward the end of its useful life); or (*d*) the present value of minimum lease rental payments is equal to 90 percent or more of the fair market value of the leased property less related ITC retained by the lessor.

Capital Structure   The financing mix of a firm. The more debt in relation to equity, the more financial leverage or gearing the firm is said to have.

Capitalized Leases   Capitalizing a lease (not already capitalized under *FAS 13*) is the same as finding its debt equivalent. The principal portion of a lease (the capitalized value) can be determined by discounting all remaining lease payments at an appropriate interest rate.

Carve-Out Refers to a production payment carved out of a larger production payment or a right to a specified share of production from a certain mineral property.

Casualty Value See Stipulated Loss Value.

Certificate of Acceptance A document whereby the lessee acknowledges that the equipment to be leased has been delivered to it, is acceptable to it, and has been manufactured or constructed in accordance with the lessee's specifications.

Certificate of Delivery and Acceptance Same as Certificate of Acceptance.

Claw Back A British term to describe a taxpayer paying back to the government an amount equal to tax benefits previously claimed, such as depreciation deductions.

Closed-End Lease A true lease in which the lessor assumes the risk of depreciation and residual value. The lessee bears little or no obligation at the conclusion of the lease. Usually a net lease in which the lessee maintains, insures, and pays property taxes on the equipment. The term is used to distinguish a lease from an open-end lease, particularly in automobile leasing.

Code In a leasing context the Code generally refers to the Internal Revenue Code of 1986. (Formerly the Internal Revenue Code of 1954.)

Co-Generation Facility A plant that produces steam to generate electricity and residual steam or heat for other uses.

Collateral Assets pledged as security under a loan or lease. Under a lease, collateral is the equipment that is leased. However, caution should be exercised in using the term *collateral* in a true lease, because this term might provide an excuse for a court to decide that a lease is not a true lease but rather a lease intended as a security document, subject to all the provisions of Article 9 of the Uniform Commercial Code. A neutral term such as *equipment* seems more desirable.

Commencement Date The first day of the basic lease term.

Commercial Bank A bank that both accepts deposits and grants loans and, under certain stipulations in some countries such as the United States, pays interest on checking accounts.

Commercial Paper Short-term fixed-rate notes used to raise funds in the United States.

Comptroller's Ruling In a leasing context the interpretation of the U.S. Comptroller of the Currency (12 CFR 7.3400) defining the leasing activities in which national banks and their subsidiaries may engage.

Conditional Sale A transaction for purchase of an asset in which the user, for federal income tax purposes and perhaps also for state tax purposes, is treated as the owner of the equipment at the outset and throughout the term of the transaction. Also called a conditional sale lease or a lease intended as security.

Conditional Sale Lease A lease that in substance is a conditional sale. Sometimes called a hire-purchase agreement, a money-over-money lease, or a lease intended as security.

Construction Contract Assignment See Purchase Agreement Assignment.

Contingent Rentals Rentals in which the payments of rents are dependent on some factor other than the passage of time.

Conventional Leveraged Lease A leveraged lease of the type contemplated by Revenue Procedure 75–21.

Corporate Financing Vehicle A corporation interposed between a partnership and a debt investor in order to create a corporate obligation within the meaning of laws and regulations restricting investments of insurance companies and other investors on certain kinds of obligations.

Cross-Border Leasing A lease transaction in which the lessee is located in one country and the lessor is located in another country.

Debt Service Payment of principal and interest due lenders.

Default An event defined in a lease agreement as a default, such as failure to pay rent or perform some obligation required under the terms of a lease.

Defeasance A defeasance of a lease that has been capitalized by a lessee. If the incremental borrowing rate assumed by the lessee in capitalizing the lease is less than interest on U.S. Treasury bonds that can be used to set off against the transaction, a trust can be set up for this purpose using the principal amount of bonds to provide funds to service lease payments, thus reducing the balance sheet liability and supplementing income.

Deferred Tax Liability An estimated amount of future income taxes that may become payable from income already earned but not yet recognized for tax reporting purposes.

Deficiency Agreement An agreement to guarantee revenues will be received or expenses paid, to make up a short fall needed to pay debt.

Depreciation The allocation of an asset's cost for tax or management purposes over a period of time based on its age.

Direct Financing Lease Under *FAS 13,* a nonleveraged lease by a lessor (not a manufacturer or dealer) in which the lease meets any of the definitional criteria of a capital lease, plus these two additional criteria: (*a*) the collectibility of minimum lease payments must be reasonably predictable and (*b*) no uncertainties surround the amount of unreimbursable costs to be incurred by the lessor in a direct financing lease.

Direct Investor Refers to the lessor in a direct financing lease.

Direct Lease A nonleveraged lease. Same as Direct Financing Lease.

Discounted Cash Flow A cash flow occurring some time in the future that has been discounted by a given discount factor on a compounded basis; the present value of a future cash flow.

Discounted Leases Leases sold or assigned at discounted face value to a bank or finance company. The discount rate reflects the interest rate and the collection risk.

Disqualified Leaseback or Disqualified Long-Term Agreement As defined under Section 467 of the Internal Revenue Code, an agreement in which the principal purpose of providing increasing rents (that is, uneven low-high rents) is the avoidance of tax and in which the property is leased to either (a) a person that had an interest in the property within the past two years or (b) for a term in excess of 75 percent of the specified statutory recovery period (the applicable ACRS period) for such property.

The Code provides that tax avoidance will not result where (a) rents increase by reference to a standard beyond the control of the parties, (b) rents are based on a percentage of the lessor receipts (common in real estate leases to retail stores), (c) there are changes in the amounts paid to third parties or in floating debt (in a leveraged lease, insurance charges, property taxes, for example), or (d) reasonable rent holidays are involved.

Where Section 467 is violated, rents are reallocated using the normalization method of accrual.

Double-Dip Lease A lease that uses significant tax or funding incentives from two sources, usually situated in two countries.

DRA Deficit Reduction Act of 1984.

Economic Life of Leased Property The estimated period during which the property is expected to be economically usable by one or more users, with normal repairs and maintenance, for the purpose for which it was intended at the inception of the lease.

Equity Kicker A share of ownership interest in a project or a potential ownership interest in a project in consideration for making a loan or lease. The kicker may take the form of stock, stock warrants, purchase options, or a percentage of profits.

Equity Participant An equity participant is the same as an owner participant, a trustor owner, or a grantor owner.

Equity Warrants Equity warrants may be included with either leases, bonds, or equity issues. An equity warrant gives the holder the right to buy shares in the company at a fixed price at some time in the future. The lower the exercise price for the shares, the more valuable the warrants will be because the holder has a greater chance of exercising his rights profitably.

ERTA Economic Recovery Tax Act of 1981.

Estimated Residual Value of Leased Property The estimated fair value of the property at the end of the lease term.

Event of Default A circumstance defined as a default.

Evergreen Renewal A renewal of a true lease at the end of the base term and any fixed renewal terms based on an appraisal of the value and remaining life that is made shortly before the conclusion of the fixed term and renewals. The lessee can renew the lease for a term that is consistent with a remaining useful life at the end of the renewal term of at least 20 percent of the original useful life. Stated another way, the lease term can be renewed such that the sum of the base term and fixed-rate renewals do not exceed 80 percent of the reappraised useful life.

Excepted Liens Those liens that a lessee may suffer to exist on the leased property without being in default on its general obligation to keep the leased property free of liens. Typical excepted liens include the lien of the mortgage in favor of the indenture trustee, the rights of the owner participants under the owner trust agreement, and mechanics', materialmen's, and tax liens to the extent that amounts secured thereby are not yet due and payable or are being contested in good faith.

Excepted Payments This refers to payments required to be made by the lessee under indemnity clauses in favor of the equity participants or the owner trustee that are not subject to any lien in favor of the indenture trustee or the loan participants. The scope of "expected payments" is customarily a matter for negotiations between equity participants and loan participants.

Extended Term Agreement An agreement to renew a lease, commonly used to describe a guaranteed renewal of a lease by a third party.

Fair Market Purchase Option An option to purchase leased property at the end of a lease at its then fair market value.

Fair Market Rental Option An option to rent leased property at the end of a lease at its then fair market value.

Fair Market Rental Value The expected rental for equivalent property under similar terms and conditions.

Fair Market Sales Value The expected selling price in an arm's-length transaction between a willing buyer and a willing seller for equivalent property under similar terms and conditions.

FAS 13 Technically, *Statement of Financial Accounting Standards No. 13,* "Accounting for Leases" (Stamford, Conn.: Financial Accounting Standards Board, November 1976). Sets formal financial accounting standards on accounting for leases.

FASB Financial Accounting Standards Board.

FAS-Bee Another name for FASB and sometimes for *FAS 13.*

Fed Funds U.S. dollar funds that are transferred between banks through the Federal Reserve system and are credited for use immediately or on the same day.

Fed Wire A wire transmission service established by the Federal Reserve to facilitate the movement of funds of member bank accounts at the Fed.

Finance Lease A type of equipment lease originally authorized by TEFRA, commencing January 1, 1984, but postponed effective March 7, 1984, until January 1, 1988, by the Deficit Reduction Act of 1984. A finance lease is similar to a true lease except that a finance lease may contain a purchase option equal to 10 percent or more of the original cost of the equipment and/or the leased equipment may be limited-use property. Finance leases were repealed effective January 1, 1987, except for property eligible under certain transition rules.

Financing Agreement An agreement between the owner trustee, the lenders, the equity participants, and the lessee that spells out the obligations of the parties under a leveraged lease. Also called a participation agreement.

Financing Statement A notice of a security interest filed under the Uniform Commercial Code.

First-Loss Provision A guarantee that is measured by some percentage of the total liability. The guarantor suffers the first loss up to that amount.

First User The person that first places equipment into service. The tax benefits associated with original ownership of new equipment flow to the owner at the time of first use.

"Fish or Cut Bait" Provision Where a technical default occurs and is not remedied, this provision requires the indenture trustee (at the direction of the loan participant) to either accelerate the maturity of the indebtedness or resume transfers of funds not needed to service debt to the equity participants. Without such a provision the indenture trustee might be able to build up a collateral cushion of cash at the expense of the equity.

Floating Interest Rate An interest rate that is adjusted upwards or downwards during the term of a loan as short-term rates move upwards or downwards.

Floating Rental Rate Rental that is subject to upward or downward adjustments during the lease term. Floating rents are sometimes adjusted in proportion to prime interest rate or commercial paper rate changes during the term of the lease.

Foreign Leasing As used in international leasing, foreign leasing refers to a lease in which the lessor is an entity domestic to the lessee's country but is owned by an entity located outside the lessee's country.

Foreign Source Income Income earned overseas (net of depreciation and other expenses allocable to such income) as reported for U.S. federal income tax purposes.

Full-Payout Lease For *FAS 13*, a lease that qualifies as a direct financing lease or a sales-type lease. The definition of a full-payout lease depends on the context in which the term is used. Generally, the term *full-payout lease* refers to a lease in which the cash flows from firm rents and an estimated conservative residual value will return to the lessor an acceptable return on investment and the cost of the leased equipment after payment of the cost of financing and overhead.

Full-Service Lease This type of lease obligates the lessor to provide maintenance, repair, and insure the leased equipment. The lessor also pays the property taxes. Full-service leases are nearly always true leases in which the lessor owns the equipment at the end of the lease.

Future Value The value of an initial investment after a specified period of time at a certain rate of interest.

Gearing Debt-to-equity ratio.

Goodwill The intangible assets of a firm, calculated at the excess purchase price paid over book value.

Grandfather Lease A lease that qualifies for treatment under prior law under a transitional rule for a limited period of time. For example: ERTA safe-harbor leases of certain transit buses were grandfathered when safe-harbor leases were repealed by TEFRA. Equipment on firm order as of a certain date continued to be eligible for ITC under TRA.

Grantor Trust A trust used as the owner trust in a leveraged lease transaction, usually with only one equity participant. The Internal Revenue Code refers to such a trust as a grantor trust (see Section 671). A grantor trust with more than one equity participant is usually treated as a partnership.

Gross Lease Opposite of a net lease. The lessor pays property tax, insurance, and maintenance costs on a gross lease of equipment.

Guideline Lease A lease that meets the requirements of the Internal Revenue guidelines for a leveraged lease set forth in Revenue Ruling 75–21.

Haircut A discount.

Head Lease In a wrap lease, the head lease is the investor's lease that is wrapped around the user's lease.

Heat Supply Contract A nuclear fuel lease.

Hedge In foreign exchange, a method whereby currency exposure (the risk of possible loss due to currency fluctuations) is corrected or offset for a fixed period of time. This is accomplished by buying or selling foreign currency at a prearranged cost or earnings. Hedges are also used for commodities following similar procedures.

Hell-or-High-Water Clause A clause in a lease that reiterates the unconditional obligation of the lessee to pay rent for the entire term of the lease, regardless of any event affecting the equipment or any change in the circumstances of the lessee. The term is derived from provisions that are common in unconditional long-term leases of ships (bareboat charters).

High-Low Debt Leveraged debt with higher payments early in the lease.

High-Low Rent A lease in which rents are higher early in the term.

Hire-Purchase Agreement Same as Conditional Sale Lease.

Hurdle Rate Minimum acceptable rate of return on investment (cf. acceptance criterion, cost of capital).

Inception of a Lease The date of the lease agreement or of the lease commitment, if earlier. (For technical application, consult *FAS 13* and subsequent amendments.)

Incipient Default An event or condition that, after the giving of notice or the lapse of time or both, would become an event of default under a lease or a mortgage, entitling the lease to be terminated or the mortgage to be foreclosed.

Income Statement A report of a company's revenues, associated expenses, and resulting income for a period of time. The profit and loss statement.

Incremental Borrowing Rate The interest rate a person would expect to pay for an additional borrowing at interest rates prevailing at the time.

Indemnitee   A term used to describe the class of persons (typically the equity participants, the loan participants, the owner trustee, the indenture trustee, and the trust estate under the owner trust agreement) entitled to indemnification from the lessee under the general indemnity and general tax indemnity provisions of a leveraged lease financing.

Indemnity Agreement   When used in the context of a leveraged lease, an agreement whereby the owner participants and the lessee indemnify the trustees from liability as a result of ownership of the lease equipment.

Indemnity Clauses   Refers to the indemnity provisions in a lease. There are three standard indemnity sections in a leveraged lease financing: the general indemnity, the general tax indemnity, and the special tax indemnity. In leveraged leases, the tax indemnity clauses can be quite lengthy and are sometimes contained in a special supplement to the lease agreement or in a separate agreement.

Indenture   An agreement between the owner trustee and the indenture trustee whereby the owner trustee mortgages the equipment and assigns the lease and rental payments under the lease as security for amounts due the lenders. (Occasionally, particularly in maritime financings, the owner trustee will mortgage the leased property to the indenture trustee under a maritime mortgage instrument, separate from but subject to the indenture of trust.) Same as a mortgage or a security agreement.

Indenture Trust   Same as Indenture.

Indenture Trustee   Some leveraged leases have a separate indenture trustee in addition to an owner trustee. The indenture trustee holds the security interest in the leased equipment for the benefit of the lenders. In the event of default, the indenture trustee exercises the rights of the lenders. The indenture trustee is also responsible for receiving rent payments from the lessee and using such funds to pay the amounts due the lenders, with the balance being paid to the owner trustee. The indenture trustee sometimes verifies that correct filings are made to protect the security interest of the lenders, although the lessee is usually obligated to cause the delivery of annual opinions of counsel as to continued perfection. The bond register is maintained by the indenture trustee, which also acts as the transfer agent.

Independent Lessor   Any leasing company investing in leases; also, brokers without funds to invest in leases sometimes prefer to call themselves independent lessors rather than brokers.

Indexed Loan   A loan with debt service repayment tied to some standard calculated to protect the lender against inflation and/or currency exchange risk.

Inflation Premium   The increased return on a security required to compensate investors for expected inflation.

Initial Direct Costs   Costs incurred by a lessor directly associated with negotiating and completing a transaction. These include commissions, legal fees, costs of credit checkings, documentation costs, allocable sales expenses (including salaries other than commissions), and similar expenses, but specifically exclude supervisory, administrative, or other indirect or overhead expenses.

Initial Term The initial period of time, exclusive of renewals, for which equipment is leased.

Inspection The lessor usually has a right to inspect leased equipment on the lessee's premises to determine its condition and location.

Institutional Investors Investors such as banks, insurance companies, trusts, pension funds, foundations, and educational, charitable, and religious institutions.

Insured Value A schedule included in a lease that states the agreed value of equipment at various times during the term of the lease and establishes the liability of the lessee to the lessor in the event the leased equipment is lost or rendered unusable during the lease term due to a casualty loss. However, parties to a lease sometimes object to the term *insured value* since owner participants and lessees may, because of inflation, insure leased equipment for amounts substantially in excess of the stipulated loss value, at least toward the latter portion of the lease term. Accordingly, the use of the term *insured value* as a substitute for the term *stipulated loss value* contains an implication that may be contrary to the facts and should perhaps be avoided.

Interest Rate Implicit in a Lease The discount rate that, when applied to minimum lease payments, causes the aggregate present value at the beginning of the lease term to be equal to the fair market value of the leased property at the inception of the lease.

Interest Rate Implicit in a Lease (as used in *FAS 13*) The discount rate that, when applied to minimum lease payments (excluding executory costs paid by the lessor) and unguaranteed residual value, causes the aggregate present value at the beginning of the lease term to be equal to the fair market value of the leased property at the inception of the lease, minus any investment tax credit retained by the lessor and expected to be realized by it.

Interim Rate Daily rental accruing from delivery, acceptance, and/or funding until a later starting date for a basic lease term. Often used when a number of items of equipment to be leased under a single lease are delivered over a period of time.

Interim Term The term of a lease between the delivery of equipment and the start of the base term. This sometimes occurs where a number of deliveries of equipment at various times are to be later combined into one lease.

IRC Internal Revenue Code.

IRR Internal rate of return.

Irrevocable Letter of Credit A letter of credit that cannot be changed or canceled without the consent of all parties involved. Most letters of credit today are irrevocable; however, if not specifically labeled as such, letters of credit are understood to be revocable.

IRS Internal Revenue Service.

ITC Investment tax credit. The ITC is a credit against taxes due which at the time of publication of this book is equal to 10 percent for equipment with a recovery period of five years or more and 6 percent for equipment with a recovery period of three years. ITC was repealed effective December 31, 1985, unless subject to firm contract as of December 31, 1985, in which case a calendar year taxpayer can claim 100 percent of otherwise eligible ITC in 1986, 82.5 percent in 1987, and 65 percent in 1988 and subsequent years. A basis adjustment is required for the full amount of ITC. To be eligible under this transition rule, transition property must be placed in service by the following dates: Less than 5 years, 6-30-86; at least 5 but less than 10 years, by 12-31-86; at least 7 years but less than 20 years, by 12-31-88; and 20 years or more, by 12-31-90.

ITC Strip Lease A lease in which the lessor claims only the ITC and not ACRS deductions. The lessor "strips" the ITC from the transaction.

Kamikaze Bid A bid by a leasing company on a competitive transaction that is substantially below the market.

Keep-Well Letter A form of guarantee in which the guarantor agrees to keep the recipient of the guarantee well by injecting capital as needed. Sometimes called a maintenance of working capital guarantee. If properly worded, equivalent to a formal guarantee.

Lease Intended as Security A lease in which the lessee is considered the owner for both state law and federal income tax purposes. A conditional sale or installment purchase for income tax purposes.

Lease Line A lease line of credit similar to a bank line of credit that allows a lessee to add equipment to a lease, as needed, under the same basic terms and conditions, without negotiating a new lease.

Lease Multiple The number of lease payments due a lessor against which a lender is willing to lend. The lease multiple reflects the lender's assumptions as to interest rate, cash flow, yield, credit, and other variables.

Lease Rate Usually refers to a percentage determined by dividing the monthly (or quarterly, semiannual, etc.) lease rental by the cost of the equipment. (Not the same as Interest Rate Implicit in a Lease.)

Lease Term The fixed, noncancelable term of a lease. Includes, for accounting purposes, all periods covered by fixed-rate renewal options that for economic reasons appear likely to be exercised at the inception of the lease. Includes, for tax purposes, all periods covered by fixed-rate renewal options.

Lease Underwriting An agreement whereby a packager commits firmly to enter into a lease on certain terms and assumes the risk of arranging any financing.

Legal Lending Limit A limit under the United States National Banking Act which states the total obligations to any national banking association of any person, co-partnership, association, or corporation shall at no time exceed 10 percent of the amount of the capital stock of such association actually paid in and unimpaired and 10 percent of its unimpaired surplus fund. There are numerous qualifications and exceptions to the limit.

Legal Reserves The portion of its deposits which a bank is required by law to maintain in the form of cash or readily available balances to meet the demands of the depositors.

Lessee The user of the equipment being leased.

Lessee Group Includes the lessee, any shareholder of the lessee, or any related party under Section 318 of the IRC.

Lessee's Incremental Borrowing Rate The interest rate that the lessee at the inception of the lease would have incurred to borrow over a similar term the funds necessary to purchase the leased assets. In a leveraged lease the rate on the leveraged debt is normally used.

Lessor The owner of equipment that is being leased to a lessee or user. (Legal title under the Uniform Commercial Code may be in the lessee in finance leases and non–tax-oriented leases.)

Letter of Credit A guarantee limited as to time and amount.

Level Payments Equal payments over the term of the lease.

Leverage An amount borrowed. A lease is sometimes referred to as 100 percent leverage for the lessee. In a leveraged lease the debt portion of the funds used to purchase the asset represents leverage of the equity holder.

Leveraged Lease A true lease or a finance lease that meets the definitional criteria for a direct financing lease or a capital lease, plus all of the following characteristics: (a) at least three parties are involved: a lessee, a lessor, and a long-term lender; (b) the financing provided by the lender is substantial to the transaction and without recourse to the lessor; and (c) the lessor's net investment typically declines during the early years of the lease and rises during the later years of the lease if a residual value is contemplated.

Liability An obligation to pay an amount or perform a service.

LIBOR The London interbank offered rate of interest.

Lien A security interest on property to secure the repayment of debt and the performance of related obligations.

Limited Partnership A partnership consisting of one or more general partners, jointly and severally responsible as ordinary partners, by whom the business is conducted; and one or more limited partners contributing in cash payments a specific sum as capital and who are not liable for the debts of the partnership beyond the funds so contributed. Leases in which individuals act as lessors or investors are frequently structured as limited partnerships. In theory the investor's liability in a limited partnership is limited to his investment. However, the at-risk rules limit deductions to the sum at risk, thus necessitating recourse on the leveraged debt by individual investors. Limited partnership participation may be arranged as private placements or public offerings.

Limited-Use Property   Same as Special-Purpose Property.

Line of Credit   A fixed limit of credit that a bank or business will provide to a customer for a specified period of time. The amount of credit, as well as the conditions under which it is provided, is established by agreement.

Liquid Asset   Any asset that can be quickly converted to cash without significant loss of value.

Liquidation   The process of closing down a company, selling its assets, paying off its creditors, and distributing any remaining cash to owners.

Liquidity   A measure of how easily assets can be converted into cash.

Loan Certificates   Debt certificates, notes, or bonds issued by the owner trustee to lenders to evidence nonrecourse leveraged lease debt.

Loan Participant   A lender in a leveraged lease; a holder of debt in a leveraged lease evidenced by loan certificates, notes, or bonds issued by the owner trustee.

Lowball Bid   A bid to enter into or to arrange a lease transaction that is purposely priced below market or with terms not acceptable from a tax or accounting standpoint, with a view to renegotiation of a higher price and/or more expensive terms at a later date. Once the bid has been awarded, the other interested lessors may no longer be available. Typically, the lowball bidder raises the price or strengthens the terms when it is too late for the lessee to seek other leasing sources.

Low-High Debt   Leveraged debt with lower payments early in the lease.

Low-High Rent   A lease in which rental payments are lower early in the lease.

Maintenance Bond   A bond to provide funds for maintenance and repair of equipment or a facility. Maintenance bonds are used in connection with construction contracts to ensure that a contractor will repair mistakes and defects after completion of construction. The bond is used in lieu of the contractor leaving a portion of the contract price on deposit with the employer to ensure performance.

Majority in Interest of Participants   The term typically used in leveraged lease indentures to indicate those persons who are entitled to instruct the indenture trustee to take action under the indenture. Prior to the occurrence of an event of default (or sometimes an incipient default), the indenture trustee may normally act only on instructions from a stated percentage (at least 51 percent and, not infrequently, 66⅔ percent or more) of both the equity participants *and* the loan participants (measured by percentage interest in the owner trust or by outstanding principal amount of the loan certificates, as the case may be). After the occurrence of an event of default (or an incipient default), the indenture trustee is normally entitled to act solely on the instructions of a specific percentage of the loan participants (except as to particular matters, such as insurance, in which the equity participants may have negotiated specific continuing rights).

Mandate   Authorization from a potential lessee or borrower to proceed with arranging a financing.

Manufacturer's Bill of Sale   The bill of sale in favor of the owner trustee from the manufacturer or supplier of the property to be leased, usually containing the manufacturer's warranty that the owner trustee has received good title to the equipment being purchased by it.

Marginal Cost of Capital   The incremental cost of financing above a previous level.

Market Value   The price at which an item can be sold.

Master Lease   A lease line of credit that allows a lessee to add equipment to a lease under the same basic terms and conditions without negotiating a new lease contract.

Master Limited Partnership   A publicly held fund or pool to invest in assets including leases, sometimes called "asset funds," "income funds," or "blind pools."

Mezzanine Financing   An unusually structured transaction, usually with an equity kicker offered in order to get better terms from investors. Typically the financing ranks between equity and senior debt in the event of liquidation.

Minimum Investment   For a lease to be a true lease under Rev. Proc. 75-21, the lessor must have a minimum at-risk investment of at least 20 percent of the cost of the leased equipment when the lease begins and ends and at all times during the lease terms.

Minimum Lease Payments for the Lessee   All payments that the lessee is obligated to make or can be required to make in connection with leased property, including payments for residual value guaranteed the lessor and for bargain renewal rents or purchase options.

Minimum Lease Payments for the Lessor   The payments considered minimum lease payments for the lessee plus any guarantee by a third party of the residual value or rental payments beyond the lease term.

MISF   See Multiple-Investment Sinking Fund Method.

Moody's   A credit rating agency.

More Likely than Not Opinion   More likely than not opinions by attorneys indicate a better than even chance that some event will occur. This term is generally used in connection with individual tax shelter schemes to avoid fraud or negligence charges against a promoter.

Mortgage   Same as Indenture.

Multicurrency Bonds   Bonds payable in more than one currency at the discretion of the investor.

Multinational Corporation   A firm with significant operations outside its national borders.

Multiple-Investment Sinking Fund Method   A popular method of leveraged lease analysis that breaks down the net cash flows into nonoverlapping investment and sinking fund phases.

Negative Pledge   Undertaking by a borrower not to offer improved security arrangements to other lenders of a similar status without offering the equivalent security to the instant lender.

Negotiable Instrument Any written evidence of a payment obligation which may be transferred by endorsement or by delivery, such as checks, bills of exchange, drafts, promissory notes, and some types of bonds or securities, and of which the transferee may become a holder in due course.

Net Lease In a net lease the rentals are payable net to the lessor. All costs in connection with the use of the equipment are to be paid by the lessee and are not a part of the rent. For example, property taxes, insurance, and maintenance are paid directly by the lessee. Most capital leases and direct financing leases are net leases.

Net-Net Lease Same as Net Lease.

Net-Net-Net Lease Same as Net Lease.

Net Worth The same as Shareholder's Equity.

NIC Lease A tax-oriented lease in which the leased equipment does not qualify for ITC. Hence, there is no ITC available. (Compare with PIC Lease and RIC Lease.)

Ninety-Day Window Lease See Window Lease.

Nominal Rate A stated rate that is usually subdivided for compounding purposes, resulting in a higher effective rate.

Nonpayout Lease A lease in which cash flows from rents and nominal residual value are insufficient to cover the cost of financing and administration of the lease. The lessor relies on a renewal or release of equipment to recover its investment and realize a profit.

Nonseverable Improvements An improvement to leased equipment by a lessee that does not qualify as severable. The circumstances under which a lessee can make a nonseverable improvement to leased property without generating taxable income to the lessor are fairly limited, although improvements amounting to less than 10 percent of the original cost of the leased equipment are permissible.

Normalization Method of Accrual The normalization method of accrual is the amount that if paid at the conclusion of each lease rental period would result in a stream of rent payments whose present value discounted at 110 percent of the applicable federal rate—under Section 1274(d)—would equal all payments due under the lease. The excess of rents allocated to periods in which they were not paid is taxed as imputed interest income.

Offering Circular Also called a prospectus. The offering circular contains a complete description of the terms of the lease or securities being offered, together with financial information relating to the borrower and any guarantor.

Off-Taker The user taking the product produced by a project. The term is often used in connection with a take-or-pay contract.

Open-End Lease A conditional sale lease in which the lessee guarantees that the lessor will realize a minimum value from the sale of the asset at the end of the lease. If the equipment is not sold for the agreed residual value, the lessee pays the difference to the lessor. If the equipment is sold for more than the agreed residual value, the lessor pays the excess to the lessee. The lease is called an open-end lease because the lessee does not know the extent of its liability to the lessor until the equipment has been sold at the end of the lease. The lessee's liability is open-ended. The term *open-end lease* is commonly used in automobile leasing. Individual liability under open-end leases is limited by consumer protection laws.

Operating Lease   The definition of this term depends on the context in which the term is used. For financial accounting purposes, under *FAS 13,* an operating lease is a lease that does not meet the criteria of a capital lease or a direct financing lease. The term is generally used to describe a short-term lease whereby a user can acquire the use of an asset for a fraction of the asset's useful life. It is also used to describe a lease in which the lessor provides services, such as maintenance, insurance, and the payment of personal property taxes. The term is derived from short-term leases of equipment in which the lessor provided an operator, such as leases of trucks and construction equipment.

Opportunity Cost   The rate of return on the best alternative investment that is not selected.

Optimized Debt   A variation from the traditional level payments of principal and interest on the debt in a leveraged base. Optimized debt is designed to optimize the lessee's lease rental rate. In a leveraged lease optimized debt payments typically equal rental payments during the early years of a lease.

Owner Participant   Owner participants are the beneficial owners, usually under an owner trust of equipment that is the subject of a lease in which legal title to the property is held by the owner trustee/equity trustee, which may issue trust certificates to the owner participants as evidence of their beneficial interests in the leased property.

Owner Trustee   Also sometimes called a grantor trustee. In a leveraged lease the primary function of the owner trustee is to hold title to the equipment for the benefit of the equity participants. The owner trustee issues trust certificates to the equity participants, maintains a register, and acts as transfer agent for such certificates. The owner trustee issues bonds to the lenders, receives distributions of rental payments from the indenture trustee, pays trustee fees due itself and the indenture trustee, and disburses amounts due the equity participants. The owner trustee makes appropriate filings to perfect and protect the interest of lenders in collateral. Compliance certificates and other information required from the lessee under the lease are received by the owner trustee and distributed by the owner trustee to the other parties. This definition contemplates that a separate indenture trustee will be named to perform duties for the leveraged debt holders. Some leveraged leases have one trustee performing both functions.

Packager   A name used to describe the leasing company, investment banker, or broker that arranges a leveraged lease.

Packer   Same as Packager.

Participation Agreement An agreement between the owner trustee, the lenders, the equity participants, the manufacturer, and the lessee that spells out the obligations of the parties under a leveraged lease. Also called a financing agreement.

Partnership A business entity by two or more persons (or corporations) and conducted for a profit.

Payback Period The amount of time required to recover the initial investment in a project.

Payment Stream In a lease, the rentals that are due.

Payout Lease A lease in which the lessor expects to recover its investment, plus interest, over the life of the lease from any or all of the following: rentals, cash flow from tax benefits, and a modest expectation of residual value.

Performance Bond A bond supplied by one party to protect another against loss in the event of default of an existing contract.

Permitted Liens Same as Excepted Liens.

Permitted Transferee Those institutional investors and other persons to which an equity participant is permitted to transfer its interest in the trust estate without the consent of, for example, other equity participants or loan participants.

Perpetuity An annuity forever; periodic equal payments or receipts on a continuous basis.

PIC Lease A tax-oriented lease in which the lessor passes the ITC through the lease to the lessee. (Compare with RIC Lease and NIC Lease.)

Present Value The current equivalent value of cash available immediately for a future payment or for a stream of payments that are to be received at various times in the future. The present value will vary with the discount (interest) factor applied to the future payments.

Principal A sum on which interest accrues; capital, as distinguished from income. Par value or face amount of a loan, exclusive of any premium or interest. The basis for interest computations.

Private Debt Placement A placement of debt securities to a limited number of sophisticated investors in the United States, as opposed to a public placement. SEC registration requirements are much easier in a private placement of debt.

Private Ruling A ruling by the IRS requested by parties to a lease transaction that is applicable to the assumed facts stated in the opinion.

Profit Motive The lessor in a true lease or a finance lease must be able to show that the transaction has been entered into for profit apart from the transaction's tax benefits (that is, without consideration of the tax deductions, allowances, tax credits, and other tax attributes arising from the transaction).

Prospectus A document giving a description of a loan offering or securities issue, including a complete statement of the terms of the issue and a description of the issuer as well as its historical and latest financial statements.

Public Utility Property As defined in the Internal Revenue Code, public utility property includes property used predominantly in the trade or business of furnishing or selling (a) electrical energy, water, or sewage disposal businesses, (b) gas or steam through a local distribution system, (c) telephone services or other communications services if furnished or sold by Comsat, or (d) transportation of gas or steam by pipeline if the rates for such furnishing or sale have been established or approved by a state (or political subdivisions thereof), by an agency or instrumentality of the United States, or by a public service or public utility commission.

Purchase Agreement Assignment Where the lessee has entered into a contract to purchase equipment to be leased prior to the arranging of the financing, some or all of the lessee's rights under the purchase agreement (always including the right to take title to the equipment) are normally assigned by the lessee to the owner trustee pursuant to a purchase agreement assignment prior to the delivery of the property by the manufacturer. There is usually annexed to the assignment a consent of the manufacturer or supplier that confirms the availability to the owner trustee of the rights of the purchaser under the contract. In the case of a facility, also sometimes called a construction contract assignment.

Purchase Option An option to purchase leased property at the end of the lease term. In order to protect the tax characteristics of a true lease, a lessee's option to purchase leased equipment from a lessor that is granted at the beginning of a lease cannot be at a price less than its fair market value at the time the right is exercisable.

Put An option that one person has to sell certain property to another person at a set price at some established point in time in the future. In lease agreements, a lessor sometimes negotiates an option to sell leased equipment to the lessee or to some third party at an established price at the end of the lease term. The IRS guidelines set forth in Revenue Procedure 75–21 provide that the lessor may not have a put to any party. A lessor may also negotiate a put to a third party as a hedge against future loss on the sale of the asset, although such an arrangement is contrary to IRS advance ruling guidelines.

Rating Agencies Agencies that study the financial status of a firm and then assign a quality rating to securities issued by that firm. Standard & Poor's and Moody's are leading rating agencies.

Recovery Property Property eligible for ACRS.

Refinancing Repaying existing debt and entering into a new loan, typically to meet some corporate objective such as the lengthening of maturity or lowering the interest rate.

Regulation Y A Federal Reserve Board regulation that sets forth business activities in which bank holding companies and their subsidiaries are permitted to engage. Permitted leasing activities are described in some detail in Regulation Y.

Regulation Y Insurance Residual value insurance to permit a bank holding company subsidiary engaged in leasing to comply with Federal Reserve requirements for residual exposure on a lease.

Related Parties In leasing transactions an affiliate, a parent and its subsidiaries, or an investor and its investees, provided the parent, owner, or investor has the ability to exercise significant influence over the financial and operating policies of the related party.

Renewal Option An option to renew a lease at the end of the initial lease term. In order to protect the tax characteristics of a true lease, a lessor's option to renew a lease of equipment from a lessor that is granted at the beginning of a lease must be at a price equal to the equipment's fair market value at the time the right is exercised. Other renewal option periods are counted as part of the lease term for guideline purposes.

Rent Holiday A period of time in which the lessee is not required to pay rents. Typically, the rents or interest on the cost of the equipment are capitalized into the remaining lease payments.

Required Rate of Return The minimum future receipts an investor will accept in choosing an investment.

Residual or Residual Value The value of leased equipment at the conclusion of the lease term. To qualify the lease as a true lease for tax purposes under Rev. Proc. 75-21, the estimated residual value of the leased equipment at the end of the lease term must equal at least 20 percent of the original cost of the equipment, without regard to inflation. (However, the lessor is not required to book any residual for financial accounting purposes.)

Residual Insurance An insurance policy stipulating that leased equipment will have a certain residual value at the end of a lease. In the event that the equipment does not have such a residual value, the insurance company agrees to provide part or all of the difference between the amount specified in the residual value insurance policy and the actual value of the equipment. Residual value insurance is also used to allow bank subsidiaries to comply with Federal Reserve regulations or Comptroller's Ruling 7.3400, as well as for other purposes.

Residual Sharing An agreement between the lessor and another party (such as a broker) providing for a division of the residual value between them. Care must be taken in any such agreement lest the tax benefits be lost and the lessee become liable under the tax indemnity clause.

Return on Investment A formula to compute the return on actual or assumed investment after taking expenses and recovery of investment into account.

Revenues Sales or gross receipts from operations.

Revenue Procedures In leasing this term is commonly used to refer to IRS Revenue Procedures 75-21, 75-28, and 76-30, that set forth requirements for obtaining a favorable federal income tax ruling that a particular leveraged lease transaction is a true lease. Generally the IRS issues Revenue Procedures on various subjects as a form of regulations.

Revenue Ruling A written opinion of the Internal Revenue Service requested by parties to a lease or business transaction that is applicable to assumed facts stated in the opinion. Published IRS rulings have general applicability.

RIC Lease A tax-oriented lease in which the lessor retains the ITC. (Compare with PIC Lease and NIC Lease.)

Risk Instability; uncertainty about the future; more specifically, the degree of uncertainty involved with a credit, a project or investment.

Risk Adjusted Discount Rate A discount rate which includes a premium for risk.

Risk Premium An additional required rate of return that must be paid to investors who invest in risky investments.

ROE Return on equity. Not to be confused with lease yield.

Safe-Harbor Lease A type of lease authorized in 1981, 1982, and 1983. Safe-harbor leases were authorized by ERTA and modified and repealed by TEFRA. Except for leases of mass-commuting vehicles, including transit buses, safe-harbor leasing was repealed December 31, 1983. Safe-harbor leases were leases of new Section 38 property by corporate lessors in which the lessees and lessors agreed to be covered by the safe-harbor rules. A safe-harbor lease did not have to be a true lease, but the lessor under a qualified safe-harbor lease could, nevertheless, claim the ITC and tax depreciation. A safe-harbor lease could be either a direct lease or a leveraged lease of new personal property.

Sale-and-Leaseback A transaction that involves the sale of equipment by the owner and a lease of the same equipment back to the original owner, that continues to use the equipment.

Sales-Type Lease The same as a direct financing lease except that manufacturer or dealer profits are involved. A lease that meets the definitional criteria of a capital lease under *FAS 13,* plus two additional criteria: (a) collectibility of the minimum lease payment is reasonably predictable and (b) no important uncertainties surround the amount of unreimbursable costs yet to be incurred by the lessor under the lease.

Samurai Lease A yen-denominated lease to finance equipment located outside Japan. The original Samurai lease was funded from domestic Japanese yen with the rate subsidized by MITI.

Sandwich A lease with an additional party between the lessee and the lessor (a lease and sublease, for example).

Sawtooth Rents Rents that vary throughout the term of the lease, usually to match debt payments and tax payments in a leveraged lease so as to lessen the need for a sinking fund.

Schedule A listing that describes in detail the equipment that is to become subject to a lease. The schedule may reflect the lease term, the commencement date, and the location of the equipment and be incorporated into the basic lease agreement by reference.

Scheduling Date The commencement date of the base lease term.

Secondary Lease   Another name for a lease that is to commence upon the conclusion of an initial lease.

Section 38 Property   Refers to property described in Section 38 of the Internal Revenue Code and generally may be defined as tangible personal property used in a trade or business and located in the United States, with certain limited exceptions in the case of aircraft, ships, and offshore rigs. For property to be eligible for ITC (where otherwise available) the property generally must be new Section 38 property.

Section 467 Rental Agreement   A lessor or lessee that is party to a Section 467 rental agreement must report rental income or deductions using the accrual method of accounting, regardless of what method of accounting is used for other tax purposes. A Section 467 rental agreement includes a lease of equipment in which (*a*) some amount allocable to the use of property during a year is to be paid after the close of the calendar year in which such use occurs or (*b*) there are increases in the rental payments under the agreement. In other words, where rentals increase, the lessor must report rental income and deductions using an accrual method of accounting.

So long as no tax avoidance motive is deemed to exist, a "modified accrual" method is used to reallocate rents under a Section 467 agreement. Under this method, the amount of rent accruing during any taxable year is determined by (*a*) allocating rents in accordance with the lease agreement and (*b*) taking into account on a present value basis any rent to be paid after the close of the taxable year.

A Section 467 rental agreement can also be a disqualified leaseback or a disqualified long-term agreement in which the principal purpose of the increasing rents is the avoidance of tax.

Secured Creditor   A creditor whose obligation is backed by the pledge of some asset. In liquidation, the secured creditor receives the cash from the sale of the pledged asset to the extent of his or her loan.

Security Agreement   An agreement between the owner trustee and the indenture trustee in which the owner trustee assigns title to the equipment, the lease, and rental payments under the lease as security for amounts due the lenders. Same as Indenture or Mortgage.

Senior Debt   Senior debt is generally defined as all debt, both short and long term, which is not subordinated to any other.

Sensitivity Analysis   Analysis of impact on a lease, a plan, or forecast of a change in one of the input variables.

Separate Phases Method   Same as Multiple-Investment Sinking Fund Method.

Service Lease   A short-term lease accompanied by service such as maintenance and insurance.

Severable Improvement   Improvements to leased equipment owned by a member of the lessee group that are readily removable without causing damage to the leased equipment.

Shareholder's Equity The book value of the net assets (total assets − total liabilities) is called shareholders' equity or net worth. Accounts that comprise net worth are preferred stock, common stock, paid-in capital, and earned surplus (retained earnings). Deferred accounts and reserve accounts such as reserve for pensions, while generally not thought of as true liabilities, are not considered equity.

Shirt-Tail Lease Another name for a secondary lease or a consecutive lease that is to commence upon the conclusion of an initial lease.

Shirt-Tail Period In leveraged leases of facilities, the 20 percent remaining useful life at the end of the base lease during which the lessor needs support rights to prevent the leased equipment from being deemed limited-use property.

Shogan Lease A cross-boundary loan (characterized as a lease or installment sale) offered by Japanese leasing companies, that can be utilized as leveraged debt in a leveraged lease or simply utilized as a private placement.

Short-Term Debt An obligation maturing in less than one year.

Short-Term Lease Generally refers to an operating lease.

Single-Investor Lease Same as Direct Lease or Direct Financing Lease.

Sinking Fund A reserve or a sinking fund established or set aside for the purpose of payment of a liability anticipated to become due at a later date.

Sinking Fund Rate The rate of interest allocated to a sinking fund set aside for the future payment of taxes (generally applicable only in leveraged leases).

SLV Stipulated Loss Value.

Sources and Uses Statement A document showing where a company got its cash and where it spent the cash over a specific period of time. It is constructed by segregating all changes in balance sheet accounts into those that provided cash and those that consumed cash.

Special-Purpose Property Property that is uniquely valuable to the lessee and is not valuable to anyone else except as scrap. A lease of special-purpose property will not qualify as a true lease because the lessee controls the residual value. Also referred to as limited-use property.

SSF Standard Sinking Fund Method of Analysis.

Staged Payments Refers to payments of equity in installments, which are typically annual payments timed to coincide with the receipt of tax benefits. The promoter or broker makes or arranges a loan for the equity investment at the outset of the lease. The loan is paid off in staged payments as tax benefits are realized.

Standard Sinking Fund Method A method of leveraged lease analysis that assumes that all negative cash flows after the initial investment will be paid out of a hypothetical sinking fund.

Standby Letter of Credit A letter of credit that provides for payment to the beneficiary when the beneficiary presents a certification that certain obligations have not been fulfilled.

Step Rentals   Rentals that change during the lease term, usually from lower amounts at the beginning of the lease to higher amounts during the later period of the lease. In order to avoid violation of the level payment provisions of the IRC, rentals under a true lease may not vary more than 10 percent during the lease term unless they are tied to an index or floating rate debt or unless the variations arise from some reason other than tax avoidance.

Stipulated Loss Value   A schedule included in a lease that states the agreed value of equipment at various times during the term of the lease and establishes the liability of the lessee to the lessor in the event the leased equipment is lost or rendered unusable during the lease term due to a casualty loss.

Story Credit   A credit that looks poor from the standpoint of its financial statements but that looks more favorable in light of the "story" about its prospects for the future.

Straight Debt   A standard bond issue or loan lacking any right to convert into the common shares of the issuer.

Straight-Line Depreciation   Depreciating an asset by equal dollar amounts each year over the life of the asset.

Strip Debt   Debt in connection with a leveraged lease, arranged in tiers with different rates, maturities, and amortization to improve the lessor's cash flow and reduce the lessee's cost.

Sublease   A transaction in which leased property is released by the original lessee to a third party, and the lease agreement between the two original parties remains in effect.

Subordinated Creditor   A creditor holding subordinated debt.

Subordinated Debt   All debt (both short and long term) which, by agreement, is subordinated to senior debt.

Subpart F Income   Foreign income earned by a foreign corporation which is subject to U.S. income tax on the income tax return of a U.S. stockholder owning more than 50 percent of such corporation, even though such income is not distributed or paid to shareholders by such foreign corporation.

Take-or-Pay Contract   A take-or-pay contract is a long-term contract to make periodic payments over the life of the contract in certain minimum amounts as payments for a service or a product. The payments are in an amount sufficient to service the debt or lease payments needed to finance the project which provides the services or the product and to pay operating expenses of the project. The obligation to make minimum payments is unconditional and must be paid whether or not the service or product is actually furnished or delivered.

Tax Benefit Transfer Lease   Authorized by ERTA and modified and repealed by TEFRA. A kind of leveraged safe-harbor lease in which the lessee provided leveraged debt. Debt payments on the leveraged debt were exactly equal to rental payments and were offset against each other so that the only payment changing hands was a payment by the lessor to the lessee for tax benefits. Tax benefit transfer leases continue to be available for mass transit vehicles such as buses, subway cars, and transit railcars.

Tax-Exempt Bonds Bonds issued by political subdivisions which bear interest exempt from U.S. income tax.

Tax Lease A lease in which the lessor claims the tax benefits associated with equipment ownership. Same as True Lease.

Tax Shelter For purposes of the registration requirements of Section 6111 of the IRC, a tax shelter is any investment (1) with respect to which any person could reasonably infer that the "tax shelter ratio" for any investor as of the close of any of the first five years ending after the date on which such investment is offered for sale may be greater than 2 to 1 *and* (2) that is (*a*) required to be registered under a federal or state law regulating securities, (*b*) sold pursuant to an exemption from registration requiring the filing of a notice with a federal or state agency regulating the offering or sale of securities, or (*c*) substantial in size (that is, the amount of equipment exceeds $250,000, and there are expected to be five or more investors).

Tax Title The title held by a corporate lessor under a finance lease or a safe-harbor lease. Tax title under such circumstances need not be identical to legal title and is determined without reference to state law requirements for legal title.

TBT Lease Same as a Tax Benefit Transfer Lease.

TEFRA Tax Equity and Fiscal Responsibility Act of 1982.

Term The period of time during which a lease is in effect.

Term Loan A business loan with an original or final maturity of more than one year, repayable according to a specified schedule.

Termination Date The last day of a lease term.

Termination Schedule See Termination Value.

Termination Value Leases sometimes contain provisions permitting a lessee to terminate the lease during the lease term in the event that the leased equipment becomes obsolete or surplus to the lessee's needs. In a true lease, the equipment must be sold or transferred to some third party unconnected in any way with the lessee. The liability of the lessee in the event of such termination is set forth in a termination schedule that places values on the equipment at various times during the lease term. The values specified are designed to protect the lessor from loss of investment. If the equipment is sold at a price lower than the amount set forth in the schedule, the lessee pays the difference. If it is sold at a price higher than that amount, the excess belongs to the lessor. The termination schedule is not the same as the casualty value schedule, the insured value schedule, or the stipulated loss value schedule.

Tolling Contract Another name for a take-or-pay contract.

Tombstone An announcement placed in a financial newspaper or journal that announces a lease financing or performance of some financial service.

TRA Tax Reform Act of 1986.

TRAC Lease A lease with a terminal rental adjustment clause. This term is used in automobile leases to describe an open-end lease. TRAC leases of over the road vehicles that otherwise meet true lease guidelines are entitled to be treated as true leases by lessors even though the residual risk is shifted to the lessee.

Transition Property Property eligible for tax benefits under pre-TRA law because it was contracted for or ordered prior to a qualifying date by a firm contract which has continued in effect.

Triple-Dip Lease A lease that uses significant tax or funding incentives from three sources, usually situated in at least two countries.

Triple-Net Lease Same as a Net Lease.

True Lease A transaction that qualifies as a lease under the Internal Revenue Code so that the lessee can claim rental payments as tax deductions and the lessor can claim the tax benefits associated with equipment ownership, such as ACRS deductions and the ITC.

Trust Certificate A document evidencing the beneficial ownership of a trust estate of an equity participant (or an owner participant, a trustor owner, or a grantor owner) in an owner trust.

Trust Supplement In a lease financing with multiple deliveries of equipment to be held as part of the trust estate under a single owner trust agreement, it is customary for the owner trustee to execute and deliver a trust supplement with respect to separate delivery of leased property, confirming that the owner trustee has acquired such property for the benefit of the equity participants and that such property is subjected to a security interest or a mortgage in favor of the indenture trustee or the loan participants.

Trustee A bank or trust company that holds title to or a security interest in leased property in trust for the benefit of the lessee, the lessor, and/or creditors of the lessor. A leveraged lease may have one trustee performing all of these functions or may divide them between an owner trustee and an indenture trustee.

Trustee Fees Fees due either the owner trustee or the indenture trustee.

Trustee Owners The trustors. The equity participants that are the beneficial owners under an owner trust. A trust owner is the same as an equity participant, an owner participant, or a grantor owner.

UCC The Uniform Commercial Code, which has been adopted by every state except Louisiana to govern commercial transactions.

UCC Financing Statement A document filed with the county (and sometimes the secretary of state) to provide public notice of a security interest in personal property.

Underwrite An arrangement under which a financial house agrees to buy a certain agreed amount of securities of a new issue on a given date and at a given price, thereby assuring the issuer the full proceeds of the financing.

Undivided Interest A property interest held by two or more parties whereby each shares, according to its respective interest, in profits, expenses, and enjoyment and whereby ownership of the respective interest of each may be transferred, but physical partition of the asset is prohibited.

Unguaranteed Residual Value The portion of residual value that is at risk for a lessor.

Unrestricted Subsidiary A defined term in a loan agreement. Typically a subsidiary of a debtor company that is free from loan covenant limitations on amounts of debt and lease liability. However, the parent debtor company cannot guarantee the debt obligations of the unrestricted subsidiary, and the total amount the parent can invest in such a subsidiary is limited by loan covenant.

Useful Life The period of time during which an asset will have economic value and be usable. The useful life of an asset is sometimes called the economic life of the asset. For a lease to qualify as a true lease, the leased property must have a remaining useful life of 20 percent of the original estimated useful life of the leased property at the end of the lease term and a useful life of at least one year.

Vendor Lease A lease offered by a manufacturer or dealer to its customers for financing its products. The manufacturer or dealer is the vendor.

Vendor Leasing The term used to describe vendor leases offered by a manufacturer, a dealer, or a third-party leasing company under a working relationship between the third-party leasing company and the manufacturer or dealer.

Wash Lease A TBT safe-harbor lease in which the rental payments by the lessee exactly equal the payments due on leveraged debt from the lessor and offset each other.

Wet Lease A lease in which the lessor pays property tax, insurance, and maintenance costs and may even provide persons to operate the leased equipment.

Window Lease Property will qualify as new equipment for a true lease provided the lease commences within three months of the date on which the property is originally placed in service. This is important in the case of property otherwise eligible for ITC. Property placed in a state of business of availability for a specified identified function is deemed to be placed in service. Equipment originally acquired by a lessee and later acquired by the lessor and leased back to the lessee within three months of being placed in service qualifies.

Wintergreen Renewal Similar to an evergreen renewal except that the renewal term is limited to fixed periods.

Wrap Lease A lease in which the lessor leases equipment at a rental rate that amortizes the investment over a longer period than the term of the initial lease. The lessor in a wrap lease is at risk to arrange one or more additional leases at the end of the initial term to recover its investment.

Wrapper A broker that arranges wrap leases.

Yield The interest rate earned by the lessor or equity participant in a lease, that is measured by the rate at which the excess cash flows (including tax benefits) permit recovery of investment. The rate at which the cash flows (including tax benefits) not needed for debt service or payment of taxes amortize the investment of the equity participants. Yield is expressed on a pre-tax basis but is computed on an after-tax basis. A lease yield is computed differently from ROE.

Appendix A

Historic Milestones in Equipment Leasing

A brief review of key milestones in the history of equipment leasing is helpful in gaining a perspective on equipment leasing as it is conducted today.

Year	Milestone
3000 B.C.	First record of equipment leasing along with other commercial transactions in the ancient Sumarian city of Ur.
1750 B.C.	Record of equipment leasing in the Code of Hammurabi.
200–600 B.C.	Records of leasing of personal property in Egypt.
200 B.C. et seq.	Records of ship charters (leases) from time to time when governments permitted ship operations as a private commercial activity.
250	The Roman Justinian Codes referred to leases of both equipment and real estate.
1200	The concept of nonrecourse debt in limited partnerships commenced in the city states of Italy.
1750 to 1850	Drayage leases of horses and wagons in the United States. Development of the laws relating to "bailments for hire."

Year	*Milestone*
1860s	Development of the "New York Plan" for financing railway rolling stock as a forerunner of equipment trust certificates drafted in the form of leases intended as security.
1870s	Development of the "Philadelphia Plan" for financing railway rolling stock as a more sophisticated forerunner of equipment trust certificates drafted in the form of leases intended as security.
1880s	Singer Sewing Machines sold to consumers for $5 down and $5 a month on an installment sale similar to a conditional sale.
1908	Short-term leases of railcars commenced by GATX Corporation.
1920s and 1930s	"Monopoly leases" of machinery by manufacturers to control use and resale.
1930s	Short-term leases of trucks and construction equipment with operators, called operating leases.
1941	Automobile finance leasing commenced in Chicago by Zolly Frank.
1941	Lend-Lease Act to supply war equipment to World War II allies.
1941–1945	Leases used as a method of writing off equipment over cost plus contracts during World War II. Leases of equipment from the government to defense contractors.
1945	Enactment of 150 percent declining-balance depreciation increased tax benefits of equipment ownership.
1945	U-Haul Corporation started by L. S. Shoen.
1947	*Crane* v. *Commissioner,* 331 U.S. 1, held that an owner could include in his tax basis amounts borrowed nonrecourse secured by the value of the property. This decision is the cornerstone of leveraged leasing.
1949	The Accounting Standards Board issued APB 38, calling for the disclosure of long-term leases in financial statements of lessees.
	Equitable Life Assurance Society entered into a leveraged conditional sale type of net lease to a railroad.

Year	*Milestone*
	Provisions of the Uniform Commercial Code relating to leasing were drafted.
1950 et seq.	Fleet leases of automobiles became popular.
1954	Enactment of the Internal Revenue Code of 1954 which provided additional methods of accelerated depreciation.
	U.S. Leasing Corporation was formed and commenced business.
1955	IRS Revenue Ruling 55-540 was issued which provided rules to differentiate a lease from an installment sale.
1955 et seq.	The rapid growth of air transportation commenced and fostered rapid growth of the rent-a-car business. Hertz, Avis, and National Rent a Car consolidated and rapidly expanded.
1956	Boothe Leasing Corporation was formed. (Later acquired by the Greyhound Corporation in 1960.)
	Enactment of the National Banking Act permitting banks to engage in a broader range of businesses.
	The Bank Holding Company Act of 1956 was enacted.
1957	Chandler Leasing was formed. (Later acquired by Pepsi-Cola in 1968.)
1958	General Electric Credit Corporation and Commercial Credit Corporation commenced leasing activities.
1962	The American Association of Equipment Lessors was formed by 13 lessors in Chicago.
	The Revenue Act of 1962 liberalized depreciation guideline lives and authorized 7 percent ITC which substantially increased benefits of ownership.
	Accounting Principles Board Study No. 4 was issued recommending lessees capitalize leases on their balance sheets.
1963	The Comptroller of the Currency issued Interpretive Ruling 7.3400, which allowed banks to engage in equipment leasing. Leases were held to be equivalent to an extension of credit.

Year	*Milestone*
	Bank of America, CitiBank, as well as other banks, commenced leasing equipment.
1964	APB 5, with regard to reporting of leases in financial statements of lessees, was issued and required leases to be capitalized if the lease contained a bargain renewal option or bargain purchase option. Additional disclosures were suggested.
1966	APB 7 was issued providing lease accounting standards for lessors. The finance method and operating method of lease accounting were defined. Manufacturers' profit recognition was permitted on finance leases.
	ITC was repealed; tax leasing was curtailed.
1967	Seven percent ITC was again authorized by the Restoration Act of 1967. This was in response to a decline in capital spending after the repeal of ITC in 1966.
	Approximately 65 leasing companies of significant size were formed to engage in computer leasing.
1968	The Computer Lessors Association was formed.
1969	ITC was repealed by the Tax Reform Act of 1969, and leasing activities and capital spending were again curtailed.
1970	Congress amended the Bank Holding Company Act of 1956 to permit bank holding companies and their subsidiaries to engage in certain non-banking activities.
1970	ICC Ex Parte Order 252 was issued providing incentive per diem on boxcars and set the stage for railroad car leasing by short-line railroads.
1971	The Federal Reserve Board amended Regulation Y to permit bank holding companies to engage in personal property leasing.
	The Revenue Act of 1971 restored 7 percent ITC and shortened tax depreciation lives through the ADR class life system. This was in response to a decline in capital spending after ITC was repealed in 1969.
	The rules for individuals claiming ITC were tightened in the Revenue Act of 1971, so as to

Year	*Milestone*
	make it difficult for individuals to claim ITC when acting as lessors. This legislation made leasing an unattractive tax shelter for individuals until ERTA was passed in 1981.
1972	APB 27 was issued describing accounting for lease transactions by manufacturer or dealer lessors and clarified when manufacturer/dealer company could recognize profit on lease type sales.
	The SEC indicated in ASP 132 the investment community needed additional information regarding lessee commitments as encouragement to anticipated FASB statements on lessee accounting.
	The first of several commercially marketed leveraged lease yield analysis programs became available to lessees and lessors. The reduction in time required to analyze the cash flows of a lease permitted more detailed analysis and greater sophistication of lessors and lessees. Standardization of lease analysis facilitated communication.
	The U.S. Navy leased a fleet of oil tankers, thus enhancing the respectability of equipment leasing.
1973	APB 31 was issued requiring disclosure of minimum and contingent rental expense for the current year and for succeeding years.
1974	The SEC served notice on the accounting profession in ASP 47 and public statements that APB 31 was inadequate and required a disclosure of the present value of finance commitment and capitalized leases.
	The Federal Reserve Board issued specific rules under Regulation Y spelling out guidelines to be followed by bank holding companies or their nonbank subsidiaries in engaging in leasing personal property.
1975	ITC was increased from 7 to 10 percent by the Tax Revenue Act of 1975.
	IRS Revenue Procedure 75–21 was issued providing guidelines for obtaining tax rulings on

Year	*Milestone*
	leveraged lease transactions constituting true leases. Revenue Procedure 75–21 was further clarified by Revenue Procedure 75–28.
1975 et seq.	Several short-line railroads were organized to engage in short-term railcar leasing.
	Lloyd's Insurance began issuing "J" policies insuring the residual value of IBM 370 computer mainframes. This encouraged a new wave of leasing IBM 370 computers on operating leases by third-party leasing companies.
1976	The Federal Reserve Board authorized banks to assume residual value risk in excess of 20 percent on leases of automobiles.
	The Financial Accounting Standards Board issued *FAS 13* setting forth accounting standards for lessees and lessors. Among other things, *FAS 13* provided stricter classification of operating leases and financing leases, rules for recognition of profit on deferred sales-type leases, and separate accounting rules for direct and leveraged leases.
	Revenue Procedure 76–30 was issued restricting leases of special-use property.
	The Internal Revenue Code was amended by the Tax Reform Act of 1976 to make certain "at-risk" rules applicable to equipment leasing by individuals.
1977	The M&M Leasing Company Case, 563 Fed. 1377 (9th Circuit, 1977) certiorari denied 98 S. Ct. 3069 (1978), was decided which affirmed the general authority of national banks to engage in equipment leasing essentially equivalent to an extension of credit.
1979	IRS Revenue Ruling 79–48 was issued restricting lessee investments for modifications or additions to leased equipment.
	The Comptroller of the Currency issued detailed guidelines to be followed by national banks or their subsidiaries in leasing personal property. These regulations were nearly identical to Regulation Y. 12 CFR 7.3400.

Year	*Milestone*
	The Association of Equipment Lessors transferred its headquarters to Washington, D.C., thus improving its lobbying capability and national presence.
1980	The ITEL bankruptcy arose out of business decisions mostly related to leasing activities.
	It became apparent that IBM 370 computers would have little residual value. Lloyd's faced huge losses on their "J" policies. Third-party leasing companies speculating on computer residuals began incurring large write-offs.
1981	The Economic Recovery Tax Act of 1981 (ERTA) was passed creating a new type of lease called a safe harbor lease. Such leases lacked economic substance and were, in effect, sales of tax shelters. The passage of ERTA was followed by an orgy of sales of tax shelters.
	ERTA also established ACRS tax depreciation resulting in increased depreciation deductions in most instances.
	ERTA vested 10 percent ITC in five years and 6 percent ITC in three years, at the rate of 2 percent per year.
	Changes in depreciation laws made leasing of equipment more attractive to individuals than in the past and resulted in individual limited partnerships becoming an important factor in the market.
	Leases of undivided interests were permitted by an IRS tax ruling.
	The OPM (Other People's Money) scandal and bankruptcy.
1980–82	A business economic recession resulted in severe credit problems for many lessors. These included: the oil patch financial reverses, the changes in per diem allowances for boxcars, the oversupply of boxcars, the financial reverses of short-line railroads, airline deregulation, and the numerous truck company bankruptcies resulting from deregulation.
1982	Enactment of TEFRA, the Tax Equity and Fiscal Responsibility Act of 1982, which repealed

Year	*Milestone*
	safe harbor leasing and authorized a new type of tax-oriented leases called "finance leases" commencing January 1, 1984. This was in response to what Congress described as the public perception that TBT leases resulted in unfair benefits to TBT lessors and lessees. TEFRA permitted trac lease structures for vehicles (leases with terminal rental adjustment clauses) subject to Internal Revenue regulations.
1982–1983	Development of wrap lease structures, particularly for financing computers.
1984	Enactment of the Deficit Reduction Act of 1984, postponing the effective date for "finance leases" until January 1, 1988, and restricting leases to tax-exempt and governmental entities and to foreign lessees not subject to U.S. income tax on 50 percent of their earnings.
	Equipment leasing as a tax shelter for individual lessors was made somewhat less attractive by several restrictions adopted by Congress and the Internal Revenue Service.
	Trac leases were authorized for vehicles.
	Committee language prohibited the Treasury Department from liberalizing the requirements for true leases.
1985	The Administration submitted several proposals for tax simplification to Congress. The House of Representatives passed a tax bill that reduced tax rates, eliminated ITC, and reduced depreciation deductions.
1986	Congress passed the Tax Reform Act of 1986 (TRA) that reduced corporate and individual tax rates, repealed ITC, changed depreciation deductions, and imposed a complex alternative minimum tax (AMT) on corporations. As a result of changes in tax laws affecting individuals, equipment leasing ceased to be an attractive tax shelter investment for individuals.
	A new Uniform Commercial Code section with regard to leases of personal property began to be adopted by many states.

Year	Milestone
1987	The corporate tax rate dropped to approximately 40 percent from 46 percent. Tax-oriented equipment leasing continued to be a popular and viable method of financing equipment as most companies which had leased prior to enactment of TRA continued to lease. Companies subject to AMT were unable to utilize tax depreciation deductions efficiently and were consequently motivated to lease equipment. As a result of the new AMT, some companies which had not leased extensively in the past found leasing attractive.

Year and *Milestone* are column headings.

1987 milestones continued:

Lessors subject to AMT were no longer able to offer competitive pricing for true leases.

Short term leases of commercial aircraft by highly leveraged leasing companies became the new vogue.

The National Bank Act was amended to permit subsidiaries of national banks to engage in less than full payout leases.

FAS No 91 amended FAS 13 and FAS 17 relating to accounting for initial direct costs and bad debts, to change the definition of initial direct costs and to require capitalization of such costs instead of recording as an immediate charge to unearned income, effective for fiscal years beginning after December 15, 1987.

Publicly held master limited partnerships formed as "asset funds" or "income funds" began acting as lessors.

1988   The Corporate tax rate was reduced to 34 percent.

The FASB required industrial companies to consolidate their leasing and financial subsidiaries for financial reporting, effective for years ended December 31, 1988, and thereafter.

Appendix B

The Time Value of Money: Future Value, Present Value, and Yield

---

Throughout this book we have used the concepts of present value and yield in analyzing the economics of leasing. This appendix explains these concepts. We also will illustrate how the effective interest cost of a conditional sale agreement or secured loan disguised as a lease (that is, a money-over-money lease that does not qualify as a true lease) can be determined.

THE TIME VALUE OF MONEY

The notion that money has a time value is one of the basic concepts in finance. Money has a time value because of the opportunity to invest money received at some earlier date at some interest rate. As a result money to be received in the future is less valuable than money that could be received at an earlier date.

The procedure for determining how much money must be received at an earlier date to be equivalent to money to be received in the future is known as *discounting*. Before explaining the process of discounting, the concept of compound interest will be explained.

Compound Interest

One of the wealthiest bankers, Baron Rothschild, was once asked whether he could name the Seven Wonders of the World. Although he answered that he could not, he did tell his questioner what he thought was the Eighth Wonder of the World. "The Eighth Wonder should be utilized by all of us to accomplish what we want," he stated. "It is compound interest."[1]

The bequest of 1,000 pounds (approximately $4,570) that Benjamin Franklin willed to Boston dramatically demonstrates the ability of money to multiply itself by means of compound interest. On June 1, 1790, the then town of Boston accepted a bequest of Dr. Franklin, who had died on April 17, 1790. The will stipulated that the sum be allowed to accumulate for 100 years. At the end of 100 years, part of the accumulated funds was to be spent for public works, with the balance reinvested for a second 100 years. By 1891, the end of the first 100 years, the fund had grown to $322,000. From the fund, the Franklin Institute of Boston was started. The balance was reinvested for a second 100 years. By 1970, the sum reinvested for the second 100 years had grown to $2,307,694. All of this on an investment of approximately $4,570!

The concept of compound interest is very simple. When a principal is invested, interest is earned on the principal in the first period. In subsequent periods, interest is earned not only on the original principal invested but also on the interest earned in previous periods. Thus, interest is being earned on an amount that is increasing over time.

For example, suppose that $1,000 is invested today at 8 percent *interest compounded annually*. The amount at the end of one year will be $1,080 ($1,000 times 1.08). The $80 represents the interest earned for one year. If the principal and interest are reinvested for another year, the amount at the end of the second year will be $1,166.40 ($1,080 times 1.08). The amount at the end of two years can be broken down as follows:

Original principal	$1,000.00
First year's interest	80.00
Second year's interest on original principal	80.00
Second year's interest on interest ($80 times 0.08)	6.40
	$1,166.40

Reinvestment of $1,166.40 for a third year would produce $1,259.71 ($1,166.40 times 1.08). The third year's interest of $93.31 ($1,166.40 times 0.08) is composed of $80 interest on the original principal of

---

[1] Loraine L. Blaire, *Your Financial Guide for Living* (Englewood Cliffs, N.J.: Prentice-Hall, 1963), p. 62.

$1,000 plus $13.31 interest on the $166.40 interest earned in the first two years.

It is the interest on interest that explains the snowballing effect of money to multiply itself with compound interest. To highlight this point, suppose the $1,000 is invested for 50 years at 8 percent interest compounded annually. The amount at the end of 49 years would be $43,427. Just how this amount is determined will be explained later. At the end of 50 years, the amount will be $46,901 ($43,427 times 1.08). The interest in the 50th year is $80 interest on the original principal plus $3,394 interest on the $42,427 interest earned in the first 49 years.

Had interest been based on simple interest, the principal invested would not have grown as much compared to compound interest. With simple interest, only interest on the original principal is realized. Interest is not earned on the interest earned in previous years. For example, if $1,000 is invested earning 8 percent simple interest for two years, the amount at the end of the second year will be $1,160. The amount is composed of the original principal of $1,000 plus two years of simple interest of $80 per year. Recall that if interest is compounded, the amount at the end of the second year is $1,166.40. The difference between simple interest and compound interest is only $6.40 in this example. However, as the time period over which the principal is invested increases, the difference between the amounts resulting from simple and compound interest is no longer trivial. For example, at the end of 50 years, simple interest will produce an amount equal to $5,000 ($1,000 plus 50 times $80), while the amount assuming compound interest will be $46,901.

To determine the future value of a principal invested today, the following formula is used:

$$FV = P(1 + r)^n$$

where

$$FV = \text{Future value}$$
$$P = \text{Principal invested}$$
$$r = \text{Interest rate}$$
$$n = \text{Number of periods}$$

The expression $(1 + r)^n$ means multiply $(1 + r)$ by itself n times. For example, if n is 4, then the expression $(1 + r)^4$ is

$$(1 + r) \text{ times } (1 + r) \text{ times } (1 + r) \text{ times } (1 + r)$$

Illustration 1

What is the future value of $1,000 invested today earning 8 percent compounded annually for three years?

In terms of the formula for future value, P is $1,000, n is 3, and r is 8 percent. The expression $(1 + 0.08)^3$ is (1.08) times (1.08) times (1.08). The value of the expression is therefore 1.2597.

Hence,

$$FV = \$1,000 \ (1.2597) = \$1,259.70$$

End of Illustration 1

It can become quite tedious to compute the value for the expression $(1 + r)^n$. Most preprogrammed calculators have an option that computes this value. Alternatively, there are tables available that give the value of $(1 + r)^n$. Exhibit 1 shows the future value of $1 for various interest rates and periods.

Illustration 2

What is the future value of $100 invested for 20 years if 10 percent interest compounded annually is earned?

Looking down the first column of Exhibit 1 to 20 periods and across to 10 percent interest, the future value of $1 or, equivalently, $(1 + 0.10)^{20}$, is 6.7275. Hence, the future value of $100 at the end of 20 years is

$$FV = \$100(6.7275)$$
$$= \$672.75$$

Compounding More than One Time per Year

Our illustrations have assumed that interest is compounded annually. When interest is compounded more than one time per year, the formula or Exhibit 1 can still be used. It is only necessary to adjust the interest rate and the number of compounding periods. The interest rate becomes the annual interest rate divided by the number of times interest is compounded per year. Multiplying the number of times interest is compounded per period by the number of years gives the number of periods that should be used. For example, suppose interest is assumed to be compounded quarterly for five years. The interest rate to be used in the formula or the exhibit is the annual rate divided by 4. The number of periods is five years times 4, or 20.

Illustration 3

Instead of assuming annual compounding in Illustration 1, suppose interest is compounded quarterly. The interest rate is 2 percent (8 percent divided by 4). The number of periods is 12 (3 times 4). From

EXHIBIT 1 Future Value of $1 at the End of n Periods

Interest rate

Period	1%	2%	3%	4%	5%	6%	7%	8%	9%	10%	11%	12%	13%	14%	15%
1	1.0100	1.0200	1.0300	1.0400	1.0500	1.0600	1.0700	1.0800	1.0900	1.1000	1.1100	1.1200	1.1300	1.1400	1.1500
2	1.0201	1.0404	1.0609	1.0816	1.1025	1.1236	1.1449	1.1664	1.1881	1.2100	1.2321	1.2544	1.2769	1.2996	1.3225
3	1.0303	1.0612	1.0927	1.1249	1.1576	1.1910	1.2250	1.2597	1.2950	1.3310	1.3676	1.4049	1.4429	1.4815	1.5209
4	1.0406	1.0824	1.1255	1.1699	1.2155	1.2625	1.3108	1.3605	1.4116	1.4641	1.5181	1.5735	1.6305	1.6890	1.7490
5	1.0510	1.1041	1.1593	1.2167	1.2763	1.3382	1.4026	1.4693	1.5386	1.6105	1.6851	1.7623	1.8424	1.9254	2.0114
6	1.0615	1.1262	1.1941	1.2653	1.3401	1.4185	1.5007	1.5869	1.6771	1.7716	1.8704	1.9738	2.0820	2.1950	2.3131
7	1.0721	1.1487	1.2299	1.3159	1.4071	1.5036	1.6058	1.7138	1.8280	1.9487	2.0762	2.2107	2.3526	2.5023	2.6600
8	1.0829	1.1717	1.2668	1.3686	1.4775	1.5938	1.7182	1.8509	1.9926	2.1436	2.3045	2.4760	2.6584	2.8526	3.0590
9	1.0937	1.1951	1.3048	1.4233	1.5513	1.6895	1.8385	1.9990	2.1719	2.3579	2.5580	2.7731	3.0040	3.2519	3.5179
10	1.1046	1.2190	1.3439	1.4802	1.6289	1.7908	1.9672	2.1589	2.3674	2.5937	2.8394	3.1058	3.3946	3.7072	4.0456
11	1.1157	1.2434	1.3842	1.5395	1.7103	1.8983	2.1049	2.3316	2.5804	2.8531	3.1518	3.4785	3.8359	4.2262	4.6524
12	1.1268	1.2682	1.4258	1.6010	1.7959	2.0122	2.2522	2.5182	2.8127	3.1384	3.4984	3.8960	4.3345	4.8179	5.3502
13	1.1381	1.2936	1.4685	1.6651	1.8856	2.1329	2.4098	2.7196	3.0658	3.4523	3.8833	4.3635	4.8980	5.4924	6.1528
14	1.1495	1.3195	1.5126	1.7317	1.9799	2.2609	2.5785	2.9372	3.3417	3.7975	4.3104	4.8871	5.5347	6.2613	7.0757
15	1.1610	1.3459	1.5580	1.8009	2.0789	2.3966	2.7590	3.1722	3.6425	4.1772	4.7846	5.4736	6.2543	7.1379	8.1371
16	1.1726	1.3728	1.6047	1.8730	2.1829	2.5404	2.9522	3.4259	3.9703	4.5950	5.3109	6.1304	7.0673	8.1372	9.3576
17	1.1843	1.4002	1.6528	1.9479	2.2920	2.6928	3.1588	3.7000	4.3276	5.0545	5.8951	6.8660	7.9861	9.2765	10.761
18	1.1961	1.4282	1.7024	2.0258	2.4066	2.8543	3.3799	3.9960	4.7171	5.5599	6.5435	7.6900	9.0243	10.575	12.375
19	1.2081	1.4568	1.7535	2.1068	2.5270	3.0256	3.6165	4.3157	5.1417	6.1159	7.2633	8.6128	10.197	12.055	14.231
20	1.2202	1.4859	1.8061	2.1911	2.6533	3.2071	3.8697	4.6610	5.6044	6.7275	8.0623	9.6463	11.523	13.743	16.366
21	1.2324	1.5157	1.8603	2.2788	2.7860	3.3996	4.1406	5.0038	6.1088	7.4002	8.9491	10.803	13.021	15.667	18.821
22	1.2447	1.5460	1.9161	2.3699	2.9253	3.6035	4.4304	5.4365	6.6586	8.1403	9.9335	12.100	14.714	17.861	21.644
23	1.2572	1.5769	1.9736	2.4647	3.0715	3.8197	4.7405	5.8715	7.2579	8.9543	11.026	13.552	16.627	20.361	24.891
24	1.2697	1.6084	2.0328	2.5633	3.2251	4.0489	5.0724	6.3412	7.9111	9.8497	12.239	15.178	18.788	23.212	28.625
25	1.2824	1.6406	2.0938	2.6658	3.3864	4.2919	5.4274	6.8485	8.6231	10.834	13.585	17.000	21.230	26.461	32.918
26	1.2953	1.6734	2.1566	2.7725	3.5557	4.5494	5.8074	7.3964	9.3992	11.918	15.080	19.040	23.990	30.166	37.856
27	1.3082	1.7069	2.2213	2.8834	3.7335	4.8223	6.2139	7.9881	10.245	13.110	16.739	21.324	27.109	34.389	43.535
28	1.3213	1.7410	2.2879	2.9987	3.9201	5.1117	6.6488	8.6271	11.167	14.421	18.580	23.883	30.633	39.204	50.065
29	1.3345	1.7758	2.3566	3.1187	4.1161	5.4184	7.1143	9.3173	12.172	15.863	20.624	26.749	34.616	44.693	57.575
30	1.3478	1.8114	2.4273	3.2434	4.3219	5.7435	7.6123	10.062	13.267	17.449	22.892	29.959	39.116	50.950	66.211

Exhibit 1, the future value of $1 assuming 2 percent interest compounded per period for 12 periods is 1.2682. Hence,

$$FV = \$1,000(1.2682)$$
$$= \$1,268.20$$

When interest was assumed to be compounded annually, the future value was found to be $1,259.70. Compounding more times per year results in more interest on interest and, therefore, a greater future value.

End of Illustration 3

Since compounding more times per year results in more interest on interest, the effective annual interest rate is greater. For example, if 8 percent interest is compounded quarterly, then the effective annual interest rate is 8.24 percent. This rate is found by computing $(1.02)^4$ and subtracting 1 or subtracting 1 from the future value of $1 using 2 percent interest and four periods in Exhibit 1. Similarly, 10 percent interest compounded semiannually, that is, twice per year, results in an effective annual interest rate of 10.25 percent.

Determining Present Value

The process of determining the amount that must be set aside today in order to have a specified future value is called *discounting*. The amount that must be set aside today in order to have a specified future value is c called the *present* or *discounted value*. The formula for the present value is

$$PV = \frac{FV}{(1 + r)^n} = FV \left[\frac{1}{(1 + r)^n} \right]$$

where

$$PV = \text{Present value}$$
$$FV = \text{Future value}$$
$$r = \text{Interest rate or discount rate}$$
$$n = \text{Number of periods}$$

Note that the formula for the present value is derived by solving the formula for the future value for the principal, P.

Illustration 4

A firm projects a cash need of $20,000 four years from now to replace a truck. The firm expects to earn 8 percent after taxes compounded annually on any sum invested today. How much must the firm set aside today if it wishes to have $20,000 four years from now?

Using the formula for present value, we have FV = $20,000, r = .08, and n = 4. The expression $(1 + 0.08)^4$ is found either by multiplying (1.08) times itself 4 times or by using Exhibit 1. In either case, $(1.08)^4$ is 1.3605. Hence, the present value is

$$PV = \frac{\$20,000}{1.3605}$$
$$= \$14,700 \text{ rounded to the nearest dollar}$$

By placing $14,700 into an investment that earns 8 percent compounded annually, the firm will have $20,000 at the end of four years.

End of Illustration 4

To find the value for the expression $(1 + r)^n$, Exhibit 1 can be used. This value is then divided into the future value to obtain the present value. Alternatively, present value tables are available. Exhibit 2 shows the present value of $1 which is found by dividing 1 by $(1 + r)^n$. The columns show the interest or discount rate. The rows show the number of periods. The present value of $1 obtained from Exhibit 2 is then *multiplied* by the future value to determine the present value.

Illustration 5

The present value of $20,000 four years from now assuming 8 percent interest compounded annually is

$$PV = \$20,000(PV \text{ of } \$1 \text{ from Exhibit 2})$$
$$= \$20,000(.7350)$$
$$= \$14,700$$

End of Illustration 5

You should note two facts about present value. Look again at Exhibit 2. First, select any interest rate and look down the column. Notice that the present value decreases. That is, the greater the number of periods over which interest will be earned, the less must be set aside today. Next, select any period and look across the row. As you look across, the interest rate increases and the present value decreases. The reason is that the higher the interest rate that can be earned on any amount invested today, the less must be set aside to obtain a specified future value.

The present value concept is extremely important because most business decisions involve costs and benefits that will be realized over long

EXHIBIT 2   Present Value of $1

Discount rate

Period	1%	2%	3%	4%	5%	6%	7%	8%	9%	10%	11%	12%	13%	14%	15%	16%	18%	20%
1	.9901	.9804	.9709	.9615	.9524	.9434	.9346	.9259	.9174	.9091	.9009	.8929	.8850	.8772	.8696	.8621	.8475	.8333
2	.9803	.9612	.9426	.9246	.9070	.8900	.8734	.8573	.8417	.8264	.8116	.7972	.7831	.7695	.7561	.7432	.7182	.6944
3	.9706	.9423	.9151	.8890	.8638	.8396	.8163	.7938	.7722	.7513	.7312	.7118	.6931	.6750	.6575	.6407	.6086	.5787
4	.9610	.9238	.8885	.8548	.8227	.7921	.7629	.7350	.7084	.6830	.6587	.6355	.6133	.5921	.5718	.5523	.5158	.4823
5	.9515	.9057	.8626	.8219	.7835	.7473	.7130	.6806	.6499	.6209	.5935	.5674	.5428	.5194	.4972	.4761	.4371	.4019
6	.9420	.8880	.8375	.7903	.7462	.7050	.6663	.6302	.5963	.5645	.5346	.5066	.4803	.4556	.4323	.4104	.3704	.3349
7	.9327	.8706	.8131	.7599	.7107	.6651	.6227	.5835	.5470	.5132	.4817	.4523	.4251	.3996	.3759	.3538	.3139	.2791
8	.9235	.8535	.7894	.7307	.6768	.6274	.5820	.5403	.5019	.4665	.4339	.4039	.3762	.3506	.3269	.3050	.2660	.2326
9	.9143	.8368	.7664	.7026	.6446	.5919	.5439	.5002	.4604	.4241	.3909	.3606	.3329	.3075	.2843	.2630	.2255	.1938
10	.9053	.8203	.7441	.6756	.6139	.5584	.5083	.4632	.4224	.3855	.3522	.3220	.2946	.2697	.2472	.2267	.1911	.1615
11	.8963	.8043	.7224	.6496	.5847	.5268	.4751	.4289	.3875	.3505	.3173	.2875	.2607	.2366	.2149	.1954	.1619	.1346
12	.8874	.7885	.7014	.6246	.5568	.4970	.4440	.3971	.3555	.3186	.2858	.2567	.2307	.2076	.1869	.1685	.1372	.1122
13	.8787	.7730	.6810	.6006	.5303	.4688	.4150	.3677	.3262	.2897	.2575	.2292	.2042	.1821	.1625	.1452	.1163	.0935
14	.8700	.7579	.6611	.5775	.5051	.4423	.3878	.3405	.2992	.2633	.2320	.2046	.1807	.1597	.1413	.1252	.0985	.0779
15	.8613	.7430	.6419	.5553	.4810	.4173	.3624	.3152	.2745	.2394	.2090	.1827	.1599	.1401	.1229	.1079	.0835	.0649
16	.8528	.7284	.6232	.5339	.4581	.3936	.3387	.2919	.2519	.2176	.1883	.1631	.1415	.1229	.1069	.0930	.0708	.0541
17	.8444	.7142	.6050	.5134	.4363	.3714	.3166	.2703	.2311	.1978	.1696	.1456	.1252	.1078	.0929	.0802	.0600	.0451
18	.8360	.7002	.5874	.4936	.4155	.3503	.2959	.2502	.2120	.1799	.1528	.1300	.1108	.0946	.0808	.0691	.0508	.0376
19	.8277	.6864	.5703	.4746	.3957	.3305	.2765	.2317	.1945	.1635	.1377	.1161	.0981	.0829	.0703	.0596	.0431	.0313
20	.8195	.6730	.5537	.4564	.3769	.3118	.2584	.2145	.1784	.1486	.1240	.1037	.0868	.0728	.0611	.0514	.0365	.0261
21	.8114	.6598	.5375	.4388	.3589	.2942	.2415	.1987	.1637	.1351	.1117	.0926	.0768	.0638	.0531	.0443	.0309	.0217
22	.8034	.6468	.5219	.4220	.3418	.2775	.2257	.1839	.1502	.1228	.1007	.0826	.0680	.0560	.0462	.0382	.0262	.0181
23	.7954	.6342	.5067	.4057	.3256	.2618	.2109	.1703	.1378	.1117	.0907	.0738	.0601	.0491	.0402	.0329	.0222	.0151
24	.7876	.6217	.4919	.3901	.3101	.2470	.1971	.1577	.1264	.1015	.0817	.0659	.0532	.0431	.0349	.0284	.0188	.0126
25	.7798	.6095	.4776	.3751	.2953	.2330	.1842	.1460	.1160	.0923	.0736	.0588	.0471	.0378	.0304	.0245	.0160	.0105
26	.7720	.5976	.4637	.3607	.2812	.2198	.1722	.1352	.1064	.0839	.0663	.0525	.0417	.0331	.0264	.0211	.0135	.0087
27	.7644	.5859	.4502	.3468	.2678	.2074	.1609	.1252	.0976	.0763	.0597	.0469	.0369	.0291	.0230	.0182	.0115	.0073
28	.7568	.5744	.4371	.3335	.2551	.1956	.1504	.1159	.0895	.0693	.0538	.0419	.0326	.0255	.0200	.0157	.0097	.0061
29	.7493	.5631	.4243	.3207	.2429	.1846	.1406	.1073	.0822	.0630	.0485	.0374	.0289	.0224	.0174	.0135	.0082	.0051
30	.7419	.5521	.4120	.3083	.2314	.1741	.1314	.0994	.0754	.0573	.0437	.0334	.0256	.0196	.0151	.0116	.0070	.0042

periods of time. In order to compare the future value of money from different periods of time, the present value must be determined.

So far, the present value of a single future value has been illustrated. The principle is the same, however, if there is a series of future values at different points in time. Each future value must be discounted to obtain its present value. Then the present values are added to obtain the present value for the series.

Illustration 6

A firm forecasts cash receipts from the sale of a product to be $10,000 at the end of each of the next four years. Assuming that the firm can earn 8 percent compounded annually on money invested today, what is the present value of $10,000 per year for the next four years starting one year from now?

The present value for each future value and the present value for the series are computed below.

End of year	Future value	Present value of $1 at 8%	Present value of future value
1	$10,000	0.9259	$ 9,259
2	10,000	0.8573	8,573
3	10,000	0.7938	7,938
4	10,000	0.7350	7,350
Total	$40,000	3.3120	$33,120

Thus, the present value of cash receipts of $10,000 per year for the next four years beginning one year from now is $33,120 assuming that 8 percent interest can be earned compounded annually.

Present Value of an Annuity

When the future value for each year of the series is the same, the series is referred to as an *annuity*. The future value series in Illustration 6 is an example of an annuity. For an annuity, it is not necessary to calculate the present value for each year. A shortcut can be employed. Tables are available that provide the present value of an annuity of $1 per period. An abridged table is shown as Exhibit 3. The present values shown in Exhibit 3 were constructed by summing the present values in Exhibit 2 over the corresponding number of years. For example, adding the present value of $1 for the first four years in Exhibit 2 assuming an interest rate of 8 percent gives 3.3120. This agrees with the present value of $1 for a four-year annuity in Exhibit 3 of 3.3121. The difference of 0.0001 is due to rounding.

EXHIBIT 3   Present Value of an Annuity of $1 per Period for *n* Periods

Discount rate

Number of Periods	1%	2%	3%	4%	5%	6%	7%	8%	9%	10%	11%	12%	13%	14%	15%
1	0.9901	0.9804	0.9709	0.9615	0.9524	0.9434	0.9346	0.9259	0.9174	0.9091	0.9009	0.8929	0.8850	0.8772	0.8696
2	1.9704	1.9416	1.9135	1.8861	1.8594	1.8334	1.8080	1.7833	1.7591	1.7355	1.7125	1.6901	1.6681	1.6467	1.6257
3	2.9410	2.8839	2.8286	2.7751	2.7232	2.6730	2.6243	2.5771	2.5313	2.4869	2.4437	2.4018	2.3612	2.3216	2.2832
4	3.9020	3.8077	3.7171	3.6299	3.5460	3.4651	3.3872	3.3121	3.2397	3.1699	3.1024	3.0373	2.9745	2.9137	2.8550
5	4.8534	4.7135	4.5797	4.4518	4.3295	4.2124	4.1002	3.9927	3.8897	3.7908	3.6959	3.6048	3.5172	3.4331	3.3522
6	5.7955	5.6014	5.4172	5.2421	5.0757	4.9173	4.7665	4.6229	4.4859	4.3553	4.2305	4.1114	3.9976	3.8887	3.7845
7	6.7282	6.4720	6.2303	6.0021	5.7864	5.5824	5.3893	5.2064	5.0330	4.8684	4.7122	4.5638	4.4226	4.2883	4.1604
8	7.6517	7.3255	7.0197	6.7327	6.4632	6.2098	5.9713	5.7466	5.5348	5.3349	5.1461	4.9676	4.7988	4.6389	4.4873
9	8.5660	8.1622	7.7861	7.4353	7.1078	6.8017	6.5152	6.2469	5.9952	5.7590	5.5371	5.3282	5.1317	4.9464	4.7716
10	9.4713	8.9826	8.5302	8.1109	7.7217	7.3601	7.0236	6.7101	6.4177	6.1446	5.8892	5.6502	5.4263	5.2161	5.0188
11	10.3676	9.7868	9.2526	8.7605	8.3064	7.8869	7.4987	7.1390	6.8052	6.4951	6.2065	5.9377	5.6870	5.4527	5.2337
12	11.2551	10.5753	9.9540	9.3851	8.8633	8.3838	7.9427	7.5361	7.1607	6.8137	6.4924	6.1944	5.9177	5.6603	5.4206
13	12.1337	11.3484	10.6350	9.9856	9.3936	8.8527	8.3577	7.9038	7.4869	7.1034	6.7499	6.4235	6.1218	5.8424	5.5831
14	13.0037	12.1062	11.2961	10.5631	9.8986	9.2950	8.7455	8.2442	7.7862	7.3667	6.9819	6.6282	6.3025	6.0021	5.7245
15	13.8651	12.8493	11.9379	11.1184	10.3797	9.7122	9.1079	8.5595	8.0607	7.6061	7.1909	6.8109	6.4624	6.1422	5.8474
16	14.7179	13.5777	12.5611	11.6523	10.8378	10.1059	9.4466	8.8514	8.3126	7.8237	7.3792	6.9740	6.6039	6.2651	5.9542
17	15.5623	14.2919	13.1661	12.1657	11.2741	10.4773	9.7632	9.1216	8.5436	8.0216	7.5488	7.1196	6.7291	6.3729	6.0472
18	16.3983	14.9920	13.7535	12.6593	11.6896	10.8276	10.0591	9.3719	8.7556	8.2014	7.7016	7.2497	6.8399	6.4674	6.1280
19	17.2260	15.6785	14.3238	13.1339	12.0853	11.1581	10.3356	9.6036	8.9501	8.3649	7.8393	7.3658	6.9380	6.5504	6.1982
20	18.0456	16.3514	14.8775	13.5903	12.4622	11.4699	10.5940	9.8181	9.1285	8.5136	7.9633	7.4694	7.0248	6.6231	6.2593
21	18.8570	17.0112	15.4150	14.0292	12.8212	11.7641	10.8355	10.0168	9.2922	8.6487	8.0751	7.5620	7.1016	6.6870	6.3125
22	19.6604	17.6580	15.9369	14.4511	13.1630	12.0416	11.0612	10.2007	9.4424	8.7715	8.1757	7.6446	7.1695	6.7429	6.3587
23	20.4558	18.2922	16.4436	14.8568	13.4886	12.3034	11.2722	10.3711	9.5802	8.8832	8.2664	7.7184	7.2297	6.7921	6.3988
24	21.2434	18.9139	16.9355	15.2470	13.7986	12.5504	11.4693	10.5288	9.7066	8.9847	8.3481	7.7843	7.2829	6.8351	6.4338
25	22.0232	19.5235	17.4131	15.6221	14.0939	12.7834	11.6536	10.6748	9.8226	9.0770	8.4218	7.8431	7.3300	6.8729	6.4642
26	22.7952	20.1210	17.8768	15.9828	14.3752	13.0032	11.8258	10.8100	9.9290	9.1609	8.4881	7.8957	7.3717	6.9061	6.4906
27	23.5596	20.7069	18.3270	16.3296	14.6430	13.2105	11.9867	10.9352	10.0266	9.2372	8.5478	7.9426	7.4086	6.9352	6.5135
28	24.3164	21.2813	18.7641	16.6631	14.8981	13.4062	12.1371	11.0511	10.1161	9.3066	8.6016	7.9844	7.4412	6.9607	6.5335
29	25.0658	21.8444	19.1885	16.9837	15.1411	13.5907	12.2777	11.1584	10.1983	9.3696	8.6501	8.0218	7.4701	6.9830	6.5509
30	25.8077	22.3965	19.6004	17.2920	15.3725	13.7648	12.4090	11.2578	10.2737	9.4269	8.6938	8.0552	7.4957	7.0027	6.5660

There is also a general formula that can be used to compute the present value of an annuity of $1. The formula is

$$\text{Present value of an annuity of \$1 at } r\% \text{ for } n \text{ periods} = \frac{1 - \dfrac{1}{(1 + r)^n}}{r}$$

To illustrate the use of this formula, let us compute the present value of an annuity of $1 for four years assuming 8 percent interest compounded annually. Substituting $r = 0.08$ and $n = 4$, we have

$$\frac{1 - \dfrac{1}{(1.08)^4}}{0.08} = \frac{1 - 0.7350298}{0.08} = 3.3121$$

Illustration 7

Compute the present value of the annuity in Illustration 6 using Exhibit 3.

The present value of $1 per year for the next four years beginning one year from now assuming 8 percent compounded annually is 3.3121. The present value of an annuity for $10,000 is

PV = $10,000 times ($PV$ of an annuity of $1 from Exhibit 3)
= $10,000 times 3.3121
= $33,121

The discrepancy of $1 between the present value found here and in Illustration 6 is due to rounding.

End of Illustration 7

The present value of an annuity shown in Exhibit 3 is computed assuming that the first amount will occur at the end of the first period. Such annuities are called *ordinary annuities*. In some cases, particularly lease agreements, the first amount is due immediately. In such cases, the annuity is called an *annuity due*. Although tables are available for an annuity due, we can still use Exhibit 3 by making a simple adjustment. All that need be done is reduce the number of periods by 1 and add $1 to the present value of an annuity of $1 shown in Exhibit 3. For example, the present value of an annuity due for four years assuming 8 percent interest compounded annually is $3.5771, found as follows:

Present value of $1 for an ordinary
annuity for three years   = $2.5771
Plus $1   = <u>1.0000</u>
Present value of $1 for an
annuity due for four years   = $3.5771

Note that the present value of an annuity due is greater than the present value of an ordinary annuity. The reason is that with an ordinary annuity there is one less year (or period) for interest to be earned since the first amount is due immediately.

Illustration 8

In Chapter 3 it was explained that if a lease is classified as a capital lease, the lease must be capitalized. The capitalized value required under *FAS 13* is the lower of (1) the present value of the minimum lease payments or (2) the fair value of the leased asset. The lease used to illustrate the accounting treatment of a capital lease in Chapter 3 was the January 1, 19X1, hypothetical lease between Best Dress Company and American Leasing Corporation. The minimum lease payments are six annual payments of $54,291, with the first payment due January 1, 19X1. Let's now compute the present value of the minimum lease payments. The discount rate to be used is 12 percent.

Since the first lease payment is due immediately and each payment is for the same amount, we have an annuity due. The present value of $1 for an annuity due for six years using a discount rate of 12 percent is $4.6048, as shown below:

Present value of $1 for an ordinary
annuity for five years   = $3.6048
Plus $1   = <u>1.0000</u>
Present value of $1 for an annuity
due for six years   = $4.6048

The present value of the minimum lease payments is then

PV = $54,291 times ($PV$ of an annuity due of $1)
= $54,291 times 4.6048
= $249,999.99, rounded to $250,000

Recall that the leased asset had a fair value of $250,000. In this case, the fair value of the leased asset and the present value of the minimum lease payments are equal.

Illustration 9

The capitalized value of a leased asset is sensitive to the selection of a discount rate. In Chapter 3, it was stated that if Best Dress Company discounted the minimum lease payments by 15 percent instead of 12 percent, the present value would be $236,285. Let's show how this was computed.

The present value of $1 for an annuity due for six years assuming a discount rate of 15 percent is $4.3522, as shown below:

Present value of $1 for an ordinary
    annuity for five years   = $3.3522
Plus $1   = 1.0000
Present value of $1 for an annuity
    due for six years   = $4.3522

The present value of the minimum lease payments if a 15 percent discount rate is used is then

PV = $54,291 times ($PV$ of an annuity due of $1)
    = $54,291 times 4.3522
    = $236,285.29, rounded to $236,285

Illustration 10

RJ Enterprises leased a machine from GS Leasing Company. The lease agreement called for 10 annual payments of $2,000. Moreover, the agreement specified that upon early termination of the lease agreement by the lessee, the lessee must pay the lessor the remaining lease payments discounted at 9 percent interest less the agreed-upon market value of the machine when returned to the lessor.

Suppose that the fifth lease payment is due today and that RJ Enterprises wishes to terminate the lease agreement. The lessor has informed RJ Enterprises that the current market value of the machine is $3,000. How much must RJ Enterprises remit to GS Leasing to terminate the lease agreement?

There are six lease payments, less the market value of $3,000, that RJ Enterprises must remit. Since the fifth payment would have been due today, we have an annuity due. The present value of $1 for an annuity due for six years assuming 9 percent interest is $4.8897, as shown below:

Present value of $1 for an ordinary
    annuity for five years   = $3.8897
Plus $1   = 1.0000
Present value of $1 for an annuity
    due for six years   = $4.8897

The present value of the six lease payments of $2,000 per year is then

$$PV = \$2,000 \text{ times } (PV \text{ of an annuity due of } \$1)$$
$$= \$2,000 \text{ times } 4.8897$$
$$= \$9,779.40$$

The amount remitted to GS Leasing would be $9,779.40 less $3,000, or $6,779.40.

Discounting when Payments Occur More Frequently than Annually

In our discussion of compound interest, it was explained that interest may be compounded several times during the year rather than once per year. To determine the future value, Exhibit 1 could be used by a simple adjustment of the interest rate and the number of periods. When discounting of future value is required, however, multiple compounding within a year requires a more complicated adjustment of the interest rate. The number of periods is still found by multiplying the number of years by the number of times compounding is assumed during the year. To find the interest rate that should be used in discounting when compounding is more than one time per year, the following formula should be used:

$$r = \sqrt[m]{1 + R} - 1$$

where

r = Interest rate to be used for discounting when compounding occurs more than once per year
R = Effective annual interest rate
m = Number of times compounding occurs per year

The symbol "$\sqrt[m]{}$" means that the mth root of $1 + R$ should be taken. By mth root we mean that when $1 + r$ is multiplied by itself m times, it will equal $1 + R$. For example, if the effective annual rate is 6 percent ($=R$) and interest is compounded quarterly ($m = 4$), what value for r will produce 1.06 ($= 1 + R$) when we multiply $1 + r$ times itself four times? If we try $r = 0.0147$, then

$$(1.0147)^4 = 1.0601091, \text{ or approximately } 1.06$$

Therefore, if $100 is to be received nine months from now, its present value if compounding is assumed quarterly and the effective annual rate is 6 percent is

$$\frac{\$100}{(1.0147)^3} = \$100\,(.9572) = \$95.72$$

Finding the root of a number is explained in elementary algebra books.

YIELD ON INVESTMENT

Generally, management discusses the profitability of an investment in terms of its yield. Alternative names for yield are internal rate of return, time-adjusted rate of return, or, simply, rate of return.

The lessee must understand the yield computation because *FAS 13* requires the selection of an appropriate discount rate to compute the present value of the minimum lease payments of a capital lease. The discount rate to be used is the lower of the interest rate implicit in the lease and the lessee's incremental borrowing rate. The former rate is nothing more than the yield that the lessee believes the lessor will realize from the lease arrangement.

The yield is defined as the discount rate that will equate the present value of the investment's cash flow to the initial investment.[2] The cash flow from an investment is defined in the next appendix.

Illustration 11

Bill Watson wishes to purchase land as an investment. The particular site he is considering costs $63,550. This includes the cost of the land and all legal expenses. After four years Mr. Watson feels that the land can be sold at a price to generate $100,000 after taxes and expenses. Should he acquire the land, what is his expected yield?

The yield is the discount rate that will equate the present value of $100,000 (the investment's cash flow) to $63,550 (the initial investment). From the present value analysis, we know the following:

$$PV = FV \text{ times } (PV \text{ of } \$1)$$

In the above relationship, we know PV is $63,550 and FV is $100,000. Therefore, ($PV$ of $1) must be .6355. What discount rate produces a present value of $0.6355 if $1 is to be received four years from now? To find out, look at Exhibit 2. Look at the row representing four years and continue across until you find a present value equal to .6355. This present value appears in the 12 percent column. Hence, 12 percent is the expected yield on the investment.

Illustration 12

Suppose Bill Watson were able to negotiate a price for the land such that after legal expenses his investment would be $55,230. What will his expected yield be if he believes he can obtain $100,000 after taxes

---

[2] Some pocket calculators have a preprogrammed package to provide the yield.

and expenses four years from now? Using the present value analysis, we have:

$$PV = FV \text{ times } (PV \text{ of } \$1)$$

We can express this as

$$(PV \text{ of } \$1) = PV \div FV$$

Substituting the known values into this last expression, we find

$$(PV \text{ of } \$1) = \$55,230 \div \$100,000$$
$$= .5523$$

From Exhibit 2, 16 percent produces a present value of .5523 for $1 to be received in four years. Hence, the expected yield is 16 percent.

End of Illustration 12

In Illustrations 11 and 12 the computation of the yield was quite simple. This is always the case when an investment generates a single cash flow in the future. The only complication that arises is the determination of the yield when the present value is not given exactly on the present value table. For example, suppose the initial investment had been $56,387. The present value of $1 we seek is then .56387. Yet this value is not shown in the row representing four years in Exhibit 2. An expanded table can then be consulted.

Illustration 13

Tucker Corporation was offered the opportunity to make an investment that would engender $100,000 each year for the next three years starting one year from now. The firm is required to invest $240,180. What would the yield be on this investment?

The present value relationship for an ordinary annuity is

$$PV = (\text{Annual annuity}) \text{ times } (PV \text{ of } \$1 \text{ of an ordinary annuity})$$

or

$$(PV \text{ of } \$1 \text{ of an ordinary annuity}) = PV \div (\text{Annual annuity})$$
$$(PV \text{ of } \$1 \text{ of an ordinary annuity}) = \$240,180 \div \$100,000$$
$$= 2.4018$$

Since the investment produces an annuity, Exhibit 3 is used. Looking across the row for three payments, the *PV* sought, 2.4018, is in the column under 12 percent. The yield on Tucker Corporation's investment therefore would be 12 percent since this discount rate would equate the present value of the annuity of $100,000 (cash flow from the investment) to the initial investment ($240,180).

Illustration 14

The interest rate implicit in the lease between Best Dress Company and American Leasing was stated to have been 12 percent. Let's see how the rate was determined.

Recall that the interest rate implicit in the lease is the yield that the lessee believes the lessor will earn. The lessor's cash flow is the minimum lease payments (excluding executory costs) plus the unguaranteed residual value accruing to the benefit of the lessor. The minimum lease payments were $54,291 per annum for six years. No residual value was assumed. The first lease payment was due immediately.

The yield can be found by employing the present value relationship for an annuity due.

$$PV = \text{(Annual annuity) times } (PV \text{ of \$1 of an annuity due)}$$

or

$$(PV \text{ of \$1 of an annuity due)} = PV \div \text{(Annual annuity)}$$

The annual annuity is $54,291, and the lessor's net investment was assumed to be $250,000. Substituting into the expression above, we have

$$(PV \text{ of \$1 of an annuity due)} = \$250,000 \div \$54,291$$
$$= 4.6048$$

Exhibit 3 provides the PV of an ordinary annuity; therefore, we must convert the PV of an annuity due so that Exhibit 3 can be used. To convert, 1 is subtracted from the present value of $1 of an annuity due and one less period is examined in Exhibit 3. To find the yield then, the PV of $1 of an ordinary annuity equal to 3.6048 for five years is sought on Exhibit 3. This value appears under the 12 percent column, indicating that this rate is the interest rate implicit in the lease.

End of Illustration 14

When an investment produces a series of cash flows that are not all equal, the computation of the yield requires a trial-and-error approach, as demonstrated in the next three illustrations.

Illustration 15

Green Corporation made an investment of $36,880 three years ago. The investment generated a cash flow of $10,000 at the end of one year, $15,000 at the end of two years, and $20,000 at the end of the third year. No additional cash flows will result from this investment. What yield did the Green Corporation realize on this investment?

To find the yield, the cash flow of $10,000, $15,000, and $20,000 must be discounted trying different discount rates until a present value for the cash flow of $36,880 is found. For example, if the cash flow is discounted at 7 percent, the present value of the cash flow is $38,773. Since 7 percent produces a present value for the cash flow that exceeds the investment of $36,880, the yield must be greater than 7 percent. Discount rates of 8, 9, and 10 percent were tried. The results along with the 7 percent discount rate are summarized below:

		Present value at			
Year	Cash flow	7 percent	8 percent	9 percent	10 percent
1	$10,000	$ 9,346	$ 9,259	$ 9,174	$ 9,091
2	15,000	13,101	12,860	12,266	12,396
3	20,000	16,326	15,876	15,444	15,026
PV of cash flow		$38,773	$37,995	$36,884	$36,513

The discount rate that produces a present value closest to the initial investment of $36,880 is 9 percent. The yield is therefore 9 percent.

Illustration 16

Lysle Construction Company's management intends to purchase a machine that would require an initial investment of $61,598. The machine is expected to last five years. The cash flow that management projects will be generated from the machine in the next five years is as follows: year 1, $22,000; year 2, $21,296; year 3, $20,667; year 4, $20,148; and year 5, $23,367. What is the expected yield from this investment?

Since uneven cash flows result from this investment, the yield must be determined by trial and error. The present value of the cash flow using various discount rates is presented below:

	Cash	Present value at				
Year	flow	14 percent	18 percent	20 percent	22 percent	23 percent
1	$22,000	$19,298	$18,645	$18,333	$18,033	$17,886
2	21,296	16,387	15,295	14,788	14,309	14,077
3	20,667	13,957	12,584	11,966	11,387	11,112
4	20,148	11,930	10,392	9,717	9,095	8,803
5	23,367	12,137	10,214	9,391	8,646	8,300
Total		$73,709	$67,130	$64,195	$61,470	$60,178

The discount rate that comes closest to producing a present value for the cash flow equal to the initial investment of $61,598 is 22 percent. The yield is therefore approximately 22 percent.

Illustration 17

In Chapter 3, it was stated that the interest rate implicit in a lease is sensitive to the estimate of the residual value. The interest rate implicit in the lease is the minimum lease payments (excluding executory costs) plus the unguaranteed residual accruing to the benefit of the lessor. When no residual value was assumed, the interest rate implicit in the lease between Best Dress Company and American Leasing was found to be 12 percent (see Illustration 14). For an assumed residual value of $43,723, however, it was stated that the interest rate implicit in the lease was 16 percent. The computations to verify that conclusion are presented below:

Present value of minimum lease payments at 16%
= $54,291 times (*PV* of $1 of an annuity due for six years)
= $54,291 times (3.2743 + 1.000)
= $232,056

plus

Present value of unguaranteed residual value at 16%
= $43,723 times (*PV* of $1 six years hence)
= 43,723 times (.4104)
= $17,944

Total: $232,056 + $17,944 = $250,000

Since the sum of the minimum lease payments and unguaranteed residual value accruing to the benefit of the lessor when discounted at 16 percent produces the fair value of the leased asset ($250,000), 16 percent is the interest rate implicit in the lease.

EFFECTIVE INTEREST COST OF A LOAN

For consumer loans federal law requires that the lender disclose the effective interest cost of the loan. The disclosure is not required for business loans. The purpose of this section is to demonstrate how the borrower can compute the effective interest cost of a loan.

The effective interest cost of a loan is the discount rate that equates the present value of the repayment schedule to the initial proceeds received. The procedure is the same as in the computation of the yield on an investment. The procedure is demonstrated in the following two illustrations.

Illustration 18

Very Best Hats Company obtained a three-year loan for $10,000 from Fair Deal Loan Company. The loan arrangement called for simple annual interest of 8 percent, or $800 per year. The total interest for the three years is $2,400 and is called *add-on interest*. Repayment of principal and interest is made with equal annual payments starting one year from now. What is the effective interest cost of the loan arrangement?

Very Best Hats Company receives $10,000 and pays three annual installments of $4,133.33 ($10,000 plus $2,400 divided by 3). The effective interest cost is the discount rate that equates the present value of the three annual payments of $4,133.33 to the initial proceeds received of $10,000. The required discount rate is determined as shown below:

$$(PV \text{ of } \$1 \text{ of an ordinary annuity}) = PV \div (\text{Annual annuity})$$
$$= \$10,000 \div \$4,133.33$$
$$= 2.4194$$

From Exhibit 3, the *PV* of $1 of an ordinary annuity for three years using 11 percent is $2.4437, while for 12 percent it is $2.4018. The effective interest cost to Very Best Hats Company from the loan arrangement, therefore, is between 11 percent and 12 percent. In general, with add-on interest the more frequent the payments, the greater is the difference between the simple annual interest and the effective interest cost.

Illustration 19

Very Best Hats Company had the opportunity to obtain a three-year loan from Friendly Loan Company. The loan would have been for $10,000 with simple interest of 7 ½ percent. The total interest of $2,250, however, would have been taken out in advance by the lender. The interest of $2,250 is called *discount interest*. Very Best Hats would have therefore received $7,750 and repaid $10,000 in three equal installments of $3,333.33. What is the effective interest cost of this loan arrangement?

The same procedure is followed as in the previous illustration to determine the appropriate discount rate.

$$(PV \text{ of } \$1 \text{ of an ordinary annuity}) = PV \div (\text{Annual annuity})$$
$$= \$7,750 \div \$3,333.33$$
$$= 2.3250$$

The *PV* of $1 of an ordinary annuity for three years using 14 percent from Exhibit 3 is $2.3216. Since this is approximately equal to 2.3250, the effective interest is 14 percent for this loan arrangement.

End of Illustration 19

Note that in the two loan arrangements available to Very Best Hats Company, the lender that offered the lowest simple annual interest, 7 percent, charged the highest effective interest cost. The illustrations demonstrate why a borrower must not rely on the simple annual interest rate when shopping around for a loan.

EFFECTIVE INTEREST COST OF A CONDITIONAL SALE OR SECURED LOAN DISGUISED AS A LEASE

The majority of the "leases" written are actually conditional sale or secured loan agreements. Should a lease arrangement be determined to be a pseudolease, the so-called lessee is entitled to a tax deduction of the interest and depreciation, not the lease payment.

Since a pseudolease is nothing more than a conditional sale or secured transaction, management will want to compare the effective interest cost of the "lease" with the effective interest cost of funds that can be obtained from other sources, such as commercial bank loans. The evaluation of a true lease, on the other hand, involves a different kind of analysis because of tax implications. The analytical framework for evaluating a true lease is explained in Appendix C.

It is not common in lease arrangements for the "lessor" to disclose the effective interest cost. The "lessee," therefore, must be able to compute the effective interest cost. The discount rate that equates the present value of the lease payments and the present value purchase option price to the cost of the leased asset is the effective interest cost of a pseudolease. Lessors refer to this rate as the *lease rate*.[3]

The procedure used to compute the effective interest cost of a pseudolease is the same as that used in the determination of the yield on an investment and the effective interest cost of a loan. The computation is demonstrated for four hypothetical leases in Illustration 20.

Illustration 20

The West Corporation wants to acquire a machine that costs $40,000. Four leasing companies have proposed the following lease arrangements:

Reliable Leasing: Four annual payments of $11,472, with the first payment due immediately. At the end of the fourth year, the machine can be purchased for $1.

---

[3] Some lessors refer to the effective interest cost as the *running rate*.

Luxury Leasing: Four annual payments of $11,080, with the first payment due immediately. At the end of the fourth year, the machine can be purchased for $2,000.

Quick Leasing: Eight semiannual payments of $5,653, with two advance payments due immediately.[4] At the end of the fourth year the machine can be purchased for $1.

Fine Leasing: Sixteen quarterly payments of $2,806, with four advance payments due immediately. The machine can be purchased at the end of the fourth year for $1.

Assuming that the four proposed lease arrangements will be treated as a secured loan for tax purposes, what is the effective interest cost of each pseudolease?

Reliable Leasing

The effective interest cost of this proposed lease is the discount rate that equates the present value of an annuity due of $11,472 (lease payment) for four years plus the present value of $1 (purchase price) at the end of four years to $40,000 (cost of the leased asset). That is,

$$PV = \text{(Annual annuity) times } (PV \text{ of \$1 of an annuity due})$$
$$+ \; FV \text{ times } (PV \text{ of \$1})$$
$$\$40{,}000 = \$11{,}472 \text{ times } (PV \text{ of \$1 of an annuity due})$$
$$+ \; \$1 \text{ times } (PV \text{ of \$1})$$

Since the last term is trivial, we can omit it. We then have

$$\$40{,}000 = \$11{,}472 \text{ times } (PV \text{ of \$1 of an annuity due})$$

Solving for the unknown, we have

$$(PV \text{ of \$1 of an annuity due}) = 3.4868$$

Subtracting $1, we have

$$(PV \text{ of \$1 of an ordinary annuity}) = 2.4868$$

Exhibit 3 can be used to determine the discount rate that produces a *PV* of $1 of an ordinary annuity for three years of 2.4868. The value 2.4869 is found in the column corresponding to 10 percent. Hence, 10 percent is the effective interest cost of the lease.

---

[4] When advance payments, or security deposits as they are often called, must be made by the lessee, some lessors permit the funds to be placed in a negotiable instrument such as a certificate of deposit. This will reduce the effective interest cost of the lease.

Luxury Leasing

The discount rate that equates the present value of an annuity due of $11,080 (lease payment) for four years plus the present value of $2,000 (purchase price) at the end of four years to $40,000 (cost of the leased asset) is the effective interest cost of the proposed lease. Unlike the lease proposed by Reliable Leasing, in this lease the present value of the purchase price is not trivial; therefore, the effective interest cost of the proposed pseudolease must be computed using the trial-and-error approach, as demonstrated in Illustration 16. When 10 percent is tried, the present value is $40,000, as shown below:

PV of an ordinary annuity for three years at 10% = 2.4869
Plus $1 = 1.0000
PV of an annuity due for four years at 10% = 3.4869
 PV of lease payments = $11,080 times (3.4869) = $38,635
PV of purchase price = $2,000 ($PV$ of $1 four years hence
at 10%)
= $2,000(0.6830)
= $1,366

Therefore, the effective interest cost of the pseudolease is 10 percent because the present value of the lease payments ($38,635) plus the present value of the purchase price ($1,366) equals, for our purposes, the cost of the leased asset ($40,000).

Quick Leasing

The effective interest cost of the proposed lease is the discount rate that makes the present value of the lease payments ($5,653) paid semi-annually and the present value of the purchase price ($1) equal to the cost of the leased asset ($40,000). As in the lease proposed by Reliable Leasing, the $1 purchase price is to all intents and purposes zero and therefore need not be considered.

The effective interest cost can be found using the "annuity" approach as in the Reliable Leasing case. There will be a total of eight semiannual payments. Two advance payments will be made immediately. It should be realized that the present value of the two advance payments of $5,653 each is $1111,306. Recall that the present value of $1 now *is* $1. This means that the present value of the remaining lease payments must equal $28,694 ($40,000 minus $11,306).

We then have

$28,694 = $5,653 times ($PV$ of $1 of an ordinary annuity)

or

$$(PV \text{ of } \$1 \text{ of an ordinary annuity}) = \frac{\$28,694}{\$5,653} = 5.0759$$

Since there are six future payments, Exhibit 3 is searched until a value close to 5.0759 can be found in the row corresponding to six periods. In the column corresponding to 5 percent, the present value is 5.0757. This is sufficiently close, so that 5 percent is the discount rate.

Since our comparisons of effective interest costs will be based on annual rates, it is necessary to annualize the 5 percent semiannual rate. A 5 percent semiannual rate is annualized as follows:

$$(1 + 0.05)^2 - 1 = 1.1025 - 1$$
$$= 0.1025, \text{ or } 10.25 \text{ percent}$$

As a side note, the reader should recognize that the definition for the effective interest could have been defined as the discount rate that equates the present value of the lease payments *excluding* any advance payments plus the present value of the purchase price to the amount of financing provided by the lease. For example, the lease proposed by Quick Leasing provides financing of $28,694. A 5 percent discount rate equates the present value of the six semiannual lease payments to $28,694. Let's use this approach to determine the effective interest cost of the lease proposed by Fine Leasing.

Fine Leasing

The amount of financing that would be provided by this lease proposal is $40,000 minus four advance lease payments of $2,806 each, or financing of $28,776. The purchase price of $1 is insignificant and need not be considered. The discount rate that equates the present value of the 12 lease payments of $2,806 to the amount of financing, $28,776, is found as follows:

$$\$28,776 = \$2,806 \text{ times } (PV \text{ of } \$1 \text{ of an ordinary annuity})$$

or

$$(PV \text{ of } \$1 \text{ of an ordinary annuity}) = \frac{\$28,776}{\$2,806}$$
$$(PV \text{ of } \$1 \text{ of an ordinary annuity}) = 10.2552$$

From Exhibit 3 the discount rate that produces a present value of an ordinary annuity of $1 for 12 payments is between 2 percent and 3 percent. A detailed annuity table would show that the present value of an ordinary annuity of $1 at 2.5 percent for 12 payments is 10.2578. The quarterly rate is therefore 2.5 percent. The annualized effective interest cost is then

$$(1 + 0.025)^4 - 1 = 1.1038 - 1$$
$$= 0.1038, \text{ or } 10.38 \text{ percent}$$

Relevant information about the four lease proposals is summarized below:

	Reliable	Luxury	Quick	Fine
Number of lease payments	4	4	8	16
Number of advance payments	1	1	2	2
Payments per year	1	1	2	4
Amount of financing provided	$28,528	$28,694	$26,694	$28,776
Effective interest cost	10%	10%	10.25%	10.38%

None of the lease proposals provides 100 percent financing of the machine. All proposals except for the one by Quick Leasing provide for approximately the same amount of financing. The first two proposals have the lowest effective interest cost. Suppose West's management is able to negotiate a loan using the machine as collateral. The effective interest cost of the loan can then be compared to the effective interest cost of the lowest cost "leasing" arrangement, available from Reliable Leasing and Luxury Leasing. The amount of financing provided by a commercial loan depends on many factors, such as the borrower's credit rating, the prevailing economic conditions, and the nature of the collateral. If a loan can be obtained in which $28,000 to $29,000 of financing is provided for four years, West's management can then select the financing arrangement that is the least costly.[5]

[5] Some lease agreements permit the lessee to skip lease payments at predetermined time periods. The principle for determining the effective interest cost of a lease agreement that permits payments to be skipped is unchanged. The trial-and-error approach used to determine the effective interest cost of the lease proposed by Luxury Leasing would be used when skipped payments are permitted.

Appendix C

A Framework for Analyzing the Lease versus Borrow-to-Buy Problem

---

Several models have been proposed in the finance literature, as well as in promotional material circulated by lessors, as to how to evaluate whether an asset should be purchased or leased. Although some authors and lessors lead their readers to believe that the analysis is quite simple, consider the following statement by two researchers:

> Perhaps no other issue in financial management, with the exception of the debate surrounding the existence of the firm's optimal structure, has inspired such sustained interest in the academic literature as the lease versus purchase decision.[1]

As an indication of the frustration of financial experts over the lease versus purchase models proposed in the literature, consider the following statement by Professor Myron Gordon of the University of Toronto:

> At various times over the last 20 years I have presented classes in finance with cases involving the choice between buying or leasing in acquiring

---

[1] Paul F. Anderson and John D. Martin, "Lease vs. Purchase Decisions: A Survey of Current Practice," *Financial Management,* Spring 1977, p. 41.

a capital asset, and invariably, I have been unhappy with the solutions proposed in the solutions manual and literature as well as the ones presented by the student.[2]

It is not the purpose of this appendix to delve into the nuances of the various models that have been proposed in the finance literature. Fortunately, this valuable service has been provided by Professor Richard Bower of Dartmouth College. In his 1973 review article Professor Bower highlights the major areas of agreement and disagreement among the alternative models proposed in the literature.[3]

The model presented in this appendix is that suggested by Professor Stewart Myers of the Massachusetts Institute of Technology.[4] The model is appropriate when the firm is in a taxpaying position and can realize in each year the entire tax shield associated with the expenses for a lease or borrow-to-buy decision. In the last section of this appendix, the model is extended to instances where the firm is currently in a nontaxpaying position but expects to resume paying taxes at some specified future date.[5] It bears repeating that these models are appropriate for valuing a *true* lease. A conditional sale disguised as a lease agreement should be analyzed by the method discussed in Appendix B.

The key concept in the lease versus borrow-to-buy decision is the need to neutralize the financial risk between the two alternative financing methods. The steps in the lease versus borrow-to-buy decision are as follows:

1. Evaluate the acquisition of an asset under normal financing. That is, the usual capital budgeting procedure for evaluating whether an asset is profitable to acquire should be performed.
2. If it is profitable to acquire the services of the asset, then determine the economic value of all the lease proposals that may be available to the firm. At least one economically attractive

---

[2] Myron G. Gordon, "A General Solution to the Buy or Lease Decision," *Journal of Finance,* March 1974, p. 245.

[3] Richard S. Bower, "Issues in Lease Financing," *Financial Management,* Winter 1973, pp. 25–34.

[4] The model was developed in Stewart C. Myers, "An Exact Solution to the Lease vs. Borrow Problem" (Working paper, London Graduate School of Business Studies, 1975). An application of the model is presented in Stewart C. Myers, David A. Dill, and Alberto J. Bautista, "Valuation of Financial Lease Contracts," *Journal of Finance,* June 1976, pp. 799–819. For a further discussion of the model and of alternative models that can be used, see Richard Brealey and Stewart C. Myers, *Principles of Corporate Finance* (New York: McGraw-Hill, 1981), Chapter 24.

[5] See Julian R. Franks and Stewart D. Hodges, "Valuation of Financial Lease Contracts: A Note," *Journal of Finance,* May 1978, pp. 657–69. The authors also provide a simplified pedagogical derivation of the lease valuation model derived by Professor Myers.

lease arrangement will justify the acquisition of the asset's service by leasing.

3. If in the first step the acquisition of the asset was not economically justified but an attractive lease arrangement is available, then the entire package should be evaluated to determine whether the services of the asset should be acquired. An attractive lease arrangement in and of itself, however, does not warrant the leasing of an asset.

In the three steps discussed above, reference was made to the "economic attractiveness" or "profitability" of an asset. Several techniques can be employed to evaluate the economic attractiveness of an investment proposal. The technique employed in this appendix is the *net present value* technique. The same technique will also be used to value a leasing arrangement. The next section illustrates the net present value technique and explains why it should be employed for capital budgeting purposes. How the technique should be used to value a lease arrangement is then explained.

Before discussing the net present value technique, it should be pointed out that some assets whose acquisition a firm is considering may not require Step 1. Management may have decided that the services of the asset must be acquired using some other criterion. For example, management may recognize that certain assets such as a telephone system or a computer must be available for operations, or a governmental agency may mandate that a firm acquire the services of an asset. In such cases the only issue is whether leasing or borrowing to purchase is the more economically attractive alternative.

CAPITAL BUDGETING USING THE NET PRESENT VALUE TECHNIQUE

Capital budgeting is concerned with the ways in which firms evaluate the economic attractiveness of long-lived investment proposals and rank those proposals that have been found to be economically attractive. By a long-lived investment proposal, it is meant that the economic benefits and costs associated with the proposal are not immediate but are spread over time. The conventional cutoff point for defining a long-lived investment proposal is that the economic benefits and costs are expected to extend beyond one year.

Long-lived investment proposals may involve the acquisition of physical assets such as a machine or a building. Or they may involve an intangible such as expenditures for the expansion into a new product line or a new advertising campaign. When assets acquired are expected to provide economic benefits and costs over a period of less than one year, such investments are commonly referred to as working capital decisions. An example of a working capital decision is the determination of the level of inventory to be maintained. The principles of economic evaluation used in capital budgeting decisions, however, are just as applicable to working capital decisions.

Since leasing involves the acquisition of long-lived assets, it requires an understanding of the techniques of capital budgeting. Several techniques for evaluating investment proposals are available to the decision maker—payback period, accounting rate of return, net present value, internal rate of return, and index of profitability. These techniques are discussed in all textbooks on financial management. The last three techniques are called discounted cash flow techniques since they take into consideration the time value of money. The importance of the time value of money was discussed in Appendix B.

The technique that financial theory suggests should be employed to evaluate investment proposals is the net present value technique (NPV). The theoretical rationale for this technique is described below. First, the technique will be illustrated.

Illustration 1

Let's begin with a simple case. Suppose that the Barten Corporation is considering an investment proposal that would cost the company $14,000 today. The investment will return $20,000 after taxes to the firm the next day with absolutely no risk. Should the firm undertake the investment proposal?

The answer is obvious in this case. In one day the firm will realize an after-tax profit of $6,000 on a $14,000 investment. The investment proposal should be undertaken. The problem is more complicated, however, if the $20,000 is expected to be received at a more distant time in the future.

Illustration 2

Suppose the investment proposal that the Barten Corporation is considering will return $20,000 after taxes four years from now rather than the next day. Is the investment proposal still profitable? In terms of dollars, the project seems to be profitable since it is returning $6,000 more than the investment dollars expended. However, from our discussion of the time value of money, it should be recognized that dollars to be received in the future cannot be compared with dollars spent today. In order to properly analyze the investment proposal, the dollars to be received in the future must be discounted at an appropriate rate to determine the present value of those dollars.

Determination of the present value of $20,000 to be received four years from now requires the use of a discount rate. The firm's after-tax cost of capital[6] is the appropriate rate if the risk associated with the investment proposal is identical to the risk of an "average" project undertaken by the firm.[7] When the risk associated with an investment proposal differs from that of the "average" project, the firm's after-tax cost of capital is inappropriate and the techniques to adjust for risk suggested later in this appendix should be employed.

Let's suppose that the management of Barten Corporation believes the investment under consideration has the same risk as that of the firm's "average" project. Let's suppose further that management has determined the after-tax cost of capital to be 8 percent. The present value of the $20,000 to be received four years from now can be found by using the present value of $1 from Exhibit 2 in Appendix B. The present value of $1 four years from now using a discount rate of 8 percent is .7350. Hence, the present value of $20,000 is $14,700 (.7350 times $20,000). Thus, if the Barten Corporation sets aside $14,700 today earning 8 percent, it would have $20,000 four years from now.

Now we are in a position to evaluate the investment proposal. The firm wants to earn at least 8 percent on any money it invests because that is the after-tax cost of capital to the firm. However, instead of having to invest $14,700 to realize $20,000 four years from now, the firm need only invest $14,000. By investing in this project, the firm will realize a profit in terms of present value of $700. Alternatively, this is equivalent to saying that the firm will earn a return greater than 8 percent.

How to Compute the Net Present Value

The steps for computing the NPV are precisely those steps used to evaluate the investment proposal considered by the Barten Corporation in Illustration 2. Let's recapitulate the steps.

First, the present value of the dollars to be received four years from now using the after-tax cost of capital was computed. Second, the present value was compared to the initial outlay of $14,000. The difference is the profitability of the project in terms of present value.

---

[6] The after-tax cost of capital is the weighted average of the component after-tax costs of debt, preferred stock, and common equity. The costs are based on the cost of raising an additional dollar of funds in the future, *not* the historical costs of raising funds in the past. The cost of capital is tied to the firm's market value. If the firm earns less than the cost of capital, its market value will decline. Earnings greater than the cost of capital will increase the market value of the firm.

[7] See Stewart C. Myers, "Interactions of Corporate Financing and Investment Decisions: Implications for Capital Budgeting," *Journal of Finance*, March 1974, pp. 1–25.

We can now generalize the procedure for the computation of the NPV.

1. Determine the after-tax dollars to be received in future years. This is more commonly referred to as the future cash flow from the investment. The cash flow is understood to be the after-tax cash flow.[8]
2. Compute the present value of the future cash flow by discounting at the after-tax cost of capital.
3. Determine the initial net cash outlay. This is the so-called investment made by the firm. Tax credits, if any, and other inflows such as the after-tax proceeds from the sale of an old asset that the new asset is replacing or outlays for additional inventory must be considered.
4. Subtract from the present value of the cash flow determined in Step 2 the initial net cash outlay found in Step 3. *The difference is the net present value.*

Illustration 3

To illustrate the computation of the net present value, suppose that the initial net cash outlay and future cash flow for a machine that the management of the Lysle Construction Company might want to acquire is as follows: An initial net cash outlay is $59,400 with future cash flows for the next five years of $16,962, $19,774, $20,663, $21,895, and $26,825, respectively. Assume that the firm's management has estimated the after-tax cost of capital to be 14 percent. The net present value following the four steps is shown below:

Step 1: Determine the future cash flow from the investment. This is given above.

Step 2: The present value of the future cash flow using the after-tax cost of capital of 14 percent is computed below:

End of year	Cash flow	PV of $1 at 14%	PV of cash flow
1	$16,962	$.8772	$14,879
2	19,774	.7695	15,216
3	20,663	.6750	13,948
4	21,895	.5921	12,964
5	26,825	.5194	13,933
	Present value of future cash flow		$70,940

[8] The cash flow for a given period is the difference between the *additional* dollars received and *additional* dollars paid out if an investment project is undertaken. Cash

Step 3: Determine the initial net cash outlay. The initial net cash outlay for the machine is assumed to be $59,400.

Step 4: Subtract the initial net cash outlay from the present value of the future cash flow to determine the net present value.

Present value of the future cash flow	$70,940
Less: Initial net cash outlay	− 59,400
Net present value	$11,540

Decision Rules Using the Net Present Value Technique

Once the NPV is computed, this measure is used (a) to determine if the project is profitable in its own right and (b) to compare mutually exclusive investment proposals.

The rule to determine whether the investment proposal is attractive is as follows:

- If the NPV is greater than zero, it is an economically attractive investment.
- If the NPV is less than zero, it is an economically unattractive investment.
- If the NPV is equal to zero, it is neither economically attractive nor unattractive.

Note that the economic attractiveness of the investment proposal depends on the after-tax cost of capital. Therefore, a project that is economically unattractive at a certain after-tax cost of capital (that is, has a negative NPV) may be attractive if the after-tax cost of capital falls. The reverse is also true.

Mutually exclusive investment proposals are investment proposals that represent alternative means of accomplishing the same objective. For example, suppose a firm is contemplating the construction of a factory in either Hicksville, Long Island, or in Jericho, Long Island, three miles away. The firm does not need two factories. Yet suppose an economic analysis using the NPV technique indicates that the NPV is $1.4 million if the factory is constructed in Hicksville but $1 million if it is constructed in Jericho. How does the firm select between these two mutually exclusive projects using the NPV technique?

The rule for selecting the best investment from among economically attractive mutually exclusive investment proposals is to select the in-

---

flow is *not* the same as net income after taxes as would be computed for financial reporting or tax purposes. For an explanation of how to compute the cash flow of an investment and an illustration of why it is not the same as book income or tax income, see: Ralph S. Polimeni, Frank J. Fabozzi, and Arthur H. Adelberg, *Cost Accounting: Concepts and Applications for Managerial Decision Making* (New York: McGraw-Hill, 1986), pp. 666–67.

vestment proposal with the highest NPV. Therefore, in our example in which the firm must decide between building the factory in Hicksville and building it in Jericho, the choice would be to build it in Hicksville since that is the alternative with the greater NPV.[9]

The reader should realize that the lease versus borrow-to-buy decision represents a decision in which a choice must be made among mutually exclusive investment proposals. As indicated in the introductory remarks to this appendix, the selection will be based on the NPV for each of the financing alternatives.

Why the Net Present Value Technique?

The net present value technique is one of three discounted cash flow techniques that can be employed to determine the economic value of an investment proposal. Why is this technique theoretically preferred to other techniques?[10]

Financial theorists have shown that under certain conditions the NPV technique is logically tied to the firm's objective of maximizing the wealth of the owners of the firm. For a firm whose shares are publicly traded, the market value of the shares should increase when a project with a positive net present value is accepted.[11] The use of the NPV technique, therefore, is not simply a convenient choice from among several techniques that take into consideration the time value of money but is a technique that provides theoretically correct decisions consistent with the maximization of shareholder wealth.

The three discounted cash flow techniques—NPV, internal rate of return, and index of profitability[12]—will reach the same conclusion

---

[9] Sometimes management determines that a certain service or performance is required even though it may not have a positive NPV. If there are mutually exclusive investment proposals that satisfy the service or performance required by management, all of which have a negative NPV, the proposal with the highest NPV (that is, least negative) should be selected.

[10] For a more detailed explanation, see Charles W. Haley and Lawrence D. Schall, *The Theory of Financial Decisions* (New York: McGraw-Hill, 1979), Chapter 2. For a graphic description, see Brealey and Myers, *Principles of Corporate Finance*, Chapter 2, or Polimeni, Fabozzi, and Adelberg, *Cost Accounting*, Chapter 17.

[11] For an explanation of why the NPV of a project will be reflected in the market value of a share, see Brealey and Myers, *Principles of Corporate Finance*, pp. 61–62. Because numerous factors influence the market price of a firm's share, in practice it is not possible to observe the market response to the acceptance by the firm of an investment with a positive NPV.

[12] In the literature various names have been used to describe the same technique. Yield, time-adjusted discount rate, rate of return, and marginal rate of return have been used in lieu of internal rate of return. Other names for the index of profitability are the benefit-cost ratio and the profitability index.

about whether an investment proposal is profitable.[13] Conflicts may arise, however, when a selection must be made from among mutually exclusive projects.[14] Thus, suppose a firm is considering three mutually exclusive investment proposals, A, B, and C. Each investment proposal is found to be profitable by each of the three discounted cash flow techniques. It is possible to find that A is the most attractive by the NPV technique, that B is the most attractive using the internal rate of return technique, and that C is the most attractive using the index of profitability technique. The existence of such conflicts does not negate the superiority of the net present value technique. Because there are problems with the internal rate of return and index of profitability techniques, in particular, both are affected by the dollar size of the investment proposal, the net present value technique should be employed.[15]

VALUING A LEASE

To this point we have discussed how the net present value technique should be applied to evaluate an investment proposal. Investment proposals with a positive NPV are attractive and may be made even more attractive by an economically beneficial leasing arrangement.

An unattractive investment proposal (that is, a proposal with negative NPV) may be turned into an attractive investment proposal if the combined NPV under normal financing (that is, the usual NPV capital budgeting analysis) and the NPV of the leasing arrangement is greater than zero. For example, suppose a tool salesman demonstrates a tool that you believe may be economically beneficial for your firm to acquire. The financial analyst of your firm performs the NPV analysis assuming normal financing and ascertains the NPV to be −$10,000. The financial analyst will recommend that the firm not acquire the tool based on her analysis. Suppose that upon being told that your firm is not interested in purchasing the tool, the tool salesman offers to lease the tool for most of the tool's expected life. Your financial analyst then evaluates the lease, using the lease valuation model presented below, and determines it to have an NPV in excess of $10,000.

---

[13] It should be pointed out that even though future cash flows and an initial net cash outlay may be available for an investment proposal, an internal rate of return may not exist. Moreover, multiple internal rates of return may be observed for an investment proposal.

[14] Reasons for the conflict are discussed in Eugene F. Brigham, *Financial Management: Theory and Practice,* 2nd ed. (Hinsdale, Ill.: Dryden Press, 1979), pp. 378–82.

[15] See Harold Bierman, Jr., and Seymour Smidt, *The Capital Budgeting Decision,* 5th ed. (New York: Macmillan, 1980), Chapter 3; Brealey and Myers, *Principles of Corporate Finance,* Chapter 5; Brigham, *Financial Management,* Appendix B of Chapter 11; or Polimeni, Fabozzi, and Adelberg, *Cost Accounting,* Chapter 17.

Acquiring the economic benefits expected to be provided by the tool using the salesman's leasing arrangement would then be economically attractive because the combined NPV (NPV assuming normal financing and NPV of the lease) produces a positive NPV.[16]

As noted at the beginning of this appendix, several economic models for valuing a lease have been proposed in the literature. The model used here requires the determination of the net present value of the direct cash flow resulting from leasing rather than borrowing to purchase an asset, where the direct cash flow from leasing is discounted using an "adjusted discount rate."[17] The model is derived from "the objective of maximizing the equilibrium market value of the firm, with careful consideration of interactions between the decision to lease and the use of other financing instruments by the lessee."[18]

Direct Cash Flow from Leasing

When a firm opts to lease an asset rather than borrow money to purchase the same asset, this decision will have an impact on the firm's cash flow. The consequences can be summarized as follows:

1. There will be a cash inflow equivalent to the cost of the asset.
2. The lessee may or may not forgo some tax credit. For example, prior to the elimination of the investment tax credit by TRA,

---

[16] The decision rule presented in this appendix is absolute; that is, if the value of a lease is positive, it is more economically attractive than borrowing to purchase. The reverse is true if the value of a lease is negative. In practice, however, a small positive or negative value may mean that the firm will be indifferent to the two financing methods. Management must decide what the minimum absolute value of a lease must be so that a clear-cut choice can be made. For example, suppose equipment with a purchase price of $25 million is found to have an NPV of $8 million. Management can lease rather than purchase the equipment. Suppose the value of the lease using the methodology to be explained in this appendix is −$1,000. Although leasing is not economically attractive because the value of the lease is negative, the magnitude of the lease value is small. Management may in this case be indifferent with respect to the two financing alternatives. Moreover, noneconomic factors must be considered.

[17] The adjusted discount rate technique presented in this appendix is fundamentally equivalent to and results in the same answer as is obtained by comparing financing provided by a loan that gives the same cash flow as the lease in every future period. This will be illustrated below.

Although the adjusted discount rate technique is fundamentally equivalent to calculating the *adjusted present value* of a lease, it is less accurate. The adjusted present value technique takes into consideration the present value of the side effects of accepting a project financed with a lease. (The adjusted present value technique was first developed by Myers in "Interactions of Corporate and Investment Decisions.") The reason for a possible discrepancy between the solutions to the lease versus borrow-to-buy decision using the adjusted discount rate technique and adjusted present value technique is that different discount rates are applied where necessary in discounting the cash flow when the latter technique is used. (For an explanation of the adjusted present value technique, see Brealey and Myers, *Principles of Corporate Finance*, Chapter 19. The application to leasing is given in Chapter 24, pp. 534–35.)

[18] Myers, Dill, and Bautista, "Financial Lease Contracts," p. 799.

the lessor could pass through to the lessee the investment tax credit.

3. The lessee must make periodic lease payments over the life of the lease. These payments need not be the same in each period. The lease payments are fully deductible for tax purposes if the lease is a true lease. The tax shield is equal to the lease payment times the lessee's marginal tax rate.

4. The lessee forgoes the tax shield provided by the depreciation allowance since it does not own the asset. The tax shield resulting from depreciation is the product of the lessee's marginal tax rate times the depreciation allowance.

5. There will be a cash outlay representing the lost after-tax proceeds from the residual value of the asset.

Illustration 4

In Illustration 3, we considered the capital budgeting problem faced by the Lysle Construction Company. The company is considering the acquisition of a machine that requires an initial net cash outlay of $59,400 and will generate a future cash flow for the next five years of $16,962, $19,774, $20,663, $21,895, and $26,825. The NPV for this machine was found to be $11,540.

Let's assume that the following information was used to determine the initial net cash outlay and the cash flow for the machine:

Cost of the machine	= $66,000
Tax credit[19]	= $ 6,600
Estimated pre-tax residual value after disposal costs	= $ 6,000
Estimated after-tax proceeds from residual value	= $ 3,600
Economic life of the machine	= 5 years

Depreciation is assumed to be as follows:[20]

Year	Depreciation deductions
1	$ 9,405
2	13,794
3	13,167
4	13,167
5	13,167

[19] We use a tax credit in this illustration to show how the model can be applied should Congress decide to introduce some form of tax credit in future tax legislation.

[20] The depreciation schedule used in this illustration is not consistent with the tax law at the time of this writing.

The same machine may be leased by the Lysle Construction Company. The lease would require five annual payments of $13,500, with the first payment due immediately. The lessor would retain the investment tax credit. The tax shield resulting from the lease payments would be realized at the time that Lysle Construction made the payment. No additional annual expenses will be incurred by Lysle Construction by owning rather than leasing (that is, the lease is a net lease). The lessor will not require Lysle Construction to guarantee a minimum residual value.

Exhibit 1 presents the worksheet for the computation of the direct cash flow from leasing rather than borrowing to purchase. The marginal tax rate of Lysle Construction is 40 percent. The direct cash flow is summarized below:

			Year		
0	*1*	*2*	*3*	*4*	*5*
$51,300	($11,862)	($13,618)	($13,367)	($13,367)	($8,867)

EXHIBIT 1   Worksheet for Direct Cash Flow from Leasing: Lysle Construction*

			End of year			
	0	*1*	*2*	*3*	*4*	*5*
Cost of machine	$66,000					
Lost tax credit	(6,600)					
Lease payment	(13,500)	($13,500)	($13,500)	($13,500)	($13,500)	
Tax shield from lease payment†	5,400	5,400	5,400	5,400	5,400	
Lost depreciation tax shield‡		(3,762)	(5,518)	(5,267)	(5,267)	($5,267)
Lost residual value						(3,600)
Total	$51,300	($11,862)	($13,618)	($13,367)	($13,367)	($8,867)

* Parentheses denote cash outflow.
† Lease payment multiplied by the marginal tax rate (40%).
‡ Depreciation for year multiplied by the marginal tax rate (40%).

End of Illustration 4

In Illustration 4, the direct cash flow from leasing was constructed assuming that (1) the lease is a net lease and (2) the tax benefit associated with an expense is realized in the tax year the expense is incurred. These two assumptions require further discussion.

First, if the lease is a gross lease instead of a net lease, the lease payments must be reduced by the cost of maintenance, insurance, and property taxes. These costs are assumed to be the same regardless of whether the asset is leased or purchased with borrowed funds. Where have these costs been incorporated into the analysis? The cash flow from owning an asset is constructed by subtracting the additional operating expenses from the additional revenue. Maintenance, insurance, and property taxes are included in the additional operating expenses. There may be instances when the cost of maintenance differs depending on the financing alternative selected. In such cases, an adjustment to the value of the lease must be made.

Second, many firms considering leasing may be currently in a nontaxpaying position but anticipate being in a taxpaying position in the future. The derivation of the lease valuation model presented in the next section does not consider this situation. It assumes that the tax shield associated with an expense can be fully absorbed by the firm in the tax year in which the expense arises. There is a lease valuation model, however, that will handle under certain conditions the situation of a firm currently in a nontaxpaying position. The generalized model is explained and illustrated later.

Valuing the Direct Cash Flow from Leasing

Because the lease displaces debt, the direct cash flow from leasing should be further modified by devising a loan that in each period except the initial period engenders a net cash flow that is identical to the net cash flow for the lease obligation; that is, financial risk is neutralized. Such a loan, called an *equivalent loan*, is illustrated later. Fortunately, it has been mathematically demonstrated that rather than going through the time-consuming effort to construct an equivalent loan, all the decision maker need do is discount the direct cash flow from leasing by an adjusted discount rate. The adjusted discount rate can be approximated by the following formula:[21]

Adjusted discount rate
= (1 − Marginal tax rate) times (Cost of borrowing money)

The formula assumes that leasing will displace debt on a dollar-for-dollar basis.[22]

Given the direct cash flow from leasing and the adjusted discount rate, the NPV of the lease can be computed. We shall refer to the NPV of the lease as simply the value of the lease. A negative value for a lease indicates that leasing will not be more economically beneficial

---

[21] As noted by Brealey and Myers, *Principles of Corporate Finance,* "The direct cash flows are typically assumed to be *safe* flows that investors would discount at approximately the same rate as the interest and principal on a secured loan issued by the lessee" (p. 529). There is justification for applying a different discount rate to the various components of the direct cash flow from leasing.

[22] Brealey and Myers, *Principles of Corporate Finance,* p. 534. The formula must be modified, as explained later, if the lessee believes that leasing does not displace debt on a dollar-for-dollar basis.

than borrowing to purchase. A positive value means that leasing will be more economically beneficial. However, leasing will be attractive only if the NPV of the asset assuming normal financing is positive *and* the value of the lease is positive, *or* if the sum of the NPV of the asset assuming normal financing and the value of the lease is positive.

Illustration 5

In order to evaluate the direct cash flow from leasing for the machine considered by the Lysle Construction Company in Illustration 4, we must know the firm's cost of borrowing money. Suppose that the cost of borrowing money has been determined to be 10 percent. The adjusted discount rate is then found by applying the formula:

Adjusted discount rate = $(1 - 0.40)$ times $(0.10) = 0.06$, or 6%

The adjusted discount rate of 6 percent is then employed to determine the value of the lease. The worksheet is shown as Exhibit 2. The value of the lease is $-\$448$. Hence, from a purely economic point of view, the machine should be purchased by the Lysle Construction Company rather than leased. Recall that the NPV of the machine assuming normal financing is $11,540.

Concept of an Equivalent Loan

The value of the lease considered by the Lysle Construction Company was shown to be $-\$448$. Suppose the firm had the opportunity to obtain a $51,748 five-year loan at 10 percent interest with the following principal repayment schedule:

End of year	0	1	2	3	4	5
Repayment	0	$8,757	$11,039	$11,450	$12,137	$8,365

(Recall that the firm's marginal borrowing rate was assumed to be 10 percent.)

Exhibit 3 shows the net cash flow for each year if the loan is used to purchase the machine. In addition to the loan, the firm must make an initial outlay of $7,652.

The net cash flow for each year if the machine is leased is also presented in Exhibit 3. Notice that the net cash flows of the two financing alternatives are equivalent, with the exception of year 0. Therefore, the loan presented above is called the *equivalent loan for the lease.*

EXHIBIT 2   Worksheet for Determining the Value of a Lease: Illustration 5

End of year	Direct cash flow from leasing	Present value of $1 at 6%	Present value
0	$51,300	1.0000	$51,300
1	(11,862)	.9434	(11,191)
2	(13,618)	.8900	(12,120)
3	(13,367)	.8396	(11,223)
4	(13,367)	.7921	(10,588)
5	(8,867)	.7473	(6,626)
Value (or NPV) of lease			$ (448)

We can now understand why borrowing to purchase is more economically attractive for Lysle Construction. The equivalent loan produces the same net cash flow as the lease in all years after year 0. Hence, the equivalent loan has equalized the financial risk of the two financing alternatives. However, the net cash outlay in year 0 is $7,652 compared to $8,100 if the machine is leased. The difference, −$448, is the value of the lease. Notice that the lease valuation model produced the same value for the lease without constructing an equivalent loan.

Comparison of Alternative Leases

The potential lessee may have the opportunity to select from several leasing arrangements offered by the same lessor or different lessors. From a purely economic perspective, the potential lessor should select the leasing arrangement with the greatest positive value. This requires an analysis of the direct cash flow from leasing for each of the leasing arrangements available.

Illustration 6

A firm has two leasing arrangements available to lease a given asset. The direct cash flow from leasing is shown below for each alternative:

End of year	Direct cash flow from leasing	
	Lease 1	Lease 2
0	$42,000	$45,800
1	(15,000)	(13,000)
2	(15,000)	(16,000)
3	(15,000)	(18,000)
4	(1,000)	(4,000)

EXHIBIT 3 Equivalent Loan for Lease versus Borrow-to-Buy Decision Faced by Lysle Construction: Illustration 4

Period	0	1	2	3	4	5
Leasing: Cash flows:						
− Lease payments	$−13,500	$−13,500	$−13,500	$−13,500	$−13,500	$ 0
+ Tax shield	5,400	5,400	5,400	5,400	5,400	0
Net cash flow	$− 8,100	$− 8,100	$− 8,100	$− 8,100	$− 8,100	$ 0
Purchasing: Cash flows:						
− Purchase cost	$−66,000					
+ Tax credit	6,600					
+ Residual value						3,600
+ Depreciation tax shield	0	$ 3,762	$ 5,518	$ 5,267	$ 5,267	5,267
+ Loan	51,748					
− Principal repayment	0	− 8,757	−11,039	−11,450	−12,137	−8,365
− Interest on loan	0	− 5,175	− 4,299	− 3,195	− 2,050	− 836
+ Interest tax shield	0	2,070	1,720	1,278	820	334
Net cash flow	$− 7,652	$− 8,100	$− 8,100	$− 8,100	$− 8,100	$ 0
Loan account:						
Previous balance	$ 0	$ 51,748	$ 42,991	$ 31,953	$ 20,503	$ 8,365
Principal repayment (+ loan)	+ 51,748	− 8,757	−11,039	−11,450	−12,137	−8,365
New balance	$ 51,748	$ 42,991	$ 31,953	$ 20,503	$ 8,365	$ 0
Value (NPV) of lease*	$ −448					

* Difference between the net cash flows in year 0 [−8,100 − (−7,652)].

The value of the lease using an adjusted discount rate of 6 percent and 8 percent is summarized below:

Adjusted discount rate	Value of	
	Lease 1	Lease 2
6%	$1,109	$1,015
8	2,663	2,818

When the adjusted discount rate is 6 percent, both leases are economically beneficial. However, Lease 1 is marginally superior to Lease 2. The value of both leases increases when the adjusted discount rate is 8 percent. In this case, Lease 1 is slightly less attractive than Lease 2.

ANOTHER APPROACH TO LEASE VALUATION

Rather than determining the net present value of a lease, many lessors use a different approach when attempting to demonstrate to potential lessees the economic attractiveness of a particular leasing arrangement. The approach is a comparison of the after-tax interest rate on the lease with the after-tax cost of borrowing money. Surveys of lessees also indicate that this approach is popular.[23] The reason this approach appears to be popular is that management finds it easy to comprehend a rate concept but difficult to appreciate the net present value of a lease concept.

The after-tax interest rate on the lease is found by determining the discount rate that equates the direct cash flow from leasing to zero; that is, it is the discount rate that makes the value of the lease equal to zero.[24] The after-tax interest rate on the lease is then compared to the after-tax cost of borrowing money. When the after-tax interest rate on the lease exceeds the after-tax cost of borrowing money, borrowing to purchase is more economical than leasing. Leasing is more economical when the after-tax cost of borrowing money is greater than the after-tax interest rate on the lease.

---

[23] Anderson and Martin, "Lease vs. Purchase Decisions."

[24] The procedure is identical to finding a yield on an investment or the effective interest cost on borrowed funds as illustrated in Appendix B. There it was stated that the yield is the discount rate that equates the cash flow to the investment. The effective interest rate is the discount rate that equates the funds received in the initial period to the repayment of principal and interest over the term of the loan. The after-tax interest rate on the lease could have been stated in an analogous manner. The discount rate that equates the value of the lease to zero is the discount rate that equates the direct cash from leasing in the periods after the initial period to the direct cash flow from leasing in the initial period.

Illustration 7

Exhibit 1 shows the direct cash flow from leasing for the lease arrangement available to the Lysle Construction Company. To determine the after-tax interest rate on the lease, the direct cash flow from leasing is discounted at rates between 6.0 and 6.4 percent on Exhibit 4. The discount rate that produces a present value close to zero for the direct cash flow from leasing is 6.3 percent. Hence, the after-tax interest rate on the lease is about 6.3 percent.

When the after-tax cost of borrowing is 6 percent, the lease arrangement is not attractive. However, when the after-tax cost of borrowing money is 8 percent, the lease arrangement is attractive.

End of Illustration 7

In the previous illustration, the determination that was made as to whether the lease was economically attractive was precisely the same determination that was made when the net present value lease valuation model was used. The identity of result is not peculiar to this illustration. The two approaches will always produce the same result.

The advantage of the net present value lease valuation model presented is that it permits interaction of the investment and financing decisions. As a result it is simple to determine whether an investment proposal that has a negative net present value assuming normal financing can be made economically attractive by a favorable lease arrangement. With the after-tax interest on the lease approach, this is not done as easily. That approach requires management to revise its estimate of the cost of capital when the after-tax interest rate on the lease is less than the after-tax cost of borrowing money and then to reevaluate the investment proposal with the revised cost of capital. This is an extremely complicated and awkward approach since it requires a continuous revision of the cost of capital as attractive lease arrangements become available. No simple solution to this problem has been proffered in the literature.

The rate approach will not always provide the same solution as the net present value approach when lease arrangements are compared. Differences in the selection of the best lease arrangement may result when the number of advance payments is different, when the lease payments are not uniform, or when the tax credit is handled any differently.[25] The best lease arrangement is the one with the greatest

---

[25] The situation is analogous to conditions in which the yield technique in capital budgeting may produce rankings conflicting with those produced by the net present value technique.

EXHIBIT 4 Determination of After-Tax Interest Rate on the Lease: Illustration 7

Year	Direct cash flow from leasing	PV of $1 at 6.0%	PV at 6.0%	PV of $1 at 6.1%	PV at 6.1%	PV of $1 at 6.2%	PV at 6.2%
0	$51,300	1.0000	$ 51,300	1.0000	$ 51,300	1.0000	$ 51,300
1	(11,862)	.9434	(11,191)	.9425	(11,180)	.9416	(11,169)
2	(13,618)	.8900	(12,120)	.8883	(12,097)	.8866	(12,074)
3	(13,367)	.8396	(11,223)	.8372	(11,191)	.8349	(11,160)
4	(13,367)	.7921	(10,588)	.7891	(10,548)	.7861	(10,508)
5	(8,867)	.7473	(6,626)	.7437	(6,594)	.7402	(6,563)
Value of lease			$(448)		$(310)		$(174)

Year	PV of $1 at 6.3%	PV at 6.3%	PV of $1 at 6.4%	PV at 6.4%
0	1.0000	$ 51,300	1.0000	$ 51,300
1	.9407	(11,159)	.9398	(11,148)
2	.8850	(12,052)	.8833	(12,029)
3	.8325	(11,128)	.8302	(11,097)
4	.7832	(10,469)	.7802	(10,429)
5	.7368	(6,533)	.7333	(6,502)
Value of lease		$(41)		$ 95

NPV. Therefore, if conflicts arise when comparing lease arrangements by the two methods, the decision should be based on the NPV of the lease.

UNCERTAINTY AND THE LEASE VALUATION MODEL

The lease valuation model presented assumes that the appropriate discount rate that should be used to discount the direct cash flow from leasing is the after-tax cost of borrowed funds. However, when management believes that any components of the direct cash flow from leasing have a degree of risk different from that of the cash flows from borrowing, a different discount rate for each component is justified. Furthermore, the use of the after-tax cost of borrowed funds assumes that management believes that leasing displaces borrowing on a dollar-for-dollar basis. In this section these issues are examined. We also illustrate how management can test the sensitivity of the proposed solution to the lease valuation model to changes in the values assigned to factors in the model.

Alternative Discount Rates and the Uncertainty of Cash Flows

In the lease valuation model presented, all components of the direct cash flow from leasing are discounted at the same discount rate—the adjusted discount rate. The adjusted discount rate is the after-tax cost of borrowing money. It is found by multiplying the cost of borrowing money by 1 minus the marginal tax rate. Yet there is theoretical justification for discounting some components of the direct cash flow series at different discount rates.

In general, the discount rate applied to a cash flow should reflect the riskiness inherent in realizing the cash flow. The greater the risk, the greater is the discount rate that should be employed. If the cash flow is as risky as the cash flow from the firm's "average" project, then in the NPV analysis used in capital budgeting assuming normal financing, the appropriate rate is the firm's after-tax cost of capital.

However, when the cash flow is riskier than the cash flow from an "average" project, one approach to handle the uncertainty is to discount the *expected value of the cash flow* by the *risk-adjusted discount rate*. Two new concepts are introduced in the risk-adjusted discount rate approach. First, by expected value of the cash flow we mean the cash flow weighted by its likelihood of occurrence. For example, if there is a 50–50 chance of the after-tax proceeds from the sale of an asset being

$2,000 or $5,200, then the expected value of the cash flow is $3,600.[26] Second, a risk-adjusted discount rate means that a premium is added to the after-tax cost of capital to discount the cash flow in capital budgeting analysis under normal financing and that a premium is added to the adjusted discount rate in valuing the lease. From a practical point of view, just how much of a premium is appropriate is often difficult to quantify.

A pitfall of the risk-adjusted discount rate approach is that it lumps together in the valuation process the time value of money and risk attitudes, thereby resulting in the compounding of risk over time.[27] Because of this drawback, another approach to the treatment of uncertainty is recommended within the context of NPV analysis. The approach is known as the *certainty equivalent approach*. Whereas the risk-adjusted discount rate approach adjusts the discount rate, the certainty equivalent approach adjusts the cash flow in a very special way. The certainty equivalent is the amount the decision maker is willing to accept with certainty to forgo the risk of receiving the uncertain cash flow.[28] In essence the certainty equivalent converts the expected value of the cash flow into a cash flow that the decision maker is willing to accept with certainty.

For example, suppose management believes there is a 50–50 chance of the after-tax proceeds from the residual value being $2,000 or $5,200. As noted before, the expected value is $3,600. To determine the certainty equivalent, management must estimate how much it is willing to accept with certainty rather than face the possible cash flow in-

---

[26] The expected value of the cash flow is found as follows:

$$0.5 \text{ times } \$2,000 + 0.5 \text{ times } \$5,200 = \$3,600$$

For a discussion of the techniques used to elicit probabilities and the experience of researchers in eliciting probabilities, see G. R. Chesley, "Elicitation of Subjective Probabilities: A Review," *Accounting Review,* April 1975, pp. 325–35.

[27] See A. A. Robichek and S. C. Myers, "Conceptual Problems in the Use of Risk-Adjusted Discount Rates," *Journal of Finance,* December 1966, pp. 727–30; and H. Y. Chen, "Valuation under Uncertainty," *Journal of Financial and Quantitative Analysis,* September 1967, pp. 312–26. For other problems, see William L. Beedles, "Evaluating Negative Benefits," *Journal of Financial and Quantitative Analysis,* March 1978, pp. 173–76.

[28] Strictly speaking, it must be noted that to marry the certainty equivalent approach to the net present value rule, management must apply the approach in a manner that prices market risk and not individual attitudes toward risk. Recall that the foundation of the net present value rule is that it measures changes in market value and, therefore, the wealth position of the owners. Now if the certainty equivalent approach is to be used to measure changes in the net present value (and the market value) of the firm, then it must be based on market parameters and not individual (subjective) ones. Thus, a "market" certainty equivalent is needed, *not* the certainty equivalent reflective of the individual decision maker's risk aversion or personal position.

volved. That is, suppose management can enter into a contract now to sell the asset at a preestablished price when the firm expects to dispose of it. How much must that preestablished price be? If management is willing to accept $2,900, then $2,900 is the certainty equivalent of receiving $2,000 or $5,200 with a 50–50 chance.

Once the certainty equivalent of the cash flow has been determined, the certainty equivalent cash flow is discounted at the risk-free rate. The risk-free rate is the appropriate discount rate because there is no uncertainty, by definition, in the certainty equivalent cash flow. The risk-free rate is measured by the rate on U.S. government obligations.

In practice the risk-adjusted discount rate approach is probably more commonly employed. Many practitioners find it easier to determine a premium for the risk-adjusted discount rate than to estimate the certainty equivalent.

Because some of the components of the direct cash flow from leasing may be known with certainty, some financial theorists argue that the appropriate adjusted discount rate should be the after-tax risk-free rate.[29] That is, the adjusted discount rate should be computed using the following formula:

Adjusted discount rate
= (1 − Marginal tax rate) times (Risk-free rate)

The three components of the cash flow that may be known with certainty are the after-tax lease payments, the depreciation tax shield, and any tax credit. The lease payments constitute a fixed charge, and hence there is no uncertainty about the cash outflow. The depreciation tax shield can be used even though in some years there may be no taxable income generated by the asset under consideration. The depreciation tax shield can be used to offset income from other projects. Even if there is a net operating loss, the loss may be carried back for 3 years and forward for 15 years. Depending on management's expectations about future operations and the resulting tax liability, the probability of benefiting from uncertainty in such instances pertains to the timing, not the amount, of the tax benefits. The present value of the tax shield provided by depreciation then depends on when the benefits are included in the direct cash flow from leasing.

The effect of the discount rate selected on the outcome of the decision to lease or borrow to purchase can be analyzed by employing sensitivity analysis, which will be illustrated later in this section.

---

[29] Haim Levy and Marshall Sarnat, "Leasing, Borrowing, and Financial Risk," *Financial Management*, Winter 1979, pp. 47–54; and Haim Levy and Fred A. Arditti, "Valuation Leverage and the Cost of Capital in the Case of Depreciable Assets," *Journal of Finance*, June 1973, pp. 687–94.

Residual Value and the Lease Term

If the residual value is anticipated by management to have a zero or trivial value at the end of the lease term, then the problems associated with discounting the residual value no longer exist. This suggests a way of coping with the treatment of the residual value. Management should select a lease term such that at the end of that term it expects the residual value to be insignificant.

The question then is, will there be a lessor willing to lease the asset for the length of time sought by the lessee? Within reasonable limits, there are lessors willing to bet that the asset will have a greater residual value than is expected by the lessee when the asset comes off-lease. Lease packagers are particularly helpful in finding lessors that believe more will be "left on the table" than lessees believe will be left.

Debt Displacement and the Lease Valuation Model

When illustrating the lease valuation model previously it was always assumed that one dollar of leasing displaces one dollar of debt. Yet some managers believe that leasing can increase the firm's debt capacity. Although it is doubtful that management can continually fool lenders by using lease financing in lieu of debt financing, there may be certain circumstances in which a lease arrangement does not displace debt on a dollar-for-dollar basis.

When this occurs, the adjusted discount rate used to discount the direct cash flow from leasing must be modified. The adjusted discount rate, in general, is equal to:

Adjusted discount rate
= [1 − (Marginal tax rate × Debt displacement rate)]
× Cost of borrowed funds

For example, if the cost of borrowed funds is 10 percent and $1 of leasing is assumed to displace only 60 cents of debt (that is, a debt displacement rate of 60 percent), the adjusted discount rate is

$$[1 - (0.40 \times 0.60)] \times 0.10 = 0.076, \text{ or } 7.6 \text{ percent}$$

In the model presented earlier in this appendix, we had the special case of the above formula when the debt displacement rate was 100 percent. When the debt displacement rate is less than 100 percent, the adjusted discount rate will increase. For example, the adjusted discount rate is 6 percent in the previous example when the debt displacement rate is 100 percent. Since the direct cash flow from leasing will be discounted at a higher adjusted discount rate as the debt displacement rate increases, the value of the lease will increase. This is illustrated later in this section.

Sensitivity Analysis

It is not uncommon in economic models to find that the proposed solution is sensitive to changes in the factors of which the model is composed. The lease valuation model, for example, depends on the accuracy and certainty of such factors as the borrowing rate, the marginal tax rate, the timing of the tax shields, the estimated residual value, and the appropriate rate to discount the residual value and any additional operating expenses. The capital budgeting model assuming normal financing depends on additional factors that may not be known with certainty.

Uncertainty about the value that should be assigned to one or more factors in an economic model may reduce the confidence management has in the proposed solution generated by the model. To assist management when the values of one or more factors are uncertain, sensitivity analysis can be employed. In sensitivity analysis the values of the factors not known with certainty are altered to assess the effect, if any, such changes will have on the proposed solution. The following illustrations demonstrate how sensitivity analysis may be useful for the lease versus borrow-to-purchase decision.[30]

Illustration 8

The direct cash flow from leasing to the Lysle Construction Company used to illustrate the lease valuation model was:

Year	0	1	2	3	4	5
Direct cash flow from leasing	$51,300	($11,862)	($13,618)	($13,367)	($13,367)	($8,867)

To determine the sensitivity of the value of the lease to changes in the adjusted discount rate, the direct cash flow from leasing is discounted using adjusted discount rates between 3 percent and 15 percent. Exhibit 5 reports the value of the lease for adjusted discount rates at 0.25 percent increments. Assuming a marginal tax rate of 40 percent, which was assumed in computing the direct cash flow from leasing, the cost of borrowing associated with each adjusted discount rate is also shown in Exhibit 5.

---

[30] Although the illustrations are within the context of the net present value lease valuation model, sensitivity analysis can be used if the after-tax interest rate on the lease approach is employed. The uncertainty usually focuses on the residual value. An after-tax interest rate on the lease is then computed for different possible residual values expected by the lessee.

EXHIBIT 5 Sensitivity of the Value of a Lease to Changes in the Adjusted Discount Rate: Illustration 8

Adjusted discount rate (%)*	Borrowing rate (%)†	Value of lease ($)	Adjusted discount rate (%)*	Borrowing rate (%)†	Value of lease ($)
3.00%	5.00%	−$4,811	9.25%	15.42%	$3,701
3.25	5.42	−4,425	9.50	15.83	3,998
3.50	5.83	−4,044	9.75	16.25	4,292
3.75	6.25	−3,667	10.00	16.67	4,583
4.00	6.67	−3,294	10.25	17.08	4,872
4.25	7.08	−2,925	10.50	17.50	5,157
4.50	7.50	−2,559	10.75	17.92	5,440
4.75	7.92	−2,198	11.00	18.33	5,720
5.00	8.33	−1,841	11.25	18.75	5,997
5.25	8.75	−1,487	11.50	19.17	6,271
5.50	9.17	−1,137	11.75	19.58	6,543
5.75	9.58	−790	12.00	20.00	6,812
6.00	10.00	−448			
6.25	10.42	−108	12.25	20.42	7,079
6.50	10.83	227	12.50	20.83	7,342
6.75	11.25	560	12.75	21.25	7,604
7.00	11.67	888	13.00	21.67	7,862
7.25	12.08	1,214	13.25	22.08	8,119
7.50	12.50	1,536	13.50	22.50	8,373
7.75	12.92	1,855	13.75	22.92	8,624
8.00	13.33	2,170	14.00	23.33	8,874
8.25	13.75	2,482	14.25	23.75	9,121
8.50	14.17	2,792	14.50	24.17	9,366
8.75	14.58	3,098	14.75	24.58	9,608
9.00	15.00	3,401	15.00	25.00	9,848

* The lost residual value is discounted at the adjusted discounted rate.
† The borrowing rate associated with the adjusted discount rate is found by dividing the adjusted discount rate by 60 percent, which represents 1 minus the 40 percent marginal tax rate.

The value of the lease increases as higher adjusted discount rates are applied. The value of the lease ranges from −$4,811 to $9,848. The adjusted discount rate at which management would be indifferent between leasing and borrowing to buy is the rate at which the value of the lease is zero. From Exhibit 5 it can be seen that the value of the lease changes from a negative value to a positive value when the adjusted discount rate changes from 6.25 percent to 6.5 percent. Hence, the break-even adjusted discount rate is between 6.25 percent and 6.5 percent. This means that if the cost of borrowing to the Lysle Construction Company is between 10.42 percent and 10.83 percent, the company would be indifferent between leasing and borrowing to buy.

Notice that when the sensitivity analysis technique is used to determine when the value of the lease is zero (that is, the indifference rate between leasing and borrowing to purchase), this point is the after-tax interest rate on the lease. Recall that the after-tax interest rate on the lease is the discount rate that equates the present value of the direct cash flow from leasing to zero. For the leasing arrangement under consideration by Lysle Construction Company, it was shown that the rate was about 6.3 percent. From sensitivity analysis we found that the rate is between 6.25 percent and 6.5 percent. Had the discount rate been increased by 0.1 percent rather than 0.25 percent, we would have found the indifference point to be about 6.3 percent.

Illustration 9

Suppose Lysle's management does not believe that leasing displaces debt on a dollar-for-dollar basis. It believes that leasing does use up debt capacity, but it is not certain of the amount displaced.

To determine the sensitivity of the value of the lease to the percentage of debt displaced by leasing, the direct cash flow from leasing is discounted using debt displacement rates between 0 and 100 percent, at 10 percent increments. It is assumed that the cost of borrowed funds is 10 percent and that the marginal tax rate is 40 percent. The results are shown in Exhibit 6.

The value of the lease becomes more attractive as the amount of debt assumed to be displaced by the lease decreases. If management believes that leasing displaces less than about 90 percent of debt, then leasing is more economical.

EXHIBIT 6　　Sensitivity of the Value of a Lease to the Amount of Debt Displaced by Leasing: Illustration 9

Debt displacement rate(%)	Adjusted discount rate (%)*	Value of lease ($)
0%	10.0%	$4,583
10	9.6	4,116
20	9.2	3,641
30	8.8	3,159
40	8.4	2,669
50	8.0	2,170
60	7.6	1,664
70	7.2	1,149
80	6.8	626
90	6.4	93
100	6.0	−448

* Assuming that the marginal tax rate is 40 percent and that the cost of borrowed funds is 10 percent, the adjusted discount rate is:

$$[1 - (\text{Debt displacement rate} \times 0.40)] \times .10$$

Illustration 10

Suppose Lysle's management is uncertain about the estimated residual value of $3,600 it expects to realize five years from now if the machine is purchased. Management has estimated the firm's after-tax cost of capital to be 14 percent. The risk associated with the residual value is greater than that of cash flows associated with the firm's "average" project. Yet management is not certain how much riskier.

Management has determined the direct cash flow from leasing to be as follows:

Year	0	1	2	3	4	5
Direct cash flow from leasing	$51,300	($11,862)	($13,618)	($13,367)	($13,367)	($5,267)

Without the residual value of $3,600, the cash flow in year 5 is − $5,267.

Exhibit 7 shows the value of the lease discounting the residual value at discount rates from 14 percent to 20 percent at 1 percent increments, while discounting the other components of the direct cash flow from leasing at 6 percent. The greater the uncertainty about the residual value, the more economically attractive is the lease alternative. In our example leasing is attractive for any discount rate greater than or equal to 17 percent.

EXHIBIT 7   Sensitivity of the Value of a Lease to the Estimated Residual Value: Illustrations 10 and 11

Discount rate for residual value (%)	Value of lease when other components of direct cash flow from leasing are discounted at an adjusted rate of	
	6.0%*	4.8%†
14%	$373	− $1,149
15	453	− 1,069
16	529	− 993
17	601	− 921
18	669	− 853
19	734	− 788
20	796	− 726

* The adjusted discount rate assuming a borrowing rate of 10 percent and a marginal tax rate of 40 percent.

† The adjusted discount rate assuming a risk-free rate of 8 percent and a marginal tax rate of 40 percent.

Illustration 11

Lysle's management believes that although the residual value is uncertain, there is absolutely no uncertainty about the tax shields and the tax credit associated with the direct cash flow from leasing. Management has estimated the risk-free rate to be 8 percent and, as noted above, the after-tax cost of capital to be 14 percent.

Exhibit 7 shows the value of the lease when 4.8 percent (8 percent times 1 minus a 40 percent marginal tax rate) is used to discount the direct cash flow from leasing, excluding the residual value. The latter component is discounted at the various rates shown on Exhibit 7. Assuming the discount rates represent a reasonable range within which to discount the residual value, it can be seen that the leasing arrangement will never be more economically attractive in this case.

GENERALIZATION OF THE LEASE VALUATION MODEL

The lease valuation model we presented is appropriate when the firm anticipates that it can fully absorb the expenses associated with either financing alternative as they arise. In this section we present an extension of the lease valuation model. The model is appropriate for a firm currently in a nontaxpaying position but believes it will commence paying taxes at some specified future date.

Julian R. Franks and Stewart D. Hodges extended the lease valuation model formulated by Professor Myers and presented earlier in this appendix.[31] The model is generalized to cover the case where a firm is currently in a nontaxpaying position but expects to resume paying taxes at a specific future date. Expenses in the nontaxpaying years are assumed to be carried forward as tax losses. This tax benefit, along with any tax credit, which can also be carried forward, is then assumed to be absorbed in a single year. The extended model is useful because many firms considering leasing are, or expect to be, in such a position.

The procedure to compute the value of the lease is considerably more complicated in such cases. This procedure is explained and illustrated below.

The following assumptions and notations are employed in calculating the value of the lease:

1. Year H is the last year of cash flow consequences.
2. The firm is currently in a nontaxpaying position.

---

[31] Franks and Hodges, "Valuation of Financial Lease Contracts: A Note." The mathematical representation of the model is offered in footnote 3 (pages 666–67) of their article. The explanation of how to compute the value of the lease and the extension to consider any tax credit and the residual value are our own.

3. The firm expects to resume paying taxes in year G (where G is less than or equal to H), having a "tax holiday" from year 0 to year $G - 1$.
4. The firm will pay taxes from year G to year H at the same marginal tax rate.
5. All expenses incurred during the "tax holiday" are carried forward as tax losses and *fully* absorbed in year G.
6. Any tax credit is carried forward and fully utilized in year G.

Using the following 14 steps, the value of the lease can be determined.

Step 1: Compute the present value of the lease payments from year 0 to year $G - 1$ at the pretax borrowing rate.

Step 2: Compute the present value of the sum of the (1) after-tax lease payment, (2) depreciation tax shield, (3) any tax credit, and (4) lost residual value for years G through H at the after-tax borrowing rate. When discounting, treat year G as year 0.

Step 3: Compute the difference between the depreciation tax shield and the lease payment tax shield for the years 0 through $G - 1$. Add up these differences.

Step 4: Add up the amounts computed in Step 2 and Step 3.

Step 5: Find the present value of the amount in Step 4 for G years using the pretax borrowing rate.

Step 6: For years 1 through $G - 1$, multiply the lease payment by

$1 -$ [Present value of $1 using the pretax borrowing rate for t years]

where t corresponds to the year and varies from 1 to $G - 1$.

Step 7: Sum for years 1 through $G - 1$ the amounts computed in Step 6.

Step 8: Multiply the amount in Step 4 by

$1 -$ [Present value of $1 using the pretax borrowing rate for G years]

Step 9: Add the amounts computed in Step 7 and Step 8.

Step 10: Divide the sum in Step 9 by

$1 -$ (Marginal tax rate)[$1 -$ Present value of $1 using the pretax borrowing rate for G years]

Step 11: Multiply the amount in Step 10 by the marginal tax rate.

Step 12: Compute the present value of the amount in Step 11 using the pretax borrowing rate for G years.

Step 13: Add the amounts in Step 1, Step 5, and Step 12.

Step 14: Subtract from the purchase cost the amount computed in Step 13. The result is the value (NPV) of the lease.

Illustration 12

Let's apply the generalized lease valuation model to the lease considered by the Lysle Construction Company assuming the firm is currently in a nontaxpaying position but anticipates commencing tax payments in year 3 (that is, $G = 3$). All tax benefits are assumed to be carried forward and fully absorbed in year 3.

Step 1: Compute the present value of the lease payments from year 0 to year 2 at 10 percent. Since $13,500 is paid in each year, the present value is

$13,500[PV of $1 of an annuity due for three years at 10%]
$13,500[1 + 1.7355]
= $36,930

Step 2: Compute the present value of the sum of the (1) after-tax lease payment, (2) depreciation tax shield, (3) tax credit, and (4) lost residual value for years 3 to 5 using a 6 percent discount rate. For discounting purposes, treat year 3 as year 0.

Year	After-tax lease payment	Depreciation tax shield	Tax credit	Residual	Total
3	$8,100	$5,267	$6,600	$0	$19,967
4	8,100	5,267	0	0	13,367
5	0	5,267	0	3,600	8,867

Computation of present value:

Year	For discounting purposes	Total	PV of $1 at 6%	PV
3	0	$19,967	1.0000	$19,967
4	1	13,367	.9434	12,610
5	2	8,867	.8900	7,892
Total				$40,469

Step 3: Compute the difference between the depreciation tax shield and the lease payment tax shield for years 0 to 2. Add these differences.

Year	Depreciation tax shield	Lease payment tax shield	Difference
0	$ 0	$5,400	$ −5,400
1	3,762	5,400	−1,638
2	5,518	5,400	118
Total			$ −6,920

Step 4: Add the amounts computed in Step 2 and Step 3.

$$40,469 + (-6,920) = 33,549$$

Step 5: Find the present value of the amount in Step 4 for three years using 10 percent.

33,549[PV of $1 three years from now at 10%]
33,549(.7513)
= 25,205

Step 6: For years 1 and 2 multiply the lease payment by

$$1 - [\text{PV of \$1 for } t \text{ years at } 10\%]$$

Year	Lease payment	PV of $1	1 − PV of $1	Lease payment times (1 − PV of $1)
1	$13,500	$.9091	$.0909	$1,227
2	13,500	.8264	.1736	2,344

Step 7: Sum for years 1 and 2 the amounts computed in Step 6.

$$1,227 + 2,344 = 3,571$$

Step 8: Multiply the amount in Step 4 by

1 − [PV of $1 for three years at 10%]
33,549[1 − .7513]
= 8,344

Step 9: Add the amounts in Step 7 and Step 8.

$$3,571 + 8,344 = 11,915$$

Step 10: Divide the sum in Step 9 by

1 − 0.4[1 − PV of $1 for three years at 10%]
11,915/(1 − 0.4[1 − .7513])
= 11,915/0.9005
= 13,232

Step 11: Multiply the amount in Step 10 by 0.4.

$$0.4(13,232) = 5,293$$

Step 12: Compute the present value of the amount in Step 11 for three years at 10 percent.

$$5,293[\text{PV of }\$1\text{ for three years at }10\%]$$
$$5,293(.7513)$$
$$= 3,977$$

Step 13: Add the amounts in Step 1, Step 5, and Step 12.

$$36,930 + 25,205 + 3,977 = 66,112$$

Step 14: Subtract from the purchase cost the amount computed in Step 13.

$$66,000 - 66,112 = -112$$

The value (NPV) of the lease is $-\$112$. When it is assumed that the tax shields and the tax credit could be fully utilized at the time of recognition, the value of the lease is $-\$448$.

End of Illustration 12

The generalized model assumes that the entire tax shield can be carried forward and fully absorbed in a single year. There are limitations as to the number of years a tax loss and any tax credit may be carried forward. The model can accommodate this situation by modifying the following four steps to allow for tax losses that may be carried forward from year F to year G:

Step 3: Compute the difference between the depreciation tax shield and the lease tax shield for *years F through $G - 1$.* Add up these differences.

Step 6: For year F' through year $G - 1$, multiply the lease payment by

$$1 - [\text{Present value of }\$1\text{ using the pretax borrowing rate for}$$
$$(t - F' + 1)\text{ years}]$$

where F' is the greater of 1 and F[32] and t varies from F' to $G - 1$.

Step 8: Multiply the amount in Step 4 by

$$1 - [\text{Present value of }\$1\text{ using the pretax borrowing rate for}$$
$$(G - F' + 1)\text{ years}]$$

---

[32] For example, if F is year 5, then F' is 5 since it is greater than 1. If F is 0, then F' is 1 since 1 is greater than 0. Note that when F is zero, we have the case where all tax benefits can be carried forward.

Step 10: Divide the value in Step 9 by

1 − (Marginal tax rate)[1 − Present value of $1 using the pretax
borrowing rate for $(G - F' + 1)$ years]

Illustration 13

To illustrate how the model can be used when some of the tax shields cannot be carried forward, let's change the tax law. Suppose Lysle Construction is currently in a nontaxpaying position but expects to resume paying taxes in year 4. The tax credit cannot be carried forward, but tax losses in years 2 and 3 can be.

The value of the lease is $1,372, as shown below.

Step 1: Compute the present value of the lease payments from year 0 to year 3 at 10 percent. Since $13,500 is paid in each year, the present value is

13,500[PV of $1 of an annuity due for four years at 10%]
13,500[1 + 2.4869]
= 47,073

Step 2: Compute the present value of the sum of the (1) after-tax lease payment, (2) depreciation tax shield, (3) tax credit, and (4) lost residual value for years 4 and 5 using a 6 percent discount rate. For discounting purposes, treat year 4 as year 0.

Year	After-tax lease payment	Depreciation tax shield	Tax credit	Residual	Total
4	$8,100	$5,267	$0	$0	$13,367
5	0	5,267	0	3,600	8,867

Computation of present value:

Year	For discounting purposes	Total	PV of $1 at 6%	PV
4	0	$13,367	$1.0000	$13,367
5	1	8,867	.9434	8,365
Total				$21,732

Step 3: Compute the difference between the depreciation tax shield and the lease payment tax shield for years 2 and 3. Add these differences.

Year	Depreciation tax shield	Lease payment tax shield	Difference
2	$5,518	$5,400	$118
3	5,267	5,400	−133
Total			$−15

Step 4: Add the amounts computed in Step 2 and Step 3.

$$21{,}732 + (-15) = 21{,}717$$

Step 5: Find the present value of the amount in Step 4 for four years at 10 percent.

21,717[PV of $1 four years from now at 10%]
21,717(.6830)
= 14,833

Step 6: For years 2 and 3, multiply the lease payment by

1 − [PV of $1 for $(t - 2 + 1)$ years at 10%]

Year	For discounting $(t - 2 + 1)$	Lease payment	PV of $1	1 − PV of $1 at 6%	Lease payment times (1 − PV of $1)
2	1	$13,500	$.9091	$.0909	$1,227
3	2	13,500	.8264	.1736	2,344

Step 7: Sum for years 2 and 3 the amounts computed in Step 6.

$$1{,}227 + 2{,}344 = 3{,}571$$

Step 8: Multiply the amount in Step 4 by

1 − [PV of $1 for $(4 - 2 + 1)$ years at 10%]
21,717(1 − .7513)
= 5,401

Step 9: Add the amounts in Step 7 and Step 8.

$$3{,}571 + 5{,}401 = 8{,}972$$

Step 10: Divide the value in Step 9 by

1 − 0.4[1 − PV of $1 for $(4 - 2 + 1)$ years at 10%]
8,972/(1 − 0.4[1 − .7513])
8,972/0.9005
= 9,963

Step 11: Multiply the amount in Step 10 by 0.4.

$$0.4(9{,}963) = 3{,}985$$

Step 12: Compute the present value of the amount in Step 11 for four years at 10 percent.

> 3,985[PV of $1 for four years at 10%]
> 3,985(.6830)
> = 2,722

Step 13: Add the amounts in Step 1, Step 5, and Step 12.

> 47,073 + 14,833 + 2,722 = 64,628

Step 14: Subtract from the purchase cost the amount computed in Step 13.

> 66,000 − 64,628 = 1,372

Because Lysle Construction loses the tax credit and cannot carry all tax losses forward, leasing has become attractive. The value of the lease is now $1,372 compared to −$448 when all tax benefits are fully absorbed as they arise and −$112 when all the tax benefits can be carried forward and fully absorbed in a single year by a firm currently in a nontaxpaying position.

End of Illustration 13

For a firm that is currently in a nontaxpaying position and does *not* expect to receive any of the tax benefits, the value of the lease is easier to compute. The following two steps provide the value of the lease.

Step 1: Compute the present value of the sum of the (1) lease payments and (2) lost residual value before taxes at the pretax borrowing rate.

Step 2: Subtract from the purchase cost the amount computed in Step 1.

Illustration 14

Suppose the management of Lysle Construction is not presently paying taxes and does not expect to receive any tax benefits associated with either financing alternative. Applying the above two steps, the value of the lease is $5,981, as shown below:

Step 1:

> Present value of the lease payments at 10 percent:
> 13,500[PV of $1 of an annuity due for five years at 10%]
> = 13,500[1 + 3.1699]
> = 56,294

Present value of the residual value before taxes:
6,000[PV of $1 for five years at 10%]
= 6,000(.6209)
= 3,725

Total present value = 56,294 + 3,725
= 60,019

Step 2:

Value of lease = 66,000 − 60,019
= 5,981

Index